CRITICAL RESPONSE TO GERALD ROSEN'S BOOKS

"[*Blues for a Dying Nation*] is *Catch 22* with all the stops pulled out . . . .
An honorable attempt at the great American novel."

New York Times

"Gerald Rosen has written a terrific book . . . A book which is deeply rooted
in American popular culture, a book that reveals a remarkably acute
understanding of both New York and California, a book that is both hilarious
and devastating, *The Carmen Miranda Memorial Flagpole* is an exceptional
novel."

New York Times

"[*Growing Up Bronx*] is a humorous, touching novel."

New York Times

"[*Blues*] is the best novel of its kind in several years."

Milwaukee Journal

Blues For A Dying Nation was selected as one of the ten most interesting
novels of the year in an article that appeared in six major newspapers.

"Gerald Rosen is nothing less than a tender, passionate Philip Roth."

Western American Literature

"This novel [*Carmen Miranda Memorial Flagpole*] has a way of creeping
up on you. It begins with laughter, one-liners and wise-guy '50s slapstick,
progresses by engrossing the reader . . . and somehow all this silly, raucous
stuff becomes touching and wonderful."

San Francisco Chronicle

"[*Bronx* is] a charming and beautifully written memoir . . . From this whim-
sical prose there comes forth a bittersweet childhood that mixes humor and
tears."

The Baltimore Sun

"Rosen is a master of comedy."

Berkeley Barb

"Rosen is a poet of the one-liner."

San Francisco Bay Guardian

"Gerald Rosen knows what's going on and he writes about it with vitality
and eloquence."

James Leo Herlihy (author of *Midnight Cowboy*)

"Gerald Rosen counts his literary influences as Cervantes, Tolstoi, and Henny Youngman . . . you can't help but smile, sing along, maybe get up and dance as you read this eminently funny and useful book. "
Chicago Daily News

"[*Carmen Miranda*] is the Annie Hall of books . . . not to be missed."
Pacific Sun

"There's madness here, and fun, and a great deal of love . . . . [*Dr. Ebenezer*] is a warm and tender and funny book about a man who does what he can to keep the dream of love alive in a difficult time."
Baton Rouge Advocate

"[*Dr. Ebenezer* and *Carmen*] are pithy, black humored and admirable for their attempts to hurl one liners at life's pain; for his characters' courage in cracking jokes at the difficulties of finding love in the world while continuing, desperately, to attempt to do so."
San Francisco Chronicle

"Can anything be more perfect? . . . [In *Mahatma Gandhi*] Rosen's portrait of a more innocent time is touching and highly readable."
Library Journal

"Rosen writes about his characters with clarity and wit. The end result is a thought-provoking and ultimately upbeat book."
New Age Journal

"[In *Bronx*] Rosen demonstrates his mastery of the one-liner and accurately recaptures the nuances of childhood, which readers will recognize and remember with pleasure and perhaps some trepidation."
Publishers Weekly

"[*Dr. Ebenezer*] is a novel to amuse, amaze"
Charleston Post and Courier

"[*Bronx*] is a relaxed, smiling, altogether nice evocation of middle-class Jewish New York, 1945-55."
Kirkus Reviews

"*Dr Ebenezer* dispenses his booze and books to highly original, exciting characters . . . splendid entertainment."
South Bend Tribune

COLD EYE, WARM HEART
A Novelist's Search for Meaning

COLD EYE, WARM HEART
A Novelist's Search for Meaning

by

Gerald Rosen

"You are not your body, you are not your mind."
A Hindu Saying

Calm Unity Press
ISBN 978-1-882260-18-8

This book is dedicated to my wife Marijke Wittkampf. Marijke does not appear very often in the book because she came into my story a year after the time period that it depicts, but the day I met her was the luckiest day of my life.

It is also dedicated to the women jazz musicians I listened to back in the day, unsung pioneers who gave so much to the world. (Lil Hardin Armstrong, Bessie Smith, Billie Holiday, Ella Fitzgerald, Helen Humes, Anita O'Day, Mary Lou Williams, Sarah Vaughn, Dinah Washington, June Christy, Melba Liston, Carmen McRae, Terry Pollard, Marian McPartland, Dakota Staton, Toshiko Akiyoshi, Jutta Hipp, Gloria Lynne, Jeri Southern, Helen Merrill, Lorraine Geller, Beverly Kenney, Nina Simone, Alice Coltrane, Annie Ross, Carla Bley, Jackie Cain, Betty Carter, Chris Connor, Astrud Gilberto, Morgana King, Cleo Laine, Betty Roche, and Shirley Scott among others.)

Cold Eye, Warm Heart

GETTING PUBLISHED

I grew up in a curious and probably unique culture in which the majority of the brightest people had come to equate death with eternal darkness and nothingness. The strangest aspect of this belief was that somehow those who held it thought that it was scientific, although there was absolutely no evidence to support it.

Joseph Campbell jokingly defined mythology as "other people's religion." This belief in ultimate nothingness was our culture's religion. This was our mythology.

When I was in my twenties I realized that even though I was very successful, I could no longer live in this culture. Every day it sucked up my energy and spit it out. I felt like a fish dropped off a truck, struggling to breathe by flapping against the wet cobblestones.

This is the story of my search for a way out.

BRRRNNNNGGGGG!

Funny, but when that phone call you've always been waiting for finally comes, the one that will change your life forever, it doesn't sound that much different than a call from the bill collector.

BRRRNNNNGGGGG!

I had just come out of the metal shower stall in our kitchen. It was fall of 1969. My wife Charlotte and I lived in a $65 a month, sixth-floor walkup, a tiny Lionel trains railroad flat on Grove Street in Greenwich Village, across from Hart Crane's place and Emma Goldman's, around the corner from Edna St. Vincent Millay's little house, and down the block from Tom Paine's.

I hurried toward the back of the apartment, toweling as I moved. There was no need for me to put on clothes. The windows were opaquely curtained, turning their backs on a dusty (lack of) airshaft. I was alone in the apartment except for my dog Shep. He didn't give a damn about what I wore. He spent his days lost in marijuana-fueled fantasies in which he defended his property from huge outsiders. Like many Americans he had a self-esteem problem. Too much self-esteem.

Shep imagined himself as being bigger and tougher than he really was. This led him to commit foolish attacks on other dogs in which he was usually mauled. He reminded me of my father in a way.

1

[Although to be fair to my father, he did calm down some in the years before he died unexpectedly at age fifty-six. He no longer attempted to run anyone over in fights about Bronx parking spaces, after that night when the intended victim leaped aside, then lunged toward my father and choked him through the window of his car. My father was lucky in that I heard him making a kind of loud, gargling sound and ran downstairs to pull the guy off him. And my father didn't beat me up anymore since that time when I was seventeen, returning home late and happy from the only party I had ever been invited to. My father leaped out of his bed, half asleep and crazed. He chased me around the apartment in his jockey shorts, hitting me with a shoe. I tried to escape by rushing into my room and holding the door closed but he was quicker than I had supposed and unfortunately I slammed the door on his head.]

BRRRNNNNGGGGG!

Sitting naked at my desk, I picked up the phone.

"Hello."

"Is this Gerald Rosen?"

"Yes."

"This is Robert Gottlieb at Knopf."

I didn't know what to say. Robert Gottlieb was the Editor in Chief of prestigious Knopf, the house that had published authors like Gide and Kafka in the Twenties. Gottlieb (the future editor of *The New Yorker*) was arguably the most powerful editor in the world. He edited authors I admired like Doris Lessing and Bruce Jay Friedman and he had worked personally with Joseph Heller on *Catch 22* for years.

Joseph Heller was one of my idols. He had saved my life when I was a suicidal Army officer. I had come to believe that all the other 12,000 people on the base were crazy. Thus, by definition, I concluded *I* was crazy. But after reading *Catch 22*, I realized that all the people on the base actually *were* crazy. This helped me immensely.

"Liz Long gave me your manuscript."

"Oh, yes . . . yes . . ." I improvised brilliantly.

How could this be happening? Not only had I never published anything, I had never sent anything out. I had not taken any writing courses. I hadn't even officially been an English major. Liz Long, a friend of Bruce and Riki Kuklick, my pals from grad school at the University of Pennsylvania,

2

had trailed along with them to visit me one day. She said she had heard I had written something and asked to take a look at it. I had given her a copy of the manuscript and forgotten about it. I had written the 500 page manuscript in six weeks of fevered work. Then I got a flu for two weeks, collapsed, rose from the ashes like Phoenix, Arizona, rewrote the book in eight weeks, gave it to her, collapsed again and forgot about it.

I had been living a crazy life in the Village, completing an Ivy League Ph.D. in American Studies at Penn in Philadelphia, while running my dead father's liquor store on the edge of Harlem, dropping acid, studying Buddhism and Hinduism, and rioting against the war while wearing my old Army officer's uniform. Then this book had somehow poured out of me.

"Gerald? Are you there?"

"Yes."

"Well I wanted to tell you that I like your book. I like it very much. Now Joe has it. He likes it too."

"Joe?"

"Yes, Joe Heller."

This presented me with the first dilemma of my new life. Should I call Joseph Heller "Joseph " or "Joe"?

"I'm glad you both like it," I said, finessing the situation.

"I'd like to talk to you about it. Do you think you could make it up here next week? Say Thursday. At . . . 2:30."

"Sure," I said. I had no appointments. I didn't even have an appointment book. My only fixed dates were the riots and they would kind of appear every once in a while like hallucinogenic mushrooms. You didn't need a secretary to keep track of them.

"Wonderful. I'll look forward to seeing you then."

I floated, stunned, into the kitchen to tell the news to Shep but he was pre-occupied, trying to get a whiff of some possible intruder under the new steel door.

Our building still hung the old fragile wooden doors from the beginning of the century. No lock-picking or sophisticated entry maneuvers were needed to rob us. The downstairs entry door was unlocked. On a weekday afternoon, thieves would just stroll in carrying an ax, climb the stairs, chop a door down and take what they wanted. You just hoped you weren't home when they arrived.

I had recently purchased the steel door. My wife and I had nothing of value but I was afraid that Shep would attack the thieves and they would chop him up with the ax. Our pal Mara down the hall had a fire escape that led to the roof so the thieves didn't even have to chop her door down. She was robbed so many times that every day when she went to work she would hide her last valuable, her clock radio, in her oven.

Mara worked at CBS at a similar job to the one Mary Tyler Moore had on her TV show. But while Mary Tyler Moore had a beautiful house, Mara could only afford our cockroach-infested, please-rob-me, tenement dump.

Mrs. Battista, the old Portuguese widow, lived across the hall from us. As I feared, she had come up the stairs just when they were installing the door. She still wore her black widow's weeds although her husband had died back in the time of Vasco Da Gama.

I respected Mrs. Battista, courageously living her lonely life, but unlike the great poet of her people, Fernando Pessoa, she had only one personality, so I knew exactly what she was thinking. I tried to soften the blow. "It's an iron door, Mrs. Battista. This way, if they come, they won't kill my dog."

"No. Now they come and chop down my door instead," she said, dolefully.

"Why don't you get one for yourself, Mrs. Battista?"

"My husband, he never tell me to get no steel door."

She never did anything that her husband hadn't told her to do.

She shuffled across the hall, disappearing into her apartment like a dark ghost, the weight of a thousand Iberian tragedies on her black-shawled shoulders.

WHAT ARE WE PROTESTING?

I bounced off the stoop like a Spaldeen, turned east toward Sheridan Square, and was immediately engulfed by a flurry of young people swelling down the street and spilling onto the sidewalk behind me. They were frantically turning over ash cans and hurling anything they could grab at the riot police who were chasing them, picking off stragglers, throwing them down to the pavement, kicking and punching them, swinging their heavy clubs at the heads of the kids who leaped over the hoods of parked cars to avoid the blows and cursed back at them as they fled.

I shifted into high gear and dashed down the street with the rioters. I didn't know them but there would be no time to explain to the stampeding cops that I was a Ph.D. with a liquor store. They would see my long hair, my unshaven visage, my torn jeans, my pot-smoker's eyes like Mars with its faint red canals, my Army fatigue uniform shirt with the silver first lieutenant's bar and the medical insignia still illegally affixed to the collar. There would be no time to explain to the cops that the shirt was mine. That I was a vet, a former Army officer. I joined the rioters and ran for my life toward the east.

I thought of shouting to the girl running beside me, "What are we protesting?" but it didn't matter. I knew what we were protesting. When Henrik Ibsen, old and bruised and famous, returned to his native Norway after decades of self-imposed exile, the students sent a delegation to see the great man. They said, "Honored Sir, we want to change the world. Can you tell us what is wrong?" Ibsen considered this for a second. Then he replied, "Everything."

That's what we were protesting: Everything. It didn't matter who these particular kids were: Students, leftists, socialists, communists, hippies, yippies, Maoists, Taoists, Buddhists, nudists, acid heads, pacifists, the "Up Against the Wall Motherfuckers," an anarchist gang from the Lower East Side, Black Panthers, White Panthers, Gray Panthers, escaped mental patients, whatever. The cops would know I was with the kids. It was the High Sixties. We rioters all shared the same invisible tattoo on our foreheads that could only be read by anyone representing The Authorities and their war: A resounding "NO!"

But it was not just no to the war. It was no to the way of life that was causing the war. It was no to what the American people were becoming and no to what our government was doing around the world in our name. We were threatening the adults with the only power we had: the power not to pass on their culture.

At Sheridan Square I ducked into the IRT subway station. The rioters and the cops ran by me down toward the Stonewall Bar, the site, a few months before, of the riot now famous as the courageous Alamo of the

5

gay rights movement in America. I was proud that the Stonewall was right down my street, just beyond Tom Paine's house.

MY LIQUOR STORE

I was riding the Broadway IRT to my late father's liquor store. Gottlieb's call had left me with a surplus of energy so I thought I might as well go up to 135th Street and pay the bills. My father had died on January 12, 1967, on the very day I had bought the notebooks and index cards to begin my doctoral dissertation. He had been crushed like a fly by a wanton boy, in this case, Governor Nelson Rockefeller, who, to avoid a minor political embarrassment, did away with the state-enforced, fixed pricing in liquor stores and thereby rendered worthless my father's investment and toil over twenty years.

Novelists can invent symbolic action, so why can't the Gods? What could be more significant than a Rockefeller, born with a silver spoon in his mouth (talk about a tough labor!) crushing an orphan from the lower East Side, population density higher than Calcutta, who had had to leave school in the tenth grade to sweep movie theaters to help support his family. Rockefeller had also destroyed the ancient black neighborhood around Green Street in Albany. When I was studying engineering in nearby Troy, we used to go to Green Street to hear great jazz in little clubs on tiny Revolutionary era brick streets—young Dave Pike, Wilbur Ware, Elvin Jones, Nick Brignola, J.R. Montrose, fifty cents a beer and midget hot dogs for a dime—and classic local r & b bands like Bill Gorry and the Meadowlarks (in which baritone sax, trumpet, and small organ blended such sweet harmonies it was like Hindus chanting to Shiva with a harmonium, just a few chords but they were so beautiful you wished they would play them all day). Rockefeller had leveled this entire neighborhood just behind the state capitol building (he called it "Urban Renewal;" we called it "Negro Removal") to erect a $2 billion monument to himself, a huge self-portrait of sterile office towers and freeway interchanges that kept black people out of the downtown Albany area.

My father had worked up to ninety hours a week, to pay off the debts he had incurred to buy the monopoly the governor erased overnight. (In

Stephen Crane's story, "Blue Hotel," after the Swede stubbornly gets himself killed in a bar, Stephen Crane focuses on a sign on the cash register: "This Registers the Amount of your Purchase.") Shortly after my father's hopes were eradicated, he toppled over dead on *his* cash register. Nelson Rockefeller went on to become the vice-president of the United States. He died while fucking his young assistant. His wife's name was Happy.

Nelson Avenue, our street in The Bronx, chanced to be aligned so that if you were playing stickball in the traffic you could see the Empire State Building seven miles to the South. When I learned that my father died it was like looking down Nelson Avenue and seeing the Empire State Building falling. Whatever was left of my belief in work-aholism and capitalist justice was swept away in the downdraft as a huge structure of permission arose in its place. [I wrote this paragraph three months before 9/11.]

Suddenly I realized I no longer had to stay at the University of Pennsylvania in Philly. Why not move to New York and write my doctoral dissertation there? Why close the store as my mother intended? It wasn't completely worthless. It could continue to modestly support three Puerto Rican families. My mother could take a small check each week and I could as well. The bowling pins of my life kept tumbling over like a slow-motion strike from the Jersey side. Why not move to forbidden Greenwich Village? Why not become a hippie? Why not run the store with my left hand, as Gurdjieff puts it, and live my real life downtown, giving into my wayward heart at last? Where was the authority that prevented this? Where was any real authority, public or private, now that my father and the American dream had come crashing down?

I knew my wife wouldn't mind. Charlotte was a beat girl from Idaho. We'd met in Seattle in summer 1961. She had arrived on a freight train after being kicked out of a convent in Kansas. She had wanted to marry Jesus, but the nuns, who were already married to him, decided against the idea, and they were right. But she had shown up on the jazz scene with her Thomas Aquinas, her port wine, her talk about God and Love and her time in a reformatory, and her love of black music, although she no longer played trombone. No, she wouldn't mind moving from Philly to Greenwich Village. She was no longer a teacher of kids in the Philly Head Start program. The mothers in the ghetto had complained about the lack of neatness in her attire so she quit. She was working for Chubby Checker's shrink in West Philly. Charlotte liked New York, but with the laxity of the Sixties her own purchase on reality was becoming fragile. She was loosening her grip and would soon begin decades of clinging to a safety rope woven out of the finest hemp.

My brother was a lawyer in the Army. My mother was in a state of convenient collapse which prevented her from doing things she considered below her status in life, such as trying to balance her checkbook, one of many such tasks which had devolved upon me, so why not keep the store open, continue to support three Puerto Rican families, take a few dollars for my mother and myself, and run wild?

The IRT subway racked and swayed and jackknifed under Broadway and I moved with it, like Charlotte on the freight to Seattle, you had to rock with it, that was the story, on the subway or off. It was the High Sixties. The Fifties' dreams of smooth sailing on a luxury yacht had sunk. The deck of the ship of state had cracked, revealing that it was actually being powered by poor dark-skinned people down below, rowing.

Even my hometown, The Bronx, where my extended family had invested their money in real estate was gone. My grandfather had advised his children that even in a depression people would need a place to live. He didn't tell them what to do if the tenants had guns and were setting fires. Our Bronx was being burned down by a vicious melange of desperate landlords, crooked building inspectors, insurance frauds, pyros, crackpots, vengeful lovers, junkies, welfare rip-offs, teen-gang firebugs and Robert Moses.

On the subway, I thought about the mixed feelings I had about giving my book to a mainstream publisher. In past times it would have represented the American dream come true for me. But this was not normal times. This was the High Sixties. I hadn't cut my hair in years. I wore old torn clothes so as not to participate in the American economy. I rarely ventured above Fourteenth Street. Wouldn't this be selling out to the establishment? A kneeling at the same altar as the people who were sending ghetto teenagers half way around the world to kill other poor teenagers?

I was also a little scared. When I was growing up in The Bronx, I had never imagined that one day I could become a novelist. Novelists lived in Manhattan. They summered in the Hamptons and studied abroad and spoke French. We had had no books in our apartment. We summered at Ha Ya Bungalows, forty shacks on two acres of land in Nyack. My mother's parents were illiterate immigrants from "Austria" which was a euphemism for Poland. My father's parents had come from Russia. They were already dead when I was born. No one would tell me exactly which town my ancestors came from. I guess their history was too dreadful to be remembered.

I had never met anyone who was famous or successful. The only professional I knew was my Uncle Lenny who lived upstairs and was an armed robber. He led a gang of black men from Harlem with Tommy guns in a series of famous holdups of nightclubs in the Baltimore-Washington area. He was also the local Cub Scout leader. He volunteered for this position because he was the only man on the block with free time. He was bald and big, like the guy on the Halvah wrapper. He would come out in his huge Cub Scout uniform and lead the boys in hikes across the George Washington Bridge to show them what a tree was. He was a good-natured guy, popular in the neighborhood. Everyone was sorry when the cops caught him and he died in federal prison.

Our block was filled with my relatives, but besides my Uncle Lenny, only my mother's cousin Al Corn made it into our newspaper, *The Daily News*. Al was a nice guy, a vet who drank at the American Legion on Boscobel Avenue, the street that led down to Yankee Stadium. When they built the legion post after World War II, they changed the name of the street to Edward L. Grant Highway. Eddie Grant was the first ballplayer killed in World War I. They had a big celebration with marching bands and speeches by immortal politicians whose names no one can remember. I learned then that if you wanted to build a highway in The Bronx the cheapest way was just to chose a street and change the name to "Highway" on the signs.

Our cousin Al Corn was in the paper after he fell three floors down an elevator shaft into the IRT subway. Somehow he was not seriously injured, just a couple broken legs. He recovered fully, becoming the father of two boys, Edward Spencer Corn and Mason Douglas Corn.

[Now, whenever ESPN reports the Alcorn State basketball score on TV, I say to my wife, "They named that school after my cousin Al Corn in the Bronx."]

TRANSMUTATION

"What is the purpose of working and living? To find freedom from the bondages of misery and death. There is no other purpose."
Swami Prabhavananda

Who am I? Is this happening to me? How could I be living in a Greenwich Village tenement and married to a beautiful beat girl? How could I be running my father's liquor store and dropping acid and rioting against the government?

For a Bronx kid, I had been making a great success in America. I had a degree in electrical engineering from Rensselaer, a top engineering school, and an MBA from Wharton, where I was arguably the best student in the best MBA program in the world. In those days it was rare to couple an engineering degree with an MBA. At twenty-two, I had been the only Wharton student selected by Boeing for their elite Executives of the Future Program. They flew me out to Seattle and paid me a high salary for a summer job in the hopes that I might consider working for them when I graduated. It was my task to decide whether to use Japanese transistors on America's best ICBM, the Minuteman Missile, the cornerstone of our defense.

Then I had returned to Ivy League University of Pennsylvania after the Army and had taken an MA and a Ph.D. in American history and literature in order to become a professor and try to serve humanity for spiritual reasons. I had changed my path again and again. I felt that my balance on the bobsled of this culture was tenuous. If I didn't find the right life path I would die. I couldn't bear to live like so many of the men in The Bronx. The ones who passed away in their fifties, never having figured things out. But now I was a longhaired rock and roller, a student of Buddhism and Hinduism and all the contemporary arts, a stoned anti-war rioter and metaphysical explorer. When Wharton sent me a survey to track their recent students, I threw it away. I liked Wharton. They had let me pursue my interests in history and economics instead of holding me to pure business courses. I didn't want to break their curve and bring down the average pay. I doubt there were many of their grads who were running a liquor store on the edge of Harlem and earning $55 a week.

After high school most of my friends in The Bronx had continued in their same cultural mode. Some went to local colleges for a few years, most quickly took jobs, married, moved to Queens and spent their spare time at the trotters or betting on Knick games. One pal, Albee, went directly from high school to a job in a lamp store, marriage and a couple kids. When I returned to New York from Philadelphia, I invited him down to the Village. He proved to be extremely uncomfortable among the hippies. Couldn't understand why I was there. As we walked along colorful Macdougal Street, Albee blurted out, "I can buy and sell any one of these guys."

When he left that night, I knew I would never see him again. This was painful. I liked Albee. But there was no turning back. As the Zen masters say, I had a tiger by the tail.

OUT-OF-TOWN-COLLEGE

"Science is always necessary, never sufficient; we are starving for beauty and where charity is lacking, nothing else is of any avail."

George Sarton

When it had come time for me to select a college I had no one to turn to for guidance. I knew nothing about universities or power jobs. I did know I wanted to go to an out-of-town-college. That was where all the smart kids wanted to go. Not the free city colleges which everyone saw as less desirable. You would be there with other poor New Yorkers. How could you make the right connections? Meet the friends you dreamed of—smart, good looking, sophisticated, and at home in America. In short, Protestants. What was the point of paying high tuition except to get away from the insular Bronx with its Jews and Catholics, to lose your New York street accent, and to spend the rest of your life as an imitation Protestant. And where else could you meet classy girls? Girls who grew up in real houses not tight dark apartments. Girls who had lawns and who had been to Paris. In short, girls who weren't like yourself.

This was the first of my moves toward finding a way out of my dead-end life. I didn't want to struggle under the legacy of our Lower East Side antecedents—the fear of actually starving, of falling through the cracks into some subterranean realm you couldn't climb out of. I needed to leave

11

the raucous, tumbling street life of the immigrant Bronx for a world like I saw on TV. The outside world had to be different from The Bronx. I was too isolated and lonely. I couldn't stand this kind of existence.

I yearned to become successful and to show up on the block in a Thunderbird convertible, and there beside me is The Blonde, possibly even Jewish, as long as she has obvious class and the right clothes, and we're coming into the city to visit the folks, and we have the tennis rackets in the back, and I have the expensive sweater wrapped around my shoulders with the sleeves tied around my neck, and up at all the windows the yentas are stirring, they're calling their husbands, "Barney, look at this! Look at his wife. And the car." They would know I was making it in America and thus my parents and I would know it, too. And this was going to finally make me happy. No more fleeing from our apartment where my parents were fighting about money and going around the corner to sit morosely by myself on the steps of the Gilman sisters' drugstore, naming the passing American cars ("Chevy, Hudson, Buick, Nash"), watching as drunken fans drove back from a Yankee game to their homes in New Jersey, while I sat there in sadness, feeling like there was no hope for me, that in the world in which I was growing up, even though I had friends, I would somehow always be miserable and lost and alone.

When I was eleven I went to the 1950 NIT basketball finals at the Garden with my friend Marty Licker and the men from Ha-Ya Bungalows (my father was working). I couldn't bear it that CCNY was going to win both the NCAA and NIT championships. CCNY had local players. Bronx guys. Guys who played in our school yard. I was the only person in the Garden rooting for Bradley. Bradley came from some place out in America. They were led by Paul Unruh, a tall thin American guy with a crew cut. It frightened me that our block could be better than anywhere else in America. Even though CCNY won, I went to Sol the Barber the next day and got a crew cut. And I walked to the freezing empty schoolyard every evening that week, chipping ice with a shovel so I could practice lonely jump shots there in the dim light, lost in my American dreams.

I knew nothing about college. I had seen a guy with a Harvard T-shirt that said "VE-RI-TAS." I thought it was the name of a fraternity. I could suggest a private college because my father, after years of spine-crushing work and scalding debt payments, had entered the brief period when he would be making good money. But before I applied to college, my father required me to have a reasonable career plan. The men on the block would kid him if I just studied liberal arts or something. I needed a professional goal. But what were the professions? I didn't really know. Doctor? Not for me. Lawyer? Not for me. Indian Chief? Not qualified. Dentist? Not for me. What else was there that I couldn't study as well at a free city college? Then it came to me: Engineer. That was it. I didn't have the vaguest idea of what an engineer actually did. I knew it had something to do with math and science, subjects at which I excelled. My mother lit up when I suggested it. Even my father couldn't hide a spark of interest. "Yeah, I'll be an engineer. That's it." I could see my father dreaming already. The same dream—The Thunderbird, the blonde, the tennis rackets, the envious neighbors.

I chose Rensselaer Polytechnic Institute although I was accepted to MIT as well. MIT had no football team and sat in a large city. I wanted to be in a small city, and to be a star quarterback like Frank Merriwell of Yale whom I had followed as a kid on the radio every Saturday morning along with Archie Andrews and Frank Luther who sang songs like, "We say please and thank you, it's the only proper thing to do . . . ." Of course, I couldn't actually go to Yale. I would have been scared stiff. People like me didn't go to Ivy League schools. I didn't even know what footnotes were, much less how to use them. This caused me trouble at RPI when I decided to do extra research on Thomas Wolfe in the library for a paper for freshman English, my favorite class. I was certain I'd receive an A but was KO'd by a left hook F instead. It turned out that all the knowledge I had found and included in my paper in my efforts to be the best in the class was somehow considered by the crazy *goyem* to be cheating. Well, live and learn, as they say.

My dream of being a football star was short-lived even though I had picked the right team—during my four years there, RPI only won two games. Although I had never played high school football, I knew I would be the quarterback; they were the handsome, brainy ones named Rick and Chet who got the girls, but after a few days' practice the coach took me aside and said he wanted me to play fullback.

"Fullback! But coach, I only weigh 167 pounds!"

He shrugged wearily. "I have eight quarterbacks. Three of them played high school ball. I only have two fullbacks." He looked away as he said, "Just take the ball and run up the middle with it. You'll see. You'll like it."

I didn't like it. One of the first times I ran the ball I was tackled by eight guys at once and they nearly wrenched my arm off. The trainer came out and froze it with some kind of chemical spray. This wasn't my dream. Quarterbacks didn't run up the middle and get their arms frozen. And this was different from TV. This **hurt**!

I decided to go out for basketball instead. I thought I had made the team but was the last one cut. That hurt even more. And when I tried out for baseball, I realized that although I was a good softball player, they played hardball. On grass. I wasn't good on grass. I had played stickball in the gutter, sewer to sewer, and softball on burned garbage ashes and broken glass at the Foundies, an old city dump a block from my house. I didn't know how to slide. No one but my crazy pal Marty Licker ever tried to slide at the Foundies. If you slid at the Foundies you shredded your pants and half your leg. Even though I had once filled in as batboy for the Giants and before the game waved Willy Mays off, "I got it Willy," and caught a fly ball in centerfield at the Polo Grounds, that was hardly the stuff of what real careers are made of.

"A Jew of the usual objectionable type."
William Carlos Williams

I decided to be a fraternity intramural athlete and live in my dreams. And it turned out I excelled at this. I had found my level. Among the smart guys, I was actually good. And we won the highly contested sports trophy for the twenty-eight fraternities. It gave me great satisfaction to beat the Christians who had not admitted us to their fraternities because we were Jewish. I was shocked to learn a thing like this could occur in 1956 at a top college. It left a scar on my dream of America that never quite healed. (Although the individual Christian guys remained my close friends. They'd been kept from admitting us by their national fraternities which had threatened to expel them.)

Besides the opening to a respectable career, I'd also **had** another goal at RPI, a dream about science. I was hoping to learn some **clean** way to arrive at the Truth. I despaired at the interminable arguments among the people around me in The Bronx, adults who could go on forever in impassioned voices debating a thousand topics from business to baseball; they knew few facts and merely gave vent to various biases and intuitions and desires. There had to be some clean way to settle all this. Some scalpel-like method that would precisely cut away the tendentiousness and uncertainty.

Science. That was going to be the way. The American way. I would study science and then I would return and make peace. I would settle matters scientifically, though I didn't yet know exactly what this meant. I would bring back stainless steel methods from the world of hard-edged scientific distinctions that I would enter at Rensselaer.

But I hadn't anticipated the drinking. How liberated I would feel to finally be out of my family's apartment with my father chasing me around in his underwear, hitting me with a shoe if I stayed out late. My kid brother, who was to become a top Wall Street lawyer, the boss of a 250-person law firm with offices at the top of the Woolworth Building and then die of cancer at forty-eight, said that the transition to the Army was no problem for him: "I felt I had been in the Army all my life."

A SEASON IN HECK

> *"Paint what you really see, not what you think you ought to see."*
>
> Claude Monet

At RPI there were no parents. There weren't even any adults outside of class. Merely 3,000 horny, stressed-out guys in a world before grade-inflation. At the first assembly they would tell you to look to your left, look to your right—one of you three isn't going to make it. Like virtually everyone else, I was no longer one of the two or three best students. In fact, I began to realize that I wasn't cut out to be an engineer at all. I was always good in chemistry so I had majored in chemical engineering. Then I found that I didn't like the way the chemistry labs smelled. I was better in the abstract, mathematical, less odiferous aspects of the program, but I was very unlike most of my dorm-mates who had been building radios and tinkering with cars and fixing mechanical gadgets around the home for their entire lives. Brilliant techies like Hank Warren who built a radio station in his dorm room and illegally broadcast classical music to east Troy, until one day he went ice skating and fell through the ice and we had to revive him when they carried him in, shaking and blue.

I had never built a ham radio or owned a car. And I'd never fixed a single thing in our apartment in The Bronx. After all, what was the "Super" for?

I switched to Electrical Engineering, which required mostly work in math on paper and in your head. Then I teamed up in a co-dependent arrangement with my fraternity brother, Dave Friedman, who was a genius in science and math but had weaker interpersonal street skills in which I excelled. We made an unspoken pact. The night before an exam, he would identify the relevant material and teach it to me. After the quiz we would go to tough bars and get totally blotto, and then I would endeavor to get him home and to keep him alive until the next exam.

All the students felt the pressure. You couldn't bullshit your way through an engineering exam. If the answer was 47, that was it. You couldn't weave in your knowledge of Shakespeare from another course to get a C. And the college was focused on exams. After Christmas vacation there were continuous semi-final exams for two weeks. Then a week of three hour finals. People completely cracked up.

As freshmen, we lived in three-story modern dorms with flat roofs. During winter exam weeks a freshman named Scott made a key to the locked door to the roof from a wax impression, then set the roof on fire. When the firemen arrived to save the dorm, he locked them on the burning roof. That was it for him at RPI.

My friend Lyle, a very bright New Englander, big, ungainly, conceited, had run wild being away from home, trying to fashion a new, suave, devil-may-care personality. He spent the spring semester cutting classes, falling behind, drinking at seedy bars; when he returned each night he would chase Eddie Johnson, a laughing flautist, around the dorm, hitting him with a broom. Lyle had great pride. He kept telling us he would catch up to us during the exam weeks. But on the first night of his finals study marathon, he was lured off to see Mickey and Sylvia at the ballpark in Albany. Nonetheless, he took his exams. He continued to believe he had shown us all up. We fools had studied all semester while he had been carousing, and now he would get the As, because he was a genius. When he found that he had failed all his classes and flunked out of school, he realized his career was over. His family was poor. He had been lying about his grades to his stern old grandfather who sponsored him, paying for the high tuition, the drinking, the preppy clothes and all. Now Lyle was shamed in front of all of us.

As soon as he saw his grade report, he seized a hockey stick and smashed out all the windows in the room. He ran out of the dorm and returned dragging large paper grocery bags of food. Mostly colorful liquids, ketchup and mustard, prune juice and mayonnaise. As we all gathered around, he set the bags down and began to fling all the bottles and jars, breaking them against the cinder block wall at the end of the hallway. He was going berserk. A kind of crazed Jackson Pollock, action-painting the dorm. Reds and yellows, soy sauce and milk. After the first grocery bag was empty he ran into his room and returned with the pile of expensive suits his grandfather had bought for him. He hurled them onto the soggy heap at the end of the hall, then smashed his phonograph records on top of them. Back in his room, he raised up the elements of his stereo and heaved them through the broken window, speakers, turntable and all, smashing them against the ground below. He lugged more clothes into the hallway—sweaters, underwear, ties and shirts—along with his slide rule, his expensive engineering books, and he threw them all into this abstract expressionist agglomeration at the end of the corridor. When his room was finally empty, he went to the second and third grocery bags, the orange juice, the cranberry nectar, the grape jam and marmalade, smashing them bottle after bottle on the palette of the wall above the soggy clothes and resplendent books and records, making a kind of fauve sandwich of all his wrecked possessions until he finally ran out of food in a delirium of sweaty exhaustion. We were all laughing like crazy. We had never seen anything like this before. It expressed everything we would have loved to have done if only we were crazy enough, but at the same time there was a hint of fear in our laughter as well.

Lyle never looked at us. As if this was solely between him and the goods his grandfather had bought for him. Yet in reality his psyche needed this one last magnificent gesture to mask his loss of face and to make him appear larger than we were. Finally he turned, walked down the hall and out the door. None of us ever saw him again. A year later, a rumor spread around campus that he was working on a banana boat, but none of us really believed it.

This was the way it was at engineering school in the late Fifties. 3,000 guys isolated in thirty below weather. RPI was officially co-ed but (except for one professor's daughter who lived at home) girls didn't apply and they weren't encouraged. There were no dorms for them. The girls were at the colleges around us, Russell Sage, Skidmore, Bennington, or even Vassar and Smith if you wanted to drive a little farther. On the weekends the roads to these schools were like icy demolition derbies. Most of the girls had to be in at eleven during the week and one o'clock on the weekends. The curfews were designed to keep the young women safe, but they actually had the reverse effect, a mad car race at the last moment, everyone drunk out of their minds, careening down the dark, narrow roads, often sliding on ice or fishtailing through a blizzard, stopping to pick up friends and their dates who were drinking from bottles of hooch beside their wrecked cars.

Once, in May, I spent an evening drinking with my pal Lori Blank. [Lori has now worked at El Al (Israeli Airlines) for twenty-five years, is married to renowned jazz saxophonist Charles Davis, and is famous among the African-American jazz musicians of New York for her annual Passover *Seder*. The great jazz pianist Cedar Walton attends the *Seder* but he calls it "a Cedar."] We staggered into her dorm at Skidmore just in time, but the dorm mother, on loan from an Edith Wharton novel, docked Lori anyhow, having it in for her because she was dating Little David, an articulate, young, black, R&B singer we all liked who wore a cape and performed in the red light district in Albany. The dorm mother marched her up to her room, leaving me steaming downstairs until I realized she had left the lounge unguarded. I had a "brilliant" drunken image of revenge: I hoisted a brand new modern easy chair over my head, carried it outside and sat in it at the curb. It seemed like a good idea at the time. I remember lolling there in the clear spring air looking up at the nearby stars. When a friend came by in a convertible, we set the chair in the back and drove it home. The next morning I regretted it, but what I was to do? To protect Lori I was forced to keep it and to take it with me to my various apartments around the country for decades.

When I first came to Troy, I drank on weekends, thrilled at the chance to be out on my own in a funky locale. I loved Troy. It was dying. It had once been like another planet, outside the gravity of New York City. I loved the fact that it had its own defunct opera house. My roommate Harvey Braun and I would go out each Friday night to River Street along the Hudson River in the old warehouse area. The bars here were attended by the more adventurous students as well as locals and sported a few bar whores to add romance.

We especially liked one bar which featured a musician called Tony Madonia. Tony was a short Italian sax player with a funky, white rock and roll band that played all the old grungy favorites, songs like "Honky Tonk," the national anthem of dives. Harv and I would each drink fifteen vodka and tonics at fifty cents apiece. Then, toward end of the evening, Tony Madonia, short, hairy, apelike, with thick stubby arms, would leap up into the air, grab the rafter and he would hang by one arm like a chimpanzee while playing "Night Train" on his sax, swinging there, honking, above us. This was the craziest thing we'd ever seen. We told our friends. We would all go every week, get completely drunk and then, as the time approached, we would shout, "Hang from the ceiling, Tony Baby!" and up he would go, into the rafters, as everyone cheered wildly and ordered more drinks.

We didn't treat the locals like they were completely human, but the "urchins," as we called them, weren't very courteous to us either, always ready to jump you on a dark empty street and bash your head against the cobblestones. They knew we were leaving for a different world, and that any of their local girls who could catch a ride would join us. The best and most likely catch for a female urchin was a member of the Spanish-speaking fraternity whose downtown house was the site of continuous conga drumming and frequent all-night wild parties thrown by the brothers, the sons of rich Latin American families who took the easiest major, industrial engineering, and drove the girls around in Porsches and Maseratis, and sometimes married their favorite and took her back to the mansion in Paraguay or Nicaragua.

Troy was beginning the decline that would lead to a loss of almost half its population of 72,000. Many of the young urchins were bailing out. The rest, who were settled in Troy or incapable of leaving, stayed behind, watching the shirt factories going south, the steel mill closing, even the huge Fitzgerald Beer plant on River Street being ultimately victimized. Their legendary factory water fountains had dispensed free beer. The employees, who spoke in a kind of drunken gargling, crawled out of the plant at the end of each day to the taverns where they could continue with small glasses of beer and ale called "dimies." (All the local bars served Fitzgerald on tap. The city government saw to that.)

After a while we left the college bars and moved up to drinking dimies with the Fitzgerald employees and the milkmen who came early in the afternoon and got wasted before dinner.

It didn't help matters that in the spring of our fourth semester we entered the world of modern physics. This was a disaster for my hopes of finding a clear, secure, intellectual world through science. We knew nothing of science history. We had been given the laws of Newton as if they were the laws of Moses, passed down on stone tablets from God to some old guy centuries ago. Everything we learned was based on these laws. We would learn some of Newton's calculus on Friday and then apply this new knowledge to Newton's physics on Monday. All the classes were coordinated that way. We used to say we hated Newton, but this was like hating your supportive but demanding father.

Then Einstein appeared. And Bohr. And Heisenberg. Suddenly we had lost our innocence and entered history. We realized finally that what we were studying was a changing model of the universe devised by fallible men. Even Newton wasn't perfect. Then I found out (we were never taught this) that half of Newton's writings were in astrology and numerology and such. In our classes on relativity we followed Einstein's path, going along the route of the same mind-experiments and mathematical equations that he did. Suddenly we were in an Alice in Wonderland world of slowing clocks and shrinking space ships in which people who left Earth and returned a century later had only aged ten years. And it got worse. We followed Neils Bohr as he was forced to come up with the idea of quantum mechanics to "explain" paradoxical phenomena. Now we were in a universe of probabilities. All that was solid melted into thin air. Then we did the math for Heisenberg's uncertainty. Of course. It made sense when you understood the equations. But what had happened to the rock-hard certainty I was going to use to sharpen my thinking so I could help humanity?

[As a young man Herman Melville had lived on the outskirts of Troy but this was never mentioned in our four years at RPI.]

20

The scientific picture continued to become bleaker. We studied the structure of the atom, Rutherford and Thompson and those other killers. It turned out that matter was a few bits of almost mass-less particles in a vast sea of empty space. Then Einstein showed us that light had the qualities of particles, photons they called them. And then, for me, the worst: DeBroglie appeared with his notion of matter having a wave-like nature. I took all this personally. I would hit my desk as I studied, exclaiming, "This is a wave?"

I waited tables and refereed basketball games to pick up a few bucks, but mostly my parents paid the bills, and it turned out that they had spent thousands of dollars to shatter whatever stability my worldview had once had. In some way I was worse off than I had been in The Bronx. Now I didn't even have my dream that science would provide the supportive answers I could use to adjudicate arguments between people and make peace among nations.

By the third year I had to admit that engineering wasn't for me. Once I learned how a TV was designed, I was no longer impelled to learn how the material world worked. If you were to be any good at this, you couldn't just cram for an exam here, memorize an equation there. You had to integrate all the knowledge. You had to care. And I didn't. Formulas and mathematics weren't even going to approach the dangerous rapids of my anxiety and help me to attack my sense of meaninglessness.

MY BEAT FRIEND

I had grown up with a friend, Marty Licker, who was a year older than I. Marty had taken another path. He'd transformed himself into a proto-beat. The role model flameout. That was the way rebels often proceeded in the Fifties. Montgomery Clift as Prewitt in *From Here to Eternity*, Marlon Brando in *The Wild One*, James Dean in *Rebel Without a Cause*, Chet Baker in an Italian jail. To rebel was to be infinitely lonely because there was too great a chasm between hip and conformity. Yet most of the rebels couldn't completely let go of their World War II loyalties to a dream version of America. You didn't have to punish them. They would do it to themselves.

Often the person who was going to succeed in changing his life was challenged and driven out there by a self-destructive friend who acted like

21

the "rabbit" in a track meet, the guy who goes all out and burns out fast but gets you moving more quickly as you are forced to struggle to keep up with his pace—Kerouac had Neil Cassady; in Kerouac's *On the Road*, Sal Paradise had Dean Moriarity; Verlaine had Rimbaud; Lenin had his older brother Alexander who plotted to kill the tsar and got himself executed; all the jazz musicians followed Charlie Parker while the comedians had Lenny Bruce-- the guys that drove too fast and attracted the chicks and the cops. Even Jesus had John the Baptist.

Marty joined the Marines after seeing *From Here to Eternity.* When he finished his tour he moved to the Lower East Side and became a heavy doper. Marty would take any drug in any amount. If you held out a handful of pills to him he would swallow them without asking a question. At the same time he was reading like a madman, all these hip authors I hadn't had the time to read because of my years of studying the assigned subjects— Celine, Nietzsche, Sartre, Gurdjieff, Ouspensky, Freud, Jung, Wilhelm Reich—and some others that I had read a little of on my own—Alan Watts, Kerouac, Camus, D.T. Suzuki. Marty had opted out sometime in high school. I had been studying for years and getting top grades; I had had few dates as a teenager because I was shy and I was determined to focus on a proper education and to attend a good university. But how had it come about that my ne'er-do-well friend Marty who never did what he was supposed to, who was considered by all the adults on our block as a failure and crackpot, who attempted yoga *asanas* on the sidewalk of our block and got beat up for it, who brought a chess set into the local Irish Bar and was lifted up by the patrons and literally vaulted into the street, who was always stoned and perhaps actually crazy, that Marty seemed to know more about the actual meaning of things—the deep, subjective, personal, essential inner and spiritual aspects of life—than I did.

And time was dripping away. Because everyone seemed to agree that these were the best years of our lives, the years we would talk about until we died, when we became mature adults like our parents, and had "selfish kids" like me, and worked seventy hours a week and worried the rest of the time.

I had no sense of a successful American adult life after college. For example, how could I find Miss Right at a corporation, when I couldn't even come close to locating her among the thousands of smart women in the colleges that surrounded us? I had no idea that it was I who was preventing Princess Charming from materializing. How could she appear when I was changing so quickly and was so unhappy with who I was? When I did meet a woman who liked me, I became frightened by dreams of home and family and drank myself unconscious. And when I met a woman that I liked, why would she like me? I was ignorant, untutored, uncouth, acne-driven, and out of control. I found one girl I liked who fit my fantasy exactly: Kathy, an actress at Bennington, a blond, intelligent, pretty girl, a Jewish doctor's daughter with a swimming pool inside her house in a classy town in New Jersey. And she liked me, as did most of the girls who could see I meant well but who kept a certain distance because I was drowning in my own suffering and splashing it on everyone who came near. So finally Kathy asked a friend to tell me she didn't want to see me anymore. Of course, she was right. How could I compete with the guys from Yale with the guitars and the guys from Williams with the sports cars and the expensive crew neck sweaters? Two years after graduation Kathy dropped her Jewish surname for an Irish one, and was playing a featured role in a drama on Broadway.

I began to date less and to drink more. Somehow I fancied myself like my idol, Charlie Parker. I would burn out gloriously like summer fireworks and die at thirty-four like Bird. I began to buy half gallons of Gallo Port and to drink them in my room listening to Bird with strings while everyone else partied in the fraternity living room. Then I would adjourn to the upper bunk and vomit down into my roommate Harvey's shoes.

> *"The one sin of which a Tarahumara Indian is conscious of is that of not having danced enough."*
> Jessie Weston

It was maddening to think that the end of my free life was approaching. That's the way it felt. I was drinking because that was the only way I might get out of my ordinary panicked consciousness from which I kept watching myself fall further behind in my understanding of the courses. The house of cards of my life-saving career was becoming unstable. I studied not to retain or understand but to learn by rote from Dave Friedman and pass the exam, and then drank to rocket out of my troubled mind. I didn't know that

I was yearning for ecstasy, to be catapulted out of my frenzied ego (from the Greek *ecstasis*: to be out of place, outside the normal self), even though sometimes I could almost achieve it, especially when we hired black R&B bands from the red light district in Albany to play at the house.

This was one of the real achievements of my friends and I, and I am proud of it still. When I arrived at Rensselaer I was astonished to find that colleges were still under the sway of a 1920s white sensibility. I had gone to DeWitt Clinton High School with kids from Harlem who were inventing Rhythm and Blues every day, singing in the school bathrooms and then on the dark street corners at night. Marty Licker and I listened to Allen Freed religiously on WINS. We knew all about the late and great Johnny Ace, and Robert and Johnny, and "Mr. Earl," and "Smoke from Your Cigarette," by Lillian Leach and the Mellows, still one of the all-time unknown greats. Our entire school, white and black, was crazy about this music. Frankie Lyman went to school right across the narrow Harlem River from my house. When Elvis Presley appeared and all the white kids went wild over him, I saw this from the same acute angle as Alice Walker. He wasn't a true musician who put the music first. He was packaging black music for white kids, covering black numbers. Success was his muse and it served him well. For a while.

Since I'd been sixteen, I trailed Marty to Birdland and Basin Street, the big jazz clubs around Times Square, to see Miles, and Coltrane, and Stan Kenton's Big Band blowing the roof off little Birdland with its low ceiling. Once, standing near the bar at Basin Street to see Duke Ellington's band, we watched as a rotund black man made his way through the crowd, and Marty said to him as he passed, "Whatta say Bill?" and he gave Marty a quick, wide, generous smile, and I said to Marty "Who was that?" and Marty said, "That's Count Basie," and I said, "You called him Bill," and he replied, as if it were obvious, "All his friends call him Bill! I read it in *Downbeat*."

At the fraternity, I found that we had an entertainment budget. We could hire bands to play in our own house. Yet whom did we hire? College kids playing white Dixieland. All the fraternities did this. Or, on some weekends there would be no band and guys would play bridge with their dates and then gather around the piano in their white college sweaters and sing slightly risqué ancient college songs. How could this be? This was so uncool. It threatened what little positive identity I had built up. And it ignored the one source I had found for beauty and honest feeling.

My friends and I and our pal Lori began to hire black bands from Green Street in Albany for all-night dance parties. And amazingly, the bands liked to come to our house. They would bring their friends. They wanted to be part of the college scene and to be accepted like anybody else, even if it was just drunken white fraternity guys living out their few years of rebellion.

The bands would bring half their neighborhood with maracas and other rhythm instruments, and when they would play "Fever" and you were completely drunk with that sweet Gallo port in your belly, and you swayed to the music with a sweating, happy girl up against you, a sweet cinnamon scent wafting off her hair, you knew you were finally happy too, and since you knew it couldn't last, that you were dripping time, you were also sadder than you had ever been.

Once I got drunk with the Trinidad Steel Band, and they tied a big steel drum to me and taught me a few licks, and I appeared on stage with them to the amazement of the audience. On a Sunday afternoon I saw Dizzy Gillespie in concert at the Armory and the word spread that Coleman Hawkins was playing at a roadside dive in Schenectady, so we drove up there and Dizzy showed up as well, and we begged him to sit in and he finally did, but on drums. America had forgotten Coleman Hawkins in the Fifties, but we hadn't. At a Dakota Staton concert at the Armory (with Sahib Shahab on alto), I went to the men's room and there was a guy in there taking a shower in a tuxedo. This became the fashion. My friend Al Skopp bought a tuxedo for twenty-five cents at the Salvation Army. At every party he would get drunk, shower in his tux, and then go outside and sleep in a tree.

We had no drugs. We had to use rough alcohol. But because of the incredibly difficult workload, the pressure of grades and time, we struggled to force moments of tender feeling and humor and desperate beauty while we still had a chance, for who could imagine a father or mother of a family, a respectable engineer or housewife in the Fifties going for the moon, for ecstasy, rocketing out of their cotton-picking minds without completely wrecking their lives and destroying themselves.

Even Charlie Parker had destroyed himself. I loved the legendary stories about Bird. How he died at thirty-four but the doctor thought he was sixty-eight because he never slept. How he was dying of whiskey, beer, speed, heroin, rot-gut wine, twenty other kinds of abuse, and at the end, when he was vomiting up blood while lying on the bed of the jazz baroness Nica Van Koenigswater, her society doctor came in to examine him and said, "Do you drink, Mr. Parker?" and Bird replied casually, "Oh, now and then a sherry before dinner."

My friend Lori Blank was in love with my pal Tom Baruch, our Marlon Brando, with the dark hair and the unpredictable leaps off the house roof into the snow, once landing between two cops who had dragged a brother home after he had been caught pissing off a three story billboard into downtown Troy. Lori turned me on to the other Parker I loved, Dorothy, half-Jewish, also a drunk; she had tried to kill herself a couple times. That was the way to go. What was the difference? Life was meaningless. I was ready to hand back my ticket.

As we approached the end of the four year college carnival, the merry-go-round began to spin too fast. Pieces sliced off in deadly tangents. The Delta Tau Delta fraternity crossed over the line. Our house continued to attempt to be the best students, the best athletes, the best party givers. "To have it all!" But the Delts! They drank every day. The whole fraternity. They began to throw strange destructive parties in which they would all vomit and wreck their house. That was the theme of the party. To smash through the walls of their empty lives. With chairs, tables, what ever was at hand. Finally, their house became a dangerous shell as the structure was revealed and proved to be vulnerable as well. The college had to close the fraternity down and disperse the students.

THE WOODCHUCK

Dave Friedman and I and my other roommates, Tom and Big Harv, began to drink at the Woodchuck, the toughest bar in Troy. No college guys showed up here. Located in the decrepit part of town, it stood next to an ancient wino movie theater that showed reruns of movies in which would-be Tab Hunters played to an audience of would-be Peter Lorres. The Woodchuck was owned by the Five DeBonis Brothers. They stood behind the bar like fire hydrants in aprons, T-shirts over their big hairy arms, ready to stomp anyone who went out of bounds. But where were the bounds? It was difficult to tell. The waitresses seemed to have come from West Virginia, with missing teeth and chipped lives. The juke box would blast "You Cheated" by the Shields, and the dance floor would be filled by low-slung, pear-shaped alcoholics with glazed eyes and hanging bellies and lolling tongues who would rub their crotches against each other while emitting strange grunts.

Of course we loved the place. I can't say they loved us. Once, my roommate Big Harv, my pal from the Bronx, was crazily going into the alley to fight a tough drunken urchin who had challenged him, a guy who had nothing to loose except his few remaining teeth and probably the knife he carried, but somehow I managed to break it up. (Big Harv went on to be a director of Deloitte-Touche.) Another roommate, Tom, would get drunk at the Woodchuck and then take his bullet-nose little Chevy on country roads at night and knock down mailboxes, one by one, smash one, back up, floor it, smash another, back up, floor it, etc. Once he ran full speed into a telephone pole and was almost killed. (Today he sits on fifteen corporate boards of directors.)

A couple younger guys joined our fraternity and began to follow us around and emulate us. Mike Herman was always drunk, day after day. I thought he was a goner. I didn't know he would become a multi-millionaire, then president of the Kansas City Royals baseball team, bring them to profitability in the interests of the charity which received the money, and then give a million bucks to RPI who awarded him an honorary doctorate and let him make the graduation speech. Another was his buddy, my "little brother" in the fraternity, Jim Saunt, who would be thrown out of the fraternity and the college. (How can you get thrown out of a fraternity?) He went on to become a junkie and was arrested for shooting up heroin in the men's room at Macy's.

A third younger guy in the fraternity was Eddie Murrell, a quiet African-American who was tall and thin and swift as a deer. When our football team was in trouble I would split him out to the right and tell him to run down field as fast as possible. I would throw the ball as high and far as I could and somehow he would run under it. Eddie gave up engineering not long after graduation, taught school in a black neighborhood, and wound up living and meditating in a house in the woods in northern California with his dog.

My southern pal, a "lady's man," Jerry Ellisberg took some extra time to graduate but not for lack of trying. One night he dressed in black, took a flashlight and broke into the Metallurgy Department office but he couldn't find the next day's exams. After he graduated he went on to be set up by the cops and arrested for selling pot in New Orleans, a serious offense at the time, but luckily his father was able to pay off someone and the evidence disappeared. Then he became a professional gambler in Charleston, South Carolina until he was shot in the head. This quieted him down a bit. He took over the family department store in Raleigh, but was arrested for running a gambling operation in his home. He proudly sent me the front page of the Raleigh *News and Observer* which headlined "Local Clothier Arrested" and quoted him as saying, "The day that a respectable businessman can't have a toy roulette wheel in his home, I might as well be living in Russia." (The scene in *Blues for a Dying Nation* in Charleston is based on a visit to him.)

My pal Dave Freidman continued to teach me the material the night before an exam. Once we aced a Dynamics test in the morning after an all-night cram, drank our lunch at the Woodchuck, and then returned completely drunk for a Thermodynamics lab. Our third partner was my pal Walt Towslee, a member of the Christian fraternity I had wanted to join. Walt was also a drinker. He was famous for having found a way to get free ice for parties. There was a huge free-standing ice machine the size of a small truck off Hoosick Street. Walt would put in a quarter, and when a bag of ice cubes slid down, he would hold open the door, climb up the chute completely into the ice machine, and pass down all the other bags. One day though, he did this when already too drunk and he allowed the door to close behind him. What were we to do? Walt was drunk and trapped in an ice machine? He tried to open the door from the inside but in the darkness he couldn't make any headway. We had visions of Walt freezing to death until my pal Dave, with a stroke of his usual genius, saw the solution. He put a quarter into the machine, the door opened, and Walt came sliding down the chute.

In the Thermodynamics lab, I drunkenly kicked a large engine which wouldn't function properly, breaking off a large piece of it. I panicked, jumped out the window, ran frantically across a field to the Student Union, dashed up the stairs, scurried into the lounge, and to the amazement of the students studying quietly on the rug or chairs, I flashed across the room, leaped over the top of a sofa and hid between the couch and the wall for twenty minutes, afraid the instructor might be chasing me. I avoided the lab for two weeks but I finally got back into the class by making up a story that my grandmother had died and I had become addicted to diet pills in my grief.

> *"Emotional disturbance, then, is to be valued not for itself, but because it is the only way to break through the culturally inherited orientations which screen us from reality."*
>
> Morse Peckham

Dave Friedman was going over the line. He declared war on his head. If ever he couldn't understand some equations the first time through, he would begin to punch himself left right left right on the noggin. You could hear the sounds of his poor head all over the library, Bonk, Bonk Bonk. He kept trying to accomplish greater intellectual feats. Perhaps to surpass his dead father who had been a Ph.D. in Chemistry from Harvard where he had roomed with Harold Land. Family legend had it that Dave's father had invented the Polaroid camera, not Land. Dave hadn't yet learned the lesson that all novelists know—it is impossible to compete with the dead. Our imaginations can hang any clothes we want in their closets.

Dave began to make a public event of his studying for big exams. He vied to become a virtuoso of cramming, a toreador of the test. He would not read the material until the night before. Dave would lock himself in his room, read each page once, then tear it out of the book and pass it under the door where we would put it in the fireplace.

He was determined to be special. Not just the smartest, but also a cool, daring, wild guy. He was not the stereotypical tech nerd but he was as big as I was, about six feet, 175 pounds, and he was strong. He didn't play team sports, but he was an excellent golfer and had famously strong legs. He did wear thick glasses and had wild, unfocused, eyes which signaled that he might do anything at any moment.

Once when we were in the Woodchuck I came out of the men's room and saw a sight that terrified me. Dave was playing for money on the disc-bowling machine with "The Dummy." The Dummy! The toughest guy in Troy. Even the DeBonis brothers didn't mess with him. His strength and viciousness were legendary. We all stayed away from him and never met his eyes. It would be like meeting Sonny Liston drunk and in a bad mood in a rowdy dive. You kept your distance and kept saying to yourself, "I'm in another dimension, he can't see me, I'm not really here."

Now Dave, very drunk, was bowling The Dummy for money. I wanted to leave, but Dave was my friend. Not to mention my ticket out of college. I had to stay. I approached the machine. The game was tight. Dave had the last shot. He had to make a spare to win. I was praying, "Please, God, don't let him make it."

Dave missed. I was thanking God as I began to breathe again. The Dummy reached for the money. And then, Dave screamed out, "Motherfucker" and leaped up onto the machine and threw himself down the waxed alley, head first, crashing into the pins.

For a second there was stillness. This was so far beyond the realm of possibility that no one could believe it. Then a riot broke out, in the confused way riots grow at boxing weigh-ins. The Dummy (thank you God!) didn't join in. He was picking up his money. The DeBonis brothers and several other human tanks stalked toward Dave. Melees erupted all around. I saw my life going down the drain with the spilled beer. I stepped in front of Dave and faced the mob and began to talk. I didn't know what I was saying but I talked as fast as I could. "Listen, this is crazy, right? And this guy here he's off his rocker, but he's not a bad guy, he's just a little nuts you see, anyone can see that, he's a little nuts, but his mother loves him and he does crazy things, but there's no reason to kill him, he's a good guy actually, and I know how you feel (I grabbed Dave with my arm behind me and shoved him towards the door) "and you see he's the kind of guy that'll do crazy things sometimes, but as far as things go in the long run . . ." Somehow this crazy torrent of words seemed to stop them like a fire hose. They had never seen anyone who could talk this fast and improvise in this way. I was amazed. And after all, we were now harmless, but there were fights breaking out all around us that the DeBonises needed to stop, so while they were distracted I flew out the door after Dave and we were saved again.

I knew that Dave was the kind of guy who might actually have charged the DeBonises in that situation. That had been my real fear. Once, several years later, in Plainfield, New Jersey, right after the deadly race riots there in the Sixties, Dave went into an off-sale bar in the ghetto to buy a six pack while I waited, double-parked outside. He came running out carrying the beer and laughing like crazy with this wild look in his eyes. "Rosie, listen, you gotta hear what happened." He continued to cackle as he envisioned it. "Listen, the bar was crowded. It was nuts. I was the only white person there. Then this black man on a barstool, he says to me in a crazy drunken voice, 'Am I in your way?' 'No,' I said, 'you're OK.' So he says, 'No, I means it. If I'm in your way, **knock me down!**' So I looked at him, Rosie, and I knew he meant it, you know what I mean? I could tell he was a good guy, he was as drunk as I was, you know what I mean? We were on the same wavelength."

"So what did you do?" I said, already knowing the answer.

Dave roared with laughter, his eyes tearing, and he said, "Rosie, I knocked him down! I pushed him over with his tall barstool and all. I knocked him down, on the floor, Rosie." Dave continued to laugh like a maniac.

"What happened!?"

"I don't know. Suddenly, the whole bar was still and the guy was on the floor kind of under the bar, and then, Rosie, listen, he started laughing. We both started laughing. The whole bar started laughing. Rosie, it was the funniest thing any of us had ever seen," and Dave just sat there with a huge smile on his face, thinking about this amazing event, pleased with one more amazing success in the exam of life.

Dave continued to get straight As at school, but most of his skewed actions still involved his head. Once at a party of a Christian fraternity we all liked, with music furnished by a band of older guys who came up there for every big weekend, "Joe Assito and his Jersey City Stompers," a working class band that looked exactly like an older version of Leo Gorcey and the Dead End Kids, a band that was not just liked, but revered, (especially for their rendition of "Your lips tell me no no, but there's *oui oui* in your eyes,") Dave thought it would be hilarious to slide across the floor and have his head go through the bass drum. Fortunately, he miscalculated and he only knocked the drum over. Again a scuffle ensued and I stepped forward to protect him; in some ways the drunken fraternity brothers were almost as dangerous as the DeBonises, they were murderously furious.

The Jersey City Stompers were their sacred tie to the street guy self-image they were bargaining away for success. I pushed Dave toward an open window, hissing "Jump!" and Dave, looking confused (What happened? I thought this would be so funny and everyone would love me.) leaped out, as I held off the brothers (my pals) with the same kind of crazy talk I had used at the Woodchuck. Fortunately Barbara Dingman, the drunkest of the three Dingman sisters, everyone's favorite residents of Troy, took a header right down the huge *Gone With The Wind* main staircase behind us. Everyone ran over to see if she was still alive and Dave survived again.

Dave came up with one last trick to punish his head. He worked out a routine where at every party the drummer would give a drum roll, calling people to gather round and Dave would announce he was going to kick a field goal. I would kneel and hold an imaginary football while he would approach and "kick" it, throwing himself forward and up in the air with his strong legs until he was completely horizontal and then he would come crashing down flat on his back, the rear of his head smashing against the hard floor. To gasps from the audience, he would rise, dazed, his eyes unfocused, but with a little smile on his face. Once again he had proven that he wasn't just a genius. He was the life of the party.

Dave went on, as I expected, to use his scientific and mathematical abilities to do breakthrough work in computer-aided design. He was one of the three founders of a Fortune 500 company, based on his ideas, worth billions of dollars. He donated much of his money and his valuable consultation time to the Technion, the premier science and technical university in Israel.

[In his senior year, Dave married Davi, a childhood family friend from Binghamton, New York. Shortly after I met Davi she introduced me to her mother. Her mother said, "Are you a friend of my daughter?" "Yes." She indicated Davi who looked fearful and said, "Why would you want to be friends with a person like that?" I quickly replied, "Davi is my friend and she'll always be my friend." My prediction proved correct. Not long after this, Davi's mother died. Her father married Dave's widowed mother. So they became Dave'n Davi, husband and wife, and brother and sister. They are still together after 45 years.]

A SECOND CHANCE

> *"Limits*
>
> > *Are what any of us*
> > *are inside of."*
>
> Charles Olson

Somehow we proceeded towards graduation. My father bought me an old clunker car. The transmission dropped. The car would only go in reverse. I drove it into the junkyard backwards. The owner said, "You got a problem?" It seemed like a metaphor for my life.

One of my fraternity brothers, "Tulip" Greenberg, had an old Nash Rambler that died. He parked it on the lawn, inserted a steel bar, and used it as a closet. I didn't have enough clothes to need another closet. I hardly noticed what I wore.

I liked the elective subjects. We were allowed one per semester. I took "Music Appreciation." The course struck fear in me. I knew nothing about classical music. But when the professor began with Bach I knew I was going to be OK. It sounded like Dave Brubeck. Without knowing it, I had been prepared for counterpoint and fugues by Brubeck and Paul Desmond. And Gil Evans had set me up for Prokofiev and Shostakovich. And Monk, Eric Dolphy and Ornette Coleman for anything else that might appear. I had learned the history of music backwards. Once again driving in reverse.

Next semester Dave and I took "Directions in the Contemporary Arts" as our free elective. Again, I had little background, but the works we studied fascinated me: T.S. Eliot, James Joyce, the Surrealists, atonal music. I was nothing if not contemporary.

> *"Outlook is proportional to insight."*
>
> Arthur Koestler

As I became less moored and more frightened about my future, I saw my success dreams dissolving. My pal Lori Blank from Skidmore was also lost. We commiserated drunkenly with each other. The only viable career path we could envision for ourselves was to become Raelettes and sing back-up to Ray Charles.

I was living in purgatory and time was running out. What was I to do to save my crazy life? I talked nonstop to anyone who would listen, trying to reassure myself that I would be fine. I drank more seriously, sometimes operating just this side of a stupor. One night after midnight, after leaving Yezzi's, a madhouse bar in Albany where I had seen a couple making out in a urinal, I ran away from my friends and hid in a dark house that happened to have an unlocked front door. I entered the living room and crouched down behind the couch, laughing to myself, "Ha Ha, they'll never find me here." The next day I realized I could have been shot.

After a party at the fraternity, alone in the basement party room, I watched myself throw a glass through the mirror behind the bar. I felt no emotion as the mirror fragments cascaded down. It was as if someone else had done it.

Late one night after another party I had an idea that it would be funny if I turned all the furniture in the fraternity dining room upside down and made it look as if someone had wrecked the place. The next day I had forgotten about this when I went over to breakfast and was surprised to find a commotion. It seems someone had wrecked the dining room.

Once our fraternity cook, Earl, told me that I had skied down the back staircase into the kitchen with a salad bowl on my head, but I could hardly remember it, and it seemed implausible since the staircase was circular and I couldn't ski.

Finally my old pal Big Harv saved the day. Harv and I had roomed together for four years joined by various other friends for a semester here and there. We had met at DeWitt Clinton High School in the Bronx and decided to go away to college together and we've been pals ever since.

Harv was the strongest guy I knew. He had almost won a garbage can lifting contest with Tommy Magliario, a mook and one of the toughest guys at Clinton. At the fraternity he had held the top of the main staircase for ten minutes against seven guys trying to rush him. Harv was also the funniest. Whenever he was nervous about an upcoming exam he would regale us with stories of his family in The Bronx. About his grandmother Rose Simutitsky who came here from Europe and changed her name to Rose Levine. "Why **Levine**?" Harvey would say. "That's what mystifies me." And he claimed his talent for football was genetic. "My Grandmother had a brother who was an All-American," he declared. "Red Grange Simutitsky."

Harv was having his own problems trying to envision a future for himself in Metallurgy, his major, and it was affecting his behavior. He was in love with Sue, who went to school at Brandeis. (They've been married now for 45 years.) One big weekend in our senior year, as he was waiting for Sue to arrive from Massachusetts, he drank a half gallon of red wine in two hours on a Friday afternoon while playing a tee square as if it were a saxophone to Lionel Hampton's "Flying Home." When Sue arrived, he was unconscious.

Harv had a favorite, rare, make-out record he cherished: Jeri Southern. He claimed this record made him irresistible and was the key to his success with women. While Sue was far away, he hung around with a nurse from Albany State named Karen Burke, a hard-drinking, fun-loving, big, earthy, wild girl, incredibly the daughter of a teacher at a high-class prep school. Karen continued to resist his advances, wouldn't go "all the way," so finally Harv played his ace; he took Karen to the dark dance room next to the fraternity bar and put his Jeri Southern record on the phonograph. It skipped immediately. He moved it to the second and third cuts. It continued to skip.

Karen had been frustrating him, and now this. Big Harv flipped. He lifted the record over his head and smashed it. He continued to smash and mangle all the pieces while Karen looked on, scared to see this generally good-natured, big Teddy-bear of a man enraged and out of control. She had seen him sometimes when in his cups march around singing "The Teddy Bears' Picnic," emphasizing the beat and knocking over any of the brothers in his path, and she had heard about the football game where an obnoxious guy on the other team had infuriated him by kidding him unrelentingly about his size until, blocking for me on a running play, Harv had run right over the guy who somehow broke his leg, but Harv was usually self-deprecatory and funny.

Finally Harv calmed down and set another record on the phonograph. It began to skip. It was the phonograph that was broken, not Harv's rare record which he had needlessly destroyed. Karen looked at his hapless expression and began to laugh. Harv had to smile a bit, but he floated off by himself for a while. Karen adjourned to the bar, as was her wont. Later, when I happened to wander outside, I saw her high in a tree, upside-down, hanging by the back of her knees like a trapeze artist. No one could talk her down. Until she fell headfirst into a concrete birdbath, completely demolishing it and tearing her dress off. She flipped her dress over her shoulder and ran off doing cartwheels down the dark street. We who were present (Harv wasn't there) watched her disappear in the distance. She would calm down and come back soon. After all, she didn't know the area and her dress was torn off.

It turned out this wasn't the case. After a couple hours we realized she had never returned. Harv and I drove slowly down the deserted residential street looking for her in the shadows. A few blocks away we reached a fraternity, lit up, a party going on inside. Bill Anderson, my friend from Computer Design class, came out of the house.

"Have you seen a blonde girl, big, by herself?" I asked.

He smiled. "A really drunk girl with a bruise on her head and her whole dress torn off?"

I nodded.

"She's down at the bar. Don't worry," he laughed, "she's having a great time."

GRAD SCHOOL

"Buying is much more American than thinking."

Andy Warhol

It was Big Harv who saved me by coming up with a way for us to proceed with our lives. He decided to go for a master's degree in Industrial Engineering.

"Is that possible?" I asked.

"Yeah. They love guys like us because they're turning to Operations Research and statistics and we can do the math."

Harv was from the North Bronx, a private house. His family had more money than mine did. But if I could swing the extra expense, this might be my ticket back to life. I wasn't interested in Industrial

36

Engineering. I was finished with engineering, but why not apply to the Wharton School of Business at the University of Pennsylvania? Wasn't that supposed to be the best? I would apply for grants and loans, as much as I could get, and study like crazy to win more, but I would still need some help from my family. I knew if I could convince my mother, she would convince my father. They would come through. They always had in difficult situations. My mother would sense I was in trouble. And my father was the world's champion of deferred gratification. He would understand if I put off being independent for two years to open up a wider and more lucrative career. He was like the hero of Kafka's "The Hunger Artist," who was so good at fasting because he had never found a food he liked.

My mother argued my case and finally my father agreed. I applied to Wharton for an MBA. It would be worth a lot more than just the EE degree alone.

"We see only what we are ready to see."

Jean Martin Charcot

What the hell, I thought. Life was meaningless. Cream of nowhere. Now I was certain of it. You had your few years in the sun or the rain and then you were finished. Back to the black Void. I had learned this as a side effect of studying science in college. The only wise choice was to make a good amount of money to lessen the pain and then buy good seats for the symphony.

I certainly didn't think of religion as a possible source of meaning. Religion to me meant Judaism. My late grandfather and his pals from the old country mumbling in an ancient language I didn't understand at their storefront synagogue in their old clothes and beards and prayer shawls, the women in a special section over on the side. Religion for me couldn't mean Catholicism, the faith of the other, more outgoing residents of our neighborhood. By my lights the Catholics were even crazier than we were. They disliked the Jews, yet they believed a Jewish man was God. They had inherited the Jewish notion of the Messiah without the Jewish tradition of suspicion toward anyone who claimed to be the Messiah. The Catholics! With their pope in Rome who had a direct hot-line to God, and their knives and guns! They feared no one except their priests and their nuns, covered up like Muslim women, gliding along the street like sailboats in a silent movie in black and white.

I couldn't go back to Judaism and The Bronx. At RPI I had progressed from the age of superstition to the age of reason. I had met Jews who owned sports cars and skis. I had dated girls with first names like Hadley and Madison. I had eaten exotic foods like squash and zucchini. No way could I return to the Bronx angle of looking at the world.

And certainly not *shtetl* type culture. I didn't need to see *Fiddler on the Roof*. I had grown up on the roof. Tar Beach we called it in the summer. I avoided popular music that employed fiddles (ditto clarinets or accordions). And where was all the ancient Jewish wisdom when my grandfather died? When the whole family fell apart and my grandmother went catatonic. They had lived above us in the apartment house that my grandfather, an illiterate former baker, co-owned. As soon as my grandfather returned to oblivion, my grandmother collapsed; she had to be cared for by a nurse, and didn't speak for the rest of her short life. And then my mother's unmarried sister, Helen, who lived next door to us, gave up and followed her parents to the grave at thirty-nine. My mother's brother Mac became an alcoholic and philanderer, drinking a quart of scotch a day. And then my father began to crack under the responsibility and to attack people, trying to run them down with his car, attempting to strangle the tenants and running after my uncle Mac with a hammer. It was like living with Mike Tyson. Where was God in all this?

Judaism seemed something out of the past. No one would tell me anything about our family's European heritage; it was the ballast my parents' generation was struggling to release. After my grandfather died, the little Orthodox storefront faded and we switched to one of the large, brick, Conservative synagogues that my parents' generation was building all over the Bronx. We went twice a year, on the High Holidays. It was a matter of form, of silencing the neighbors who would talk against us if we didn't. I remember once asking my mother, "If you could get a really good job by renouncing your Judaism, would you do it?" She thought for a while and then answered, "It depends on the job."

Once my grandparents were gone, my mother, like her friends, stopped making an effort at keeping kosher. Slowly she let ham and

38

bacon in the house and gave up on the two sets of dishes for meat and dairy. Pork was the only obstacle. It was not only religiously forbidden, but worse, it was also potentially unhealthy. There were finely graded distinctions of households depending on their relation to pork. Some never ate it. They were the most prestigious and let everyone know about this often. Some only ate it at restaurants but didn't allow it in their house. They were next highest. Then came people like my family. We let it in the house but only if it had been barbecued by Chinese people. No one that we knew ever actually cooked pork. That would be left to the kids of my generation.

My parents were not highly educated but they were born here. They spoke to their parents in Yiddish and to us in English. My mother's generation changed their names—Esther and Minnie and Dora and Rosie and Fanny became Estelle and Muriel and Doris and Rosalind and Phyllis. Suddenly I was living in a small time Shakespeare Company. They gave their own children, my friends and I, American names at birth. The boys were no longer Abe and Benny and Izzy and Moishe. They became Alan and Barry and Ira and Mark. And the girls were now Arlene, Carol, Marilyn, and Barbara. (One called herself Barbra, but she lived in Brooklyn.)

I loved it at Ha Ya Bungalows when all the men would come up from the city on Wednesday nights, and we kids would sit with them in the dark under the stars outside Irving Siegel's bungalow and have long Talmudic discussions, employing our heritage of thousands of years of textual analysis and debating skill to painstakingly analyze the relative merits of our illustrious centerfielders, Mickey Mantle, Willy Mays, and Duke Snyder. Which one was the greatest? How did one decide? It was a mystery like the stars. A great mystery, never to be solved.

But I got the message. I refused to attend Hebrew school after regular school let out. I was an American. I needed the time to practice stickball in the street so I could play for the Yankees. They were the glamorous beings the adults were interested in. You didn't see any rabbis honored on the plaques in centerfield at Yankee Stadium, the home of champions, which was located down the street from our house.

The Hebrew teachers were the lowest paid and least prestigious men in the neighborhood, especially if they spoke English with accents. We had one in our building. When I fell in the street and broke my arm and he came over to help me up, my mother became convinced that he had broken my arm. There was no talking her out of it even though I denied it and Stanley, the Polish super who had witnessed it, backed me up.

Of course I took a certain pride in my heritage. I was proud of all the famous Jews around the world: Albert Einstein, Milton Berle, Sigmund Freud, Piper Laurie, Leonard Bernstein, Tony Curtis. And I took a kind of reverse pride in coming from uneducated street roots. When my fraternity brother Art Spector visited and said he loved the colorful environment and the friendly informality of our house, I swelled with delight. Art came from Brookline, Massachusetts. He drove a new convertible. His mother was the president of the national Jewish women's organization, B'nai Brith. At his house they had people like Golda Meir over for dinner. We never had anyone over for dinner. Not even my father most of the time. We ate in the kitchen, my mother, my kid brother Mark and myself, home-cooked food like a meal of hamburgers coated with matzo meal and fried, along with three vegetables: mashed potatoes, Franco American spaghetti and Del Monte creamed corn. My mother claimed to serve the freshest canned-food on the block. The only place we ever ate out was at the Horn and Hardart Automat. Or we brought Chinese food into the house on a Sunday night if my father had won his baseball bets—the Won Ton soup, the Chow Mein, the Fried Rice and yes, the Barbecued Pork.

My college friends who had had to define themselves against the ocean of gentiles surrounding them, the Jews who lived in rich suburbs or isolated in small out-of-the-way cities, had kind of a romance around the dream of an idealized Jewish community and were more attached to the notion of a homeland in Israel than some of us who'd actually grown up amidst thousands of poor Jews.

My principal concern was social class. The immigrant German Jews who came here first, the rich Jews from Manhattan with their hot-shot rabbis who affected what they thought was a high class American accent but actually sounded more like Billy Graham, the Jews who dropped the names of fabled hotels in Miami like "The Sans Souci" that we couldn't translate, much less afford to go to.

I never once thought of going back. The Jewish-American novel has a requisite arc—the young Jewish protagonist has his fling, he goes to the Apollo theater, he dates a *shiksa*, he sows his wild oats, but it is required that he return home as a sign of his growing into maturity. He sees where the real values are, the values of tradition, family and community, and he returns to his Jewish roots. (Cf. even rebellious contemporary Jewish novels like *Jew Boy* by Bronx beat writer Alan Kaufman and Allegra Goodman's delightful Jewish-hippie novel, *Paradise Park*.) This wasn't turning out to be my story. My father didn't pay thousands of dollars to RPI so that I could know less about things than the men of his generation. I was wise to what was coming down. Life was a joke. You live, you have a few good times if you're lucky and then you head for oblivion in as dignified a way as possible. There was no old man with a beard in the sky who had a special relationship with our people. We weren't chosen, even though we did well on the College Boards. If we had any doubts about this, Auschwitz put them to rest. Even my parent's generation knew this. The old connection was broken. We were here now for better or worse, in America, facing west.

My Uncle Mac worked in an Army-Navy store and drove a Lincoln. He drank scotch after every sale, came to our house on Sunday nights and sang "Dinah" accompanying himself on the piano using only the black keys, waxed his mustache, wore cologne, and dressed like a Hollywood star. Once he actually traveled to Hollywood riding some crazy dream he couldn't have explicated clearly himself. The closest he got to stardom was on a studio tour when they actually encountered Mickey Rooney on a set. My uncle pulled out a letter from his pocket, announced "Telegram for Mr. Rooney," left the tour and walked over the barrier to Mickey who looked puzzled. My uncle whispered in Mickey Rooney's ear, "It's no telegram, Mickey. I just didn't want you to think that I'm one of those Abners here on the studio tour. I'm no hick. I'm Maxie Berger from the Bronx." Mickey Rooney cracked up. The old show biz pro. You couldn't rattle him. When my uncle asked Mickey for his autograph he signed it: "To Maxie Berger from the Bronx. He's no hick." And he shook my uncle's hand. One of the unforgettable moments of my uncle's life.

My Uncle Mac died at 89, broke, despondent, Prozacked, at the end catatonic. He had begun to pray and to attend synagogue as he aged, but I remember him at the age of 85 singing and playing, "If you like ukulele baby . . ." on the ukulele he had kept with him for 70 years.

41

He could never go back. Vaudeville and the movies were his religions; Georgie Jessel and Clark Gable his rabbis.

And I had traveled further than he had.

WORKERS OF THE WORLD

> *"We are suffering from a metaphysical disease and the cure must therefore be metaphysical."*
>
> E.F. Schumacher

A life whose meaning centered on social idealism, world politics and public affairs was also not an option and never arose for consideration. No one in my neighborhood was a socialist. We weren't middle-class enough. After we had made our millions we would share some, funding a hospital wing or giving to Sister Kenny for the polio cripples, but that wasn't our concern when I was growing up. The last organization we would trust would be a government. We just wanted to avoid starvation, fit in, and have a fair chance somewhere after 2000 years on the road.

And the communists were the worst. They were hated by the real Americans and many commies were Jewish. They gave us a bad name. They stood out like the Hasidim who were also not on our dance card. I understood virtually nothing about these macro theories and their history. I didn't know who Leon Trotsky was, much less that he was Jewish and had lived in the Bronx for a while when he was on the run.

In the sixth grade my teacher, Miss Feingold, was reputed to be a Communist; she was less sensitive to other people than any other teacher I'd ever had, embarrassing me in front of the class so badly that I stopped going to school for a while. I knew that Senator McCarthy was after the commies, that he was having a beef with a rich guy named Alger Hiss who was probably a well-meaning spy, but I never got a handle on the details. We didn't want the commies screwing things up for us. As for McCarthy, anyone could see that he was an asshole and he became the butt of many jokes on the block, everyone doing imitations of him clearing his throat while stuttering, "Uh Uh Mr. Chairman, M M M Mr. Chairman . . . p p p point of order" in his nasal junkie drone.

Most of my fraternity brothers weren't much more politically conscious than I. They were liberals for the most part, especially in the area of civil rights. There was a feeling that we minority Jews should support any other minority that was being stomped. I can't remember hearing much talk of politics in my four years at RPI. Some of the brothers probably watched the news once in a while, and I know some of the younger guys imitated voices from the Yogi Bear TV show but no one watched television regularly. We had more homework than it was possible to do, and we were surrounded by women's colleges with thousands of intelligent young coeds whose parents were hundreds of miles away. Why watch TV?

Our fraternity admitted anyone we liked regardless of racial or religious or ethnic qualifications. If the few black students on campus were shut out of most fraternities, they knew they were welcome at ours. I had become involved in the civil rights struggle in high school when my pal Marty alerted me to the Montgomery Bus Boycott and Rosa Parks. Marty asked me to join him in sending money to Martin Luther King which it was my pleasure to do. But I knew little of world history, nothing about American radicalism or red diaper babies and what little I knew about the political left in America was filtered through Bronx street prejudices that made the radicals seem to me like an impractical group of folk dancers pretending to be Latvians or something. Too Jewish, too European, too white. Way too uncool for those of us who were pretending to be black.

As I waited to hear from Wharton, school continued to unfold in the usual manner. I drank a pint of Southern Comfort and was thrown out of a sold-out hockey game by the police as the crowd cheered, but till this day I have not been able to ascertain what I did. We drove down to Bard College, a quaint school to us, composed of loose women and folk dancers. As with most reports of loose women, there was a small measure of truth to it but my southern pal Jerry Ellisberg was the only one who could find them. This was really his major, not metallurgy, and it would become his life's work.

At Bard Dave Friedman got drunk and dove headfirst through a large hi-fi speaker. A commotion ensued, like a Bobby Knight press conference, and a campus policeman appeared, a kind of "Pop Beloved" guy who was eighty-six years old. Bard only needed a symbolic police presence; they were not that amenable towards the presence of regular cops on campus. The old rent-a-cop had probably never had any real encounters before—folk dancers were generally not a rowdy lot. But suddenly the situation cohered. Everyone stopped pushing and shoving as Dave and "Pop Beloved" squared off against each other, ready to duke it out, each in a kind of ancient John L. Sullivan boxing stance.

I quickly stepped between them to break it up. Dave moved on to something else, his eyes unfocused, probably working out integral calculus equations in his head, but it took me quite a while to calm down the elderly cop. He was like Bob Dole on Viagra looking at Brittany Spears. It was one of the great moments of his golden years and he was in no hurry to let it go.

I took an elective in Abnormal Psychology with my roommate Big Harv. Due to illness, I missed the field trip to a mental hospital in Massachusetts. I asked Harv, "Anyone interesting?"

"Yeah, there was one guy named Henry. Every twenty minutes he would go over and piss against the wall."

"What'd they say about him?

"He was a schizophrenic. But they said that about everyone. To me, it seemed like they were missing out on what he really was. I mean as an individual."

"What was that?"

"A Pissing Henry."

NEARING GRADUATION

>*"I perceive the teachings of the world to be the illusion of magicians."*
>
>   The Buddha

In our junior year we studied the great electromagnetic field equations of James Clerk Maxwell, one of the monuments of the human mind. Some of the courses were interesting enough, but it was like trying to study the language of the Hittites while you were drowning. As seniors we EEs took an interesting course we called ROPS, which considered mathematically the response of actual physical systems involved in electrical design and devices. Electrons could be considered abstractly. They had virtually no mass and seemed almost ethereal, but the actual systems, the wheels and capacitors and such, had inertia and temperature and momentum and in this course we built mathematical models to include these factors. Dave Friedman often averred, "This is so beautiful. Don't you see it?" At times I did, but it was an austere, Antarctic beauty. Nonetheless, one couldn't help but admire the great scientists. We would arrive at the same place they did, puzzle over where to go, and then marvel at their elegant breakthrough solutions, like brilliant, unorthodox moves by a Jose R. Capablanca in a chess championship.

We studied semiconductor theory, the basis of transistors. We were still in the age of the vacuum tube and we learned them from scratch and at length, but we were moving toward the world of transistors, which was mushrooming up around us. We also learned the theory of computers, which I found interesting, the Boolean Algebra on which their logic was based, and how to design a mainframe computer, again starting from scratch. We took theory of metallurgy, electrical machine theory, and a class in feedback control systems which take a small portion of the output of an electrical device and reverse it to negative, sending it back into the input to act as a governor, a delicate and often unstable operation. I was entering an arcane, specialized world that would be of no possible use to me. I felt like thousands of wriggling differential equations were trying to bore themselves into the tender flesh of my brain. I tried to hang in there, watching the mail box for news from Wharton, struggling to concentrate on the head-crackingly difficult material.

"The normal is a tightrope over the abyss of the abnormal."

Witold Gombrowicz

As I look back I am fascinated by the strange knuckle-ball arcs of lives. No one was immune from the spells of madness. I remember two of my friends, Len and Vern, who drove towards Bennington drunk in a convertible, crashed and hurtled through the air. When they got out of the hospital a week later, they began to argue about who had flown the furthest, so they went back to the spot with a tape measure. (Len would soon become Dean of Students at a prestigious university.)

In the spring another freshman Hell Week arrived. I always avoided these ceremonies. When we were freshmen, my friends and I were attracted to Phi

Sigma Delta, in part because they told us that unlike the other fraternities, they had no Hell Week. Then, in the middle of the night, they came for us, dragged us, half asleep, to the fraternity house, and sat us in a dark room with bright lights shining in our faces so we couldn't see the "drill sergeant," an alumnus we didn't know, who sat at a desk in the dark in front of the brothers, and called us "shits" while everyone laughed.

We rebelled. Walked out. Confusion. Almost a couple fist fights. After a night of negotiations, we agreed to return. We pledges decided we would end Hell Week when we became brothers ourselves. The next year I brought this to a vote. Virtually no one joined me. I was astonished. They said, "We went through it, now they can go through it." I made an impassioned speech: "This is like saying, 'We were in the Army, so now they should be in the Army.'" No one agreed. I felt very lonely that night. During the Hell Week, I hung around the pledges, making sure the pranks didn't go too far.

[Now, whenever a group of our old friends get together, everyone looks back fondly on the Hell Weeks, laughing warmly at the insults, the shit calling, the absurd tasks and all-night hazing. I don't object, but I find I still can't join in.]

Finally, the admittance from Wharton arrived. I had made it. I collapsed. There was one month to go till graduation. I would crawl there somehow. Suddenly the strain I had been under surfaced. I had been fighting for my life for years. It had been impossible for me to fail. One summer I had worked in Lower Manhattan for Western Electric. A boring job that drove me crazy, but the real killer was the long subway inferno back to the Bronx. I owned two cheap lightweight suits. Each night I would cram myself into the sweltering subway, an obscene unisex steam bath, and when I reached home, I would wring out my dress shirt, hang up my wet suit to dry for a day, take a shower and collapse in our un-air-conditioned apartment, ready for a sleepless night of wandering the floor searching for oxygen, listening to the shuffling sounds of other exhausted ghosts in the steamy structure around me.

I couldn't live that life. It was simply not possible. I would die. I could not fail at RPI. I couldn't disappoint my family and humiliate myself. But all the studying, what had it been for? What had I learned?

I slept for twenty-four hours. I couldn't arise. I slept another day. I made it to class but then came home and slept again for sixteen hours. This became a pattern. Six or eight hours dragging myself through the motions of a life, then sixteen to eighteen hours sleep. I went to the infirmary. They said my blood was horrible. Incredible. They thought I might have some kind of mono but it wasn't exactly mono. It was worse. They didn't know what I had. It was beyond the parameters of a name. They told me to rest and keep returning for blood tests. The test results kept getting grimmer. They were sinking to the bottom of unexplored seas. I was sleeping twenty hours a day.

Somehow I made it to the end. I had no choice. But I thought I might be dying. The doctors were mystified. The Senior Weekend arrived; the one we had all looked forward to for years, classes done, a couple days before graduation. I lost hope. I had slept for a month. I gave in. I decided that nothing I did made any difference, my blood levels were in the Guinness Book of World Records anyway, I might as well go down with glory, get drunk and die. On Friday I snagged a ride to Bennington with friends and I began to drink. I partied and drank for three days, sleeping on the grass of the beautiful Vermont campus. I broke into the Bennington orchestra studio with my pal Betsey Dingman. There was an entire symphony set up with no one around. It seemed like an hallucination. I helped my friend Steve (future physician) avoid arrest by talking skillfully to another old rent-a-cop after Steve had punched out a window with his bleeding fist. I rode around southern Vermont with a mailman on his deliveries for some reason I couldn't understand.

Sunday night my friends carried me home and I collapsed. Monday morning I went in abashedly for a blood test and the terminal news. The nurse looked at me with dread in her eyes. Each of my blood tests had been worse than the last and this was the final outrage to their efforts. ""Your blood!" she exclaimed. "What have you been doing?"

I couldn't answer. I stood there mute as she exclaimed, "It's normal. For some reason, your blood has gone completely normal over the weekend. None of us have ever seen anything like this."

I was terribly hung-over. I could hardly call up any emotions to respond. This crazy event folded into my crazy life. I thanked the nurse and, bemused, put the month-long, potentially life-threatening illness behind me and headed off to my graduation.

WHAT I "KNEW"

I was twenty-one years old, an electrical engineer who had graduated in the top quarter of his class at one of the best engineering schools on the planet. The world before I was born was pretty much a blank slate to me other than some scientific laws and procedures in physics and chemistry that hadn't been superceded.

I had grown up in New York City at the height of its influence and creativity, and I had managed to pick up some contemporary knowledge on my own. My father stopped his education after the ninth grade due to poverty and my mother, age ninety-one as I write, always avoided any knowledge that might prove unpleasant (which may be one of the secrets of her longevity.) I knew about black music, my consolation and opening to street beauty—rhythm and blues, jazz, and rock. I had come to like abstract painting and begun to travel down to Manhattan to see foreign movies. I'd been to a Broadway musical and decided it was not a form for me. I knew about sports and that the greatest baseball team in the world, the Yankees, played down the street and represented our neighborhood, and that they had recently been led by two dead immortals, Babe Ruth and Lou Gehrig, the Father and the Holy Ghost, and that I had seen the Son, Joe Dimaggio, play center field.

I knew about the civil rights struggle and did what I could to be a part of it. I reached out to black people and black culture, traveling out of my neighborhood on the subway to attend a high school with kids from Harlem. I attended the Apollo Theater many times, often by myself, and shopped across the street from the Apollo in a hip record store where the manager had taken an interest in me and taught me about jazz chord changes.

I knew that life was meaningless and dangerous. I had been born into a time of depression and chaos and lived for my first seven years in a world completely at war from pole to pole, people bombing, stabbing and shooting each other, soldiers and noncombatants, women and children, culminating in Hiroshima and Nagasaki which fried entire cities (I didn't know about Dresden). I knew people could be crazy and mean, even entire nations. I knew the Nazis had wanted to kill me and all the Jews, but I believed America was good to the Jews, had done everything it could to stop the slaughter and save the Jews of Europe, and had protected me and my family from a Nazi invasion. I knew that the Jews had formed a nation in Israel and I was happy for them, but I didn't see this as affecting my life in any profound way.

I knew the Communists might A-bomb us and destroy New York which was their number one target. I had participated in air raid drills at Junior High School, and was fearful whenever a loud crash of lightning and thunder shook me out of sleep. I worried about my father. I might survive in the Bronx, but what would happen to him in an attack, down there in Manhattan where the real carnage would be?

I had known no place of security in my life. America and the Jews had been potentially under attack when I was a child, aware of air raid sirens and blackout curtains; RPI had been a continuous test where I actually felt my life on the line. I had been subject to violence at home in the cash-poor frenzy of my parents who needed to borrow to the max and save every penny to realize their dreams of upward-mobility and, at the same time, to spend every penny to keep up with the neighbors, leading to a situation in which I was often the designated victim when the contradictions surfaced in even a minor financial earthquake. And I wasn't safe on the Bronx streets either, amidst unconscious teenagers who already knew they were going nowhere in life and were beginning to get guns. I came to enjoy the excitement of going to a high school where there were weekly gang fights and individual fights; you never knew what was going to happen; one day at school I saw the two deans holding a kid against the wall while the principal worked him over with a series of rights and lefts to the midsection.

I knew the old ways of my grandfather's generation were superstitious and outmoded. I knew the world had been formed in a Big Bang, that we were made of protons and electrons, that the Bible was a tribal fiction translated into a weird pretentious English that I could hardly understand. I knew that prestigious colleges and corporations had Jewish quotas, and that I was an uncouth lower-class Jew who would always be uneasy in polite middle-class society and would never have an equal chance at making my way in the world. But I hid my desperation beneath a smile and a joke.

I knew that I was a nice guy. My mother explained that my father held the anger of the family while she and I loved people. My mother often said, "When I worked at the Woolworth's they used me to sell any junk that no one wanted to buy. I could sell people anything. Any *dreck* they were stuck with in the store people would buy from me. And you know why? Because people knew I loved them. I could sell people anything because they could see I loved them."

I knew nature was good. I knew nothing about nature. I loved dogs. I talked and begged my family to get me a dog. I promised I would take care of her. They took me down to Gimbel's one day and bought me a pedigreed cocker spaniel. We registered her name as Princess Ali Bey. I took advantage of my father's workaholism and let him take care of her.

I loved my father even though he had a short fuse and would sometimes attack me. I enjoyed it when he attacked someone else and got beat up, or when the tenants pushed him down the stairs.

I knew I was lucky. I had gone to a great college. I had unique and loving family and I lived in the greatest country in the world. America wasn't perfect but we were different from other countries. They all went around the world oppressing people and looking out for their own pocketbooks, but we valued liberty and we were interested in spreading freedom and democracy around the world. The old colonial powers were cynical and greedy, but we had never had any colonies. The Russians were materialists but we were idealists. We believed in God and freedom, and we intervened to protect human rights in other countries even if it might sometimes cost us some of our own lives.

I knew our Army was different from other armies. It was a people's army, and the small number of professional soldiers were under the control of democratically elected civilians, and they were Americans too, trained professionals, doing what they could to further human values in a difficult world. I remembered the World War II movies where each patrol represented all of America, the Brooklyn street guy, the black guy, the Texan, the Midwesterner, the Southerner, fighting together for humanity, a kind of United Nations. I knew everyone had an equal chance in much of America, and we would soon clean out the pockets of resistance to this in the South.

I knew that science was, like America, different from its rivals. Scientists were disinterested scholars in search of a truth that they would experimentally verify, a real truth, not like other explanatory systems that merely served their proponents' egos or self-interest.

I knew that people were good at heart. That we in America were going to help humanity through progress fostered by dedicated scientists and engineers like my friends, and I knew education was the key to this new world, and that professors were like priests of education, people who had studied selflessly and taken lower paying jobs so they could have a chance to serve humanity and have a voice in its future.

I knew we were going to die, and I wondered how everyone, even smart people like my fraternity brothers, could go on with their normal lives in the face of this fact which caused me to feel forever alienated from other people and somewhat frightened of them because they all seemed to be capable of living in a group hallucination, a kind of strange dream in which they ignored the basic facts of life right in front of their faces.

I knew my fraternity brothers really were like brothers to me, the greatest bunch of guys I had ever known, who would in one way or another always be special to me, many of them the closest friends of my life.

THE CLASS OF 1960

> *"Personality is only a persistent error."*
>
> Max Jacob

We were the class of 1960. We stood on the beach, at the end of solid ground, the water beginning to lap at our toes. We knew we were privileged, especially those of us who were Jewish; we believed the rhetoric and ideals of World War II, and we supported the Civil Rights movement for Negro freedom in the South. We didn't realize that we were beginning to release frightening exuberant energies. Energies that had been projected onto other cultures in the past were emerging in ourselves. We were giving something to the Negroes and the workers, and they were also giving us something. I would later understand that the old white, Protestant, work-ethic personalities which had served this country so well when it needed hard work, savings, and investment, were now superfluous in a world that required lack of restraint and hedonism to keep the factories running. Energies that had been structured and bound for centuries were now escaping. Old style personalities were leaking, the ancient pressures being released, causing new tensions to emerge, the products of personal change.

Conservatives bemoaned this new lassitude in their speeches while their corporations encouraged it in their ads and credit policies.

We were learning how to dance.

Dostoevsky had Ivan Karamazov say that if there is no God then anything is possible. We could see the limitless horizons offered by an empty sky, but we were not yet wise enough to understand that Dostoevski had foreseen the horrors of our terrible century, and that Ivan had made this statement with great sadness and foreboding.

We were the class of 1960. There were twenty-three of us in the fraternity. In a few short years three would die violent deaths—one would commit suicide, one fall under a commuter train, one become a Marine fighter pilot and then crash as a test pilot for Israel.

In our last days at RPI the school held an election for the most inspiring student. I nominated myself and ran for the position. I wanted to exemplify the hip modern student; I wanted to show that the election was a fraud, that none of this high-pressure torture was inspiring, that our experience had been a stupid meaningless exercise and that we were doomed to lead dead lives in plastic bureaucracies. Meaning and inspiration were dead words clutched at by hypocrites and hicks. Scores of my friends promised to vote for me.

The winner was a nice guy, Richie, a vet, who had courageously made it through while holding a night job and living in a metal Quonset hut with his wife and two kids. I received one vote. My own. I was shocked that none of my friends had voted for me. But afterwards, thinking about what a decent guy Richie was, and how hard he had worked, I wasn't sorry that he had won. I wished that I had been able to vote for him myself. But it was too late for that.

THE WHARTON SCHOOL

"You can't get enough of what you don't really want."
                                                                    Eric Hoffer

I liked Wharton and was excited to be in Philadelphia. I loved 19th century commercial and industrial cities. When I was young, I had visited my cousins in Washington, D.C. where they owned a grocery store in a rough part of town. I looked forward to the train ride for months, writing down each little town we rolled through on the Pennsylvania Railroad with its big, dark-green, electric locomotives. I especially liked passing near the Philadelphia baseball stadium, ancient, storied Shibe Park, visible from the train near the elevated North Philadelphia station. Philadelphia was a romantic city to me, where unknown people led different lives, but so was Wilmington, Delaware, and Newark, and Trenton, New Jersey, ("Trenton Makes, the World Takes" said the electric sign running along a bridge over the Delaware River) and fabled Baltimore, with its rows of white steps, the seventh largest city in America.

Wharton defined management as "Getting things done through people." At last people were part of the equation. I respected the effort of scientists to keep out the personal. There was something clean and self-abnegating about a method that sought to keep one's hand off the scale, to search for a public truth by public means, by making hypotheses which could be tested and then having the tests repeated by others with less interest in the results. But I came from the Bronx, a people hive. My very block had more inhabitants than most towns. I wanted to understand the social world in which I lived. I wanted to understand my wooly and mysterious self.

Wharton was not unscientific. All major American universities are based on the scientific method. Even English Departments mimic the scientific method by using footnotes that attempt to make the process of gathering evidence and arriving at conclusions public and repeatable by others.

Karl Popper said a truth couldn't be scientific unless it provided means for its own falsification. They taught us this at Wharton. They taught us Marxism as well.

I took a small seminar co-taught by William Gomberg, the labor mediator and Peter Drucker, philosopher turned management guru. We read many interesting books, including *The Communist Manifesto* and Joseph Schumpeter's *Capitalism, Socialism and Democracy.* The professors explained that Marx claimed to be scientific, but that his prediction of a future revolution by the workers could not be falsified and thus could not be considered true in the scientific sense, and I thought this made sense. (I still do.)

Wharton, the business school of the Ivy League University of Pennsylvania, was not a caricature of a university, a trade school showing us means for making money. The professors often spoke of knotty problems such as the departures from democracy in a large bureaucracy, or a lack of worker control over the workplace, or the increasingly diminished power of stockholders in corporations. We learned theoretical economics, and the history of business as well as current practice.

[Recently I read with some shock that certain distinguished professors at Wharton were being honored for a lifetime of using the latest mathematical and statistical knowledge and operations research to do things like get fat people to buy more Frito-Lays than the people wanted to. This kind of amorality didn't disturb me when I was a student there. I just avoided their classes. "You can't fight City Hall," was what I believed back then.]

There were six of us from RPI in the two year MBA program. We all did well. Wharton was easier than RPI. Less abstract, less distant from everyday life, less cumulative so that a missed class would not prove fatal at some unmarked crossing further down the line. We had to work hard to catch the economics majors who came from Yale and Princeton, and the business majors from Dartmouth and Harvard, but Wharton ran at a much higher speed than any undergraduate program and we accelerated quickly up to pace.

I did not feel that I was entitled to my parents' aid. I had jammed my allocation of freedom into my undergraduate years and felt compelled to excel here to win a scholarship for my second year. I worked as hard as anyone at the school, up at the library in the morning and often there when it closed.

When the library closed at night, sometimes I would run downtown to hear jazz at the Negro clubs—Miles or Shirley Scott or Benny Golson at the Showboat or John Coltrane at Pep's—which were located on the South side, about a mile from the University. Penn was surrounded by largely black neighborhoods that provided other venues for good music. I went by myself to hear James Brown and the Famous Flames at a small arena under the elevated train structure and was pretty much the only white person there among the black teenagers; I would sometimes go to a funky movie theater on Market Street for a third-run feature matinee with the black kids or to amateur night at a local black theater on Baltimore Avenue. I liked being in a black environment, I felt more comfortable there than with upper-middle-class white people. This was before the black power years of rage; everyone understood that the brightest, hippest people of both races were reaching out to each other and the white people who showed up were always welcome at black venues. At least that was my experience.

> *"One must have chaos within oneself to be able to give birth to a dancing star."*
>
> Friedrich Nietzsche

I excelled in my studies. But it was a lonely life that was leading me. All day at the library, home to my little room for further study, day after day, until the pressure would drive me to get really drunk. I didn't date much at Penn. I liked many of the girls there, but they had the same problems with me as the girls around RPI. I didn't behave like a normal college boy. I patronized bars that students didn't attend. One of my favorites, a wild, distorted, Eugene O'Neill kind of place that I called Dante's Inferno, was in a basement, so when the bartenders tossed someone out into the street, they had to throw him *up* the stairs. I liked that idea, that I was drinking in a bar so low they had to throw people *upstairs* to leave them lying drunk on the sidewalk.

I also felt out of place at the Wharton mixers. Everyone there seemed so accepting of the success railroad which speeded through the suburbs to the cemetery. I didn't know what I was looking for; a part of me was miserable in spite of my ascendancy. In fact, the closer I came to real success, the more I thought about all the deaths in my family, and the confusion and despair which followed. When I tried to speak of this with my dates, they didn't understand. Why focus on the negative when I was beginning such a great career at a great school in a free country? I had to admit they were right, but it just made me lonelier and thus more prone to dousing my mind in alcohol.

When my friend Marty Licker showed up it didn't help matters. Marty was out of the Marines now and going full-tilt crazy, a pill-filled hipster whom I let stay with me in my room for a month or two until my father found out and had me evict him. I loved Marty. I felt his pain and admired his courage for living an honestly psychotic lifestyle while I was always compromising. I would read in my spare time and I admired the beats—

Kerouac, Ginsberg, Snyder. They had more courage than I. Kerouac wrote *The Subterraneans* about an actual affair he had with a black woman while I could only approve of it, spending my days in the citadel of capitalism. Yet what was the alternative? I wasn't an artist. If I didn't succeed at Wharton I was afraid of going insane at an ordinary low-level job or of actually starving. I didn't realize I was starving for meaning. So I kept trying to fit myself into a square hole.

Marty ended what chance I might have had for a social life at Penn. I would bring him along to parties and he would always fuck up, even though the students, like all college kids, tried to be tolerant of aberrant behavior. Like he would climb up on a table with all the food on it and make a speech about Ouspensky or Nietzsche, and the table would collapse leaving all the food and the carpet ruined, and we would be thrown out, and I would sympathize with the host, but I would also feel for Marty, too, because he was dying for God's sake. My pal. I felt so bad for him. Yet we had good times together on our own, living like two Kafka cockroaches in my tiny, roach-motel room, hanging out at the black bars in West Philly where we would find diamonds on the streets. Like the time I happened to hear beautiful piano music coming out of an ordinary black bar on West 52nd Street on a Saturday afternoon, and I recognized that, unannounced, it was Junior Mance, the great jazz pianist. I ran home to fetch Marty, treated him to drinks, and I saw that it gave him some rare sweet happiness. He was so proud of me; he had no one else in the world, he was even more alone than I was, and he was smiling for a change. All he could say, again and again, was a warm, "My Man" with an elder brother's pleasure as the pearls of his life slipped softly through his fingers.

(A couple years later Marty's mother called me and asked me if I would attest to the fact that he had been crazy since he'd gotten out of the Marines and thus had a service connected disability. I agreed. Marty didn't want a pension. He was proud of his honorable discharge from the Marines, even though he'd been in the brig for a while, but I felt America had made him crazy, a would-be shaman stuck in a Kelvinator ad, and America could afford to pay him a few bucks so he didn't starve. After all, they paid rich people not to farm, and he wasn't farming, was he? He was writing poems like "Salami and the Seven Veals," line after line of meat puns clacking by like Charlie Parker runs, like rackety freight cars in the American night.)

I was even more out of place at Bryn Mawr out on the Main Line. The girls there liked me in a way, but they kept their distance. Perhaps that was their attraction for me. They were intelligent, and more Protestant, cooler, less experienced and more fragile than most of the girls I knew. One night I drove out there by myself and appeared on campus very drunk. Where was everyone? I saw the poster. Brendan Behan was speaking in the auditorium. Brendan! One of my heroes. I had followed his adventures, his drinking himself to death in public, in the papers. Brendan Behan at Bryn Mawr! An Irish bull in the China shop of America's colleges!

I dashed full-speed toward the hall. Cut across a lawn and hit a thigh-high steel wire that was intended to keep people off the grass. I folded over it in the air. It almost cut me in half. But I managed to rise and, breathless, ran again.

When I entered, Brendan was doing a hilarious impersonation of a Bing Crosby- Barry Fitzgerald movie from a real Irishman's point of view, doing all the voices, running around the stage with his sport jacket pulled over his head to impersonate a nun. And he was sober. I was so glad to see that he wasn't drunk. I had read in the Philadelphia *Bulletin* that he was trying to save his life by staying on the wagon. I had seen his play *The Quare Fellow* in which, at the end, the dead get up and dance, but I wanted him to stay alive.

Brendan told the girls that he and his wife had one child: Him! He told a story about his uncle, gone to Liverpool to burn down the Park Hotel for the IRA. But the cab driver would not take his uncle to the Park Hotel. The cabby wanted Brendan's uncle to stay at the cabby's brother-in-law's hotel. No matter how much the uncle pleaded and cajoled, the cabby would not take him to the Park. Finally, the uncle had an idea. "Your brother-in-law's hotel, is it as big as the Park?" "Oh, yes. Bigger." "Is it as modern?" "Oh, yes." "Does it attract as fine a class of people?" "Oh, definitely. Better." "Then take me to your brother-in-law's hotel," said Brendan's uncle, relaxing into his seat in the back of the cab.

I loved Brendan. I felt no longer alone in the world. So of course, when the speech was over, I ran to the front and leaped up onto the stage to thank him. Immediately the authorities responded, but Brendan took in the entire situation with a glance and said, quickly, "He's with me." He signaled me to follow him backstage. They told him he had a few minutes before he would take questions from a select group of students in a smaller room.

I followed him to a small, windowless, ill-lit dressing room. He deflated onto a straight-back chair; it was as if all the wind had been punched out of him. His public persona melted and he sat there, small and infinitely weary in front of a make-up mirror. At that moment I saw who he was: the tired, sensitive, awkward boy in a cell. The Borstal Boy.

"I . . . I'm sorry, Brendan. I just wanted to thank you. I better go . . ."

He took a breath. Life came back into his face. "No, no, have a seat, lad. Please . . . ."

"But you need to rest. I shouldn't . . ."

"No. It's fine, lad." I could tell he meant it. He didn't want to be alone in the cell. Somehow he felt comfortable with a bright, drunken boy who felt he didn't fit at this posh gathering. With me.

I sat on another straight back chair and the strangeness of the situation struck me: I was alone with Brendan Behan and he was completely sober and I was roaring drunk. He was the first writer I had ever met. And he liked me. I could see it.

"What's your name, lad?" He spoke in the deepest brogue I had ever heard. He emphasized each word as if he were making a pronouncement in a foreign language.

"Jerry."

"Jeddy." He nodded and brightened as he reached into his jacket pocket and pulled out a huge cigar, which he held out toward me. "Well, have a seegarrh, Jeddy me boy. "

"No thanks, Brendan," I said shyly. "I don't smoke."

"Oh, what a pity." His face lit up into a beautiful mischievous smile, and he enunciated slowly, "Amurrica has such good seegarrhs. And they are so easy to steal."

Suddenly we were both laughing together. Two lunatics in a tea shoppe.

"What is that you do, Jeddy, me boy?"

I told him my story. RPI. Wharton. My search for meaning. My unhappiness. He was easy to talk to. Not an "author" but more like a pal. I offered again to let him rest but he shook his head no.

"Why is it you stay at Wharton, Jeddy?"

"I don't know," I said shyly. Then I added, "I figure if you can't beat them, join them . . . . For a while," I added and he laughed.

Some old people came to the door and told him it was time for the small session. I followed him into another room with about 30 girls seated in a kind of circle. He took the easy chair at the center. Again he looked weary. I stood at the side.

For a half hour he answered questions from the students. Then one sensitive-looking co-ed said, "Is it hard for you, Mr. Behan? Not drinking, traveling around from city to city, putting on these shows for students, answering all these questions?"

Brendan thought for a moment and then said, quietly, "As a friend of mine once said, 'If you can't beat them, join them . . . . For a while.'"

The audience chuckled. Brendan turned and gave me a little conspiratorial smile.

A couple weeks later, in Toronto, a student spiked his drink and Brendan fell off the wagon. Not long afterwards I read that he had drunk himself to death.

God's blessing on you Brendan Behan. Some thought you were too gross for the literary life, but actually you were too fine.

I returned to Bryn Mawr, completely sober, on an evening a week later. As I entered the dorm lounge I had visited a few times before, two girls I knew hurried up to me. "You can't come in," one said, looking over her shoulder for the housemother who wasn't there at that moment.

"You've been banned from campus," the other said.

"Banned? For what?"

"They said you disturbed the speaker last week." She shrugged, showing me she didn't agree. "That you interrupted his period of rest between the talks."

"But it was exactly the opposite. He wanted me there."

They both shrugged uneasily. "We're not supposed to talk to you."

"You better go," the second one said. "If they see you, they'll call the campus police."

I saw the guilty, helpless looks on their faces, as I turned and left Bryn Mawr for the last time.

TASTE OF SUCCESS

Before I gave Marty a few bucks and he lugged his ancient, Ellis Island suitcase onto a bus to New Orleans, one of the turning points of my life occurred, almost in spite of my efforts to prevent it. I won the best summer job in America. I was the only one at Wharton selected for the Boeing Executives of the Future Program. They would fly me across country and pay me a large salary to work on the Minuteman Missile, the cornerstone of America's defense for a generation. This was the job everyone coveted, the culmination of my exertions since I was five years old, the greatest success of my life. They had singled me out. I would be groomed to run a major corporation.

Yet the strangest part of this was I had been awake most the night before the interview reading Kerouac's *The Dharma Bums*. I couldn't put it down. I was captivated by the grandeur of the American west, the mountains, the pine forests, the Zen Buddhism, the wrestling with the great questions of life, the freedom! It was set on the Olympic Peninsula, near the Boeing plant in Seattle. I had thought I had killed any chance I had for the job. I had gone crazy during the interview, ranting about the beauties of the great evergreen trees around Seattle, about how soulful it would be to make chocolate pudding in the snow on Mt. Rainier. I had never been west of Pennsylvania, but it all seemed true to me.

Somehow, I won the Oscar of jobs. But I quickly experienced the teeth of success. When I gleefully told Marty, he was surprisingly unmoved. He gave me a stern lecture on selling out my birthright of freedom for a mess of porridge. Deserting the Dharma for Mammon. I promised him I would cash in my airplane ticket and drive across the country following Kerouac's route. I would go to Larimer Street in Denver and search for Neal Cassady's father. But he would hear none of it. He spun around and walked out of my little room, no doubt to cop neon street drugs from strangers.

I called my mother in The Bronx. After all, this was the apex of her life as well; she and my father had backed me all the way. But she told me my father had just been in a fight with Felix Elkin, a tenant, who had pushed him down a flight of stairs. And my mother was troubled by the job offer. She thought someone was trying to cheat me. "How could you be the only one at Wharton they gave a job to?"

"Because I deserved it, Ma. I won it fair and square. Aren't you happy?"

"Did you give him any money? The guy who said he was from Boeing?"

"Money? Why should I give *him* any money? He's giving *me* money, Ma. Don't you see? This is the greatest day of my life. This is what we've prepared for all those years."

"I don't know, Jerry. I know you're a smart boy, but this doesn't make any sense to me. You're too good-hearted. I think we should get Mr. Schoen, your father's lawyer for the buildings, to investigate this guy."

"Mr. Schoen? Investigate? Ma, what're you talking about? Can't you see? I won! Me. Jerry Rosen. I got the great job."

"Look, Jerry, just don't send him any money, OK? Let's leave it at that. And don't tell your father. I don't want to upset him."

AN EMBLEMATIC WEEKEND

Sometimes events in one's life assume the shape of a clear symbol on their own. On St. Patrick's Day weekend, the schizoid structure of my life lit up in a way that was impossible to misunderstand.

After my pal Marty left, I couldn't shake his presence. Something of his anarchic spirit clung to me like my shadow. I had been reading Zen Buddhism and feeling even greater confusion and alienation from the life around me. On St. Patrick's Day weekend, I invited a couple friends of mine down. Tex, a pal from RPI, was originally from El Paso. He was going for a doctorate in Aeronautical Engineering; soon he would design aspects of the Lunar Excursion Module for NASA's moon shot. My other friend, Eddie, was from my block in The Bronx; soon he would be analyzing the trotters at Yonkers Raceway.

I had been up late on the night before they came, studying Keynesian economics. I liked the way Keynes' mind worked, his knife-thrower equations, his ability to juggle four graphs at once. Like Einstein he was able to locate the simple within the immensely complicated. I had to smile when he said that the government didn't need to spend a lot on defense to prolong prosperity. In economic terms it would be just as effective to pay half the people to bury money in bottles and then allow the other half to dig it up.

On Friday night, St. Patrick's Day, I steered Tex and Eddie to a dance at a nursing school near the Philadelphia Museum of Art. I smuggled in a pint of hooch. After I finished it, I felt more isolated than ever. The dance featured a horrible band in an ugly, echoing room with a large dance floor that was mostly unoccupied. It all made me terribly sad. I felt so bad for all of us, trapped in second-hand lives of hidden discontent and woe in a milieu in which fake music in a dead room was supposed to offer us relief. I felt sorry for the nurses, standing around, hoping that some rich guy would show up and take them away, or some nice guy would give them a chance for love. It was obvious that most of the guys who'd shown up just wanted to get into their pants, since nurses were supposed to be hot, nudity was nothing to them, they were exposed to it all the time.

It was all so hopeless. How could there be so much unacknowledged suffering in the world?

I sat down on the floor in the Buddhist position, over on the edge of the dance area, far from the few couples who were attempting to move in synch with the harsh, beat-less music. I closed my eyes and meditated, watching my sorrow rise up over the walls of my defenses.

Until the cops came. They asked what I was doing. I said I was just sitting there, catching my breath, getting myself together, meditating a bit because I felt sad. They said the floor was for dancing. I said I wasn't in anyone's way, which was true. They said I had to be dancing to be on the floor. I said this *was* my dance. They threw me out. They locked the doors behind me. They wouldn't even let me go back in to get my coat.

I drove my pals down deserted Chestnut Street in downtown Philly's posh shopping area. By now I was terribly drunk. I felt very dizzy. I heard the sound of a siren. Red lights were flashing in my rear view mirror. I pulled over and stopped. I realized that I must have been driving about five miles an hour and weaving.

The policeman, a very tall man in crisp uniform came up to my window and ordered me to exit the vehicle. I attempted to comply, but when I tried to get out of the car, I fell onto my back in the gutter. When I focused my eyes, I saw the cop standing above me. He looked like a skyscraper from my angle, lying on my back in the street. I had to think fast. I had to seem classy, not just a common drunk, so I began, while lying at his feet, to speak in an English accent, and I said, in a jaunty, aristocratic, Oxford locution, "Terribly sorry, officer. I hope this won't affect my career."

There was a long silence. And then, incredibly, everyone started laughing—my pal Eddie from the Bronx, my pal Tex, and yes, the cop. The cop was laughing. Tex stepped into the breech and said to the cop, with a knowing, complicitous smile, "St. Patrick's day, officer. I'm afraid he had a couple too many."

The cop looked down at me, then back to Tex. The cop couldn't keep a smirk off his face.

"OK," he said. "Can you drive?"

Tex nodded.

"Just take him home," the cop said, shaking his head. "Keep him away from the wheel."

"Yes, sir," Tex said, and he helped me up out of the gutter.

The next night we had a party at my flat with some wild girls I had met from a Philadelphia art college. These were small town Pennsylvania girls who'd come to the city to run wild and maybe do some art in the process. I liked them. They were completely unpretentious and you never knew what they would do next. On the night of the party, one of them, Joan, showed up with a gun. A pistol loaded with blanks, but when she shot them off it sounded exactly like the real thing. We were all dancing to loud rock and roll music so we didn't pay much attention when Joan climbed out the window onto a roof and began to shoot the gun off. Soon after she came back into the party, a loud knocking sounded on the door. I moved to answer it. "Let's scare them," Joan giggled, as she ran past me. "Open it, and I'll shoot the gun at them. They won't know it's blanks. I'll scare the shit out of them."

Some deep Bronx instinct scuttled up onto the shore of my shrinking island of consciousness. I grabbed her arm and snapped, "No! Put it away!" When I swung the door open, there were two Philadelphia cops there, hands on their guns.

Because I told them I went to Penn, they believed me when I explained that we didn't know anything about the report of gunshots, and we got away with just a warning to keep the stereo down.

I realized with a chill that we could have been killed.

A little later, my neighbor came to the door. Ron was a crazy Russian major and jazz drummer whose room was almost filled by a set of drums on which he would pound for hours each day while shouting and groaning to maximum volume Blue Note jazz records, his drums in the center of a mess of old, unsheathed, Philly Jo Jones records strewn all over his floor. Ron was drunk, and carrying a bowling ball. The girls giggled and asked him teasingly what the bowling ball was for. Ron turned toward the straight, double-length staircase behind him, and flung the ball crashing down the whole flight of twenty stairs. At the bottom, the ball kept flying forward and made a kind of explosion as it smashed right *through* the closed front door of the building.

It all seemed part of the plan, the normal sweep of events at that crazy time in my schizoid life.

SEATTLE

> *"The commonest, one might call it the natural rhythm of human life is routine punctuated by orgies."*
>
> Aldous Huxley

In May I cashed in the Boeing plane ticket and set off for the frontier, on the road in an old Dodge. I was traveling two different paths, following the route of Jack Kerouac toward the mythical American west while simultaneously heading to a job working on an atomic missile; I was traveling not with Neal Cassady but with an economics major heading for the San Francisco Federal Reserve Bank. Yet it was a step forward. For a while, at least, I had jumped off what I saw as the Cemetery Express.

America was not yet completely drawn and quartered by the Interstate Highway System. We drove through small town main streets on two lane roads, an America of John Muir and Edward Hopper rather than cement and glass and steel.

I took the beat, jazz lover's route, stopped in Denver to look for Dean Moriarity's father, went to see Anita O'Day there at a club on the strip. She was drunk and sang beautifully. When a man from the audience called out, "Sing 'Tea for Two,' like you sang it last night," she laughed and said, "Mister, I don't even know what town I was in last night, much less how I sang 'Tea For Two.'"

Somehow I ended up at a Negro after-hours club. I guess the police raided, because at one point everyone rushed into the men's room and leaped out the window, so I jumped out the window too and fled down the street with a large group of drunken people who dissipated into the Denver night.

The Rockies! The great mountain passes with large mammals loose in the woods.

The Painted Desert. The Grand Canyon at dawn. Hauling through the Nevada desert with a water bag slung over the sludgy radiator of my old Dodge City Dodge. Las Vegas. Hitting a jackpot on the slots and being amazed to find that the bartender was a mathematician from the University of Nevada. LA and Shelly's Manne Hole jazz club with Shelly himself playing drums. The Lighthouse jazz club on Hermosa Beach. San Francisco. North Beach. The Co-existence Bagel shop. Beat poetry readings on Grant Street with me sneaking whiskey into a tea pot and afterwards being thrown off a cable car up on Hyde Street for trying to ride while hanging on the outside.

Then Portland. A commune with one guy living in the closet. Everyone up for days on speed and a beautiful grand piano in the living room owned by the son of the director of the Portland symphony.

And then beautiful Seattle! So much further away then. No square, glass, high rises. No freeway through the center. Just the Alaska Highway. (Alaska!) Seattle was still outside the loop of easy jet travel and mass tourism. A distant northwest American port. Loggers, fishermen, West Coast jazz, people living on boats, Native Americans. Where the residents didn't fear starving, or freezing to death, or winding up on the Bowery in winter. Where men in their thirties and forties didn't have careers and didn't seem to care, but somehow were content with temporary jobs and free time and boats and saxophones.

Where I hung out with divorced people for the first time.

Upon arrival I stepped from my car outside the Y, intending to rent a room, feeling my anonymity, my freedom. The air sparkled, fresh and tangy and new. I had left my world behind. I had left my old self behind. I was thousands of miles from home and family, from the ballast of my bourgeois identity. I could get arrested and no one would know. I could change my name. I could make up a fictitious past.

I was an immigrant from another country with a different language. The Statue of Liberty should have been set here, in Puget Sound. I could finally breathe free.

As I stepped out on the sidewalk, amazingly, someone called my name. A friend from RPI. He and another RPI friend, temporarily in jail, were engineers at Boeing. He offered me a suite in their house with my own living room and a view for $35 a month. It was all magic.

On my first day at Boeing I sat next to my future wife at orientation. I didn't realize it at the time, but in Charlotte Mayer I had found the one woman in the United States who was least likely to please my parents. Charlotte was not only gentile, she was Catholic, a practicing Catholic, a *German* Catholic, a poor farmer's daughter from a nowhere town, Lewiston, Idaho, who had been committed to a kind of reformatory as a teen, been thrown out of a convent for reading Sartre and Bertrand Russell, had shown up in Seattle on a freight train, and was now studying theology at the Jesuit University of Seattle.

Yet, from another angle, a tall, thin, pretty young woman who loved Negro music and hung out on the jazz scene. A kind of Catholic beat (like Jack Kerouac) who feared the middle class. She knew she couldn't please them, not the daughter of "Hog Joe," so she wrote them off. A girl with one good dress and no pretensions who had dropped out of pre-med at University of Washington because she said she couldn't see any reason to keep people alive before she found out the meaning of life.

Now I knew why I had had no luck with the girls back East. I steered by a completely different compass. Like Charlotte, I was not comfortable in middle class society. I was an outsider. I, too, was searching for meaning. I could not live in a world in which the one who accumulates the most toys wins and then you die. Like Charlotte, I was haunted by death and the fear of being rejected.

I had found a girl like me. A girl who was the opposite of the girl of my dreams. Or were they my parents' dreams?

Immediately upon reporting at Boeing I learned the score which Charlotte already knew. I would have to punch a time clock. I had such low status that I was assigned to a parking lot almost in Tacoma. I worked in a huge undivided room, rows of desks under plastic light the color of the fake cream they gave you in little cups on airplanes. No one had remembered that I was coming. The project for which I had taken a programming course, to computerize the purchasing for the Minuteman Missile, was already completed. My boss didn't know what to do with me. He improvised a project. I would decide whether to put Japanese transistors in the missile. We both knew this was impossible. I wrote a series of letters to Japan and then waited three weeks for a reply. I had to kill time and stay out of the way. It was easier to do this when I had a hangover. Or when I was drunk. Or when I repaired with Charlotte, who worked as a secretary in the building and was often drunk herself, to the airplane repair hanger below our offices and made out with her in torn-down Boeing 707s from around the world.

Charlotte began to take summer courses in theology at the Jesuit University of Seattle and was conscientious about studying, so I had plenty of time to meet people. I joined the jazz world with the other lonely alienated people who were trying to form a multiracial society based on hymns of the night and the sacrament of alcohol. I hung out with Warm Springs Indian women who dug Charlie Parker. My roommates and I traveled to Vancouver where we listened to jazz at The Cellar and then partied with the musicians afterwards. My future friend, the English-Canadian poet David Bromige, was hanging at The Cellar that summer and going to the parties afterwards, and he is certain we met. Perhaps he's right. I remember loving Vancouver, another Portland-Seattle new town on the far edge of the world. We had a bass player, Virgil Washington, sleeping in our living room. We had met him at a bar one drunken night. He played bass by humming through his nose better than he played on an actual instrument. Once he lost his shoes at The Cellar. I loved the way he played his nose.

After an evening of jazz in Vancouver, we were eating breakfast at the piano player's house and he said to me, "I'm not a complete pacifist, I was on the beach with the Canadian Army on D-Day, but I'll be damned if I would spend my life making missiles." I had no answer.

In August, my second roommate, long out of jail, quit his job and joined the Marines to become a fighter pilot. Here was someone who had accomplished the RPI-Boeing success trip and was throwing it away.

Of course, my relationship with Charlotte was impossible beyond the summer, but when I returned back east, after this adventure outside of the vault of major ambition, it was equally impossible to fit into my old Wharton uniform.

I had learned a lot from Charlotte, with all her talk of Jesus and Love. I saw another side to Catholicism beyond the Bronx tough guys. Charlotte was wrapped up in Aquinas. She gave me books about Abelard and Heloise, books by Gabriel Marcel and Jacques Maritain, and *The Pastoral Symphony* by André Gide. She spoke of taking back Christianity from St. Paul and returning it to Jesus. (I improvised to hide the fact that I knew little about this. I told her that St. Paul was Jewish. That his name was not Paul but Saul. Saul of Tarsus. I told her that if ever the twin cities of Minnesota came up in conversation, I would appreciate it if she would refer to them as "Minneapolis and Saul.")

Charlotte was poor. Her family had paid for her brother to go to the University of Idaho where he was Phi Beta Kappa in math. He was now in the Navy, a possible future astronaut, writing a book on space navigation with an admiral before taking fighter pilot training. Her parents said they didn't have the money to pay for her education as well. I told her this didn't seem fair to me, but she shrugged; this was her life. She was working full-time by day to pay her tuition. I didn't know girls like this. I respected her.

She kept saying that Jesus' love was needed to complete and complement the justice of the God of the Jewish Old Testament. I could never be a Catholic, but, like Jack Kerouac, I did see that center of mercy and forgiveness for sinners at the heart of the best of Catholicism. I remembered that Kerouac had asked Gary Snyder (when they were talking about Eastern religion and meditation and Zen koans at Kerouac's house) whether their ardent conversation was any more spiritual than Kerouac's mother quietly making their dinner in the kitchen? Salinger in *Franny and Zooey* would also come back to Jesus, as did Tolstoy and Dostoevsky, so you had to respect that shining core of Catholicism even though it had been used at times to burn the Jews.

In Seattle, I had thrust myself on the other side of the curtain, on stage with the musicians and poets and Zen students and out-of-control would-be saints. To Charlotte and the other girls in Seattle, I was the insider, the hip guy from "back East." For them, "back East" began at Denver. There was a music of yearning blowing within me that was drowning out the voice of my normal reasoning.

Why did I feel so alone in the normal world? I had had a nice childhood. I had a father who worked hard and fulfilled his obligations in the world, and I had a mother who was a warm-hearted, saintly woman whose only fault was that she was too nice to people. I knew this was true because she told me so herself. And I was fulfilling my dreams of success. The Boeing program wasn't all worthless. Once every week or two they took us to labs and lectures, showing us the wind tunnel facilities and a full-size wooden mock-up of their forthcoming new airplane, the 727. They provided a couple dinners with executives who weren't really bad people. So why did I feel uncomfortable except when I was drunk with other freaks and misfits, people like myself, with ticks and secret dread, all moving their bodies to the beat of jazz or Negro rhythm and blues?

I felt like I had a disease I couldn't begin to treat, because I couldn't give it a name. It seemed urgent that I confront this anxiety, because for some reason that I couldn't rationally explain, I was afraid my eternal soul was at stake. It was more than a matter of life and death.

AMERICA THE BEAUTIFUL

I drove back east on the northern route. I loved America so. I wanted to know every inch of her. To caress every state and county and town and city. I drove across wide Montana. You could drive all day and still be in Montana. A kind of Anti-Bronx. You drove for twenty or thirty miles without seeing a person. Then a little town with a gas station and a Ford dealer and a café. Then into the open spaces again. Montana! They even had the biggest mosquitoes! And then North Dakota. Where entire communities did not yet have electricity or telephones. It was so wonderful to drive on the two lane roads that gave the countryside a chance to slowly yield to you, to snake your way through the center of fabled towns and cities. Bismarck and Fargo! I had always heard of them, but now I could really see them and be inside them.

I continued down through the fabled twin cites, Minneapolis and Saul, to Madison with the great university beside the lake, to Chicago to catch Gene Ammons, recently out of jail, playing along with Sonny Stitt at a black club on the South Side. This was my country. I was a native born

American. This was the legacy I had been promised and was now inheriting as I came of age.

Back at Wharton, I talked them into allowing me to take a course, "America in the Twentieth Century," from Professor Thomas Cochran. Finally, an Ivy League liberal arts course! In the Graduate School of Arts and Sciences. Professor Cochran had begun as a historian of business and economics. He had a background in science. He followed William Fielding Ogburn whose book, *Social Change*, in the twenties, had asked the question: "Why does a culture change?" Why doesn't it simply repeat itself as cultures did for thousands of years, some of them, stone-age cultures, still around today? Ogburn said the driving engine was science and technology.

Professor Cochran taught the story of a culture rather than the story of older white males directing wars and making governmental decisions. History included women, labor, art, inventions. Suddenly my knowledge, which was limited to science and technology and business, seemed very relevant to understanding the world. A culture was a system of shared values. New technology led to new values. The Model T Ford was related to sexual mores of teenagers. We lived in a culture with a dubious sense of a future because of atom bombs made by science. Our world and our perceptions were shaped by the birth control pill, and by epidemic diseases, and by novels. Advertising followed the arts and attempted to co-opt them by using their forms. The Civil War did not speed up industrial growth as everyone believed. Everyone thought World War I changed everything, but the Armory Show, which demolished American assumptions about art, took place *before* the war.

Now I had a role model. I wanted to understand the world around me. Since I was formed to a large degree by this world, these studies might be a path to understanding myself. What was I, if not a lonely American? What had occurred before my appearance on Earth and what momentum had it left behind to deflect and impede our purposes?

And since I was reading Zen Buddhism in my spare time, it was natural to ask: Who was I before I was an American? Before I was socialized into a culture.

I was so miserable. I was hurting for time to think. To study life and meaning. Perhaps to meditate. I didn't know where it would lead. I needed to tap into the thoughts of the thousands of artists and scholars and holy people who had been here before me. My life was wasting. I was dying.

I decided to become a teacher. I would trade away money for time. I would study liberal arts. I would go for an Ivy League Ph.D. Having taken Dr. Cochran's class, I believed I could do it. I would try to live a life in which I followed what the Buddha had called "Right Livelihood." A life of study and service to mankind. Whichever path I wound up on, I knew that a life of service would not prove an impediment.

I would ask Charlotte to marry me. Once I made this decision I began to feel better. My life had a direction and a purpose at last. I knew I had finally chosen correctly.

My whole body broke out in horrible boils. I had to go to New York every week for painful treatments.

But I persisted.

In March, Charlotte came to Philadelphia and we were married, twice, in a Catholic Church and in a Bronx County office. My parents somehow went along with it. They kept themselves under control for two months until we visited them in May, and Charlotte walked on Nelson Avenue without shoes, and they found out that I was serious about leaving my career and serving mankind. They threw us out of the house.

By then I had signed my papers for the Army.

UNCLE SAM

Supposedly the original Uncle Sam came from Troy, New York. At least that was what they said. Somehow, shortly after my Wharton graduation, with no ROTC training, I found myself to be an Army officer.

My last challenge at Wharton had been the MBA orals which happened to be scheduled right after the steel companies raised the price of steel by six dollars a ton. JFK was leaning on them to withdraw the increase. I knew the orals board would quiz me about this. It was a classic Wharton issue. When they asked, I was prepared.

"The steel companies raised the price as a defense against Communism," I said.

The three professors awoke at the smell of blood. Finally, after a never-ending day of tedious orals, a student was going to shoot himself in his private enterprise zone.

"Against Communism?"

"Yes," I said, with a straight face. "You know, Karl Marx said, at the end of the *Communist Manifesto*, 'Workers of the world unite. You have nothing to lose but your chains.' Well, at these prices for steel, what worker can afford to lose his chains?"

There was a second of shocked silence. Then, simultaneously, they got it. It was a joke. A crazy student had told a joke at the crucial moment in his Wharton career. Yet, after a long, monotonous day, it was kind of fun. Refreshing actually. They all began to chuckle.

I had survived again.

A LUCKY GUY

My first Army assignment was a couple months at Fort Sam Houston in San Antonio. I had never been to Texas. I looked forward to the trip to the Southwest, the cowboys and the Alamo. Unfortunately, I had not heard the "South" in "Southwest." Driving down through Arkansas from St. Louis, I saw, for the first time, the rural poverty of the Negro south. The unpainted, rotting, one-room shacks in rows along drainage ditches. Could this be America? Then, in San Antonio, I was astonished to find that Charlie Williams, a black friend of mine among the new officers, could not sit downstairs in movie theaters and was not allowed in the better restaurants. An American Army officer! In Texas! In 1962!

One mysterious event occurred in Texas. We weren't given the full basic training but we did undergo an abbreviated version. When I was fourteen, there'd been a horrendous accident in training at Fort Dix. Every soldier had to crawl under live machine gun fire. If you stood up you would be cut to pieces. Something went wrong. The bullets were directed too low, and they tore up a large group of young men. This frightening image stayed in my mind for years.

In high school, I dreaded that the Korean War might continue until I was drafted. I knew little about the war. I didn't even know how to tell a North Korean from a South Korean. But I feared death in Korea less than being shredded on the machine gun range. Somehow, I got it into my head that this irony was to be my fate.

In Texas, I was surprised to learn that we would have to crawl under the machine guns, and not just once but twice. The moment that had haunted me for years had arrived. I was shocked to see that as they fired over our heads we had to crawl under rows of barbed wire, while charges of dynamite, surrounded by little fences, would be going off among us.

I made it got through the daylight trial, though you could hear the bullets whistling by. The night was tougher because you could see clearly the tracers going right over as you lay on your back to crawl under the barbed wire by holding it up with your rifle. But I survived. After eight years of nightmares, I made it through. Then I heard someone calling my name. I turned back. It was a friend of mine, Frank, a pharmacist from Fordham University. He was caught in the barbed wire. He was beginning to panic. He called to me with short breath, "Help! Help me Jerry! I'm stuck."

"Shit!" I thought. But I found myself shouting, "Don't get up! Stay down!" And then, with great apprehension, I crawled back under the machine gun bullets to help him.

I disentangled him from the barbed wire. We crawled back out together. We never spoke of it again. Later I wondered, how could I have done such a thing? I knew I was a coward. I had always backed away from fighting and I hated pain. I guess it just seemed impossible not to do it.

Driving to Fort Devens, Massachusetts at the end of the two months, I entered the Deep South. This happened to be the week that James Meredith, a black man, was attempting to register at the University of Mississippi. The South erupted, spewing hot lava on everyone. President Kennedy had to send troops to protect Meredith and to force the university to admit him.

The Southerners viewed this as an invasion. A continuation of the Civil War. I heard and felt the heat of their fury wherever I stopped. At times I was in real danger. People would see my New York license plates and scream at me. When I stopped for a Coke in a small town north of Atlanta, an old farmer in worn overalls passed me on the town square and, not seeing my car, just defining me as another white man, said, nonchalantly, as a kind of greeting, "Well, they let the nigger in."

In New Orleans, the restrooms were labeled, "Men," Women" and "Colored." The whites had new water coolers. The blacks were forced to drink at chipped little fountains. New Orleans! The cradle of jazz, home of Louis Armstrong and King Oliver.

I was shaken. Like actually being in an earthquake for the first time, rather than merely reading about it. How could I square this with my picture of America, the land I loved?

And how could I think about the fact that my parents had thrown us out, with little money and no place to go, when I'd only intended to show Charlotte the city for a week and to be with them before I went into the Army where I might be killed. How could I integrate all this?

It made me think about a time as a kid, to be repeated more than once, when my father lost money on a baseball bet, and he begged my mother not to buy clothes for a month so he could pay the notes on the building and the liquor store, and my mother, a shopaholic, moved the blame to me, saying that I needed shoes and a new suit, things I didn't want. I protested. "That's OK, Dad, I don't need them." It pained me to see my father practically begging like that, almost crying. But my father snapped, "Don't contradict your mother," and my mother said, "I am entitled to be supported in the manner to which I have become accustomed," which I guess she had heard in a movie and memorized. My father got a look of despair on his face that quickly turned to anger, like he wanted to slap my mother who was impervious to his pleas, but he couldn't hit her because her father was taking him into the real estate business. He flipped out, and, like a rabid dog, he turned on me and begin to growl and beat me with his belt, and my mother screamed, and I tried not to cry, although I was terrorized, for if I cried he would beat me harder, and then later, as I lay in my room in the dark, my mother brought me a big slice of cherry-cheesecake and told me he was an animal and she couldn't understand why he would act like this.

My father was addicted to adrenaline, that big rush of living at 299 of 300 possible stress points; at the slightest tremor, he would crack. Later, this would help me as a novelist in my observation and understanding of people. I was forced to be precise in my estimations of his mood. Was he at 299 points today, or 295? If I misbehaved, would it result in my facing a reprimand or in my being attacked by a maniac?

Yet, I knew I was fortunate to be living in America and to have a stable and loving family, parents that worked hard for me and would later sacrifice to send me to an out of town college. I was one of the luckiest guys in the world. My parents were respected around the block. My mother always said to me, "You and me, we're not common people like your father and his family. Grandpa, my father, is a landlord. You know what a landlord is? He's the lord of the land. And I'm his daughter."

My mother was generous. Anyone who came to the door—cancer, polio, Lou Gehrig, the Girl Scouts— she would give to.

She had a zest for life; she was pretty, she would get a joke and possessed a vital spirit. She kept a scrapbook with her varsity letter in basketball from Morris High (later to be Colin Powell's alma mater) and photos of her on docked ships with her skirt up ("Show Biz Hopeful"). She had gone off to Boston to dance in a nightclub in her late teens.

And though my father had a screw loose, people knew he would only attack men whom he felt had wronged him, perhaps once or twice a year. Since he wasn't that big and often wound up getting thrown down a flight of steps, the other men had a certain affection for him, finding him more amusing than dangerous. He added spice to life on the block. Of course, he wouldn't turn down an offer to buy a hot TV, but who would? He was reliable, a hard worker, kept his word, would do you a favor, and he was intent on becoming middle class, a goal which everyone respected.

And I loved my little brother Mark, four years younger. He was already showing signs of the ability that would make him a top lawyer. Lively intelligence, quick wit, agility in verbal sparring, lack of illusions about the human race.

But he wouldn't eat. When I was ten I began to blow up like a Macy's parade balloon, while Mark continued to be the tiniest, thinnest, most frail kid in his class. My mother called him a "skinny merinck." Together, he and I looked like a midget Laurel and Hardy. He would sit guiltily at the table, staring at his food, while I nervously gorged myself, quickly grabbing everything within reach, voraciously stuffing it all into my mouth. My mother had to watch to make sure that I didn't accidentally swallow my brother as well.

Mark grew up to be a normal sized man, with a love of good food and wine. One of his light-hearted ambitions was to eat lunch at every restaurant in Chinatown. He achieved this goal just before he died.

My family and I were hungry for status and respect in America. They were a launching pad pointed toward success and everyone respected them for this.

75

Yet the skin of the rocket, my ego, my defense system, was beginning to reveal microscopic fissures. The early signs of stress fracture.

THE ARMY

"Military Intelligence is a contradiction in terms."
Groucho Marx

I had mixed feelings about the Army. I wouldn't have called them if they hadn't called me, but I did carry a residue of patriotic feelings left from World War II. A Jewish kid, I had seen the American army as defending me from the Nazis. I felt that the military would be a step toward my Americanization and my manhood.

When my draft notice arrived, unlike my friends I didn't opt out by taking a critical skills deferment as an engineer. This was my first penalty for leaving the corporate world. But I discovered that because of my Wharton MBA, I could receive a direct commission as an officer in the Medics if I signed up for three years. This suited me fine. I would be helping people instead of killing them. I could put Charlotte through college, study like crazy, and save from my officer's pay to finance my Ph.D. studies when I returned to Penn.

My uncle Mac had never been in the Army but he gave me two pieces of advice:
1- Don't try to get out by claiming you're nearsighted or they'll put you up front.
2- Don't believe anything the recruiter said.

But the recruiter was a nice guy, a regular American who assured me that I would not regret my lack of ROTC training. I would probably be in a management position in a large metropolitan hospital. I might not even wear a uniform.

Wrong! In six weeks I found myself alone at night in Texas rattlesnake country, trying to make my way home by compass which no one had taught me how to use. Not long after, at Fort Devens, Massachusetts, I became troop commander of the hospital, leading 180 men in a parade. Fortunately, I had been a Boy Scout for six months in the Bronx. I pretended I was our scout leader, Normie Pincus, and I shouted orders to the men, some of whom had fought at the Battle of the Bulge. At one point I had to turn the men to the left to pass in review before the generals. I shouted out, "Column right." That was what I remembered them shouting out in war movies, "Column right . . ." The men behind me hissed, "*Left! Left*, sir! *Left!*" Quickly I cried out with authority, "I take it back! Make that a *left!*" and we managed to turn just before we all crashed into the reviewing stand.

My incompetence was remarkable. I didn't even know how to speak on an Army radio. I remembered Able, Baker, Charlie, Dog, from the movies, but what if the letter E or F came up? All this could be comical at times in Massachusetts, but I was subject to being sent to Vietnam at any time.

The older soldiers were good-natured about my inexperience. They knew that I wasn't going out of my way to bother them, and that somehow I was now their superior and could put them in jail. Fortunately, about this time, a program came on TV called "The Lieutenant." I watched every show and during the following week I did whatever he did. These shows had to have technical advisors who knew the rules. Since everyone else on the fort took their standards from the show, the enlisted men raised their opinion of me.

Most of the soldiers lived on the fort, but we rented a dumpy flat about half hour away in Fitchburg, Mass., a likeable hilly mill town composed of French Canadians who lived in a section that looked like a little Montreal, Finns with their saunas, Italians with their restaurants, and Fitchburg State College, where Charlotte was majoring in English to be a high school teacher. She had feared going to school with East Coast kids, but the professors were delighted to have this West Coast wild girl with the unkempt look who wrote papers about her search for the meaning of life. She quickly became a 4.0 student.

The professors had no contact with the soldiers, but one English professor, Louis Shepherd, and his wife Ruth were very kind to us. Louis was a brilliant madman with one published novel and eleven unpublished. He knew everything about World Lit.

He lived in a house filled from floor to ceiling with books, records, paintings and grotesque little gargoyles he collected at Woolworth's. Raised in hotels by his mother, an actress, Louis had a theatrical quality that was new to me. He bought winter clothing for his poor students and jogged along country roads always carrying a loaded pistol. He had evenings at home for us and our friend Richard DeLisle in which he would show hours of movies he had made from his car, at random, as Ruth drove him around the countryside. He plied us with gallons of cheap wine and played loud Wagner records while shouting exuberantly, "This is great! It's really great!" at the appearance of every new gas station on the little screen. Once when I went with him to the liquor store, I was surprised to hear the clerks call him, "Father." Later he explained, "Somehow they got the idea that I'm a priest, and I never saw fit to disabuse them of that notion because they give me a clerical discount."

Louis was a powerful influence on me. I had never been friends with a professor, much less an artist. I was astonished that he was interested in me. He seemed to admire the fact that I was an Army commander who understood calculus, possessed a Wharton MBA, yet was interested in pursuing the liberal arts. He helped me to see myself as someone who might be an interesting person in my own right, even though I knew I had always taken the safe route of ambition and security.

Richard DeLisle was Charlotte's classmate. His parents, Desneiges and Raybo DeLisle, took us into their large French-Canadian family. Raybo was a short, round man, with a goofy smile. Once he told me if I wanted to get a cheap car, to go to Worcester and make a low offer to a Jew car salesman on Monday morning. "The Jews never refuse their first offer of the week. They think it's bad luck."

"But Raybo," Richard said, abashed, "*Jerry's* Jewish."

"So?" Raybo shrugged, with a smile. "I'm just trying to get him a good deal."

I liked Raybo and Desneiges. He meant well and she had a heart pure as snow.

I bought college text books in history and liberal arts to try to get the equivalent of a BA on my own so I would be prepared to compete at the graduate school level: History of Civilization, of Art and Architecture, of Philosophy, of Political Theory, History of Science, of the City, of American Literature, of English Poetry. It was difficult work because I didn't have the cross-references I needed. I was studying the history of poems I hadn't read. But I ploughed on. Beginning with the pre-Socratics and the Egyptians and Greeks and Romans was a good idea, because there was not yet a long background of recorded previous events that I didn't know. I studied like crazy. Yet I worked seventy hours a week, sometimes thirty-six-hour shifts with no time off to compensate, so my life continued on its fissured path.

One night I turned on a Boston radio station and heard the Censor of Boston explaining why he had closed the theater where Edward Albee's play, *Who's Afraid of Virginia Woolf,* was being acted. Furious, I called in long distance and found myself on the air with the Censor. "What's the basic idea behind this?" I asked, innocently. "That exposure to pornographic material may warp a person's mind and cause him to commit lewd and lascivious acts?"

"Yes, I think that's a fair summary," he said.

"Well, then," I said, "who among the entire population of Boston has had the most exposure to this kind of material. *You!* It's your job. You watch it all day."

He sputtered and shouted in an angry confused manner until the host stepped in and, laughing, said he agreed with me but the hour was over.

One of Richard's sisters was married to a Fitchburg cop. On Friday night I might study till ten and then go to a drunken party with the Fitchburg police, then on Saturday study until midnight and then drink opiated cough syrup with my pal Gus, a big Greek guy who lived in the dump above us. Gus drove a huge Lincoln and ran errands for the Mafia.

One night Charlotte and I were in a crowded, rowdy, workers' bar and an old drunken Finnish woman expatiated at length to me on the merits of Jean Sibelius. Then an almost unconscious fat woman with absolutely no teeth turned on her barstool and said to me, "I wanna bite the world."

I began to dread going to the fort every day. I had believed in the America I saw on TV, a kind of anti-Bronx that would offer me some American hope, a place where people like Robert Young, and Ozzie and Harriet, and Jimmy Stewart, and Southern Methodist all-American Doak Walker led clean, fair, ungrubbing lives. I had bought an idealistic view of America that I thought the Army was going to represent for me, with its aristocratic ideals of bravery and honor and freedom, but instead I found the Army to be shockingly similar to the Bronx, just lacking our street irony and Jewish humor.

The military proved to be merely the world's second largest bureaucracy, not so different from the Soviet Union that, in theory, it opposed. We bought our food at the government commissary. We shopped at the PX, a kind of government Kmart. We dined at the Officer's club, bought our gas at the government gas station, and our liquor tax-free at the base liquor store. We couldn't be fired and were guaranteed free medical care and a pension for life if we signed on and made a few small sacrifices—our freedom of speech, our privacy, our freedom to choose where we lived and how we dressed. I thought the lifers' hatred of the Soviet Union was a kind of reaction formation to their own attraction to that way of life.

Although I knew the allure that security, a big mother for life, could offer, I quickly came to hate the Army. I couldn't understand why no one else could see that everyone around us was crazy. Every once in a while a drafted enlisted man would flip-out and do something like throw a typewriter through a thin hospital wall, and I would have to punish him. This was difficult because a secret sharer in me sympathized with him. Some lifers rebelled unconsciously by destructive drinking. One sergeant, O'Reilly, began to binge right before his twenty years were up. That was the dangerous time, the months before one left mother and returned to the world. That was when they began to steal and destroy things so as to be put in jail, safely near mother still. O'Reilly wasn't a bad guy, just a passive, sleepy NCO with a huge belly. I knew that if the colonel caught him he would ask me to reduce his grade before he retired so his pension would suffer for the rest of his life. I hid O'Reilly out of the way in the laundry room. But astonishingly, the colonel showed up for inspection. O'Reilly hopped out of his chair and snapped to attention with a sharp salute, but his momentum carried him backwards and he toppled over into a laundry cart. I didn't have the heart to break him, so I fined him quickly, hundreds of dollars. Then when the colonel called me in, as I expected, and told me to break him, I was not legally able to. That would be double jeopardy. I saved him thousands.

But what was my problem? At Boeing? In the Army?

The people who committed to these lives weren't bad guys for the most part. Especially those on the bottom of the ladder, the minority soldiers and the draftees. It seemed that it took a certain blindness to one's own faults, a lack of self-consciousness to be a leader of men. And this often led to bad endings. Even the Duke of Wellington, who wound up with a title and the general approbation of history, took a mistress with literary pretensions who wrote a memoir about him that made him the laughing stock of Europe. And for every Wellington, there was a Stalin who made it to a (probably) natural death only to be cursed by history's kiss, and a Napoleon who ended up alone on chilly, damp St. Helena, a rock in the South Atlantic, or a Hitler who committed suicide in his bunker amidst the warmth of Berlin in flames, or a Mussolini who sang his last aria while hanging by his heels from a lamppost north of La Scala.

But the officers I had contact with were not on this scale of warped genius and grandiose evil. They were simple civil servants, trying to get a new auto tire by trading some aspirins from the pharmacy to the motor pool, or engineering a way to use hospital TVs in their house on the base. One bright young doctor, just serving his time, played golf with the general who was in charge of the defense of New England. I asked the doc how he would evaluate the general's competence compared with executives outside the Army. He thought for a second, then said, "Well, I'll put it this way: If you owned a nice gas station on the edge of a small town, you might allow him to run it . . . but maybe not."

The colonel in charge of the hospital was a doctor who had taken his degree abroad long ago and had gone into Army hospital administration. He tried to avoid anything to do with medicine but was forced to take one patient: the general. The general refused to be treated by the crack young docs just drafted out of Harvard Medical School. No, he was the general. He wanted the colonel to treat him. This terrified the colonel but what was he to do? Some of the wise-guy young docs used to sit in on these sessions which they enjoyed because they said it was like finding a text book on medicine from early in the century.

The other career Army doctors weren't much better. They decided they should wear red or green pins to distinguish the surgeons from the other doctors, but they had to give up on the idea after fighting for weeks. Each side wanted the red pins.

The colonel went one step beyond relating to the Army as mother archetype. He actually moved his aged mother into a private room in the hospital and let her make the big decisions. He was terrified of her, as were we all once she seized the power behind the throne and took command.

I began to believe that all the normal people who ran things were asleep. But I couldn't find anyone to talk to who was awake.

"We look at the present through a rear-view mirror.
We march backward into the future."

Marshall McLuhan

The military always prepares to fight the last war. I arrived at Fort Devens in September of 1962 just in time for the Cuban Missile crisis. We all went to bed each night wondering whether there would be a world in the morning. But the sergeants were elated when the orders came down to give all the men yellow fever shots. Yes sir, the Big Chief in Washington was serious, that's for sure. And when they began to pack up the hospital and ship it south, the sergeants' spirits rose again. This was going to be a great adventure. The generals always say that no one hates war as much as the military because they have to fight it, but nothing is more boring than the peacetime army, and the lifers were excited by a chance to leave wife and kids and pick up where they had left off in World War II, with cheering *señoritas,* and rum to drink, and goods to "liberate" after the immediate victory. Like President Kennedy, they believed their own propaganda. They visualized this as a short war, an invasion of a little Caribbean island. The Cuban people were not going to fight for Dictator Castro. They would welcome the chance to go back to a pre-revolutionary state of freedom, with American tourists, and gambling, and nightclubs, and chorus girls, and whores, and the Mafia, and illiteracy, and no health coverage, and a different dictator. And like President Kennedy, the soldiers were shocked when someone pointed out that Cuba, laid out on a map of the U.S., would stretch from New York to Chicago.

It was like President Johnson would later say, "I don't want to go down in history as the man who started World War III," as if there would be a history to go down in after World War III.

But the Cuban invasion hadn't occurred. Why was I going crazy now, months later? Why did I feel that at any moment a bell might go off and everyone around me might start killing people, and then another bell would ring and they would all return to what they were now, nice enough guys, with no memory of it, like nothing had happened.

Why couldn't I be like one of my assistants when I was Deputy Management Officer of the hospital, Corporal Kravitz from Chicago? Kravitz was a twenty-two year old, overweight, Jewish accountant who didn't like the Army, but merely because he could be making more money outside, and he could go to "Mee-ami" in the winter. Every time it snowed he would whine, "I shouldn't be here, Lieutenant. I'm an accountant. I should be in Mee-ami." Kravitz didn't mess with Captain Stigh, our boss, jowly, fat-waisted, five o'clock shadow that arrived about noon. He looked like the illegitimate child of Richard Nixon and Flem Snopes.

But the captain messed with me. Rural, uneducated, he'd been in the Army since Bunker Hill, and he had only advanced just a little higher than I had. He envied me and feared my education, so he made sure I feared him. He would berate me in front of the enlisted men if I forgot to call him "Sir" in each sentence. He thought I might sign on for life and take his job. This was a scenario from the movie "Fat Chance."

He kept ribbing me in the office, pretending he'd heard that I wanted to join the paratroops. Finally I said to him, in front of everyone else, that I had considered joining the paratroops, but then I discovered you had to jump out of airplanes.

I had wanted to stay out of the way for three years, to study for my return to the university. He screamed at me like my father and kept me there every night, working for hours after he went home. (Suddenly I realized my father had worked in administration in a veteran's hospital before World War II.) In a terrible cosmic irony, just at the moment I was beginning to read assiduously to learn who I was, I fell into the power of an angry father who prevented me from studying and who hated me because I knew his secrets, that he was in a job above his head, and that he made long distance calls to his mother on the office phone at night to brag about how big his budget was.

Vietnam was heating up. At any minute I might be sent over there to kill people. Our whole civilization seemed to be based on murder. And now it was my turn to go to the other side of the world to stab and shoot people. I feared that when I returned, I would be stained with blood and as unconscious as everyone else.

"A mind is metaphysical in so far as its position within reality appears to it essentially unacceptable."

Gabriel Marcel

I was reading books on Buddhism, Hinduism, Christianity, and Judaism. Zen and Vedanta fascinated me. I was also passionately reading the Existentialists. They spoke to me directly. A philosophy that began with alienation and hopelessness!

The living Paris existentialists had an authenticity that couldn't be denied. They were trying to come to terms with what they had experienced in the occupation of World War II, where Sartre said they had come into contact with an evil that was irredeemable. I didn't think that Dostoevsky wouldn't agree that anything was irredeemable. I remembered that he had said that if Christ said two and two made five, he would say it as well. I felt this was relevant to the question but I wasn't sure exactly how.

I couldn't completely understand the existentialists. I didn't know what they were reacting against, or how they related to the scientific tradition, but somehow I recognized they were talking to me, to my plight in the Army, to my "nausea."

Maybe I was less pessimistic than they were because I was an American and surrounded by a nebula of unconsciousness that was only just beginning to condense into a dark star. I pondered for weeks what Sartre said about existence preceding essence. I knew these words had a context, a long history I was unaware of. It was exciting when he said that you could define who you were by your own free, day to day, decisions. But I was stuck in a desperate situation without the knowledge or background to make the right decisions.

Their key words, freedom, responsibility, dread, *angst*, their refusal to take anything on authority, enthralled me. Yet, ultimately, they proved depressing. Camus's statement, "I rebel therefore I am," and his assertion that when Sisyphus pushed that rock up the hill it yielded him a certain stubborn satisfaction, were thrilling. I loved Camus, but he and Sartre didn't give me the answers I needed to guide me through the minefield of my daily life on the post.

I turned to the existentialists with a religious bent like Soren Kierkegaard, the Russian Nikolai Berdyaev, and the Frenchman Gabriel Marcel. Much of this was over my head, but their passion, their honesty, their emphasis on subjectivity, on the freedom of the unique suffering individual, resonated with something inside me. Yet I still didn't know how to apply these new thoughts to my life.

When D.T. Suzuki, the man who brought Zen to modern America in the way that the Bodhidharma had brought Zen to China in the Sixth Century A.D., wrote that the existentialists say that life has no meaning and they dress in black and are depressed, but we Zen Buddhists say that life has no meaning and we smile, I was fascinated. I thought about this every day. But I didn't know why he wasn't depressed.

> "...*nothing burns in hell but the self.*"
> Theologica Germanica

Charlotte was happy going full-time in English at Fitchburg State. I was working seventy hours a week and was often too tired to study after a thirty-six hour shift. But I plugged on. I read relentlessly in every spare moment I could make. I barely ever slept. Nothing was going to stop me. But soon I began to wear down. I sank into a suicidal despair. Charlotte and Marty Licker (on the phone) were telling me to be like Jesus. To let go of my desires, to move beyond my ego, and to love everything and everybody. This was easy for them to say—they had no jobs, they possessed little and had achieved little, so letting go for them was not difficult. Still, I knew they had a point. Dostoevsky had defined Hell existentially by saying that Hell was the inability to love. I was certainly in a state of Hell. Yet, although I felt guilty about it, I found I was unable to love everyone at work. There were deadly plutonium particles of bureaucracy floating in the air there, killing every sign of independent life.

But I tried. I tortured my soul when I couldn't love everyone. I wanted to be like Jesus. Or like my mother. I saw my father as a just Old Testament God and my mother as a New Testament source of mercy. Like the Virgin Mary.

> "*I believe the time is not far off, when one will experience, perhaps dearly enough, that one has to start, if one wants to find the Absolute, not with doubt, but with despair.*"
> Soren Kierkegaard

I received orders making me defense counsel on courts martial for the fort. It would be up to me to keep people out of jail. But I knew nothing about law. I went to the Judge Advocate General and said to him, "There must be some mistake, Sir. I'm not a lawyer." He responded cheerfully, "That's OK, the prosecution isn't a lawyer either."

"There is but one truly serious philosophical problem, and that is suicide."

Albert Camus

I became more desperate. I thought about going AWOL but that was a trap. When they found you, they added your jail time to your Army stretch so you would have to stay longer.

I would sit at my desk each morning watching the clock tick, each second a little razor slicing into my life. My spirit was dying just when I felt a new vision promising to open up for me. Something was very wrong with everything. I had to find out what it was before I killed myself, or worse, killed someone else for the wrong reason.

What was really bothering me was that there was no consciousness on the base. And the base, to me, represented America. I had to give up protecting my men at the hospital from going to jail, because I found that often they would push things until they *were* punished. If I gave them a fine instead of jail time, they would do something even more outrageous and wind up in a worse fix.

And there was a kind of arrogance in the career Army. The weapons at their disposal were much more powerful than I had imagined. They would take an eighteen-year-old who isn't allowed to drive the family car and put him in a tank. I had seen one pound of dynamite shake the earth; I brooded about a 2,000 pound bomb dropped from seven miles high; about a 20 million ton bomb.

These soldiers, many of them unthinking, self-satisfied, drunk on what they had achieved in World War II (or often just drunk), were in possession of the most powerful weapons ever devised by man. Weapons thought up and manufactured and turned over to them by smarter people. People like my friends at RPI. People like me. I felt like I was sitting in an oily pool made up of hubris, dynamite, and "innocence." It smelled like napalm. I didn't know it, but I was getting a whiff of Vietnam.

But no one else seemed to see this. Or care. Now I was really isolated.

My American dreams had turned dark and toxic but I was insistently clutching them to me.

I was terrified to let go of them or of my straight life. I planned to kill myself. I began to act in a crazy manner. One day in my despair I left the fort and drove down the road ten miles to the deserted old Concord graveyard where I lay down on Thoreau's grave, my head against the little stone. "Henry help me," I cried. "I don't know what to do. I'm really lost and I don't know what to do." There was no answer. The only message that came reminded me that now a hot dog stand stood on the shore of Walden Pond.

I was haunted by images of violence. How it would feel to shoot an Asian teenager in the face. President Kennedy was sending more troops to Vietnam. I couldn't exactly place Vietnam on a map. If I were sent into battle, I would be running a company aid station near the front lines. I had no idea how to do this. I would be carrying a rifle I didn't know how to use. Were we supposed to be able to break down and clean the weapon in the jungle? I didn't know anything about surviving in the jungle. When I was Duty Officer at night, I would walk the hospital perimeter and practice how it would feel if young people were in the woods wanting to kill me. How would it feel to fight for my life? To put a bayonet into a Vietnamese teenager's belly and then to pull it out while he looked into my eyes asking, "Why?"

I feared dying less than I feared being maimed. Life was intolerable already. How could I endure it after stepping on a mine or being shot in the balls?

Memories of World War II that I had sequestered in the basement of my mind flooded up over me. Terrible questions that had haunted me throughout my childhood. How could the world have gotten into such a situation? What was there that was worth killing a child or blinding a person you didn't know? What could possibly justify such acts? Why wasn't anyone talking about this?

People were animals but more dangerous. With bigger brains turned toward abstractions of greed and power. I was surrounded by zombies with secret purposes unknown even to themselves. How had I ever chosen to work at Boeing on hydrogen bomb delivery systems in order to buy a better hi-fi system?

My first sergeant, Lopez, had gone into hock to buy a fabulous stereo. He took me to his home to play it for me. But he didn't like music. He owned just a couple records. Racing cars. He played them at full blast. I sat there listening to the cars roar across the room in stereo. "That's great," I lied. "Just like the real thing." I'd never heard the real thing. He beamed with pride.

I had reconciled with my father to some degree. He was no help. He had avoided the army in World War II but he kept repeating to me, every time we spoke on the phone, "Just remember, an officer deserves respect, regardless of who he is as a person. When you salute an officer, you're saluting the uniform, not an individual."

He couldn't get it into his head that *I* was an officer.

Was I a pacifist? I would have fought against the Nazis. But how did you fight without becoming an animal yourself? Tolstoy was a pacifist. He said you didn't need a church or religious authority, just follow the example of Christ, so he was excommunicated. But when he was my age he had fought at the Battle of Sebastopol. Later, when he advised students to resist the draft, he wasn't giving up a career. He was famous and had already proven he wasn't a coward.

The Fort Devens Hospital had been built in World War II to last for five years but it was still being used twenty years later. Lights would explode in surgery during operations. Designed as a wide-spread grid on a single floor to minimize the damage of aerial bombing, the large structure was set on wood stilts three feet high so the dampness wouldn't rot the cheap wooden floors. But the floors were rotting and warping. One day the legs of a patient's bed crashed through the floor leaving him in the air for a split second before he fell, like in the cartoons.

The hallways were narrow, quarter-mile long, and tunnel-like, seriously warped, twisting and buckling. A German expressionist insane asylum. Dr. Caligary. You never knew if you were hallucinating or merely seeing accurately. You couldn't see the end of the tunnel.

I was losing my grip. Finally I surrendered. I went to see a shrink. All I wanted was a free pass out of the Army. But he refused. He thought I should not give in and should fight this battle right now. I knew he had X-ray eyes. He could see into me, all my secrets—my cowardice, my lack of macho, my perpetual horniness, and the fact that my father had been right when he used to call me a "selfish pig." But what else could he see? Sewers inside me that I wasn't even aware of, frightening pits and latrines.

I went to him for three sessions. I knew little about psychiatry. I focused on Freud's Oedipus complex. I babbled on, defending myself against his unspoken accusations. I told him I had read that Freud's truths weren't universal but were only applicable to particular milieu, middle-European Jews at the turn of the century in the Austro-Hungarian Empire. Then I realized that my family were middle-European Jews from the turn of the century Austro-Hungarian Empire. Oedipus was the last guy I wanted to hear about.

Although the shrink was actually a nice guy, I believed he was trying to get me to adjust to being in the Army. I didn't want to adjust to the Army. I believed that the Army was trying to turn me into an unconscious murderer. It was wounding me at the core, in a place that treadmill tests and angiograms still can't reach. I resigned from the treatment. I had nowhere left to turn. My problem now wasn't getting through the three years, it was surviving the next day.

My center wasn't holding. One Saturday afternoon I went to an enlisted men's jazz jam session at a local roadhouse. Towards the end, to my astonishment, I leaped up and began to play the piano. Only I didn't know how to play the piano. I threw fistfuls of crazy "chords" at the keys, like a maniac. I was so drunk, it actually sounded good to me. Like Monk. The musicians were startled at first, but then they swung along, laughing. They were drunk too. I was acting out their subconscious fantasies. I was moving jazz ahead by twenty years. I was going out of my fucking mind. Who cared?

APPROACHING THE TERMINAL

"You aren't what you are protecting."
                                        Ram Dass

The next day, when Charlotte went to Mass in Fitchburg, I decided to go with her. I was desperate, at my mind's edge. Every road I could imagine led to a dead end.

89

Charlotte attended Mass every Sunday, though she wouldn't take communion because we were using birth control. This seemed ridiculous to me. Why did communing with God require one to overpopulate the Earth? But she said, "You want to play in their game, you play by their rules."

I thought this punished people for being honest. In Charlotte's case it seemed especially unfair, because her father, at the age of thirty-eight, had divorced his wife to marry Charlotte's mother, a poor girl singing in taverns, as I heard the story. Then, believing they were living in sin, they went to their priest who said their only chance lay in bringing up their kids as good Catholics. This put pressure on Charlotte, since her brother was the "good one." Rod did everything right. He even figured out a way to be patriotic while topping the Hell's Angels by becoming a navy fighter pilot and one day diving his Phantom jet into the valley, practically landing on Main Street, then pointing its nose up and kicking it into overdrive, shaking every building in town with a huge ROAR, making the bikers' big Harleys look like kids' toys.

But Charlotte played the Church game straight. There was no talking to her about it. I argued that the ban on birth control was just a way to have more Catholics to contribute to the Church. I challenged her to provide instances of when the Church had stood for morality *against* its own interests. She just kept going to Mass every Sunday.

The church was a small, undistinguished building in the Italian section of town. A statue of Jesus hung from the wall behind the altar. I sat alongside Charlotte in the half-filled pews, thinking of ways to kill myself. There was no way out. But every lethal method seemed less inviting than the last. It was like the Dorothy Parker poem, acids stain you, nooses give. I sunk into a black hole from which no light could escape.

And then it hit me. I could die right there. I would stop my heart and never walk out of the church. This was it. It was all over. My life.

I focused on my heart and willed it to stop. I tightened the center of my chest and focused every laser of energy I could summon right down into my heart. I listened to it beating. I slowed the beat. I was finished. The long struggle was over. I watched my heart slow down and waited for it to kill me.

But it wouldn't stop. My desire to live had completely collapsed. I had no thoughts of future or of consequences. I just wanted to cash in my chips and die right there. But my stubborn heart wouldn't quit. Something inside me wouldn't give in, in spite of the fact that I had surrendered.

I sat there, in agony, fighting to stop my heart. Almost in tears at the frustration. I felt like ripping myself to pieces in my anguish.

And then it came to me. Who was "I"? How could I want to die and not be able to? Who was controlling my body? My life? I watched with amazement as my little heart pumped away, obstinately following another agenda, and in a flash I realized that my idea of myself was all wrong. I was much larger than this little "I" that had been suffering so, lost in its own conflicting desires: The desire to live. To be holy. To be good. To end it all.

Something within me exploded. Something burst and I began to weep. Right there in the church, I began to bawl like crazy. I couldn't stop. In spite of myself, all this crazy gratitude was pouring out of me. The fever had broken. I looked up at the statue of Christ. It floated out towards me. The statue of Jesus was alive. He looked so kind. He was looking into my eyes and flooding me with love. The light in the church glowed electric with a tint of lapis lazuli.

Everything was vibrating with a fullness of color I had never seen, as if it were all lighted from within. Something larger than me, something lighter, and brighter, and glowing, and more forgiving had made an appearance when I had let go, when I had given up all desire, even the desire for life. Something wonderfully vibrant and sympathetic had taken control, something that loved me more than I loved myself.

I sat there weeping, soaked in gratitude.

Up at the rail, people were kneeling to take communion. I looked up at Jesus. He wanted me to take communion as well. I walked slowly forward. I knew my life had changed. I would never be the same again.

I knelt at the rail and opened my mouth. The priest put the wafer on my tongue. I felt it melting and I suddenly understood. The miracle of the Eucharist was taking place in my mouth. A dead wafer was being transformed into living flesh. Into my flesh.

We were all sons and daughters of God. That was what Jesus and all the saints and gurus I had been reading had wanted me to see. We would all be forgiven and resurrected. We hadn't been forgotten. Everyday life itself was a miracle.

I knew I was blessed.

How had I been so blind?

I walked slowly back to my seat. I continued to weep, but now softly, with gentle happiness. The dark night of the soul was over. I could begin again now. I was on the right path. I had jumped blindly out of the burning building and somehow had landed in a safety net I hadn't known was there.

Now I understood.

I wanted to go outside into the sunlight. I followed Charlotte up the aisle. She didn't look back. I couldn't wait to tell her what had happened. I had been reborn, not as a Christian, I was way beyond that, but reborn nonetheless, in her church. I was going to live.

The air shone crisp and refulgent. She turned around on the sun-bright sidewalk and glared at me with a stare of abject horror. Her jaw fell and her mouth hung wide open. Her eyes dilated in disbelief. She looked as at me as if I had turned into a werewolf right in front of her eyes. And then she began to scream, a kind of "AGGGGGGH" right there in front of the exiting parishioners.

My heart dropped. Quickly I said, "Jesus told me to do it."

She spun and walked away, her mouth still open as if she had seen a ghost.

"Let me tell you what happened . . . ." I called after her.

She turned back for a second and shouted at me, "YOU SHIT ON MY BELIEF!!!"

"WHOSE CHURCH IS THIS?!!" I shouted back at her as she stomped off.

POST

> *"And priests in black gowns were walking their rounds,*
> *And binding with briars my joys and desires."*
>
> William Blake

My spiritual experience had occurred inside a church but I knew Catholicism did not subsume it. I was way beyond any Thomist or essentialist method of thinking. I was not going to yield to any established religion. I used to joke that I believed in Jesus but not the Bible.

What did my rebirth experience have to do with a Bible or a bureaucracy or a man in Rome? I didn't see this in Christian terms at all. More in Zen terms or Vedanta. This was bigger than the ordinary mind and its books and words. I had been catapulted out of my identification with my ego instead of my Self.

I kept thinking of the existentialist theologian Paul Tillich who had said that God is who appears when you become absolutely certain there is no God. That was as far as I was willing to go in defining the experience.

On a simple level, my life force had broken out of the religious chains. There was a Nietzschean or Blakean quality about it. Surprisingly, I found that when I returned to daily life, I was less concerned about morality and self-sacrifice. After all, I had already been graced with a religious experience. I had let go of my life and had been touched by God. What did I have to prove or earn now?

I reconciled with Charlotte. When she heard what had happened to me, and realized that I had been suicidal while she had been enjoying her life at college, she joined me in moving the Dodge of our lives forward and letting that run-over garbage can in front of the church fade into the distance. She herself had had her days, the times when she had thrown open the door of our moving car and threatened to jump out during arguments, or the time she had punched her fist through our bathroom wall shortly after she arrived in Philadelphia.

I returned to the post and shifted into Bronx gear. If these rubes wanted to be unconscious, so much the worse for them. I contacted the young career officer who split the defense counsel duties with me. He *liked* being counsel. It gave him a sense of power and offered him a chance to further his career by performing in front of a board of senior officers. I gave him a gift. Almost all my cases. He was delighted. I told him he merely had to keep quiet about this arrangement.

Shortly afterwards, I walked into the management office and Captain Stigh nonchalantly asked me over his shoulder, "Raining hard?"

"Not too bad," I said, setting my jacket on a hook.

He flipped out, screaming at me in front of everyone, "NOT TOO BAD?!!! NOT TOO BAD, *SIR*!" He was completely out of his mind, right in my face, shouting with his sewer breath, "DON'T YOU EVER TALK TO ME LIKE THAT AGAIN LIEUTENANT. DON'T YOU EVER! IF

YOU EVER SAY ANYTHING LIKE THAT TO ME AGAIN WE'LL GO RIGHT DOWN TO THE COLONEL AND WE'LL SEE WHAT HE'LL SAY ABOUT IT WHEN I REPORT YOU FOR INSUBORDINATION TO A SUPERIOR OFFICER."

I don't know what happened, I never made a conscious decision, but something in me snapped. I thrust myself into his face and shouted back at him, as loud as he had been shouting, "ALL RIGHT! ALL RIGHT GODDAMN IT! IF YOU WANT TO GO TO THE COLONEL, LET'S GO TO THE GODDAMN COLONEL. LET'S GO DOWN THERE RIGHT NOW." I spun around toward the door when, astonishingly, I saw a look of yellow, abject fear on the captain's face. And then I understood for the first time. He was terrified of me. I had nothing to lose. What could they do to me? They weren't going to severely punish an officer for shouting a couple sentences. It would look bad for all the officers. We had to seem to stick together. But the captain had a whole career on the line. He was dealing with a very smart, out of control, enraged Bronx guy who might say anything. I might know things about his job performance that he had never even thought of. I might ruin him.

He said, suddenly quiet, "Well, listen, Jerry, don't get all excited. Come into my office and we'll talk this over." He moved toward the door, touching his arm on my shoulder, saying softly, "Who said anything about going to the colonel?"

A couple days later we both agreed it would be a good idea for me to be Troop Commander of the hospital. The colonel took the captain's recommendation and moved me to my own office, about a thousand yards from anyone else, way down in the corner of the hospital near the enlisted men's barracks. Now I could completely stay out of the way. I wouldn't get the floating assignments that were given to the first officer the colonel ran into. I had my own fiefdom. I carried a huge forty-five pistol to protect the payroll when I paid the men in cash each month, and I controlled the company recreation funds. I immediately took a small amount and subscribed to several magazines I knew the men would be interested in reading: *The New Yorker, The Atlantic Monthly, Harper's.* I instructed the first sergeant to make sure I received them as soon as they arrived. The sergeant smiled. He was proud of me. I was getting the idea.

94

We were in charge. I turned over most of my duties to him. He smiled again.

Shortly thereafter I went to the colonel and volunteered to be Postal Officer for the hospital. The colonel was impressed and agreed. Now I had a key to the Post Office. Now I could take everybody's magazines and read them before they were distributed a day or two late. I knew that this was against the thinking of Immanuel Kant. Fuck the categorical imperative. I'd had enough tsuris from that quarter already.

Once, when I was asked to give company instruction hour, to speak that week on "Courage," I lectured to the men on Plato. They looked puzzled but actually were somewhat interested. Who knew what the crazy lieutenant might say? It was a hell of a lot better than the usual lecture by some sergeant on keeping your toothbrush clean. When we inspected the men every week, I knew they had two toothbrushes, the dirty one they used, and the immaculate one they kept for inspections. I didn't care. Fuck their teeth. They were adults. I had enough on my mind.

I decided to become a Regular Guy. I drove into Worcester, 20 miles south, to go to the fights at the old Mechanics Hall. I drank shots of whiskey and smoked cigars and cheered and booed like everybody else. After a couple times, this got old, so I began to go to see foreign movies there, at a moldering, old theater some mad idealist had re-opened on a side street off downtown. Years later I learned his name was Abbie Hoffman. The theater was decrepit, just the way I liked it, but apparently few others agreed. There were usually only six or seven other people there and soon it closed.

Somehow the Worcester Museum became one of the venues for the first major show of Pop Art. Charlotte and I were enthralled. Then I drove down each week for a class in early American history at Clark University, a good small school where Freud and Jung spoke on their only trip to America in 1909 when G. Stanley Hall ran the psych department.

One time in class a student asked the professor whether the political machines in early America were the first in the world. The Professor replied, "What about the machines in Greece?" and I quickly shouted out, "And what about the grease in the machines?" There was a sickening silence for a second and then the professor looked at me and laughed like crazy. I knew I had won him over.

When Charlotte graduated from Fitchburg State in May 1964, she took a job for the fall teaching high school English near the post. There was no longer any reason for me to commute to Fitchburg, so we moved into a large, new, ranch house in the officer's quarters on the post. Now I could really study. I kicked in the after-burners. I would read most of the night, every night, and then, after lunch the next day, I would leave work "to go to see the prisoners in the jail, to prepare a defense," and return home to sleep. No one was the wiser. They thought I was being conscientious. I was promoted to First Lieutenant on schedule.

When one of my men was arrested and put in jail in Maine, like a good commander I put my men's welfare before my own. I left my office and drove an Army car all the way to Maine by myself to get him out and bring him back. All my men thought this was great. What a guy! I was forced to drive leisurely up the lovely, salty, rocky coast of Maine for the first time.

I was reading books in psychology and sociology, Erich Fromm and Paul Goodman's *Growing Up Absurd*, along with novels that asked the big questions: Tolstoy, Kazantzakis, Herman Melville, Kafka, Celine, Dostoevsky. And contemporary American novels: Heller, Pynchon, Barth, Bruce Jay Friedman, James Purdy, Terry Southern, Flannery O'Connor, Carson McCullers, Norman Mailer, Mary McCarthy, Gore Vidal. Saul Bellow's *Herzog* was brilliant, but somehow static and difficult to finish, although his *Dangling Man* was obviously relevant.

Where Camus found the universe to be absurd in that it presented an irrational world that could never really be understood by a human being whose very heart cried out for clarity, Paul Goodman was less pessimistic. He saw our *culture* as absurd. He claimed that a worker on an assembly line who put the fins on a Cadillac knew that his work was meaningless. And that the impoverished juvenile delinquent who steals a Cadillac is fulfilling the culture's mandate just as surely as the person who buys one; the kid has no other way of possessing what the culture values so he takes a shortcut to the sanctioned goal.

I held a special fondness for Jack Kerouac and J. D. Salinger. Years later I realized that although the critics and scholars didn't see it, they were the two writers who were introducing Buddhism and Eastern thought into the American novel. I didn't understand this consciously at the time but somehow must have sensed it. In fact, Holden Caulfield's story is structured exactly like the archetypal story of the Buddha. A young person, privileged and in a protective environment, comes into contact with sickness, old age and death, realizes that the adults in his life have not given him any way to cope with this sad information, and goes off in search of an answer.

The Catcher in the Rye was the first real novel I discovered and read. I was thirteen, driving with my parents and brother from Montreal to the Thousand Islands. My family was making a ten day summer auto trip. For the rest of the summer we would swelter in the concrete pre-air-conditioned Bronx. And this was when summers were still summers. Before the New Ice Age. When people would sleep on fire escapes to try to catch some air.

We had never traveled. I didn't want to be on this trip. I wanted to be in summer camp where my friends were being coached in sports. I'd never had any coaching. My parents said they couldn't afford to send me to camp. They wanted me to understand that I had to put the family first and enjoy the countryside. But I didn't want to understand. I was grumpy and selfish.

I had never read a novel. I had started *Ivanhoe* in Junior High but this reinforced every prejudice against art that I had grown up with. Books were for the rich. They were written in some strange language I could barely understand. They concerned girls named Rowena and people who called each other Thee and Thou. What did this have to do with me? With Pinhead Brady who stole my lunch money every day on the way to school? With Miss O'Hare, the attendance officer, who nabbed me for playing hooky for a month while going to the Museum of Natural History every day to see the dinosaurs? The dinosaurs were the only people I could identify with. They were obsolete. They couldn't make it in the modern world.

Somehow I had bought a copy of *The Catcher in the Rye*. I don't know why. Maybe the cover attracted me. Reading this book was like opening a door to a world in Technicolor. How could I return to a world in black and white, a world that everyone I knew seemed to think was the only world?

The Catcher in the Rye showed me that books could speak to me. They could be written honestly in the living language of the New York streets. They could speak to my deepest questions of meaninglessness and death, issues which trailed me like the tides trail the moon but which no one else seemed to notice. Books might be a way for me to connect with adults who were funny and smart and kind. For the first time I had found a hope that there might be other people out there like me. That there might be a reason to live. At the very least, I was no longer alone.

As I lay reading on the motel bed near the Thousand Islands (the perfect location, on the border between two countries), my father said it was time to go on the boat tour. I said I would pass. He said I had to go. I said I didn't want to go. I would stay there reading. He snapped and began to pummel me. I found myself running around the room with my father trying to slug me. My mother screamed, "Sol, Sol, not on his head. Don't hit his head!" My father was growling and swinging away. I ran into the closet, seized the doorknob, and held it. My father grabbed it from the other side and tried to twist it open. "Sol, are you crazy?" my mother shrieked. My father shouted back as he tried to get at me, "I paid a thousand bucks for this goddamn trip, and this kid is going to see these goddamn islands if I have to kill him."

Finally I relented. I knew that even if I stayed in the closet for a week, my father would still be there, twisting the knob, and then he would be really angry.

"I'll go. I'll see the islands.

My father relaxed. "You're goddamn right you'll see these goddamn islands."

They *were* right of course. I did like the islands. But when we returned to the motel, once again I walked through the door that had been opened for me that afternoon. The gateway into the world of literature.

AT THE FEET OF WISE MEN

> *"The powers have to be consulted again directly—again, and again, and again."*
>
> Heinrich Zimmer

In the fall of my third year in the Army, I applied to the University of Pennsylvania in American Civilization and crammed for the GRE exams. I studied like a madman. I was fighting for my life. The normal college students didn't stand a chance. I broke the national curve. Thirty points above the ninety-ninth percentile.

Then, in spring, the letter arrived from Penn. I had won a scholarship that I hadn't applied for. One that hadn't existed earlier but just had been awarded to the University by the Defense Department. A National Defense Education Act (NDEA) Fellowship. I would have free Ivy League tuition for three years. They would pay me a monthly salary to go to school. If my doctorate took longer, the GI Bill would kick in.

I didn't know it at the time, but this award was one of the supreme ironies of my life. The Defense Department had given Penn this fellowship because they thought that a more accurate history, done mathematically, might contribute to our national defense. Penn's department of American Civilization was going to devote itself to mathematical history. They were going to make history into a science.

I was the ideal candidate. I was not only an Army officer, but I was a science graduate, with an A in advanced calculus. They didn't know I was headed in exactly the opposite direction. I had had it with the Army and national defense. I was sick of engineering and science. I was finished with higher math. I was entering graduate school to get away from exact science and to move toward the inexact liberal arts. I was more interested in discovering who I was and in saving my soul than in participating in some vast attempt to stretch the cloth of science over even more of our lives.

I accepted the fellowship with joy. I knew I would be a good student. I knew, in some crazy paradoxical fashion, that I had earned it.

The next day I took a long lunch and drove into Harvard Square where I purchased a book, *The Cycle of American Literature,* by Robert Spiller. Professor Spiller was the acknowledged dean of American literary historians. He taught at Penn. Soon I would be studying with him.

As I walked around Harvard Yard, students made snide remarks about my uniform for the first time. Nothing threatening, merely unpleasant asides as they passed. I wanted to respond, "Soon I'll be with you. I'm an Ivy Leaguer, too." But I didn't see why they should be so hostile.

Gerald Rosen

AN EXISTENTIAL MOMENT

Richard Brautigan's daughter, Ianthe, once told me that, as a boy, Richard had returned from school one day to find that his family had moved without telling him. This was the way that I felt when I learned that President Kennedy had been assassinated.

It was during the break from a court martial trial. My response was more disbelief than sadness. I couldn't take in the news. It was coming from credible sources but it was not credible.

Norman Mailer had defined an existential act as one that changes the assumptions under which we live and whose end is unpredictable. No one understood exactly what was occurring. Was this a *coup d'etat*? A communist invasion? A military takeover?

It was all happening too fast. There was not even time to come up with reasonable narratives. The murderers were at large. The fort went on alert. Even professional sports closed down. Then a suspect was apprehended. Who was he? Had he been to Russia? Cuba? Mexico? Then someone shot him on TV. A man named Jack Ruby. Something to do with strip clubs. Mafia? What could all this mean? These questions have still not been satisfactorily answered forty years later, so how could we put all this together at the moment?

Presidents and public figures weren't assassinated in America. This wasn't Argentina or the Congo. This was a venerable democracy. This couldn't be happening. Especially to Jack Kennedy. The Kennedys were numinous figures. We didn't look at their faults. They were archetypes, gilded symbols of youth. We didn't know Jack had been fucking Marilyn Monroe. And fucking (I won't say "making love to") a hundred other Marilyns. We didn't know he was having a kind of contest with his rival Frank Sinatra to see who could fuck the most chicks. We didn't know he was fucking the girl friend of a Mafia boss from Chicago in the White House while Jackie was shopping, that the Mafia had given money to Jack's father to help him carry the West Virginia primary, and that Jack and Bobby were in league with the mob in making attempts to kill Fidel Castro.

To us, the Kennedys were young gods, eternal and shining, who had come down from Olympus to help us in an aristocratic spirit of noblesse oblige. They stood for youth and adventure, hipness and daring, class and sophistication and romance. We had voted for them to retire the old grandfather, President Eisenhower, who had led us through the old war and had come back to steady the ship through the inner turmoil of the Fifties, a period of wealth and conservatism and consolidation—a President from Abilene who watched westerns on TV while eating TV dinners on little tables in front of the TV set with his wife.

Now it was time for America to move forward again. It was time for the country to grow up into its new sophistication. New York was the capital of the art world now, not Paris. New York was abstract expressionism and modern jazz and Broadway theater, and fashion and the novel and Wall Street.

Of course, it didn't hurt to have a first lady who was beautiful and the height of fashion, who knew about art and addressed the French in their own language, still the sign of sophistication. The Kennedys were Ivy League. That was my new dream. The Army, the old America, science, they had all failed me. Now the dream was the Ivy League. Kennedy had graduated from Harvard. He had written a book. Kennedy's advisers were from Harvard and Yale, scholars like Walt Rostow and John Kenneth Galbraith (we had studied their work at Wharton) along with Walt's brother Eugene Rostow, McGeorge Bundy, a dean of Harvard, his brother William Bundy, Arthur Schlesinger, Robert McNamara, Dean Rusk, Rhodes scholars, intellectuals, the "best and the brightest."

The Kennedys were vital and energetic. Eisenhower played golf; they played touch football. We had a pregnant first lady in the White House. The life force had returned to America. The lights were on again. Sargent Shriver, a brother-in-law, was head of the Peace Corps. Peter Lawford, the actor, another brother-in-law, was a member of the Rat Pack goddamnit! This wasn't Lawrence Welk. This was Frank Sinatra who had recorded with Count Basie. Pablo Casals was playing in the White House now.

Jack appointed Bobby Kennedy Attorney General. People who said he was inexperienced and too young for the job didn't understand—youth and energy was what this was all about. He was a Kennedy! That was enough. Death and tragedy had been banished.

The full appeal of all this became apparent to me in Fitchburg in the fall of 1962. One night Teddy Kennedy came to town to speak in the

Town Square. He was running for the U.S. Senate. He had no experience, indifferent grades; he was just turning thirty, the minimum age. I was suspicious as were many, though another vote for the Kennedys would give more power to the smart, good guys.

The bandstand was filled with seedy Massachusetts politicos, like Boss Tweed's men in a Thomas Nast cartoon, only worse dressed. Short pugs you couldn't tell from petty crooks, jokers who had crawled up from a gutter in which such distinctions didn't exist. As Teddy Kennedy arrived, the bosses didn't realize the mike had been turned on. The whole crowd could hear them discussing the nuts and bolts of politics in harsh street grunts, totally cynical, something old and dead inside of each of them being thrust into the light, like hearing a bugged Mafia meeting. Teddy Kennedy strode up to the platform, and he could hear it too. The citizens of Fitchburg were horrified, although shame was not a word in the bosses' lexicon. Teddy looked down toward the embarrassed crowd and he began to laugh, a big hardy, infectious laugh. HaHaHaHa. Teddy's vibrant, good-natured energy steam-rolled over that old corrupt world; he was so far above these sewer rats, they were merely something laughable to him. He was physically a head taller than all of the bosses, wearing a fabulous, hand-made suit and with a great build, his face unlined and glowing with a rich man's suntan. Surprisingly we all found ourselves laughing along with him; we were now above them too. And at that moment it seemed like a special golden spotlight beamed down on him, a light coming from somewhere above us, somewhere in the sky.

A RENDEZVOUS WITH DESTINY

"Meet the new boss
Same as the old boss"
The Who

Voting in the election of November 1964 was a simple choice. Barry Goldwater, a Republican militarist madman who might get us into a land war in Asia, or Lyndon Johnson, a Democrat who had kept on the Ivy League advisors of President Kennedy, and who, like them, stood for peace and restraint. I voted for LBJ who won by a landslide.

Shortly before, LBJ and his advisors invented a fake assault on the American Pacific Fleet by two North Vietnamese torpedo boats and started the process of sending hundreds of thousands of troops to Vietnam. We didn't know that the Tonkin Bay Resolution that enabled this was based upon a fictitious attack. Later I would realize that this series of events was the best evidence that Franklin Roosevelt hadn't invited the attack on Pearl Harbor to get us into the war in 1941. If you wanted to engage in a war in the Pacific you didn't have to sacrifice the whole Pacific Fleet. A small fictitious attack would do.

The number of troops authorized to be sent to Vietnam kept being doubled. There seemed to be no limit. The government was following the perennial American philosophy: If something doesn't work, try twice as much.

The telexes came in from the Pentagon. Every morning I read them to see if I was required to go myself or to send any of my men. They didn't ask for a specific soldier, just an MOS (military occupation specialty.) They might want a company aid man, to be sent up front into the fighting. It would be my task to choose who would go. How did you decide? The First Sergeant wised me up. Specialist Wills was a perfectly good driver on his time off, but he had purposely failed his ambulance driver's test three times so he wouldn't have to work weekends. The men were furious, but he just smiled slyly. I couldn't fine him, there was no concrete proof, so I gave him the death penalty.

The orders continued to arrive. The decisions about who to send were not always so obvious. I thought about this at night when I wondered if I would be sent there as well. There was talk they might extend all of us. Just when I was hoping to finally be able to find out what things were all about.

The tension level rose as my discharge date approached. One morning, from outside the hospital, I saw one of my men, Specialist Faragano, speed toward the front of the hospital in one of our old big box ambulances, lose his brakes, fly up the ramp and into the air, shearing off the columns that supported the porch and bringing it down, the whole ambulance smashing right through the front wall of the hospital, ripping off part of the roof and winding up at the information desk in the lobby, as if it wanted to ask a question. I knew I should hustle over there, but I saw doctors already running to the scene. Instead, I found that in spite of the possible tragic implications I couldn't stop laughing. I kept looking as the ass-end of the ambulance visible through the hole in the front of the wooden hospital, the ridiculous wounded building up there on stupid three-foot stilts, the roof crushed, the lobby now outdoors, everyone running around like crazy, and all I could do was laugh. I laughed and laughed, howling and roaring uncontrollably. I laughed until I doubled over, and even when my stomach ached, I still couldn't stop laughing.

FAREWELL

> *"You used to be worried because you had no faith; why aren't you happy now that you have it?"*
> Sonya Tolstoy [to Leo]

Just before the end, Charlotte's brother Rod came to visit us. He was now a fighter pilot on the aircraft carrier Independence. He wanted to say goodbye for a while. They were heading for Vietnam.

Rod flew an F-4 Phantom Jet. I asked him how big a bomb it could carry. "I can't say." He was silent for a couple seconds, then he added, quietly, "Very big."

I liked Rod very much. He was a shy, responsible guy, mathematician, honest, soft spoken. He was six foot four with the unconscious stoop of the tall lean guy. I thought he was too tall for a fighter pilot, but apparently not.

I asked him if he wanted to go to Vietnam. "Not really," he said softly. "But I love to fly. I like the Navy. I hope to make it my career. The Navy paid millions of dollars to train me to do this and I agreed to it. That's the contract." He stood there quietly, then added, "I have nothing against the Vietnamese. I wouldn't go on my own. I don't know much about it. But I made a deal and I'll keep it. I'll do my duty. I love my country and I'll do my duty just like the next guy."

"Funny," I said, "but that's pretty much the way I feel. I don't like the Army, but if they extend me, and send me over there, I'll go. I don't know much about the war either, but I'll do my duty like everyone else."

Rod stayed with us for a couple nice spring days. We took him over to

Concord and to Gloucester and Rockford over on Cape Ann. He told us he had met a girl in Virginia and they had decided to marry when he returned from Vietnam. He showed us her picture.

Four months later he was dead.

IVY LEAGUE

> *"One repays a teacher badly if one always remains nothing but a pupil."*
>
> Friedrich Nietzsche

On a beautiful fall day in September 1965, I glided into my first Ivy League literature class, Early American Lit, taught by Professor Robert Spiller. What joyous exhilaration! Sitting in a large lecture hall in one of the older campus buildings with about 100 other students waiting in anticipation for the famous scholar to enter. It was for this that I had toiled in all my free time for the last three painful years.

The Ivy League was the polar opposite of the mindless Army. It had to be. I was running out of options.

When Professor Spiller entered, the students quieted and reached for their notebooks. He set his briefcase down next to his desk on the podium, peered up over his half glasses, asked the class to pass up their IBM cards. The students sent their cards forward; the professor sat at his desk and counted them. My heart pumped faster. Charlotte and I had arrived in June, I had taken a couple summer courses, but this was the signature moment. I had survived the Army. I had achieved the goal I had worked so hard for, to study liberal arts at the feet of wise men at a great university. I released a deep, proud, satisfied breath that seemed to say, "At last."

Professor Spiller looked up with an irritated expression on his face. He counted the students in the class one by one. "There are 95 students present but I count 94 cards."

I raised my hand.

"I guess it's me, sir. I'm an American Civ major. I'm just starting in the program and I didn't realize I had to bring in my IBM card. I can bring it to you tomorrow if you like."

"You don't have a card?"

"I have a card, but it's at home. I'll be glad to bring it in. I had no idea that we had to bring these cards to class. I thought there'd be a roster or something."

He scrutinized me with deepening annoyance. Then he said in a sleepy monotone, "I'm afraid you'll have to leave. You have to have a card to take the class."

"But I have a card. At home."

"I said you have to leave." He was becoming angry.

"Leave?"

"Do I need to make myself more plain? Leave." He nodded toward the exit door.

"But sir, I've just got out of the Army. I studied for three years to take this class. I'm in the program. You can ask some of the other students here who know me from the summer classes."

"Then go home and get it."

"But I'll miss half the class. The syllabus and so on."

"Am I not getting through to you? Leave!!"

I turned to the other students for help. They began to murmur but Spiller stayed firm.

He said with determination, "Don't you understand English? I'm not going to start this class until you leave." He sat stubbornly on his chair, his arms across his chest, ready to wait there for the hour and forty minutes. With his large bald brow and his reddened face he looked like a pouting baby.

Before I knew what I was doing, I said back to him, "Well you might as well call the police because I studied three years for this class and I'm not leaving."

We glared at each other. I continued to stand there. The clock ticked away. The showdown continued. After a minute or so a student I knew shouted out, "He's in the program."

"Yeah, let him in."

"Are we gonna sit here all day. He's in the class."

"Yeah, let's go."

Now angry students were cursing and shouting irritably at him from all sides of the room.

Finally he looked at me balefully and he grumbled through tight teeth, "You better bring that card in tomorrow."

"I certainly will," I said.

Professor Spiller took out his notes and began to talk about Literature. This was what reading all 29 of James Fenimore Cooper's novels had led to.

I already knew Professor Spiller's theory of the four stages of our national literature: the letters home; the practical writing of guidebooks, treaties and laws; the imitative literature which followed the forms and language of the old country, in our case, England; and then the beginnings of a true native literature, exemplified in the writers of the American literary renaissance of the 1850s: Poe, Emerson, Hawthorne, Thoreau, Melville, Walt Whitman, and later, Mark Twain, whose *Huck Finn*, Hemingway said, was the real beginning of the American novel, the first serious long work of fiction written in the American language.

I had read a book about this: *The American Renaissance*, by F. O. Mattheissen. I didn't know that Matthiessen had committed suicide.

PACKMAN

In June 1965, Charlotte and I had moved into a dump on Walnut Street, not far from the Penn campus. The landlord, Mort Packman, appeared to own half the old buildings in the area. He had been my landlord when I was at Wharton. His office had been in my building, right next to the front door that my crazy friend Alan had smashed with a bowling ball three years before on the night we were almost shot by the Philadelphia police. On the Monday morning after that party, when Packman saw the damage he just laughed.

You had to like Packman. He was a kind of Zen master in this way. Nothing phased him. He thought all the chaos of life around the university was hilarious, and besides, he had already added an amount to our rents to cover things like this before they occurred.

You've heard perhaps of a motel chain called "Motel Six" that used to charge six bucks a night for a room. Packman's rooms contained used furniture that appeared to have been purchased from "Motel Two."

I had met Dr. Garvan, the Chairman of the American Civilization Department, when signing up for a couple summer classes. He seemed to quack when he talked. He pressed me into auditing a third class at my own expense. I was afraid to say no. "Nineteenth Century American Bridge Construction" taught by a friendly visiting professor. It wasn't the most popular class in the University. I thought I would make the best of it but the needle of the class got stuck in the groove of trusses, every day a new truss, day after day, truss after truss. The class had turned into Hernia 101. I faded away.

The American Civilization Department had four faculty supplemented by professors in other departments, like Thomas Cochran in History and Robert Spiller in English. I had little further contact with the Chair, who specialized in colonial artifacts. I would be studying with the three other professors, Murphey, Leonard, and Flink, two of whom were teaching that summer.

"The universe is made of stories, not atoms."

Muriel Rukeyser

I signed up for "History of Early American Science" with Professor Murray Murphey and "American Forms and Values I" with Neil Leonard. The classes were everything I had hoped for.

Professor Murphey was a polymath, a walking encyclopedia and a deep, rigorous thinker about matters scientific, philosophical, and social scientific. With his friendly, slightly unworldly smile, alabaster skin, and shock of carrot hair, he was the whitest person you could imagine. We all instantly loved him and looked up to him.

He began the course by teaching us the Aristotelian notion of the four causes. I had never thought about causality before, much less that there could be a scheme in which one of the causes of an action could be the purpose, "the final cause." But Murphey was nothing if not thorough and he was trying to put us into the mental framework of the Puritans so that we could see they weren't simply wrong, just different. They were not against science and the observation of nature; they believed there were two books in which to read God's laws and will: first and foremost, the Bible, and second, nature. They believed that God intervened in human affairs, especially if humans violated his laws. If a Puritan's house were struck by lightning, he would likely pray and ask God what he had done wrong.

Then along came another kind of Boston boy, Ben Franklin, who invented the lightning rod. What now of God's vengeance and awesome power, if a local lad could stick up a pole to tame it? This was the beginning of the end for that kind of metaphysical thinking.

Murphey was the driving intellectual force behind the department's move toward social science and mathematical techniques in the service of history. He was severely honest even when the truth made it more difficult for him. He turned us on to one of the most valuable and jarring books I've ever read: *The Structure of Scientific Revolutions* by Professor Thomas Kuhn of Princeton.

Professor Kuhn said that in normal times science proceeded as we usually conceive of it—scientists worked within the governing paradigm, the global idea like Newtonian physics which governed their total picture of the world, while researchers attempted to devise experiments to explore the implications of this paradigm, to clarify dark corners, add to or test the smaller laws which it had suggested. However, no global theory could explain all results and experience. As scientists worked within a paradigm, certain results would arise which Kuhn called anomalies, data that could not be fitted into the theories exfoliated from the basic paradigm. A perfect example would be the Michaelson-Morley experiment on the speed of light. These anomalies are usually put to the side and ignored for various reasons, including the difficulty of obtaining funding to do research which might explode our fundamental understanding of the world, collapsing the old "house" within which people had made their careers by mapping particular rooms.

Kuhn said that these anomalies build up until some young scientist focuses on them and comes up with a different paradigm that includes them at the expense of other data; this begins the process all over again. Thus, he was quietly saying that science is not truly progressive (its primary claim to be considered different from other forms of knowledge). That is, in a scientific *revolution* outside of the accepted paradigm and its normal, small-scale science, global paradigms are not dropped because evidence falsifies them, rather they die when the scientists who grew up with them, and worked within their assumptions, pass away, and a group of "young Turks" arises desiring a new paradigm to explore and work within. This new paradigm addresses the hidden anomalies which have been ignored, bringing them to the surface like splinters under the skin, but ultimately it produces anomalies of its own.

This was astonishing to me. It also justified to a degree my negative beliefs about the department's attempt to make history into a social science. If *physical* science had a kind of subjective element, what hope was there for a value free, objective, *social* science? Professor Murphey was of course aware of all this, and he was trying in his way to measure the error or degree of reliability of historical assertions.

We all learned from him. The best of us developed a horror of bad scholarship which was based on unexamined sampling techniques. You could prove anything if you biased the sample you examined. This was a special problem for history because you couldn't rely on many of the techniques of the other social sciences—interviews, questionnaires, current data, etc. You were stuck with the sparse data available. Why had it survived? Was it representative? It seemed to me that social science itself, in the present, was on shaky enough ground. Applying it to fragmentary data from the past seemed to be stretching the evidence too thin. You could see the rents in the fabric.

Professor Murphey taught some of us with math backgrounds a course in advanced statistical techniques. In a way there was something quixotic about this attempt to push science onto the data of the past, yet like the great Don, something noble besides. Murphey allowed some of us to substitute a challenging statistics exam for a second language requirement for our PhD. It became apparent to us that he had reached the limit of advanced statistics; it couldn't give him what he wanted, so, amazingly, he had mastered the field and was attempting on his own to develop the new statistics that he needed.

We all became better scholars because of his determined quest on the frontier. In a way his aim resembled my original goal in going to college, to understand the world of human affairs scientifically, to finally settle the world's disputes in a rational manner that everyone could agree on. But I was no longer interested in this. I had changed. RPI, the Minuteman missile, the Army, the hubris of science, the Vietnam War, had given me another kind of education. I respected Dr. Murphey's efforts, but it was not an area in which I wanted to spend my life. Science and statistics were all right as far as they went, but they kept to the sober horizontal plane; they lacked a dimension of magic, of whimsy, and perversity, and coruscating laughter, and the blazing spirit that burns off the protective sheath around your naked, unborn soul.

I wondered about the theories beneath these methods as well. If you wanted to study the aggressiveness of confederate generals and correlate it to the violence of their childhood upbringing, and you had just a few diaries of their childhoods, how could statistics ever give you the solidity you required? Especially since these kind of questions were ultimately generated by deep theories, like those of Freud, and how much reliance could we place on these theories?

I once asked Murphey about Carl Jung. He burst out laughing and rolled his eyes; from a scientific point of view, I could understand why, yet from a more speculative, intuitive angle, Jung, in spite of his dubious character, was a great originator of ideas. To my mind, Sigmund Freud, who was considered much more scientific, and perhaps was, was actually a kind of novelist. When I read *The Psychopathology of Everyday Life*, virtually every statement and connection Freud made seemed arbitrary to me. I couldn't believe how unscientific he was.

> *"My fundamental premise about the brain is that its workings—what we sometimes call mind—are a consequence of its anatomy and physiology, and nothing more."*
>
> Carl Sagan

[Carl Sagan, a fine scientist and amiable pot-head, presented a TV series called "Cosmos," in which he always stood close to the camera with a picture of the universe behind him so he would appear to be the larger of the two.]

Professor James Flink was a mid-westerner who had toured playing saxophone in a dance band when he was younger, the opposite of staid Ivy League. (Although a true believer in the social sciences, he never did fit in and wound up out west, at UC, Irvine.) I once asked him what the aim of all this social science history was. "Someday we're going to be able to put a tractor in Africa and know what the result will be." But I was concerned about who the "we" would be that was putting the tractor in Africa. What were their values? Science desired to get to the objective facts, but was it possible to distinguish clearly between facts and values? Where did you draw the line?

Wasn't that a value judgment in some way? I asked this of the philosopher Elizabeth Flower in a lecture I attended, and she agreed.

I was afraid that the ultimate aim of all this—to predict what humans would do—denied, in its assumptions, the element of human freedom. Perhaps there would be a way, as in quantum mechanics, to predict the overall behavior without predicting the behavior of each individual entity; but I kept thinking of Dostoevsky, when he observed that the goal of people was freedom of action. That people would behave irrationally, rather than in their own interests, if that was the only way they could assert their freedom. I remembered that Dostoevsky had defined man as the "spiteful biped." Scientific scholarship was admirable but only up to a point; I was also attracted to an area of mystery and indeterminacy in all human affairs. I liked the idea that some character would always behave "irrationally," if only to tap dance when alone in an elevator, or laugh out loud for no reason, or put water each day in an offering bowl before a statue of the Buddha.

I felt that a serious problem in the modern bureaucratic world was that no one would take responsibility for his actions or for the results of corporate behavior. It was hard to find the responding human within those bureaucratic structures of roles with their scripts and buck passing. It was beginning to be difficult to get through the phone trees and reach a human being on the telephone when you called a large corporation. Sometimes I couldn't tell if I was speaking to a person or a recording. What was happening to the personal in human interactions? Every once in a while a corporate locomotive would come crashing through the terminal decapitating people and it was never easy to figure out whom to blame.

I worried that the trend toward explaining human behavior by heredity was another way to avoid responsibility. But the opposite liberal position, blaming it on environment instead, led to the same result. Somehow all this explaining was leading to an inhuman world. A world in which people were seen as programmed machines. Yet the people who argued these theories seemed to present *themselves* as responsible for their ideas, not as machines.

Perhaps the popular science fiction theme about robots becoming human was the opposite of what was really happening to us—we were beginning to see *ourselves* as robots. But under these mechanistic assumptions, why should one respond toward humans with a higher morality than toward machines?

ART IS PART OF HEART

Professor Neal Leonard was the arts man in the department. He knew all about sculpture, poetry, painting, classical music and such, but he specialized in jazz. He had written a book, *Jazz and the White Americans*, that I quickly bought and read. The hot new record among hip jazz fans at the time was by an alto player from San Francisco, John Handy, *Live at the Monterey Jazz Festival*. It consisted of two long tracks, each a complete side, featuring a driving rhythm section augmented by a jazz violinist, Mike White, who played in a fierce percussive style, way beyond the old (but wonderful) Stephane Grappelli. Professor Leonard won me over when I asked him if he had heard, "If Only We Knew," the hit side and he lit up and said, "Yeah, it's great, isn't it? But have you heard the other side, 'Spanish Lady'?" This was exactly what I had felt, but had hesitated to say since the first side, also terrific, was the one everyone knew. I had found a friend.

Professor Leonard was an outsider in the department, symbolized to me by the fact that his office was in another building. He was trying to fit into the tight, tweed jacket of the social scientist but his unruly elbows kept wearing through the sleeves. In a social science-oriented department, his sympathies were with artists and he rebelled in a passive-aggressive fashion. For example, writing about jazz as myth and religion, he spoke of "Troeltshean metaphors" and jazz sects which are "liminal" or "limonoid" and he wrote of play aspects in jazz, commenting, "Jazz had Cailloisian *agon, alea, ilinx*, all balanced between *paidia* and *ludens, . . .*" but then he followed up by quoting a drummer saying to Hampton Hawes, "You one bad motherfucker." He was a quiet, feeling man, with no pretension in relating to his students. But I wondered what the presence of all this toxic language in our systems would do to us over time.

Dr. Leonard was a specialist in the diffusion of forms from the arts throughout the culture, for example through the cannibalism of advertising, and he taught the ways in which ideas in science, philosophy and the arts influenced each other and changed the values and perceptions of the culture at large or, more likely, were co-opted by the culture. We thought in terms of "culture" in the American Civilization Department. Culture in the sense defined by anthropologists: "A system of values and beliefs communicated through language." What defined a people as distinct from other cultures? We approached American history as if we were anthropologists trying to locate the underlying values that made the whole system cohere. We tracked the way these cultural forms and values changed over time and why they changed. What made us Americans? What assumptions did Republicans and Democrats unconsciously share? In which ways were we different from Europeans, and why?

I saw culture as a kind of hypnosis that left us gyroscoped with limited, structured vision and secret guilts. It seemed to me that the aim of Zen, for example, was not be become like the Japanese, but to be free of all cultures. To my mind, that was the path toward becoming liberated.

The department focused on the Puritans because they were the most homogeneous culture in America (excluding native-American cultures). [Dick Gregory said that Columbus was the only person to discover a country that already had people living it. I quoted this in a book review once and received hate mail.] The Puritans were very close to an isolated, unified culture. We spent weeks studying their values, customs and ideas; they were more interesting than I had supposed. Especially because of the religious experience I'd had in Massachusetts. The Puritans centered their world on religion and in reading their original documents I could see that the religious experience they described, the one that they had (at first) required for a person to receive membership in their churches, was just like mine. This affirmed for me, beyond doubt, that my own religious experience was authentic and had historical precedents.

Later, I took a course in American Social and Intellectual Thought from an older, funny professor I liked, Wally Davies, who fulminated against the fundamentalists; he once shouted out that we blamed everything screwed-up in America on the Puritans but that this was wrong. After a beautifully timed pause, he added that everything had actually been screwed up by the

Baptists and the Methodists.

Davies was a popular professor. He was the opposite of cool, but his neuroses, his honesty and passions and wit endeared him to the students. Once, when a student asked him about the American transcendentalists, he confessed that he couldn't understand them either and that he always scheduled his lecture on them for the last class of the semester, hoping he would get sick for a week so he wouldn't have to teach it.

Another favorite professor was Robert Lucid, a pal of Norman Mailer who appointed him his literary executor. He taught Modern American Lit: Dreiser and Stephen Crane, Dos Passos, Eliot, Hemingway, Fitzgerald, Steinbeck, Mailer, etc. Lucid was one of our idols. He would come into class on Saturday morning with a hangover, looking like Rick in *Casablanca*. He never took attendance. He was beyond attendance. Some of the people there weren't even students at the university.

Professor Lucid's philosophy was that if you would show up every week at nine o'clock Saturday morning to hear literature lectures, he would speak to you, whoever you were. And we loved the way he spoke. About "arenas of discourse" and "stuttering styles" and "worlds of fragments." Once, he lost his composure and shouted desperately at the class, "Don't just suffer all this for nothing! At least make art of it!" I never forgot that injunction.

They worked us unconscionably hard. We were assigned reading of about 1500 pages a week, plus we had to write papers, prepare for a language test, as well as research and write an MA thesis. We read all the time, every day, while we ate, almost while we slept. I pretty much stopped drinking. I couldn't afford the time for hangovers. Besides, although always tense and pressured, I felt like I was moving downhill now, without the depression and the exhaustion of all those wasted hours in the Army. And I was learning at a greater rate than at any time in my life, the type of knowledge I respected most—the kind that helped you to put different fields together, to integrate them, to try to comprehend the infinite variety and connections of the vast and mysterious life around us.

Perhaps all groups think they're special, but I thought my friends in the Am Civ program were. Bill Issel from San Francisco went on to write books on urban history and a history of the U.S. since World War II, Bob

Jones became a professor at the University of Illinois in religious studies and edited the Emile Durkheim journal, Mel Hammarberg went on to be a professor at Penn. My pal Joe Skerett, a witty, bright, African-American student, had told me he was having trouble with a famous literature professor, an old Southerner who, Joe said, wryly, "didn't like people of my complexion."

Joe was sensitive and fun to talk to. Once, he took me home with him to a family barbecue in Queens, where we had a wonderful afternoon, all the generations dancing together on the back lawn. Several years earlier, along with a group of disgruntled, waggish, graduate students from northeastern universities who wrote subtly ironic letters of praise to idiotic public figures, Joe had been one of the founders of The Dirigible Society, "dedicated to bringing style and grace back into American life." He invited me to a gathering of the society in a small town north of New York City; standing in the middle of the town square, we joined in singing the plaintive anthem Joe had written, "Lighter Than Air Are We." Joe printed up stationery with a dirigible on it, and whenever he read about a particularly stupid, racist speech by some Southern yahoo, he would write to him in our name, and in flowery language congratulate him on his insight, eloquence, and perspicacity. The bigots would always take these compliments seriously; Joe kept their grateful replies in an archive.

To avoid hierarchy and a competition for leadership posts, all members of the Dirigible Society served as presidents simultaneously, and were addressed as such. Disturbed by the American Civilization Department's social science emphasis, President Skerett, a lover of literature, transferred to take a PhD in the Yale English Department.

My two closest friends were Bruce Kuklick, the best student among us, and Rochelle Gatlin, a San Francisco proto-hippie radical leftist. She showed up with her husband Ken Gatlin, a quiet poet from Northern California who crashed Robert Lucid's lectures.

Bruce Kuklick was a phenom, reaching for two PhDs at the same time, Am Civ at Penn and Philosophy at Bryn Mawr. He was from Philly, the son of a laborer at the water works. Of German descent, he was very American in his love of the Phillies (he later wrote a book about Shibe Park), but his German inheritance surfaced in his blond hair and his inexorable work ethic. Bruce would be at the library door every morning when it opened. If there was a blizzard, if he had 103 degree fever, he would be there.

Bruce had been an undergraduate at Penn. His wife, Riki Kuklick, also went to grad school at Penn, studying sociology and urban planning. She came from a prominent, wealthy, Jewish liberal Philadelphia family. While I had sent Martin Luther King my allowance when I was a kid, they'd been having him over to fundraising dinners at their classy house in Northwest Philly.

The Kuklicks were far ahead of me intellectually and politically. They lived downtown behind Independence Hall in a Revolutionary War brick house with one room on each floor. When Bruce first told Riki he had invited to their party a guy he had met at school whom he liked, an ex-Army officer, engineer, Wharton MBA, with a crew cut and a wife who was a former nun, she looked at him like he was crazy. Riki and Bruce and I were to become lifelong friends.

While I had been waiting for autographs as a teenager outside Yankee Stadium, Bruce had been studying Marx and Lenin in a radical political group, led by a friend's Old-Left parents. While I collected Martha Reeves and Dave Brubeck and John Coltrane records, Bruce and his friends were accumulating FBI records.

The Kuklicks stuffed their little house with windup talkers at the parties. Grad students, young profs, leftists, intellectual friends from Philly like Gloria Simon, the witty daughter of a famous newspaper columnist. Gloria and her husband Bob, an artist, had a pet skunk that slept all day and paced compulsively back and forth along their flat's rear wall like a marine sentinel at night. Bob drank all night when he wasn't making beautiful paintings of saints on wooden plaques in the old Siennese style. For some reason he had built a scale-model North African village that filled a whole room of their flat.

Gloria told me, laughing, that she had a friend, a classical organist, who was leaving on a concert tour of Russia. Gloria remarked to her that at least it would be easier to travel there since Stalin was dead, but her friend had never heard of Stalin.

I was learning new things about art and intellectual life every minute, hanging out with these people who, except in the areas of black music and dance and pop culture, and Eastern thought, were much more sophisticated than I. When someone brought up the name of Dr. Sam Shepherd, the unconvicted murderer, and Gloria quipped, "Character is fate," I didn't know what she was talking about.

Bruce Kuklick loved to debate philosophical questions. Though he worked like a fiend, he had a lightness, a brightness, an easygoing temperament and a wonderful laugh; he was tall and you could see his blond head across the room and hear him almost giggling with joy as he said to a philosophy student, with amazement, "But you've got Kant all wrong! He was saying just the opposite." Bruce loved to talk about ideas and he loved anyone who would oppose him. I knew he was going to be a great teacher. I was not surprised when, after postdoctoral work at Oxford, he took a position at Yale, wrote a book, *The Rise of American Philosophy*, which won the Phi Beta Kappa award as the best scholarly book in its field that year, and became editor of *American Quarterly*, the premier journal in American Studies, all while still in his twenties. He has since written a bouquet of significant books, and now holds a prestigious Chair in History at Penn where he was voted the students' favorite professor.

Charlotte was not comfortable at these parties, not being a glib talker or academic. She and taciturn Ken Gatlin, the two Northwesterners, would sit on the stairs by themselves, quietly having their own party.

When the Kuklicks discovered that I had come to the university to seek wisdom by sitting at the feet of wise men they looked at me with astonishment. Their jaws actually dropped and they were speechless. It was like Caspar Hauser had arrived in Philadelphia, a world class naïf, raised in a basement out of touch with mankind.

They were also amazed that I was not vehemently opposed to the war in Vietnam and they began to make my education in this area their project. I did not support the war, I admitted that America was flawed, but I didn't like the Communists either, and I towed around a certain Bronx suspicion of radical intellectuals whom we had seen as fashionably anti-American and somewhat impractical in the gangster dominions of the real world. Surely America couldn't be *that* bad.

Soon after I met Bruce, Charlotte's mother called from Idaho with the news that Charlotte's brother Rod had been shot down. His navigator/ bombardier and he had ejected. One rose off the ground and was immediately captured. The other just lay there. That was all we knew. Rod was either dead or a prisoner.

This woke us like the unexpected touch of a cold knife on a hot day. I had not had much time to follow world events. In the Am Civ program there was no way to keep up with the assigned work. Charlotte had worn a dark veil of fatalism between herself and the world since she had experienced how people treated a poor girl like her in Idaho. She kept her distance from world events and separated herself from endeavors that involved large numbers of human beings.

But somehow she began to attend a weekly teach-in on Vietnam run by a professor of Chinese history, Jonathan Mirsky. She would come home and fill me in on what had been said. It didn't take long for her to turn against the war. I couldn't fit her reports into my diagram of America and the world. There was a kind of dissonance, a mental astigmatism that fuzzed up the data. I was no longer sure exactly what I believed; I tried to be fair to both sides, but something was disturbing me, like the almost subliminal sound of a persistent bass line from a neighbor's stereo, bleeding through the walls.

I decided, in the scientific fashion, to change my hypothesis; as an experiment, I would attempt to believe for a while that America was wrong and see where it led me. I went with Charlotte to a couple of the teach-ins. Immediately, certain anomalous facts emerged from the shadows. I was astonished to learn that it was the U.S. that had violated the Geneva Accords of 1954 by preventing free elections in Vietnam because President Eisenhower rightly believed that Ho Chi Minh would win. We were there to prevent democracy.

This war had been going on for decades with Ho Chi Minh leading his people against the Japanese, the French (who had colonized the country for a century), and now the U.S. I hadn't known that Richard Nixon, when vice president, had brought up the idea of giving the French the atom bomb to use in Vietnam. I hadn't known that Ngo Dinh Diem, the President of South Vietnam, had spent their war of liberation against the French in New Jersey, at a Catholic seminary. And that he had been put in place as President of South Vietnam after reactionary Cardinal Spellman of New York had suggested him to the Kennedys. And thus the war was not just a war of capitalists versus communists, but a war of nationalists against the imperial powers who were trying to regain the colonies they had lost in World War II, and also, in a way, a war of Catholicism against Buddhism.

The electricity of these facts jolted me. Why weren't they reported in the mainstream media and known by all? But most significantly, once I put on my new hypothesis, my role of opponent to the war, all the day to day news reports from Vietnam suddenly began to cohere and make sense, as did the rest of American foreign policy.

I had tried to be a reasonable, mature, middle-of-the-road liberal, but the middle ground was being carpet-bombed daily by Boeing B-52s. You had to move to the Left or the Right.

My mother-in-law moved toward the Right. She spoke on patriotism and gave out rifle competition awards at the Idaho high schools. She wanted to continue the war to affirm "the principles Rod had fought for." My own mother also supported the war. This shocked me. I thought that everywhere in nature, the motherly instinct would be strong enough to overpower social conditioning. An eagle would have said, "Stop the war. Bring home my chick before they torture him to death." But apparently, with humans, this was no longer the case. Humans learned too quickly. The hypnosis was too strong.

Charlotte and I moved to the Left, although this was still more a personal matter than active opposition. Charlotte pretty much retreated back into her personal life, and I, although paying more attention to the war than I had before, returned to the shelter of my frenetic studying.

I felt a certain guilt at being a student. I was twenty-seven years old. Why didn't I have a job? Going to RPI had been a luxury, and Wharton was already beyond what I had been allotted. How could I have gone back to school, become a professional student, as my family and friends in the Bronx saw it? Why wasn't I beginning the career my family had paid for, taking my place in society as an adult and supporting a family?

I had the rational answers, but the old conditioning etched away at me. I had to work from morning to night to justify myself.

Even though I needed to study harder than the other students who had been predominantly history majors as undergraduates, the program was fascinating. Finally I was taking courses that related directly to the world around me and thus to my understanding of myself, since I had been formed by this world around me.

I loved the way the courses came together. Our principal class was a yearlong Am Civ Pro-Seminar with Professor Jim Flink, a passionate teacher. A protégé of Professor Cochran, he specialized in the automobile and its effects on American culture. Now, we were going back to the organization charts I had studied at Wharton and learning how they had been improvised and worked out by Alfred Sloan and others when they were trying to figure out how to run mega-corporations like General Motors in the Twenties.

Professor Flink was knowledgeable in all fields of American civilization. He taught us the Puritans for weeks; he was a kind of puritan himself, a zealot of social science, lecturing to us on his various theories, his ideas about the connections between technology and values and history. By coming to university late and from a lower social class, he was a kind of convert, pleading with us to see the truth, cajoling, almost preaching to us, sometimes leaving the class in hot tears when he felt he hadn't gotten his point across.

We had stirring class discussions led by Bruce Kuklick on our side, laughing with joy as he engaged in these debates that he cherished so. Bruce, who knew more philosophy than Flink, would be happily standing up and quoting from C.I. Lewis and W.V. Quine and other modern philosophers to back up his ideas about leaving room for a modicum of uncertainty when proscribing what was true or not true in human society.

I loved when the courses complemented each other. We might attend Murphey's class on science history and be fed the background for Darwin's theory of evolution, learning about his grandfather Erasmus Darwin and Larmarck and the geologist Charles Lyell and how the revolution he sparked in nineteenth-century geology led to the new biblical criticism, shook the picture of a stable, short-lived human past, and thus contributed to the zeitgeist which enabled Darwin. Then we would go to Dr. Leonard who would be talking about the effects of Darwin's ideas on the arts, how they demolished the accepted idea of man as a special creation, separate from the animal kingdom, the crown of God's handiwork, and what this did to the received notion of the artist as a respectable, somewhat unworldly man who had a privileged access to the domain of ideals, a mediator between the heavenly and the earthly realm, a man who could be trusted to educate and enlighten the daughters of the rich. Suddenly artists were going downtown, to the disreputable, to the Bowery, to the unconscious and the vital downtown regions of the body.

Then Professor Flink would talk to us about Social Darwinism, how Darwin's ideas of struggle for existence and survival of the fittest seemed to his contemporaries to be an accurate picture of the unstable, industrializing world that they found themselves swimming in; businessmen and conservative thinkers used these ideas to justify the benefits of untrammeled competition, claiming that government intervention and social programs would only retard the progress of the species and the evolution of society.

Professor Flink drew two curving parallel arrows on the black board and excitedly explained to us that the "fittest" only meant the fittest to survive and reproduce in a particular environment, there was no moral connection to it at all. Whichever "curve" of genetics and behavior happened to conform to the changing "curve" of the environment was "the fittest." Then we discussed Prince Kropotkin, the Russian anarchist who opposed Herbert Spencer and the Social Darwinists by pointing out that man had no powerful teeth and long claws and that humans had prospered and survived by *cooperating*!

Then Dr Leonard would talk about Freud, how his ideas slowly leaked over to America until they combined with an underground literary tradition (E.W. Howe, Edward Eggleston, Hamlin Garland) that had opposed the traditional American biases toward rural values and mythically good small towns, and thus helped to produce a twentieth century masterpiece, Sherwood Anderson's *Wineburg, Ohio*, which depicted the underground, inner, lonely, sexually frustrated life of the American heartland.

Professor Murphey would talk to us about Einstein and relativity; Dr. Cochran would talk about the physicist Leo Szilard prodding Einstein to suggest making an atom bomb to F.D.R.; Dr. Leonard would describe the parallels between Einstein and the arts, multiple perspectives in cubism, how Faulkner combined Freud and Einstein in *The Sound and The Fury*, showing the action from multiple points of view and characters driven by unconscious forces; Dr. Flink would talk about conglomerates, and immigrants, and unions, and riots and Pinkertons—all the multiple, out-of-control forces that collided in the chaotic American market place at the turn of the twentieth century.

It was all too exciting to bear. Everything was coming together. I had been right in going back to school. It was possible to learn about the world in a way that enhanced and clarified one's life. This was the way I was going to spend my time on earth. Teaching and learning like my mentors. Working to raise human consciousness.

I was not at all interested in a successful power career in academia. Years later when I asked a young friend studying economics at Berkeley how he was doing, he told me excitedly that he had already kissed up to two famous professors; he'd hung around their offices, read their books, did favors for them, and been invited to their houses. This, he said, would eventually lead to excellent recommendations to Harvard grad school and would help him to form a network to attain a top academic job.

He made me see how impractical I'd been by ordinary standards. I had given no thought to this kind of manipulation as a student. I saw teaching as an alternative to the career path. I assumed this to be the view of my peers in grad school. It surprised me when I learned that many saw themselves as stuck with liberal arts degrees and were using a Ph.D. as their ticket to the suburbs and the station wagon.

TIME AND MOTION

"The nature of history and all that it contains is such that nothing perfect can be realized in time."
Nicholas Berdyaev

I wrote my MA thesis on Fredrick Winslow Taylor, the father of scientific management at the beginning of the twentieth century (and thus, indirectly, the father of business education and schools like Wharton.) Taylor analyzed the steps of factory work, breaking them down into motions and figuring out the one best way to perform every task and how to perform more than one action at once. His ideal would have been a one-man band playing all the instruments quickly until he collapsed. Then you could get another man to replace him.

It was the assembly line refined and brought down to an individual level. (Charlie Chaplin's *Modern Times* eloquently shows some "collateral damage" of this procedure.) This was the beginning of time study and the efficiency engineer. These ideas swept through the world, making Taylor one of the leaders in creating the texture of modern life. He was praised by American industrialists, but also by Lenin. Here was the common root of the entire modern, bureaucratic, industrial world, its rituals, assumptions and pacing, communist as well as capitalist. He had sculpted our world in his image.

Yet he was incredibly neurotic. As a student at Harvard, he went blind. When he returned home, as he had desired, his blindness vanished, thus was probably hysterical. He ran his life the way he ran a factory. No false moves. An incredibly tight person, he suffered repeated nightmares. He analyzed them and found that they occurred when he slept on his back. He built a contraption, a kind of S&M device that wrapped around him and tortured him if he slept on his back. This seemed to me a succinct image of the worker in the world he was creating.

The Taylor material fit the program perfectly, connecting industry and science with forms and values of daily life. Professor Flink had been hammering into our heads Dr. Cochran's notion that between the Civil War and WWI, entrepreneurs had made the major cultural decisions, not presidents and generals. It was business decisions that determined the quality and rhythms of daily life for millions of Americans during this time. Entrepreneurs were the initiators of accelerating social and cultural change. George Washington would have been more at home in the world of the ancient Romans than in America a century after his death. It was more important to study the character and value system of Andrew Carnegie and J.P. Morgan than Chester Arthur's vote totals and the dates of battles.

What kind of values were required to succeed in America then and now? We had gone from an inner-directed culture in which people of inflexible values lived in a stable world they saw as shaped in mysterious ways by God's purpose, to a world in which God was an unnecessary, uneconomical hypothesis; increasingly, the world could be explained more concisely by eliminating references to Aristotle's fourth cause—purpose or design.

We lived in a chaotic, quickly changing environment in which success required flexibility, loosely held values, situational morality. I listened very carefully here, because this was the world that had made me sick. Dr. Flink himself noted that under these assumptions, Jay Gould would have been more "fit" to survive than Jesus.

Fredrick Winslow Taylor's work created a fad for efficiency and applied science in every area of American life. The schools had to be efficient. The teacher's work was to be broken down into separate tasks, measured, timed and scientifically evaluated, as was the work of everyone from the garbage man to the housewife. The correct scientific methods of running a home were taught in home economics classes. Taylor even invented a "better" tennis racket, an idea which seemed totally crazy to me, but it turns out he was merely ahead of his time.

These ideas led to the notion of impartial experts directing life in all areas, and even to the Technocrats, a somewhat influential third party in the Depression, who advocated rule by experts according to objective standards, instead of biased politicians. This seemed a wonderful dream on the surface, but I kept thinking of my friends at RPI, the future scientists and engineers of America. Were they objective and coolly impartial? What about the people who ran Boeing? I couldn't forget my guilt over my vision that people like me had given the world's armies, and even Hitler, their weapons. I am not a moral relativist. Call me old fashioned, call me out of date, but to this day I still believe that it is wrong to be a Nazi.

It didn't occur to me at the time but now it seems clear that the American Civilization Department's attempt to apply scientific methods to American history was a late flower on this oleander tree.

I was not opposed to science. I saw what was bothering Professor Murphey about sloppy history. But students like Bruce and Riki Kuklick, Rochelle Gatlin and myself were in the forefront of a generation that was going to question the assumptions of a value free science and to voice doubts about the authority of scientists outside their narrow field of specialization. Riki Kuklick would become the Chair of the Department of History and Sociology of Science at Penn. The idea that science could be studied sociologically was a new and radical one that would have been considered heresy in the time of Fredrick W. Taylor. It stemmed from a breakthrough doctoral dissertation in the Thirties by the sociologist Robert Merton that demonstrated that science and innovation had flourished better under the Puritans in England and in Protestant societies in general than in Catholic cultures. Before this, science tended to be seen as beyond culture, a pure method of ascertaining truth that was above the influence of particular societies. The next step was to question the assumptions and cultural biases of the *social* sciences. Riki Kuklick did her major work on the attempt of the early scientific anthropologists to be objective in studying Africa. She showed that they came equipped with all the racial assumptions of the European cultures of their time which believed that species evolved on a scale that continued upwards from bacteria to animals to colored people to white people. In certain cases, an anthropologist coming upon beautifully developed art or craft in Africa invented a fictitious incursion of white people to explain the high level of civilization he found. Bruce Kuklick did similar work in the history of archeology.

Beside all this talk of knowing what would happen if we put tractors in Africa, or of bringing mathematical certainty to historical studies, I wondered what the purpose of my life was and how all this scientific thinking could contribute to it. I had put my spiritual life on the back burner for lack of time. I kept recalling the state of my being before my vision in the church in Massachusetts, how all this exposure to scientific and modern thinking had led me within a hair's breadth of a dead end. What tissues deep inside ourselves would we have to violate to attempt to find out what would happen if we put a tractor in Africa? Outlook was proportional to insight. I hungered to educate my feelings, to raise my consciousness, to refine my sensibility, to approach questions of ultimate meaning. I began to question the whole modern project itself.

> *"the ultimate of all objectifying acts: murder."*
>
> Roland Barthes

But my feelings were disjointed. It was as if I were driving an old touring car with the luggage rack on the roof, and now, along with all the mental baggage I had accumulated over my life, I had added a couple new suitcases crammed with doubts about Vietnam and about science. I kept these bags sealed and separate, as if they contained something shameful, like the infected sheets of sexual disease

From another angle, there was so much coming at me so fast it was like being in one of those floods in Missouri that we saw on television, half the town coming down the rampaging river, whole houses, dead cows, farmers, barns, the works. Only here at Penn I was swimming in a flood of propositions, half-baked notions, brilliant hypotheses, scintillating theories, facts, living ideas, carcasses of dead arguments and a whole floating TV store with screens showing simultaneous biographies: Andrew Jackson, Frederick Douglass, Robert Fulton, Jim Fisk, Boss Tweed, U.S. Grant, the failed drunk who became president, Harriet Beecher Stowe, Elizabeth Cady Stanton, Andrew Carnegie, Emma Goldman, Gene Debs, Frank Norris, Thomas Edison, Emily Dickinson, scores of faces and facts rushing by, soaking my clothes and threatening to pull me under as I tried to absorb it all.

I continued to respect the wonderful education I was receiving from my brilliant and dedicated teachers. My scholarship was rising to the high level that was demanded. I saw the advantages in their notion of minimizing the old narrative history, the old stories with heroes and villains, and instead concentrating on social science history, which, like a poem, could comprehend all sides of the matter, and employ the rich new statistical data about education, economics, family, race, demography and so on, in order to explain the dynamic of what had occurred in cultural terms.

I wrote two publishable scholarly papers in grad school. One was for Dr. Cochran: "Broadcasting: The Invisible Revolution." My thesis was that the entire structure of the television industry had been designed, authorized, and constructed for a weaker medium, radio, and later was simply passed down to TV which was seen as merely a radio with pictures. Yet around the time of World War I, when broadcasting was introduced, and these momentous decisions were begin made, radio was still envisioned as a telephone without wires. That's why it was called "wireless." It was defined in relation to what had come before. The fact that everyone could listen in to a signal was seen as a disadvantage. No one had the slightest idea that radio would be of any importance except to supplement the telephone in situations where wires were impractical such as ship-to-shore telephony or on trains. I proposed that perhaps all revolutionary technologies tended to be seen as merely new ways of performing old functions.

In science, Kuhn had asserted that a revolution occurs not when the evidence disproves a former theory, but when the older people who grew up with it and did their work within the old paradigm die. In the case of radio, it took a young man, David Sarnoff, to see that the "weakness" of radio, that it issued forth in broadcasting rather than narrowcasting, was actually the clue to the beginning of a new industry. Sarnoff had been the telegraph operator who became famous as the boy wonder who contacted the ships in the *Titanic* disaster and funneled the news to a curious nation. Not long afterwards he was the president of a new corporation: RCA

I hoped to make this thesis the subject of my doctoral dissertation under Dr. Cochran, but for a seminar paper for his class I decided to simply prove the first assertion, that the introduction of radio was invisible, and that its structure and revolutionary consequences were never debated. I turned to social science sampling methods. I posited that the *Reader's Guide to Periodical Literature* would have no reason to be biased in this case and would present a fair and random sample. I found that they listed 207 articles on Wireless from 1895, the year of Marconi's invention, to 1920, the year of the beginning of continuous radio broadcasting in America (on KDKA, Westinghouse in Pittsburgh.) I scoured the libraries of the East Coast and found over 200 of the original 207 articles. Sure enough, I was proved right. There was scarcely a mention of what would become the real future of radio (and television). Only three or four articles. Yet two years after KDKA's initial broadcast, the whole world of broadcasting was set in concrete—who would own it, who would pay for it, who would get the rights to the limited air waves, corporate control, networks, "the whole shebangle" as my pal Rigo Lopez (who later helped me run my liquor store) would say.

Dr. Cochran was impressed with the paper and told me to send it to the editor of the major scholarly journal on the history of science and technology. The editor liked the article but suggested I compare radio to the introduction of the railroads, which was probably his own hobbyhorse. I hardly had time to bathe, much less to sidetrack my studies into this new field of research, so I let it go. I decided to flesh out the article and compare it to other fields, railroads, or more aptly, the laser, after I did my dissertation.

"Most modern plays are concerned with the relation between man and man, but that does not interest me at all. I am interested only in the relation between man and God."

Eugene O'Neill

I also wrote a paper on Eugene O'Neill and Lorraine Hansbury for my American drama class with Gerald Weales, drama historian and theater critic for *The Reporter* magazine. He suggested I send it out for publication in a scholarly drama-history journal. Professor Leonard suggested that an idea I had about Faulkner might be sent to the "Notes and Queries" section of the principle journal for American Literature, but I had no extra time. I felt like I was driving a car that would explode if I slowed down below fifty miles per hour.

Professor Murphey was drilling us in historiography. If we wanted to approach objectivity in understanding the historical past we had to understand that all that we had to work with was material in the present— writings, artifacts, etc.—that had survived and still existed. We had to project this surviving material backward and in a sense create a past using the limited resources we possessed which tended to become thinner as our field of inquiry moved back in time. Professor Murphey attempted to replace data that hadn't survived with other data that correlated with it statistically. But statistics didn't yet have the power to assure him that this result was objectively true. He filled the boards with equations. I was back in the land of capital Sigmas, the primary operators in our Integral Calculus classes at RPI. The letter Sigma seemed to be following me in spite of myself.

When we were tested on all this, in our first dreaded final exam that fall in Dr. Murphey's basic essential Historiography course, something went awry. We were asked to explain the high level of nineteenth century geographical mobility in America. We filled our pages with all the new history, the equations, the Sigmas, the normal curves, the abnormal curves. Poor Rochelle, we worried about her afterwards; she had little math and she had merely suggested looking at the diaries of pioneers, the old history at its worst.

Then we studied all night for the monster final the next day, Dr. Flink's horrifying Pro-Seminar exam. As we waited for the test to begin, Dr. Murphey appeared. He announced that all but two of us, about 30 of 32, had failed his exam. Rochelle had passed. How could this be? Her answer was simple common sense, the answer we would have given in high school. Was this what all the high powered statistics we had been studying had come to?

If we had already failed our first final, what kind of ground beef would Dr. Flink make out of us? Many of us had taken great risks to return to school. I couldn't go back into business. I would die.

Bill Issel, the future honored historian, cracked first. He was responsible for a growing family. He muttered curses, threw his exam book down and stomped out of the room. A bright young woman followed, weeping.

We all spit out our protests. The professors looked fearful. What would happen to the department if they failed us all in a required class? If several more of us walked out? There would be a scandal. The department might sink.

It was decided that we would all rewrite Murphey's exam at home that night, which was a farce since by now we all knew the desired answer. We all received Bs. The ship remained afloat. In due course everything was swept under, smoothed down, patched up, covered over. For a while.

> *"The moment when you realize that you are out there as far as anyone has ever been. Beyond maps, beyond radio contact, beyond the manual of instructions, Holy Mary, Mother of God, pray for us."*
>
> Timothy Leary

The waters were deep and there was no small sum of hubris in the department's quest for unassailable methods. The hunt for the Great White Truth had its perils as Melville had seen. Now the American Civilization Department is no longer extant, deconstructed, filleted and eaten by the University. Some years after we graduated, the whole department crashed into post-modernism and came down.

Professor Murphey had become chair by then. He moved toward making the department in his image. He hired another student, Mel Hammarberg, instead of Bruce Kuklick when Bruce returned from his post-doc at Oxford. Bruce didn't talk to Murphey for two years. He had idolized Murphey. Bruce dreamed of excited daily debates about the foundations of knowledge, a peripatetic school that would discuss the great questions of epistemology on the way back from lunch, everyone stimulating each other by probing, salient questions, but this wasn't Murphey's idea. He wanted a student who would accept the paradigm and work within it. Mel had been a minister in Minnesota before coming to the city. Bruce said Mel was looking for another religion which Murphey's program fulfilled. This was true in a way. Murphey sought to lead a band of puritans setting out for a higher truth in a new land. A city on a hill in academia.

I knew Mel had a good heart and I liked him though he was still a little naïve about metropolitan ways. He worried continually about the great black riots, the burning and the sabotage in North Philly that continued for days. We could see the smoke from campus in West Philly. One day he turned to me at lunch and said, with a troubled expression, "I think I know why the blacks are rioting." "Why is that, Mel?" "I don't think they're happy with their lives."

Mel would go on to do some good work on mathematical manipulation of nineteenth century data. Dr. Garvan would retire. Dr. Flink would bail and head for California. Dr. Murphey would hire others dedicated to the same ideals, a band of brothers following him into the wilderness. But then sisters appeared. The department had to hire women. As I heard about it, over time the sisters began to insist on the unique experience and viewpoint of women and lesbians. The original purity of the program was compromised. Skirmishes broke out between the brothers and the "Indians." The fashions turned away from science and white male authority. The confrontations turned to all-out war. The next generation turned against the purity of the founding fathers. The fighting shook the department and began to spread, involving the university. Finally, the department was capsized when our continent was hit by a huge new wave of the various post-structural and post-modern approaches which had begun to grow all the way over in France. The original Mayflower of idealists was fractured, dismantled and sunk. The University stepped in and distributed the remains to other departments. All that was left was Professor Murphey, floating alone in a vast sea of information on a large capital Sigma.

But what a teacher and scholar he was, and how much we all owe him! Later, when I began to sail strange acid seas, beyond bibles, beyond science, beyond reason, inhabiting the visions of different cultures and different times, soaring beyond the limits of all cultures into other dimensions, to vast universes of dreams within dreams, I thought of him and the other great teachers at Penn. They had somehow, by forcing me to confront their attempt at objectivity, unwittingly prepared me to question the scientistic worldview in which I had been socialized. Ultimately, a sense of fidelity to my own experience led me to take off the dark glasses of our inherited conceptual-perceptual system and to accept what I saw myself.

LOVE AT FIRST SIGHT

"We have put art on a reservation."

Claude Levi-Strauss

On July 4, 1967, Bruce and Riki Kuklick asked Charlotte and me to accompany them to an anti-war protest. I had never participated in such an activity before. I remember the temperature was over 100 degrees with humidity and no breeze. Riki had hoped that we might jump in her mother's pool afterwards, but her mother wouldn't have the four of us scruffians outside the house while she was entertaining a group of African diplomats inside. Riki had once said that in the Thirties her mother hadn't known there was a Depression until some people tried to eat the grass on her lawn. I had assumed the story was apocryphal, but now I wasn't so sure.

We joined a couple thousand people outside Independence Hall. There were speeches and a folk song or two. Just a nice lazy afternoon in the torrid holiday heat with a crowd of people I enjoyed being with. And then it happened. A disturbance up ahead of us. The police were running forward. I stood on my toes but couldn't see what was going on. Then the word was passed back through the crowd.

"Some guy chained himself to the Liberty Bell. The cops can't figure out what to do. They're trying to get some metal cutting equipment to cut him off."

I began to laugh. But what emerged went beyond laughter. I had to hold myself together to keep from crying. This seemed to me to be so significantly beautiful. The most improbable and perfect gesture. An incredible piece of folk art. At the cradle of the American Revolution, Independence Hall, in Philadelphia, on Independence Day, the anniversary of the signing of the Declaration of Independence, written by Benjamin Franklin and Thomas Jefferson, some rebellious young American had chained himself to the Liberty Bell.

I was a goner. It was love at first sight.

Talk about putting your body on the line. The Philadelphia police always crouched somewhere between the law and anarchy. They were like salivating German police dogs, straining at the leash. Their Chief, Frank Rizzo, challenged by days of black riots, had vowed to "make Attila the Hun look like a faggot." Not long afterwards he was elected mayor.

But now the police were mystified. There was no procedure for handling this. No one had ever chained himself to the Liberty Bell before. This was life as metaphor. We laughed and laughed while the police stood there, outwitted by a way of thinking more nimble than theirs. This agile, symbolic manner of responding to the authorities would be our model in the years to come.

TRAVELING LIGHT

"I asked my plumber, he's from Bombay, how old he was and he didn't know. I guess they don't have age in India."
                                                                        Paulette Long

One hot morning I woke up and drifted into the living room of our apartment to find three of our landlord's repair elves going through my pants' pockets. I was pretty loose about student-style housing but this was a bit much. Of course, Mort Packman found this hilarious. He put his arm on my shoulder, taking me into his space in a kind of Aikido move, and

133

said, grinning, "You know I offered these jobs to Penn medical students but for some reason they wouldn't work for minimum wage."

I had to smile with him but Charlotte and I decided to move to Lansdowne, just over the city line.

Before we left, my old pal Jim Saunt from Cleveland, who had been thrown out of the fraternity and RPI, showed up with his new girlfriend, Paulette, who was to become my lifelong pal. Paulette had an MA in art history. She was an Italian girl from Cleveland, one of those independent young women of the time who had taken a walk on the wild side, climbing over the fence between the races to a new land of jazz, rock and roll, and multiculturalism. Like Charlotte in the Philly ghetto, she was teaching in the Head Start program in the heart of the Cleveland hood, Hough, site of major riots over the years.

Paulette was visiting Jim in New York City for the summer. Jim had escaped the draft because of problems with hard drugs, uppers and downers. He was working in a record store in Manhattan where he was amassing a major record collection, blues, rock, jazz, and classical. Whether his boss knew about this was not clear. Jim had grown up hearing the great Cleveland Orchestra under George Szell at Severance Hall. He knew a good performance in every genre of music—Chicago blues, Stax-Volt, Motown, Blue Note jazz, Johannes Brahms.

I admired people who led a freer life, outside the social institutions that determined what was proper and legal. I didn't focus on the fact that Jim was living a split life. A street life of drugs and illegal activities along with a parallel existence in which he would go home to Shaker Heights on every major Jewish holiday, sleep in his boyhood bed, and dress up in a suit and tie for synagogue and dinners with his straight Hungarian parents. (None of us could have imagined that twenty years later Charlotte would be Jewish, married to Jim, stoned, and playing in the Shaker Heights Symphony.)

We took Jim and Paulette to a bar across the street from the university. Verna's was half a flight down, dark, with an art deco look to it inside, a square underground bunker with a round bar at the center, a low ceiling, just space for a few booths along the walls, and a huge juke box that blasted rock music at foghorn levels. Verna had all the great records of the day—the Temptations, the Four Tops. These were Jim's favorite groups.

He began to throw down boilermakers. I had stopped there now and then for a couple beers after leaving the library, and each time there was a near riot in progress. Verna's was like a hellish pre-mosh-pit, jammed with students dancing in a human heap to the rocking jukebox. Pretty, dark-haired, and still in her twenties, Verna was said to have inherited the place from her older husband who was in a mental hospital. She seemed to be sailing on that course as well. Not up to becoming the requisite authority figure, she would get gloriously drunk and at some point she would jump up onto the bar and shout, "Let's wreck this fuckin' place, boys!" She would fling her beer mug against the wall and thus would begin the general smashing and the breaking as the crowd sang along with Eric Burdon and the Animals, "We gotta get outa this place," and wrecked the bar.

Afterwards, as we strolled drunkenly home with Jim and Paulette, we passed a monstrous pit where the university was building a gymnasium. Jim became convinced he could drive the huge earthmover sitting a couple stories below us at the center of the ditch. He climbed over the fence, made his way down there, and attempted to climb onto the huge machine. After an intense struggle he nearly succeeded, lost his balance, hung there for a couple seconds. Then there was a loud ripping sound and he crashed down into the dirt.

Bruised but unbowed he made his way back up to us on Walnut Street. He was OK, but when we looked down, we saw that he had no trousers.

The next morning I donated a pair of jeans so he could return to New York. He was not the kind of guy who traveled with luggage. Soon they would be off for San Francisco and the summer of love.

WHERE HAVE YOU GONE, JOE DIMAGGIO?

I took a summer class in Constitutional Law focusing on the history of civil liberties in America. Began to wonder where was "America" if this was our history, Dred Scott and all the rest. I watched a Muhammad Ali fight, against some white guy (Joe Bugner?) at a local tavern. The patrons were shouting, "Kill the Nigger!" at the TV. I wondered where "The North" began. This was supposed to be the Quaker State, the "City of Brotherly Love." If you went north of Pennsylvania, you'd be in Canada.

In September, Bruce asked me to join him in a class on American foreign policy about which I knew little. The teacher was Gabriel Kolko, another professor who was to make a change in my life. Kolko was the first avowedly radical professor I'd ever had. In a manner of speaking, he had chained himself to the Liberty Bell as well.

There had been some riotous activity at Penn, in connection with a think tank on campus that was doing research for the CIA. The students arrived at dawn to chain shut the doors of a campus building, locking the administrators out. Professor Kolko, commenting on this in class, suggested wryly that they should have waited a couple hours and then chained the administrators *in* the building.

He was a wonderful teacher, stirring us into thinking in modes and about materials that were not available to us in the general culture and media. He had written a classic book, *The Triumph of Conservatism,* about the Progressive era at the turn of the century, in which he showed convincingly that the reforms of Teddy Roosevelt, the various commissions and regulatory agencies such as the FDA, the FTC, the ICC, and the FCC, were put into place not to curb business, as we had always been taught, but at the request of businessmen who were themselves frightened by the growing chaos as millions of obstreperous immigrants came here from non-Protestant, non-northern-European countries—emotional workers, who often voted socialist, rioted, tried to form unions, etc. The businessmen decided that rather than attempting to control an angry populace, it would be wiser to have commissions appointed to give the appearance of government control over business, and then to control the commissions.

I had never heard this angle on events, stated clearly and with cogent evidence. It shook me, not just because of what it was saying about the Progressives, but because of what it was saying indirectly about my previous education and about the weakness of the American media.

We read Lenin on imperialism. His ideas were mostly derived from J.A. Hobson, an English economist; Lenin made sense. Capitalism needed to keep expanding and one method was to colonize third world countries to insure new and larger markets for manufactured goods, inexpensive and reliable sources of raw materials, and cheap labor. Professor Kolko explained that America had colonized the western United States and then had adopted what seemed to be an anti-colonial stance because most of the good places overseas were already taken; the American leaders understood that it would be in our interest to advocate open markets in places like China where we had been shut out.

We read William Appleman Williams, *The Tragedy of American Diplomacy*, and other critics of America foreign policy; slowly I lost my sense of American exceptionalism. The US was not the worst country in the world. It was just not very different from any other colonial power, talking in terms of freedom and responsibility while pursuing its own selfish interests.

Then we read about neo-colonialism, in which major powers like the United States learned that rather than directly colonizing third-world countries it was now easier to put local people in charge in our stead, and to control them by providing or shutting off capital while training and arming and backing up their military forces.

All this led up to Vietnam, but this is not the place to re-fight the Vietnam War. Our government will do that for us in other lands.

It was all fascinating stuff but coming almost too fast for me. I couldn't integrate it all as yet. I was still hoping to live a quiet life, a college don on a small campus, outside of major academic ambition, sharing ideas with the students, and finding time to study and to meditate.

BORIS KARLOFF BOWLING

I grew a beard and bought a pipe. Joe Academic. I'd had it with cheap student digs and petty crooks and city traffic on busy Walnut Street outside our window. Lansdowne would be an adult location, quiet, serene, home of police and firemen in attached neat row houses.

I built bookcases and had Charlotte take a photo of me in front of my wall of books, smoking my pipe, like my mother taking photos in front of her Cadillac.

We were enjoying the peace on the first night in our new suburban apartment on the top floor of a small, neat, two-story row house, when I dropped a book on the floor. BANG BANG BANG BANG. Crazy banging surging up from below, banging that threatened to come right through the thin floor. Charlotte looked at me terrified, and I didn't blame her. This was insane gonzo banging, way too loud and insistent for the occasion. We didn't know what to make of it.

The next morning as we left the house, we found out. Our neighbor below came out and introduced himself. He looked and moved like Frankenstein's monster. Like Boris Karloff bowling. His name was Mr. Randall. He said he was a policeman, and he had a gun and a plate in his head, and that the walls of the house were thin, and if he heard any loud noises he couldn't stand it, and he was going to get out his gun and shoot himself, but first he was going to take some people with him.

"Well, we'll certainly try to be quiet in the future," I said, quietly.

Call me cowardly but this made me uneasy. We did see him later that week going off in a uniform. He didn't seem quite human. He was tall with a stiff, immobile face. He looked like a Nazi who had wandered into a delicatessen. He began to write letters to our landlady in Florida telling her we were anarchists and were wrecking her house. She wanted us to move which seemed not such a bad idea except school had begun.

Where would I find the time? Yet whenever we dropped something on the floor Charlotte and I would hiss "Mr. Randall!!" and jump up on chairs and freeze, our arms pressed tightly against our sides, trying to make ourselves as narrow as possible, looking down at the floor and waiting for the bullets to start flying through his ceiling. This wasn't the way we had planned to live when we had decided to become normal American adults in the suburbs.

Fortunately, fate intervened. Mr. Randall didn't show up for days. His apartment remained dark. We ventured to the beauty parlor in the next house and they explained that he wasn't a policeman. He was a bus driver who thought he was a policeman. Last week, he had not approved of the behavior of some of the people on his bus. He had left his route and driven into Philadelphia with all his passengers, in effect kidnapping them. He had kept them on the bus until he reached the West Philadelphia Police Station where he had "arrested" them.

Mr. Randall would not be bothering us any more. He was no longer living in the area. We were free of him. Except that every few years, wherever I was living around the country, I would receive a postcard saying, "I haven't forgotten you. I know where you live. I'll get you– Mr.

Randall." But I could tell by the handwriting that the note had been written by Bruce Kuklick, by then a Professor at Yale or Penn.

IF YOU'RE GOING TO SAN FRANCISCO

> *"thus I turn my back. There is a world elsewhere."*
> William Shakespeare, *Coriolanus*

The third member of our trio, along with Bruce Kuklick and myself, was a young woman who had shown up from San Francisco, Rochelle Gatlin. Something was happening in San Francisco, and Rochelle, who had been living with friends in a big flat in a neighborhood called something like "The Haight-Ashbury," was eager to tell us about it. And we were eager to listen.

Rochelle was not a theorist or mathematician. She was more of a proto-hippie, a socially concerned historian, open to using social science where it applied, but mostly interested in changing the world and excited about the undercurrents of thought that were surfacing. Rochelle was raised in LA, a working class woman, the daughter of Russian Jewish grandparents, with a father who was a union man; their family home sat in Torrance, one of those nowhere suburbs that exist inside LA, near the airport so the movers and shakers could move and shake your house when they landed their jets at LAX.

Rochelle had courageously moved to San Francisco, hooked up with a wild group of friends on Page Street, and made herself into another person—a hip, hard-working scholar. When we all wrote twenty page course papers, she would write sixty pages. She loved books, loved to hold them close to her thick contact lenses, loved to be surrounded by them, piles of them, rooms of them, all of them read completely and underlined.

She carried a huge shoulder purse, filled with books and papers; she looked like she should have been of the generation of Emma Goldman, reporting angrily on the Triangle fire of 1912 or picketing the trial of Sacco and Vanzetti with Edna St. Vincent Millay. She was an early feminist but she always claimed that the Sixties gave her the strength to follow the imperatives of her incorrigible heart. Later, she would write a fine book, a history of women in America since 1945, that embodied these views of the Sixties as a liberating time for women.

She showed up in Philly with her husband, Ken Gatlin, a serious, intelligent poet with a quiet wit. Ken was a pacifist, excused from the draft, so he worked for the Quakers as a movie projectionist. Oddly, in spite of their wild San Francisco environment, Ken had never had a single drink of alcohol. Each day he would walk home from work, passing the student bars, and never step inside.

Towards the end of the first year, I bumped into him on Walnut Street and noticed he seemed a little bouncier than usual. "I've had a drink," he bubbled. "I feel good. I think I'll stop in and have one each day on my way home from work."

Ken began to have two or three drinks. Then they went to San Francisco for the summer. In the fall of 1966, Rochelle returned without him. It seemed things were picking up in the Haight. It was The Summer of Love. Incredibly, Ken had become an acidhead. He was having an affair with their friend Beverly who also lived in the communal Page Street flat. Rochelle didn't seem to mind. She was absorbed in her studies and took up with another student friend of ours, a tall, athletic, mid-westerner, Bob Jones, who would wind up a professor of religious studies at the University of Illinois. Bob looked like a defensive end, but he was a gentle giant and Rochelle just moved ahead with no regrets.

After Mr. Randall had gone berserk we feared that some other suburban looney tunes might materialize in his apartment, so we moved Rochelle in below us as soon as she arrived. She had brought back fabulous news from San Francisco. Just as she was leaving she heard that it was possible to get legally high in a manner the government couldn't block. The answer: smoking bananas.

We quickly walked to the market. This was so cool. United Fruit would never let the government ban bananas. It was an answer from God. (It never occurred to us that if this proved possible, our government might put poison on the banana skins—that was completely outside our radar until a few years later when the Americans sprayed the Mexican pot fields with Paraquat.)

But now here we were, in 1966, a time of hope and innocence. We lit candles. We played one of Rochelle's Jefferson Airplane records. Rochelle had been baking the banana skins for hours until they dried up. We chopped up the remains and rolled our joints. Charlotte and Rochelle and I. All grinning conspiratorially as we smoked bananas.

"Do you feel anything?"

"I don't think so."

"I don't really feel anything."

"Here, try another hit."

"I still don't feel anything."

It didn't work. Donovan's "Mellow Yellow" was a pipe dream. United Fruit was safe. But we weren't discouraged. We knew there were thousands of hip chemists and budding Pasteurs out there who were willing to test their serums on themselves. Someone would find a way. In the meantime, there were hundreds of pages of assignments to read.

SUICIDE IN SLOW MOTION

On January 12, 1967, I had stopped on the way home to buy office supplies to begin my dissertation. When I opened the door to our house, Charlotte was standing in the shadows at the top of the stairs. "Your Uncle Ike called," she said, cautiously. "Your father's dead."

"My father's dead?"

"Yeah. We have to go to New York right away. The funeral's tomorrow."

But my father hadn't been sick. How could he be dead?

We drove to Yonkers where my parents had moved not long before. The apartment was filled with people. They were uncomfortable with my beard. Several of them joked lamely, "We thought you were the Rabbi." I tried to smile.

When the real Rabbi arrived he said it was customary to tear a piece of clothing when a father died. He was holding a small pair of scissors. I was wearing one of my few respectable pieces of clothing, a new sweater.

"Here, cut my sweater."

"Are you sure you want me to? I can just cut something else."

"No, cut my sweater." What did a sweater matter in the face of death?

A couple months later I would look at my cut sweater and wonder why I had been so foolish.

The funeral was held on 167th Street in our old neighborhood in the Bronx which has since been partially burned down. I would dream about that haunted block again and again. Twenty years later I would recognize it as the location for the dark Bronx "Inferno" scenes in the movie, *Bonfire of the Vanities*. It seemed to be following me.

I decided to keep the liquor store open. I studied at Penn during the week, drove to New York each Friday in my ancient VW bug. With its ineffective heater and no gas gauge, it appeared to have been manufactured in Germany around the time of the Thirty Years War. I wrapped my legs in a blanket and struggled to navigate up the freezing Jersey Turnpike.

In May we moved to Greenwich Village.

LIGHT MY FIRE

> *"What you are looking for is who is looking."*
> St. Francis of Assisi

"The time to hesitate is through." That's what they were playing everywhere in Greenwich Village that spring. I could hear Jim Morrison's Declaration of Independence spilling out of every bar as I walked along Seventh Avenue, breathing.

Ever since our whole class had almost been failed in Historiography, I had been living on a continuum of uneasiness. I harbored unspoken doubts about our academic gurus' worldliness and practicality outside the cult of knowledge. We were given hour after hour of extra exams—Master's Comprehensives, Doctoral Qualifying, Statistics, French— before our difficult spring finals. We were caught in the thresher of objective measurement. I was suffering the nagging symptoms of an influenza of distrust.

In Lansdowne I strolled alone on the dark empty streets at night and witnessed a hundred hunched-over Ed Sullivans staring at me from every window in every row house.

In Vietnam we were increasing the maiming and the napalm. There was still no word about my brother-in-law Rod. Robert McNamara and his brilliant assistants were using statistical measurement techniques to determine "kill-ratios" and "bang for the buck." It would not be long before the tonnage of the bombs we had dropped on Vietnam would exceed the total of all the bombs that had ever been dropped by all the countries in all the wars in the history of the world. All this on an impoverished country the size of New Jersey.

The time to hesitate was definitely through.

IT TAKES A VILLAGE

What kind of mulligatawny stew of hormones and ideals enticed or impelled me to move to Greenwich Village, I couldn't have said. If a trolley car named Desire had trundled through The Bronx, it would have headed for the Village. But the Village was also a center of spiritual thought, of underground philosophies, secret amber knowledge and arcane spells, sandalwood incense and lilac perfumes.

One evening in 1960 I had met my pal Marty Licker at his hangout, a dingy café way over on the Lower East Side, between Avenues B and C, just beginning to morph into the funkiest corner of the East Village. A chilly night on a dark tenement street vacant of other shops. Someone was giving a talk on P. D. Ouspensky, the follower and chief explicator of George Gurdjieff, the late Caucasian mystic who had attracted a following in the Twenties in Paris and the U.S. Katherine Mansfield had moved into his Center in France when she knew she was dying. Gurdjieff had worked out a world system of Eastern spirituality, esoteric mathematics, and Sufi psychology that offered a schema of the universe and a guide to daily life centered on "Self-remembering" along with various dances and music based on his physics and metaphysics. The Russian Ouspensky's books, *In Search of the Miraculous*, and *The Fourth Way*, were the rage in advanced underground circles such as the one that Marty had hooked up with in the East Village. As the talk turned into a fascinating and difficult philosophical discussion among the denizens of the dark café, a fight between local gangs erupted outside on the deserted street. The sounds of screaming and chains and blows and the thuds of kicks landing.

My old Bronx instincts kicked in. Mainly fear. I was with a bunch of stoned alchemists and unworldly philosophers. We were defenseless. My first thought was: "Call the cops." But this became the subject of debate. Was it proper for anarchists to call in the organs of the state? A Socratic dialogue ensued, at a leisurely pace, pro and con. I sat there terrified. We couldn't see outside through the painted-over dirty windows. Shouts and screams continued. I kept looking toward the door. Finally, after about the length of World War II, the violent noises and shouts subsided.

But I left fascinated by the new ideas I had heard. I had been keeping in touch with a pure underground stream of alternative thinking and Eastern religion since I was a teenager. While in high school I had read Huston Smith on world religions and was amazed to learn of these very different ways of seeing the world, paths followed by billions of people since ancient times. In the late Fifties, at college, the beats had turned me on to Zen Buddhism. I loved the verbal sparring of Zen, the jokes and sharp thinking.

I read Alan Watts, an Englishman, ordained minister in The Church of England, who had studied Zen in Japan and somehow wound up a hip guru and philosopher on a houseboat in Sausalito. At RPI and after, I had often turned to his books for the intriguing puzzles and skewed insights that hinted of making sense in a way I couldn't quite grasp. I was also intrigued by Taoist wisdom about flow and change. Lao Tsu and Chuang Tsu, two old Chinese jazz musicians toking beside the River of Being in ancient Asia, watching it all drift by. I continued to stay in touch with the original Zen masters as well, with their double somersaults and twists, their koans like, "What is the sound of one hand clapping?" and "What was your original face, the one you had before you were born?" I chewed on them for years, unable to completely digest them, but always returning for sweet tastes of the sacred juice.

I had no spiritual practice. I merely thought, attempting to crack the antediluvean codes and to apply this wisdom to my life. Then I met Charlotte, who pierced my side with the arrow of Catholic mysticism, Jesus, and St. Theresa, and St. John of the Cross. In the Army, after I ran into trouble, I turned to Hinduism, especially Vedanta, through the English writer Christopher Isherwood, student, collaborator and translator of Swami Brahmananda, himself a student of Swami Vivekananda (a living disciple of Sri Ramakrishna, the Hindu saint). Swami Vivekananda had brought this Indian thinking to the U.S. at the turn of the century when he amazed people at the World Fair in Chicago, showing them a swami who didn't fly on carpets but presented a coherent, deep, and intellectually satisfying philosophy for another way of life, a path toward inner peace. I

144

learned from Aldous Huxley and Gerald Heard as well, Isherwood's fellow English pacifists in LA, who contributed to his *Vedanta for the Western World.*

[Strange how the colonized get their revenge by converting the brightest children of their conquerors, smart young Englishmen turning to Indian thought; the Vietnam War bringing Buddhism to the non-Asian United States.]

In the Army, I came back to Gurdjieff and Ouspensky, reading them avidly, while mining Tolstoy and Dostoevsky and Berdyaev for their religious insights; they all hailed from that same frontier area where East meets West, the Eurasian, Caucasus, Middle East-Far East mix. I came to love the tradition of Asian thought, seeing echoes of it in Thoreau and Emerson and Whitman before I learned that they had actually been reading the same basic texts that I was, ancient holy books like the Hindu *Baghavad Gita.* The Americans in nineteenth century New England were gleaning the seeds of their philosophies from the German romantics who were also reading the holy books from India.

I loved *Zen Flesh, Zen Bones,* with its beautiful little tales, heart piercingly lovely stories that made you question the aim and method of the more intricate, outward, and wordy Western short stories.

It was only at Penn in the past couple years that I had lost touch with this beautiful salving resource, my opening to the Heart at the center of the universe.

I had survived a long tense twenty-eight years in the world. Even when I would attend a Giants' football game at the Polo Grounds for the fifty cents high school student rate in the bleachers, I would bring my French text and study on the freezing bench before the game, while around me the men who had walked over from Harlem would be joking and laughing steam and drinking shots of Four Roses from pint bottles in their old overcoats. I always carried my super ego around with me like a portable penitentiary. Every once in a while I would break out and get staggeringly drunk, but I knew they would find me and bring me back the next day.

Greenwich Village was to be a kind of spa after all this effort. But there were still the ridiculous Ph.D. orals, the twelve hours a day of cramming, the preparing of my mind like a body for the doctors' measurement. I was speed-eating material I would never keep in; I would shit it out at the orals and then forget it, just for spite, in my anger at this method of forced feeding, like young veal in a little cage. Each day I was tugged in two directions, the absurd black and white cramming versus the Technicolor Sixties parade on the local streets. Fortunately there were more than twelve hours in the day. I could stroll the avenues and trawl the bookstores in the evening, but it was like taking off Frida Kahlo's full-body cast each night, and then having to strap it back on the next morning.

A double life. A few hours a day of reaching for freedom. Maybe this was the way most people lived.

From the viewpoint of Highbridge where I grew up, Greenwich Village was a kind of anti-Bronx. Composed of anti-matter. Where anti-parents with anti-morals lived under anti-laws and became anti-respectable and anti-repressed.

The Village was dangerous and ecstatic, art and orgies, black Sabbaths and desecrations of the sacraments, sex and hallucinations.

The Village was bohemia. Colorful like Paris, or Rome, or Mexico, or other places we could only imagine, while The Bronx was gray in its heart, gray streets and gray lives covered with gray dust, gray buildings, gray concrete under gray skies.

The Village was charming old crooked lanes with pretty little Left Bank trees, impracticality, exuberance, recklessness, booze, jazz, wild women, exotic drugs, poets reading in coffee houses, intellectuals up all night arguing philosophy, communists, folk singers, nudists.

And gay people. The first time this came to my attention in The Bronx, I heard a guy from the next block, about seventeen, three years older than me, Freddie Morrisey, not the brightest light bulb in the package, bragging to a bunch of guys my age on the street, "I wen downa Village last night. I really tied one on. You shoulda checked out the chicks down there. What a bunch a locks! But listen, this guy comes up to me in the men's room and he makes a fuckin pass. At *me!* I coulden believe it. This fuckin fruit makes a fuckin pass at me. Jeez."

"What'd you do, Freddie?" little Torpedo Clapman said.

"Whattid I do? I cold-cocked him." Freddie's loose head bobbed as he laughed through his chipped front teeth. "Just like anyone woulda done. I laid the fuckin fag out, right there in the fuckin toilet."

Everyone nodded with respect. I thought, "What a fuckin moron!" I walked away by myself along the treeless street between the naked apartment houses at dusk, feeling lonelier than ever.

We would read about the Village in the *Daily News*. Always some drug murder or crazy poet gone off his rocker or a picture of some wild *shiksa* in a leotard. One morning I was on the El train on my way to high school when I saw in the paper that there was a Miss Beatnik contest at noon in a bar down there called the College of Complexes.

Miss Beatnik! This flipped a lighted match into the sewer gas of my imagination. I leaped up, slipped out the door to the southbound platform and headed for the Village. Fuck school! Who could resist? A contest. Beat girls! I'd never been down there before, but somehow I found the almost deserted bar. I tried to look like I knew what I was doing. Sat down with about five other guys across from where they had a long table for three judges. Two photographers were taking pictures of three young women, one in a leotard. This was so great. Sin City. The Casbah. I was anonymous. Impersonating a Village guy. I could be lost down here for weeks. No one would find me. But what adventures I might have.

I was going out of my mind. The bartender approached us carrying a tray of small glasses of fruit juice. I took one with what I hoped looked like confidence. Raised it to my lips. And then I felt a chill. I stopped. Suppose it was drugged. Maybe that was the way they did things down here. Suppose everyone was going to get high on drugs and I couldn't handle it and they would find me down by the docks, my parents recognizing my picture in the *Daily News*, tortured in some weird sexcapade.

I subtly set the glass down in front of me. I wasn't going near that shit. I looked over at the bartender. I wondered if he was the kind of guy who would drug people. How could you tell?

The contest was idiotic. Even I was embarrassed. They asked the women questions like, "What is a short?"

"A sports car," the bored contestant would say.

The judges would nod and make a mark on a paper.

I was rooting for the leotard. She came in second. Afterwards they took some more photos. I wondered why the women would subject themselves to this crap. I guess this was what it took to build a career or something. At the same time, standing right there, was a real beatnik in a leotard. Everyone stood around making idle chatter, sipping on the drugged fruit juice. I was drugged on my own juices, swimming in a tropical sea of hormones. I went up to the leotard. She was tall. About twenty-two.

"I thought you shoulda won," I said.

"Thanks" she said.

"They don't know what they're doin'."

She smiled perfunctorily.

What was *I* doing? I didn't even date Bronx girls yet, much less Village beatniks. If she had said, "Want to have a cup of coffee?" I would have run out the door. But the heart (so to speak) has a will of its own.

I was shy with girls. I had been a year or two late to puberty. That meant I had lived not merely with the prospect of delayed puberty, but with the fear of no puberty at all. I had been preparing for an isolated life as a short fat kid, avoiding locker rooms where I had already learned the true cruelty of teen age boys, even your best friends, too many times.

When our family doctor retired and he was passing the baton to his replacement, I went to his office with my father during the transition and our doc said to the new doctor, "This is that impuberty case I was telling you about." I was mortified. He said this in front of my father. I was "a case"! Doctors were talking about me behind my back. Our doc gave me a shot of something, and I left contemplating my future as a castigated freak.

Then, in one year, I grew nine inches taller and entered the Israel I had prayed for: puberty. Suddenly, I was a tall thin guy, ravaged by terrible acne. I was often ashamed to go into the street. My face looked like a pizza.

It was hard to let go of my sense that I was going to be a freak. And that all the girls knew this. But inside the equatorial caves of my body, my new hormones were whoring and moaning, although I was still living like a monk, trying to hide my insecurity from everyone.

The College of Complexes sagged sadly in the gray afternoon light. Sawdust and stale beer. I was still running out of control. I found myself trying to commiserate with the leotard. I didn't know what to say. Finally, with relief, I saw her smile at me and turn to talk to a photographer, leaving me standing there.

What was I to make of this day? I knew the contest wasn't about beatniks but about publicity and sex and some second-rate guy taking a copyright on "Miss Beatnik" and crazy dreaming that it might lead to money for him down the road from horny guys like me. Couldn't he see it was a completely hopeless notion? Could it be that this guy knew less about the world than I did in some way?

Before I went back to the subway I entered the bar's men's room nervously. Luckily no one was in there. Above the urinal someone had scrawled, "Only a square could love anything but jazz of the coolest and chicks of the most."

I kind of liked that. It was very anti-Bronx.

BANK STREET

It was impossible for a neophyte to snare a rent-controlled apartment in the Village. The few that weren't passed to friends were advertised in the *Village Voice*, but we later learned that you had to wait in line at the news stand across from the office of the *Voice* in Sheridan Square, the first place in the city to get the paper each Wednesday; you quickly read the ads as you ran to one of the public phone booths with your change in your hand.

We took a studio apartment in a six-story, 1940s, elevator building on Bank Street, a block from the Hudson River in the northwest corner of the Village. Bank Street had a distinguished association with the arts. In past decades Willa Cather and John Dos Passos had written books there, and in the near future Diane Arbus would commit suicide a couple blocks to our left, and Sid Vicious would OD over to our right. Our building was solid but unpretentious, across from some tenements, next door to a famous acting school, near the danger of the docks. Quickly I divided the one large room by raising up my tall bookcases, filled them with my load of books, hooked up my stereo, put on some Miles, set out my pipe and tobacco. I wore black shoes and button-down Oxford shirts.

Charlotte found a part-time job as secretary to a local lawyer, an older Jewish man who lived with his wife in the Village and painted in his spare time. Strangely, Charlotte's predecessor, Marquel, was another hip, pretty, young woman from Idaho who knew Marty Licker. The lawyer owned a few tenements. Five months later a rent-controlled apartment opened up for us in an old building on Grove Street. Somehow, Charlotte had backed into a power job, dispensing rent-controlled apartments. She could have taken kickbacks for thousands of dollars under the table. There was a code word for this in the ads: "Furniture available." That meant you paid a thousand bucks for an old kitchen chair. We never did this.

My view of the city had changed when I was sixteen. With my pal Marty Licker, a year older, in the lead, I began to travel for inner sustenance to the area north of Times Square: Birdland, and Basin Street East. Jazz had shown me the healing miracle of art. It was not long before I was venturing down to the Village in pursuit of the heart and beauty of jazz music, its blue jewels of craft and meaning. I had quickly located forbidden oases in the desert of my life, The Village Gate, Café Bohemia, The Village Vanguard, The Half Note down on Hudson Street, The Five Spot, clubs where John Coltrane, Billie Holiday, Dave Brubeck, Paul Desmond, Charlie Mingus, Chris Connor, Al Cohn and Zoot Sims, and dozens of others were dispensing their cool absolution. Sometimes I would subway down on a Sunday afternoon and shyly listen to the folk singers in Washington Square. I was beginning to see the Village as a place where I could be comfortable with people who were like myself only more courageous. They had risked everything and followed their dreams. I was just a visitor, always lugging around the weighty backpack of my career, like a heavy gold bar that was going to keep me from ever being sucked into my parents' nightmare of becoming old and broke on the Bowery in the winter of January America.

But now that Charlotte and I had moved to the Village in 1967, I was still being torn apart by the opposing gravities of my divided self. I was so close to the Ph.D. that would enable me to teach and to learn for the rest of my life. But oh I loved walking along Bleeker Street and looking at the girls and listening to the sounds and gazing in the windows of the dozens of unique shops. Of course, I never shopped in any, but it was nice to have them there. My map of the Village highlighted bookstores and movie theaters. There were eight cinemas in walking distance. Most showed foreign movies and repertory. And there were the jazz clubs and little legitimate theaters. I hungered to make up what I had missed. I wanted to immerse myself in Italian Neo-Realism and French New Wave. I wanted to read books that weren't assigned, books about saints and foreign policy. I wanted to see all the plays I had missed, Brecht, and Chekhov, and Lorca, and Moliere and Strindberg. The Village was like a permanent repertory festival going on all around me.

Sometimes when I studied at night I would take a break up on the roof and look down at the Village like a winking tiara studded with self-lit stars, and I knew if you set it on your head and strolled along the street you would feel like Krishna, and people would look at you with astonishment but they would not be frightened.

New York was a great place to live if you were rich or poor. In the blocks around us there were always free events, free classical concerts of high quality along with poetry readings by Edward Field or Allen Ginsberg or May Swenson, or you could hear Yusef Lateef at our tiny, local library, as well as distinguished scholars talking about socialism at Cooper Union and wild, new off-off-Broadway plays in bars and lofts and tiny theaters; it seemed half the world of experimental dance lived in our neighborhood. And the streets themselves! The streets were so alive, when you walked along it was like surfing because the new spirit carried you.

But each evening I watched the war on television. I watched newscast after newscast. I thought of Rod, my brother-in-law, perhaps being tortured. I looked carefully at the GIs on the screen. Did I know that one? Had he been one of my men? And that one, torn apart by a mortar. Was that Smithson? With his crazy laugh and his funny impersonations. And that one? Had I sent him there?

I possess a vivid imagination. I envision future scenes; characters talk to me in my mind. I am always trying to think of the worst before it happens so I won't be surprised. I live in the future. I'm the guy who pulls into the right lane a mile before the exit.

Now I was jolted back into the imagination of disaster. My Army mind. My walking on duty behind the hospital at three a.m. checking the woods, imagining Vietcong there, waiting to kill me. Practicing whether I would kill them if I saw them. Whether I would blow the face off a teenager fighting for his ideals, in his country, against us, the rich white guys from the other side of the world. The white guys with the big weapons.

Throughout the High Sixties you could always smell the scent of burning bodies in the air. The fun, the concerts, the demonstrations, the walking down the wavering street on foam rubber acid feet, the riots, confronting danger with your brothers and sisters, dancing all night, smoking dope with your pals, the best times in the world, but they always took place on the banks of the river with the burning bodies of the dead on the ghats, smoldering, reminding us to seize the day, reminding us that people were being murdered at that very moment, by us, once the good guys, and that our communal hippie dancing was really in a long American tradition, the desperate dancing of Native Americans trying to overcome the superior fire power of the crazed white people who wiped out the buffalo for sport, frenzied shaman dancing, the casting of spells, the appealing to the Gods to stop these rabid Americans running wild, to stop their madness in the interests of both sides. What else could we do?

BUT SHE'S NOT THERE

> *"The Italians have as much right to take Ethiopia from the coons as the coons had to take it from the boa constrictors."*
> Wallace Stevens, 1935

Every day my orals appeared to be more irrelevant. In comparison to what was happening around me each day on the streets, and to the murderous daily slaughter on TV the American Civ Department down there in Philadelphia looked like a teapot in a tempest.

But I trudged on. Resentfully. I took the Pennsylvania Railroad to Philly and studied in a hotel all night before the orals. Late August. The students hadn't arrived yet. I waited by myself in the dim hallway outside the American Civ office. A dark afternoon. Thunderstorms threatening

Dr. Murphey opened the door. I walked inside. The four professors sat facing me but not looking up from behind an old wooden table in the weathered, dark, wood-walled office with the high ceilings. After years of intimate contact, I had not seen these men for several months. I smiled.

No one changed his dour expression. I felt like I had died and this was my funeral and they were looking at my corpse. I had anticipated some greeting, a little sense that this was a necessary hurdle for all of us to climb over, some acknowledgement that I had worked with them all for two and a half years and had done A work, even better, written publishable papers, been a class leader, always prepared, month after month, had been through the department ups and downs, and those outside of class as well, the Philadelphia riots with all the killings, the feeling of danger throughout the city, the smell of smoke in the air, and the department parties with their own more subtle dangers.

I looked at them again. Nothing. I felt like a comedian bombing in Peoria. Professor Murphey began to read a statement, the rules of the engagement, in a dead voice like a zombie. No one would meet my eyes. A team of unconscious doctors was transforming me from a sacred feeling subject into the object of an examination. I knew about unconscious doctors. I remembered them from Germany in the war.

I had left the bureaucracy of the Army for its opposite, the Ivy League. Now the Ivy League was proving to be merely the Army and water. I had believed that when JFK was elected and he picked all those brilliant Ivy League professors as his top advisors that we would never get into another stupid goddamn war. Now the Ivy Leaguers were running the stupid goddamn war.

I had a flashback to when I had entered this office when I was fairly new in the program. I had walked in to see the Department Chair, Professor Anthony Garvan. A group of professors stood right where we were today, gossiping, talking about the Chair. Did you hear? Tony said this, Tony did this, Tony thinks this. When they stopped for a second, I nodded toward the door of the Chair's office and said, "Is Tony in?"

Their heads snapped back. A student had called Tony, Tony! Heaven forfend! I saw immediately I had committed a mistake. I might have recently been wearing a gun, commanding 180 men, some of whom had fought at the Battle of the Bulge, I might have been working in a hospital, in charge of dead bodies at night, assisting in emergency procedures, sending people to jail or to their deaths in Vietnam, but now I was no longer an adult. Once again I would have to pretend to be smaller than I was.

I had gained an enormous library of knowledge in my head at Penn, but I had lost something as well.

I thought of this as I answered the routine questions on the orals. I noticed quickly that the orals weren't about me. They had nothing to do with me. They were about the professors trying to impress each other. The younger ones showing Dr. Cochran they had been good boys and passed along his teachings to me. Each of them preening before the others. I had wandered into an academic thicket and was cutting my face on twigs and branches of tenure, and promotions, and questions of prestige among one's peers. There were only four players in the room. I was the shuttlecock they were batting back and forth to show off their games.

I'd been studying for months. Up all night. My nerves were shot. I began to heat up. I found that all I had to do was give them back the ideas they had given me. I could even phrase it in the same words and that would satisfy them. But was this all they wanted of me? Why not just play tape recordings of themselves to themselves? I could no longer go along with this. This was all too small. I didn't want them to be so small. I was having a premature ejaculation of spite. Like the end at RPI when my body rebelled a month too soon and I became seriously ill, something was bursting out of me one step before completion. I was not going to shrink myself and participate in this farce.

They asked me about history writing centered on wars versus history centered on culture. This was the basic metaphor of their entire project. I moved to World War I, the chief symbol and example of their procedure. I quickly repeated to them the shortcomings of traditional history with its emphasis on great men and presidents and battles, agreed with their objections to it but only in a couple paragraphs. Then I began to move to the edges and penumbras of their thinking. I dredged up examples they weren't comfortable with. I was challenging their entire lives. I spoke about what the actual artists who participated in the Great War thought of it. I admitted the points the professors had taught me, but I qualified them by asking whether Hemingway, and Dos Passos, and E. E. Cummings and Erich Maria Remarque, and Wilfred Owen had not seen themselves as changed by the war? I asked whether these great writers were wrong about their own experience. Did the war do nothing to Aldous Huxley, now throwing away his literary reputation by taking mescaline; however modern Huxley (the grandson of Thomas H. Huxley, Darwin's defender) had been before the war, did they not think that some of his extreme and rebellious behavior afterwards was influenced by the fact that three-fourths of his class at Oxford had been killed in France?

All hell broke loose. In spite of the fact that I had been careful to show that I knew their arguments and basically agreed with them, the orals disintegrated. They kept trying to "save" me, to move me back on course, and I kept agreeing, showing them my grasp of the materials and then respectfully pointing to anomalies.

Finally Professor Neil Leonard, the jazzman, seeing my predicament, moved the orals to literature and I began to talk directly to him, giving him the answers he wanted because I agreed with those answers and I wasn't angry with him.

At last, after four years in the trenches an armistice was declared. I was asked to wait outside in the dark, deserted hallway. I knew I had annoyed them, but I felt certain I had shown a real mastery of the material and that they couldn't ignore the years I had worked with them. Surely they would see I had tried to kick the orals up a notch to make them interesting to all of us.

But no one emerged from the office. I could hear mumbled debate inside. I sat there as the debate continued. Oddly enough, I had no idea until I wrote this memoir as to what had really motivated and enraged me at that moment, when the questions had touched upon the importance of the war in changing young people's outlook and values. It was not until thirty-five years later that I was able to see that I had been speaking about myself. The war was shattering *my* values. I did not yet consciously realize that I was holding on by a thread to the system, to the culture and the personality it had created in me. I was on the verge of blasting out. The accommodation that I had struggled so hard to maintain was crumbling.

The war in Vietnam was an earthquake, a series of shocks that had just started and that were going to destroy the structure of my life as I had known it. Except for the radical historian Dr. Kolko, who had wound up not only at another university, but in Canada, so far as I remember not one professor had ever mentioned Vietnam in any of my classes. Except perhaps once or twice to say that it wasn't that important. It was one ship on the ocean of culture.

But I was beginning to touch the slightest wisp of my personal truth. I wasn't going to emerge from Greenwich Village with my pipe and my sport jacket after having merely gained a veneer of culture and post-modern thought. I was not embarking on a kind of Wanderjahr, a time to fill in my background in the arts, to loosen the binds and relax a little after years of study. I could not yet clearly understand that, in reality, the ties that had been constricting me had actually been holding me together.

I was beginning to fall apart.

AMERICA, YOU BROKE MY HEART

> *"From my point of view, General Fuller [who called himself a Fascist, and called for a Fascist Britain] has as good a title to call himself a 'believer in democracy' as anyone else."*
> T.S. Eliot, 1939

I had always enjoyed the railroad trip between Philadelphia and New York, but now that I had become acquainted with the films of Michaelangelo Antonioni, I could see the true beauty of the old factories that lined the tracks, the piles of gorgeous gold and copper and saffron colored industrial powders, the shapes and textures of twisted and broken machinery rusting there for decades in the snow and rain. Antonioni would frame environments like this as abstract art and then he would put elegant Monica Vitti in front of them, the rich, gorgeous, dissatisfied, industrialist's wife, and he would shoot her blond hair against the beautiful complimenting colors of the conical piles of raw materials, and he would have her husband ask her in desperate loving frustration what exactly it was that she wanted, and she would reply slowly, in huge close-up, without any expression on her face, "Everything and everybody."

I passed the orals. By the skin of my body. They told me they were very disappointed in my performance, but perhaps I had had a bad day, and after long debate they had decided to let me go ahead, since they knew I understood the material, but that I hadn't really passed on that afternoon.

I was shocked at first. As if I were still alive but had been swatted across the room by a lion. This was another bitter lesson. I was just beginning to perceive that everything in my life was going to be worse than I had imagined. I staggered out of there. But now, heading north on the train, a beer in my hand, looking at the post-industrial wreckage of New Jersey outside, I thought, "Fuck it." After all, I had gotten what I wanted. I didn't sell out and I didn't fail. I had cut it as close as possible and I had passed. I would never have to take another class. I would write my dissertation and move on with my life. Fuck it.

But I knew that I hadn't gotten what I had really wanted.

That night on Bank Street I mixed up some martinis for Charlotte and myself. My secret recipe: Gin and dry vermouth. We strolled over to a little Spanish restaurant hidden down by the docks. With adult waiters from Spain who were polite and efficient but maintained their dignity. An orderly place for the war veterans, the only people that Hemingway trusted. We chose a good white wine and paella.

Tomorrow I would begin my new life of frugality and morality. I would get some dope and join the rioting against the war.

THE DOMINO THEORY

In the Sixties an entire generation went crazy, wouldn't listen to reason, turned to violence and almost wrecked our nation.

That was the adults.

Fortunately we young people, impressed by the long tradition of non-violent resistance that went all the way back to the Buddha and Jesus, passed down to us through Henry David Thoreau, Leo Tolstoy, Mahatma Gandhi, and one of our inspired leaders and examples, Martin Luther King, resisted the selfish, aggressive proclivities of our leaders and parents and attempted to stop the war and save the soul of our republic by the use of largely non-violent means.

The operant principle behind our nation's aggression was that if we "lost" Vietnam, all the other countries in the area would fall like dominoes to the Communists. This philosophy was often summarized as: "If we don't stop them in Vietnam, we'll have to stop them in San Francisco."

Somehow this never made sense to me since North Vietnam didn't have a navy. Whenever I heard this statement, I always conjured up images of thousands of Vietnamese soldiers showing up one day under the Golden Gate Bridge on inflated inner-tubes, paddling backwards with their arms in the water, their rifle straps in their teeth, trying to keep their weapons dry.

The war was obscene and depressing but I was optimistic about ending it. I could understand how the American people might trust their government and be hesitant to stand against their country that had fought for freedom in World War II. After all, I had been in that position myself not long ago. And the average person didn't have the advantage of a top education, disillusioning experience as an Army officer, and the time and freedom to change his opinion as quickly as I did. Our job was to bring the lessons that I had learned home to the people. To show them that their children didn't want to fight this war, that the war was unjust, bad for America as well as Vietnam, and against America's traditional values. We would take the American people along the same path that had led me to change my position and to come out for peace.

Unfortunately, I would soon find that it was not going to be that simple. What I discovered was that the domino theory really was true in a sense, but as a projection of what was actually an internal process: once you turned against the war, all your other beliefs in this society came tumbling down like a row of dominoes. If the war was wrong, and America actually was an aggressive, amoral, imperialist power, then you were being lied to every day from every direction; you could no longer rely on government spokesmen, print journalists and columnists including the *New York Times* and *Washington Post*, TV newscasts, weekly news magazines, professors, pundits, liberal politicians and intellectuals. The vaunted American "free press" was actually serving as a de facto public relations machine for the American government and capitalism. This knowledge crushed the structure of the world you had thought you were operating in and left your former identity lying there shattered on the floor.

It was not a process that the mature and the established were willing to endure.

FREE AT LAST

But it was September in Greenwich Village and I was liberated. I still owed Penn a dissertation, but that would be at my own time and pace. No more exams for a lifetime, no more cramming for courses or orals, forcing information into my weary brain like stuffed derma, all those years of striving day after day to get out of The Bronx and to locate a path that wouldn't bore me to death or endanger my soul.

The Village was so alive. So different from Lansdowne. We're not in Kansas anymore, Toto. I strolled the colorful, free streets, made even more resplendent by the costumes people were wearing: blue jeans, denim workshirts, flowing Elizabethan dresses, theater usher uniforms, tie-dyes, old army fatigues, purple velvet Robin Hood shirts, yellows, oranges, carmines, bright light blues and indigoes. I dawdled on Eighth Street, the movies, bookstores, delis, sometimes meeting the eyes of my fellow villagers and secretly signaling, "I'm with you now. I actually live here. I've stepped outside. We're gonna change the world. I know it." The hopeful, sunny scene made even more vibrant by the weed I had purchased from Noel.

Noel was five years younger than I. He had grown up on my block, a close friend of my pal Marty Licker's younger brother, Irwin. Noel worked in a stained-glass lamp store on Fourth Street, a kind of funky atelier, where they made the lamps and sold them while continuously playing the latest rock music, Jimi Hendrix, Jim Morrison, John Mayall on a small phonograph that sat amidst the litter on the old wood floor.

He dealt a little weed on the side from his apartment way over at the far end of the East Village. Noel was about six feet three, with a wispy goatee and a gaunt aspect that made him look like a dangerous, dark Russian out of Dostoevsky, a brooding Raskolnikoff. He wasn't a gentle hippie by any means, but more of a street hipster. Noel always gave Charlotte trouble, making her wait for days for weed, forcing her to walk over to his decrepit block and then not being home. That was the way guys like Noel treated "chicks." Charlotte didn't like it, but she liked her weed more than she disliked these encounters. Usually I would go instead.

But I remembered Noel as a lonely kid on the block. His mother, a sweet, round nurse who tried to raise him on her own, one of the few kids in the neighborhood without a father. I always had a soft spot for Noel because of those memories.

I recalled how once, Noel, probably coming off a three day speed run, showed up at Marty Licker's house at Friday dinnertime, stumbled right past Marty's mother who had opened the door, basically fell down the dark hallway toward the little room Marty and Irwin shared and wound up crashed and out cold on Irwin's bed. Marty's mother, Evelyn, was dumbfounded, but they let him sleep. Marty slept on the other cot and Irwin slept on the floor between them.

The next morning Marty and Irwin went in to breakfast, but Noel slept on. Evelyn, becoming worried, went inside and shook him. "Noel, the family's going in to breakfast now." Noel just grumbled, "Yadda Yadda," still asleep, and turned away. At Saturday lunch, Evelyn tried again. "Noel, the family's having lunch now." "Yadda Yadda." No response. That evening, she woke him again. "Noel, the family's having dinner now." Noel just rolled away and went back to sleep.

Finally at bedtime, Marty, frustrated by his mother's inability to just let Noel sleep, went over and woke Noel himself. When Noel groggily looked up, Marty said, "Noel, the family's going to sleep now." Then Marty turned out the light and went to bed.

Marty Licker's brother Irwin was six years younger and repeated his every move. When Marty had become the only Dodger fan on the block, Irwin became the second. When Marty moved to the East Village, Irwin followed a few years later. When Marty turned into an aficionado of jazz, Irwin followed here too, becoming infatuated with Miles Davis. The birth of the cool.

Irwin did not go to college. Instead he bought a trumpet and studied Miles' records. He imitated Miles' manner as well, always walking with his shoulders up as if it were too chilly. Irwin made a fetish of his trumpet. He carried it with him wherever he went, the little case under his arm like a fragile crack baby. No one could touch his trumpet.

He became pretty good at it. Sometimes, when I would return to New York from the Army or college, Marty and I would meet at Irwin's pad. We would buy some cheap wine, smoke a little weed, turn out the lights, and lie on the threadbare rug or on the old couch, while Irwin would go into the next room and stand there in the dark, playing muted, soulful, faraway, Miles-like melodies that seemed to condense out of the air.

Irwin had always been a good kid, much easier to deal with than Marty. I'd known him for his whole life and had always liked him. I didn't know then, that he would soon head for San Francisco, take a place on the lower, funkier end of Haight Street, and die at twenty-nine. Marty would live a couple years longer and be found dead in New Orleans at thirty-eight.

Since college, I'd smoked a little weed here and there, usually in connection with Marty or Irwin. Weed was not available at RPI. Sometimes a joint or two would turn up, from my pals or Jerry Ellisberg, my southern roommate who was later arrested for selling pot in New Orleans. Jerry liked living on the edge of the law, a kind of southern cavalier in the Christopher Marlowe line. He knew Marty and they got along for a while, but there would always be trouble. Once, when Jerry lived in New York for a couple months, Marty crashed with him and one night smoked all Jerry's dope, a huge amount. Dope was not easy to get in those days. Jerry threw him out, and told me, frustrated but unable to keep from smiling, "He always says whenever *he* has something he shares it with everybody, but goddamn it man, he never *has* anything!"

[Once Marty showed up at Jerry's parent's house in Raleigh, looking really beat. Jerry brought him in for dinner to the suspicious looks of Jerry's wealthy father. When the black maid brought his food, Marty thanked her profusely and gave her a kiss. After dinner, Jerry's father bought Marty a ticket to New Orleans on a bus leaving immediately.].

Weed was a big deal in those days. Normal middle-class people weren't exposed to it and wouldn't go near it. It was dangerous to possess as it could lead to long prison sentences. Only in the High Sixties did weed begin to be generally available and to be used as a sign of membership in the counterculture. I liked weed, but being a control freak, tightly wound, I had farther to unroll when I unraveled. Smoking in public made me nervous at first unless I was around people I trusted. I was afraid of straight people when my defenses were down and my brain went on vacation, which it always did, taking the first flight to Jamaica as soon as I began to toke. I loved to smoke on my own at night, when the straight people were asleep. I didn't smoke that often in the daytime because I still was working on my dissertation, and I couldn't read on dope since my mind, tortured for so many years, once off its leash refused to remember anything abstract or related to work.

When the Beatles' *Yellow Submarine* movie came to the Twelfth Street Theater, it was reputed to be a doper's event. Everyone was getting ready for it. We were living on Grove Street and we got really loaded. Too loaded in a way. As Charlotte and I made our way over the ten blocks to the theater, we could barely navigate down the street. But then, when the movie came on, tragedy struck: the screen was only the size of a postage stamp! I had been anticipating this moment for weeks and now I couldn't see the damn screen! But the stream of light overhead, slicing through the cigarette and pot smoke in the theater . . . it was *sooo* beautiful! It was so incredibly pleasant to lie back in my seat and float downstream, just watching the variations in the flowing colored light beam overhead, while listening to the Beatles on a fabulous sound system. So much more relaxing than having to follow some silly plot. I had a wonderful time, although I never did find out what the movie was about.

The draconian dope laws were way out of step with the mores of the new generation, but they came in handy for the government when the anti-war activities heated up. Unfortunately for the authorities, the courts still held that it was illegal under the Constitution to arrest people for speaking out against the war, although polls showed that many, if not most, of the American people would have gladly voted against the Bill of Rights if given the chance. Yet there *were* the dope laws. And virtually every leading and outspoken anarchist and hippie and anti-war activist smoked dope. So if you were after a radical young person, you could just bust his apartment and then send him to the penitentiary for years under the marijuana laws. And if he didn't have any dope on him at the time, how hard was it to drop a joint into his jacket pocket? After all, he probably had smoked pot at one time or another.

THE ATTACK ON THE PENTAGON

> *"I went thus through the 'inner catastrophe'. . . I had literally come to the end of my conceptual stock in trade. I was bankrupt intellectualistically, and had to change my base."*
>
> William James

With my orals behind me, the war became my life. I seemed to live in the war, not beside it. I centered my days upon it. Protests, lectures, civil actions, draft card burnings, Whitehall Street (the induction center), Wall Street, Columbia, NYU, Tompkins Square, Washington Square. I had a vivid imagination that personalized everything and I felt guilty at my past behavior. As if I had repeatedly walked by a murder in progress every day, in order to attend to my personal affairs.

Now I had few personal affairs. I could do the liquor store in one afternoon a week if there was no trouble there with the employees or the cops. I loved being with the young people and radicals. This generation was so informal. Somehow they seemed to see the world from the same angle I did. Often I liked to just go over to the park and talk to people. Everyone was hopeful and energized. Everyone was reading like crazy and excited about the new music.

Once I walked to The Peace Eye Bookstore in the East Village. This was owned by Ed Sanders, who was somewhat famous as a beat-hippie poet and member, with scruffy poet Tuli Kupferberg and others, of a poetic, funky, rock band called the Fugs. When I entered the store I was astonished to find it was manned by Ed Sanders himself. He seemed to live in a room behind the store. And he was nice to me, a relative nobody. This was not the way famous people behaved. He was some kind of archeologist by trade; he knew all about ancient religions and he talked to me about the plans to levitate the Pentagon.

How could I not go?

It was almost Halloween, so I was quickly able to purchase a rubber skull on a pole to carry with me to ward off the demons. On Saturday, the buses left unconscionably early for the five hour trip, so I stayed up all night and dropped a dexy with breakfast. I donned my army fatigue shirt with ROSEN printed over my right breast, my fatigue hat with the silver first lieutenant's bar affixed to it, stowed a half-pint of brandy in my pocket and set out for the deadly nerve center of the machine, the robot factory of unconsciousness whose poisonous emanations had almost driven me to suicide back in the Army.

Charlotte was not going. She had retreated back into a familiar cave of social despair. You couldn't deal with the straight people. They had been mean to her in Idaho. Mean because she was poor and pretty and smart and different. There was no way to change them.

She began to center her life on horror movies. Each week she would go through the *TV Guide* and circle every horror movie. There were no VCRs. Most horror flicks were shown late at night. She would set alarms.

I would see her out there at four a.m., in her old nightgown, smoking dope and watching ghouls and vampires and werewolves and righteous burgers. Her sleep patterns were completely irregular. She began to lose weight and to look a bit like a gaunt Halloween creature herself.

The war was becoming unimaginably worse. Every day it tore off another layer of my skin. At the protests I functioned as an individual, not as part of a group. I had never been a joiner. I didn't trust clubs. Clubs were things they beat you with. I remembered in James T. Farrell's great trilogy, Studs Lonigan always wandered around the Chicago streets alone, lost, a victim, dying, but seeing himself as "Lone Wolf Lonigan." That was the way I fancied myself. "Lone Wolf Lonigan." Whenever I would go to a protest, I would go alone and I would repeat to myself aloud, with determination, as I walked over and readied myself for a beating or jail, "Lone Wolf Lonigan."

But I had never been to anything like *this* before. The Pentagon. This was going to be huge! People on the bus were laughing and filled with energy, singing and sharing food and drinks. I was nipping at the brandy. At each entrance to the Jersey Turnpike, more buses pulled on alongside us and we all waved to each other. Newark and North Jersey were on board. Rutgers and Trenton. As we approached the familiar Philadelphia entrance I wondered if we'd meet any more buses. And suddenly, there they were, good old Philadelphia, an unending row of buses entering the Turnpike, everyone waving to us and shouting and making peace signs. Yes, I had known New York would support this, and Boston with Harvard, and BU, and BC, and MIT, and Northeastern, and Radcliffe, and Tufts, and Emerson, and Simmons College and the rest—I knew they'd be there, but now Philly was on board, one bus after the other as far as the eye could see, probably all the way back to Walnut Street where I used to live. The cradle of American independence, the home of the Quakers. Good old Philly was on board!

We had taken over the Jersey Turnpike! The whole highway was filled with buses. They seemed to stretch without stop from Washington to New York. There were literally a thousand of them. All filled with people who were going to attack the Pentagon. Tens of thousands of people who were going to put their lives on the line for something true and right and beautiful. This was the day I had dreamed of, the day I had known I would never see in my lifetime.

He tried to hide it, but as he sat there by himself in the back of the bus, "Lone Wolf Lonigan" began to weep.

I DECLARE THE WAR IS OVER

We parked on the mall below the Capitol Building. I had never seen so many buses, parked in long lines as far as I could see. I joined the growing mass of protestors heading toward the reflecting pool between the Washington and Lincoln Memorials.

I was moved by this historical location. Lincoln. Washington. Jefferson. (The Vietnam Memorial for the more than 50,000 dead GIs was not even imagined yet.) This had been the site of Martin Luther King's "I have a dream" speech.

We were the true Americans fighting for the great tradition that we had inherited, America as the last best hope. We held the true American dream. Jefferson had said that each generation might have to make a revolution. I knew this is what he meant. I knew Jefferson and Franklin and John Adams would have been here with us.

I wanted so much for the American experiment to work. I wanted all the old corny images, the soldiers being welcomed with flowers by the people we were really liberating, and they would be happy to have the Americans there because they knew we would be fair, I wanted a good society in which people really saw the other person beneath the color of his skin, I wanted America to still be the country that had let in my ancestors and all the poor, Jews and Italians and Poles and Irish and all the rest of them, the melting pot, the country that had taken in the radicals and free thinkers after they were kicked out of Europe in 1848, I wanted to believe what the French had put on the Statue of Liberty when they sent it over to us as a gift because they loved the American revolution, that poem by Emma Lazarus about send me your tired and poor, your huddled masses yearning to be free, I wanted this country to be an example to the world that a good life was possible here on the earth, with liberty and justice for all, I wanted to believe all the old images, the spacious skies and the fields of waving grain, I wanted them to be true. I really wanted this to be a country that God had shed his grace upon. I wanted to be proud to be an American, and I wanted America to be a gentle giant, an honest broker among nations, respected by people all over the earth. I really did.

The air sparkled on a brisk fall day. Everyone was charged up by being with so many others of similar views. It was like being part of a *sangha*. The spice of danger suffused the sharp air. I could imagine how it felt to be here in Washington when the city was threatened with attack after the battle of Bull Run in the Civil War. I wondered how many of the kids were thinking about the fact that some of us might not be alive by nightfall. I had known the Army mentality too well for too long. I knew we weren't going to be running around inside the Pentagon, gaily tearing up papers and turning over desks and spray painting peace signs on the walls.

I knew they would kill us first.

I moved toward the Lincoln Memorial. The crowd stretched all along the sides of the reflecting pool. I'd never been with so many fellow believers before. I felt a shiver move up my spine. A black man was holding up a sign: NO VIETNAMESE EVER CALLED ME A NIGGER. I laughed. Yes, that was it, force them to see that the war for "freedom" was being fought mostly by the poor and blacks who couldn't even vote in much of the country.

Someone was making a speech about peace and freedom. An excited man jumped into the reflecting pool. I laughed along with everyone else. I was supremely happy and proud to be there. I was joining those throughout history who had risked something in the cause of consciousness and humanity.

The speeches droned softly in the background like Musak as we all checked each other out, invigorated by a vibrant, festive spirit. Those who were going to march on the Pentagon were forming up on a road down behind the speakers' platform. I walked over to join them.

At the front was a kind of preface, a platoon of marshals and other young organizers. Behind them stretched the wide, low, horizontal parade banner, followed by the first group to march. The writers! I quickly moved toward them. I didn't know why. If I was going to die I wanted to die with the writers for some reason. They were the ones I really loved, the ones who were mad for freedom and beauty, like Lord Byron who died for freedom in Greece, like Tolstoy who spoke out against the draft in Russia and was excommunicated for it, and Thoreau who went to jail for tax refusal during the Mexican War. Writers like Emile Zola, who stood up for the Jew, Dreyfus, and, it now appears, was murdered for it by a right wing fanatic who blocked his chimney and asphyxiated him.

I spotted Robert Lowell in the first row. Out of the bin for a while between his manic runs. I recognized Dwight Macdonald whose criticism I liked, standing next to him, looking like an extremely intelligent penguin. There was William Sloane Coffin, the anti-war chaplain of Yale, and just beyond him, looking tall as a stork, Dr. Spock. Half the country blamed him for all the ruckus on the campuses. [Yes, that was the cause of the problem, Henry. It had nothing to do with our napalm setting fire to people's skin, and our toxic agent orange killing all the trees on the hills so the Vietcong couldn't hide under them and already beginning to run down to the valleys with the seasonal rains, destined to continue to do so for decades and to cause horrible birth defects in future generations of Vietnamese. It had nothing to do with our burning of grass houses with extended families in them by GIs with cigarette lighters or our carpet bombing from B-52s, bombs as heavy as Volkswagens, leaving huge craters in the earth, it had nothing to do with the millions dead. That's right Myrna. That's why the kids were turning to violence and not cutting their hair. We were too good to them, that's why, and all because out of the goodness of our hearts we listened to that Red, Dr. Spock. Yes, Henry, that's what all the authorities and psychologists are saying on TV. I heard the Pulitzer Prize poet Karl Shapiro saying it just the other night. The kids were turning to violence because we were too good to them.]

And immediately at the center, right behind the low, wide, horizontal banner, there was Norman Mailer. I had heard Mailer on TV talking about coming here and I had admired his bravery because I knew he would be the target. Not old Dr. Spock. Mailer attracted nuts and guns like honeycake at a Jewish sheriffs' picnic. We were pointed toward Virginia where the Pentagon sat. George Lincoln Rockwell and his American Nazis were headquartered in Virginia. The Far Right was up in arms over this march. This wasn't Harvard or Yale. This was the fucking Pentagon! On our side, we young poets and idealists saw it as a traditional five-sided geometric symbol for evil, but we knew very well what they saw it as symbolizing.

And yet here was Mailer, in front, in tie and jacket, probably a bit in his cups, at the center of the bull's-eye.

I thought of "Kit Carson," from Saroyan's play, *The Time of Your Life,* the motor-mouth, old-timer, the bull-shitting spinner of tall tales who somehow in the end comes through, standing up to evil just like he said he would in all his fantastic, baroque, silk-spinning verbiage. Good old Mailer. In the end he actually *was* the guy you wanted next to you in a foxhole.

The parade gathered its energy, took a deep breath and got ready to set out toward the Potomac River Bridge to Virginia. I stepped in right behind Mailer. If the Nazis attacked him, I was going to fight. I wasn't going to let him go down alone. He was taking a courageous chance with his life. He deserved help. If he were assaulted or shot at, I couldn't not help him. This was the moment I had waited for.

Back at the reflecting pool they introduced the fine folk singer, Phil Ochs. The older people, the moderates, SANE and so on, God bless them, they were going to remain there. And as our long column began to move, we could hear Phil Ochs (bless his soul, he was soon to commit suicide), his high pitched, beautiful voice singing his sweet, powerful anthem, "I declare the war is o-ver," and we began to move toward Virginia.

I trailed right behind Mailer all the way to the Pentagon parking lot. Amazingly, there was no sign of violence along the way. We were herded into a side lot beside the main one. We were penned in here by a chicken wire fence. Immediately some of the more excitable brothers and sisters attacked it and began to stomp it, to tear it apart and demolish it. Quickly it was obliterated and the advance guard stepped over the mangled wires and moved toward the main lot in front of the Pentagon itself where we could see the troops with their rifles and bayonets.

A flatbed truck stood at the center of our original space. I saw Ed Sanders and the Fugs and the hippies dancing around on it. I climbed up and joined them. I was waving around my skull on a pole, pointing it toward the Pentagon and dancing like a maniac on the back of the truck with all the other participants in the sacred levitation ceremony, as people were shouting "It's rising. It's levitating. It's going up," and helicopters were circling overhead as hippies were beating drums and shaking rattles, and Ed Sanders was on the back of our truck waving his hands like wands and chanting some crazy litany into a microphone, "In the name of Toth and Isis and Osiris, in the name of The Great Mother, in the name of Zeus and Hera, in the name of Goddess Athena, and Artemis and Aphrodite, in the name of Baal and Cybele and Ishtar and Astarte, in the name . . . ," crazy chanting, his head full of these names of archaic gods and goddesses that he could run off like a Charlie Parker solo, and we were all dancing like Native Americans and we chanted toward the Pentagon, "Rise!" Again and again we chanted repetitively, "Rise up! Rise Up!" We all danced around and I couldn't help but shout wildly as loud as I could, "Levitate! Leave the earth and levitate!"

Whether the Pentagon actually levitated or not is still a matter of debate. In the end I guess it was a question of what you had for breakfast.

When the ceremony ended, I jumped off the truck and joined the tens of thousands who were making their way through the trampled fence and heading for the front of the building itself.

And there it was. Set back maybe a hundred feet on a plateau, about ten feet higher than our level. The Pentagon!

Goya said that the sleep of reason breeds monsters, but what happens when reason never sleeps? This was the world's 24/7 nightmare, the Sumerian Juggernaut of technology, the Egyptian pyramid that our whole culture supported, the Chartres Cathedral of materialism, the Jerusalem temple of consumerism, the concrete octopus with tentacles that reached all around the world, never dozing, never resting, overseeing the bringing back of a third of the world's resources to be made into deodorant and Cadillac fins, the Pentagon.

Between us and the plateau sat a broad stone staircase. On either side of the stairs stood stone walls, perhaps ten feet high, protecting the upper level. At the foot of the stairs were soldiers with M-16s held across their chests, the shielded bayonets pointed up toward the sky.

> *"Brothers and sisters, you have no mother and father to take care of you. If you will not take care of each other, who else, I ask, will do so?"*
>
> The Buddha

I moved closer to the huge crowd along with the rest of the young people who had been dancing in the levitation ceremony. I was surprised by the number of young women. The women were joining us in facing the guns. They were dressed functionally, wearing jeans and denim jackets or sweat shirts, clothes they had been encouraged to avoid at college in the Fifties. These were a different kind of young women. I saw in a second that this meant the end of housemothers in college dorms. This meant the end of curfews and the myth that college girls couldn't be responsible for taking care of themselves, the end of the Miss America ideal, of the ball gowns, and the fake hairdos, and the plastic surgery. These were the young people I had been yearning for but had never expected to see. They were walking toward the guns with me. They were my sisters and brothers. For the first time in my life I was in a crowd of people and I was not alienated.

Once again I began to weep. Not only was this the greatest day of my life but I knew of this greatness *while it was occurring!*

At that moment, I knew my life had changed forever. These were my people. I would go to the end with them. I would die for them. Finally, it was possible for me to feel at home on the earth.

We could see faces at the Pentagon windows, and we could see the military sharpshooters on the roof, and we could see the troops on the steps and the federal marshals massed beside them, and the cops and sheriffs and all the rest of them scattered all over the place. Quickly I moved to the front of the huge crowd, toward the troops at the steps. I walked up to the young soldiers with the bayonets and I found that it was dangerously impossible for me to fear them. I had recently been commanding these troops every day for three years. I knew their fears and their ignorance. I knew their deference to officers like myself.

Being afraid of them would have been like being afraid of a dog that had been obeying your commands for years. I almost felt outraged they would hold a loaded rifle up near me. I felt like swatting their rifles aside and snapping, "Don't you dare hold that weapon up to me, soldier." Young women were approaching and putting daisies in the barrels of their automatic rifles. The women in front were talking to the young soldiers, saying, "We're not your enemies, we're young like you, we're on your side, we don't want you to get killed for nothing."

The officers behind the troops were cajoling, "Look smart, soldiers. Eyes straight ahead! Don't listen to them." But some of the young kids couldn't help turning their eyes subtly to look at the pretty girls who were now chastely kissing a couple of them on the cheeks and laughing. The soldiers were mostly country kids, draftees, recent high school grads. This was beyond them. They appeared confused. They wanted to be hip and impress the girls but now the girls were telling them to put down their rifles and "Join us!"

The whole crowd took up the chant. "Join Us! Join Us! Join Us!" The soldiers looked scared. Then we began to chant at the Pentagon, tens of thousands of us in unison, "OUT DEMONS, OUT! OUT DEMONS, OUT!" And all kinds of people were doing witch dances as the force of the vast crowd of voices swept over us toward the building itself, "OUT DEMONS, OUT!" and we all looked at the faces in the Pentagon windows, and they appeared to be amazed at the whole spectacle, as fifty thousand of us danced around and swayed our arms as if sending spells toward them, "OUT DEMONS, OUT!" and I danced right in front of the troops, waving my skull on a stick at the building like a wand and shouting, "OUT DEMONS, OUT! OUT DEMONS, OUT!" and the soldiers stared at me, puzzled, because they could see my officer's shirt with the lieutenant's silver bar on the collar and the metal silver bar on the cap, and they didn't know what to think, but the silver bar acted as an amulet to keep them off balance and they did nothing as I continued to wave my skull at the building behind them and to chant, "OUT DEMONS, OUT!" feeling the intense relief and joy of having so many of my old army demons and fears rushing out of me at that moment and watching them fall at my feet, harmless.

I was high as the sky, winged by a happiness that welled with the hope of community and a risky moral quality that quickened my heart. Both sides quieted down into an extended stalemate. Military helicopters circled overhead menacingly. Sharpshooters maintained their positions on the roof. Soldiers came and went on the plateau which stood between the Pentagon itself and the wide steps. I kept wondering what the people looking out of the windows in the Pentagon were thinking.

About a decade after he had courageously released the Pentagon Papers, Daniel Ellsberg telephoned me in San Francisco. He had liked my little book, *Zen in the Art of J.D. Salinger*. He introduced himself and invited me to his house across the bay.

Ellsberg was a very bright and highly energetic man, very open, encouraging frank talk. At one point over lunch, speaking about the assault on the Pentagon, he told me that he had been watching us from inside the building that day, standing next to Robert McNamara, the Secretary of Defense. He said that we would have made more of an impression on them if we had not fooled around and had been more serious. I smiled and said, "Maybe," tentatively. Later, pondering this, I realized that although consciously I had been hoping to convince the American public and those in the Pentagon that we were not just a few oddballs but that we were millions and we were right and we hoped they would see this and join us, a certain unspoken word within me already knew this was hopeless. That we were not going to be able to convince the Americans on moral grounds. We were not going to be able to fight our way through the media to get a fair hearing and even if we did, the authorities knew that while there were millions of us protesting, there were tens of millions watching us on TV and hating us no matter how we behaved.

In a sense, this march would prove a turning point in the Sixties. The liberal Sixties, the Kennedy Sixties, with the hope for peaceful change, the Civil Rights movement, the belief in the Democratic Party, the Labor Unions, the college presidents, the intellectuals and the liberal commentators on TV, this Sixties was beginning to fade and the High Sixties, the uncompromising Sixties, the radical Sixties, the belief in the need for a counterculture that opposed every aspect of the American culture as it had developed was coming to the surface. The black rage, the post-capitalist, post-modern, post-Christian, acid visions, were beginning to arise just below the skin and would soon erupt.

I walked over to the side of the building and saw, to my astonishment, not just more soldiers with rifles, armed and waiting, but soldiers with tear gas dispensers that looked like flame throwers! I walked back to the base of the steps and looked out over a lake of people. In spite of the guns and cops and MPs and marshals, there was a kind of exhilaration in the air, a beautiful football Saturday in October America with the college students sitting around, eating and drinking and smoking dope together not unlike a game day crowd at Yale or Franklin Field. I looked back toward the Pentagon and became apprehensive. There was a disjunction between the students and the soldiers in defining the situation. I wondered about the difference between a game and something that was not a game?

I thought of the Belgian Johan Huizinga's book, *Homo Ludens*, where he reconceptualized most human experiences as games; social institutions (e.g. the Catholic Church) were enclosures where "games" were played according to rules which only applied within the agreed confines of the arena of the institution. I would ponder this for months until I came up with my favorite sentence in my first novel, *Blues For A Dying Nation*: "When the gun goes off, the game is over." That is, when death enters the picture, we are no longer in the land of games as we define them.

Over to my right a disturbance was beginning. A squad of perhaps thirty helmeted U.S. marshals was marching right into the crowd, for some idiotic reason disturbing the stasis that had ensued. The marshals, wielding batons, remained in formation, butting into the huge crowd like a truck, knocking young people aside. The kids in the crowd who were being trampled pushed back. The marshals bashed their heads and shoulders with their blunt heavy clubs. The students were furious. A melee erupted. I saw for the first time, what I would see so frequently in the future: Again and again the government initiated the violence. And in violent situations, the most violent people on both sides moved toward the front.

The soft peace had dissolved. Everyone was lifted by adrenaline. Objects were flying at the marshals who beat people harder. Fights broke out. The marshals backed up, flailing away. Confusion reigned. All kinds of shit was flying at them. Angry officers ran up to the young troops on the steps and ordered them to point their rifles down toward us. The most violent in the crowd surged toward them. Others, like myself, formed a wall in front to keep the kids from the troops. On the right, the marshals retreated. Both sides quieted momentarily, but the battle had begun.

When the soldiers pointed the rifles at me, in my face, I almost snapped, "Are you crazy, soldier?" But now the students were shocked into a kind of madness. How could this be happening? How could the U.S. Government be pointing rifles down into a crowd of thus far fairly peaceful college students? The girls who had been putting daisies in the soldiers' rifles when they had been pointed upwards were replaced by hotheads who began to throw the flowers, hard, at the young soldiers, in their faces. No more chants of "Join us, join us!" Now the whole crowd in the area around me, almost up against them on the steps, chanted fiercely, "Shoot! Shoot! Shoot your sister!" as the firebrands continued to hurl the flowers. At that moment the liberal Sixties died. The game was over.

You had to feel sorry for the soldiers. They wanted to be rock and rollers, too, but they also wanted to fight for their country, John Wayne and all that. The situation had swelled beyond the reach of their previous conceptions. They were frozen in place, embarrassed and scared.

Yet it was not impossible that one would pull the trigger.

The students continued to rail at the soldiers. "Leave the GIs alone!" I shouted. "They're not in charge, here." Everyone was screaming different advice and ideas. The flowers were gone now and bullhorns came out in various areas of the crowd. You could take a bullhorn and shout into it and a debate ensued between the bullhorns, street democracy at its purest and most raw. But the debate centered on whether we should charge up the steps into the formation of the soldiers with the rifles and bayonets.

At that moment I saw it. I saw what happens when two different definitions of shared reality collide. The students were treating this as an out-of-control college rally. They could not conceive of the mentality of the people they were opposing. They expected the guys in the Pentagon to play fair. To recognize their middle-class status and to behave like the students thought reasonable Americans should behave toward them.

At that moment I saw Kent State and Jackson State. I saw that at some point down the road the students were going to move forward trustingly, and the government was going to massacre them. In America! The American government was going to shoot down its own students and kill them. I have never recovered from that moment.

A wild-looking, slightly older, Old-Left type guy grabbed the bullhorn, and pointed it out toward the masses and shouted, "Trotsky told us don't charge up the steps! We tried it in Odessa in 1905!"

Suddenly we were in a different dimension. We young Americans had stepped over a rise and entered the plain of history.

"Fuck Trotsky!" came the new-left response from several bullhorns.

I grabbed the mike. "He's right!" I shouted. "This isn't a college rally. This is the Mafia we're dealing with. These guys are murderers. That's why we're here. They'll murder you. I know this. I was an Army officer. They're killers. And whatever you do, don't charge *UP* the steps!"

"Fuck that!" came the response from a bullhorn from the right side of the steps. "Let's charge. That's why we're here. To get into the fucking Pentagon."

But on the other side, on our left when we faced the steps, someone had come up with an outrageous flanking movement. The Army had counted on the ten-foot high walls to funnel us toward the heavily guarded steps where the armed troops would hold us off the plateau which surrounded the Pentagon, but they hadn't conceived of the possibility that some madman would bring along medieval grappling hooks. Incredibly, there were several ropes spanning the walls and the students were scurrying up them and heading toward the actual doors of the Pentagon itself.

I could hardly believe this but I was merely learning another astonishing lesson— we were smarter than the Army. We were much crazier, more unpredictable, more flexible and more creative than the cops and marshals could ever be.

We had innumerable mad geniuses who were falling out of the known culture, no longer playing by the old rules and free now to think on the run. To improvise. To ransack world history for weird and beautiful pre-historic and multicultural responses to the predictable bureaucratic authorities. There were tens of thousands of us. No one in the world could predict what we might do. We didn't know ourselves. The authorities were going to have a much tougher time handling us than they expected.

And then the moment I had never believed possible happened. The vanguard of the students flung open the big doors and entered the Pentagon itself! But there the authorities had the better of it. They had come up with a crazy plan, perhaps accidentally. Behind the large doors, they had the entrances to the building packed with thousands of paratroopers, ready to spring out and attack. But because our attack had been from the flank and so unexpected, they hadn't had a chance to deploy. They were crammed into the hallways behind the doors, jammed against each other. There was no way to enter the Pentagon. It was like trying to attack a subway train in rush hour. A scuffle ensued. The mad students flung themselves at the paratroopers who clumsily untangled their arms and beat the students back by bashing in their heads with their rifle butts. The doors finally shut closed again, bloody students lying outside or inside arrested.

I ran from the stairs over to the wall where a fat young woman was stuck on a rope, in danger of falling. A couple of us got under her behind and pushed her up the rope until someone at the top could finally pull her over. Then the tear gas came down. We retreated backwards. This is the tear gas that the papers said the next day, citing government authorities, was not used. We moved back and tied hankies across our faces. Skirmishes continued to break out all across the huge field as various authorities attacked and students countered.

> *"The world only goes forward because of those who oppose it."*
> J.W. Goethe

I wasn't arrested. I later read in Normal Mailer's *Armies of the Night* (which I can attest was highly accurate so far as the events I witnessed with him were concerned) that as soon as we reached the Pentagon he stepped over a rope line and gave himself up to be arrested peacefully. He said he had a cocktail party to go to that night, but he found out the government wasn't going to be as considerate as he had hoped.

I had no hope for the Army. I was never arrested in all the demonstrations and riots I attended. Passive resistance, lying down and being carried off to jail was not for me. The government had had me in "jail" for three years in the Army. If they were going to get their hands on me again it was not going to be with my cooperation.[Twenty years later I still would not take the public road across the Presidio Army base as a shortcut with my fellow San Franciscans. Everyone thought I was nuts, and maybe they were right. I explained myself by saying, "If a war breaks out, they'll close the gates and they won't let you out till it's over." This usually brought a laugh but I wasn't completely joking.]

On the bus back to New York that night I sat next to an older African-American man, a survivor of the Thirties Old-Left. We talked for a while. He was excited, tired, and happy, as I was myself. He had been through these wars before and there was a battered lamp lit in his eyes. "Wasn't that a great moment?" he said to me, warmly. "I'll never forget it. Young workers and old workers, student workers and regular workers, men workers and women workers, all heading over the walls and entering the Pentagon itself." I nodded and smiled. I knew I would never forget that day either.

I had almost replied to him, jokingly, "Are you kidding? No one on our side *works!* The workers were the ones in the Army." But I didn't have the heart to interrupt his great moment. As a black radical in America, he deserved the scarce moments of satisfaction that came his way every few decades. I preferred to sit there with him and share the profound feeling that had swept over us, as we enjoyed our brief time of well-earned peace along with our fellow happy, bloody and gassed revelers, on the old dark bus heading back to Greenwich Village, toward the wilder and more angry protests and riots which would inevitably erupt in the coming weeks.

"SHADOWS OF AGENT ORANGE
THIRD GENERATION OF VIETNAM VICTIMS"
"At the residential treatment center ... all of the 30 boarders and nearly half of the 100 day students are suffering from its effects: twisted or stunted limbs, bodies covered with tumors, some blind or deaf children, others with faces in perpetual pain."
Gail Bensinger— *San Francisco Chronicle* 2003

Charlotte was waiting up for me. I saw the relieved look on her face when I trudged in the door. She hugged me long, then exclaimed with a big smile on her face, "I saw you on TV. The national news. Huntley-Brinkley. You were dancing around on a truck with that skull of yours." She couldn't hide her pride.

We smoked dope and drank a couple beers as I related the exciting events of the day. She told me many more protesters in Washington had since been beaten and arrested after I'd left. "The government's going to shoot down the students in the streets." I said, "I know it. I see it. America is going to shoot down its students."

Stupid me, I began to choke up. I turned my face to the side to hide the tears coming into my eyes. I wiped them with the back of my hand, pretending they were merely irritated by something in the air. I was beginning to understand that cutting America out of myself was going to be a life-threatening operation.

I stood there silently, gathering myself together. Then I said, "You should have seen the young women! It was so beautiful! They were right there beside me. Right up against the bayonets. God, I'll never forget them. They were so brave." I paused for a second, then added, "And you know something amazing? They aren't even eligible for the draft."

"You aren't either," Charlotte said, quietly.

" . . selfishness looks virtuous when expanded into patriotism . . ."
Edmund S. Morgan

FALLING DOMINOES

I couldn't believe how fast the dominoes of my beliefs were crashing down. As you moved outside the culture you could see the inside more clearly. Norman Mailer had said that if this war wasn't wrong then the distinction between right and wrong no longer had any meaning. But the war was worse than wrong. It was obscene. In 1969 James Purdy, bringing his powerful novelist's imagery to bear, would say to me that it's like watching a gorilla rape a child while the whole nation applauds. Later we would learn it was even worse than we feared.

Two flash forwards— Twenty years later I am talking to an American, a former Navy Seal, in and out of mental hospitals since the war. I ask him, "What did you Navy Seals do there that bothered you so?"

He said that he joined up to be a good American, like his father and grandfather before him. He wanted to take a risk for freedom, not to take what he had inherited for granted. He wanted to do the right thing. Even joined the Seals, a dangerous assignment. He meant well toward America and the world. But then little by little he had found himself crossing small boundaries, step by step, until he found himself in strange geography, ill lit and morally perverse, yet he still was able to think of himself in some way as a "good man." It was only when he returned to the States and he saw what he had done in the more stable light of his old injunctions that he cracked up.

"Give me an example?"

"Well, they'd find out that some young guy, a printer, was asked by the Vietcong, which means guys he went to high school with who were fighting the great war machine of the U.S. and taking tremendous casualties, well we'd find out that they asked him to make an identity card for one of his buddies. Then we would go to arrest him, but he'd be gone. To prevent this in the future, to teach them a lesson, we would go to his thatched hut at night, where he still generally lived with his extended family, grandparents and little kids and all, and we would set it on fire with them sleeping inside and we would kill them all."

My friend was in a platoon headed by an officer who was now a state governor. He showed me a letter from the governor. I was surprised to read the warm tone. The governor said if my friend was having trouble he should come to the governor's mansion and he could stay there until he straightened out.

I had always believed that the reason that more GIs were being brought home during the war for heroin addiction than for war wounds was because of the innate conscience of the young American soldiers. They couldn't bear to live with what they were being asked to do.

Flash forward #2. I recently read Dan Ellsberg's extremely frank and brave memoir, *Secrets*. My jaw fell open when he wrote that even in 1969, after the years of Kennedy and Johnson, when Ellsberg was still working for the government, this time for Richard Nixon, he learned for the first time while working on the Defense Department history of the war, the secret Pentagon Papers, that the Geneva Accords of 1954 had not set up two separate countries, North and South Vietnam. He and everyone he knew, all the Ivy Leaguers in the government, believed Dean Rusk's story that the North had violated the Geneva Accords and invaded the sovereign Republic of South Vietnam. All these bright guys pursuing the war with all their great intellects and knowledge and no one had taken the trouble to find out why the war had started and why we were there in the first place. Dan Ellsberg had the courage to admit, after years of Pentagon and battlefield duties, that his notion of the war had been completely wrong.

I was not amazed to learn these facts about the Accords. We had known about this before he found out in 1969. We kids outside the Pentagon, the rag tag and bobtail, the urchins, and angry students, and dopers, we had known more about the war than the brains trust inside, the Rhodes scholars and Harvard professors who were justifying the war and pursuing it.

STEPPING OUT

> *"Bliss was it in that dawn to be alive,*
> *But to be young was very heaven!"*
>
> William Wordsworth
> *("French Revolution")*

It was the best of times, it was the worst of times. Back in the summer of 1967 intimations of loss and mortality were already beginning to sound softly on the timpanis, but I had taken a break from studying for my orals to go with Charlotte over to the East Side. A new nightclub was opening on St. Marks Place: The Electric Circus. A free block party with the hard rocking black band, the Chambers Brothers, playing out on the street.

I had some trepidation about this. I knew what these affairs in poor neighborhoods at night were like. The initial electricity, the resentment by the local hoods that their turf was being invaded, the drinking, the anger, the fistfights over pretty girls in tight red dresses, the escalation into ethnic violence, the stompings and the stabbings, and if you were lucky, the cops breaking it up before a real riot erupted with gun shots and chaos and everyone running away down dark, bandaged streets.

Charlotte was in a top mood as we approached the crowd. I looked warily for a sign of the danger that was to come. There was no sign. People were dancing joyfully in the gutter. The speakers were blasting rock music, the Beatles, the Stones. The women were dressed simply, jeans decorated with embroidery, work shirts or tops knitted by hand.

The old tenements that lined both sides of the street were brightly illuminated by dazzling light shows projected to the opposite sides of the street from light machines on fire escapes. Spotlights set on the street flashed across the tenements and into the sky. Colored lights on the roofs splayed down on the heads of the revelers. The speaker system pounded out Motown, that big rocking sound that heals the soul and seals the hole. If your body doesn't move to Motown music, you're legally dead in forty states. Charlotte immediately began to dance in the gutter. I joined her. Something was missing here. The smell of violence. The local guys were drinking beer but they were laughing as the hippies passed them joints. Everyone was passing around weed and laughing. All the West Side Story vibes, the horny macho guys, the fiery sex-blazing chicks, were absent.

Hippies lining the rooftops were floating large colored balloons and rainbowed streamers onto the dancers below. The air carried the sweet smell of incense and pot. The Chambers Brothers set up on the back of a flat bed truck. The began to play their hit single, "Time." The crowd cheered and moved forward dancing at the edge of the truck. Still no hint of the dark vibes that any New York street kid could pick up blocks away.

A thrill of happiness rolled over me. You could see that violence was now unfashionable. Violence was what the adults did. The old culture. Violence was stupid. And somehow even the street gangs picked this up. Hippie girls were dancing with the Puerto Rican guys. The local Ukrainian guys were smoking dope with the students. The local Polish guys were doing crazy dances with the college girls. Everyone was having a great time. The Chambers Brothers were smiling and laughing along with everybody else. There was no hard edge to the celebration.

It was like heaven only better. Bright Eden blossoming amidst the tenements and gang turf of the Lower East Side.

There was only one arrest. A large black man, overcome by the rapture of the shared good spirit, had climbed onto the hood of a parked car to photograph the dancing revelers. The police tried to get him down. He kicked at their hands as they grabbed at him. I looked closely as the cops took him away. It was Charlie Mingus. The great bass player and composer. He had played at the classic Massey Hall concert in Toronto, in the irreplaceable quintet with Charlie Parker and Dizzy Gillespie, Max Roach and Bud Powell. They'd played "Salt Peanuts" and "All the Things You Are." I'd worn the record out. The cops were putting him in a paddy wagon.

"The major advances in civilization are processes that all but wreck the societies in which they occur."

Alfred North Whitehead

ROUGHER TIMES

The old days of protest, the peaceful marches in the spring of '67 in New York, the friendly police and the polite dissidents out on Fifth Avenue, the sunny, hope-scented halcyon days were gone. Now the police were turning vicious. I had a certain dogged fondness for the individual New York City patrolman. Most were New York street kids from the outer-boroughs like myself, trying to move up in class, to make an honest living on the tough pavements and in the hoods without a college degree. Their job was a kind of college, with departments of thuggery, thievery, bunko, foreign languages, psychotherapy, and cultural anthropology.

There was a quality about the good cops that was shared by the best of shrinks, a sense that you couldn't surprise them, they'd seen it all, and in many cases this led to a kind of acceptance that sometimes stretched into compassion.

But in groups at protests the cops were different. They had grown up on these streets and they were not about to lose control of them to a bunch of middle-class college kids, nerds and dope fiends who challenged their masculinity, rich suburban kids who were mocking them by turning their backs on the cops' life goals. The worst cops moved toward the front and they began to beat the kids with clubs, to beat them in order to hurt them, to bloody and punish them until they yielded. Once a riot combusted, all the other cops would join in.

And the firemen were becoming worse. As the months passed they would turn violent as well; flying large American flags on their fire trucks, they blew their obscene horns and careened around the city, ultimately organizing know-nothing pro-war demonstrations, joining with the workers from the Longshoreman's Union to beat up students.

These were working class guys from the streets. Yet the ideologues, the Stalinist and Maoist extremists, the old left Marxists could not get it into their heads that the workers supported the government. This was not Europe. Every worker in America saw himself as a future capitalist.

We protestors were trying to follow in the footsteps of our non-violent role models, Mahatma Gandhi and Martin Luther King. Most of us maintained this stance. Yet as the despair spread among us, the more volatile would strike back, although we continued to try to distinguish between violence to property and violence toward people, a distinction the adults, not only the cops but the liberal intellectuals and the press, seemed unable to comprehend.

Robin Williams has said that if you remember the Sixties, you weren't really there. With so much turmoil and so many actions they do seem to blend into one another in memory, but I recall two protests from that time that stand out.

I remember standing in the street on the Upper East Side, I believe near the U.N., with thousands of others when Martin Luther King, looking so human, so vulnerable, a walking target, spoke out against the war. His advisers had told him not to. Everyone had told him not to. He would be diluting his support on the racial issues. He would be losing moderate supporters who funded his cause. He would be going off message, alienating middle-America and fuzzing up his own issues. But they all ignored one thing: The war was wrong. It would be wrong not to speak out. So there he was, just a fragile person, subject to being shot just like Gandhi or anyone else, putting his life on the line for a moral principle that could be said to be against his own interest. This is something that has been lost in the world, among the presidents, and popes, and prime ministers, and all those who live in a parallel universe of information counselors and speech writers and spin doctors: The power of the authentic word. The power of taking a moral position against one's own self-interest. How it elevates and energizes one's followers. Seeing this happen, this unbelievably beautiful and courageous event, how could we not put ourselves on the line as well? How could we be any less fervent and honorable in proceeding? Martin Luther King wasn't perfect. And yet he risked it all. He spoke out from his heart and spoke eloquently. That was why we loved him.

DINNER AT EIGHT

There was a joke I liked that was supposedly going around Russia at this time: Under capitalism man oppresses man, but under communism it is exactly vice-versa.

The Soviet Union was officially a materialist nation as was China. Dialectical materialism. But so many Americans seemed to be suffering from our own corporate-driven materialism. There were Christian materialists, Jewish materialists, atheist materialists, liberal materialists, conservative materialists, born-agains with credit card problems.

I knew the Soviet Bloc was neither democratic nor free. But how had it come about that they were the ones who were providing support for most of the national liberation movements in poor countries around the world, while we tended to be supporting corrupt dictators or agents of the imperial powers? (I was now finally coming to understand that we were late to the worldwide imperial banquet because we had three million square miles to conquer and scores of native tribes to dehumanize and decimate right here in our own backyard.)

On the second night of protest that stands out in my memory, Dean Rusk, the Secretary of State, who, according to Daniel Ellsberg had been lying to Congress while under oath, spoke at the Waldorf Astoria Hotel. Rusk was going to address a formal dinner of major corporate leaders, bankers, and financiers in the heart of Manhattan. This was putting it right in our face and brought out the more vociferous and angry of the demonstrators. We massed, thousands of us, in the street outside the Waldorf. The police on horseback amped up the tension by sidling their huge animals into the crowd, trampling some of those in front.

As the limos pulled up to the curb at the awning, and the corporate leaders stepped out, the crowd boiled over. Hot heads threw newspapers and empty cups at them and screamed, "Killer! Killer!" The cops went after those who threw things and beat them with their heavy clubs. I recall the expressions of surprise on the businessmen's faces. This was one of the crowning events of their lives. They and their wives or mistresses were important enough to be asked to the Waldorf, the King of American hotels, where the Secretary of State would expound upon his policies to *them*. They had worked for years to shine in these honorific moments. And then these ingrates, these hippies, and beatniks, these refuseniks, these cowards and . . . and failures! were bleating and shouting and cursing while the police and Waldorf staff attempted to protect the invited guests from the missiles by hurrying them into the hotel like craven dogs. This wasn't the way it was supposed to be at all. How could young people connect them to the war? How could the crowd accuse them of killing babies and selling napalm?

Twenty-five years later, I thought of their expressions, that look of shock that quickly turned to outrage, when I chanced upon a TV show of a dinner for the Man of the Year thrown by a Cleveland civic club. Here they had the best people in Cleveland all gussied up in tuxedos and gowns, national TV on C-Span, everyone ready for a civilized evening in the company of other distinguished people, and then the kids, the students and the punkers and ragamuffins appeared at the door and had to be restrained by the police as they cursed and threw blood at the guests and screamed and almost broke through the police lines to get at the Guest of Honor, the Cleveland man of the year, a local physician who had been doing outstanding research for the betterment of mankind by chopping off the heads of chimpanzees and trying to replant the heads on the other chimps' bodies. When things quieted down, I recall how profusely the chairman at the dais apologized to the honoree for the "uncivilized" behavior he had been forced to confront on his way into the civilized gathering.

After the guests were guided safely inside the Waldorf, the rowdier elements of the crowd began to run through the streets chased by the police. Perhaps it was because I came from The Bronx where we had always been a kind of audience for the "real" events which took place on the stage of Manhattan, or perhaps it was because I had been a repressed good boy for so long, the student and Army officer, that I found it quite a rush to be chased through the streets of Manhattan by the Tactical Patrol Force, the biggest, meanest cops with the boots and the biggest clubs who would stomp you if they caught you or smash in your skull without a second thought. It did wonders to focus the attention. One had felt so powerless in the face of the war and outside the Waldorf. All we could do was attack the corporate leaders' self-image. Otherwise we were impotent. But in the streets our youth and intelligence did give us a certain weight—the power to tie up Manhattan. The power to scare the straight, pro-war, tourists from the Midwest. The power to outsmart, outrun, and frustrate the cops. The power to create disorder in a society that saw itself as orderly.

Now we were evolving new tactics. No more sit down and be arrested and appeal to the society's conscience. Now the plan was simply to run amok in every direction. Or, more correctly, the plan was not to have a plan. This puzzled the authorities. They thought in terms of the Old Left whose organization mirrored their own. They might have been Commies, but one thing you had to admit, they were disciplined and orderly. But these new kids, this New Left . . . The authorities kept trying to figure out our plan. To find the mastermind leaders, the conspiracy that was directing all this. But our secret weapon was that we had no direction.

We just ran wherever the cops weren't. The cops would decide we were headed to the U.N., so they would send a force to the east of us. We would run to the west. They would send reserves to the west. We would run to the north. Yet there was something unsettling about all this for me. My old friends from RPI were moving into power positions in the corporate world. They might be inside the cabs and limos that we were tying up in traffic. Where did I fit in all this? Who was I? What was I becoming? But there was no time to think. Not if you wanted to keep the cops from smashing in your head. I ran along with everyone else. And I felt a new exhilaration.

That night our side actually began to do some damage to property. Throwing garbage cans over into the street and setting fire to them. Torching wooden newsstands closed for the evening. Breaking windows. Breaking the glass protecting the posters at Radio City Music Hall and throwing garbage in the lobby. That was the idea: trash the sacred symbols of popular American culture.

I simply ran along. I was still non-violent, even toward property. I was sorry when some hothead torched a newsstand. I thought of my older pal back in The Bronx, Joey Scharf, an emaciated World War II vet who had a hard time getting started after suffering pneumonia in the war so he played stickball with us every day in the schoolyard, a sweet guy with a slow pitch he called his "epis" pitch, and a cocker spaniel named Shane D. ("pretty" in Yiddish) who carried his Phil Rizzuto glove in her mouth. After years of unemployment Joey had finally found steady work at a newsstand. (He and I used to sell newspapers together in The Bronx on the street when the candy stores were closed for the Jewish holidays.) I knew poor people made their living at those newsstands. I tried to stop the rioters from setting fire to them but with no luck. The situation was out of control.

In my heart, I was saddened and scared that things had come to this. I had hoped to enter mainline civilization and I had worked so hard for my whole life to earn my place in it. I wanted so badly to be a success in America. And now we had tied up all of midtown Manhattan. Everywhere you looked there were flames and trashings and fire trucks and sirens and red lights and police cars. I cherished reading and stability. I would have liked it so much more if I had been able to protect my native city, to love it and live in a time of peace. But apparently this chaos was what it took to stop a mass murder and to save what little was still left of our nation's soul. It was heartbreaking.

We ran north in the direction of Carnegie Hall. I was a conservative person in many ways. I subscribed to the World Symphonies Series at Carnegie Hall. The Moscow Symphony. The Prague Philharmonic. I saw some beautiful concerts with great cellists like Jacqueline du Pré shortly before she died at the age of forty-two. As she played, the music poured through her, tossing her about like a helpless rag doll in a flood until you wanted to shout to some referee in the sky, "Stop it! Stop it!" but then she would gather her forces and she would respond with a ferocity that almost embarrassed her and then you wanted to shout, "Don't stop it!" And Mstislav Rostropovich. When he came out onto the stage and sat down behind his cello he looked like a frog, but when he started to play he turned into a prince. You wouldn't want to be thrown against the wall by this man, or to try to move him against his will. You could see the fires of the defenders of Stalingrad in his eyes. He played on the sword edge between perfect control and being completely and dangerously out of control.

But now I was running away from the cops after the Dean Rusk speech, and our momentum led us south to Times Square. We flocked towards the Times Building where the news in lights circled the block, another famous American landmark and symbol of our free speech, and we chanted by the hundreds, "Bullshit! Bullshit!" at the electric headlines circling, while the tourists looked at us in terror, and the wildest among us began to smash windows and set more small fires, and you could hear sirens all over this section of Manhattan, and see squad cars and paddy wagons running the wrong way on one way streets until they located us and it was time for us to run away again.

Of course the next day our behavior was reported as disgraceful by both the liberal and conservative media. Some of the sisters had been trampled by the huge police horses outside the Waldorf, some property trashed and burned, and the cops broke some heads, but not one person had been killed or permanently maimed during that wild night in New York, while on that very day the U.S. Government had killed hundreds of Vietnamese people. Yet we were the ones who were defined as "violent."

We were skating on thin ice over Lake Despair. We had to keep moving.

IVY TOWER

Charlotte and I moved to Grove Street at the end of November 1967, in the center of the old Greenwich Village, around the corner from the Theater De Lys on gay Christopher street, a couple blocks from the great Circle in the Square and two other leading off-Broadway theaters in Sheridan Square. O'Neill, Lorca, Chekhov, Strindberg, Arrabal, these were our new neighbors.

We lived in a two-room apartment at first, across the hall from Victoria and David and their three kids, a boy, seven, and two girls, five and ten. David was a freckled, slightly overweight, light skinned black man, about my age; sweet tempered, intelligent, he worked in a good bookstore over on Eighth Street and was liked by everyone, but he seemed overwhelmed by it all and he slept most of the time. Victoria was older with a thin, hawkish face and wild red hair, a speed freak who wandered around the Village picking up discarded junk and bringing it home to their two room flat. She looked like the archetypal witch. The junk now reached up near the ceiling. The kids had cut a path through it to their mattresses on the floor in the bedroom. There was no longer a way to reach the refrigerator. It had been buried for months. Later, when they moved, the handymen cleaning the apartment opened the refrigerator and vomited. There had been a cooked chicken incubating in there through the torrid New York summers. The kids lived on take-out food and what we neighbors gave them. We all looked after them. In a sense the building as a whole raised them; they drifted from apartment to apartment, each child beautiful, with freckled copper skin and a spunky life force. It takes a Village.

I was working furiously on getting through my dissertation. After my orals, I decided I didn't want a power career in academia. I would never give a doctoral orals. I would work in a state college where the emphasis was on teaching and the classes were offered democratically to practically anyone who walked through the door. I wouldn't teach the children of the elite but rather people from backgrounds similar to my own.

I also decided I had had it with "objective" social science. There had to be some correlation between what was happening in Vietnam and the detached unemotional attitude of the social scientists; I could feel it. There was nothing in their program that encouraged them to work on themselves. Many of them were afflicted with the American hypnosis, the unquestioned belief in progress through technology at whatever expense to the earth and to powerless people and other cultures around the globe.

Once again, I was to find later that my intuitions had been right. As one example, shortly afterwards the students at Penn erupted when they learned that a professor had been doing experiments on sanity and madness by torturing dogs. He would teach a dog how to avoid electric shocks and receive food, and then he would confuse the dog by continually changing the rules and shocking the dog when he did the "right" thing until the dog was finally driven out of its mind while the professor carefully took notes and measured the variables. This professor had become widely respected and received major grants. The university authorities couldn't understand why the students were so disturbed.

The *New York Times Magazine* printed a little essay by Dr. John Dollard, Professor of Psychology at Yale. "Safety Doesn't Permit Attack on the Powers of Government," read the header. Dollard was the darling of the social science historians. At Penn, we had been assigned his book on the South. He was the future, one of the most highly regarded psychologists in the United States; they were counting on him to broaden historical knowledge by bringing to it his deep understanding of human behavior and psychiatry and psychological theory.

Professor Dollard said he was optimistic about the future and that "the seeming disorder is of minor importance." [This in 1967 with black and anti-war riots (forty-one dead in one black riot alone in Detroit) and worldwide university takeovers and turmoil, the chaotic revolutionary year of 1968 two months away.] He believed that scientific advances would soon make energy virtually free and that the world's needs for food, clothes, shelter, machines and even luxuries would be freely met. "We will level mountains, water Saharas, warm the tundra and harvest the sea." Dr. Dollard saw the Vietnamese war as necessary to check "Communist China's second aggressive thrust in Asia in twenty years." [The fact that China and Vietnam had been fighting with each other for centuries was not on his radar.] He expected to see a worldwide representative government created, under which there would be no right of civil disobedience. "It seems to me that essentially the same argument applies now to the United States," he wrote.

There was little one could say about this logic. The sad part to me was that it was coming from Yale and the *New York Times*. That fall I impulsively changed my dissertation topic to literature. This was career suicide since I'd hardly had any courses in literature, but I'd had it with social science and with major universities. I couldn't represent the social science project as I had experienced it. Literature often explored the rugged terrain of the mysterious self, the author's included, which social scientists seemed to simplify and take for granted. I felt this was where the work needed to be done.

But what to write about? I thought I might consider the work of three somewhat overlooked Jewish-American novelists of the Thirties: Nathanael West, Henry Roth, and Daniel Fuchs, all of whom went beyond the simple naturalism of the Thirties fiction, sold few books and gave up writing fiction. West went to Hollywood and was killed in an automobile accident, Roth moved to Maine and became a duck farmer in his depression over the fate of the Spanish Civil War, and Fuchs moved to Hollywood and wrote screenplays. I stayed with this for a month or so but found it hard to get a handle on the material.

Then I decided to try black humor in American fiction as a topic. I loved black humor, existential, gallows, sick humor, Lenny Bruce and the novelists like Terry Southern, Bruce Jay Friedman, Joseph Heller, John Barth, J.P. Donleavy, Thomas Pynchon, and the rest. Finally I settled on James Purdy, who had published seven books and was still alive, residing in Brooklyn. I loved Purdy's work; he was a "writers' writer," little had been written about his work, and the rubric of black humor was a convenient jumping-off point to organize the dissertation.

I did all this reading and selecting in a few months while continuing to riot and run the liquor store while availing myself of the cultural life around me. Like most of the protestors, I was finding the path steep and rocky and it was making me furious. It was becoming apparent that the government did actually represent the majority of the American people, liberals and conservatives who basically had the same life-style. I couldn't face the imperatives of this as yet, but I found myself becoming angrier in my daily life. On Thanksgiving I almost punched out a dentist:

HE: All of Vietnam should be destroyed as quickly as possible.

ME: Including the children?

HE: I wouldn't give a slice of this turkey for all the kids under Communism. I'm an American, an American first! What do you care about our enemies' children? Aren't you an American first?

ME: I'm a *human being* first!

He was stumped. He had never thought of that before. He had been preoccupied all evening with whether there was garlic in the turkey dressing. I guess garlic has a long half-life and he had patients to treat the next day.

I imagined that he was very concerned about painless dentistry, for Americans.

Black humor was humor in which nothing was out of bounds. It was wild, unbounded humor that expressed outrage. Unlike white humor, liberal humor, the kind of humor of the *New Yorker*, it contained real, naked anger. Anger like this wasn't permitted in the *New Yorker*. It didn't go with the ads. Black humor highlighted the rage in outrageous. It mirrored that structure of radical versus liberal. It went beyond liberal. The liberals needed the conservatives in the way that CNN needs Fox News. Liberals put good taste up against the yahoos. Black humor was insistently in bad taste. Bourgeois was the word that kept appearing in my journals to designate the Other. My morality had been formed during World War II. I knew when I grew up that the one thing I wasn't going to be was a "good German." That was how we now saw the bourgeoisie: Good Germans. In the New York intellectual world, it didn't matter how you lived. Only what you said. We wanted to walk our talk. The liberal world had suddenly become, in our eyes, a world of brilliant talk. But only talk.

Marty Licker had first turned me on to James Purdy's novel, *Malcolm*. Now it seemed that I was backing into Marty's world. Marquel, from Idaho, who had held Charlotte's job, was leaving town. It was her apartment we had taken. Victoria and David across the hall were Marquel's pals. Marty knew them all. Now I was buying dope from Noel, who was connected to many of Marty's village pals.

Oddly enough, after I had put Marty on the bus to New Orleans from Wharton, he had somehow wound up in Montreal. I had visited him twice. Once, in the Army, I took a bus up there for a couple days and stayed with Marty at a Yoga Center north of the city in the Laurentians where he was living. It turned out his teacher was Swami Vishnudevananda who was a friend of Swami Satchidananda who was to become one of my teachers. Marty and I independently found our ways to two disciples of Swami Shivananda, spiritual brothers who taught roughly the same tradition. They both had senses of humor as well. Swami Vishnudevananda got a pilot's license and he billed himself as the "first flying Swami." [Later Swami Satchidananda would say, in his heavy India accent, "You can't take your money with you. No one has ever come here with a wallet, and no one has ever left here with a wallet. That's why they call a man the 'undertaker.' When you die, he reaches *under* you, and he *takes* your wallet before the police come."]

I was impressed by the way Swami Vishnudevananda was kind to Marty, although Marty was, as always, difficult. The Swami understood him and had a certain sympathy for his pain. Some weeks later Marty acted out and the Swami had to ask him to leave. Marty defended the Swami when I inquired about it. He said, "The Swami is a good man. He was right. I messed up." Marty could surprise you in this way. He was very loyal to anyone he respected.

Once, before Marty joined the Marines, in the year Marty was failing out of Hunter College because he listened to the radio personality and great storyteller Jean Shepherd for six hours each night, after listening to Alan Freed and Symphony Sid, one of Marty's former teachers, the jazz historian Marshall Stearns introduced the Count Basie Band at Basin Street. I turned to Marty and said, "Isn't that the jerk who failed you at Hunter?" and Marty quickly responded, "No. He's not a jerk. He's OK. I didn't do the work. I deserved to fail." Sometimes Marty could carry this respect too far. Like the time he almost got into a fight with someone who insulted General Sarnoff, the President of RCA, because Marty claimed that Sarnoff was somehow a distant cousin and Marty felt he had to stand up for his family.

Marty had been getting himself into trouble throughout those years. Once, at about age twenty, he began to obsess about a girl, Diane, whom he had had a crush on in the first grade. He remembered where she had lived, five blocks from our house on a street we had never entered, but on a Friday night he walked over there, found her family name on the mailboxes, walked upstairs and rang her bell, looking like a wild-man as always. An older man answered the door, no doubt Diane's father. Over the man's shoulder Marty could see the family seated for the Sabbath dinner, and sure enough there was Diane, whom he recognized after fourteen years, along with her mother and two big guys, one probably her brother and another perhaps her fiancé. Marty rushed past the father, and shouted, "Diane, I love you. I've always loved you." He tried to take her hand and kiss her cheek as he shouted, "Marry me. Please. I love you." By then the father had tackled him and the family beat the living shit out of him and threw him down the stairs.

The second time I visited Marty in Montreal, right after my orals, he was living next to McGill University where he had a following of local French kids. Marty liked Canada, although he said he missed all the black people and it was thus too tame for him. The Canadian kids had never seen anything like Marty before. Now he had his pension from the Marines, and he had changed his name to Raspberry Mahogany. The French kids were amazed by him and called him, "Framboise."

I took the train up from New York. When I arrived at his apartment at the appointed time, of course he wasn't there and hadn't left a note. I spoke to his neighbors. They told me to look in the McGill Dining Hall. That was where he ate at this time of day. Sure enough I found him there, going around and eating the food off students' plates as soon as they left.

Marty showed me the beautiful city. I remember a café where they kept playing John Lennon's "Norwegian Wood," a lovely song that would ensure I never forgot the poignant feeling of this trip. One night we were walking along a deserted dark alley, heading home from downtown, when a police cruiser spun around the corner and pinned us against the wall. The two French policemen told us to get into the back of the car. My hair was long and Marty was dressed almost in rags. I knew what this was about. The stock exchange had been bombed recently. This was not something the Canadians were accustomed to. They were picking up anyone suspicious. I was scared. Cops, longhairs, an alley. Even if we weren't arrested, I knew we were going to get beat up. We were sitting on the back seat of the cruiser. They turned to Marty, and speaking in a thick French accent, one said, "May I see *votre carte d'identité.*" Marty looked at him for a tense moment and then he replied, "Mister, I don't even have underwear, much less identification."

I jerked my head back, expecting a blow, but when I looked, unbelievably, the French police where laughing. Somehow they found Marty amusing. This was not New York. They turned to me. Asked me for identification. I showed them my old Army officer identification. Told them I was visiting my friend here, a former American Marine, who was living in Montreal.

The police examined my ID. They looked at me. They smiled. They appeared to be embarrassed. They said, talking to me, ignoring Marty, that they were terribly sorry, could they drive us home? I was astonished. They drove us home like a taxi. This was definitely not New York.

We had another run in with French-Canadian officials a couple nights later. Marty took me to a party at an art school that occupied the two floors over a tavern in a small building. People were drinking wine, viewing the student paintings on the walls. A three-piece rock band was playing against the far wall. I walked over to listen to the band. A red light facing the front side of the base drum seemed to flash in time with the music. Then the band played, "Light My Fire." Incredibly, the drum flashed red just like it was on fire. What a realistic effect! Then I realized, to my horror, that the drum *was* on fire. Was this part of their act? The band was playing nonchalantly. Then flash, the fire consumed the drum and licked up the wall and set a couple oil paintings ablaze. "Fire!" I shouted, and people began to scream and run for the stairs but Marty ran forward like a demon with a blanket he had picked up somewhere and began to fight the flames. I and many of the guests joined him and we managed to quench it before the fire department arrived. The bar patrons below were now in the street watching the excitement as the French firemen ran up the stairs with a hose. They took care to extinguish the embers and wet down all the charred paintings and walls. When they were ready to leave, I thought, Oh, oh, here we get it, disturbing their evening and almost burning down the house because of a negligent rock band at a decadent party, but no, I was surprised again. The owner of the gallery brought out some good French red wine and quickly the firemen were joking and drinking with us in the midst of the ruined flat.

Later, when they left the room, the firemen turned back to us to smile and wave, and one said, laughing, (in French) "See you next party!"

No, this certainly wasn't New York City.

On my twenty-ninth birthday, December 24, 1967, I began to keep a journal. The next day, on Christmas, Marty called. I will now begin, from time to time, to quote in italics from my journal and letters in my own voice as I saw the events at the time.

Just got a call from Marty in Montreal. Third time he called me and ran out on the bill. The operator asked where he worked and I told her he didn't. "'ow can 'e not work?" she said in a thick French accent. "He's a hobo." "An oboe?" "No, a hobo. That's someone who doesn't work." She laughed and said, "'E told me 'e was a convict." [The French-Canadians! They were beginning to win my heart.] I declined to pay for the long call. He had called Saturday and said he got a job as the weak man in a circus. Marty lives near a church which had a bloody crucifixion outside which has been hidden for Christmas by a nativity scene with cows, etc. This appeared to enrage him. He later told me that he went to church on Christmas Eve, and as people approached the communion railing he played the Marine Chow Call (Come and get your beans boys) on his kazoo. Charlotte thinks that Marty feels if one sends a letter then the letter should be answered. He is down to sending empty envelopes with just a few words on the back so he'll receive your obligatory letter. Apparently he's feeling lost and lonely, having sent envelopes to Noel, Irwin, Marquel, Jean Shepherd, and Swami Vishnudevananda and received no answers. He said to Charlotte, "They're not children anymore. They're responsible adults and they should answer their mail."

DETACHMENT

Reading about comedy, humor, laughter. In Western theory this most basic and universal of human responses was always a step-sister to the other, more painful forms and emotions. Yet I thought comedy might be seen as a higher form than tragedy.

Most totalizing Western philosophers and psychologists wrote about comedy as an afterthought, realizing they had to say something about it since humor and laughter were so widespread and basic in all people and cultures. They merely inserted it into their theories at the end, so as not to leave it out. For example, Freud loved jokes, but his *Wit and The Unconscious*, although not wrong, tailored comedy and wit to fit into his overall schema of human behavior. Henri Bergson as well; viewing comedy from his own framework of life as vitality enmeshed in machine-like behavior, Bergson defined the comic as a living being repeating himself and thus behaving in an unconscious manner like a machine. This is certainly true but it is not the complete story. Bergson made many valuable comments on humor in the process, for example that it takes a certain anesthesia of the heart to laugh at human misfortune. This was another way of talking about comic distance or detachment. For example, if you slip on a banana peel, it isn't funny, it hurts; if your child slips, it also isn't funny because you are emotionally involved; if Hitler slips on a banana peel it is funny because you have the necessary emotional detachment. Another way of approaching this is embodied in the saying that for the person who feels, life is a tragedy, for the one who thinks, life is a comedy.

Tragedy, a literary form we've inherited from the Greeks, includes seeing as well as suffering. In the World Lit textbooks, the tragic hero is traditionally said to progress through the "three Ps": Purpose, Passion (suffering), and Perception. Sometimes the suffering leads him to see what his own responsibility was in bringing on his pain, but often it is too late for him to change or to be saved. One corollary of this is the idea that it is only through suffering that one can see or learn. (Anyone who has children will understand this part of the learning process.)

Comedy is a more hopeful form. It doesn't even have to be funny but rather simply eventuate in a happy ending. Comedy descends to us from spring rebirth rituals. There is a saying: "In tragedy the father is right; in comedy the son is right." Comedy is about the young person, not the foolish father, getting the girl, and it usually ends with a marriage. This is again a legacy of the old spring fertility rituals, with sacred orgies to magically induce babies and good crops, planting the seeds, and celebrating the death of the winter. Easter is set in the spring for this reason, it is a rebirth ritual, marked by flowers, and thus is a comedy, although it seems to me that Christianity (especially in its iconography) too often seems to forget this and to stop at the tragic-seeming Good Friday. Dante called his great Christian drama, *The Comedy*. [Later generations called it *The Divine Comedy*]. He saw the universe as a comedy because it had a happy ending.

Comedy lends itself to many different theories, particularly because it is possible to write long tomes distinguishing between comedy, satire, jokes, wit, puns, laughter, etc. That's not a path I want to tread here but I will say that one distinction I like was made by the critic J. D. Sutherland who said that comedy serves as the attorney for the defense of the human race, while satire serves as the attorney for the prosecution.

Beneath all these different angles on the matter I kept coming back to references to comic detachment. At the same time I was reading Buddhism and Hinduism. It had begun to seem to me that if we were to have peace in the world we would need to approach the world with peace in ourselves. I especially liked to quote the Christian pacifist, the Reverend A. J. Muste who said, "There is no way to peace. Peace is the way." I often remembered my spiritual experience in the church in Massachusetts though I knew I could never be a Christian, not after the centuries of suffering they visited upon the Jews, and the misfortune the Christians had brought to so many other people and cultures around the world for millennia. There had to be something wrong or shortsighted in a worldview that caused centuries of unnecessary suffering and death for so many whose crime was simply disagreeing with the Christian story.

I found myself more urgently seeking for a direction in my life in Eastern thought as my grip on my old values slipped. And here too, strangely enough, as in comedy, I kept running into the notion of detachment. Buddhist detachment, Hindu non-attachment. There was a certain distance toward worldly events required in the Eastern view of the wise life, as opposed to the passionate involvement valued by those of us raised in the West. I remembered that when the Bodhidharma brought Buddhism to China in the sixth century, he said his philosophy was, "No holiness, vast emptiness [openness?]." No holiness! That was an interesting take on a religion. It seemed to me if you wanted to find out what you defined as "holy," you could ask yourself, "What can I not joke about?" So in a way, if you wanted to find your "attachments" in the negative Eastern sense, you could ask yourself, "What couldn't be joked about?"

Since they both spoke in terms of detachment, could there be a relationship between the attitude, the approach required by comedy and that of Eastern religion? There certainly was much humor in the Zen tradition. The old Zen masters were often quite witty in dealing with their disciples. Like the Zen story where the master and his disciple meet a beautiful, lightly clad young woman stuck on a street which is flooding. The Zen master lifts her up, carries her through the waters, and sets her down on the other curb. Later as they walk on, the disciple, troubled, turns to him accusingly and says, "You're supposed to be a Zen Master, yet you lifted up that beautiful lady and held her against yourself while you carried her across the street." The Zen Master responds, "Yes, but I put her down back there. Are you still carrying her?"

Or the Zen Master (in civilian clothes) with his disciple in a mountain inn, and the waitress comes up and says, "It will be such an honor to serve you, a Zen Master in our little inn!" When she leaves, the disciple says, impressed, "Wow! You didn't even say a single word and she recognized that you're a Zen Master," and the master says, "Yes, I wonder what I'm doing wrong."

I loved these little stories and found them humorous as well as edifying. Even Horace said, back in ancient Rome, that the function of poetry (art) was to educate and amuse. When I looked at the first "P" of tragedy, "Purpose," I thought of the Buddha saying that the root of suffering was desire. And that the way to reduce suffering was to reduce desire. I also thought of the anthropologist Jules Henry, who in his excellent *Culture against Man*, pointed out that the motto of Madison Avenue was: "Create More Desire."

I found much to think about here, stoned and sober, as I worked on the dissertation and in the decades afterwards. In a way, it all came down to whether you saw life as having a happy ending or not, a question which almost cannot be asked any longer if one hopes to be taken seriously in our benighted culture.

1968

1968 was the pivotal year. As it was happening, you knew the numbers 1968 were going to be an insignia of something in future world history, like 1789 and 1848, but you weren't sure what they would signify.

Events were happening too quickly to integrate. The ambulance of modern history was bowling down the street in fast-forward with siren crying and garish lights blazing, knocking down everything in its path. Even the sidewalks were not safe. For months without intermission every day gave birth to new atrocities or to outrageous hopes. Something would lift your spirits to a new height one day and then fling your body down onto the concrete floor the next, so hard you felt things breaking inside you, vital organs and bones that couldn't be repaired.

The year began in a worldwide paroxysm of hope, an international TV spectacular in which events fed off each other as radical and rock and roll images flung themselves around the globe at the speed of light. The year ended in a despair for compromise and for change from within the system.

During 1968 I lost my faith in the Kennedy consensus, in liberal intellectuals and writers and academics and journalists, I lost faith in my family, in the American government, in the American people, in my former worldview and my cherished American ideals. Then I began to take LSD regularly.

How can one recreate the context in which we lived in that astonishing year so as to make it real for someone who was not there? How can one describe what it was like to see beloved leaders assassinated, a simmering and flaring up of civil war in scores of black communities, with the National Guard in the streets with tanks, and blacks shooting at them from nighttime rooftops, burning and looting in hundreds of locations, TV shots of troops with machine guns behind sandbags on the U.S. Capitol Building, while a large part of Washington D.C. burned in the distance, stoned young people with foot-long hair screaming about peace through electric guitars in a new kind of music whose power rivaled the whistle of incoming shells, while the sirens outside in the streets were also screaming.

What was it like to see hundreds of universities closed down by their students and to see the police breaking the heads and smashing the faces of young people on TV every day? To see Buddhists in Vietnam setting themselves on fire in the lotus position in the street? To see images from Vietnam—a young girl, naked, terrified, howling, running toward the camera, her clothes burned off in a napalm attack; a South Vietnamese General executing a man, blowing his brains out with a pistol in front of the camera. To see our troops dropping burning napalm on villages? To see them coming home by the thousands with heroin addiction or mental illness?

As Vietnam vet and future U.S. Senator John Kerry would later testify to Congress: American troops "had personally raped, cut off ears, taped wires from portable telephones to human genitals and turned up the power, cut off limbs, blown up bodies, randomly shot at civilians, razed villages in fashion reminiscent of Genghis Khan, shot cattle and dogs for fun, poisoned food stocks, and generally ravaged the countryside of South Vietnam." He also testified that massacres of civilians like My Lai were "not isolated incidents but crimes committed on a day-to-day basis with the full awareness of officers at all levels of command."

[Preceding quotes from, *Lies My Teacher Told Me,* by James W. Loewen.]

January began with disruptions around the world. The Czechs confronted the Russians by putting reformer Alexander Dubcek in power. Students rioted in Birmingham England, shut down the University of Madrid in Franco Spain, protested in Poland, confronted the culture minister in France. Japanese students mounted huge demonstrations against the U.S. 300 arrested. Martin Luther King began the poor peoples' campaign. Dr. Spock and Rev. William Sloane Coffin of Yale were indicted for counseling draft evasion. Then the month ended with a bang. Robert McNamara, Secretary of Defense, testified before the Senate Armed Services Committee that the Vietcong was losing it. Their combat efficiency and morale were falling. They had pretty much lost their power to launch sustained and coordinated attacks. Later that day, the Vietcong launched the Tet Offensive, attacking thirty-six cities, sending the South Vietnamese army scurrying away along a 600 mile front. Chaos and vicious American counter-attacks followed. The Vietcong captured much of the American embassy compound in Saigon. In the next four days we suffered 281 dead and 1195 wounded. The South Vietnamese lost 632 dead. We used artillery and bombing to level crowded areas of Saigon. 1,000 civilians were killed there and 1,500 wounded. Air power reduced eighty percent of the city of Hue to rubble in order to recapture it. Another 1,000 civilians killed. The entire countryside was filled with confused and desperate refugees. The Pentagon declared the Vietcong's Tet Offensive to have been a complete failure. Then they sent thousands more soldiers to Vietnam, increasing our forces there to over half a million.

But what were we to do? Ordinary Americans like myself. We would have to open the eyes of the people. TV wouldn't do it. We would have to do it ourselves, changing people's minds one by one. As Chairman Mao said, the journey of a thousand miles begins with a single step. And he knew what he was talking about. He had led the Long March for well over a thousand miles.

According to his doctor's memoirs, afterwards, Chairman Mao, at this moment, was holding old Imperial Tea Dances in Beijing. While we were assaulting the bourgeoisie for their retro taste in music, and attacking the Waldorf Astoria, Mao was emulating the Waldorf Astoria, complete with formal dress and Lester Lanin-type society orchestras. Mao would have loved to dance at the Waldorf Astoria, to show off his steps. While the most extreme radicals among us were citing Mao, he was having the wealthy Chinese dress up their teenage daughters in the antique silk outfits of the aristocracy, with more personal attendants working on them than even Hollywood divas, and then Mao would choose his favorite each week and show off his dance steps with her, and then retreat to his private quarters off the dance floor and fuck her. And Mao had venereal disease and refused to acknowledge this or treat it. It was a sign of influence and pride for the powerful in China to have a daughter who had fucked the Chairman and had his venereal disease.

But the Chairman's supporters here didn't know this at the time. People change.

HE'S LEAVING HOME

I would convince my mother about the war. That was the way. My mother and my uncle "Hollywood" Mac, her older brother, and the rest of the family as well, the aunts and the cousins and the neighbors (including her friend Fay, who somehow had come to believe that North Dakota didn't exist.) My mother would surely come on board the peace train. After all she had always told me when I was a kid that she was a good person who only lived for others, too good for this world, she didn't have a mean bone in her body. She said it was my father who was the problem. He was the violent one. She told me back then that she was like me, we were both high class, sensitive individuals, and she regretted marrying my father when she could have married a dentist or a lawyer who had been courting her.

My mother was living in the north end of Yonkers now, a garden apartment. My father had never been comfortable in Yonkers during the couple years he had lived there before he died. He would skulk around like a mongrel at a dog show, lost and confused. He had never done anything but work. Living in a garden wasn't for him.

Now we would meet at my mother's place occasionally on a Sunday evening, cousins, aunts, chunks of the extended family, Uncle Mac, always the center of attention, with his Clark Gable looks, his trimmed mustache, his eye for the women, the scotch on his breath, his ukulele, his playing the piano on the black keys, and his stories, always his stories. He was my mother's guru, her older brother, she idolized him; he taught us all how to tell one-line jokes, and funny stories. He was our Homer and our Virgil, relating to us again and again his oral history, the funny family Bible, his Odyssey in which he outsmarted fools, swindled his immigrant father, cheated the dim and outflanked the angry. The angry often included my own father who several times went after him and had to be restrained by the police.

Mac told us for the twentieth time about when he had a cab driver in the store to buy a leather jacket but there was only one in stock, too large. The man was turning it down when Mac took out a stick of chalk and somehow convinced the man to lie on the floor. Mac drew his outline on the ground the way the police do with a corpse on the street, and then helped the man up, laid the jacket over the drawing and said, "There, you see, a perfect fit. You can't argue with that. That's scientific."

And the story about the time he put a huge sweater on a "balagoola" [literally "stable boy" but used here metaphorically] and the guy claimed he wanted to look at himself in the mirror so Mac held up a tiny automobile rear view mirror and the guy said, "I can't see, it's too small, move back," so Mac moved back and the guy kept saying it was still too small until Mac moved all the way onto the sidewalk and then the guy was yelling, "I can't see, you're too far away." Mac returned to the store, indignant, saying, "I can't please this guy whatever I do," and the guy felt bad and bought the sweater. These stories seemed like hyperbole until you actually worked with Mac in the Army-Navy store, as I had done before holidays when I was a teenager, and saw him retreating to the Irish bar for a shot of scotch after every sale, and getting wilder as the day wore on. Once I saw him bring up a pair of jeans from the cellar with green mold all over them and when the customer exclaimed, "What's *that*?" Mac dusted it with his hand and said, seriously, "That? That's nothing. It's penicillin. It'll keep you healthy."

My mother was a great laugher and could get a joke and could tell a funny story herself. I had thought after my father died she would move up in class as she had always said, but instead, she found it tough going in the middle class. She had never read or followed the news or paid attention to anything cultural. She had shopped for clothes and lived in a dream of fame and celebrity that she had once had a shot at when she was young. But when push came to shove, she began to date Charlie Rosenberg, a guy about a dozen years older than she was who was just like my father only less accomplished, not as successful, not as good looking, not as smart.

Charlie was of retirement age and had dedicated his life to material pursuits, but he had wound up with no money so he was forced to keep working at a convertible bed store. He was broke but he did have a huge black Caddy. Charlie was odd looking; his head seemed squashed somehow, as if God had dropped something heavy from heaven and it had landed on him. His body wasn't pear shaped, he had no shape really, a kind of parade balloon with a round head set on top of it without a neck.

Charlie had no culture or conversation and he envied my Uncle Mac when Mac would begin his show business routines at family gatherings. Charlie never spoke at all, never laughed, never responded to the life around him. He would ensconce himself in a soft chair and look out of slitted eyes at Mac, balefully. He reminded me of the alligator at the Bronx Zoo. He would just keep staring at you under those heavy eyelids without moving for hours. You couldn't tell if he was awake or asleep, but you wouldn't want to put your hand in front of him.

One evening Charlie amazed everyone by not only speaking, but actually standing up and declaiming. Mac had been telling my mother slightly off-color jokes since she was ten years old. Mother was a Bronx street girl and she and her brother had a bond of street talk and showbiz patter that had lasted for decades. They were a team against my grandparents and their Old World values and morality. My mother fancied herself American upper class, a kind of celebrity the world didn't know about yet; she kept plastic covers on the living room furniture that never came off except when Queen Elizabeth II came to visit. I guess things were pretty busy for the queen over in England in the aftermath of World War II, because she hardly came over to see us anymore.

So without a second thought, Mac, drunk and on a roll, as he had been doing since I was a kid, told us all a joke that had the word "shit" in the punch line. At this Charlie popped out of his seat like a jack-in-the-box, fiercely irate. We were all astonished. He took a stand at the center of our circle, turned toward Mac, Charlie's face scrunched up with fury, pointing his finger in Mac's face, and he said, emphasizing each single word with a jab of his finger, "Don't you *ever*, and I mean *ever*, don't you *ever* say that word in front of Eve again." Then he rolled back down into his chair and returned to his silent, lidded scowl.

Mac, like the rest of us, was flabbergasted. But Mac was not off balance. Like a fencing master with an upstart pupil, he turned toward Charlie, and with a triumphant smile on his face, he said to the rest of us, as if making a case in court, "Is *that* a mind!" He pointed toward Charlie's weird face and he repeated," Is *that a mind*!" Then he paused beautifully, for the exact hundredth of a second necessary, and he added, slowly, "You take that mind and you put it in anyone else's head, it'd be worth a million dollars."

Charlie sat there grimacing as we all laughed without stop. That was the last time I remember him speaking.

We had some laughs, but as the months went on, I realized I was getting nowhere in my attempts to make my family see the war. They didn't watch the news. They avoided reading anything. There was no way I was going to get them to go against their government. My mother was convinced she loved people and she trusted the government, even though if someone called on the phone and asked her opinion for a survey, she would make up an excuse and hang up. She trusted her government, but she wasn't going to give her opinion on the phone.

I began to see that people like Mac and my mother and Charlie had made a deal with the government. Mac drove a Lincoln. Charlie had a Cadillac. Even when Mac had only worked in a small Army-Navy store, before his father died, he still drove a Lincoln and wore only the most expensive hand-tailored clothes, our own Beau Brummelstein. He and my mother felt they were doing pretty good in America. Most American's felt the same way. The government was not acting against the will of the people. The government was actually representing the wishes of the majority of Americans. The citizens had made a bargain with the government. "Don't ask, don't tell." You leave me alone and let me have a house or a big car, or hope to have them, and you can do whatever you want to the balagoolas around the world. I'll look the other way.

[My cousin who works on Wall Street said laughing to me just after the start of the bombing in Iraq in 2003, "I don't want civilian casualties, but let's face it, if there *are* going to be civilian casualties, better them than us."]

As the crazy year of 1968 unfolded, I was forced to see that the American people were not going to be convinced by reason or morality. The news they saw on TV was stacked in favor of the war, the same corporations that owned the politicians owned the networks, and even if by some miracle a fragment of the truth did come across the airwaves once in a while, the people wouldn't see it anyway.

YOU CAN'T GO HOME AGAIN

The Bronx is a lot like Venice except for the canals and the pretty houses. The Bronx was sinking in my estimation. I couldn't return to the old ways of thinking. I had burned my 155th Street Bridge behind me. It was so obvious. My family were imperialists. I couldn't even root for the Yankees anymore. They were the monopoly-capitalists of baseball. How had I not seen this? How had I come to root for the cowboys against the Indians at the movies when I was a kid? How had Hollywood painted the Indians as villains in a thousand westerns?

And what was happening to my hopes for a civilized life in Manhattan?

The negative epithet that kept appearing most frequently in my journals at the time continued to be "bourgeoisie." This was natural for me, since I came from a rather aristocratic background. My family had not been in trade for 400 years. (If you don't count pushcarts.)

> *"when we decide to practice peace, what we encounter is everything that is not peaceful in us."*
>
> Trudy Goodman
> *Insight* [Buddhist] Journal

I had hit a nerve of fury in myself. Every journal paragraph I wrote was studded with insults directed at the bourgeoisie. Of course, these were also directed toward my craven bourgeois self. I hated the fact that I was still working feverishly on my doctoral dissertation, *James Purdy's World of Black Humor.* Why couldn't I just drop out and pursue the revolution and become a real writer, which was my new goal? With all the bombing and death on TV, and the rioting and drugs around us, graduate school at Penn was coming to seem completely irrelevant.

Nonetheless, I continued to dredge away at the dissertation. Every morning I went down into the mine and picked at a vein. Yet I was falling apart. My anger was my way of not feeling the sadness at what I was losing. I had sacrificed so much, tied myself up in knots of self-discipline for so many years to remake myself as a civilized person. Even smoking dope was not easy for me, although it was a sign of membership in the counterculture. But I had succeeded in the regular culture. I had so much more to lose than Marty Licker or Charlotte or the young kids who had dropped out of college. In my heart I kept hoping that I would wake up and this need for rebellion would all be a dream. But I knew it wasn't. Vietnam wasn't a temporary aberration. The world had been like this since I was born. Fallen. Something really deep had to be reached and changed.

My adjustment to the world was slipping, my personality cracking. Fortunately, I seemed to be splitting into two principal pieces rather than simply shattering. During the day and evening I continued to be an information-processing machine: research, writing, protesting, movies, plays, museums, concerts, hanging out with my new radical friends, exploring the bookstores, reading the papers and magazines.

Then late at night I would smoke a joint and put *Sergeant Pepper* on the stereo. Who could believe it? The Beatles, the mop-heads, poor kids from Liverpool who could have taken their millions and sold out like so many others before them, the Beatles were on acid. They had gone to India to study Hinduism and were speaking out for peace. God bless them, I thought. They gave courage to us all.

I would open my journal and give myself stoned advice. It was like I was my own big brother. I would even refer to my day self as "Jerry." Jerry do this and Jerry don't worry about that. I would spend hours analyzing my whole life from a stoned viewpoint, as if Marty Licker were there, giving me an avuncular consultation, and I would tell myself in great detail how to proceed, beginning tomorrow. The Buddha had only an eight-fold path. My path had hundreds of folds. I was merciless in my diagnosis and injunctions.

I guess that's why the next day I never read what I had written the night before. I would just drink a cup of instant coffee, and begin to work on my dissertation. Fuck my other self. The stoned one. Let him hang out with wilder guys he admired like Timothy Leary, whose father was Eisenhower's dentist, or Baba Ram Dass, whose father was President of J.P. Morgan's New Haven Railroad. My father came from the kind of people that the trains ran over. I had to prepare to make a living in case the revolution didn't work out. When I informed my doctoral advisor that although I had majored in the history side of the program, I wanted to teach in a small English department, he said, tentatively, that if I wrote my dissertation in literature, it should be possible. I could no longer teach history. I believed with James Joyce that history was a nightmare from which I was trying to awake.

I was always a student at heart. Even now, in the midst of my crazy life in this crazy year, I was preparing to teach lit by taking a course in Shakespeare at the New School that I followed with a course in the Twentieth Century English Novel. After the grad courses at Penn, I was surprised at how easy these courses were. I was also attending a series of lectures on Jewish-American fiction at the 92nd Street Y.

The liquor store drained only an afternoon a week if there were no emergencies. Every Tuesday I would finish up my dissertation work for the day and run up to 135th St. on the IRT. Sometimes I wondered which of my activities was offering the greater service to humanity: Writing a doctoral dissertation that no one would ever read, or providing good liquor at decent prices to people who really needed it?

POETRY AND BAYONETS

On the subway, someone calling my name awakened me from my reveries. Slim was a light skinned black man about forty whom I knew from the liquor store. He would come in every day and buy pints of Gallo port. I was surprised to see him in another context, wearing an old but presentable sport jacket. I was pleased that he had come over to sit next to me and chat.

Slim was famous around the store for a kind of mantra he would announce every time he came through the door. "Won'-be-long-now

. . . ." He said it in a worn-out, funny kind of way, mocking himself, but there was something artful and touchingly true about it as well, the words joined together in a slurred sing-song voice like Billie Holiday's: "Won'belongnow." Over the years I've often found myself repeating Slim's mantra when I'm lonely and my thoughts slip into a sweet longing to return to a different, happier planet.

Slim and I walked to the liquor store together. My father had always said that a day never went by without an ambulance, police car, or fire truck stopping on the block, but at that moment the street was quiet. Bare of trees. Filthy. Lined by identical six-story tenements on both sides. The air was sharp and clear, the kind of crisp day in which New York City shines. Noah Rivera waved to me from his barbershop next door. I'd known him forever. He was a great guy. An expert on opera. Come winter evenings, he would put on his Russian fur hat and head down to the Met where he knew everyone and worked as an extra.

Rigo Lopez, my manager, was in the store with his assistant, Guillermo Martinez, also from Puerto Rico. Guillermo was a sweet, lost guy, a half a foot shorter than I was, maybe five foot six, but he weighed about 220 pounds and he wasn't in great shape. He had a short thick head that gave him the overall aspect of a fireplug. The poor guy was only about twenty-eight, but he had three kids and he was still having a tough time adjusting even though he'd been in the U.S. for five years.

Rigo, who'd been my father's assistant, had come from Puerto Rico as a child in the 30s and had grown up on the block. He'd been shot in the war as a sergeant in Germany and had a plate in his head. He lived on aspirins, about twelve to fifteen a day. He was a sweet guy, very charming, with a freckled copper complexion and a ready smile, but he also had a temper, and since he'd been a boxer people didn't mess with him.

I'd known Rigo since I was a kid; I was fond of him; he was like an uncle to me. I knew if guys jumped me outside the store he'd come flying out to help. (They never did.) Some people questioned my judgment when I turned the daily responsibility for the store over to Rigo, but I trusted him. I knew he was capable of being more than a clerk. I also loaned him my father's huge Oldsmobile for occasional deliveries of cases, but also for his personal use because I knew it would be much faster and safer than the two buses he took home to the Bronx each night. I believed that with his new large salary and the car, he would see that he had a stake in the store and would do a good job of stepping into my father's shoes. He proved me right.

[I loved the idea that after working for our family for so many years, now he could take his own family for a Sunday drive in my father's big Olds.]

He lived in The South Bronx with his family whom he loved, his wife and his bright, pretty daughter Rosita who attended The High School of Performing Arts and hoped to become an actress. Rigo often expressed his love for his daughter by explaining in gory detail what he would do to anyone who touched her. My father used to give the same lectures to me, telling me what he would do to anyone who laid a hand on me. There was a certain irony to these lectures since my father was the one who was beating me up, but of course I couldn't say this to him or he would have beaten me up.

Rigo worked long hours, but everyone in the neighborhood knew and respected him and they made the store was a kind of social club. He had several girl friends including one who hung out at the store and brought him down hot meals. At least one of the little kids on the block was his. Because we were not allowed to sell beer, the store was dead in the summer, so Rigo would watch the Yankee games with his friends on my father's stolen TV.

[Crooks and con-men were always coming into the store to sell hot merchandise. I wasn't really interested in buying stolen goods. The usual con was, "I have a $100 TV in my car trunk and I'll sell it to you for $20 but I need the money up front to bail my car out of the garage." Well, I don't know about other places, but no guy from The Bronx is going to advance money to a crook for stolen goods that aren't present, especially if he doesn't know the crook. Nonetheless, I was always polite when I refused. Everyone's got to make a living.]

"Doctrines pass, anecdotes remain."

E.M. Cioran

When I entered the store with Slim, Rigo and Guillermo greeted us. Slim bought his first pint of Gallo port for the day and left. Rigo came around the counter and shook my hand. He turned to Guillermo, "Here's the man who's gonna buy us a gun!"

209

I smiled perfunctorily. This went on from week to week. Rigo wanted me to persuade my mother, who officially owned the store, to sign a permit for a gun for them.

"I told you, Rigo, if they come, just give them the money."

"We don't give anyone money. That's the way of the store. Your father wouldn't have gave them any money."

"Yeah, right. That time when you *were* held up? What happened? He gave the guy the money."

"If they come, we throw bottles. That's the code of the store."

I shook my head and let it go. We'd been down this dead end road before.

"How's Rosita doing?" I said to change the subject.

"Rosita? She's doin' great. But if I get my hands on that Johnny Carson, it'll be another story."

"Johnny Carson?" I said in amazement. "What does he have to do with Rosita?"

"I sent him her poems, that's all. She's a great poet. You should read her stuff. I sent it off to Johnny Carson to get her published."

"So what happened?"

"What happened? He didn't even answer, the son of a bitch. He didn't even take the time to answer."

"Well, Rigo, I mean, think about it, he probably gets lots of letters from all over. Hundreds every week. Maybe thousands . . ."

"Don't give me that. That's bullshit. My Rosita, she's a great poet. Johnny Carson's gonna publish her poems and say he wrote them."

"I don't know . . ."

He turned to Guillermo. "He doesn't know! Johnny Carson's gonna make a million bucks off my daughter's poems and he doesn't know."

Guillermo just gave us his usual puzzled smile. Everything about New York seemed to amaze him. Rigo opened the trapdoor and climbed down to bring up a case of some booze. I was sorry I had contradicted him but he would forget it in a minute. He knew I was just trying to calm him down so he wouldn't have to take some more aspirins. I went behind the counter and opened the books and began to write checks.

Working in the liquor store had always been my nightmare future, the one I had studied so hard to avoid. Now I took it lightly, I was only a visitor, but it still gave me a chill when I saw my handwriting continuing the columns in the books where my dead father's writing left off.

As I grabbed a couple bottles of wine and prepared to leave, I saw that Rigo, behind the counter now, was looking at me with a little sly grin.

"What?" I said. "What's so funny?"

"You notice, today, I didn't ask you so much about the gun like usual?"

I realized he was right. "Yeah. What's up?"

His face lit up like a neon sign that said, "Triumph!" He reached under the counter with his right hand and slowly pulled out a razor-sharp bayonet. With his left hand he took a stone and began to sharpen the steel blade. Smiling wickedly, he looked over the naked bayonet at me.

He had me. We both knew it. He'd won. There was no way I could keep them from having an unsheathed bayonet somewhere in the store. I could never find it. I nodded graciously in defeat. We shared the smile. Guillermo smiled, too. We all stood there grinning, watching Rigo sharpen his bayonet.

Well, at least he couldn't accidentally shoot a customer. And it would make a good story some day. Everything has two sides I thought, even Rigo's bayonet.

A couple weeks later I received a phone call from Armando, a Puerto Rican cop I liked who hung out at the liquor store.

"Jerry, come up here fast. We got a problem."

"What? What happened?"

"It's Rigo. They just took him away in an ambulance."

"*What?*"

"He was cleaning his bayonet and he fell on it. He stabbed himself in the thigh. Hop in a cab. He'll be OK. I'll stay here till you get here."

As I was rushing up to the store in the cab, I thought to myself, "Thank God I didn't get him a gun."

"Today's literature: Prescriptions written by patients."

Karl Kraus

In January of '68 I decided to take a week off to cool down. I flew out to San Francisco to see our friends. Charlotte had only been working a few months so she was unable to come.

Jim Saunt, from Cleveland, who had been thrown out of RPI and had ripped his pants off in Philly, had married Paulette Perrone and they had a little baby, Claudio. They were living in Berkeley. Rochelle Gatlin, my pal from Penn, had a rented room just over Chinatown in San Francisco. Her tribe was still in the big flat on Page Street, one block from the heart of Haight Street, but all the rooms there were occupied when she arrived.

Jim quickly pulled out a fifth of brandy when I arrived. We proceeded to drink it and stay up all night talking madly about the crazy events we participated in, our anger at the government, the great movies and memorable performances we had seen, all our hopes and plans for ourselves and the world. Jim played beautiful records all night. He was managing a record store on Market Street in San Francisco and continued to add to his collection. He was especially enamored of a recording of the Brahms *Double Concerto for Violin and Cello* by the Philadelphia Orchestra with Eugene Ormandy featuring Isaac Stern and Leonard Rose. But mostly he played electric blues and exciting new rock.

Paulette seemed happy, stoned, with her books and records and her baby, her watercolors, and crocheting, and Italian and French movies. A Cleveland girl, she was content in the January sunshine, and the gentle crazy atmosphere of Berkeley which people called Beserkley in those days. Jim had been involved in big riots in Oakland where the police apparently were rednecks, unlike the cops in New York or San Francisco, and he told me excitedly that after the police had beaten the demonstrators, the kids had released the brakes of cars, pushed them over the top of a rise and let them roll down the hill scattering the Oakland cops.

The next day Jim drove me to San Francisco. You could see the difference from New York immediately. Everything was looser and easier here. First of all, the weather was gentler. In January, people were outside in their shirtsleeves and shorts. In fact, at the freeway interchange at the foot of University Avenue in Berkeley, dozens of long-haired young people were hitchhiking, seated on the curb, many in shorts, backpacks next to them, holding up signs: SEATTLE, SAN DIEGO, RENO, LA, CHICAGO, FRESNO, MEXICO, ALASKA.

Everyone was hitching. That was the way to go. It saved fossil fuel resources, it cost nothing, and it was a chance to share with your brothers and sisters, to make new friends, to take part in the great unfolding adventure, the magical mystery tour.

And what amazed me as a New Yorker was it seemed to be working. There was very little violence and bad car trips, everyone with a car felt guilty and sought to pickup hitchhikers who were clearly the moral ones in the transaction.

The Zen masters had a saying that remains one of my favorites: "Cold eye, warm heart." In the Sixties we were most focused on the warm heart. We came, so many of us, from difficult families; we tried to create families amongst ourselves, all of us breaking the law (pot, draft card burning, rioting, etc.), all gassed and beaten by the cops; we tried to see ourselves as brothers and sisters, to take care of each other as the Buddha suggested. Of course, we went a bit too far in this direction at times. It was still too early to realize that just because a guy had been thrown out of school, committed a felony, did time in jail, sold drugs, and hated the cops, it didn't necessarily mean he was a nice guy.

But what was amazing was how well it all worked for a while. Everyone was trying to think holistically. If you used a gallon of gas that was one gallon less for your grandchildren. Acidheads like Dr. Andrew Weil, students of Hindu yogis like Dr. Dean Ornish, were learning the lessons that would later change our world.

Jim took me to his record store where he "purchased" a copy of the Brahms for me. We knocked around the city for the afternoon. But where were the adults? The whole city was overrun with stoned young people. And they seemed to be in charge. This was very different from New York. This whole city was like a Mediterranean Greenwich Village.

No wonder a movie like *King of Hearts*, in which the authorities disappear during an invasion and the inmates take over the asylum, became a cult favorite here. [As I said later in my novel, *The Carmen Miranda Memorial Flagpole,* San Francisco is the kind of city where you put nets on the baskets in the schoolyard and no one steals them.]

New York was an old tough city. There were certain ways of behaving that had survived the Darwinian tests and you were expected to follow them. If you wanted to live in poverty in New York, there were thousands of people who were ready to help you to achieve that state and to beat the shit out of you in the process. Just riding the subways at night and emerging alive was a skill that could have been the subject of a major in college. The buildings stood above you, hard and huge, intimidating you, making you feel small, like sleek pyramids from some other planet, built by giants who disdained you. The ruts were firm, the unions inflexible, the church powerful, the winter threatening, the Bowery calling like a siren song to those who got tired for a moment and took a fatal step off the ambition escalator.

San Francisco shone gaily in the sun. You were asked to come with flowers in your hair. It was like a small town to me. It seemed like a beach town, a resort with gaily-colored, flimsy wooden houses designed to bend, to flex in a quake. Life was easy here. There was no real winter to freeze you. I felt safe on the street because everyone I encountered was stoned.

The Haight bordered on Golden Gate Park which ran to the ocean where there were Dutch windmills somehow. Throughout the city, especially in the Haight, throngs of young people were on parade. Ransacking the attics and junk shops and thrift stores and costume companies, they were attired in the clothing of all ages and climates. Many had on barely any clothing at all. The hippies were functioning outside the economy of fashion of the season, and planned obsolescence, and the conspicuous consumption that was expected (especially of women).

This was a city that was built barely a century ago by gold rushers, and it invited extravagance. Settled not by families but by plungers and miners and forty-niners, gamblers and dance hall girls and women willing to go off and take a chance, along with dreamers like Mark Twain, and Brett Harte, and Jack London, and Frank Norris.

San Francisco virtually invited you to walk around stoned. You could see many were on acid. Some couldn't even get off the ground to wander around, they appeared to find the sidewalk so interesting to gaze at, but somehow everyone understood and took care of them. Haight Street was a virtual parade. Later, when the tour buses came to look at the freaks, the "freaks" held up a large mirror so the tourists would be looking at themselves.

Everything was becoming so clear to me. There was no reason to wear black like the beatniks and kill yourself with hard drugs. The straight people would never get it. Just step outside the culture. There's a whole new world waiting next door. Like in Kafka's *The Trial*, the door was open. You just had to step outside. What was I protecting? What was I holding on to?

I had wanted to be respectable and learned, to believe in things like *Time* and *Newsweek,* and the publishers, and Columbia University. But the culture's moral authority was collapsing around me every day. Soon it would lose its metaphysical authority.

(I was beginning to define a culture as a group of people who have decided not to see the same things together.)

There was a basic difference between the liberals and us. They believed the war was a political problem and could be solved by political means. I was beginning to see the abominations around me as a cultural problem, the excrescences of a decadent lifestyle and narcissistic culture that was beyond repair. Yes. What we needed was a counterculture. And it was beginning here in San Francisco where there was a free store run by the diggers on Haight Street, you could just walk in and take something or leave something for others, and where rock bands with fantastic creative names that announced their freedom from convention, their dada and surrealist inheritance, (Vietnam was our World War I), bands like The Jefferson Airplane, and Big Brother and The Holding Company, and The Grateful Dead, and the Quicksilver Messenger Service, and Country Joe and the Fish were giving free concerts in Golden Gate park and people were handing out acid on the street and *policemen* like Sergeant Sunshine *were on acid*!

That morning in Berkeley I had seen a stoned, longhaired, hippie mailman, barefoot and bedecked with beads. Later that day, as Jim drove me over to the Fillmore after dinner, we maneuvered carefully around a tripping young man playing trumpet in the middle of the street.

FOXY LADY

The Fillmore was filled with stoned young people. A square-shaped ballroom, not a theater; the bands played on a slightly elevated platform set at the middle of one of the walls. The crowd sat on the floor in front of them. There were no seats. Behind us, on another raised platform, the hippies running the light show with their color slides and spinning projectors worked their acid magic, not merely on a little screen, but on the walls around us so you felt, like Jonah, that you were inside of something and going for a crazy ride.

I saw the democratic aspects of this immediately. Everyone was on the same level. There wasn't a higher world, on stage, with private entrances and dressing rooms, a world of celebrities, untouchable, and the groundlings below them. There were no reserved seats for the richer patrons. There was no distance between the show and the audience. In fact, looking at the audience you could see that they thought of themselves as part of the show.

We sat on the floor behind a beautiful girl, maybe seventeen, wearing a lovely long, green, Pre-Raphaelite style dress. Her long black hair hung down to her waist. She sprawled on the floor and pulled out *a marijuana cigar*! She flared it up and began to blast away.

Over on the sides of the seated crowd was free space for hippie dancing. People on psychedelics or other rushes were swaying and letting their arms swing freely like birch trees in the wind. (Later, I had an idea about the origin of this kind of dancing when I watched the 1936 film of Jerome Kern's *Showboat,* where teenage Irene Dunne is hanging with the Negroes in her family's kitchen and she wants to show them she is choosing them over her parents, so she begins to do this crazy dance that she thinks is black, but it's merely a beautiful hippie dance, thirty years ahead of its time. I nearly jumped out of my seat.)

The Fillmore was inexpensive and offered an incredible line-up. Three acts: Albert King, John Mayall and the Blues Breakers, and Jimi Hendrix. The blues had been rocked and plugged into modern power by the white English kids like Mick and Keith and Eric and the rest who came upon American black music in the early Sixties and had been developing and preserving it in England while the white Americans were listening to commercial music provided by Tin Pan Alley for the corporations to market to the teenagers.

When I had first come upon this music, I couldn't believe what I was seeing. White American kids were listening to real black music! Blasted out through big speakers. And so loud! I had never heard music at this level of volume. I wondered how the bourgeoisie allowed this. They simply had no idea how loud this music was played, nor of the orgiastic feeling

216

when you were bathed by it, like sitting at the foot of Niagara. I realized the adults couldn't even imagine what was going on among the young people. They were blind to the young people. This gave them the ability to fuck over the young, but it gave the young people room to create magical, sensual environments in the interstices of the majority culture.

When Jimi Hendrix came out, I saw quickly that he was a genius. And likeable. There was something very sweet about him that you might not gather from the posters and record albums. He had realized immediately what other people who were seeing the present through the framework of the past hadn't noticed. The electric guitar was not merely a loud guitar. It was a way to hook into the power grid, a modifier and amplifier and bender and synthesizer of electricity. You didn't have to play music on it in the old linear mode with notes and scales and the rest. It provided opportunities for something new entirely. A wall of sound that you could shape and bend.

Hendrix had huge speakers set at either side of the platform. A young woman went up to the one on our left. I saw with amazement that she had somehow tied tangerines into her dark, long, unruly hair. She put her hands on each side of the speaker to support herself as she leaned forward and put her head *into* the speaker! She began to sway to the music, shaking her head from side to side as her heavy hair swung after her. The orange balls glittered in the colorful lights flashing all around us.

Jimi Hendrix was dressed in a kind of colorful soft "gypsy" outfit with a psychedelic bandana around his head. He played left-handed so he was facing in her direction and quickly he spotted her. His mouth dropped open. He looked like he was watching a car wreck. He indicated the woman by moving his chin in her direction. She had no idea this was happening. She was looking straight into the speaker, entranced, shaking her head in time to the music.

Jimi kept looking toward her in amazement and then back to the audience. We saw what he was saying. Is this OK? Is this the way they did things in San Francisco? Should he stop? Should someone intervene? The audience understood this and they laughed warmly. If she wanted to do her thing, that was OK in San Francisco. Hendrix then broke into a beautiful smile and shrugged, as if to say, Well, it's a little crazy, but if that's the way you guys do things around here, and it's OK with you, it's OK with me, and he stepped on the accelerator and took off, his guitar sounding like a big WOW as the people shouted and the car looped over the top of the roller coaster and entered free fall, wild and rocking, dazzling and soaring. His guitar seemed to be speaking, and if it was talking in a language we hadn't heard before, so much the better to us.

ROCHELLE'S HIDEAWAY

You couldn't help but admire Rochelle Gatlin. She had no idea how brave she was, there by herself, virtually penniless, in her room on a hill just over Chinatown with her bookcases full of books, all neatly underlined, working every day on her dissertation and then heading up to the Haight at night to get loaded with her pals on Page Street.

Like myself, Rochelle had switched her dissertation topic towards literature: James Agee, the southern writer who had made his way to New York, drank, and died of a heart attack in 1955 at age forty-five. Agee had collaborated with Walker Evans to write *Let Us Now Praise Famous Men*, that hymn of photos and print in celebration of the poor southerners in the depression. He had written poetry; the beautiful novel, *A Death in the Family;* the screenplay, *The African Queen;* and had invented serious film criticism in America. Rochelle had fallen in love with Agee. She would tell me about how Henry Luce hired him for *Fortune* magazine to help him out in the depression, and Agee would drink at lunch and then lie on the floor of his office with the speaker next to his head while he blasted Beethoven on his phonograph.

Rochelle had me reading Agee, including his *Letters Of James Agee To Father Flye*. Flye was an intelligent, understanding Episcopal priest who had become a mentor to the young, sensitive, despondent Agee, had saved him for life and American literature.

Rochelle had visited with us often, for days or weeks while she checked in at Penn and worked on her dissertation in New York. Sometimes along with Ward Hoalton. We all stayed with each other. Slept on couches or floors. For any length of time. At our apartment in the Village we would have people sleeping all over the place. Bruce and Ricki Kuklick would come often. Rochelle's old boy friend, Bob Jones, the gentle ex-football player would come up from Penn. Other friends from Philly and elsewhere.

To get to the bathroom you had to walk through our tiny bedroom, just barely bigger than the bed. We didn't mind. Once we had so many people there that it felt like summer camp; after we turned out the lights I came out of the bedroom and played taps on my harmonica.

That was the way we lived back then. We tried to disassociate ourselves from the culture in as many ways as possible. We saw the straight culture as blind and murderous. You had to find ways to separate yourself or you would drown in guilt. You had to jettison your old values. All of them. Good or bad.

We took each of the culture's values and turned it upside down. If it valued privacy, and competition, and being white and European, and Christian, and violent, and being tough and macho, and serious and straight, and accumulating money, and ripping people off, and expanding the economy, and materialism, and science and reason, we valued community and cooperation, and being multi-cultural, along with Eastern religions, and non-violence, and being vulnerable and open to our femininity, and conscious of the environment, and stoned, and living cheaply, and trying to be fair to others, and open to mysticism and drug visions, and ecstasy and intuition.

We were trying to kill something in ourselves. It was especially hard for people like Rochelle and myself. We had worked hard to be civilized. Now in our personal choices we were not merely deciding to disassociate ourselves from the violence, we were questioning the value of all the centuries of the project of civilization itself. We were learning that you couldn't extricate the roots of the culture in yourself without dismantling the self the culture had constructed for you, the self that you had thought was your own.

Every day we chiseled away at the hard block of our old self, hoping eventually to find the statue of a god or goddess underneath.

EIGHT MILES HIGH

The large flat on Page Street filled the entire top floor of an old Victorian house. Rochelle's pals (especially Ward) kept it extraordinarily neat, white walls, high ceilings, fresh light flooding in from the many windows. Haight Street was in continual festival mode just a block over, but Rochelle's friends somehow defined themselves against the local environment wherever they were, straight or hip. There were five or six people living in the flat, paying about thirty dollars a month each. The large living room and adjoining huge kitchen were practically bare of furniture and without books or magazines which the inhabitants kept in their individual rooms. This made Bev's wheelchair not just ornamental but practical. She never had to worry about a seat in any room she wheeled into.

Beverly Hall, a pretty woman with fair skin and long straight black hair, wore an impish smile on her stoned face. It turned out that she didn't actually need the wheelchair. There was nothing wrong with her legs. But the chair was *so beautiful*, probably a hundred years old, a large wooden contraption, handcrafted by unknown artisans who took pride in their work in a simpler, more fulfilling age.

And the chair was handy when she was real stoned or tripping and not sure she wanted to try to walk at that moment. The wooden armrests were perfect to set down your tea or ashtray with a joint in it as you visited the various agglomerations of friends throughout the house.

Ward kept the house pristine. That was his job so to speak, although it wasn't spoken outwardly, but everyone understood Ward didn't pay rent. He kept the tea going and the public rooms spotless. Ward was a kind of Zen master in his way, thin, almost gaunt and hawk-like; he hardly ate, spent virtually no money, sometimes cleaned houses to earn what he needed for bare survival. With an appealing shyness underneath a testy exterior at times, and a sophisticated elegance to him, Ward possessed virtually nothing. But he performed essential services for the others. Everyone trusted his taste in the arts. Rochelle relied upon him in this way for years. He kept up with all the reviews of art, films, music, the radio, the Haight street buzz, the library. He found books for each person to read, knowing their individual tastes; he recommended movies to go to as a group, gave a kind of ongoing seminar in pop culture, and was careful never to fall into clichéd thinking. For example, on the day I was there, Ward suggested going to a particular movie. One of the crew who actually had a job, I believe it was Betty Mullen, said, "It's Friday night. There's going to be a huge line," and Ward replied, immediately with excitement, "Oh, I luuuuv lines."

Ward loved Lytton Strachey and in fact Ward reminded me of him so far as I could imagine Strachey in life. Actually, the whole place struck me as a kind of stoned Bloomsbury, without of course the mature geniuses like Virginia Woolf and Keynes producing world-shaking works. Yet there was something crazily civilized about this drugged menage.

Ken Gatlin, still officially Rochelle's husband, lived there as well. His affair with Bev was winding down. No more the shy, tight-lipped, brilliant poet who never touched alcohol to his lips, he was now completing his period as an acid head and just staying stoned all the time with the rest of the tea-sipping group, always augmented by friends from outside, like Paul Fortino, a Jewish-Italian Bronx guy who worked as an usher at the Symphony, and Jan, his old lady, who had a couple kids and worked a day job at the phone company to support them, and David, a somewhat short handsome gay man with a blond mustache and Prince Valiant haircut who spent much of his time getting his teeth cleaned by their handsome but sadly heterosexual dentist whom David had a hopeless crush on.

The spacious kitchen was almost bare, criss-crossed all over with thin gas and water pipes. Ken Gatlin had painted them all in his acid phase, circling them with one-inch wide rings of various bright colors. He had done excellent, neat work, very professional, perfect choices of colors, kind of like a Frank Stella working in plumbing fixtures, and it added a magical Oz glow to the otherwise minimal kitchen, especially when you were stoned. Apparently, he would drop acid and then sit on the floor all day staring at the pipe until he came up with exactly the right color for the adjoining ring. I was glad to see he was no longer on the floor, but he certainly had done a good job.

Now Ken was working in North Beach at a newly opened small, unassuming boutique. As opposed to New York, San Francisco seemed to value a certain joyous amateur quality in everything you did. New Yorkers never caught onto this aesthetic. When the Cockettes performed in an old theater in San Francisco's Chinatown, it wasn't actually a "show." It was a big party with the entire audience stoned out of their minds, many tripping, and the cast in the same state, so it was a kind of open field of behavior, a satire of the stringent standards of Theater with a capital T, the opposite of classical music. And the audience understood that they were allowed, in fact encouraged, to be part of the show if they were outrageous and creative enough. Later, when the Cockettes blew into New York, the theater audience expected to see a show; they understood they were "audience" and they were paying money to see something other people with more talent had put together with much hard work and training. They waited to be entertained and both sides were horrified to see that the Cockettes weren't that "good" if you really evaluated them critically. But if you were in San Francisco where most of the populace was stoned out of their minds, and you could dress up in medieval clothes and drop acid and go down to Chinatown and leap onto the stage and dance the can-can with the cast, and shout and sing and run around in the aisles and create an atmosphere that was crazy and spacious and out of control, filled with joy and love, and perhaps wake up the next day at some place you didn't recognize, with new friends you didn't remember meeting, wasn't that better than being entertained and then going home to your daily life? In San Francisco, hardly anyone had a daily life.

When the Cockettes evolved into the Angels of Light, they realized another potential of this process: acid-Hindu pageants that existed in a loving spiritual space, playful, but reaching toward the Gods with breathtaking costumes of mirrors and jewels along with fake elephants and Indian music. Years later, when I took my six-year-old son one night, visiting from Cleveland, he was completely enthralled; at intermission he said excitedly, "I'm going to drink a lot of water so I can stay up. I don't want to miss a minute of this!"

Ken Gatlin seemed to be enjoying himself at the funky boutique in the little storefront on Grant Avenue, the center of the beat culture a decade before. One could do worse than to spend his time stoned and giggling with a gaggle of young women also stoned and trying on colorful dresses. But I worried about his poetry. I admired his skill with language, his knowledge of literature, his poems with their hard lines, terse and bumpy like knuckles.

He was no longer the tight-lipped northerner I had met in Philly. Some rubber band inside him that had kept his structure rigid had snapped.

Well, perhaps the change would be for the best. He was certainly enjoying himself, and he was making enough money to get by without really contributing to the straight economy or the war effort. That was the important thing.

BACK IN THE USSR

When I returned to New York, a garbage men's strike was in progress. 100,000 tons of garbage was piled on the streets. (No doubt diligent professors were already out there weighing it.) The counterculture was pulling at me like a second moon circling the earth, tearing me apart. But I went back to my dissertation, and not without a certain relief. I hated to admit it, but I liked the structure and goals that regular work brought into my life.

One afternoon when I returned at dusk, Charlotte was sitting quietly at our old piano, softly and slowly stroking a series of beautiful chords. She didn't hear me enter. I watched her for a while, in the wan winter light; Charlotte had exquisite timing. She could play many instruments. She was a kind of musical genius in a feeling sort of way.

Finally, she sensed me, turned her head and smiled sleepily.

"Dylan?" I said, nodding toward the piano.

"No, Bach," she said, softly.

I knew Dylan could be a fine wordsmith in a hit or miss, Rimbaud manner, but now I saw him in a new light.

Charlotte was getting back into music. Watching fewer horror movies. She bought a flute and started classical lessons at an inexpensive venerable music school a block from our house. She also took lessons in jazz techniques and theory. As she walked around the Village and befriended people, she saw that unlike Idaho, here she was no longer the freak show. In fact, it was not easy to attract attention on the streets of the Village in 1968. Loopy or stoned as you might be, there was usually someone crazier nearby. The residents enjoyed the color and variety on the streets. Especially on week days.

The Village functioned as a tourist economy. Friday and Saturday nights the sidewalks swelled with tourists from out-of-town, weekend beatniks from Queens trying to pick up girls (also usually from Queens) and kids from New Jersey taking advantage of the lower drinking age in New York to get blotto. On weekends the local inhabitants went on stage to act, played their music, or worked as waiters and bartenders to make their bread for the rest of the week. Real Villagers went out on weekday evenings. When the visitors had disappeared, the hip came out of their holes.

Sometimes I drank at a dark, semi-basement bar just down the street where Grove met Christopher, a couple doors from the Stonewall. The "55" was a narrow saloon with a great juke box and a friendly local crowd—people like Bobby Timmons who played piano with Art Blakey and the Jazz Messengers and lived around the corner from us. You could go there on weekends because there was a huge black man, maybe six foot six, built like an NFL offensive tackle who manned the door. When New Jersey suburban kids appeared he would step forward and say in a deep, no-nonsense, baritone, "Bar's full boys." They would never argue, just thank him in high voices, calling him "Sir" and leaving quickly.

Charlotte began to eat again, to come outside into the air, to let her hair grow in frizzy afro–like freedom, to add color to her used wardrobe, to stand straighter and walk the streets, stoned, with a new assurance in her stance and gait. She was practicing her flute every day and becoming happier as she put behind the grieving for her brother. The mourning for a lot of things.

You never knew whom you might meet on the Village streets. One day on our block I saw a woman, perhaps fifty years old, no doubt once a real looker, platinum blond hair down to her shoulders, wearing a tight white sleeveless sweater and tiny gold micro skirt over silver boots, walk out of an old building, take two large metal trash cans from the curb, haul them back inside, then return for more. It took me a moment to realize that she was the janitor.

Another time I was approached by two hippie-looking, high school girls who asked me to buy a flower for the Vietcong.

"The Vietcong?" I replied, laughing. "How can you get this money to the Vietcong?"

"Oh, they have an office on Twenty-first Street," one replied, perfectly serious, without missing a beat.

I was amazed, but then I thought to myself, "Who knows? Maybe the Vietcong *do* have an office on Twenty-first Street." I bought the flower.

THOU ART THAT

"What was said to the rose that made it open up was said to me here in my chest."

Rumi

My emotions were close to the surface. Often they brimmed over and I would find myself choked up over little things. I had always been easily moved by art. I often wept at the movies. I was the kind of moviegoer who reached for his handkerchief when the lion came out and roared at the beginning of the picture.

But now my defenses were shattering. Each day I had to face the loss of everything I had ever hoped for in my life. I had wanted so badly to be accepted by educated people. But they had disappointed me so many times that now I no longer cared. Strangely enough it was the rare good news that moved me. My responses to the bad news, the damaged information, the desert of hope in which we lived, had dried up long ago. But the curry of rebellious wit could always wake me up and bring forth a smile, like when Robert Rauschenberg painted his bed and hung it on the wall of a museum, or when he slung a tire around the midriff of a stuffed goat and sprinkled bright colors of paint around the goat's nose. The goat looked so soulful and sad. Like he had been carrying that silly tire since the Babylonian empire. I loved that goat. He reminded me a lot of myself.

Some small portion of unexpected beauty, some desperate vulnerability in an artist or hint of nobility or flash of courage in my fellow protestors was enough to get the waterworks going. I felt so damn lost and miserable otherwise. I kept thinking about my vision in Massachusetts. In the church. I remembered how it felt to believe that I was loved, that the universe was ultimately friendly. That somewhere I was valued and understood, and that somehow things were OK, forever, even though we couldn't see it right now.

I think that was why I was so easily moved as my cultural conditioning peeled away and personality disintegrated. I missed God. I missed being in touch with the Love at the center of the universe. I wasn't suicidal. I'd been through that in the Army. But even during the good times, I carried a deep sadness around with me. Even when I felt good, there was always the sandalwood incense of solitude, a profound loneliness only one step away.

As I wandered through the labyrinth of devastation, I held tightly to the thin thread that connected me to my spiritual vision. But how could one return to a world of meaning and beauty?

I continued to seek the answers in spiritual and Eastern thought. I thought about the "sound of one hand" and my "original face" all day and especially at night when I would get stoned by myself or with Charlotte, when the "little friend" as Don Juan called it would help me to relax and loosen the binds of my ego defense system. I found many answers, all interesting, but here I was, still in the world, still basically lonely and sad.

The Puritans differentiated between Arminians who earn grace through good works and Antinomians who believed grace was freely given by God, by visions endowed by God upon certain people for God's own reasons. I was nothing if not a moralist. I tortured myself with moral evaluations every night when stoned. But at heart I had reluctantly come to admit that, although I believed in moral behavior, I was a kind of Antinomian. Antinomians were sometimes beyond the law. At their best, they received the gift of grace humbly, without deserving it, but it was based on personal vision, on a life-shaking spiritual experience. This seemed to be my path in spite of myself back then.

I wasn't going to get the word second hand. I wondered why the *sadhus* and gurus and masters from the East were here. Why, if they were beyond desire, had they come to America like my grandparents? What were they looking for? Why weren't they living in a cave in India like the Tibetan saint Milarepa who was one of my favorites?

I could have saved time and unnecessary anguish by giving up some pride and listening to a spiritual leader with more experience than myself, and could have connected with like-minded people, but I continued to wonder: Along with what India had to teach us, didn't we have anything to teach India? Something about women's rights and democracy. Organized religions seemed to me to lack a means of feedback. This was the job of writers. Free speech was not a luxury. Nations and institutions needed it. They needed crazy writers who wouldn't be silenced, who said the emperor has no clothes. Yes, writers could be annoying. Often they disturbed the populace as well as the authorities. They created disequilibrium. But without them the system would slowly weaken and finally fall in like a rotted house. [Now we can see this was clearly the case in the Soviet Union.]

I had generally been a good boy, a fine student, respectful of my teachers, working hard to fit in and learn the systems, but that was over now. For years to come, I wouldn't trust anyone resembling a parental figure. Yet I had seen something that day in Massachusetts. And the old Eastern traditions were talking about it. They knew that sacred vision. They were plugged in to the Sun behind the sun, the Sun that was alive. I accepted this. But I carried on, trying to decipher the ancient holy texts by myself.

> *"Remember the two most important points of Vedanta:*
> *1. The world is unreal.*
> *2. I am Brahman"*
>
> Swami Sivananda

Thou art That. That was the essence of the old teachings of India. Thou art That.

This was the "koan" that I wrestled with the most and was always defeated. But I kept on.

You are Brahman. The God of Gods. You are God? How could that be? What could they mean? How could I be God?

And suppose I succeeded in losing my ego? What would be the point? I remembered back at Penn when Ayn Rand lectured. She wore her long, plain, black dress with a large dollar sign pinned to her chest. She spoke precisely to this point. If I am to give up my ego to achieve peace and eternal bliss, she said, what's the point if I'm not there? I thought about this as I tried to work against my ego. (Ego in the Eastern sense, which has aspects of what we call id.)

How could I achieve bliss if I was no longer there? What was the difference between this and the annihilation that all the secular people, the science worshippers, seemed to believe finally awaited us in the cold machine of a universe in which they believed they lived?

[As I was writing this memoir I chanced upon a panel of three men, Ayn Rand supporters, on TV. They were calling for the completely free man, a kind of Nietzschean superman, the extreme individual, soaring in glory above the cowering masses, blazing above the unexamined conventions of social life. They were dressed like "hip" professors in sport jackets and the fashionable collar-less black jerseys of the season.]

THE HELP OF FRIENDS

Charlotte gave an apartment in our building to a couple from the *Rat* newspaper and we began to hangout with their friends from the *Rat*. A group of young people, recent graduates from local colleges like CCNY, they had taken time from career paths to run the anarchic paper. Bob Eisner was a graphic designer, the art editor of the *Rat*, and his girlfriend Pat was a lovely, bright African American young woman with the sweetest disposition; you wondered what she was doing with these urban radicals, but after about a year she picked up and went off to begin a new life in Alaska. I marveled at this—just a few years before I had been involved in a near civil war in Mississippi just because James Meredith tried to enroll in his state public university, and now here was Pat, traveling across America to start again in Alaska.

Bob Eisner's brother Gil, a successful graphic designer with Milton Glaser and the like hung out with us, and Leon, a little, round, brilliant guy, future doctor, Marvin the paper's business manager and others in their crowd. Once I met Jerry Rubin at the *Rat* office, a large, unruly, loft-like space on the Lower East Side. I was surprised that he seemed shorter than on TV when he was in costume and being provocative. I liked him. I liked anyone who was on our side. He seemed a reticent young man with an appealing faint smile on his face. When you saw him like that, just one of the guys, improvising his way through the new conditions of life, you had to admire his courage. He seemed small and very vulnerable in person.

I published my first work in the *Rat*. A cartoon when Robert Kennedy was shot. Bob Eisner drew it for me. I have no talent in that direction. It was titled, "One Man, One Vote." I showed a close up of an old fashioned ballot box with a slit cut into the top for the ballots. A hand was inserting a pistol with the name "Sirhan Sirhan" written on it into the box.

But still I was somewhat isolated. I was almost ten years older than the kids at the *Rat*, and more skeptical. I remember once Leon showed me a pile of paving stones at the back of the office. "When the revolution starts, we'll be prepared," he said. I thought, as I had at the Pentagon, "My God, these guys are preparing for the Paris Commune of 1870." One guy said he thought we should go uptown and wreck Lincoln Center. I didn't answer, knowing it was just another pipe dream, but I remember thinking that the answer to irrelevant art is to create relevant art.

One gesture of mine emphasized these differences. I attended a preview of a play by Jack Gelber, *That Cuban Thing*. I had loved Gelber's *The Connection* which had been performed by The Living Theater some years back. A real eye opener to me. Junkies waiting for the man in a play that sliced through the standard conventions of theater and knocked down some of the fences that separated opposites in the culture. Among the junkies were a real jazz group, The Freddie Redd Quartet with Jackie McLean on alto. They were lying around, speaking lines like everyone else. Then every once in a while they would rise and slide over to the piano and play beautiful jazz, written for the occasion by Freddie. But were the musicians actually junkies in real life? I knew Jackie had been one. Were they really strung out? And what about the other actors? Were they junkies? And what was one to think when they came into the lobby at intermission, big rough looking guys, and begged for money for drugs in a somewhat intimidating fashion?

I looked forward to *That Cuban Thing*, a play about the middle class after Castro's revolution. It was not a miracle like *The Connection*, but a serious, interesting, balanced work with much merit. Especially compared to standard Broadway fare, which was generally served on white bread. Like Tin Pan Alley, Broadway was stumped and threatened by the Sixties. Broadway responded with two plays on the subject in 1968 (one by Peter Ustinov) and amazingly *each of them was the same*! The kids dress up like hippies and then the father, to teach them a lesson, also dresses up like a hippie and begins to hang around and say, "Yeah, man," and "That's cool," and the kids are terrified and ask to go back to the old way of doing things.

I was astonished when Gelber's play received unanimous bad reviews and closed after one night. The critics said the play was pro-Castro. So I went to the editors of the *Rat* and proposed that I write a review, correcting this injustice. They refused. They said the play was *anti*-Castro.

After Pat went to Alaska, Bob Eisner joined with another beautiful lady friend, not from the *Rat*, more like a gorgeous slim fashion model, elegant even in her jeans and old sweatshirt. She was pals with Paul Butterfield and his wife. She moved up into a little shed on their property in Woodstock. Bob borrowed a car and we drove up to see her. She was wearing old work clothes and putting the finishing insulation on the walls of the tiny cold shed which she had fixed up by herself. She was going to live in the thin-walled shed through the winter. The times were definitely changing.

Paul Butterfield was on the road, so we spent the afternoon in his house with his wife and kid. I loved his dazzling blues harmonica playing. He was not only one of the best white players, he was one of the best of all time, period. How could I be in his house? Other fences and lines were coming down, boundaries around my self-image and ideas of whom I might expect to be and associate with in my life. Paul Butterfield! When he played at the Fillmore East it was like an F16 roaring through your apartment at Mach Two and not breaking anything. Whew!

I loved hanging out with the kids from the *Rat*, often in our building. They were generous, intelligent, young people, living the life and risking a lot in the name of our ideals. I had to laugh when Mayor Daly went on TV after the 1968 Chicago Democratic convention and accused them of planning the riots. My picture of them was sitting in a circle with me, lighting a joint and passing it around until we were all wrecked and then discussing Marcuse, and Nietzsche, and the new Jimi Hendrix record. I knew they weren't into planning, not even about who would go out to get some food for our dinner.

A ROOM OF ONE'S OWN

Like many true believers, modern prophets and street corner evangelicals, Bill Graham bought an old theater and turned it into a Temple. The Fillmore East. Just below Saint Mark's Place on Second Avenue.

The Electric Circus was a relatively hip place but it was still a nightclub. The old culture trying to adjust and make a buck on the tourists and weekend hippies. The Fillmore East was different. Not quite different enough for the Lower East Side SDS affiliate, the "Motherfuckers," however. They thought the music should be free. Given away to the people. Nothing was ever quite good enough for them and they would make occasional guerrilla forays against the venue, breaking things and swinging chains and they would have to be beaten back by Bill Graham's own troops.

In fairness to the Motherfuckers, you could see what they feared and they were right in a way. They saw that rock would evolve into what it became in the Seventies and Eighties. Huge machines for money making, expensive tickets, massive stadiums, overdone effects. But the Fillmore wasn't like this.

I never had a bad time at the Fillmore. I always felt that the prices were fair, the entertainment excellently produced, and the atmosphere splendid for a rock concert. The old theater was just right, one of those Loew's theaters with a large balcony and good acoustics. It was not as democratic in form as Fillmore West. The Joshua Light Show was in back of the movie screen set up behind the band; you couldn't see the machines and the light artists at work, and it wasn't wrap-around like in San Francisco so you didn't feel you were part of the show. The musicians were on a stage, with separate dressing rooms off to the side in the old fashioned manner. But Bill Graham always took the trouble to provide great sound, all seats had decent sight lines, and the prices, though not completely uniform, were fair; if you bought tickets early enough, you would be sure to have a great seat.

The atmosphere was a large part of the pleasure for me. When you entered, you felt that you were in a different culture. As the war worsened and the culture bifurcated, it became increasingly less rewarding for us to go above Fourteenth Street. New York had a large hippie contingent, but the city was so huge it dwarfed any segment of the population. The city was not very safe, and you were always in danger of being attacked from the left, so to speak, the poor who might mug you and engage in individual redistribution of income, or the straight people who would not hesitate to call the police on you, just for some minor offense like walking around with your mind in a different world. They were always ready to "help" you by putting you in Bellevue in a ward of psychotics, or in jail to rehabilitate you, for your own good, of course. Uptown New York was not as bad as TV where you virtually never saw anyone like yourself, but once you left the Village you were generally a minority person.

Not in the Fillmore. Here, once you entered, you knew you were among friends. Bill Graham went out his way to achieve this effect. Everyone who worked for him might be sober at the moment, but they were all dopers, you could tell that. There were no dress codes for employees, quite the contrary. As you walked through the lobby there might be hippies with baskets of fruit giving out free apples. The ushers were there by choice, music aficionados. The security wore overalls and were very capable. Bill Graham did not tolerate inefficiency, but they were longhaired dopers too.

Rebelling against a culture that worshipped efficiency, it was all too easy to opt for inefficiency and sloth, but Bill Graham, in the middle of a scene that accepted and even depended to a degree on drugs and laid back attitudes, made sure everything was set up right and functioned in a first rate manner. I loved the anticipation in the darkness when all you could see were the red lights of the amplifiers, and you heard the musicians shuffle onto the stage to tune up, and the crowd cheered and hooted and howled, and then the show itself, the long sets, the encores, the whole package designed to give you the best possible presentation of this music, week after week.

It brought out the best in the audience as well. Everyone would pass food around. You weren't allowed to smoke dope but of course some would sneak in a joint or two and pass it around to set up a "straight-free zone." (My friend Raymond Mungo, small in stature, frail, big glasses, but large in heart and ideas, would do this later at Giants' baseball games with me in Candlestick Park, when he would come down for a break from his campaign for Governor of the State of Washington on a legalize pot ticket. He would go to the Giants' Club, buy a couple stiff drinks, bring them back and then proceed to get the entire section loaded on grass. If anyone suggested he be more cautious, he would reply, "Don't let the androids get you down, my friend." It made perfect sense after a while.)

[Years later, Ray would originate and orchestrate a brilliantly successful day-long writers conference at a hotel in Monterey, California, sending out the publicity, selling the tickets, greeting the guests, scoring free goodies from the local wineries and merchants—wine, food, little gifts, free hotel rooms for us writers whom he had hired. Ray wittily introduced the speakers, chaired the panels, bravely helped to break up an incipient fight when a member of the audience, much larger than himself, attempted to attack a famous critic, got drunk at dinner, took the microphone that evening, stepped up to the piano and crooned a complete torch song in the manner of Frank Sinatra, made a profit, and finally was arrested for driving the wrong way on a two-way street. When I related all this to my pal Barry Gifford, he said, "For Ray it's the perfect end to a perfect day."]

The Fillmore was our church; like a cathedral, it offered a taste of an experience in a different framework from the world outside the building. This was our own world, and the amazing thing was the music was so wonderful. It was like when Mickey Rooney and Judy Garland would get together with the other kids and say, "Hey, let's put on a show." There were no "adults" in here. We wrote the music, the musicians were loaded, as were the roadies and everyone else, and a good time was always had by all. If it cost us a few bucks to support this, it was real bargain.

I recall so many wonderful shows at the Fillmore East. I remember seeing the Allman Brothers. No one knew very much about them. I heard some talk on the radio and decided to take a chance. It was a pure hunch. They were the second act on a three-act bill. Charlotte and I had decent seats. We had gotten really stoned at home and walked over with little bottles of booze hidden in our underwear.

The Allman Brothers were like an American dream come true. Six kids from Georgia who had gotten the message, an integrated band from the South, two drummers, one black, putting down a heavy beat with Berry Oakley (soon to be dead) joining on base, Greg Allman on organ, always my favorite instrument in blues-based music, laying down the magic carpet of blues chords, and then the blue spotlights went on and caught two guitar soloists in front of the band, Dickie Betts and Duane Allman (also soon to be dead), and the band began to move, to rock the house with a music so forceful and beautiful you felt it would be made illegal if the adults found out.

The great shows at the Fillmore were about more than the music and this was one of the greatest. These kids were from Macon and they had come up to New York and they were taking care of business. It was like watching a minor leaguer step into a big-league game and pitch a no hitter. Those two singing guitars over that heavy beat playing songs like "Stormy Monday" and "In Memory of Elizabeth Reed." I thought of my black pal Charlie Williams in the Army whom they wouldn't let into the restaurants in San Antonio and here, right in front of me, was the answer. These Southern kids had gotten it, playing black music as only southerners could, and by God they were going to show New York what real music was all about. The pressure of a debut merely served to elevate their performances and a light went on in my imagination, the one that says, "ART GOING ON," and I knew I was in for one of those evenings in my life that I would never forget, and they kept getting better. Dickie or Duane would play an incredible solo, building beautifully with those salving notes, and the other one would then step forward and equal it, and all I could think was, "Please, God, don't let this end." I had a degree in electrical engineering and I knew this was what electricity was made for, to be bent and shaped into waves that moved your body and softened your heart with feeling.

And it kept getting better. There was no reason for it to ever stop, this pouring out of good feeling and love. They were having the time of their lives showing off their great band to New York City, spinning the whole tragic history of the South with all its black suffering into a source of profound good will and great art, and they kept right on that fantastic beat like a race car driver risking it all and making every turn right on the edge. There was no hard attitude about their playing, they were shockingly open. They kept looking at each other and smiling at the miracle that was occurring through them as I sat in the audience astonished.

After the show ended, the Platonic heart of the music, the sweet solos in the blue lights, the fabulous rhythm section, kept singing in my mind. As the third act began to play, a hard-edged, speed-driven, boogie band, "Canned Heat," I turned to Charlotte. "Would you mind if we went home? I'd like to leave here with that Allman Brothers' music in my head?" We walked across the Village to our little apartment without speaking, our faces brighter than the street lamps above us in the beautiful funky world outside.

I remember Elton John in his first American appearance. Playing New York meant a lot to everyone; there was always something extraordinary about the performances and this was especially true for out-of-town musicians, English guys and southerners and such. Elton John was a thin teenager with big teeth. He was so happy you could feel the radiations in the fifth row where Charlotte and I were sitting. We, as always, had gotten stoned before we came, had sneaked in a joint and I had a little bottle of brandy in my underwear. Elton just kept getting happier and happier, banging on the beautiful grand piano. This was before his irony and glam-rock and such, just music, and when the headliner, Leon Russell, walked out with a guitar and joined the band, Elton practically passed out. He turned toward the audience and said, simply, with amazement, "How can this be happening? I'm an English kid, and here I am, suddenly, playing the Fillmore East in New York City, and then my idol, Leon Russell, comes out and joins my band?" That was the secret to the Fillmore. The musicians were comfortable there. It was our space, one of the best venues in the world to play in, and the musicians were having the best time of all.

Elton kept flying higher and higher. He was going out of control. Charlotte and I were close by. We saw him begin to take off. This wasn't just show business. He began to bang on the piano while standing and mule-kicking both his legs out behind him at the same time, keeping himself afloat while in the prone position with his hands on the keys. He was high as a planet. Ultimately, he reached such a state of euphoria that he spun the big grand piano around and began to push it toward the edge of the stage! He was going to push the piano over the stage into the audience in a final *Gotterdammerung* of glee and destruction. We could see it in his eyes. At the very last second, with the big grand just about to fly off, he came to. He shook his head like a person coming out of a dream and couldn't believe what he had almost done. He grinned in the charming way the scrawny English kids had as if to say, "Whew, sorry," and moved the piano back onto the stage. Later in the evening, he came out and played with Leon Russell's band. It was the greatest night of his life. He didn't try to hide it. I turned to Charlotte, "I love this guy. He's going to be a real star."

Now when I see him dressed in Louis XIV wigs and silks, I remember that young honest English kid having the time of his life and I have mercy in my judgment.

When a great band like the original Allman Brothers cranked up and began to pour out their hearts, I would always think, "Mozart, if he was young and alive today, would be doing this, up there with these crazy generous kids," and I would marvel at their helplessness in the face of their own beauty. Taking greater risks than we did. Keeping it together enough to give us indelible performances that honored our counterculture. I rooted for them so passionately. They were the spokesmen of our new nation. They were like young Shackleton's, brave enough to accept the hard fact that the mother ship was hopelessly locked in the ice. They had set off in life boats without compass or charts, risking everything, hoping to come upon some island of consolation in a vast, freezing sea. Many of them would soon drown. Each performance might be their last.

I loved these crazy kids.

We all loved them.

One summer night Charlotte and I journeyed up to Wollman Rink in Central Park with Noel and the gang from the lamp store to see B.B. King. We all elevated our spirits on the grass outside. During the concert B.B. turned toward us and introduced a young singer to the audience. Janis Joplin. She wasn't really famous yet. We had tickets to see her a couple nights later. Janis and a few friends were sitting right in front of us. She stood, wearing a huge happy smile, delighted to have been acknowledged by a real bluesman. She wore no makeup and was dressed simply, jeans and a blouse. Her face was wide and plain and loveable. A real Texas face. Her skin rough. You could see her doing the washing outside a poor shack somewhere in the middle of East Texas. She reminded me of someone but who? Then I remembered. Janis looked like Babe Ruth.

I'll never forget how happily she shone, shouting back to B.B. in a real Texas accent, "Wanna jam tonight, B.B.?" She couldn't have been more appealing, but still, I was surprised at how plain she was. How poor and American. It warmed my heart to see her as her dream was coming true.

After the concert we got loaded again with Noel and the gang. They wandered over to the Central Park Zoo. I didn't think we should be there. I was amazed that there were no gates. No cops. No one but us and the animals in cages. A person could walk right up and put his hand between the bars. A jerk could throw things at the animals. Harm them. I kept waiting for the guards to arrive and arrest us or throw us out but no one came. We had our own private zoo. Stoned, we ambled from cage to cage. Could this be happening? In Central Park, known to be a kind of jungle habitat for the various loonies who wandered Manhattan at night? But nothing untoward happened.

On the day of the Janis concert at the Fillmore East, I awoke to a commotion in front of my house. Trailers blocked the street. Police. Assistants with lights and such. I discovered they were filming a movie, *The April Fools* with Jack Lemmon and Catherine Deneuve. *Time* magazine had recently had Ms. Deneuve on the cover, declaring her "the most beautiful woman in the world." And there she was, in the gutter, sitting on a folding chair like a beautiful doll. Her fine platinum hair that looked like some kind of frosting was being combed out by a maid. She seemed like a princess out of the court of Louis XVI. Thinner than I had pictured, somewhat brittle like civilization. I always respected her work, she was an excellent actress, but I could see why Bunuel would cast her as the ice maiden. She was very fine-tuned but didn't seem to have any blood. Perhaps she was merely withdrawn that day, picking up a pay check.

Then the crowd stirred. A gasp went up. Out of a trailer appeared Myrna Loy. After all these years. The gay guys went wild. Shouting and applauding. The whole neighborhood gave her a standing ovation and she, older but still graceful, turned to us and in the manner of Nora Charles opened into the warmest smile, taking a little bow, right there in the gutter. We were all helplessly charmed. Royalty has that power.

That night Charlotte and I went to see Janis. But when she appeared on the stage, it wasn't Janis. It was "Pearl." With makeup and a colorful dress and shawls and a boa and a vibrant smile. How could this be? This wasn't the same woman we had seen in the park. I wouldn't have recognized her. She was drunk, carrying a bottle of Southern Comfort, radiant with energy and happiness. That night we saw and heard the Janis who was never captured on record or film. [The closest is the scene in *Monterey Pop*, where they focus on her shoes as she seems about to leave the ground, or a number in the documentary *Festival*.]

She sang for hours. I was entranced. If I breathed it would dissolve. Like Coltrane, she held nothing back. I wished the concert would never end. I began to fear for her. We were right up front. I saw that she was trapped. The crowd was screaming out their adoration for her, and throwing flowers, and she was wandering around the stage like mad Ophelia, picking them up and clutching them to her, drunk out of her mind. And then she would sing again, holding the crushed flowers to her chest.

Finally, about 3 a.m., as the crowd continued to applaud and throw flowers, I stood up and shouted to her, "Go home! Janis, go home. Save some for tomorrow." But she couldn't. What was home? A lonely hotel room? How could she resist us, this lonely, alienated, small town Texas girl, with the bad skin and the big face, being sent all this love by the people of New York City. How could she leave? As I watched her wandering around her stage and singing so movingly, I realized that I had seen "the most beautiful woman in the world" that afternoon, but at this moment, Janis was more beautiful, in the living flesh, right in front of me, blood flushed and heart driven, giving everything to us, people she had never met.

A year or two later, I was seated in the Museum of Modern Art for an afternoon performance of a foreign movie. As we waited for the lights to go down, I noticed part of a huge headline in someone's folded *Daily News*: JANIS. I couldn't see the rest. But I knew the *Daily News*. I had grown up with that paper. There was only one reason that they would have the full front page covered with a huge headline about Janis Joplin. I burst out crying and rushed out into the street.

The secret to what made the great rock stars was that they gave more than they should have. They had no defenses against our love. That was why so many died. They couldn't come down out of the dream. The incredible dream that had appeared from nowhere into their lonely lives and threatened to end if they let it go.

THE WORLD TURNED UPSIDE DOWN

That was the song the British band played when they surrendered at Yorktown and effectively ended the American Revolution. It was also the theme of a play by Kenneth Patchen that we saw in a little off-off-Broadway theater in Chelsea. [I couldn't imagine that in a couple years I would be talking to his widow, a lovely woman, still beautiful, at a party in San Francisco.] The play was set at a fashionable cocktail party. Everyone is chatting and then the lights go out and there is a kind of earthquake with thunderous noises and confusion. When the shaking and convulsions cease, and the lights come back on, the chandelier is now fixed to the floor and the arm chair is now upside down and attached to the ceiling above the cast who are sprawled over the floor which now represents the ceiling. This is unnerving and disorienting at first, until they realize the world has turned upside down. But soon they adjust and they go back to their drinking and sophisticated conversation while standing on what was the ceiling.

This seemed an accurate picture of our situation in regard to the fashionable and powerful. The Adults. They appeared to be refusing to see what was happening or to see us, their children. Later, Charlotte and I would attend the American premier of The Who's rock opera, *Tommy*. It was a memorable event for several reasons, one being that it represented a larger accomplishment than merely a set of good songs; the opera had structure and development, in the line that the Beatles had begun with *Sergeant Pepper*. We sat up close. I was concerned for my ears because they had erected a wall of huge speakers on the stage of the Fillmore behind the band. Twenty seven of them, nine across and three high. I counted them. I was afraid they would blow us away, but by the end I wished the music was louder.

I remember when Roger Daltrey, as Tommy, turned to the audience in the penultimate moment and sang, "See me, touch me, feel me." That touched us all, I think, because it spoke for something we were loathe to admit: We wanted the adults, our parents, our leaders, to see us. We didn't want to accept the truth, which was that they would send us to our death for some idiotic material junk they didn't really need, as long as they could mouth a couple stupid slogans over our bodies. Luis Bunuel spoke to this in his movie, *The Phantom of Liberty*, in which the parents go to the police to report their little girl missing. At that moment the girl walks into the police station, appears before them, and tries to tell them she is there, but they just keep telling her not to worry, they'll find her, the whole police force is out searching, they're bound to find her.

How did you make a counterculture that couldn't be co-opted, that would be seen and that would alter the majority world? Was a world view contagious like in Antonioni's great film *Blow Up* where, at the end, the hippies play tennis with an imaginary ball. They hit it towards the protagonist and they look at him imploringly, until finally he joins their reality and "picks up" the imaginary ball and "throws" it back to them. Or was the problem more like Bunuel's *Exterminating Angel,* where the rich people are at a party and suddenly, like a kind of possession, they find they can't walk out the door of the room, even though it is wide open. This delusion spreads among them. Even the people who come to rescue them are enchanted by this notion and recognize the "barrier" of the imaginary door. They wait outside as the wealthy descend into chaos, fighting for the little resources that are available in their room, digging through the wall to get to the water pipes, everyone under the same spell, believing themselves trapped, all in a kind of hypnosis while the open door beckons, unnoticed.

For me, now, the world *was* upside down. I had walked out the door and thrown back the tennis ball. I was actively rooting for the Vietcong now. You had to admire their guts. They were up against the war machine that had almost killed me in the Army. America had gone crazy. A virulent cancer abroad. It would not only be better for Vietnam and the rest of the world if America lost, it would be better for America itself. I saw all the good karma earned in World War II being spent foolishly in an evil endeavor. I felt that if America did win, this would prove that humans could no longer stand up to the terrible mechanized force that scientists in their "ethical neutrality" had given to the Americans, that the human spirit has been defeated by machines. I saw a future in which America would perfect its technology further and intervene in countries all over the world to preserve our one-third share of the world's resources. I saw this leading to environmental devastation and more gross inequality than we faced today. I saw the American soul being sapped day by day.

In April "they" shot Martin Luther King Jr. They shot down a man of peace. Our beloved leader. The kind of real Christian that the Jew who had founded Christianity had envisaged. Our living link to the *arhats* and *bodhisattvas* of the ancient peace lineage.

The linchpin was broken. The wheel came off and split apart. SNCC. Southern Christian Leadership Council. Black Panthers. Eldridge. Huey. Stokely. Bobby. Julian Bond, Jesse, Fred Hampton (soon murdered by the police), NAACP, Black Muslims, Harry Belafonte, Richard Pryor, The Urban League, Angela Davis, Jimi, Rap Brown, the stepson of my pal Pearl, who raised him in Harlem. (Pearl who would come up once a week to clean my mother's house and turned me on to black music. "Rap, he used to call me 'Momma Pearl,' Jerry," she told me. "He was like a son to me.")

The last time I saw Pearl she was listening to black spirituals on the radio. "Pearl, what's with this music? What happened to your old favorites, Jocko on WLIB. The Moonglows and Jackie Wilson and Smokey?" Pearl was thin as a wire now. She opened into her big worn smile. "I'm too old for all that stuff now, Jerry. You know, you gotta move on as you get older." I never forgot this sermon. Pearl understood that the black love songs we adore descended from church music, and were once songs of love for God.

Quickly as the news of Dr. King's death spread, the blacks began to burn the country down. How could this have happened? The white people had finally gone one step too far. City after city went up in flames. Dozens, scores, over a hundred cities torched. Burn baby, burn. The blacks were setting fire to everything in sight. National Guard tanks were in the streets, whites were buying guns, white women were taking shooting lessons, no one knew where this was going to lead. I had never thought I would see the day when troops in machine gun emplacements were set up on the steps of the Capital Building in Washington, and you could see on TV the black smoke of the burning city in the background of the Capitol for days.

I had seen the harbinger of this outburst in the struggles of John Coltrane and other black artists to keep themselves together and non-violent in the preceding years. Coltrane was in the mold of Dr. King, a good man, deeply serious, not without personal demons and flaws, but searching for a way of peace and meaning. In the best black tradition, that river of endurance and Dostoevskian suffering that polished the soul until it finally shone through, Coltrane had had a religious vision in 1954, and he tried to stick to it, but again and again he admitted he had lost his way. Imagine being John Coltrane and not being allowed to enter a restaurant or hotel in much of his native country. To the degree that blacks attained civil rights, their position became more intolerable. Coltrane began to swing between passionate devotion on the one hand and a kind of daemon that drove his playing on the other. I saw him wear audiences out. You knew he couldn't keep this up and live. (Listen to his record, *Live at the Village Gate*, with Pharaoh Sanders, to hear this. I can hardly play it, the pain is so great; he is flaying himself in the way that only sinners who really have seen God can achieve.) Then he would make a record like "A Love Supreme" on which God ultimately banished the demons, but only after you first heard Coltrane's struggle in the music's anger and dissidence, and when, at last, you did ultimately see the harmony of God it was through the dirty window of a speeding el train at dawn. A peace was finally reached, but it was close to the peace of exhaustion. How could he keep this up and live? Then he died. Age forty. Dr. King was thirty-nine.

Malcolm X was forty when he was killed. He too, in his own way, was heir to this tradition of black seriousness and reaching for authenticity and prophesying. I had a fond spot for Malcolm, partly because he looked like my father. And he was gunned down near our liquor store.

On the night Dr. King was killed I fell into a grievous frenzy. My mother called. She hadn't heard of it. She avoided the news like pork chops. She wanted to ask me a question. Charlie had asked her to "go steady." She wanted my advice on what to do.

I told her Dr King was dead. She didn't really care. She knew little about him. It was just some more *mishegas* as far as she was concerned. Her real problem was whether to "go steady" with Charlie.

It was only when I told her they were burning down white businesses in Harlem that I got her attention. Then she went into a complete panic. "Do something." There was nothing I could do.

The next day I went uptown and found our liquor store unharmed. We were a few blocks from central Harlem and had been protected by the hill on which CCNY stood. I cut some beautiful pictures of Dr. King out of the paper, bought some art supplies, and had Rigo, who had much more artistic talent than I, make up a window display in honor of Dr. King.

I was being torn apart by my equivocal position in all this. That night I reported to my mother about the store but she and Charlie were pre-occupied. They had decided to go steady.

After I put the phone down, a story poured out of me. I was beginning to fancy myself as a possible writer. Every day I identified less with professors and more with artists and writers and musicians and European filmmakers. They were the people on the front lines, molding new art for mankind from the fusing fire that burned all around us. They were the madmen and wild-women who blazed with the smoke of defiance, the ones I really loved. My story centered on Dr. King's assassination. About a guy just like myself, with the liquor store, his guilt, his family's indifference. He gets more and more frenzied with guilt and grief until finally, when the store is spared in the riots, he goes uptown the next night and burns the store down himself.

ROAR LION ROAR

Columbia wanted to extend its campus toward the Harlem side and build a gym in a funky park, plans which were opposed by the Mayor and Parks Commissioner. This caused the Columbia riots of April 1968. Radicals were beginning to feel they had to move from protest to resistance. Students occupied a building. The black students wanted to be separate, especially after Dr. King's recent death. Integration and peace had also been murdered that tragic night in Memphis. Black students at Ivy League Cornell were arming themselves with guns.

The white students turned the building over to the blacks, then occupied President Kirk's Office. Hundreds of police waited nearby. A tragic clash of signs and misconceptions ensued. You could say the kids and the cops spoke different languages as long as it was understood that the languages were not French and Spanish but perhaps Welsh and Chinese.

To the cops, and the general public, Grayson Kirk was a distinguished educator and president of one of the world's great universities, holder of one of the most prestigious jobs in New York. To the students he was the member of the boards of IBM, Socony-Mobil, etc. and had turned the University into a whore of a defense contractor, a former professor who had sold out for power and money, leader of a university administration who were a clique of white, old-boy elitists who were colonizing their Harlem neighbors just as the U.S. Government was colonizing people of color around the world. The cops didn't know that President Kirk had stated in Virginia two weeks *before* the takeover that the students "had taken refuge in a turbulent and inchoate nihilism whose sole objectives are destruction." But the students knew it.

To the police and the white public, the residents of Harlem were lazy scofflaws, welfare cheats, drug addicts, and armed criminals. To the students they were a resilient underclass, the Marseillaise, descendents of slaves who had managed to create the greatest American art form, jazz, which descended from the gospel music of their deeply felt religious tradition.

To the students, the cops were a hired army of thugs, covering themselves in the mantle of the law that the capitalist imperialists used to suppress democracy wherever it raised its "ugly" head. To the cops, the students were hypocritical, rich, white kids who had no ties to the people they supposedly spoke for, privileged suburban jerks who were throwing away the precious chance for the education the cops themselves had been denied.

The cops waited nearby, salivating, rubbing their clubs up and down with their fists, tugging at their leashes until their necks began to bleed. Students smoked the president's expensive cigars, trashed university property, and destroyed faculty files, some of them irreplaceable. The police were tired of chasing the fleet kids around the streets as they mocked the officers and burned flags. Now they had the kids trapped. All it would take would be for the wise men to say the word and release them to end this farce.

Finally the wise men spoke and gave them the go-ahead. How could the result have been any different? The police waded in and beat the shit out of the students with their clubs and kicks. The ambulance shrieks sounded throughout upper Manhattan.

In her apartment near the campus Diana Trilling, "fearful that the university might be overrun or burned down by the blacks of Harlem, lived behind bolted doors sitting up late into the night, 'the unceasing campus radio at my side, straining for the unfamiliar sound on the street beneath my shaded windows, the tramp or rush or scuffle of invasion.'" (Note the high level prose, the sense details, the confluence of sound and image, the complete misapprehension of what was actually going to happen.)

[Quotations in this section have been taken from David Caute's *The Year of the Barricades, Perennial Press, 1988.*]

> *"Have you heard about the riots at Columbia? Everyone says the police were right in beating the shit out of the students (over 100 treated at hospitals) because the students are 1.-Nihilists and 2.-Disgusting."*
> My letter to the Kuklicks at Oxford, April 1968

I had wanted to believe in the Manhattan liberal culture, the classy networks like CBS and NBC. Could it be that their newscasters were merely the highest paid tedders in history? I had wanted the *New York Times* to stand tall like a lighthouse emitting a beacon that was above the clawing and gouging of our lives in The Bronx, a clear light that carried information that was true and not warped by desire or personal motive or cultural blindness. The *Times* had tried to be objective about the protests, and sometimes they were, but I came to see that ultimately they stood for the status quo. You could tell the *Times* reporters on the street. They were the earnest young men who came to the riots in jackets and ties. If there were 100,000 people at a demonstration and 100 counter protestors, the *Times* would print two photos on the front page, one of ten protestors and one of ten counter-protestors. They saw this as presenting a balanced view.

When Columbia exploded, the editors at the *New York Times* foamed at the mouth and joined the Yahoos. It's one thing to favor free expression, it's another when your daughter comes home with a black guy dressed like an American Indian. This wasn't some hick college in the sticks. This was Columbia University! *Our* university! There were too many Columbia alumni on the staff of the *Times*, too much interconnection between the *Times'* corporate board and the Columbia trustees, the School of Journalism, the Pulitzer Prize, too many friendships, too many ties of mutual interest and egos. The two great institutions were like Chang and Eng, the original Siamese twins. They shared too many blood vessels for them ever to be separated.

The liberals were not going to threaten the structure on which they had climbed to the top. I had an insight about this months later when I had become friendly with James Purdy, the subject of my dissertation. He sent me out to Queens to see Bettina Schwarzchild, a Jewish woman who had written the sole book about his work. James was unusually complimentary to Bettina. He usually was coruscatingly funny on the subject of critics and scholars. But he respected Bettina, they were friends now; he seemed to love her in a brotherly way.

Charlotte and I visited Bettina in her high-rise apartment. She had two teenage kids in school, husband at work. Your typical Jewish Queens housewife. Except, as a child, she had been one of the last Jews to escape from Germany before the Holocaust. And she had written a scholarly book, on her own, about one of the most feared and controversial novelists of our time. A good book. With accuracy and depth and heart.

There was something warm and round about Bettina. She sat us down and served us chicken soup, often opening into her big round smile. James kidded her all the time as he kidded anyone he liked, always probing, always testing, always putting his worst foot forward to see whether you were going to reject him as had so many others.

To me, he had referred to Bettina jokingly as "The whore of Woodhaven." I'm sure he had said this to her as well and they had shared a laugh since she was as far from a whore as one could imagine. She told us, smiling warmly as at a favored but disobedient nephew, that James told her she was never going to be a real writer unless she stepped out into the world and lived. "James tells me I should go to Harlem and have an affair with a black man," she said, laughing. "But I think he's just projecting. That's what he'd really like to do. Anyone want any more chicken soup?"

I asked her about her memories of Germany. She was quite open about it. "It wasn't so bad for me. I was just a girl. I remember in school, when I was the only Jew left, that it felt bad when they gave out the milk and cookies and I couldn't have any."

We talked some more about Germany and about James' work. As we were leaving, we both thanked Bettina for a lovely afternoon, and I couldn't help myself, I had to know, so I said, "You must really hate the Germans, don't you?"

"No," she said, with a sad smile, "they're just people." She thought for a second and then she added, "The Germans were tested and they failed. The Americans have yet to be tested."

We moved toward the elevator in the hall and she said goodbye, once again sending us her big round smile. I knew then why Bettina was one of the few people James really trusted and opened up to.

What I think the Manhattan liberals, the upper-West-side intellectuals, missed was the very American quality of the protesters. The intellectuals had had their experience either in Europe itself, or dealing with the issues and theories of Communism in Europe in the Thirties and Forties. This was their frame of reference which they couldn't shake. They literally saw Tom Hayden as a future Lenin and Mark Rudd as a coming Stalin. But when my angle of vision pointed toward Europe, it focused on Nazi Germany. I believe that many of the protestors thought similarly. We didn't want to be "good Germans."

Phil Ochs caught our basic viewpoint of the straight culture perfectly when he sang of people not wanting to interrupt their Monopoly game to offer help or call the police while a woman outside the window is being stabbed and raped. I felt, every day, we were witnessing mass murders, done without feeling, from 50,000 feet, for a reason no one could even articulate. I felt we protestors were fighting for the soul of America. I remember talking to one old man who said we should bomb the dikes in North Vietnam. "That will kill millions of innocent people," I said. "You call them people," was his reply.

This was the mentality that seemed to be taking over my beloved country. My dream of the "world's last best hope." I felt we protestors were risking our bodies for the honor of our country in its role as a representative of the hopes of mankind. We had sworn to ourselves on a million soft American porches and hard Bronx streets that we would never let that German experience happen here. At least that was the way I saw it.

It still surprises me that so many of the great intellectuals of America, the men and women I had worshipped and hoped to emulate, many of them driven here by Europe's insanity and strife, could not see that Tom Hayden would go to Hollywood and marry a millionaire, that Jane Fonda would become an exercise guru and move to Georgia to marry a southern billionaire, that Mark Rudd would become a junior college teacher in Delaware and Jerry Rubin would wind up on Wall Street, a small-time entrepreneur of the most American kind. How could they have missed those Abby Hoffman interviews in which he bragged that he wanted to eat in all the great and most expensive restaurants in the world, and that he gave interviews to magazines that would fly him to Paris and put him up in four star hotels and wine and dine him? Was it such a shock that he wound up with the "masters of the universe" in the world of cocaine and then killed himself? What could be more American than Rennie Davis becoming the follower of an eleven year old guru from India, or that Huey Newton should become a drug dealer, or Bobby Seale put out a book on barbecue cooking? Or that Timothy Leary should wind up in Beverly Hills, friends with the son of Elizabeth Taylor?

As the bombing and slaughter continued, a friend pointed out to me, somewhat shocked, that I had begun to refer to the Americans as "they." He said that I would declare, "Did you hear, they bombed Hue today?" or, "They killed 2,000 Vietnamese this week." I answered quickly in my New York wise-guy mode, "*I* didn't bomb anyone!" I was trying to conceal the fact that what he had said had shaken me.

BREAKING UP IS HARD TO DO

It had to be admitted that as the year went on the people on the left became increasingly fragmented and rancorous toward each other, more rigid and ideological at the extreme edge.

The blacks split off from the whites and then began to splinter and fight amongst themselves. The black community was far from monolithic. Who could claim to speak for it? The white movement shattered and splintered as well. Hippies and Yippies and SDS and moderates, socialists, and anarchists, and Leninists, and Maoists, and Trotskyites, and Lovestonites, and all the other "ites" and "ists" and the various Labor Parties with all the initials that no one besides themselves could distinguish from one another.

In the spring of 1968, Eugene McCarthy shocked LBJ by running against him and gaining increasing support. College students across the land organized to go door to door for him. They cut their hair and wore nice clothes. Their motto was "clean for Gene." I supported this and voted for Gene in the New York Primary, but it was too late for me to be "clean." I'd been the good boy long enough. I didn't believe there was any way we were going to convince the American people to leave Vietnam. But it was worthwhile to try. I think that beneath almost every kid who saw himself as a revolutionary, there was a young American who still hoped the U.S. would come to its senses.

Then, a couple months after "they" shot Dr. King, Bobby Kennedy entered the race, too late for my taste, and "they" killed him too. There was much reason for despair, yet around the world an entire generation of young people was in revolt. In Franco Spain, England, Germany, Italy, Japan, Poland, universities were shut down, thousands arrested, governments tottering, turmoil. In France, where the workers still had a revolutionary tradition, thousands of them joined the students and they shut the entire country down. No one knew what was going to happen next. In Czechoslovakia, the nation moved toward an idea of "socialism with a human face," and in "Prague Spring," they elected Allen Ginsberg, "Queen of the May."

But here in America it seemed to me the fix was on. I couldn't see any real hope in the elections. The whole process was designed to keep outsiders out, even in the Democratic Party. There were too many southern white delegations, too many politicos who were appointed without contested elections. After Eugene McCarthy had incredibly driven Lyndon Johnson to drop out and not seek another term, and after Robert Kennedy entered the race, Hubert Humphrey threw his hat in the ring, a so-called liberal who had been LBJ's vice-president and had supported the war for years. As we turned to the electoral system one more time, Humphrey avoided the primaries. He turned to the hacks and bosses who controlled the delegates of many states that were not bound by primaries, an inside job. This was the last straw. They were no longer even pretending to be democratic. It was sheer power and force now. The iron fist in the iron glove.

The Republicans had dug up old Tricky Dick, Richard Nixon, the King of the Red Baiters. He had been deemed dead after he lost to Kennedy in 1960 and had been beaten for governor of California in 1962, but somehow they disinterred him and there he was, straight from Transylvania, apparently alive once again.

What could we do? Vietnam was an American war. The whole world's youth was watching us. We had to do something to participate in the revolutionary festival that was sweeping everyone along. The blacks kept pushing us not to be privileged white kids. We knew they were right. They were actually getting shot and killed by the government that had so far limited itself to cracking our heads and gassing and jailing us. The blacks were getting guns and beginning to fight back. They kept harking back to the racism that underpins imperialism. They pointed out that Asians were actually fighting against the machine and dying. We knew the Vietnam War was largely being fought by young men of color. We had to do something, make some sacrifice, to disassociate ourselves from the war and the violent, narcissistic American culture. We had to do this to assuage our own guilt and to set an example to the people of the world, to show them that America was not totally corrupt and morally bankrupt.

But it became rapidly clear that there was nothing we could do except offer our heads to be broken in a useless manner. As I had seen at the Pentagon, the radicals were underestimating the firepower and the ruthlessness of the government and the unswerving loyalty of the American people.

In despair at getting a deep analysis or fair deal from the establishment media we created our own newspapers. In New York, the *Village Voice* had been founded in 1955 as a more liberal and personal alternative to the

Times. Now the *East Village Other* rose up as a farther-out alternative to the *Voice*. Then the *Rat* was born in a poorer neighborhood on the Lower East Side as a more radical alternative to the *Other*. Scores of underground papers sprouted up around the country, printing radical news stories, sexy underground comics, rock reviews, drug reviews, anything to disturb the authorities and bourgeoisie, while chipping away at the boundaries of the old culture and giving us a chance to see the world from outside of the establishment view of what was pertinent and permissible. My pal Ray Mungo and his friend Marshall Bloom even began an underground Liberation News Service.

The government attacked the underground press. They infiltrated it with spies who created division among the staffs. They submitted forged news stories that sowed discord among the various left groups. The FBI and CIA tapped the phones, threatened landlords until they evicted the newspapers, threatened printers until they refused to print the papers. They enlisted the local police in the crusade, encouraging them to beat up editors and reporters, to bust them for weed and put them away.

As our condition grew more hopeless, the theories came forth, the ideology, the wild leaders. It was perfectly easy to see that your opponents on the left were wrong because in actual fact, *every* optimistic theory and plan of action was wrong. There was no way to proceed. The American people were not behind us.

America had turned out to be crazier than we thought. Our plans grew more diverse and extravagant in proportion to our inability to achieve them.

And who were our leaders? Who voted for them? Virtually all the histories of the period have been written by or about the people at the top of SDS or the Yippies. The members of SDS were among the bravest, always ready to confront the police and take a beating. They saw the connections between our American lifestyle and the poverty of the third world and the declining environment. But as they moved toward violence, toward confronting the cops and the Army while wearing football helmets and hockey pads, they seemed in their earned despair to be entering a dream-like romantic space. Though one could understand their frustration as every channel of peaceful change silted up while the murder continued, I was reminded of Einstein's advice that you couldn't solve a problem by approaching it on the same level that had caused it.

How many protestors actually belonged to SDS? Not me. Just a small minority. It was actually the media who selected our leaders to a large degree. Of course they looked for the hungriest, the most violent, the most colorful and self-destructive who would make a good story.

To my mind there was something hungry and unseemly about always moving toward the spotlight, even on the left. Yet there was no denying the courage of those who stepped forward. It took someone with dreams and perhaps foolhardy bravery or out-of-control rage to work day and night to set up these big rallies and actions and to accept the FBI tail, the phone tap, the beatings, the potential long term in prison or worse.

They asked Fidel Castro for help and he told them America wasn't in a revolutionary situation. Of course he was right.

I persisted in non-violence. That was a line I wouldn't cross. But I appreciated that violence attracted the media. We needed the crazier souls on our side to act out and get us into the media. That was the paradox. I couldn't resist a feeling of enormous glee when they did it cleverly and made fools of the adults. Like when Abbie Hoffman threw dollar bills onto the floor of the New York Stock Exchange from the balcony, or when Jerry Rubin appeared before an august congressional committee dressed like a Revolutionary War soldier with a bandolier. When Jerry and Abbie formed a Yippie Party, I was glad. When the Yippies rallied at Grand Central Station and climbed up on the big clock and pulled the hands off, I was delighted, even though the cops beat the shit out of them. The cops couldn't handle a world without time.

When the Yippies ran an actual pig for president that summer, and brought him around to rallies and parades, I was with them. Though not in calling the police "pigs." I didn't like the dehumanizing over-simplicity. I wanted to keep this a tragedy, not a melodrama. But when I realized that the pig actually looked like Hubert Humphrey, I was elated.

The Democratic Convention in Chicago in August of 1968 was the final turning point. There was something fascinating and terrible about it. A once great nation cracking into pieces on TV. Here all dreams and hope for quick peaceful change died. We feared that Huxley and Orwell had been right, that we were heading toward a steady-state, self-replicating dystopia. Chicago was not New York which pointed toward Europe. New York saw itself with its sophisticated liberal mayor as an outpost of western civilization on the edge of a rude land; Chicago was a real American city, hog butcher to a nation, Al Capone and sons, and Mayor Daly a tough guy who ruled like Mussolini.

As the convention unwound into chaos on the street and the Chicago police with official support ran amok, beating up the press, delegates, protestors, and bystanders, on the sidewalks and in the classy hotels, attacking the McCarthy headquarters and beating the crap out of his campaign workers, gassing and clubbing down the outnumbered young people who chanted "The Whole World is Watching" on TV, as the police stomped the living shit out of them, mercilessly, with clubs and boots, Mayor Daly inside the convention hall shouted down Senator Abraham Ribicoff who was chastising the police violence (you didn't have to be a lip reader to understand it): "Fuck you, you Jew son of a bitch, you lousy motherfucker go home."

But as I feared, it didn't matter. My family wasn't going to watch this on TV and those who did weren't going to see what was happening right in front of their eyes. "Don't ask, don't tell." Even though the Walker Commission later would investigate and call this a "police riot," the nation was with the police and Mayor Daly by huge numbers. Mayor Daly made vague references to assassination threats without providing any evidence but, as Abbie Hoffman's biographer Jonah Raskin points out, although Hoffman was crazed, on a manic run all week, making all kind of weird and hilarious statements, the only actual threat he made was that he planned to go into the convention and pull down Hubert Humphrey's pants.

In a survey by the University of Michigan two months later, only 19 percent of the American people thought the police had used too much force. Even among the Robert Kennedy supporters only 29 percent agreed the force was excessive, and only 36 percent of the McCarthy backers. [See Caute, p322-323.]

All this occurred a couple weeks after the Russian tanks moved into Czechoslovakia and crushed the Prague Spring, the hope for a free and democratic socialism. The Czechs didn't stand a chance, surrounded by Warsaw pact nations who moved in on all sides. Only the hippies put up resistance, climbing on the Russian tanks and pleading with the bewildered young Russian soldiers to "join us." The images from Chicago were too similar to Prague. The armored vehicles, the cops and soldiers, the hippies trying to resist and being crushed.

This was not the USSR versus America. This was bureaucratic power and technocrats and violence on both sides of the iron curtain crushing human hopes and ideals. The American straight people screamed at us to move to Russia, but to us Russia was more of the same.

The debates on the left between drop-out hippies and committed street fighters intensified. It was now obvious to all that peaceful protests were not going to shortly end the war, that in fact Chicago had made us *less* popular in the nation, but what should we do? Since reality was impervious to realistic action, the old pleasure principle dreams resurfaced: Going back to the land; joining up with the American Indians and retaking the country; retreating to the ancient Hindu and Buddhist paths; joining in self-supporting communes; forming communities based on acid visions; promoting colonies of freaks in space. While on the political side, the old words reappeared with equal reification: A workers' state; proletarian revolution; helter-skelter race wars of liberation; anarchy and chaos.

It was difficult to reign in the centrifugal factions because everyone could plainly and correctly see that the other guy's plans wouldn't work. Yet something had to be done. Both major parties were running candidates who supported the war.

My sympathies at this time were closer to the hippies than the Weather Underground. I felt we had to keep protesting. I knew that we couldn't directly defeat the American military and we could no longer appeal to the conscience of the American people. That had been destroyed along with any self-discipline or ability to defer gratification by a half-century of electronic corporate advertising. This began at the start of the twentieth century when America found itself able to produce more than it needed to consume. Then, after World War I, America was suddenly the greatest industrial power in history. But how to move all those goods and keep the factories running? The answer was to turn the workers into hedonists, to destroy their work ethic, their impulse to save. To turn the entire nation into addicts. To destroy all vestiges of American's self-discipline by brainwashing them through advertising. The best Ivy League psychologists were now turning their talents over to Mad Ave for big bucks. Sigmund

Freud's nephew Edward Bernays showed up and created the field of corporate public relations, the early spin-doctors. A new level of slippage was appearing between language and reality.

Fortunately for the corporations, the Twenties saw the opening of electronic communications, radio, national networks, phonographs, movies, fan magazines, installment buying, the age of celebrity, to be followed soon by credit cards and TV. Bankruptcy became acceptable. Debt was made fashionable. Bank architecture registered this change, from stone classical fortresses that said no money will ever be taken from these vaults, to open glass structures with drive in windows that said come in, we're giving money out, just sign on the dotted line.

They built a culture based on prescription drugs and then complained that the young people were forming a drug culture. They advertised on children's TV programs and in the schools and broke down the kids' self-restraint and then complained that the kids were turning into ids.

They built a culture of mirrors. An other-directed culture based on appearance, on the fear of being out of fashion, the dread of being an outsider, a culture that kept people in the throes of desire, that de-emphasized guilt and shame. On TV, as opposed to radio, it's how you look that counts. Americans spent more time watching TV than going to school. That was where their real education took place.

Narcissists are people who are not in touch with their Jungian shadow, the unacknowledged part of their personality. They are obsessed with being young and beautiful and think they are good and only good. Any disparate information is censored out and repressed. They are self-centered and don't think other people are real, except in so far as the others are extras in their movie, instruments of their plans. Narcissists are famous in their own minds. They believe the world loves them and are shocked and angered when it doesn't. Corporate America had created a nation of narcissists; shopping was their religion and mirrors were their altars. And their defense system was the TV news that filtered out any shadow events for them. American foreign policy was narcissism run wild.

My parents' generation, the kids who grew up in the Twenties, were guinea pigs in the greatest experiment in history. They didn't know Thorstein Veblen but he knew them. They were carpet bombed with electronic advertising. They could not imagine its power and its aims.

They projected their narcissism on to us, their children. We, the Sixties rebels, protesting against consumerism, we were the narcissists, not them. But that's what narcissists do: deny their dark side and project it onto others.

Ronnie and Nancy Reagan were in this generation. Ronnie, whose legacy to American children was the lesson that image was more important than substance, that good looks and charm were superior to hard work and education and careful preparation. And Nancy, who thought that the *nouveau* in *nouveau riche* was a compliment.

And the capitalists thought they were conservatives. That was the funny part. They bemoaned the dislocation and chaos in the world, the decline of the old stable values, the selfishness of America's youth, the laziness of the young workers, the low national savings rate, the rock and roll records their corporations were selling by the billions. They refused to see that capitalism was the greatest destabilizing force ever invented by man, that it was destroying value structures built up over thousands of years, infantilizing the populace, despoiling entire third world cultures, and that it was unsustainable and had a horrendous impact on the environment in the long term. They didn't live in the long term. They acted as if they lived in a godless world and that, as Keynes said, in the long run we are all dead.

Yet Communism was also lousy.

> *"We Americans have used more of the world's resources in the past forty years than all the people of the world had used in the 4,000 years of recorded history up to 1914."*
> Fielding Osborn (1953)

I thought that since we couldn't appeal to their conscience, we had to appeal to their selfishness. We had to bother them and inconvenience them into finally leaving Vietnam. For surely they cared about their own comfort more than they cared about Vietnam. We had to block bridges and tie up traffic and keep disrupting every facet of their spoiled lives. That was the only way to reach them.

In the argument between retreating to the country or fighting it out on the streets, I took the reasonable middle way, just as I had in the debate of pot versus booze, when I had suggested a glass of wine with one's joint.

I could see no way to build a new society without working on one's self, yet we could still resist non-violently in the meantime. But I wondered if this was cowardice on my part. Meanwhile the movement was being torn apart. Even the Liberation News Service split into two factions, one stealing the office and moving it to the country, the other invading the new office from the city. It was like having another Pope at Avignon.

I recall being at a large demonstration in Washington with Ritchie Havens singing to thousands of us sitting on the grass. Ritchie was one of my favorites, a gentle man so far as I could see, a spiritual man with a deep compassion and soul. But right then a group of know-it-all Maoist young people ran across in front of us, disrupting the interlude of beautiful music before the dangerous rioting was to begin, blocking Ritchie from our view by holding up large banners and chanting an insipid "Power to the people!" "What do you think *we* are?" I shouted at them in frustration. As arguments broke out, I looked at the stately government buildings around us and I wondered to myself, "How is it possible to ever get people to agree long enough to form a stable government? How could it be that our country had been relatively stable for 100 years?" At that moment, it seemed a kind of miracle, I admit it, to have had peaceful transitions of power over a century. But this just made me angrier at what harm our national leaders were doing to this venerable structure.

I saw that we were not going to be able to change anything until we changed ourselves. I saw ego on all sides of me, "I'm right, you're wrong," old habits and imprints being played out, my own ego included. As I look at my journals from this period, I am astonished to see how little I was writing about these public events. Virtually all my writing was about my own life, my past and my psychology, the intersection of culture and economics and my personality, my thoughts about art and dope as vehicles of personal change, my anger at Penn and the liberals, my guilt at not being able to let go of my doctorate.

We had to change ourselves. To examine the *subject*. To ask questions of all sides. Why did Karl Marx raise his three daughters like proper bourgeois young ladies? Why did two of them commit suicide? Why did John Steinbeck support the war in Vietnam? (Later, I discovered that J.D. Salinger had also supported it.) Why did everything smell of death in the way that a small town smells of wood smoke on the first cold day of fall?

It seemed like death met you in every direction you turned. How could you ever be free if everyone alive was always in the power of a universal death sentence? If, as most advanced people thought, there was no God, and people were merely chemicals, and consciousness was merely an epiphenomenon, why was it wrong to kill another person? What was so bad about destroying a deluded machine?

Even the best times (and they were the best, among the best of my life) were like a party on a South Seas beach with the Rolling Stones, and sunset, and all your closest friends, and great dope, and you're all high together, and then you discover a dying whale on the next beach, and you realize that he's just about gone, and he dies, and you go back to the party, and it's incredibly wonderful, but still there's that big dead whale, beginning to smell, nearby.

How could I stop thinking about my brother-in-law, Rod? There had to be a way out. A better way to organize life. After all, our culture was pretty much the only one in the history of the world to ignore preparations for an after-life, to not provide means of contacting other spheres of being and deeper meanings. We took pride in our difference from the "primitive" past. But what had we lost?

I smoked dope each night to give me distance on these questions. A different point of view. I pondered the ancient koans. Why did the Zen masters say, "We can get you to the top of a fifty-foot pole, but we can't make you jump"? What did they mean when they advised you to cut through the illusions of the world with the sword of your intellect? How could you tell the illusions from what was actually real? Why did the Zen masters advise, "If you meet a Buddha, kill him. If you meet a Zen master, kill him"? Why should you want to kill a Buddha? And when the Buddha said, "Life is suffering," did he really mean that? Was life really suffering until you began a path? Was Buddhism like a movie theater with the marquee reading: "Life is Suffering"? No wonder few people paid their admission to that particular show. And when the Buddha said there was an answer to suffering, the noble eight-fold path, basically giving up desire, coming to an acceptance, living a sane, simple life, did it really work? Why were so many of the gurus and masters power hungry and womanizers?

I knew one thing: if our protests and attempts to build a new way of living on earth were to be effective, we would have to be honest. We would have to speak with authenticity by living our values. One way to begin was to withdraw from the American corporate economy as far as possible. We would have to live simply so we would not be taking the fruits of imperialism that our armies were stealing. We would have to live with a holistic vision of the results of the actions of each of us on the world as a whole and on future generations. We would have to drop the culture's hunger for oil, for fame, for the "freedom" a million dollars could provide. We would have to re-find a path that led to real freedom, the freedom from death. To me, this added up to some kind of spiritual trip but I wasn't sure which one or whether we might have to invent a new one.

I knew I was desperately confused, not secular and yet not Christian or Jewish. By choosing a scientific world, had we banished the awe and beauty of magic and the healing possibilities of vast openness and infinite possibility? Was I just beginning to ask the real questions and to find my real path? I did know that since my religious experience in Massachusetts, I had not accepted the common sense world of conventional wisdom. But what did it mean on a day to day basis in this violent world?

I knew that the Movement was enabling me to become more deeply in touch with other people than I had ever been before. Now I could come out of my own closet, (We each had a closet, didn't we?) and I could talk about my true ideas without holding back for fear of scaring friends or isolating myself. Now the intelligent, the scorned, and the mutilated had begun to call ourselves "freaks" proudly, to wear our alienation as a badge of distinction in the straight world; I loved to consider the effect this honesty and informality might have on life in the future (though I felt sorry for barbers, since I knew they would soon no longer be needed.) I loved discussing the books we were reading, the books that brought a puzzled smile to the straight professors and critics: Carl Jung, Herman Hesse, Doris Lessing, Paul Goodman, C. Wright Mills, Timothy Leary, Ram Dass, Allen Ginsberg, Jack Kerouac, Jane Jacobs, Antonin Artaud, Eldridge Cleaver, Kurt Vonnegut, Gary Snyder, Kate Millet, Joseph Heller, Aldous Huxley, Jean Genet, Anais Nin, Richard Brautigan and Christopher Isherwood, all the mad ones, the gay, the jailed, the ostracized.

I possessed two major personalities at that time. Number one revolved around the aim to be a saint, to follow the path of Jesus, turn the other cheek, work against the ego by working against one's selfishness, Love is the answer. But alongside it I had another, earlier personality, the Bronx street one, the one that lined up with Henry Miller and Ferdinand Celine, the one that was based on the simple motto: Fuck You, Jack.

I had a lot of work to do. That's why I needed to be a professor. I would serve the world by teaching for decades and asking the real questions. Already I felt good about having given up a multi-million dollar career. I never doubted that. I felt good about living in such a way that I was not taking more than my share of the earth's resources. I wanted to leave the earth no worse than I had found it. I thought differently now about my father, following us around the dark apartment, imploring us to turn off the lights. We had thought my father was cheap, but it turned out he was merely "pre-maturely ecological."

But mostly I felt hurt and betrayed. By my parents, my teachers, my country. Why had they not warned me? Why hadn't they taught me what to expect? Cars making nine miles to the gallon, wars over oil, sweatshops in Indonesia, democratic governments we had overthrown in Guatemala and Iran and so on? Why hadn't they told me about corporations dumping poisonous waste in Lake Erie which was now pretty much dead? Why hadn't they told me that the U.S. was a relatively safe country to live in because we exported our violence?

I FRIGHTEN HUBERT

The Chicago convention had knocked the wind out of me. But OK, it was Hubert versus Tricky Dick. We had to move on. The American people seemed to be leaning toward Tricky. They *wanted* a guy who was bad. They had projected all their own badness onto the world. They wanted a guy who was Super-Bad! They still hadn't learned the lesson of the Italian Renaissance, that when you hired the bad guys, mercenaries, to defend your city, and let them in the gates, they tended to turn on you and take over the city themselves.

Since the convention Hubert had been in hiding. The idea was, I guess, that time would heal, forgive and forget, all that crap. OK, Hubert had stolen the nomination, OK, he had supported the war for years, but now, in the face of the unspeakable, we would all come together under the big tent.

But this wasn't to be the case. There had been too much blood spilled on the streets of Chicago for them to clean it all up in a few weeks. In truth, I thought Nixon had a better fix on who he was than Humphrey. Nixon was a tough guy. He believed we lived in a dog-eat-dog world and he was going to get the biggest dog and then it was Fuck you, Jack. You knew what to expect with Nixon. If you moved toward a rattlesnake you knew the salsa music was going to start up.

Humphrey, however, still thought of himself as a good guy, a guy with a heart. I didn't trust people like that. Those who knew they were saints and thus gave themselves permission to do anything they wanted to anybody; afterward, they would just go unconscious and forget about it, since bad behavior didn't fit into their self-image. My mother was like that at times. Already she was leading Charlie toward buying her a huge diamond ring and a red Caddy that he would be working to pay off until his death in his seventies. I called her "Mother Teresa in a Cadillac," but this didn't touch her. She kept saying that she was "innocent." Later James Purdy would point out to me that the root of the word "innocent" meant "not to harm."

I feared Hubert. I would rather deal with a cynic than an unconscious narcissist. Who knew? Maybe Tricky would see that it was in his self-interest to end the war, to blame it on the Democrats and move on. I was voting for Dr. Spock.

The Democratic candidate traditionally began his presidential campaign in New York at the Labor Day Parade. I decided to go up there so that Hubert would know we hadn't forgotten. I had visions of shouting over the crowd, of booing loudly so that perhaps he would hear.

But there was no crowd. The city had emptied for the hot weekend. I stood on Fifth Avenue just above Forty-second Street with just a few other losers, maybe a person or two every ten feet along the police barriers set to keep up on the curb. A couple brainwashed labor guys. Some idiots with flags and kids. Otherwise the sidewalks were empty.

I hadn't shaved, had fat unkempt hair, torn clothes. At the head of the parade I could see them: Hubert, in all his pink porkatude, and George Meany, the head of the AFL-CIO who had turned the labor movement in support of the war. But as they came closer, I was astonished. Hubert was not a simple, sleepy, pink guy who was unconscious. Hubert was in full street-whore regalia. He was face-painted, wearing more makeup than the prostitutes who hung out right down the block on 42nd Street. Hubert had become totally fake, completely corrupted by his drive for power. You couldn't miss the symbolism. Hubert was walking in the Times Square area, dressed like a whore, cynically selling himself.

Somehow this set me off. I moved one leg between the two wooden barriers into the gutter so I could be closer, and I screamed with hate, glaring at him, just a few feet away, my fist in the air in his direction with the thumb pointed down, "NEVER, HUBERT! NEVER!!!!" I screamed in the way I had imagined I would have to shout to be heard over the crowd. But since there was no crowd I was the only one shouting, practically in his face. Hubert jerked his head toward me and I saw he hadn't forgotten Chicago either. This was his first appearance since then, and to my astonishment we locked eyes and I saw him staring at me in terror. He thought I was going to kill him. That I was his Oswald. He thought my fist was a gun.

Immediately a cop stepped in front of me, lazily. A huge, wide, sleepy New York flatfoot. Maybe six-four with cauliflower ears. He had seen what was happening and who I was. He knew I had no violent intentions. I still had one leg behind the barrier. I snapped out of it and met his eye and raised my hands in a kind of symbolic gesture of surrender to show him I understood and that I was all right. I stepped back onto the curb. He looked into my eyes and he laughed. I had to laugh as well, embarrassed. He said to me, with a Bronx accent, still smiling in a kind of amazement, "You can't do something like that, pal. You'll get yourself shot." I nodded, still smiling awkwardly. "I know," I said.

"You know better than that," he said, shaking his head to admonish me but still smiling. I nodded.

Humphrey looked away and moved along, darting anxious looks left and right. There was no reason to stay at the stupid parade but as I turned to go I heard jazz music. Coming down the street was an ancient flatbed truck. MUSICIANS UNION—Local 802. There were a couple ribbons attached to it that said, "Let's pretend I'm a float." But there was a jazz group on the back, playing great, swinging, modern jazz. As they passed, I could see them, a quartet, a set of vibes and a rhythm section, jamming away for nobody on a hot, empty morning, and there on vibes, I was astonished to recognize Milt Jackson of the Modern Jazz Quartet, arguably the greatest vibes player of all-time. He was wailing away, smoking on top of that rhythm section. And I realized how strange it is, that just when you are ready to submit the divorce papers between you and America, just when you are ready to throw up your hands and say take the house, take the kids, take it all, I want outta here, America gives you a crazy little gift to complicate matters. Milt Jackson up there on an truck in the morning on a fetid street, playing for maybe twenty bucks, playing for no one but me. And he seemed to be having a wonderful time.

THE THOMAS JEFFERSON AIRPLANE

With the new band in the White House, "Tricky and the Clones," and the American people supporting them, the Movement began to fall apart. There had always been some cracks in the fuselage of the Movement, the radicals versus the hippies, the violent versus the pacifists, the Old Left versus the New Left, but now the fissures began to propagate and spread to the wings. Once people realized this contraption wasn't going to fly, there was no reason to be rational and compromise.

Timothy Leary and Gerard O'Neill, a Princeton astronomy professor, talked about sending up a space station large enough to support and sustain an entire functioning alternative culture which would live in peace, floating lazily through the sun-filled sky. I didn't believe this was a feasible idea. In fact, it had already been tried. They had called it America.

There were feminists who wanted to break the glass ceiling at IBM; there were feminists who wanted to bomb IBM. There were women who wanted a fair chance to make decisions along with the young men in the Movement institutions; there were women who wouldn't work with men in these institutions and in some cases (the *Rat*) took them over from the men. There were men on the left who recognized the justice of the demands of the women and wanted to work with the feminists, there were other young men who made fun of them. There were women and men who saw pornography and sex as liberating and others who saw them as continuing the patriarchy. There were women who wanted to uphold the reputation of Virginia Woolf and women who wanted to hold up Brinks' trucks. There were women who followed Betty Friedan and women who said that the only true feminists should turn lesbian.

There were Puerto Rican nationalists and Puerto Rican Communists. There were those who supported Cesar Chavez's non-violent organizing of the farm workers and those who supported Mexican prison gangs. There were supporters of Native American spirituality and others who supported them in shootouts with the FBI. There were those who thought the country should be returned to the Indians. There were artists like Ed Sanders and Frank Conroy who suggested that Charles Manson was more a product of the prison system than the counterculture; there were others like Weather-person Bernadine Dohrn and Jerry Rubin who supported him as a revolutionary.

There were Jewish leftists who supported an Israel based on the kibbutz and Jewish leftists who supported the Palestinians. There were gays who put the left first and gays who complained about homophobia in Castro's Cuba. There were street-fighting macho-gays and pacifist internationalist gays. In Northern California there were gay dairy farmers who dressed like milkmaids.

Why not? The plane wasn't going to fly. It was like an inverse Pandora's box. Once you opened it, all the good causes poured out at once, swamping any unity of command and control.

The war was destroying an entire country. Ours. I wondered whether, in some warped unconscious manner, our leaders *wanted* to destroy our country.

As for the cracked airplane, some thought we should preserve it as a kind of museum for future generations, a kind of seed farm in Northern California. Others thought we should take it up one final time and crash it into a building.

My own particular solution began with a kind of yoga of psychedelic drugs.

Eve Berger (Rosen) c 1924.

Uncle "Hollywood" Mac Berger and Jerry's grandparents,
Minnie and Sam Berger.

Mother Eve Berger
in her heyday.

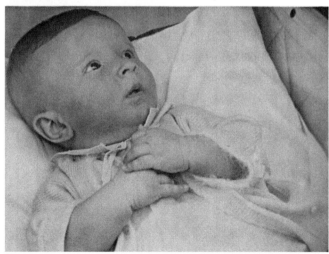

Jerry

Uncle Lenny,
the armed robber.

Jerry and Princess Ali Bey,
The Bronx.

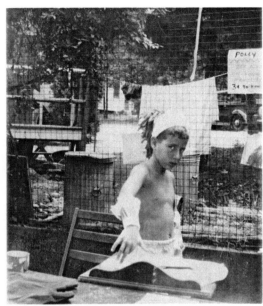

Marty Licker
at Ha-Ya Bungalows.

Jerry's Bar Mitzvah.

Jerry as batboy - The Polo Grounds, NYC.

Eve and Sol in their Bronx apartment.

Innocent days at the falls, Troy, N.Y., Harv and Sue Braun, foreground, Lori Blank, Dave and Davi Friedman.

Lori Blank

Lori Blank,
Tom Baruch

Davi and Dave Friedman, RPI.

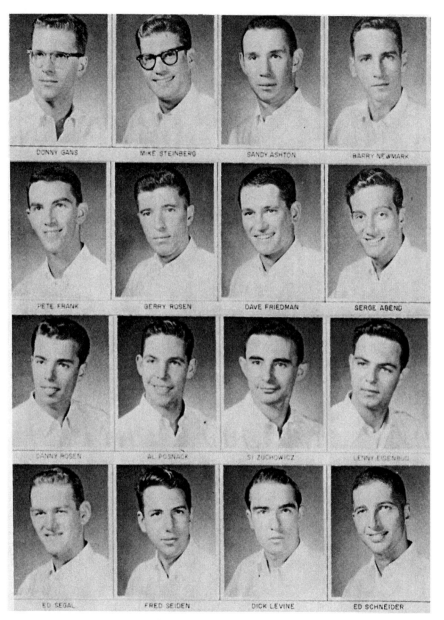

Phi Sigma Delta, RPI, 1960.

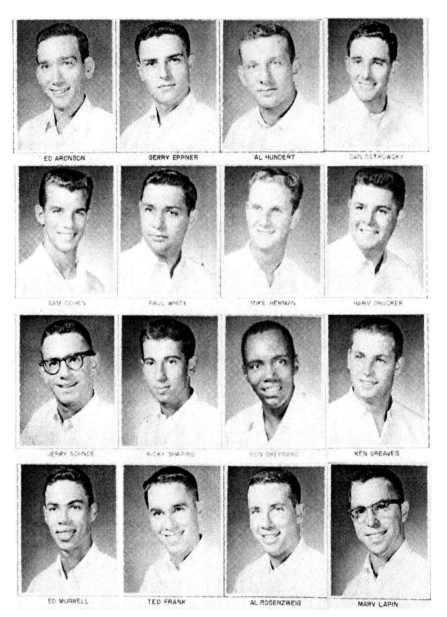

Phi Sigma Delta, RPI, 1960.

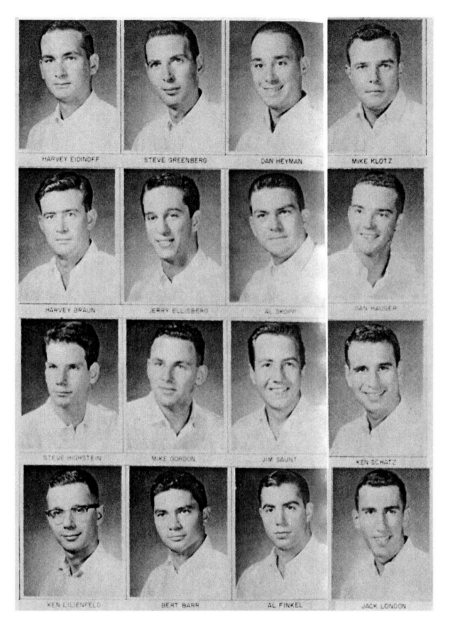

Phi Sigma Delta, RPI, 1960.

Phi Sigma Delta, RPI, 1960.

Roommates Jerry Rosen and Harvey Braun.

RPI Sports Trophy, 1960. Jerry second from right, front row.

Celebrating the trophy, RPI, 1960.

Jerry and Shep, Grad School, Penn, 1965.

Jerry as suicidal lieutenant, 1964.

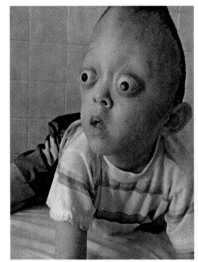

Agent Orange child, Vietnam. 2004.
(Photo by Dan Shea, Portland OR.)

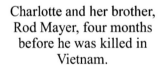

Charlotte and her brother,
Rod Mayer, four months
before he was killed in
Vietnam.

Bruce and Riki Kuklick (they divorced in 1976).

Charlotte, Jerry, Paulette, Amsterdam, 1966.

Mara Posner, Jerry, Greenwich Village, 1968.

Charlotte, Rochelle Gatlin, Ward Hoalton, Grove St., 1968.

Michael Kranish, Grove Street.

Gil Eisner, Bob Eisner of *The Rat*, a friend, Liz Long of Knopf.

Terry Kelsey

Mark Rosen, Duane Dobbs, Rozi Dobbs (Charlie's daughter), Eve, Charlie Rosenberg, Charlotte, Lucy Rosen (Mark's wife), Jerry.

Eve's Wedding, 1969.

Richard and Margie De Lisle.

Jerry in Fairfax, California, 1971.

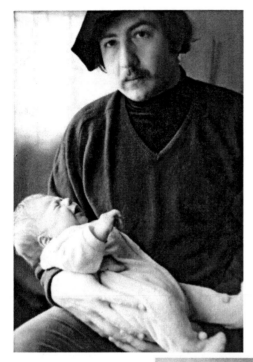

Jim Saunt and Claudio.

Bela Bartok, Paulette,
Jim Saunt, Claudio, 1971.

Jerry, Charlotte, Paulette's brother Perry, Paulette, Jim Saunt, Paulette's brother Rocco, Marin County, CA, 1971.

Rochelle Gatlin, Charlotte, Ward Hoalton, Marin, CA, 1971.

Rochelle Gatlin,
San Francsico.

Charlotte and Jerry behind their shack in Sonoma Couny, CA, 1972.

Jerry, Jesse, Rusty the Wunderkar, Sebastopol, CA, 1972.

Charlotte,
Sebastopol, CA, 1973

David Bromige

Andrei Codrescu
(photo by Roxane Lambie)

Sherril Jaffe in Jerry's office at Sonoma State University.

Ray Mungo

Judy Levy-Sender
and
Ramón Sender
Barayón

Ntozake Shange

Jerry, novelist Barry Gifford, Faulkner scholar Jim Carothers at the Chicago Art Institute on the way to Wrigley Field, 1990.

Jerry and son Jesse, Delft, The Netherlands, 1989.

Marijke and her sister Liz at the family home, Schiedam, The Netherlands, 1989.

Gerald Rosen

Retired English Professors, Sonoma State University.

A friend, Jonah Raskin, J.J. Wilson, Gerry Haslam, Cecelia Belle Bromige, David Bromige, Jerry, Helen Dunn.

"Life, like a dome of many-colored glass, stains the white radiance of eternity . . ."

Percy Bysshe Shelley

CHARLOTTE IN THE SKY WITH DIAMONDS

It is customary when writing about LSD to begin with a formulaic disclaimer that the author does not advocate that anyone use LSD. This statement is probably for legal purposes, but I really mean it. I don't want to advise anyone to drop acid. On the other hand, I don't want to advise people not to drop acid. I don't want to be responsible for people's lives in this way. Or to appear to be responsible.

Just as I don't advocate that anyone drop acid, I don't advocate that anyone become an astronaut. Being an astronaut brings value and vision to humanity and I am glad that people are permitted to do it, although it is certainly more dangerous than taking acid which also brings value and vision to humanity.

Acid is definitely risky. Everyone must be his or her own judge about whether the journey is worth the risk. However your trip goes, there is a good chance you won't come back the same person who left. In my own case, LSD has been an expensive university but I have never regretted the tuition. I learned more from acid than from any book. Acid has made me much smarter and lonelier. I don't do acid anymore, but I guess you could say I loved acid in the way you can love something that is beautiful, and wild, and dangerous, something that had you in its power, and taught you, and decided to let you live.

I do think it is important to underline that an LSD trip is not what it is portrayed to be in the media, a kind of light show that leads to crying for one's mother when hellish hallucinations of cemeteries and skulls and ghosts inevitably appear and drive one close to madness. This picture of an LSD trip can easily be disproved. If this were the usual case, why would anyone ever take acid twice? Yet many did. Including myself. A lot more than twice. And lived to not regret it.

'Tell it slant"

Emily Dickinson

295

I have avoided writing about acid directly for thirty-five years. I am actually a conservative person in many ways. Acid frightens me and writing about it also frightens me. Straight people also frighten me. The greatest danger of taking LSD comes from straight people who want to "help" you by putting you in a cage or a mental hospital.

I kept thinking about Charles Darwin. Darwin was also conservative and shy in his way, so far as I can tell. He knew what the results of his theory would be in the world, what damage it would do to a way of life and to its God. Publishing his book was like releasing Einstein's formula equating mass and energy. It would lead to many mental and spiritual Hiroshimas.

I didn't mean to compare myself to Darwin of course, but even the seagull knows something about what it feels like to be an eagle. He didn't publish for twenty years until forced to by Alfred Russel Wallace's notice that he was about to publish the same ideas without Darwin's years of documentation. Darwin was sick for much of that time, a hypochondriac, avoiding people, lying around the house with nagging illnesses and pains. A lot like my life. Hoping to avoid the telling of the secrets that God has given one to say.

GOD FOR A DIME

That was what the straight people called it, mockingly, "God for a dime." That was the way I thought of it as well. Because I knew I had *really* been addressed by God in that church in Massachusetts when I was suicidal, when I had let go of everything and had a religious experience. I thought to myself that there is something terrible to seeing God, along with the rapture. You don't want to go too close to the sun. I remember writing in my journal, "If you know God, you don't want to deal with him for a dime."

> " . . . in landlessness alone resides the highest truth. . . "
> Herman Melville

Charlotte took it first. We had always had a little unspoken rivalry about these matters. I was the success, the ambitious one, the one with the grades and the scholarships. She was the one with fewer accomplishments but also fewer attachments in the negative, Buddhist sense. She wasn't afraid of getting a bad mark on her record. She had no record. She had no ambitions. But as I came to think of myself as a possible writer, I felt a need to let go, to take chances for wider experience. So we pushed each other. But ultimately, there was no way I could compete. I was still writing an Ivy League dissertation. I was hoping to finish before I deranged my senses. I was so close to the end. While Charlotte was the one who had been in a kind of reformatory way back in high school. She had known that the middle class and the successful would never accept her. They had hurt her in Lewiston. She was the daughter of poor people. Hog Joe and Bessie Mayer. Joe was an old farmer who didn't even have his own farm but share-cropped on dangerous land on the Lewiston Hill and went into town with his overalls on. Bessie worked at the lumber mill that stunk up the entire valley.

Lewiston was one of the most isolated small cities in America, about 20,000 people in a valley at the foot of the Lewiston Hill which stood between you and Spokane, the nearest city, 100 miles away once you climbed the seven miles of switchbacks for a half hour to get to the road north. There were no colleges in Lewiston, no main highways passing through it. Everyone knew everyone else, knew who was acceptable and who wasn't. Joe Mayer wasn't. He had divorced his wife to marry Bessie, twenty years younger; she'd been singing in bars, coming out of poverty so dire there was doubt about whether she would have shoes to attend school. The Catholic girls knew about this and that Charlotte was the product of this union. They knew Charlotte's parents had a little band and Charlotte and Rod had grown up in dance halls, sleeping behind the instrument cases since her folks couldn't afford a baby sitter. She didn't have the money to join the in-girls and what made it worse, she was the smartest girl in the school which evoked jealousy. How could a poor, unfashionable girl be the valedictorian? It wasn't fair. And she attempted to make a virtue of her poverty. Her parents were well meaning, but ostracized by the Church; they tried to square themselves by raising the best-behaved children in town. That was easy for her brother, a year older. When Charlotte applied, the position was already filled. Rod was the nice, measured, quiet one who became the town hero by taking one of the most dangerous jobs in the world—flying a supersonic jet fighter off an aircraft carrier.

Charlotte attempted to fight back by ignoring the rules, the manners and styles the good girls enforced. She hung out with Neil Peters and his single-mother Billie Peters, who lived down by the tracks and were not even acceptable to the lower circles in which Charlotte might have stood a chance. Neil was the goofy, awkward, lonely, town beatnik, with his motorcycle and his Zen books, his flute and koto records from Japan, and his beautiful paintings of the sun. The police knew all about Neil. And Charlotte as well. In a way, Charlotte, by not dressing in fashion, by living simply and trying to make an honest life without money, was actually saying to her parents that they were all right. She liked the fact that they had a little band and that they taught her music; she saw life as being a spiritual journey that did not lead to the country club. She liked the fact that her mother had a genius for learning things like the piano, and designed houses that her father built and sold for almost no profit to their friends.

She saw early on that she couldn't trust the middle class, the successful. She would never outgrow this; it cost her potential friends and flexibility. She had dropped out early and now this history was imprinted on her like a number on her arm. Charlotte was ambivalent towards the women's movement. When a woman friend asked her whether she was for women's liberation, she said, pointedly, "Liberation from what?" We both had a lot to learn from the women's movement, more than we realized at the time, but Charlotte was becoming happy in the Village. People liked her, she was acceptable in this upside-down reality. She had dropped the horror films, and was putting on weight, going from gaunt to slender, a tall, striking woman with wild frizzy hair and a big smile who was getting really good at the flute. Charlotte would never submit to the pressure and judgment of the fussy people whom you had to please to be a first line classical musician, but she played Bach with a jazz feeling and intonation. She took some lessons from Jeremy Steig, the famous jazz and pop flutist. She had a gorgeous tone, big and deep, as good as the symphonic flutists, better than any jazz flutist I'd heard.

When Charlotte said, "Liberation from what?" I thought she was pointing out that she had already liberated herself from career, the corporate world, shopping, the suburbs, patriotism, contributing to imperialism, and despoiling the environment. We had no car, we lived in a dump, we wore torn clothes, we hardly had any property at all. We were saying by our lifestyle, "We can honestly protest the war, Mr. President, because we are not unconsciously asking you to bring back one-third of the world's resources for the use of 6 percent of the world's people." Charlotte was turning her poverty and inexperience in the worlds of fashion and chic restaurants and money into a virtue. Thus, she thought the women's movement should take its place among the rainbow of organizations and ideas that made up the larger anti-war movement. She wanted to limit the Movement to the people who actively protested the war and racism, opposed the middle class and the corporations. She wanted clear lines between us and the straight people, the normal, nice, suburban, middle-class people, who were addicted to shopping and wanted to lock up the drug users; she was afraid the gender issue would soften these boundaries and would allow in those who had hurt her.

Of course there were shortcomings to this view. She disdained but also feared the middle class, afraid that they wouldn't accept her. If my successful friends came to see us, she would often quietly slip away. She hadn't come to realize that people with a complete and rooted opposition to success and the values it required would have a hard time getting anything done successfully in the world, or perhaps in life in general. She couldn't function in the world unless she was stoned from morning to night. But she had a nice part-time job, she liked her boss, a lawyer and amateur painter, she felt accepted in the Village, loved her music, in fact she was probably the most content she had ever been.

Charlotte and I both felt that until one was free of the fear of death one would not be liberated. Charlotte knew instinctively that the problem we were all facing was larger than politics. When Gloria Steinem wrote a number-one best seller twenty years later announcing this revelation, that inner-life and psychology were also important for liberation, I thought of Charlotte. But I also knew that politics *was* important, and that because of Gloria Steinem and people like her the next generation of parents would not find it so easy to simply give the college money to the son and leave out the talented daughter, who, in Charlotte's case, had to ride a freight to Seattle and work as a secretary at Boeing to finance her own education.

To the degree that I was still in the system and successful, Charlotte put a lot of pressure on me since she was clearly the further-out one, the one less implicated in the corrupt and violent system. Even from a Buddhist framework it seemed one should let go, not be weighted down by attachments. The Buddha said that life was suffering and that suffering was caused by selfish desire. Once, when Charlotte, with her suspicion of any group activity beyond playing music or smoking dope with your close friends, was asked by a woman friend from the *Rat* on the day after a demonstration she had missed (though she did go to some), "What are you doing to end the war?" she snapped, "I'm praying, damn it. I'm praying!" This answer wasn't acceptable of course, but I understood her to be saying, "I am not affirming this culture. I am challenging its deepest assumptions. Assumptions about what is real and true and in the long run healing and leading toward the salvation we all hunger for."

Charlotte tended to speak in potent aphorisms, rather than in long-winded thought-out discourses like those I have been using to explain her. She would say, attributing it to Blaise Pascal, that, "Nine-tenths of the world's problems are caused by people who can't sit still." Or she'd say, "Render unto Caesar, that which is easier."

With so much invested in my education and career, I was cautious about acid. I would be the trustworthy guide. I would wait a few months until I finished my doctoral dissertation. Charlotte would drop the acid.

Yet a few days after she did, I also dropped acid. Like two jazz musicians we pushed each other to higher places. Neither would yield. Story of my life. Always say no, give a hundred well thought-out reasons of why I should be a good boy, and then do something wild anyway. (See my later description of smoking elephant tranquilizer etc.)

> *"Out beyond ideas of right doing and wrong doing, there is a field. I'll meet you there."*
>
> Rumi

Charlotte seemed very far away. Yet not unhappy. We were in our living room. It was as if she was on another TV channel and the signal had reflected off something and she had become a ghost on ours. A small smile of wonderment lit her face. When I asked her what she was seeing she said little. I couldn't reach her. She seemed fascinated but dumbfounded. Yet I knew she was OK.

When she began to return to our world, after perhaps six hours, I asked her again. She had a faraway look in her eyes that was appealing. She merely smiled and nodded her head, as if she were bewildered. She continued to have that far away aspect to her for a couple days; then she was fully back but still quiet. She just couldn't find the words to give form to her experience. When I would ask her if she hallucinated, she would kind of shrug and emit a befuddled light and say, "It's different. It's not what I expected. I can't say, really. You'll have to see for yourself."

Yet I wasn't concerned about her. She had not died or gone crazy. She was back at work and didn't seem disturbed by what she had seen. Slightly mystified, perhaps, but also fascinated. When I asked her if she would do it again, she said, quietly, "Yes."

LIVING LIGHT

> *"Just as there is good music and bad music, there are bad drugs and good drugs. So we can't say we are 'against' drugs any more than we can say we are 'against' music."*
>
> Michel Foucault

A few days later, early on an afternoon, I dropped the acid in our living room with Charlotte as the guide. A tiny, almost weightless, little transparent square, like gelatin, maybe a quarter of an inch on each side. I was surprised at how long it took to come on. I still held to the thread of my own earth-shaking experience in the church. I would judge the acid against that. I felt a little silly. This was ridiculous in a way. Encouraging an afternoon of hallucinations. After forty minutes, the light began to change. To strobe and flicker. The light seemed alive in a way. Filled with love. Beautiful and somehow holy. The light of living forever. I felt my body softening and relaxing. All the objects in the room glowed un-earthily. As if they were emitting the light. The gorgeous inviting light. Everything was happening so slowly and gently. And then the air took on a lapis lazuli tint. It seemed to buzz with a living electricity. The whole space acquired a different aspect. I felt like I was in the same room but the room was in a different novel. I was back in the space I had been in when I had my religious experience in the church. Diamonds and trust. How could this be happening? I had taken a pill and entered a real world of death and rebirth. I might never come back. It was out of my control. The space was inhabited by God in some way. This was just what had happened in Massachusetts when I had been suicidal. I was on that edge again. Between death and life. I had left the dead mechanical modern world and entered a world that was holy and dangerously alive. I felt apprehensive and blessed.

Most significantly, I saw that this was not a hallucination. I was not stoned or intoxicated. I was thinking and seeing with the utmost clarity. I had just fallen out of the preceding 400 years and into something earlier and more mysterious. More profound. More spacious and alive.

My eyes began to tear. I had entered another world, awesome and wish fulfilling, in touch with power beyond conception, power beyond all the hydrogen bombs of the countless burning stars, a holy world in which I was blessed and life had meaning and God wouldn't let people die. My rapture in Massachusetts had been receding into the sands of memory. Now, somehow I was back there.

I felt the universe was like a cradle that held me.

How big is the universe? Big enough.

[Quotations in italics without citations are from my journal at the time.]

I said to Charlotte, "You can't fall out of the universe. I see it. There's nothing to worry about. We're taken care of for eternity. But we can't stay on the earth."

I saw that I could force myself to disbelieve all this. But for what? The shallow hopeless love-starved world we had built over the last few centuries? The war and the lies and heartlessness? And not only was this alternative world more satisfying, infinitely more warm and loving than the other world, it was more real. To say this was a hallucination, I would have to lie to myself. That was not possible. This was real. This is what virtually every other culture in the history had been telling us, there was something else. Something blessed and loving.

I looked at the light which was glowing now and subtly, uncannily sparkling. Somehow the light seemed alive. I thought of Einstein. He knew light was special. I saw what genius consisted of. Genius required, besides great intelligence, the ability to let go. Almost in the Buddhist sense. To let go and not be attached to anything. I saw what Einstein had done. The Lorenz equations, the Michaelson and Morley paradoxical results were all public knowledge. Everyone ignored them. Only Einstein had the courage to let go. Of the entire Newtonian worldview. In order to accept what nature had shown us about light, he had to back into a crazy Alice in Wonderland worldview with slowing clocks and shortening rulers and bending space. Only Einstein had the courage to do this. To head toward landlessness. To leave the human community and move into another world. How lonely he must have been. Like being the first person lost in space. How impossibly lonely.

But even Einstein hadn't seen that light was alive. He was part of a community of scientists. Ultimately he would not be alone. They would be able to follow where he led. He was creating equations and laws to map the new reality and describe what necessarily would occur if the light paradoxes were followed. He had left the Newtonian universe to enter a world that was beyond common sense. But his conclusions were testable. He was still in the community of science. He had not passed to the point where God was free.

My trip was like the Michelson-Morley experiment. It couldn't be true. But it was. How could this be happening to me? I had always lacked courage. I kept one foot in the society. I was writing a doctoral dissertation. But now, right now, I was out there. I had swallowed a substance and moved toward a godly space. It was impossible. But it had happened. Was this what the communion wafer was hinting at? Now I would have to let go of my old assumptions about what was real or possible. I had to follow Einstein and the other explorers and the Buddhists and let go.

The difference between pot and LSD: On pot you say, "Wow! This is great. I am going to remember this vision and take it back with me to the real world." On acid you say, "Wow! This is incredible! I am going to remember this vision and take it back with me to the fake world."

Now I knew what acid was about. Why people gave up their careers and risked arrest and moved to India afterwards. I had tested LSD against a real religious vision. LSD really did take you to where I had been in Massachusetts. I felt a joy and a new sense of power. I had taken LSD and I knew what it was.

And then the walls began to breathe.

BEYOND THE BEYOND

> *"Have a mind that is open to everything, attached to nothing."*
>
> Tilopa

It wasn't like a hallucination or an optical illusion. Not like on pot, when with some effort you could soften your eyes and perhaps see the walls move a fraction of an inch, or was it the light? No, these walls were really moving. Slowly, oh so slowly, like the whole trip surprisingly, the acid was much more powerful but also so much more gentle than I had expected. It took you way out, but so slowly that at times you wished it would speed up and get there already, but no, the acid went at its own slow pace. It knew better than you.

The walls were really moving, slowly, gracefully undulating in and out, perhaps a foot in each direction. It was like being within some large lung or inside a whale. As I sat there watching the walls soften and breathe, I felt something melting inside myself, some internal structure that was letting go. As astonishing as this was, I realized it called into question the very notion of hallucination. My body felt like a skyscraper, a steel frame supporting the hanging flesh and organs, but now the steel had reached its melting point and was beginning to give.

I wasn't scared somehow. It felt deliciously luxuriant to simply soften and let go. After all these years of holding myself tight and erect. The walls breathing so slowly. Alive. The walls were alive. Wasn't that what the Hindu scriptures said? God took the form of the world. How much energy I had been spending to keep myself from seeing this. Holding myself rigid to keep the world in the pattern of straight lines. "Dead Matter." How could this have come about? I had been hypnotized. That was it. Since I had been born. Culture was hypnosis. Even the stage hypnotist was asking you to take the childlike posture, re-culturalizing you temporarily as a substitute parent. See this. Don't see that. Until he suggests that you come back to the majority culture. The majority hallucination.

I felt so good. The whole room was melting. Einstein. Matter is energy. Energy is matter (mass) times the speed of light squared. There it was again. The beautiful light. Magical. This world made so much more sense than the other one with its permanent death and its right angles and infinity of nothingness. This world was alive. Matter was frozen energy. God manifesting into forms. And energy was God seen from the other side. God was Love. Energy was Love.

Charlotte came into the room. She had two pairs of eyes, one over the other. She was wearing a kind of Algerian djellaba she had made, a long robe that she slid on over her head, with wide sleeves, made of a soft material of beautiful muted color, oranges and golds melting slowly into each other. And above her head there hung a halo. It was triangular, of a kind of glowing plastic with sparkling diamonds embedded. But there was no mistaking its reality. It advanced with her as she moved slowly toward me. I thought of it like a bridal veil that had been thrown back over her head. You kissed the bride and her veil became a halo of diamonds. And then, as in a TV in which the hundreds of horizontal lines that compose the picture begin to separate, or a sculpture made of mist that begins to quickly evaporate when the sun comes out, the room disappeared. The Earth was like a tiny pea a million miles away. Insignificant. On which little people were playing out a Punch and Judy show. I was loosing touch with it.

"I wanna go home."

Dorothy *(The Wizard of Oz)*

We were in empty space. No points of reference. Just Charlotte and I in the infinity of space, a kind of mental space. Like the space of a dream, only this was real. Charlotte and me. And I thought I had realized the terrible truth. We were eternal. We were alone. We were immortal. We were the original two. Male and female. God and Goddess. Yin and Yang. Isis and Osiris. We were alone and lonely and we had created the world. We had agreed to imagine it together. To forget our real condition. But we had included an escape hatch. A chemical which would catapult us out of the dream when the dream turned ugly. Now the world had become too ugly to sustain. Charlotte had eaten the magic square. The earth dream was over. Now we would be alone again. Forever.

I looked at Charlotte there next to me in space and I was convinced she was seeing and inhabiting the same novel I was. She had only one set of eyes. Now I was scared. Was this death? Had I died? At the end of your life did you continue but the world died like a dream?

"Why didn't you tell me?" I said. "Why did you let me lose the dream of the world? It's too soon. It's too lonely."

She just smiled her gentle, mysterious smile.

"Can we ever go back?" I said. "Will we ever forget this and become ordinary people again?"

She continued to smile, amazed at where my head was taking me.

"Will things ever be the same? Will I come back to the earth? Will there be a dissertation, and people going to work on the subways, and baseball games, and music?"

Charlotte looked at me for a while and then she said quietly, lovingly, "You'll come back. In a few days you'll return to your normal life." Then she added, very softly, "But it will never be the same."

She smiled. I felt lost and betrayed. After a long time, I had no idea how long, the living room began to form around us. In and out. We moved back and forth between the two worlds as the dream of the earth returned. I thought of Chuang Tsu, who said one night he dreamed he was a butterfly and he believed it was real, but now he had awakened and he believed he was a man. How was he to decide whether he was a man who dreamed he was a butterfly or a butterfly dreaming he was a man?

Strangely enough now I found I wasn't sure I really wanted to come back to the twentieth century, with its gas chambers and malls, its wars and advertising, its lack of golden living light, and eternity, and the feeling that you couldn't fall out of the universe, and that nothing that ever existed could die. I didn't want to let go of the feeling that the universe was alive, that God loved me, that everything was OK forever. But I was scared of the consequences.

I looked at the clock. I had been tripping for six hours. I snapped at Charlotte. I blamed her for killing the dream of the world. She just kept looking at me with amazement at where my big dome intellect could take me. After a while I calmed down. I felt a lot of love for Charlotte. For the world.

I asked Charlotte to play some Bach records. Then some rock. I drank a couple beers. They had no effect. I was way above beer. Charlotte was smoking a mound of dope but I couldn't tell if she was stoned or not. It was like looking at a Piper Cub down below, when you were at 35,000 feet. She could have been on the ground so far as I was concerned, she was so much closer to the earth than I was. I was overwhelmed by the experience. It was bigger than my brain. Larger than language. I looked around our living room. The walls were spongy but they had decided to stop breathing. It occurred to me that stability and natural law were God's mercy. We weren't ready to live in those other spaces yet. That's why we were here.

I listened to the music for a couple hours. It sounded like the band was really in the room. But what was real? I remember a Zen saying, "Before I had satori I chopped wood and I drew water. When I had satori I didn't chop wood or draw water. After I had satori I chopped wood and drew water."

After a while I thought of another Zen saying. "When I am hungry, I eat. When I am tired, I sleep." I decided to delay thinking about what was real. I realized that I hadn't eaten all day. I was hungry.

> *"The nature of all reality is spiritual, not material, or a dualism of matter and spirit."*
> British Physicist Sir Arthur Eddington

Charlotte led me up the street to the Riviera Bar and Grill. I felt like I was walking on foot-high foam rubber pads. I realized that I wasn't afraid of dying. Strangely, I didn't feel like a vegetarian. I wanted to eat beef. I liked having teeth. I ordered a jumbo burger rare and a good ale. The jukebox was playing Aretha's "Natural Woman," written by a Brooklyn-Jewish girl, my age, Carole King. How could this be? How could these two daughters of centuries of suffering have joined together to pass on such beauty and feeling to us?

The meat tasted delicious. I liked biting into it and chewing it. Charlotte was laughing and having a good time. The bar was filled with hippies and Villagers. I felt puzzled but good. Uncertain about where this would all lead, but somehow OK.

I knew I would never really come home. Wherever this led, I would never be able to be a straight person again. There was no going back. I would begin to study and think about this as soon as my mind straightened out. I didn't know what was real anymore, or how this figured in my life. Yet I felt powerful and brave. I had risked my life for Truth.

I couldn't tell who in the bar was stoned or drunk. I was the highest person in a Village bar. I felt I belonged with those who had risked everything, with the outcasts and rebels and poets. Finally.

I knew there was a path beyond where I was. I had wound up in a space that was narrowed down to the final Two. But I knew there was a higher space. The space of the One. There had to be. The Buddha and all the holy men and saints and visionaries were not lying. I would bet my life on it. I knew that soon I would soon take acid again and continue my journey. I knew that Charlotte's trip and mine were two ends of the same trip. That we were on this journey together. I didn't know "the truth," but I knew that in my culture all the experts and professors and doctors and commentators and intellectuals were on a path that led to a dead end.

The jukebox played "Who Knows Where the Time Goes?" Sandy Denny. Her big soulful voice. She had written the beautiful, sad song. When Fairport Convention was auditioning for a new lead singer it seemed that every girl in England had shown up. The band was worn out. Ready to give up. But they let this girl from South London give it a try. She was a bit chubby with a round face, unkempt strawberry blond hair, a sweet English rose. Well we might as well give her a shot. She sang one line in her impossibly big, kind, throaty voice. The building shook. The floor moved. The guys looked at each other with their mouths hanging open.

The auditions were over.

Where did these young women suddenly come from? Janis, Sandy Denny, Tracy Nelson ("Down So Low," "Mother Earth"), Aretha Franklin, and the rest? How could a Jewish Carole King have written songs like "Will You Still Love Me Tomorrow?" for the Shirelles? How could this be happening?

Somehow I felt safe and among friends there in the Village. I was on the path again. The journey to the East. I had broken through the glass case and was inhaling air that was fresh and clean. Air that had never been breathed before. Charlotte and I ordered a couple more ales. I was ready to meet the world again.

308

GROUND CONTROL! GROUND CONTROL!

" . . . the scrupulous fidelity to the truth of my own
sensations."

Joseph Conrad

Over the next two days I slowly came back to earth. The liquor store,
my mother and Charlie, the unceasing war. The acid manifestations let go.
But what was real? After all, didn't Swami Sivananda, a physician before
he was a swami, assure us that the world is an illusion and that "You are
Brahman [The Creator]"? I understood that it would be easy to say that I
had taken a "drug" and had "hallucinated," but I remained loyal to what I
had seen. There was no choice. Giving in meant acceding to the Spanish
conquistadores and the Church who had desired to stamp out these holy
visions (and those who held them) from the face of the earth forever and
had nearly succeeded in Latin America. And what was a hallucination?
Who determined this? Who was to say whether "reality" was not merely
the majority hallucination of a particular culture?

I knew that when I came back it was like entering slowly into a
lesser level of reality. In the same way that you know when you awake
after a night dream that the dream can be folded into the larger reality of
your day life, I had seen that the earth was a dream, part of an infinitely
larger reality. I thought that all the dream interpretations, the Jungian and
Freudian and the rest were all useful, but perhaps the real function of the
dream was simply to show us that it was possible to be in a world that
seemed absolutely real and crucial to one's fate, and then to wake up and
realize one was actually part of a larger, more real world.

Taking acid was easier in those days because the culture had lost all of
its authority. There were thousands of people risking their lives at sea in
various home-made craft. It was very easy to view the old culture as a tissue
of lies, spread like a flu by confused and angry elders who had lost their
way. Anyone looking back on this period and trying to honestly understand
it must remember the context—our government was pursuing a senseless
war that was causing an average of about ten World Trade Centers of deaths
each month, a 9/11 every three or four days for ten years. You had to do
something! Even if it seemed crazy or extreme or was doomed to fail.

"When you have found the beginning of the way
the star of your soul will show its light, and
by that light you will perceive how great
is the darkness in which it burns."

Light on the Path

Like the earth losing its hold on the astronauts, the culture had lost its hold on me. A culture not only tells you how to see the world—what is beautiful and real and good and true—it tells you who you are, it lays out the parameters of a self. I had bought every piece of clothing in the immigrant's American dream bag, and then one by one they had been stripped from me and I found myself naked and shivering in the slushy Stephen Crane Bowery of my nightmares.

I had to rebuild a self, immediately. The basic cultural novel no longer made sense to me: The majority's novel that contended that somehow, out of dumb nothing, all we could see and experience had arisen. And that it would all disappear back into nothing. And that we were the smartest beings who had ever lived. And that the whole amazing process, so beautiful and intricate and complicated that even Albert Einstein couldn't come close to understanding it, all this was the product of no intelligence. It was simply "Natural Laws." And these incredible laws had just appeared. As if this didn't simply put the whole question of the creation of mind and intelligence one step backward. Yet this view was supposed to be "rational," which meant acceptable or good. The people who believed this didn't see it as a belief. I had already been viewing the culture from the outside for several years: A strange place where people had boxes in their living rooms that lied to them.

But there were thousands of ways of interpreting our experience. Virtually every other culture in history had attempted to build or worship some connection to the starry realms of meaning and magic. Pyramids and sacred mountains, and Sumerian ziggurats and gothic cathedrals. We were alone in having sacrificed all this for technical progress and power over nature. And we had accomplished wonderful things, like reduction of pain and prevention of polio, but what had we lost?

"In my mind, the collapse of the atom was the collapse of the whole world: Suddenly the stoutest walls fell. Insecure and soft. I wouldn't have been surprised if a stone had melted into thin air before my eyes. Science seemed to have been annihilated."

Vasily Kandinsky

Why were scientists wasting their time contending with Fundamentalists? It was like playing the St. Louis Browns. Why did scientists and intellectuals and their religious opponents all equate spirituality with an angry man in the sky who reminded me of my father?

Why were acid and mushrooms and peyote called "drugs" when so many other cultures saw them as sacred medicines? If God, or the Goddess, or the Great Spirit, or the Beyond All Names, could make this entire incredible world, with the genes, and relativity, and Mozart, and gardenias, and hamburgers, why couldn't She or He have made a world in which a mushroom or a chemical could confer the power to see. I certainly didn't believe God was in the chemical or mushroom. LSD seemed to work by blocking our cultural learning in some way so that, in the language of the Romantic poets, we saw with the eyes of a child. Was that so incredible to conceive? Acid was merely an artificial version of the holy plants and sacred mushrooms which people had been relying on since the beginning of time. How could the intellectuals talk about multi-culturalism without realizing that this meant respecting the view of 99 percent of the world's cultures that believed in the reality of these acid visions?

Yet I had to be careful now. The authorities and adults were not going to allow anyone to see anything that they themselves were afraid to look at. They were like the church fathers in the old story of Gallileo. When he said that moons moved around Jupiter, which was not possible in their theories, they refused to look into his telescope. We were going to have to operate in the dark corners and crawl spaces where the reality police feared to creep. As Aldous Huxley had said to Timothy Leary at Harvard,

"Remember Dr. Leary, you are an anthropologist among a very primitive people." Dr. Leary refused to remember. He was a rogue and rascal and not trustworthy some of the time. But he was bright, and brash, and funny, and articulate, and learned, and he loved a fight. In short, he was Irish.

Eventually they put him in a cage.

Yet I was feeling strong. I was beginning to feel like someone to be reckoned with, unlike when I was in college and had seen myself as a crude oaf, a mute inglorious Milton Berle.

SPECIFIC GRAVITY

On the day after my trip, I spoke to Charlotte about her obsession with the goddess Kali, the Hindu goddess of death. Charlotte had identified with Kali, particularly since she'd begun her horror film fascination. I suggested that maybe it was time to let Kali go. Charlotte agreed. She took out a drawing she had made of Kali while I had been tripping. She put it in a pot on the stove and set the paper on fire. The burning embers lifted and swept around the room. Quickly, I set a cover on the pot and we ran around swatting at the sparks. Luckily nothing in the room caught fire.

I took the day off, smoking dope and trying to slide back into the acid space, but the gravitational tug of the mundane was reasserting itself. I was running into speed bumps on my dissertation. So far as I was concerned I had finished it, but my professors didn't see it that way. They thought Ph.D. meant "Paid His Dues," and they were going to be sure I paid mine. I had organized my work chronologically, going from book to book of James Purdy's. My advisor thought I should organize it by theme. This meant re-writing the entire dissertation in a way that seemed less effective to me.

I was dying to write a novel. The vectors of my passion were bouncing around within me. I felt like the inside of my body was larger than the outside. I was in danger of exploding, a premature ejaculation of emotion. Yet somehow I managed to rewrite the entire dissertation. Then I thought I could finally move on after a millennium of school. But my second reader read the new version and he asked me why I hadn't written it in chronological order. I blew up and told him that he should discuss this with the first reader and I would do whatever they said. I didn't care any longer. They were torturing me in the way that Dr. Martin Seligman at Penn was torturing dogs.

They agreed I should go back to the original mode of organization. Then, after a hard day of being chased around Manhattan by the police, I received word that the third reader was "insulted by my use of the comma." I was one step away from getting off what I now call the Ritalin to Prozac Railroad. That's what Rochelle Gatlin seemed to be doing out in San Francisco. She couldn't hold it together any more. She was getting stoned with Ward all the time. She had become an astrologer.

I once met a woman who had survived a serious suicide attempt two years before. "Was it in a moment of passionate desperation?" I asked.

"No, it wasn't that at all. It was just that one day I realized, in a way that seemed quite logical to me, that I simply didn't want to be alive any more."

I was sorry I had asked the question. "But I'll bet you're glad that's all in your past and over with."

"I don't think it's ever going to be completely over with. Once you're a suicidal person, you're always going to be a potentially suicidal person."

I thought of my time in the Army and I knew she was right. I had my spiritual visions to fall back on, but I needed time to develop and integrate them into my life. I had already committed suicide on my million dollar career. I couldn't dance the white, stiff-legged Peabody any longer. I couldn't do the capitalist one-step. Any normal jobs were out of the question. I could no longer be servile. I couldn't smile and wait on tables. If I had been born Christian in the Middle Ages, I might have entered a monastery. I needed a sanctuary with books and ideas. Time to meditate and think. I had conceived of the university as my place of refuge, but it had proven to be bureaucratic and part of the war effort. The Army and water. I no longer wanted a career in scholarship. I had had it with careers. I needed the Ph.D. I needed to be overqualified, so I wouldn't be pressed to publish or perish and be pushed around. I needed to be in a small college where I wouldn't have to sit on Ph.D. orals. I wanted to teach poor kids, anyone who walked in the door. I didn't want to be near the top of the pecking order. I was burned out on pecking. I couldn't be part of ignorant armies clashing by night all around me. And not only on the battlefield.

I was feeding on my dreams of a new culture and a better world because the old culture had come to seem like a permanent catastrophe, a World War I on wheels. The professors on my Ph.D. committee couldn't see this or help me. I was furious at them. They couldn't tell that I had begun my path out of The Bronx by being a good boy, always finishing what I had started, always succeeding, Rensselaer, Wharton, Boeing, the Minuteman Missile Program, Army company commander, and that I had wound up suicidal. I was losing my ability to comply.

[Now I see that I had asked two of my dissertation advisors to serve on my committee *because* they were among the most intelligent, hip, and compassionate of the professors. But they were accustomed to young, middle-class students with successful parents, not desperadoes like Rochelle and me, struggling to keep one foot in the system, drugged, exploring arcane philosophies, fighting the police, trying to find a path toward avoiding homelessness or mental hospitals by right work. They couldn't imagine that my father was one of eight kids, and that he was still the only one who owned a car. I see now that my advisors were no doubt pre-occupied with their own problems and alienation. They were just doing what professors had done at Ivy League schools for generations. But, for me, this was no longer enough. I needed some nook on the edge of civilization in which I could hide out and heal.]

I went back to the dissertation, slinging commas around like sharp boomerangs. Then I received a desperate phone call from Armando, the cop I liked up at the liquor store. "Jerry, come up here, fast. Guillermo, he went nuts. They took him to Bellevue. The store window is broke. They took Rigo to the station house. I'll hold the fort till you get here."

I hopped into a cab. I had been worried about Guillermo, Rigo's assistant for a couple months. He was built like a fireplug, a no neck nose-guard, but he was the sweetest guy in the world. He'd never adjusted completely to coming here from Puerto Rico. He looked increasingly tired each week. When I spoke to him about it he muttered something about the chickens making noises at night. I wasn't quite sure how to respond. I didn't want to embarrass him. Later I found that the country people often did raise chickens in the neighborhood tenements. But it was more than the chickens. It was the pace of life, the kids, the responsibilities for a twenty-something, uneducated guy in a new country where he barely spoke the language. It was New York. What could you say? He'd cracked.

When I arrived at the store, Miguel, Guillermo's brother who often filled in at the store on weekends and holidays, was sweeping up the glass on the sidewalk. He had stepped in and made the few sales while I was coming uptown in the cab. I knew he was afraid I would sack his brother.

Armando filled me in as Rigo showed up. Rigo looked miffed to have been taken to the station but also pleased that they had taken his word for what had happened and let him go. He took pride in his position as boss of the liquor store and felt they had respected it. I knew he told everyone in the neighborhood that he owned the store and that *I* worked for *him*. I didn't care. Whatever made him happy was fine with me.

It turned out Guillermo had gotten progressively worse over the last couple days, wandering around like he was half-asleep. Then today, after lunch, he showed up back at the store, all 230 pounds of him, riding a little kid's tricycle. Rigo watched warily from the doorway. Guillermo came up parallel to the store on the sidewalk, struggling to pedal, his knees askew, his face troubled. Then, just opposite Rigo, the puny bike flipped over the curb, catapulting him off, all his weight landing right onto his head in the gutter.

Guillermo rose slowly, dazed, holding his skull. Somehow he got the idea that Rigo had punched him in the head. He accused Rigo, Rigo laughed, Guillermo ran over to the side, picked up a full garbage can, and threw it right through the store's plate glass window. Then, of course, Rigo, the former boxer, did punch him in the head. This led to the consequences Armando had described on the phone.

Rigo was still fuming, but as he finished the story, I began to laugh and he had to laugh as well. Soon we were all laughing, except Miguel, uneasy because of his fear about his brother's job. "Look, don't worry, Miguel," I said, "I'll hold the job for him, if you'll fill in until they let him out. We all know Guillermo's a good guy. He's just trying to support his family. I'm not gonna take away his job because he blew his cork." Miguel relaxed. Then Rigo added, making a fist, "I'll blow his cork all right," but I knew he was just letting off steam.

"A mind forever voyaging through strange seas of thought, alone"

William Wordsworth

I had to step carefully in the world now. Reality was much more slippery than before. I had always been lonely but lately I had come to a place of real desolation. What would happen to me if the counterculture collapsed? I began to lead the life of a double agent. During the day I reworked the punctuation in my dissertation, the commas coming to resemble the sickles on Soviet flags. Then I would return to my shadow life. Attempting to understand the events of my recent life and to integrate this experience. Late at night I would get stoned and try to go back to the acid space. This was helpful but it never really worked because it was obvious that if I were ready to return, then I would have taken acid, not smoked pot.

I turned to the New Testament. I would never be a Christian, but I had a lasting respect for Jesus as a principle or a way into the sacred figure of God as love. Charlotte was no longer attending church or following its forms. She was still praying, but she had moved away from the Pope and the family of the Church and into the community of the stoned and rebellious. I had read the New Testament at Penn when Professor Murphey, as a brilliant assignment in historiography, had assigned us to go home and read the Gospels and write a biography of Jesus over the weekend. Of course it proved impossible. There were so many elisions and worse, outright contradictions between the Gospels. (And we didn't even consider the other Gospels, the ones that the Church had tried to destroy but which someone had found in 1946 in a cave in Nag Hamaddi, Egypt. Like the Gospel of Thomas, which leaned more toward Eastern religion, inner peace and meditation.) But when I reread the Gospels I found little that could help me. Most of the questions they were dealing with were moral, not metaphysical and certainly not about inducing and interpreting visionary experiences. The Gospels required belief. The visions and the holy words had occurred in the past. We had to have faith in these accepted accounts of them written decades after the original experiences, repeatedly translated from language to language, erratically copied, vetted by authorities, and passed down through the centuries. They were not helping me understand what was happening to me in the present.

I read the Old Testament, opening it up at random and reading passages. I knew little about it. I had always been allergic to the language but now I was shocked by the picture of God as a vengeful tribal chief. There were beautiful and holy stories, like when Abraham offers Isaac to God, which I saw as each of us offering our life and sanity, our fragile self to God as on an acid trip, there was Moses and the burning bush (which Marty claimed was marijuana), but mostly it was God telling the Jews to smite these guys and to slay those guys. Yahweh was not nearly as smart as Albert Einstein.

Yahweh seemed to me the kind of God you would come up with if you had lost the sacred, ecstatic vision and had back-engineered a Creator from merely the mundane events in the de-sacralized world.

When I turned again to the Eastern religions, though, they confirmed that I no longer saw with the eyes of the blind. They were talking about what I had seen. *They* had seen it. They knew where I was. They had been there.

In the culture around me, people professed to believe that the external world, the earth, was round, but in their inner world, their subjectivity, they were still in the era of the flat earth. You sailed along through the storms of your life, you came to the end of the earth, and you fell off. There was no vertical dimension to their imagining. No transcendence or magic. No wonder so many were hopeless and depressed and lashing out at others in their despair.

THE MAYOR

Every great block has a mayor and the mayor of our block was my best friend in the Village, Terry Kelsey. Terry was a most unusual New Yorker, having arrived a few years earlier from San Jose, California. A couple years younger than I, Terry looked like a mountain man with golden-silver ringlets hanging down over his shoulders and matching his beard. He was an inch taller than me, maybe six foot one and had played high school football, so he was big, but there was a delicacy about him, you could see it in the way he held his ever-present cigarette in his thumb and forefinger, away from himself, as if he was just about to flick an ash with his middle finger. And from the blue velvet smoking jacket he had purchased at the Salvation Army and wore over his jeans and T-shirt.

Terry had been going nowhere in San Jose, stuck in the muck of ordinary nowhere life, when he first heard Lester Young playing saxophone on the radio. Suddenly his life had a purpose. It was like Saul on the road to Damascus. This was it. This was really it.

Immediately he hitched to New York and bought a tenor saxophone. He read everything he could find about Lester Young. ("Prez.") He began to follow jazz fanatically, to hang out at the right spots and to introduce himself to the musicians and ask about Prez. Who was this big, sensitive, California mountain man? Uneducated, but with a large native intelligence and a gift for gab and a gruff voice that sounded like something between Symphony Sid the all-night jazz disc jockey and a Model T, and a curiosity about Lester, one of the legendary saints of jazz, that Terry soon backed up with a wide knowledge. At the very time that the jazz musicians were drifting toward an even greater despair than usual, as all the young people were leaving them for rock, Terry charmed everyone he met.

Now he was living a couple doors down from us on Grove Street in a decrepit tenement with his old lady, Julie Kurnitz. Julie was a big, large boned woman, an easy-going, sophisticated singer/actress with a bit of a limp and a beautiful smile. You can see her in Woody Allen's *Radio Days*, where she plays the society-lady, radio-hostess (based on Jinx Falkenberg?), but you won't see her earthiness and her sweet smile since it conflicted with the role. They had virtually no money, but were living on the cheap on an inheritance left to Julie by her uncle Harry Kurnitz. Harry had been a famous Thirties-Forties wit, playwright, bon-vivant, and popular man about town. He had written for the Marx brothers. I loved the fact that Terry and Julie were being supported by money from the Marx Brothers.

Terry held court on his stoop. His window sat just to the left of the top of the front stairs. You could see him there virtually every day, smoking a joint or sipping at a can of beer, low saxophone music in the background, presiding over the quorum who sat outside on the steps. A symposium of the stoned, the talented, the brilliant jobless, and those regretfully employed, returning from work. Terry knew all the gossip. He knew everyone. He ruled over his stoop. It was our neighborhood café, the central social institution for our side of the Village. He was like a block monitor as well. When Samuel, the sophisticated, middle-aged black man who always wore a sport jacket, was robbed and left bound and gagged, and wriggled his way down the steps across the street, it was Terry, of course, who found him, and untied him, and then told everyone for blocks around.

Julie and Terry's tenement apartment was nearly empty, just a couple pieces of old furniture around Terry's inexpensive phonograph which sat on the floor in the center of the room, a few LPs between two bricks against the wall. They lived in a kind of genteel poverty, trying to stretch the inheritance without working at straight jobs. Terry didn't work at all. He was studying records and practicing his saxophone, trying to learn to play like Prez. He had few LPs because when he bought one he would play it over and over until he had memorized the solos he judged worth keeping and then give the record away. Or he would send it to one of his friends around the country. He always directed the return address to Thelonius Monk. He said to me, in his gruff voice, "Then I know if it doesn't get to who I sent it, Daddy, it goes to Theo. That way I can't lose." Of course Terry knew "Theo" as he knew all the jazz masters, and Thelonius liked him in Theo's way. Once Terry and I went up to the Village Vanguard, to see Thelonius. Max Gordon, the owner, who had dealt with every hustle and scam possible as a long time successful night club owner in New York, knew Terry and liked him and amazingly let him in for free. Everyone knew that this crazy white boy had no money and had become a kind of encyclopedia of jazz and was giving his life to playing like Prez. They all took care of him. We went up to Monk, standing there in the corner, looking over the club slyly. Terry said, "Theo, what's happenin', Daddy?" Monk looked at him, amused, and replied, "Nothin's happenin' till it's happenin'." Terry cracked up. Monk and I both knew Terry would quote this for the rest of his life. Terry turned to me as if to say, "You see, Daddy, you see. This guy is so right on the mark every time, he's RIGHT THERE!" and Monk saw this and even Monk, normally reticent and oblique, had to smile fondly.

Terry gave me many LPs and I cherished them. He had no use for rock LPs. His attitude was that of most jazz musicians toward players who were clearly not up to their level and were making millions of dollars playing a few chords. But I liked rock music. I liked simplicity and feeling. I thought it was needed along with the intricate complexities and angry technicalities that jazz had reached. So much of jazz now was black power driven, angry and self-destructive. I yearned for simplicity at times. I liked the naive overwhelming youthful straight-ahead emotion of rock. And I liked pretty tunes like those of James Taylor and Carole King, the back-to-the-gospel unadorned harmonies that sometimes showed up in rock, like when Eric Clapton got strung out on heroin and retreated and then came back not as a huge star with his hair standing out as if he was touching a live electric wire when he played with Cream, but with a gentler, homier group, Delaney and Bonnie, and when they played the Fillmore, he hung out in the background of the band, in a white suit, just trying to be supportive and survive a while, to keep it down to earth and simple. I appreciated that. I was coming to favor quiet paintings by Barnett Newman and Ellsworth Kelly. I needed some times of separate peace.

Although, of course, I would always love jazz. I was married to jazz. And Terry knew jazz inside out and taught me so much about it. He would give me records by southwestern tenor-men like Arnett Cobb, and Don Byas, and Illinois Jacquet. He would find live records from Birdland by musicians like Art Blakey and he would circle the best cut on the jacket with red ink and he was always right. I knew he had more advanced and better taste than I did.

Once we were walking on the street and there was one of my idols, Paul Desmond. Terry of course said, "Pauldesmond," as we passed and Desmond recognized him and smiled. (Paul Desmond knew all about Terry because Paul played in the style that Prez had originated, the softer, breathy, more sensitive, "feminine" style that was followed by Stan Getz and Zoot Sims and especially Paul Quinichette, the "Vice Prez' as opposed to the big, macho tenor style of men like Coleman Hawkins and Ben Webster.) Paul knew all about Terry's stories about Prez which Terry picked up from everyone but especially from Prez's widow, whom Terry had somehow located and befriended and visited all the time. "What's happenin', Daddy?" Terry said. "Whatcha doin' these grievous days?" Desmond smiled again and said, shyly, "Oh, I'm working. Doing some arrangements for Herb Alpert." Terry said, "Herb Albert?" Terry shook his head from side to side, both as an admonishing grandfather and in sadness at the bleak state of things, and he said as we left, "He should be working for you, Daddy. He should be working for you." Desmond cracked up.

You had to laugh at this twenty-something kid from the West, looking a little like the young David Crosby, clearly a rocker by style of dress and grooming, always stoned, usually with a couple drinks under his belt, giving his maxims and advice to the jazz greats. They recognized the enormous respect and even love behind everything he said. One late afternoon he looked troubled, sitting at home in the twilight shadows.

"What's up, Prez?" I said. That always cheered him up when I called him Prez. It wasn't hard, since he had adopted Prez's unique style of playing, holding the sax out to the side from his body at a forty-five degree angle. "Bobby Timmons asked me to play with him. He wants me to come over to his pad and we'll just fool around a little."

"Bobby Timmons! Wow, that's great! When?"

Bobby Timmons was a great piano player, one of the world's best. He played with Art Blakey and had written jazz classics like "Moanin'." He lived around the corner on Bedford Street, near Edna St. Vincent Millay's former cottage.

"I ain't goin'."

"What!?"

"I ain't goin'. I'm not good enough. When I'm good enough, then I'll go over there on my own. He won't have to ask. But I'm not good enough, Daddy."

"But Terry, he knows that. He just wants to fool around. He wants to help you. He *likes* you." Terry just kept shaking his head no. He was nothing if not stubborn.

"I like to hear you play. He'll enjoy showing you a few things. He's a nice guy."

But Terry was already lighting up a joint, still shaking his head no. Then he started laughing, coughing and blowing out smoke as he often did when he spoke. "You know, Prez used to carry his grass around in a gold cigarette case. He kept it right here," he indicated his hip. "He called it his 'edis.'"

"Why his 'edis'?"

He laughed harder now. He looked like a young Gabby Hayes when he laughed like that. "I don't know, Daddy. Prez had style. When people asked him about it, he said that it was because 'edis' is 'side' spelled backwards. He had his own language, man. After he got out of the Army, he changed. He wouldn't play in the upper register anymore. He was too sad."

As I took this in, Terry laughed. I knew he had thought of another Prez story. "Listen Daddy, you know Prez called everyone 'Lady.' When he first came to New York he lived up in Harlem with Billie Holiday and her mother. He and Billie were like brother and sister. Like a family. He's the one that named her 'Lady Day.' And she named him 'Prez,' the President of Jazz. Since then Prez calls everyone 'Lady.' Like if he was here with us now, he would call you 'Lady J.'

"Anyhow, once at Newport, Prez goes out on the stage along with his quintet and he's wearin' his pork pie hat tilted to the side in his cool manner, but something's goin' on. The whole band is really drunk and stoned but especially old Joe Jones on drums. Some stupid argument about something and you know Joe Jones is always clowning and got his big smile and all, but here, somehow, Prez said something and with the booze and all he hurt Joe's feelings and Joe is pouting and 10,000 people are waiting and Prez is standing there looking frustrated but Joe Jones won't even look at him. So George Wein, the producer, he panics and he runs out onto the stage and over to Prez and he says, 'Lester, what's goin' on?' Lester shrugs. So George says, 'We've got all these fans of yours who love you and you guys aren't playing.' Lester turns to him and he nods towards Joe Jones, who is still sulking like a baby, and Prez says, 'Lady J's done got his feelins hurt. Lady J won't make tickee-boom, tickee-boom . . . . He done fucked up the rest of us ladies.'" Terry laughed like crazy, blowing pot smoke through his nose and mouth, emitting rasping snorts chug chug chug like an old steam locomotive. I was glad to see that he was happy again. Bobby Timmons' innocent offer had hurt his feelings. He had been sulking in the dark. He was sensitive that way, but now he was back home in the land of Prez legends, the country in which he really lived, and, still coughing and laughing out of control, he exclaimed once again, "He done fucked up the rest of us ladies!!" and he passed me his joint.

JAMES

"Just remember, Jerry, I'm not a person, I'm a monster."
James Purdy

When I was researching my dissertation, I had written a note to James Purdy in care of his publisher regarding using his papers at Yale. I was surprised to receive a phone call from a friend of his, Richard Hundley. In Purdy's fiction, people are often distanced from each other. They speak more in interviews rather than spontaneous interactions. Richard said that Purdy would like him to come over and interview me. He said Purdy had had one request to do a long study on him by an academic and he had denied the man permission to quote from his works. It turned out that Richard lived exactly across Grove Street from Charlotte and me. He was a classical composer and singer in the Metropolitan Opera chorus. Nervously I agreed to see him. I needed to get my union card and begin my own life. I couldn't fit into the student uniform any longer. I hadn't anticipated this potential obstacle.

[I think it's interesting that James lived modestly in Brooklyn before this was fashionable. He was always wary of the Manhattan "in-crowd" and kept his distance from them, geographically, as well as by using irony and hilarious angry satire when discussing them with me.]

Richard was soft-spoken, friendly. We immediately established the beginnings of a friendship. He assured me that James and I would get along. A week later, I received a letter from James on blue paper, the envelope sealed by a stamp on the back from the National Wildlife Federation. It was only later that I saw the humor in this. James discouraged me from expecting too much from his papers and recommended I connect with Bettina Schwarzchild. He said Bettina knew his work better than he did. He concluded, "I am pleased that you're interested in my work but I don't like the universities much better than I do the yahoos that run the *New York Times*."

James, I would soon learn, was always testing, always putting his "worst" foot forward, always giving you the chance to reject him, to reveal that you were unable to let go of the cultural orthodoxies that had hurt him.

James had come to New York as a young gay man to find his work misunderstood by the liberal intellectuals of the Manhattan book world. In my estimation he had been forced to see their limitations quickly and to reject their authority by reason of the pain they had caused him. The anti-war movement had driven me to a similar position. I was flattered to have been the recipient of a letter from an author of his caliber. I quickly wrote back telling him that Vietnam had shown me that both the *New Yorker* and the *Times* were ultimately servants of the status quo. In regard to the *New Yorker*, I took a chance and wrote: "good taste is the last bastion of the bourgeoisie."

This remark caught James' attention and he wrote back, "I liked your discussion of 'good taste' and the New York Establishment. What is really at stake, it seems to me, is something that has taste, something you can taste, and something that is without any taste, odor, or flavor. . . . One cannot call the *New Yorker* writers people with good taste or who write with good taste. They're tasteless. They live in terror that they may say something.

"Henry James is their ancestor. He seems to have known nothing about anything, and his talent was making this non-knowledge his theme. He finally gloried in it.

"I feel even Proust and especially Conrad are deceivers of a kind."

Then he added, "It's so funny, most novelists and most critics don't know anything about human beings. Most doctors ditto. They deal entirely in cliché."

How could this be happening? How could one of my favorite novelists, a major American writer, be responding seriously to something I had said? How could I be discussing Henry James and Proust and Conrad with James Purdy? It was as if I had jumped out of a theater audience onto the stage and joined in the dialogue. Surely they would find me out.

What I didn't understand was that James Purdy was becoming a role model for me, a kind of mentor. By word and example over the next few years he would show me how a pure writer lived and thought and worked. I could not have had a better teacher. James was as dedicated and honest a writer as one could encounter.

James now is the subject of a web-site run by scholars and fans and there is a James Purdy Society initiated by Joe Skerett, my old pal from grad school who had founded the Dirigible Society, but in those days there was not a lot written about him. I was reading all the reviews of his work I could locate. When I informed him of this he immediately replied to warn me that newspaper reviews "are written for the most part by very bad and even immoral men."

As we corresponded, I began to understand that James was less concerned about being rejected than about being accepted but misunderstood. Of course, James was chastised by the yahoos and the blind, but because he was clearly a dedicated, intelligent and innovative writer, the fashionable intellectuals who made a business of being more avant-garde than the public were claiming to comprehend him and attempting to fit him into the cynical, almost blasphemous spirit that prevailed among the more advanced and difficult writers and critics. James saw Susan Sontag and Ted Solotaroff as the worst offenders in this regard. Solotaroff was an authority on Henry James, Purdy's *bête noire*, and Purdy thought that to Sontag anyone who wrote about an old woman in a small midwestern town was a sentimentalist. This was precisely the subject of James' second major novel, *The Nephew*. Over time I was surprised to learn that James more passionately identified with *The Nephew*, which was close to his rural Ohio roots, than with his first novel, *Malcolm*, more famous, less traditional, more in the black humor mode. I discovered to my surprise that he vehemently denied he was a black humorist at all: "I don't know what they mean by it, but I write American English almost pure, which I suppose is a dead or dying language. Since best sellers are made by people who do not understand or speak American English, this is one of the reasons I am not read by the monied and well-heeled."

After the interchange of a few letters, I was amazed to realize that James and I seemed to be hitting it off and he began to telephone me. I looked forward to these calls. James' talk was incisive, unpredictable and often hilarious. He could say corrosively funny things about himself and other people, but every remark was softened by his tone. James knew he was funny; he had a soft, small, nasal voice, a kind of southern/midwestern drawl. He spoke slowly, in a somewhat ironic manner, so that even when he said "terrible" things, there was a quality of performance about it; he couldn't hide his delight in turning a witty phrase or in trying to shock me with his opinions. I saw him as a gentle, brilliant man, standing on a rowboat, throwing out sharp, amusing quips at the USS America as it bore down upon him.

Malcolm is a dark, funny, stylized picture of a young man who shows up on the decadent arts scene in Chicago, ruled over by the imperious Madame Girard, and her husband, the billionaire Girard Girard. Their "circle" includes Mr. Cox, an astrologer, and Kermit, a feisty midget who insists that he is "merely short." Malcolm has virtually no learning or personality or interests and he gives very little of himself. In the capitalist emotional economics which pervades our society, his holding back of his "supply" increases the demand for him and his value skyrockets. They pass him around the circle and vie for him for a while. He is even accorded the greatest "honor" of all when Girard Girard allows Malcolm to call him "Girard," but to everyone's astonishment, Malcolm doesn't even understand what he has accomplished.

The Nephew, written in a beautiful, simple American English as Purdy intended, is a novel about an old woman who learns that it's better to face the truth than to be protected from it, and that the real truth is probably not as bad as the truth imagined.

When most of the critics thought of Purdy, they thought of *Malcolm*. James felt they were missing the essence of who he was. In fact, he saw himself as a Christian. "All my books are 'Christian' in the broadest sense of the word, since I am not affiliated with any church now and don't believe in their dogma," he wrote to me, "but my books are Christian in the sense that they show that only by coming to terms with the most unlovely part of ourselves, the parts the world is ashamed of, the world in us, that is, can we be free."

This recalled to my mind Christ's, "Know the truth and it shall make you free," which is precisely the theme of *The Nephew*. James was an outsider in New York, both because of where he hailed from, rural Ohio, and the subject matter and approach of his writing. James saw the Manhattan literary world as lacking heart and compassion and infatuated with false, dead style. Thus he defended his own native language against what he saw as the show-biz language of New York and the stylized language that New Yorkers confused with good writing.

James wrote to me, "The writers who are applauded today and read are all what the communists and new left call petty bourgeois. All the New Yorker writers and the writers applauded by the molting senile Times are this or worse. [Recall that when Gore Vidal published the landmark American serious gay novel, *The City and the Pillar*, the *Times* would not take ads for it.]

James continued, "Nabokov, one of the worst writers to appear in decades certainly, is a cynical, essentially inept writer, whose bad English is applauded by those who have no inner relationship with the English language as spoken and written in America.

"The things that make great writing, passion, the unconscious, agony, and style are all missing in the writers applauded today. . . . Updike could just as easily be a Hungarian or a Dutch-Russian, as his language has no relation to a spoken or heard tongue anywhere."

In the margin James had added in pen, "Because Nabokov's English like Conrad's is completely artificial and bloodless, the antithesis of style and passion, he is acclaimed a stylist." Then he scrawled on the bottom, "Canned strawberry pop is preferred to blood fresh morning," an image which still takes my breath away.

This startled me but it made sense. I was relatively new to literature so when I had discovered that Nabokov, Updike, and Henry James were not among my favorites, I had not known why and attributed it to my inexperience in the field. Just talking to Purdy and receiving his letters was giving me a brilliant tutorial with someone who was an outsider like myself. James was endowing me with a permission to trust my own feelings about books, a confidence I had not received at the university. James gave a dignity to my alienated and radical opinions about the world since he shared so many of them himself. It seemed to me he was much more passionately involved in the dialectic between his work and his life than were most professors.

He wrote that I would have to come to grips with the critics in New York who were attacking his Christian vision. And he lashed out at that academic favorite Henry James again: "Anything not established by money made him nervous. He is the patron saint of all those who hate Christ."

I quickly responded that I understood what he was saying, but I still felt there was a core of black humor in much of his work. I thought he was taking the alienation of the existentialists and turning it into comic detachment. I thought it was possible to write black humor with feeling and spirituality. Even *Malcolm*, perhaps his "flattest," most stylized novel, had Christian overtones to my ear.

After I met with Bettina Shwarzchild, I received a note from James: "Madame Bettina . . . tells me she has told you how wicked I am." This was quintessential James, playing the wicked one, but I noticed that after Bettina's recommendation, he was more open and friendly toward me. He wrote his notes to me as "Dear Jerry," and signed as "Your friend." James trusted Bettina.

James did not attempt to be politically correct. That was a different time and it would have violated his principles as a writer, and, in fact, I would say his religious philosophy. But he was an equal opportunity insulter. He dismissed Joyce Carol Oates as misunderstanding what he was doing. When I read her review I had to agree with him; she judged him against standards he was not trying to meet, as if she were criticizing Thelonius Monk for playing "off-key." For a different reason he objected to Stanley Kaufman (whom James called "Stanley Cough-Medicine") and Wilfred Sheed, whom he considered militant heterosexuals. He sent me a hilarious little unpublished piece he had written, a "manifesto" supposedly by Stanley Kaufman, called "I, Heterosexual."

[Remember that at this time homosexuality was illegal in forty-nine states including New York.]

James wasn't going to let me kneel before any contemporary idols. He declared that Malamud and Roth were processed salami merchants. On Salinger, whose family actually *were* salami merchants, he said that his language "sounds like it was invented in a TV studio." He knew I liked the Beats so he told me that Allen Ginsberg was "an agent of Wall Street."

[I thought of this when I met Allen Ginsberg a couple years later, just outside of San Francisco at a conference in Marin County where I was giving a reading. Just to make conversation I asked him what he thought of Ann Charters' biography of Kerouac and he shouted at me, furiously, that the book was a travesty of Kerouac, how could I like it? This wasn't what I had said, I had merely asked a question, but he continued angrily, saying that since the Kerouac estate wouldn't give her permission to quote from Kerouac directly, she had had to paraphrase him and this had changed the meaning and tone of what Kerouac had written. "Don't you see, if he says, 'I climbed a mountain with a bunch of crazy guys,' he's complimenting them, but if she says, 'He climbed a mountain with a bunch of crazy people,' it's not the same?" Of course I saw that, but before I could reply he stomped away in frustration. This wasn't the gentle Buddhist behavior I had expected.

Nonetheless, that night, when I was having a drink with Gary Snyder, Ginsberg hobbled in. (He was on crutches. I believe he'd broken his leg recently.) There was something unearthily sweet about him. I still recall his innocent smile and how happy he was to see us all and to join us. I guess there were two Allen Ginsbergs, the Madison Avenue advertising man, and the angelic poet he became.

I was talking to Gary Snyder about LSD. His first words to me when we met were, with a smile, "So you're the comic Buddhist I've been hearing about." I had asked him whether he believed in the acid vision.

He thought about this for a moment, and then said, shaking his head, "I don't know. Whenever I take LSD, I believe I'm going to live forever, but the Zen masters say that nothing lasts." At the time I just resolved to think about this. Ginsberg entered and broke the thread. [Today I would say, "I believe that Gary Snyder won't live forever, but your highest Self will, and it will be more familiar to you than Gary Snyder ever was."]

James, having been so often misunderstood, sometimes feared that the New York critics might not really grasp his Christian vision because so many of them were Jewish. Once he said to me, obviously teasing (remember his soft, languid voice), "I'll never be a popular writer because the Jews don't like me." To which I snapped, "Well, why don't you teach the Protestants how to read?" James laughed like crazy. I knew he would, and that he respected me for standing up to him. Of course, we both knew that Bettina Schwarzschild and myself, the two people writing at length about his work, were of Jewish descent. I found that James had a certain fondness for the Jews from the outer boroughs, like Bettina and myself. I remember once he said to me, after halting a moment while searching for the exact way of saying what was on his mind, "I think I'm going to have to use a Yiddish word: 'Alienation.'"

He wrote to me, "Black humor is all non-Christian and much of it is . . . opposed to the great Jewish vision of a Kafka." So he wasn't opposed to the "great Jewish vision," but to my mind, merely the modern, secular, science-based, anti-spiritual, heartless materialism he associated with the New York intellectuals, many of whom were Jewish, and the worship of material goods that he associated with the *New Yorker*.

Once James wrote to me from Martha's Vineyard after Mailer had proposed New York City be declared a separate state: "I would go Norman Mailer one better and propose New York City be made a separate *nation*. It's the fount of all evil, the synthetic dynamo, and no nation should be stuck with it. Then its mooring could be loosed and it could float with its poison off to nowhere."

Whenever James presented himself as wicked or politically incorrect, I recalled that he was the person who had taken the bus all the way to New Orleans for W. C. Handy's funeral.

Since I was entertaining thoughts about becoming a novelist myself, I was concerned about James' ideas about the real American language. If, as he claimed, New Yorkers spoke an artificial language, a kind of show-biz patois, where did this leave me, since this was the language I had grown up with? Why was his language the true American language? Why not mine? I was an American, too. Where did the authority come from to declare which was the "real American language"? At the same time I could see that wisecracks and cynical one-liners could be a way to short circuit the depths of discourse. But as I thought about this over the years, I concluded that what James found sometimes wanting in this New York patter was the ability to carry the full cargo of feeling; it was easy to give in to a slick and glossy surface that was ultimately heartless. His remarks pushed me toward employing my native tongue, the street lingo of one-liners and wise guy talk, but to strive to transmute it into the language of the heart, which was at home in The Bronx as well as Ohio.

Charlotte and I had met James for the first time at a party thrown for him by Bettina Schwarzschild at the Gotham Bookmart (a midtown bookstore James liked). I noticed that he wore a fond smile when he talked to Charlotte and he always asked about her afterwards. In retrospect, I can see why. Among the people one might meet at a New York literary party, Charlotte, though tall and slim and striking with her afro-like hair, was the furthest from a fashionable Manhattanite one could imagine, with her old clothes, her Idaho accent, her exclamations of "Goll-lee!", and her quiet stoned talk about Bach and her belief that Christianity belonged to the loving heart of Jesus rather than to St. Paul. No wonder she and James hit it off. A former Spanish teacher in Cuba, he always referred to her affectionately as "Carlotta."

Shortly after we had begun to communicate, I informed James that I wasn't going to turn my dissertation into a book. I had had it with being a good boy and winning all those degrees and doing all the right things. I was moving step by step away from the "objective" world toward a subjective truth. I wanted to do something wild and dangerous. I wanted to write a novel.

I felt guilty about this because James' work deserved to have books written about it, but James understood immediately and he was always supportive of my decision. Once he even asked me to send him a story. I had never sent anything out for publication, but I did have a couple stories, so I sent him one. It couldn't have been a very good story, I was just setting out, but James told me I was right to get my university union card and move along because, "You are a real writer." How kind that was! How much that undeserved compliment meant to me, a person who felt so culturally deprived that I couldn't even begin to try to write fiction until I had achieved a Ph.D.!

To me this was the "real" James.

I remember when he sold his novel, *Cabot Wright Begins*, (about a handsome, wealthy, serial rapist from Yale and Wall Street who becomes fashionable in Manhattan), to the movies. I was relieved because I worried about him when he turned his back on television publicity and teaching jobs and such. I was actually still afraid of us starving. But James lived a risky life on the little money he could garner from his beautiful and honest books. He told me that he was sorry that his mother wasn't alive to see this sale because she would have been proud of him.

I sent him no more pages. That wouldn't have been fair to him, I thought, he was already too kind, but he continued to help me with my writing in oblique ways. He told me that every morning before he sat down to write, he played records of Shakespeare to get the language going. Once, when I had finished the dissertation and was selling my first novel, I asked him what he could tell me about the publishers and he replied in his small, slow, mischievous voice, "I still don't understand the publishers. The only thing I know about them is that they're the enemy." After my first book, when I began to receive rejections, he consoled me by saying that when he was young he had received enough rejection slips to paper the Washington Monument. When he was finishing up a later novel, *Jeremy's Version*, he confessed that he didn't like publishing his books. That he never had.

As the anti-war demonstrations proved fruitless and the Movement dissolved into greater chaos and anarchy, James would ask me for reports about what was going on with us young people. Once, when I called and asked him what he was doing, he said, slowly, "I'm sitting at my window listening to the civilization cracking outside." I like to remember one evening when I had returned from a particularly riotous day in the streets after the government had committed some even grosser atrocity than usual. James called and he said, kidding in his languid, playful tone, "Jerry, when the real revolution begins, tell your friends not to worry about the *New York Times*. I'll take care of that."

331

I shared a long complicitous laugh with him, just thinking of the absurdity of this fine novelist and gentle man, who had been so kind to me, joking about behaving in such a manner. Yet I did know that if the *Times* were to go out of business tomorrow, James wouldn't mind.

THE WRITER AS SEER

I was preoccupied with the question of seeing. It seemed to me that what you saw, on acid or not, was to a degree a function of how honestly you lived. The more you acted against your principles, the greater would be the tendency to repress the memories of these acts and to become unconscious. This was especially important to me because I was now seriously thinking about becoming a writer. I couldn't forget my foreboding at the Pentagon that the Government was going to shoot down trusting students. I wanted to write a novel to warn them. I was boiling over with feelings that couldn't be contained in the pressure cooker of my day life—the dissertation writing and the studying to be a future lit professor.

Joseph Conrad had said that he wrote to make people see. This was a statement out of the age of modernism with its sense that there was a correct way to see. This viewpoint was too comprehensive and overbearing for my generation. There had been too much murder and too many atrocities committed in the name of the "correct" ideology (or "novel") in the twentieth century. We were moving toward a multi-cultural post-modernism, a complementarity of opposing visions. The world was too small now for fundamentalist beliefs of any kind (even science), ego notions that one was possessed of the single correct way of understanding the world: The True Novel.

I was thinking in terms of novels now. Physicists tended to see things, even non-scientific subjects, in terms of relativity and uncertainty, biologists saw evolution everywhere—social evolution, evolution of thought, etc.— and I was seeing the world as a battle of "novels" to inform the imagination of mankind: the Jewish novel, the Christian novel, Islamic novel, Hindu, scientific, atheistic, and so on.

Nonetheless, Conrad had been basically right: the novelist was paid to see. (Which is why so many drank.) The novelist was a descendent of the shaman. Along with the psychiatrist, physician, poet, minister, historian, drug-dealer, etc. The shaman was the first specialist. His job was to preserve the culture's past, to watch over and pass down its forms, its stories and founding myths, its pathways to the Gods. To heal with medicines, both those that were direct acting and those psychedelic. To heal the whole person. (The word "heal" descends from the word "whole.")

I was beginning to think of myself as a shaman stuck in a sitcom. The world was too small and precarious now for single vision and Newton's sleep. I liked the honest stance of the novelist who admitted from the start that his vision was personal and idiosyncratic. Seeing the pre-scientific "primitives" as deluded barbarians was no longer possible. We had to raise our consciousness as much as we had raised the level of our weapons. That was our only hope.

But why couldn't people already see? There is a story where a person comes to the Buddha and asks him for his philosophy. The Buddha says, "I'll tell you but first go out and find a person who hasn't suffered deeply in life." The man returns after a couple years having failed to find anyone. The Buddha says, "OK, that's the first lesson."

The Buddhists situated this problem in desire. Life was suffering, but suffering had a cause and a cure. The cause was desire, selfish craving, ultimately based on the desire to live forever in the same personality. (As Timothy Leary joked, how many times did you want to see John Denver appearing in Las Vegas?) Their solution was the noble eight-fold path—basically right thinking, right meditation, right behavior, and right livelihood. The last was especially important. If your daily work didn't fit your principles, didn't in some way avoid contributing to human suffering, then you would not see clearly and would feel anxiety—you'd be serving your separate, selfish ego (or, as the Taoists saw it, you'd be out of synch with the Tao, the Way.)

This coincided precisely with my desire to leave the main culture's economy with its selfish grasping and its attachment to material advancement, both of which interfered with perception—if you drove a gas guzzler, it would be difficult to see America's foreign policy clearly. But wasn't my motivation, though admirable, still based on desire?

CIRCLE IN THE SQUARE

We are now returning to the starting point on the traffic circle of this narrative thus far, the telephone call from Robert Gottlieb, and it is time to discuss my path as a novelist. Shortly after my dissertation was accepted, in the fall of 1969, I began to write a novel. My original plan had been to teach, but I realized that I had a chance now, with the liquor store providing a small income, to attempt life outside the steel structure of institutions. I burned to drop out, to try my hand at a novel.

In writing my dissertation, I had familiarized myself with much of offbeat contemporary fiction. We young people had selected those authors, mostly from World War II, Salinger, Kerouac, Vonnegut, Heller, etc., who had seen through the common assumptions of their war and projected a sensibility that was, in many respects, congruous with our own. But wasn't it time to actually write about the momentous events that were occurring in reference to *our* war?

How to begin? The primary injunction for any behavior at that time was that it not sleepily follow the contours offered by the majority culture. Jesus had admonished us not to put new wine in old bottles. For the young novelist, the old bottle was a small, straight-ahead, autobiographical coming-of-age high school or college novel. This was out of the question.

Events were too huge, mad, jagged and dangerous to be stuffed into that innocent Christmas stocking. The government was going to shoot the students. Someone had to warn them. This was a time when anyone thinking about large events and major changes turned to books. We were, perhaps, the last generation that took our problems to the bookstores; we dragged out piles of books (including novels) that might help us conceptualize the matter and put us in touch with a long tradition of dissenting thinking that we respected. The novelists were our big-brothers and sisters. They had suffered and passed down their advice. They were not selling soap like the pundits on TV.

A battle was being fought for the imagination of the world. From one angle this could be a definition of culture: a set of forms for the imagination. Certain novelists and publishers seemed to a degree to be outside the deadly colas that saturated the corporate media. Many of the publishers were small businesses, still owned by the founders who started them with ideals that were beyond the marketplace. This was before Disney and Sea World and Viacom Cable TV and AOL and Rupert Murdoch had bought up the publishers. The word was you could still go to an editor's office after work and have a drink with William Faulkner and Malcolm Cowley. [I couldn't have dreamed that shortly before he died, Malcolm Cowley would write to me that he had enjoyed *The Carmen Miranda Memorial Flagpole*.]

Flannery O'Connor wrote that in the country of the blind you had to speak in large, exaggerated images. I decided to write a kind of dark satire, *Blues for a Dying Nation*, with exaggerated events that clarified the absurdities and outrages of our lives. I wanted to attack the Army using my experience as an officer. Strangely, I discovered that I hardly needed to exaggerate. Seen on the page, much of the daily behavior I had witnessed about me was ludicrous and almost psychotic. I portrayed the Army as a matriarchy, with the hospital run by the colonel's mother who terrified him. But this had actually been the case in my hospital, where I, as troop commander, had been given orders on how to run my detachment by the colonel's elderly mother who resided on a ward.

I did exaggerate when I had the general of the base believe that we were still fighting the Japanese, but this seemed metaphorically accurate as the Army did seem to be thinking in World War II terms and hence losing the war in Vietnam. I had the colonel, a physician who was the hospital commander, take over the fort and begin to bomb and shell the surrounding countryside because he believed it had been infiltrated by Communists. (This was in Massachusetts.) When my lieutenant tells the senile general about this, the general says approvingly, "That's the toughest decision an officer has to make. To bring artillery fire in on his own troops."

The hospital commander sends out helicopters to strafe the citizens. He says you can tell they're the enemy if they run. Sure enough, after several strafing incidents, the "enemy" does appear, since everyone begins to run. Then, as a cost-cutting measure, the colonel uses combat helicopters as med-evac helicopters as well. First the choppers shoot rockets into the local towns, then they strafe the local citizens, then they land and give the wounded and dying the finest medical care in the world. Only the young people object. They dress as American Indians, they revive the ancient

American Indian ceremonies, call themselves the "B.C." and they attack the base. The Army mercilessly shoots them down.

At this time, especially due to the writings of Marshall McLuhan, there was a fear that print was losing its influence. Too slow for the postmodern sensibility. People were programmed to expect the speed and entertainment values of TV. I attempted to co-opt TV. I would write the book in the form of a televised football game. Quarters instead of chapters. I would have "commercials," but for the government. This is how I saw the evening news, which would show an event and then have an authority figure from the administration put his spin on it. Then the shows with discussion panels would boil it down until it was limp and palatable for those without teeth.

Satire was based on exaggeration but how could one exaggerate reality any longer? I made up outrageous acts of violence and irrationality, acts which broke through the filtered TV vision of the world, and then, just when people were about to say, "That's ridiculous, impossible," I would paste in a little filler item from the *New York Times* that showed a similar incredible occurrence, only this one was true; I used these clippings as footnotes to authenticate the possibilities tossed up by my imagination. I believed these filler items told the true story of the collapse of our culture.

I interrupted the novel to switch between three "cameras" I used to "televise" the show: Camera One was Close Up, written in the present tense. Camera Two was Medium Shot, simple narrative past tense. Camera Three was a long shot, an overview or summary in the past tense.

In doing this I was following John Dos Passos who, in his great trilogy, *USA*, kept interrupting the narrative and pushing you out of your suspension of disbelief, trashing your identification with the characters just as you were beginning to forget this was a novel, an artificial creation of a writer who was maneuvering the action and puppets. That was the point, to keep people from getting completely involved and believing they were looking out a window on reality. For what was a culture but an imagined approach to "reality"? We had to expose how every view of life was imagined, mediated, somewhat arbitrary. Perhaps "reality" could be changed by transforming the way we *imagined* it. This was the job of the artist. Art had a revolutionary function.

Brecht had done this in his plays, showing the created, artificial nature of the work so the viewers would have some objective distance and they could judge it less emotionally. But I wanted to evoke emotion, I wanted the readers to identify with the characters and to be moved but also to know there was a person doing this to them, taking them on a trip, that this wasn't "real." There was something Buddhist or Hindu about this: To watch oneself watching the world even when being moved by it. Cold eye, warm heart. Perhaps the readers would see that their normal manner of perceiving and presenting "reality" was also being spun, but by those in power in their own interests. It wasn't that there was no reality. But rather that reality was like a kind of Connect the Dots game, where you had to touch each of the dots, but there were many ways and shapes of lines with which to do it. In the end there were only novels. There was always someone with interests pulling the wires above the stage.

Later, the Italian critic Franco Minganti would say that my books had a "depth of surface." This is what I was after. I believed that you could interrupt the narrative repeatedly, but in spite of this attack on the reader's suspension of disbelief, the reader would fight back, she would want to feel and believe, and thus you could still move the reader and energize her. Hadn't Cezanne done this? His paintings were still beautiful even as they came up toward the surface, acknowledging the two-dimensional aspect of the canvas. (In my second novel, *The Carmen Miranda Memorial Flagpole*, a tragedy about the end of the Sixties that was my most popular book with both the critics and the public, I had the characters speaking in one-line jokes (also a way of bringing the work up to the surface in painters' terms), but I found that many readers were still able to feel the depths of the novel. (One friend of mine, a woman Swami, Vimalananda, was left weeping in a café when she reached the end.)

I was following what the Russian critics like Bakhtin called "defamiliarizing" the encounter between the spectator and the work of art. I wanted to defamiliarize the assumptions about media and the perception of the everyday world.

Some of the fiction writers, particularly those in the Fiction Collective, were traveling this road, following the influence of the best of this group, Gilbert Sorentino (*Imaginative Qualities of Actual Things*) who was writing in the tradition that led back to the Irishman of the Thirties, Flann O'Brien (*At Swim-Two-Birds*), to Laurence Sterne in the eighteenth century, and even to Miguel Cervantes. At its avant-garde extreme this view could lead to the point where the novel was seen as being only about words (an angle more useful to poets, I thought) just as paintings were only about paint. But the Fiction Collective tended toward books that were thinly intellectual. They began on the surface and stayed there. Often the reader got the point and then had no reason to read the book.

Sometimes these writers fell off the common sense world and became entangled in the net of pure theory. One of their leaders, Ron Sukenick, questioned the assumptions behind the structure of the old novel, saying that the novel had to change because we no longer believed in the assumptions about reality that the traditional novel was built upon. This claim was true to a degree, but Sukenick, in his "real" life, turned toward Washington, joined committees, dispensed grants, networked at the source of grants and fellowships and this worked for him in a way, as he landed government support for his little magazine and three different year-long grants from the NEA. His recent ex-wife was also given a major fellowship. For a while he was largely being supported by the NEA. When the fine critic Jerome Klinkowitz told me that Sukenick had declared that time and space no longer existed, reality no longer existed, cause and effect didn't exist and the self didn't exist, I replied, "Well that's all fine, but what's he going to do if he finds out someday that the NEA doesn't exist?" [Later I heard that he wound up with a house in Colorado, apartments in Trump Tower and in Paris, and a drinking problem.]

(Whenever anyone says there is no cause and effect, I reach for a bottle of iodine and say, "Here, drink this, maybe it will make you feel good.") It seemed to me there was something grievously inauthentic about this. There *was* a place from which you could see that all these fixed points and orientations didn't really exist forever, but if you attempted to honestly live this truth then you would be navigating through your day-to-day life on an acid trip, and that was surely not the case for those directing their attentions to networking in Washington and copping grants and awards. I felt the novel had to acknowledge that we did know these new truths, but that we were also condemned to live in the shared diurnal world of time and space. There was an acid world I had visited in which money was merely green pieces of paper, and it was hilarious that everyone desperately devoted their lives to collecting them, and that these green papers were driving the desire of the entire world. Yet these notions didn't help when you saw people living in sardine cans with their unshod children on the edges of third world cities.

I always thought that words were more inherently referential than paint; nonetheless, these writers did have a point. We had to keep reminding people that all propositions and statements were provisional by nature, that the received world was already processed by the imagination (the cultural hypnosis), because to really alter the world we had to reveal the hidden assumptions beneath the acceptable way of imagining it.

Blues For A Dying Nation was soaked in hot anger and disgust. I actually felt like I wanted to throw the book at the reader when I finished. This was far from the intellectualism of many of those working in this tradition of self-referential, self-reflexive novels which fore-grounded the author, his technique, and the fact that the novel was an artifact, a product of the imagination.

> *"My erudition is no doubt an aspect of my ignorance."*
> Guillame Apollinaire

Since I had never studied writing or written more than a couple stories for my own edification, I thought the actual writing might be difficult and would proceed in staggered fits and starts like trying to drive a VW Bug up a too steep hill in the snow.

Quite the contrary. Once I began, the process was more akin to learning to ski down a too-steep slope. I felt if I stopped I would crash and lose it all. I was swept away on a tide of a wild logorrhea of learning, enthusiasm, jokes and spite. I wrote in longhand, scrawling to keep up with the words and images that flooded through me. I worked from morning to night. After six weeks I had finished the rough initial manuscript for what would become a double-spaced typescript of almost 600 pages. Then I collapsed with the flu. After two weeks, I rose and began again.

Eight weeks later I was finished with a second (typed) draft. Shortly after I recovered my balance, Elizabeth Long showed up and took the manuscript with her up to Knopf. I Xeroxed it but I gave her the original, the one with the actual clippings from the *Times* pasted onto the pages. I liked the collage effect. Braque and Picasso also used newspaper clippings; it broke down the plane between the work of the imagination and the world

(even physically because of the clipping being actually pasted on top of the two dimensional page.)

Since I was an unknown who desired to be taken seriously, and the culture confused erudition with wisdom, I put everything in the book but the kitchen sink (and I would have included the sink as well if we had a spare). I had no idea how one packed a manuscript. I bought a gray, metal, file box, about the size of the manuscript, threw out the file folders, and laid the manuscript inside. It slid down the wall and sagged there like a dead fish. But I couldn't think of an alternative.

After giving the manuscript to Liz, I returned to my "normal" life, swollen with a great feeling of satisfaction. I had written a novel. It wouldn't see print, but I would always have the manuscript and I would glow with the honor of having tried my hand at the noble task of changing the world by writing a book. I had felt like Tolstoy at times in my mania, the words spilling down through my Bic ball-point pen. I could imagine a kind of electromagnetic field that surrounded the earth, an invisible "harp' in which each mind participated, and I was reaching out to it, bending and shaping it, trying to make a beautiful music that would change the mental grid of the world. (I had written the first draft using the cheapest pen available. I loved the Quixotic idea of attempting to change the world armed with only a nineteen cent pen and the cheapest pads of paper.)

I had no idea that my wild manuscript was being read by the likes of Robert Gottlieb and Joseph Heller.

I yearned to get back to my adventures with LSD.

STRING THEORY AND VIOLINS

> *"life is a luminous halo, a semi-transparent envelope surrounding us from the beginning of consciousness to the end."*
>
> Virginia Woolf

How had I gotten so far out? Even political radicals like Noam Chomsky and Ralph Nader still appear to accept the culture's definition of reality without questioning it. Even a great writer like Virginia Woolf, so valiant and brilliant in questioning the hidden assumptions of our culture, in the statement above assumed along with the culture that consciousness has an end without seeming to realize this was an assumption. (Perhaps this had something to do with her mental illness.)

If you saw a headline in the newspaper tomorrow that scientists, using string theory, had succeeded in coming up with a Unified Field Theory, a "Theory of Everything," would it matter? Would it help get your kid out of jail or explain why your mother just tore up her long-term care policy after paying for it for twenty years? Would it convince the U.S. to get out of the country in which they were fighting the latest of the Indian Wars?

In fact, what we are witnessing in our chaotic world is a kind of return of the repressed. Everything science decided to ignore in its original assumptions is crawling out from under the nylon carpet. It turns out that in a theory of everything, "everything" means "everything that can be measured," or "everything that we scientists can possibly understand within the assumptions and exclusions of our initial viewpoint."

> *"the universe is dying, and eventually the Big Freeze will kill off all intelligent life forms. This had theological implications because what is the meaning of life if all life is doomed to freeze by the laws of physics?"*
>
> Physicist Michio Kaku

Professor Kaku, one of the furthest-out of the distinguished physicists, like virtually all scientists (including Nobel Prize physicist Steven Weinberg who writes on science and philosophy from a militantly materialist standpoint for the *New York Review of Books*) simply assumes that the viewpoint of the scientific culture about what is possible or real isn't an assumption. I don't want to single out Professor Kaku whom I respect; I quote his statement because its unconscious assumptions are typical of virtually all brilliant scientists. I could have quoted many others.

Professor Kaku can imagine that we might travel to another universe next door in a billion years and escape the big freeze. But beneath these types of statements is the idea that a billion years from now science will still be focusing on the objective world that we can see and touch and perform repeatable experiments upon, and that this will still be the only world that can be considered as real. There is not a sliver of thought given to other pictures of reality, to the realms of thought in which the earth is more like an idea than a thing, or a dream from another level of reality, or a dream within a dream, infinite dreams, or that there are other levels of intelligence creating all this, or that someday life, including ourselves, may exist on other planes where this universe is just a forgotten memory. [I would have trouble believing this if I hadn't seen it myself, but it helps to remember that of the thousands of cultures in history, our modern secular culture is virtually alone in having lost access to these possibilities.]

Yet physicists, and so many who follow the scientific road, take it for granted that the measurable reality is the only reality and not merely an assumption based on the values of a particular culture at a specific time, much less do they understand that this angle of vision leads to a shallow, impoverished world view in which most people are drastically unhappy, willing to dull their senses with various medications and addictions rather than live with the dead end implications of the modern scientific view. The truth is we are already frozen inside; that is why the universe seems dead to us and why these long term entropy hypotheses seem eminently reasonable. (Just as most people who choose cryonic suspension after death are already frozen in a part of themselves.)

The big-bang is called a "singularity," a point where the equations fail and the mathematics break down, but I would suggest it is a point where our scientific models break down and the hidden assumptions beneath them are revealed. (In a similar manner one could say that a chronic bad back is often a kind of "singularity," where allopathic medicine breaks down and the hidden assumptions behind it, of a separation between mind and body, are exposed.)

> *"Prepare thyself, for thou wilt have to travel on alone.*
> *The teacher can but point the way."*
>
> *The Voice of Silence*

Early in 1970 I decided to go out there again. The acid space. Trying to get there on pot, however interesting and helpful, was like trying to go into space in an airplane. I needed to go back to the real thing. To the infinite risk.

I am a control freak. It was self-control that got me out of The Bronx. Acid was the ultimate letting go. It terrified me. Yet I was attracted to loss of control. And to people who had less self-control than I did.

I needed to go back to the space I found in Massachusetts. As I thought about my first acid trip, when Charlotte and I were Gods, I had come to the conclusion that I had been in the space where the ancient Egyptians had stopped. Of course the Pharaoh would marry his sister. They were Isis and Osiris, eternal Gods, spending some time in the earth dream.

THE TALE OF THE TIGER

> *"All things are always changing,*
> *but nothing dies . . . "*
>
> Ovid

I dropped a purple tab of acid at 2:40 pm. I began by nervously scribbling down my feelings and speculations while waiting for the medicine to come on. Trying to stay in control. Here are a few notes written while I was on the trip:

> *3:05- I feel lighted up. The lights are brighter. Maybe the speed, if there is any in the acid, has already taken effect.*

> *3:20- Maybe this will be a Zen trip. Oh, it will, I feel it. Religion isn't so somber. It is re-ligio, re-linking up with the joy of the universe, which the harried creatures around us can't face because they don't think they deserve it.*

This is followed by babble and theories about everything. I played "Sergeant Pepper."

> *Things are beginning to happen. My hands are losing their color. God loves me. I feel nervously happy. Like on the roller coaster, "Here we go . . . "*
> *Because God loves all of his children, the good and the bad, then the more people we can love, the more we are like God.*

The Devil is God's fool.

How gentle this drug is. How slowly it takes you up. How considerate, the hours it takes to take you out there.

The world is a conspiracy against freedom, space and joy. You'll be arrested for being too happy. It is <u>the world</u> which is sorrow. It is the world which has been constructed to teach us the Buddha lesson of sorrow. Actually, Reality is proportionate to beauty. Plato was right.

3:55- Up to now I've still been on earth. Now I am entering a different world. Strobe lights are flashing. Shadows move on their own. Here, you know this world is only imagination, but you know <u>everything</u> is only imagination. The earth is imagination frozen in a single mold. It's not that the earth is a dream, but simply one form of the imagination. The static world is not more real than the fluid. It is one frame of the movie. There is no such thing as "<u>only</u> imagination."

Later- Questions belong in the earth world. That's why we have no "answer" out here in space. The real truth is that the deepest and most significant questions on earth have no meaning here.

Out here there is no "merely." "Merely" is the same as "really." It is possible to continue to live on the earth but it requires empathy. That is the difference between the saint and the madman. The saint can understand what people on purgatory (earth) are thinking. He can empathize with them. The madman cannot.

Ah the bliss!!! There is too much bliss!!!! Nothing can scare me.

The visionary must understand that his visions of ecstasy somehow, unbelievably, will be misunderstood by other people, and will scare them.

The earth exists not on a time-space continuum, but on a continuum of possibility.

Intelligence is an earth concept. The real question is who

knows and who doesn't? Who knows that Reality is boundless
and boundlessly lovely?
It's so much easier the second time. You pass a point where
you realize that the other world really is! More and more
trouble to think of earth. The diamonds here are real!

At this point I began to realize that I wasn't going to the same places as the first trip. That I knew little about LSD. That I had handed over the controls. I began to look around for Charlotte in space and I found that I was alone. I felt fine, but I was alone. And then I thought about the Hindu maxim: "Thou art That." *You* are what you are looking for. But then I made a big mistake. I confused Thou with my ego. I began to think this maxim meant that I had imagined the whole world. Not Charlotte and Myself. Just *me*! The trip had taken an unexpected and possibly bad turn. I was lost somewhere in space or in a dream space. I could still think. But I had left the freeway. I began to get worried. Was this death from the earth point of view? Had I died? Maybe the bubble had burst and the earth dream was over and I was alone, forever. I was really becoming frightened. I ransacked my learning for help. I remembered what Sartre said in *No Exit*: "Hell is other people." I was getting more frightened. I thought maybe Sartre had it wrong. Maybe Hell was the lack of other people. I didn't know how to proceed. Here's where I paid for my hatred and fear of authority which had kept me from getting help from more experienced travelers. A couple years later I would describe this moment to a Swami visiting from India, "I thought I was supposed to realize that I was God," and he smiled and said, "You are God, but only in the way a ring is gold."

I had let go of the whole world, the whole created universe and everyone in it. I began to sweat and shiver. I felt the chill of dying. Dying to my earth life. Lost and alone forever. Not merely for a million years. The Terminal at the end of the Solipsism Subway. The earth dream had burst. I had let go of everything. I had created the Earth dream to assuage my loneliness and now it was gone. The Jerry Rosen Show was over forever.

But what about Charlotte? And my brother and my mother and my friends. They needed me to bring back these messages and ultimate questions. They needed me on earth. I had to return. I began to shiver. Scared and lonely and cold. I didn't know what to do. And then, without thinking about it, somehow I began to chant softly, "Lord Buddha help me," quietly repeating it, "Lord Buddha help me, Lord Krishna help me, Lady Tara help me, Lady Kwan Yin help me, I take refuge in the Buddha, I take refuge in the Dharma . . ." Slowly, turning my life over to them, letting go of control, I began to feel better and to come down to the familiar spaceship. The Earth.

As I returned, I realized with a shudder how far I had traveled. Of course I wasn't at the ultimate goal yet: Beyond death. I knew death was the only partner worth dancing with for a lifetime. But was the dance a tragic moon-tango, or a shining golden samba with the sun? I was confused and shaken. But I had to go on. I had taken a wrong turn somewhere but I was on the right path, the ancient road. Accessing the old starry information. And there was no stability to return to in any case. Every trip in the old culture led to a dead end.

Somehow, I also felt brave. I had gone out into the space as large as dreams and returned alive. I still felt loved and supported by the universe. I knew there had to be a way to proceed. I was just beginning the great voyage. I thought of what Timothy Leary had said: "Trust the process. Don't make life-changing decisions while on acid."

Yes, I felt puzzled and lonely, but by God I also felt powerful and blessed. And determined to continue. Wisdom or death! There was no alternative. Freedom or death!

"Once you take a tiger by the tail, there's no letting go."
Zen Saying

I saw Charlotte standing there, in our spongy, breathing, living room, watching me cautiously. She offered me a beer. I began to tell her what had happened, excitedly, how I had almost died but that I realized people need me, my mother needed me, my brother Mark needed me, on and on. What I didn't understand yet was that it was I who still needed them.

I had not yet realized that there is a place in which you are beyond all need.

346

THE BIG TIME

"It is a curious anomaly that we listen to jazz, we look at modern paintings, we live in houses of modern design, we travel in jet planes, yet we continue to read novels written in tempo and style which is not of our time . . . "

Anais Nin

My usual approach-avoidance conflict over success and fame was coming to the surface again. Of course celebrity was the common coin of the realm, more fungible than money, exchangeable anywhere for all the goods and services people would gladly provide, but didn't it also lead one closer to the dangerous radiation from the social power lines?

On a Thursday in February, 1970, I went up to meet with Robert Gottlieb. His office was high in a new skyscraper over on the East Side of midtown on Publishers' Row that ran along Third Avenue. I believe Knopf had recently moved there, perhaps in connection with their being purchased by Random House.

Liz Long, who was always a good friend, (now Chair of Sociology at Rice University), had revealed to me that Bob Gottlieb had compared my manuscript to the early work of Bruce Jay Friedman and Ken Kesey, but I still felt uncomfortable going into "enemy territory," the country of big corporations and hierarchies so large that even secretaries had secretaries. I didn't know what to wear. I didn't belong above Fourteenth Street. I wasn't so much nervous as tight and wary.

When I was brought to his office Robert Gottlieb surprised me. He came out and greeted me. He was shorter than I had envisioned. I had somehow expected an imaginary Maxwell Perkins, an elderly editor of the old school, tall, lean, with a Protestant tweed jacket and an unlit professor's pipe in his mouth. Gottlieb was wearing a crew neck sweater. He wasn't that much older than I was. Of course, I suddenly realized, his name was Gottlieb, probably Jewish, and was called "the boy wonder." Still he seemed younger than his years, more like a graduate assistant at Columbia, which I knew from Liz Long, had been his university.

His large, bright, round eyes shone, wide-open and intelligent. You could see the light of intellect in them, looking right at you. The fact that he was young and smart somehow gave me confidence. In those days it wasn't clear whether having power in the society and wearing nice clothes was a sign of strength or weakness. Liz Long had told me, laughing, that Gottlieb was intrigued by me because he had always been able to pigeon-hole manuscripts and he wasn't sure where to place me.

He showed me around his modern office, surrounded by windows looking over midtown Manhattan. His office was slightly larger than my apartment, lightly furnished, uncluttered. I complimented him on the view. He said that it took some getting used to because the building was designed to sway in the wind for stability and it was unnerving at times to feel yourself moving at that height. Still wary, I wondered to myself if that was a sign of prestige—to have your office move further than another person's because you were so high up.

I kept thinking that maybe this was the scene in my life movie where someone in power says, "Boy, I'm gonna make you a star," and I sell out. I knew from the movies that selling out was the result of many incremental decisions you made before you realized you were sliding down the slippery slope to being accepted and rendered harmless.

Yet I enjoyed being with Gottlieb. I liked talking to intelligent people; you might disagree with them, but at least they understood you and you could learn from them. I didn't want to admit this in the land of overrated IQs and smart spin doctors, but it was the truth.

As he moved toward his desk and guided me to a seat across from him, he said, "Have you ever read *The Brothers Karamazov?*"

"Yes."

"That was a great book," he said, taking his chair. Then he added with a sly twinkle, "I just read it again this weekend. I kept thinking, this book is really good, but it could have been so much better if I'd had a chance to edit it."

I smiled. I wasn't sure what to say. I did know what he was telling me: This is the big time. High up in the food chain. We don't have any idols here.

I thought to myself that perhaps he could have improved it, nipped and tucked to make it move more quickly, but I wasn't sure what the side effects of that treatment would be.

I read your book," he said. "We've never had a book submitted in a file box before." He smiled. I smiled, too. I thought I was his secret sharer in a way. Acting out for him.

"I liked it," he said. "But I can't publish it as it is. I need to ask for some changes. I think it could be a good book, but you'll have to re-write it under my guidance."

I thought, here we go. The Big Sellout! I had been compromising all my life. This book was finally the product of my unhindered feeling and thought. This was to be the one thing I did in my life that was for myself, true to my soul.

"In what way?"

He thought for a second. "You have to make a novel of it."

"Who decides what a novel is?" I said quickly.

He couldn't resist a small smile. "I think you know what I mean."

I did know. Take out all the interruptions, the crazy exaggerations, the authorial interjections like where the hero's Jewish mother calls and he tells her, "You can call all day, you're not getting into my novel." He tells her to call Philip Roth. That kind of thing. I knew he wanted me to make the characters more credible and developed rather than cartoon-like. He wanted to create a book that was more accessible, more saleable, maybe even better in a way, but it wouldn't be my book. There was a difference between us. I couldn't put my finger on it right then, I wasn't ready to see it, but the truth was that just as I was reaching a pinnacle of success that was beyond my most extravagant American dreams, there was no longer a common ground between myself and the mainline audience.

"You know," he said, "one thing I can tell you is that you can't take a central character and drop her for a hundred pages and then just pick her up again as if nothing had happened."

I knew he was referring to my character Cali, the woman Army officer. And he was right. I hadn't thought of that. I knew he could help me. He was being very generous to a crazy guy like me. He did see that I had written something special though unformed. But I didn't want to make it into a "novel."

When I didn't answer for a while, he said, "You know Joe feels the same way I do. We talked it over. If you call him, he'll tell you the same thing. You want to call him and ask him yourself?" He reached for Heller's number.

"No, no, it's OK. I believe you." The thought of calling Heller frightened me. "It's just that I'm not sure exactly what you want."

I didn't say that I felt that I wasn't sure he knew what he wanted. I wasn't sure I could give it to him. I might be entering a long process that would lead nowhere. On some deep level we weren't in the same world anymore. I didn't think he could imagine that I was sitting there wondering whether I had created the world and had created this drama with him to pass the time and loneliness of eternity by myself. The end-zone of fantasies.

He was at home in the world. He was completely on earth. I could see why he was successful and I respected him. This interview was forcing me to face how far out I had gone.

The system was ultimately based on murder. After years of trying to get my old shoe in the door, the door was opening and I wasn't sure I wanted to enter. What would be the soul price? Of course, I understood what I would be giving up by turning him down. He was holding an endorsement from Joseph Heller in front of me, along with the backing and advertising and attention and reviews that having Bob Gottlieb behind the book would guarantee. It wasn't a chance in a million. It was a chance in a hundred million.

He saw my indecision. He saw everything that was going on in front of him. I was more spaced out than he. I was preoccupied with spacey visions in which this moment was a moral turning point in the journey of my soul, a drama situated in a dream that was somehow real to a degree. .

"Listen, Jerry," he said in a friendly tone, "why don't you go home and consider this?" He stood up. I rose as well. I understood that the interview was over. We moved toward the door. "Why don't you think it over. Maybe rewrite a chapter or two at the beginning and show it to me. If I feel that you're honestly trying and that we can work together, I'll write you a contract."

I was startled by this. He was actually at the point of thinking about contracts. He wanted to work with me like he had worked with Joe Heller on *Catch 22* for seven years. But I didn't want to work on the book for seven years. I wanted it out now so that young people would be moved by it, so I would have a voice in what was going on, so I could share my vision with others, so that young people would know that the government was going to shoot them down like dogs in the street.

Yet he was right, I ought to go home and think all this over. At the door to his office he held out his hand and smiled and I shook it. He looked me in the eye and said, "I can name three or four editors right now here in New York who would take this book as it is and publish it. But I won't do it. Not like it is. So think over my offer and let me know what you decide."

I marveled at how honest and considerate he was being to me. He was giving me the opportunity of a lifetime. I liked him and I appreciated it. But I knew that my job was to find one of those editors he had mentioned, an editor who would publish my book as I had written it.

> *"We've got to rip the old veil of a vision across, and
> find what the heart really believes in, after all . . ."*
>
> D.H. Lawrence

I gave the manuscript to my friend Malcolm Harkness, a member of the distinguished Harkness family of New York. (The Harkness Ballet, etc.) Malcolm was living in a tenement in the East Village. He had studied creative writing with Edward Albee at the University of Connecticut, and taken an MFA at Columbia. Now he was tripping and had become a public typist.

That was how I had met him. He had placed an ad in the *Village Voice* and I had hired him to type the clean copy of my dissertation. Malcolm was an excellent typist among other skills, and he edited and proofread as he went along. And being a full-fledged dropout and brilliant member of the counterculture, he didn't charge very much.

He was particularly interested in my dissertation because he was a fan of James Purdy. He had become interested in Purdy because of Purdy's novel, *Malcolm*. He had even corresponded with Purdy. Malcolm was often on acid. It was inevitable that we would become friends.

He lived in a tiny dump. His window was situated beside the stone stoop. He had painted the window black. He had created his own world, a moon of Jupiter, a world without daylight but not without illumination. Malcolm had surrounded himself with fish tanks around all the walls. They glowed eerily. You didn't have to know whether it was day or night outside. You didn't have to be attuned to that outside world at all.

After the dissertation was typed I would often walk over and take a cup of tea with Malcolm in the darkness amidst the humming tanks and magnificent tropical creatures. Malcolm was a couple years older than I, pale, not a large man, with long, straight black hair and funky clothing. Always bright and funny. Because of his family background he knew a lot more about the Manhattan publishing and intellectual world than I did. Often we talked about acid. Malcolm said that Edward Albee would come up to Connecticut on the train, loaded on acid, wearing all these glowing rings. That once Albee had taken acid with his students. It was hard to tell whether these stories were one hundred percent accurate or whether they were extrapolations of reality, colored somewhat by Malcolm's awed affection for Albee, for fabulous stories, and for fabulous characters in general, but I had no doubt they were substantially true. Once Malcolm pointed to a large imposing electrical plug that stood out from the wall where it sat in an electrical outlet: "I was on acid here with a couple friends. We were really out there, and we became convinced that that plug was our lifeline to the world, that if we pulled out the plug, we would die. We looked at each other, and even on acid, we all said, this is ridiculous, but when we dared each other to pull it out, none of us would do it."

Malcolm was a kind person; when I told him the Gottlieb story, and asked him how to proceed, he stepped forward and said he would do it for me. He would take the manuscript to Farrar, Strauss. That was a perfect solution for me. Now my problem was enduring the waiting until they responded. That was always the problem, the one that novelists shared with soldiers. The interminable waiting.

> *"Had I not seen the sun*
> *I could have bourne the shade"*
>
> Emily Dickinson

I began to take acid every few weeks. I wanted to give myself time between trips to integrate what I learned and to be able to function in the world again.

I did know that nothing I saw out there, no conclusion about reality that I drew, was going to make me agree that the war was right, or make me indifferent to opposing it.

My brother Mark was in the Army in Washington now, an officer in JAG. He and Lucy had a child, Lauren, and were trying to live a normal life in the chaotic time. Mark and Lucy always tried to do the right thing, to give something back to others. They opposed the war but because Mark was an Army Officer it was illegal for him to protest. In Army logic, if they caught you, they would send you to Vietnam "to get a closer look, Ha Ha." One day he had quietly slipped into a Washington peace march and soon bumped into his boss, the Colonel, who was returning from shopping. Mark pretended he was crossing the street and had been swept into the march. It wasn't clear that the Colonel believed him. Mark then had a better idea. He volunteered to be a neutral legal aid and mediator for the marches. The government had many more lawyers than the protestors, so this gave him the chance to insure that the marchers were treated fairly regarding permits, arrests and so forth. Lucy opened her house to us. When I myself, or Charlotte and I, came down to a protest, we would camp all weekend at their place.

In the summer of 1969, my dissertation had been accepted. For the first time since I was five, I was free. I had been growing progressively further from the academic mindset. Once, angry at the delays in responding by my advisors at Penn, I had gone up to the Whitney Museum where our professional organization, the American Studies Association, was having their annual meeting in conjunction with a show of American Art of the 1930s. I felt uncomfortable in the stuffy atmosphere. There was something abstract, self-important and involuted about the meeting, in comparison to the energy in the streets, the riots, drugs and rock. I repaired to the makeshift bar and joined in slurping down the white wine with an older man who looked out of place. It turned out he was one of the artists in the show and was going to speak.

The professors organized themselves, made some speeches and voted in a new president who proceeded to move some chairs so they could set up the slide projector. Drunk now, I said aloud, sarcastically, "I knew the president had *some* duties!" Everyone ignored me. I found that I had much more in common with the artist seated next to me. He was drunk as well. When it came time for him to address the members, he insulted them all. I laughed like crazy but no one else joined me.

I remembered what Barnett Newman had said when asked if he cared about the critics: "As much as the birds care about ornithologists."

I thought back to the Columbia riots. I had been following a course in Modern American History on educational TV at the time. Taught by Professor James Shenton of Columbia. I knew the material but I was curious about how he would present it and why he was the one picked for this important assignment. He was a nice guy, Professor Shenton, well meaning. When the Columbia administration had unleashed the police to remove the students and the protest had turned into a bloody police riot, I saw Professor Shenton on the evening news. He had been a kind of marshal, an intermediary. Now he was weeping as they carted the bleeding students off to the hospitals and jails. He kept saying, "Who could have imagined this? Who could have thought the police would beat the students like that?" He could barely talk. It was very moving to see him. But I thought, "I could have imagined it. Anyone who had any idea of what's been going on could have imagined it." I liked Shenton, he was a decent man and a good historian, but I saw that to be chosen to interpret recent American History on educational TV you had to know a lot, but there were some things you had to not know.

WAITING AND WANTING

While the editor at Farrar, Strauss held the book, I collapsed. It had been too much, too many days on the Tilt-A Whirl, drowning in decisions, disintegrating. I kept thinking about the book, how much I wanted to be published, and then flailing myself for being attached to career goals and fame. Friends would visit and I would talk about the book relentlessly and then tell them it didn't matter, we had everything we needed right inside ourselves, there was no point in talking about it any more. Then I would begin talking about it again. Everything had happened too fast. I had not taken a break after the dissertation, but sat right down and wrote the novel in six weeks.

I hadn't been able to integrate the last acid trip. There was too much to tie together. Too many sides of myself. When I went up to visit my family in Yonkers, I would no longer talk about Vietnam. It was like preaching in a graveyard. I wouldn't talk about acid either, but rather discourse in terms of Buddhism and Hinduism. They didn't know what to make of me. One Sunday, my uncle "Hollywood" Mac took me aside and said, in a well-meaning and somewhat worried tone, "Jerry, this religious bit. It isn't going over." I knew what he meant. I agreed to stop talking about it. But the acid soaked my clothes. I couldn't walk away from it.

I even spoke about God to three Jehovah's witnesses who had shown up at my door. They were telling me about evil and I told them that perhaps a little evil was needed in oneself, a kind of inoculation, to keep one from being open to complete infection. Unfortunately, they seemed to see me as a prospect. They showed up again to invite me to their big shindig in Yankee Stadium. I had to smile, thinking of myself in my old dream of being a rookie prospect in Yankee Stadium. I told them politely that our paths had crossed but that we were going in different directions. I told them that the Buddha conceived of the fallen world in terms of ignorance rather than evil but I don't think they were really there for a conversation.

I liked to make up silly jokes and tell them to people who were sad. I told one to the Jehovah's Witnesses. I said that I had invented a new religion, "Jewish Science." "We're the opposite of 'Christian Science.' We go to the doctor even when we're well." They didn't get it. I had also created a follow-up joke but I didn't tell it to them.

Q. What do you get when you cross a Malamute with a St. Bernard?

A. A St. Bernard Malamute.

I knew it wasn't their kind of joke.

I went to see Günter Grass speak at Columbia. I liked when he said that all countries get the government they deserve. Coming from a German, this was especially powerful. Yet when I came home, I wrote in my journal that Grass was a good man, witty and charming, but essentially a political rather than a religious writer. He provided symbols for the professors but his questions didn't go deep enough. I noted that it was easier to make sophisticated fun of Nixon than to look into yourself.

Farrar, Strauss rejected the book. I panicked. What was I doing? The straight people were not going to accept me as I was. I had no real job. I had multiple selves and they were pulling the wagon in too many directions.

I suffered heart palpitations, muscle spasms, couldn't sleep. Charlotte and I were trying to have a child but nothing had happened. We consulted specialists at a hospital in Brooklyn who had been highly recommended by a doctor we knew. They were reputed to be the best. We did all the tests. They told us gravely that I was marginal, but that Charlotte, due to an infection in college, had no chance of ever having a baby. They advised us to move toward adoption if we wanted a child. There was no other choice. They believed fully in what they were saying. We believed in their authority, their white coats, the world of science behind them. It turned out they were wrong. Charlotte would give birth to two healthy babies in her second marriage. But we didn't know this at the time.

Charlotte was damaged by the official prognosis of no children. She retreated, reading Schopenhauer and practicing her flute for two hours every day. We looked into adopting a child abroad, Mexico, Brazil. It was more trouble than adopting here. We began to take steps to adopt in New York. This proved to be another centrifugal force in my life. I feared becoming like my father. I didn't want to have a kid like myself; I felt I had been a tremendous financial burden to my parents.

Was I going crazy? I couldn't speak about all of my life to anyone. I felt I had to censor any talk about acid to the academics and had to keep a lid on my radicalism with my pals from RPI who were now in business. I was terribly lonely. Once, my old friends, Ruth and Louis Shepard, Charlotte's wild professor from Fitchburg State (who passed for a priest at the liquor store) showed up at our apartment. The steel door opened into the kitchen and we were standing by the refrigerator. They hadn't even sat down yet, when Louis immediately began a tirade about acid. I hadn't mentioned a word about it. He declared, truculently, "They say it's so far out. I get farther out when I jog. I can get higher just by jogging than any hippie can on their acid." He wouldn't stop. I reached into the refrigerator and took out a little phial with some tiny purple squares in it. I held it up to him. "What's that?" he said, still energized by his fervor. I answered quietly, "LSD." Suddenly he was still facing me but he was ten feet away. Like an electron he had flown back to another orbit without moving through the intervening space. I was astonished. I saw he was horrified. He edged forward and looked at it cautiously from a distance as if I had pulled out a snake. I put the acid back into the frig, took out a couple beers and we moved into the living room.

Academics and liberals were very touchy about so many things. You couldn't really talk to them about what was in your heart, your real hopes and confusions. I had just read a review in the *Times* of a book by the militant radical priest Daniel Berrigan. The reviewer applauded Berrigan for denouncing President Nixon, but said that when he attacked Cornell University – Berrigan had called the professors a bloodless lot without an ounce of passion amongst them – that he was going beyond the bounds of decency and heading toward anarchy.

Finally, desperate to talk to someone outside the system and beyond conventional thinking, I told all this to a friend at the *Rat*—the metaphysical-acid questions, the threat to my soul by publishing, the need to let go in the Buddhist sense, the Hindu questions, my fears of being a father, the revolutionary implications of my choices, for society, for my self, and for my eternal soul. He looked at me with dismay and recommended I see a psychiatrist.

Malcolm called. He said, "I should have known. Farrar, Strauss has never had a sense of humor." This was new to me. The idea that publishing companies could have personalities and characteristics like a sense of humor. He was considering sending the manuscript to Seymore Lawrence, at Delacorte Books, but while he pursued this option, I found another channel on my own. We had been hanging out with Mara, our friend from across the hall who worked for CBS News and hid her clock-radio in the oven. She was seeing a painter, Peter Hanssen who lived in Westbeth, housing for indigent artists that the city provided in a former Bell Telephone building over at the docks near Gansevoort Street. (The Gansevoorts were Herman Melville's mother's family, though few knew this.) Peter was doing a series of beautiful cross-hatched drawings of iconic figures- Lester Young, Gandhi, etc.- only each had Peter's face, with his beard and wild, kind eyes. Peter was a jazz fan and told me that Gil Evans lived in Westbeth. How could this have happened? The great arranger, who, with Miles Davis, had changed the direction of jazz, the birth of the cool, was now living in public housing for low income artists.

Don't complain. Don't put old whine in new bottles.

Mara's sister had a friend, Karen (CAR-wren) Kennerly, who was an editor at Dial Press. Mara said that Karen was smart and hip. She knew many of the avant-garde intellectuals. She lived in Miles Davis' house. Mara called Karen and took the manuscript up to her.

"to die is different from what anyone supposed, and luckier."
Walt Whitman

I dropped some acid. I had concluded since my last trip that I had gone off the track into ego-mania and would avoid, if I could, that lonely space in which I felt like a God, alone. I thought that I had somehow reached that place where the Zen masters say that they can get you to the top of a fifty foot pole, but they can't make you jump. But how did one jump? I knew I had cut through the illusion of the reality of the world and other people with the sword of my intellect, but I believed that I had continued to hold onto the illusion of myself. But what happened if one did let go of one's ego and fell into the bottomless void? Was that OK, because, since the void had no bottom, you would effectively be flying and would never crash? Or without your ego, were you dead from the earth point of view? Or would you return to the earth permanently mad? That was a problem with our language and culture. The only model we had available to describe what was happening to me on these trips was the psychiatric one.

I decided to avoid that solipsistic territory. I made up a mantra: "If there is no you, there is no me." Whenever I was tempted to think that I had created the world, and I was alone forever, I would chant this mantra. On this trip and the ones that followed, I wrote on my palm in marker pen: "NO YOU- NO ME."

I dropped LSD alone. I liked being alone on acid. I could go really far out. I made up a code of rules that included no going outside, no answering the door or phone, and staying off the roof. I never violated these injunctions. As the acid came on, I closed my eyes and tried to feel my way back inside myself to the source. I was presented with the image of an acorn or nut that opened up and grew into a tree. I didn't actually see this outside myself, I felt it inside. I knew it was an image, but it seemed like I was being given a lesson. I saw that this tree was the created universe, the tree of life so to speak, and that each of us was a leaf on the tree. Each of us was a particular "vibration." What we didn't normally see was that each vibration was connected to the acorn which still was whole and contained all the vibrations, like the Hindu word "OM" which is supposed to contain all sounds. I could see inside myself and down through the tree and feel these vibrations in the original "acorn" which contained them together in an eternal OM. We had forgotten this. We believed we were separate and abandoned leaves, destined to fall and wither and finally disappear. We didn't see that when the leaf of our body and separate self fell away, our souls would glide back down the tree to our home. The implications of this were immediately obvious. *The earth* was the place of separation and alienation. The earth was the place of loneliness. When you die, it isn't like leaving everyone behind and floating off into nothingness. After death you return to the center and you are CLOSER to everyone. Part of the great Chord of Being. There was something of us that had never left the whole. And when the universe dream was over, the film would run backwards and the entire tree would in-fold into the acorn. And inside the acorn everything felt full and complete and blissful. No emptiness, forever.

When I returned to normality, I wondered why I had never thought of this before. Perhaps "nothing" didn't exist. That's why we called it "nothing." Perhaps dying meant we would be closer to the ones we love. Wasn't this as possible as our accepted myth? Why did we always look at death from the point of view of the survivors rather than the deceased? All the conventional views were arbitrary and not based on evidence. Why did we always drag along the luggage of our culture's myths?

I had always been trying to figure out how something could come from nothing. I had come up with the idea that perhaps nothing split itself off into plus one and minus one which still added up to nothing. Maybe you could have a world and an anti-world and it all added up to zero. But now I began to realize that I had assumed that *nothingness* was primary. Why not assume instead that *Being* was at the heart of things. That Being, in some formless, unlimited manner, had always been here, and lasted forever, and never died.

I smoked dope regularly each night to try to imagine living in a world of universes to which there was no limit. Dreams within dreams. Space and time returning forever. No ending. It was difficult to conceive of. I was still psychologically shattered to a degree, from the stresses and changes and fatigue in my life. I found it healing to listen to Bach. Bach was not a modern person. He lived in a different "world." His notes fell like rain drops on the keys. They didn't seem to have a clear goal. They were soothing because they could go on forever without the clash of melodrama. The dope and Bach were my tickets to an older consciousness, a more merciful world; even with the knowledge of how many of Bach's children died in their youth. Especially with that knowledge.

MY "MOTHER"

"Hello, Jerr. It's me, your mother." For some reason, when she called she always said "mother" as if it were in quotation marks, the way she enclosed "mother" in quotation marks when she sent me a birthday card. "You're gonna be really proud of me. I joined in a demonstration to support you. I drove around with my lights on all afternoon and I honked my horn to support the troops."

"But Ma, that was a pro-war demonstration! That was organized by the firemen and the unions that support the war! That was to continue the war and the bombing! After all these years I've been talking to you, you don't know which side I'm on, do you?

"You haven't even taken the trouble to find out who's fighting in the war, or what side the Americans are on."

"But don't you support the troops?"

Once again, for the twentieth time, I tried to explain the war to my mother but I could feel the futility of it. I had to end the call when my throat constricted into a fist. As I sat there, I recalled an incident that I hadn't thought about in years. I was about nine years old. My mother and father thought that I was behaving badly when he wasn't around because my mother was too good to hit me. So he bought her a cat of nine tails to whip me. When she actually pulled the cat of nine tails out of the drawer and started to whip me I was so shocked that I rushed insanely toward her and wrestled it out of her hands and ran with it into the street and threw it down the sewer. I was terrified of what would happen that night when my father returned home, but no one ever mentioned it again.

POSTER CHILDREN FOR THE AMERICAN DISEASE

In late April 1970 it happened. What I had dreaded since the March on the Pentagon back in 1967. Three days after President Nixon announced a widening of the war with an "incursion" of American troops into Cambodia, the Government shot down unarmed students like dogs. On May fourth, at Kent State University, in northern Ohio, the National Guard troops fired into a crowd of students. Four students fell dead. Nine others were wounded. The rubber band that had been holding me together snapped. Immediately I called my mother. Of course, she hadn't heard about it. The reality filters were working. I screamed at her, "You finally did it! You shot me down in the streets!"

"What? I don't . . ."

"You shot me down in the streets!" I shouted.

I hung up the phone and ran over to NYU at Washington Square. A crowd of people were excitedly discussing this in the courtyard of a building on this beautiful spring day. I believe it was the Law School. I climbed up on a statue and I shouted, "This is too much! We can't take this anymore. Shut down the school. Let's shut down the school." I guess I was, in the right-wing parlance of the time, "an outside agitator." The students did shut down the school, but they would have done so without me. Students across the country shut down their schools.

I rushed up to Columbia University where I knew the real action would be. The school was already shut down. Students were milling around, rushing here and there, making impromptu speeches, debating what to do, all the old chaos that hadn't worked, the helplessness of knowing that things were just getting worse, the same speeches, the Maoists, the Leninists, the anarchists, the dejected and the lost. I wandered around from group to group in front of the Low Library. Students were organizing, committing small acts of vandalism; then everyone began to march downtown. We would follow the route of the Fifth Avenue Bus Line over to the East Side of Central Park, and then march right down Fifth Avenue. Stick it to the rich. Right in their face. Already the Viet Cong flags had appeared which pleased me. Stick it to them. Even if it was the *poor* whites who really supported the war. The rich were doing nothing to stop it. Nothing mattered anyhow. America was finished. The power that held apart the opposites, the energy that delineated the contours of a culture had collapsed. The battery was dead. The engine wouldn't turn over. The moral power of America had been shot down in Ohio. The air was redolent with a funereal lament. Something very big was dying.

I marched along with the students. The whole city was in a state of centrifugal uproar. Wherever we went, we met young people running around, causing trouble. At each neighborhood, kids joined us, fists in the air, high school kids fleeing their schools, blocking traffic, turning over garbage cans in the street, while angry straight people, senior citizens and working class louts, were screaming bloody murder at us.

I identified with everything we were doing, but suddenly something inside me exploded and lay in fragments at my feet. I was very, very tired and sad. I couldn't stand the futile heartbreak and the noise anymore. When I looked up, we were approaching the Metropolitan Museum of Art. The banners proclaimed the "YEAR 1100" show. That was where I wanted to be. The year 1100. I couldn't stand 1970 anymore. It was too hopeless. I entered the museum.

There were frightened tourists and shocked museum visitors in the doorways. This was Fifth Avenue we were trashing. I walked into the shelter of the stately, quiet museum. I was wearing a short jeans jacket along with torn dungarees and an old denim work shirt. My hair was disorganized. I hadn't brushed it that morning. I hadn't shaved for days. But I was a Ph.D. and was behaving civilly. I just wanted to be outside of disorder for a while. In a space of peace.

I had seen the power of escaping into a meditative region when Richard Albert, who had been fired with Leary at Harvard over LSD, held a public evening at a church on the Upper West Side. Albert, now Baba Ram Dass, had become a Hindu in India, taken a guru, and now had returned to spread the word. The atmosphere had been so serene in the church, supple and healing, Ram Dass and his cohorts up on the "stage," playing soft chords on Indian instruments, beautiful women in multicolored outfits and saris sitting with Ram Dass on the Persian rugs they had laid out, some of the women rising and spinning slowly, Sufi style, their rainbow robes flowing after them. Then Ram Dass spoke quietly, gently, slowing everything down, passing along the wisdom his guru had told him, telling stories about Americans in India, about living saints, about taking acid with his guru. For one evening at least, the war was over. The craziness faded into white.

That was what I needed now. I was too overwrought. Dead tired but fuming under the surface. I had lost it. I knew it. Thank God there was a space outside of the current bitter disarray.

I joined a line at the coat check counter. My heart was still beating fast. I was too warm. I would check my little jeans jacket. I waited as the line moved slowly. Ten or twenty people lined up behind me. When I reached the counter, the moron attending the coats gave me furious look. I couldn't miss the implication. The old Frankenstein mambo. He thrust my jacket back at me and said, angrily, "Too short!"

"What?"

"Too short! Can't check it," he snapped with jaw jutting forward. "Move along!"

"Are you kidding?"

He turned to the next person, a clean-cut tourist, and reached for his jacket. The last zipper of restraint within me snapped. I was an artist. I was civilized. I was a New Yorker. I had as much right as anyone else to be in our museum. I simply wanted some serenity. Was it going to be impossible to find that even in the world of art? I grabbed the tourist's jacket, held it up against mine, measuring the length, stuffed it back to him saying, "Sorry, too short. Move along." I shuttled up the line, grabbing people's jackets and measuring them against mine and then returning them, "Sorry too short, can't check it." The coat check guy shouted for the police. They came running, caught up in the dangerous energies outside. I held my hands up in the traditional gesture of surrender.

Everyone started shouting at once. With my hands still up in the air I said, quietly, "I'll go." The cops heard me. "I'll leave peacefully," I said. "I just wanted to check my coat and they wouldn't let me. I'll walk out the door if you'll accompany me."

Somehow I reached them. They walked with me, one on each side, escorting me to the doors. I didn't resist. My blood was boiling. I wanted to choke the fuck at the checkroom, but I kept myself under control. I was nonviolent by principle, by inclination, and by virtue of having lived for two thousand years among confused people who needed only the slightest excuse to join together and stomp you in the name of a God of love.

Outside the chaos and the shouting were continuing. I returned to the Village and walked over to the Lions' Head, a saloon on Sheridan Square where the journalists congregated, and I got mercifully drunk.

SOLD

One weekend I drove down to Washington D.C. to Mark and Lucy's. I joined 100,000 others in protesting the "incursion" into Cambodia. [Later, when I heard about the atrocities of Pol Pot, I would think about those days, and about the fact that we ultimately dropped almost 300 million pounds of bombs on that poor little country with less than 10 million citizens. We flattened peasant villages, destroyed the entire infrastructure and left hundreds of thousands of casualties. Soon afterwards, everyone was shocked when Cambodian society fractured and collapsed, yielding quickly to Pol Pot, becoming a behavior sink. The mainstream media never questioned whether we had anything to do with it.]

Late in May, 1970, I received a call from Mara's friend, Karen Kennerly. She liked the book and wanted to make an offer. We made an appointment for me to come up and see her. She said she would take me to lunch. Before this day, my mother and Charlie had been married. At the wedding, a former neighbor of ours from The Bronx took me aside.

"Look, Jerry, would ya explain to Howie [his son] that money is the name of the game in life."

"You think life is a game?"

He looked at me bemused and walked away. I couldn't shut up.

DIAL PRESS

The Dial Press's offices were set in a large building on Third Avenue at publishers' row. They were less luxurious than Knopf, but more so than Farrar, Strauss, down near Union Square where I had gone to fetch the manuscript when they rejected it. All the publishers had receptionists who kept you out of the offices if you didn't have an appointment. The last thing they wanted was to give would-be writers direct access to the editors.

Karen was a beautiful young woman, maybe a couple years younger than I, self-confident with intelligent eyes that sparkled with a spirit of fun, white, smooth skin and a high, round brow with long, thin, black hair that hung straight down over her shoulders. Her clothes were expensively and stylishly made of gorgeous materials but everything was subtle and understated. She introduced me to a man just rising from his seat, "Jerry

Rothenberg." I realized this must be Jerome Rothenberg, the poet, author of a well-known book, *Technicians of the Sacred*. (Of course, no mention of his achievements. Just "Jerry Rothenberg.") He was dressed in a homey, functional manner, smiled sweetly and excused himself.

Karen had a rather small but adequate office against the wall. The lesser employees, proof editors, designers, etc. were in the center space, divided into cubicles. I liked Karen from the start. She was not a hippie, but reminded me more of one of those aristocratic English women of the twenties; like Miles, she was stylish and hip. More European, more civilized than the bourgeoisie. She led me to a cool, expensive Italian restaurant on the street. I hadn't bought clothing in years, but I was glad I had worn a pair of slacks and an old Oxford shirt I had found in the closet. Nonetheless, I still felt out of place. This was a foreign country to me. I wasn't sure what to order. I had never eaten in a fine mid-town Manhattan restaurant before. I looked at the menu but immediately eliminated any fowl dishes. I didn't know how to eat chicken in a joint like this. Did you use your fingers? I wanted to concentrate on discussing the book. I looked for the item that would be simplest to eat.

"The spinach fettuccine is very good," Karen said. I liked the way she pronounced fettuccine in the Italian manner. She probably spoke Italian.

I had never had spinach fettuccine. I wasn't exactly sure what it was. Then I found it under Pasta. I had no trouble eating pasta. I went with the fettuccine.

Both of us feeling, like the Japanese, that it was impolite to begin with business. we talked about general topics for a while: Mara, Mara's mother, publishing in general. I noticed that Karen made a point not to be subservient to the company or her bosses. Dial Press had been bought by Dell Books and Karen was not going to allow anyone to forget that Dell Books had started as a comic-book company, and that Helen Meyer, the current boss, was the wife of the late comic-book king. Karen said that "everyone at Dial is terrified of Helen, but I don't kowtow to her." This was a point in Karen's favor with me. She was telling me she was not a loyal soldier of the institution. I had already concluded that I would always be an outsider because I would never be loyal to any institution, on the left or the right or anywhere.

We talked about jazz and Karen startled me by quoting something that Wayne Shorter had told her recently and speaking knowledgeably about his latest record. Then I remembered, she lives in Miles' house. Karen was definitely impressing me. At the same time, I could see that she had heard about my life path from Mara, the university degrees, the riots, the drugs, and she wanted to impress me with her independence and hipness. We both wanted to impress the other. We both wanted her to do the book.

She asked me to tell her the story of my encounter with Bob Gottlieb. I saw that Malcolm, Karen, Liz Long, everyone in publishing was fascinated by Bob Gottlieb. He was a larger than life figure, like when he said in an interview that publishing wasn't really important to him anymore, he was only passionate about the ballet. I told Karen I didn't want to make the book safer, to iron out the wrinkles I had strategically placed in the text. I was getting excited talking about the book. My fear of what she might want from me (and a couple glasses of red wine) energized me. I told her passionately, riding on suspicious, nervous energy, how I had shaped the book, worked to make its somewhat ungainly form dance; that I had invented a way to interrupt the narrative, yet to time the interruptions so that the reader's sporadic movement in and out of the main story would parallel my hero's reluctant involvement in the action. I finished breathlessly and looked into Karen's eyes. "You see, I can't just do what Gottlieb wants. I can't make this into a 'novel.'"

Karen smiled. "Jerry, you think I want to limit your freedom as an author. I want to do this book, and I hope to help you clarify it and sharpen it and make a few suggestions, but . . . (Her face lit up with mischief.) I want you to go *further* out. Let's make it *crazier*!" She poured another glass of wine. She couldn't help but giggle slightly as this rebellious side of herself came out. "Get wild," she said.

"The book is yours," I said, quietly. I didn't inquire about money, or any other arrangements. I felt that somehow I had witnessed a miracle.

Karen and I both sat there smiling happily. "Of course, she said, "it isn't a traditional best-seller type book." She handed me an interoffice memo from her beautifully crafted purse. The memo, from another editor, questioned the commercial potential of my book. But the strangest quality of the note was that although it was about money, it was written in some pretentious, affected, prose. I was astonished. This was a territory where fops wrote interoffice memos in the stylized prose of Eighteenth century belles-lettres. "But I have some support as well," Karen said. "Others like it and we'll work to convince the rest of the book's potential." She looked me in the eyes. "The artist comes first," she said, as if it were obvious.

I walked out of the restaurant glowing. We had hardly discussed the advance. As we parted, Karen brought the matter up and said she would do her best for me in that regard. Probably $2,000, which was standard for first novels at that time. [$10,000-$12,000 in current dollars]. I didn't care. I knew Karen would be fair within her capabilities at the firm. Besides, my secret was that I would have given her the book for nothing.

FREE AT LAST

I wouldn't see Karen again for six months. I would speak to her on the telephone but we didn't sit down to work on the book until about Thanksgiving, 1970. At the end of our first lunch, she had surprised me by saying she was off to Italy for a month. Like most "civilians" I had a wrong idea of the process of publishing a book. I thought that once you had a manuscript accepted, you sat down with the editor who had just read it and you went through it together, worked on it for month with her, and then they published the book. The whole business taking perhaps two months.

But once Karen explained the process to me, I understood it differently. The publishers brought out two "lists" of books each year, the spring list and the fall. Dial Press was a large corporation with hundreds of books in print. Everything had to be planned from many angles: production, sales, financial. Here, in June, 1970, the fall list had already been pitched by the salesmen who dropped in on each bookstore twice a year. The fall books were being printed. They would need to be shipped well in advance of pub date. The leading reviewers would receive books months in advance. Large corporations had to plan. To reduce future uncertainty. To balance their lists and estimate future expenses. The succeeding list, for spring 1971, would be printed, publicized and sold in the fall of 1970, and was already pretty much booked up. I would probably be placed on the fall list for 1971, over a year away.

I was disappointed to learn this. I had hoped to somehow warn the students about a Kent State eruption but unfortunately it was too late for that. In fact, nine days after that tragedy, troops had fired into a crowd at Jackson State in Mississippi, killing two black students and wounding nine. Another line had been erased. Still, I rationalized, September 1971, fifteen months away, wouldn't be that bad, especially now that I had a good editor to work with.

I spoke about this with Karen on the phone. She was sympathetic, but she said, "It won't be very time-consuming. Why not take it easy for a year and enjoy putting a beautiful book together?" That made sense to me. I was slowly coming to realize through our phone conversations that there were many decisions to be made. Karen was concerned about the book as an artifact. She wanted to fight for money to make it out of the best paper, the binding sewn not glued. We would have to choose an appropriate typescript, a jacket designer, a cover design under the jacket, a designer for the inside of the book, which would be complicated with all my quirky layouts. We would design the title pages, work out a plan for publicity and write press releases with the publicity people, try to sell it to magazines and the movies. There would be a hundred small decisions and chores before the book actually appeared. It all sounded reasonable, but . . .

When I received the contract (with a $2000 advance on future royalties, half on signing, the other half when an acceptable manuscript was turned in, by custom none of it returnable even if the book sales didn't earn it back), I realized that I didn't understand what I was doing, subsidiary rights, foreign rights, percentages of movie sales. I had to hire an agent. I don't recall who recommended Elaine Markson, but one day at one o'clock I found myself ringing her doorbell in a large, older building right across from Washington Square Park. Elaine was a Villager, living a few blocks from my house. She was just starting out as an agent. A Villager! I knew before I met her that this would be right for me. As I entered her apartment, she introduced me to her husband, David, sitting in the dark living room, eating a sandwich and drinking from a can of beer while reading from the *New York Times*. He sent me a generous smile. I liked him. Then it hit me. This was David Markson, the avant-garde writer, pal of Malcolm Lowry.

Elaine was a pretty woman, roughly my age or a couple years older. I imagined her as one of those hip Jewish girls who had made it from Brooklyn to the Village, made the big step, taken a chance. I always admired women like that. She had a friendly smile and I liked her immediately.

This was far from the world of Fifth Avenue agents with power lunches and huge rents to cover. Elaine didn't even have an office. She took me to an extra bedroom that she was using as an office, laughingly pointing out a sign on the door that her son had made for her, "LITERARY AGENT," in Crayola crayons.

Elaine was my kind of person. I didn't have to talk business with her. I knew she was smart, and somehow I knew she would be successful because writers would be comfortable with her. When she said she was more interested in the writers than the money, you had to believe her. After all, she was married to a serious, unwealthy writer herself. She would understand things from the writer's point of view. [This proved to be true. Elaine quickly became one of the most respected agents in New York. She opened an office in the Village and never moved uptown. She's still there, still the Greenwich Village girl, even with a staff of assistants, and having represented all species of writers, from Abby Hoffman to Dan Rather.] We worked together without a contract.

Now that I had an agent, I began my year of freedom. I had been doing a kind of independent tutorial in the arts since I had passed my orals almost three years before. This was an open, spacious time for the arts since all standards and rules were begging to be questioned. Artists were asking deeper questions than usual, trying to reveal the foundations, the hidden assumptions behind the inherited traditions, just as we were tussling with the same issues on a political, personal and spiritual level, trying to be more free and conscious, less blind in all areas of our development and activities. Thus in the theater, we asked who had decided that a proscenium arch should separate the audience from the actors? Who had invented the stage and why? Why wasn't the audience a part of what was happening? Did you need a script?

Theater was incredibly exciting especially at off-off Broadway theaters. One influence was Antonin Artaud. I had heard of his book, *The Theater of Cruelty*, but I thought it was a text about power and relationships which might be pushed to sadomasochism, a way to explore the impotence and fantasies of the under classes and the dispossessed by projecting them onto a symbolic, sexual plane. There was much of this, often quite interesting in the little theaters around the Village. There was an actress named Mary Woronov, connected to the Warhol people, a beautiful, six-foot tall, dark, sex goddess in many of these productions. Later, in her autobiography, she revealed that at the time she had been a virgin, living uptown with her parents.

When I did read Artaud, I saw that this was not what he was recommending. A former French film actor (e.g. Carl Dreyer's *The Passion of Joan of Arc)* who was going crazy, Artaud had traveled to Mexico in the Forties, and trudged into the mountains where he became initiated into hidden Indian psychedelic ceremonies. When Artaud returned to a crazy Europe, still going crazy himself, he came to believe that the theater must be returned to its ancient rites and power, perhaps to alter consciousness without drugs, to rip away the veils of the assumed. The cruelty he spoke of was the act of tearing these illusions from the audience, often by non-verbal means. Jean Claude van Italie was one of the contemporary playwrights who took him up on this in his groundbreaking *America Hurrah* which featured giant puppets and exaggerated, machine-like dialogue.

Sam Shepard also traveled in this direction. At that time he was putting on plays with music in little venues in the East Village, where he lived with his wife and co-star O-lan. He moved his plays up to Lincoln Center but I thought he really found himself later in his *True West*, where he has one of the two brothers, who are house-sitting for their mother, steal twenty toasters. He makes toast in all of them and the toast pops all over the kitchen floor so when the brothers revert back to the primitive sides of themselves and begin a deadly fight wrecking the kitchen right there on the stage, they are fighting on top of real toast, a perfect visceral symbol of affluence and waste and the mere veneer that is civilization.

Once again, theater was becoming an arena that was dangerous and unpredictable. This was especially the case if the audience was invited to participate. I remember one night going to *Dionysus in 69*, directed by Richard Schechner at the Performing Garage, a former auto repair shop down in the area which is now Soho. The actors ventured into the audience and tenderly began to take off some of the willing spectators' clothes, a jacket here, a shawl there. At one point, a beautiful woman in the audience began to take off an actor's clothes. Soon they were making out on the floor in the corner. Other members of the audience walked onto the stage, which was not raised, and participated in the dances, chants, and ritual action of the play. At the "curtain" (there was no actual separating curtain), the cast, many almost unclothed, took out protest signs, raised the door of the erstwhile garage and led the audience out into the dark street to block traffic. All the boundaries were coming down, the lines between theater and not-theater, reality and fiction, audience and stage. Where did the realm of fantasy and play-like behavior begin and end? No one in the audience fell asleep during the play that night.

This was not the case when I attended a performance at Lincoln Center of Arthur's Miller's *The Price*. Miller had written a well-made play, tight, powerful in the old sense, balanced, resonating with the language of right and wrong, guilt and innocence, in which members of a family wrestle verbally with questions of responsibility between the two brothers, one a cop. But the audience, although perhaps challenged to a degree by these old philosophical conundrums, were physically safe. They knew they were not going to be challenged beyond their surface ideas of what constituted theater. I noticed that many in the audience, especially the men, slid into sleep. Arthur Miller was among the best of the senior playwrights, and *Death of a Salesman* one of the handful of great American classic plays that will live forever, but in comparison with what was going on in the streets every day, the mainstream theater was in danger of becoming a safe place for tired professionals to sleep at night. Certainly 90% of Broadway plays were served on white bread. This was the theater that Artaud had assaulted before he went mad. Meanwhile, in The Village you never knew what was going to happen.

I had attended the Living Theater's return to The Brooklyn Academy of Music. They had retreated to Europe after their breakthrough performances of *The Brig*, and *The Connection*, and such, years before. Now, they had evolved or devolved into a kind of commune. They would come out on stage virtually nude, and do living statues or the like and chant, and then they would confront the audience. There were no scripts. Unfortunately, in New York the problem with the fashionable theater audience was not how to involve them in the event but how to get them to keep quiet. The performance disintegrated into shouts and arguments and nascent fights but at least it was alive and equal to the energy outside of the theater.

It was Jill Johnson of *The Village Voice* who noticed that, as a dance critic, she was finding her bus ride to the theater more interesting than most of the dance performances she reviewed. So she began to review her trip to the theater and then, her week in general. Life was surpassing art. Often the creativity released among "ordinary" people was more astonishing than that created within the accepted tradition by more organized, ambitious, and so-called "sane" people. After all, wasn't R.D. Laing, the hip Glasgow psychiatrist, *living* with his psychotic patients? And wasn't he writing that if he could turn us on, if he could blow our minds, he would? Jill Johnson could no longer pretend to stand aside and give an "objective" review of the dance. She felt a responsibility to attempt to find out who the person (Jill) was who was doing the reviewing, the filtering of the performance through the prism of an ego.

This stance not only challenged her authority, it was part of a general inclination to challenge the very notion of objectivity. Here we saw the beginning of that post-modern theme of multiple realities and standards leading to the assault on the citadel: science.

We had learned in opposing the war that it was too late to rationally debate with the liberals who had proven useless. The theater had to be large and crazier. You couldn't be subtle. In her satirical hit play, *MacBird*, Barbara Garson had virtually pictured LBJ as killing JFK. I loved the *Theater of the Ridiculous* of Charles Ludlum and his pals, in which they would mount fey, mocking productions that fell off the reality tightrope into the realm of the absurd below. Strange askew productions, mounted in awkward spaces in the East Village at midnight when the squares were asleep, sophisticated plays which ignored the line between pop and classical culture, the sacred and the profane, featuring characters like a ballerina named Birdshitskaya. The time for reason and debate had passed.

Ideas similar to Jill Johnson's were attracting the fiction writers as well. In his book, *In Cold Blood,* Truman Capote wrote a factual narrative using all the techniques of the fiction writer; in *Armies of the Night*, Normal Mailer put himself at the center of the action at the Pentagon assault, not only as drunken narrator, but as active participant. In *The Electric Kool Aid Acid Test*, Tom Wolfe, a dapper Yale Ph.D, would join the Merry Pranksters and Ken Kesey for their psychedelic ride across the country in their rainbow bus, freaking out the locals, life as art, written in a hopped-up, seemingly doped-up wacko style which was appropriate to his material. Hunter Thompson took this one step further by actually living and writing while completely wrecked on various drugs. He was out of control, the perfect person to cover political conventions or a police anti-drug convention in Las Vegas. Neither respectable nor rational, he was a wailing libido, an animal with a typewriter. He terrified the straight people.

This led to the "New Journalism" where you had to present yourself as part of the equation, dropping the stance of "objectivity" which was being revealed everyday as part of the conservative conventions of the culture. At one point the great "objective" semantics scholar turned hawk and conservative, S. I. Hayakawa, said that TV caused the inability of young people to relate to each other, which was leading them to drop out. No one questioned the fact that Hayakawa's statement assumed that dropping out (joining the counterculture, protesting the war and the system behind it) was the equivalent of not being able to relate to others. Once again, objectivity was attributed to any statement that reinforced the conventional values; social scientists and Hollywood producers thought young people were dropping out because, for some mystifying reason, they *wanted* to be miserable.

Jill Johnson brought up a question that many choreographers in our neighborhood had been thinking about: What was dance? Or rather, what wasn't dance?

A week-long avant-garde dance festival was mounted up at Times Square. Yvonne Rainer, one of our Village choreographers, took half our neighborhood up there and on a Broadway theater stage had them doing push-ups and sit-ups. It was terrific (for a while). *Epater le bourgeoisie.* And even if it went on a bit too long, it helped to bring athletic moves into the ballet.

ASTAIRE TO ASTARTE

My favorite ballet company was the Joffrey and my favorite piece was *Astarte*. The stage is uncurtained and bare except for a large, warped movie screen, like a kind of sea shell, somewhat twisted above and across the rear of the stage. A woman (goddess) comes out in a kind of brief, almost invisible, leotard and begins a sinuous dance to an excellent live rock band featuring a lyrical, howling solo guitar in the orchestra pit. Then the goddess appears on the movie screen. At first it looks like a live video image but then you see that at times the ballerina on stage is dancing *in opposition* to her image on the screen. And then one of those strange Sixties' moments right near where we were seated. A well-dressed black man in the orchestra stands and begins to remove his suit and tie. He strips down to a thong while the ballerina continues, oblivious of what is happening. And then, of course, he heads for the stage, wearing just a thong. We watch, fearful and excited. What's going to occur? Immediately he moves to dance with her. But still no one stops the ballet and calls the cops. He dances around her, improvising as he goes along. And you think, yes, this is incredible, but this is the Sixties, you swing with it, you don't call the authorities, and then, unbelievably, he appears in the film above them, dancing with the goddess while the guitar howls. And then the two of them begin to dance with the film and to dance, at times, against their images in the film on the warped screen stretched all the way across the stage. This goes on, a beautiful spacey ballet, the screaming, holy, guitar, until, just when you hoped it would never end, amazingly the screen begins to lift and disappear above, the large back doors behind the stage open up slowly revealing the busy street and the man, who has appeared to be in a trance all this time, slowly moves away from Astarte. He glides gracefully, slowly, in his thong, into the street among the pedestrians and traffic; now they are all in *our* space, part of our "reality", as he disappears into cold, night air. The line has disappeared between theater and reality, between the proper attire and behavior for the ballet and that for the streets, between trance and normality, between trip and life. Mystified pedestrians outside on the sidewalk peer in at us while the rock guitar sings and cries out and the goddess Astarte continues her trancelike dance as the lights go down.

I defined a trip as a voyage in which you begin in one place and wind up in another. The ballet had been a trip. The man began as a suit and tied spectator at a cultural event; he moved from the audience to the stage, became a participant, danced with the goddess (LSD?) and wound up naked in the streets, entranced.

Many defining lines disappeared in those days. I attended free cultural events in the local parks: Washington Square and Tompkins Square. The audience was always appreciative; the winos were perhaps even a little too enthusiastic. They wanted to help. If there was a doo-wop group, they knew, they just *knew*, that they could make it better if they could join the background singers, or if it was, say, a big band, they wished, so fervently, to add their voice in front, to sing the lyrics. That's why an essential part of producing any such concert was to employ "wino-pushers." As soon as the music struck up, the winos would appear and head towards the front. Like strange animals, they would haul themselves in one way or another up over the edge of the stage. So you needed "wino-pushers" to rush about on the front of the stage pushing them off. Sometimes, if the concert was say, Mozart, it would be distracting, but after a while you got to used to this and could enjoy it as a tableau-vivant, a kind of staged old-fashioned battle at sea with a Mozart score. It all depended on how you looked at it.

Another "psychedelic" play I saw was the San Francisco ACT's performance in New York of Edward Albee's *Tiny Alice*. They did the play as an acid trip with a large powerful organ playing chords that shook the theater when something mysterious and mystical occurred. I was in the first row, enchanted, marveling at how they'd gotten the essence of this play of houses and cathedrals within houses and cathedrals. For that was the only way I saw to respond to this play. Critics exhausted themselves interpreting or cursing the play's mysteries, but to me it was a symbolic reproduction of a trip, and there was no way to pin it down, it was merely a picture of realities within realities, universes within universes, ad infinitum. I came out of there liberated from meaning, walking on sponge shoes.

Thus I was puzzled when Albee vigorously disowned the production. I couldn't understand why he was upset. Especially after what my pal Malcolm had told me about Albee. This seemed to me one of the greatest productions I had ever seen. I still don't understand his response.

NEGATIVE CAPABILITY

Charlotte and I liked to attend the free Shakespeare in the Park on summer evenings. Just to be in Central Park on a hot, stuffy, city night quickened one's life, with the fresh ozone in the air and the living green scents of trees and grass, on the edge of a lake with boats sometimes included in the play for sea battles, and the action underlain by sweet recorders playing Elizabethan melodies; it was a way out of your sticky existence for a while. Shakespeare always seemed to me like a compatriot soul, with his horror at human violence and his fixation on premature death.

One night the show was delayed by a light rainstorm at twilight. We waited under the stands. When darkness fully arrived, the rain abated. People slowly filtered back to their seats. Then we heard a screeching of brakes. Several thuds and screaming behind the theater over where the auto road snaked through the park. Someone ran onto the stage and shouted, "Is there a doctor in the house? There's been a terrible accident." A more appropriate question might have been, "Is there anyone in the house who is not a doctor?" but only two doctors shouted out, a hippie and a young Englishman. They followed the man who ran off toward the rear of the theater.

Charlotte and I and others jogged outside after him. A fine mist still hung in the dark air. You could barely discern a car stopped in the bushes. We quickly ascertained that in the rain a car had skidded and had, at virtually full speed, ploughed into a group of elderly theater-goers. No one knew how many they were, or where they lay. Bodies stretched out on the road, possibly dead. Others were in the bushes, lying here and there where we found them. The two young doctors scurried about performing triage.

After what seemed like half an hour, ambulances arrived to find us making our way through the wet foliage in the dark, looking for more bodies. Eventually, when the carnage was cleared, some people headed back to the theater. I told Charlotte I'd had enough Shakespeare for the night. I already felt exactly the way I would feel at the end of one of Shakespeare's dark plays, like I had blood on my face and hands and clothing.

Although I rarely ventured up to Times Square to see Broadway plays, when Nichol Williamson's *Hamlet* arrived, I took a chance and bought a front row seat for a matinee. I had never seen Williamson but heard good things about him. Here again, as in *Astarte*, something shocking occurred in the theater. The stage hung no curtain. When I took my seat, I could already see the spare setting, lit only by the house lights. Then I was startled to see something unbelievable. One of the bums from Times Square had somehow made his way onto the stage of the theater. He was lying there, over in the corner of the stage, against the wall. He was almost invisible, dressed in black clothing. He wasn't moving but you could tell he was crazy. He had crazy eyes. He was angry and could turn violent. You could see it. I wondered what would happen when he was discovered but immediately the king and queen came on stage in their royal finery and the house lights dimmed as the play began. The hair on my back stood up as I watched from the edge of my chair. This was unprecedented and dangerous. Something really wild was going to happen on a Broadway stage. And it did. After a couple moments the crazy guy stood up and skulked over toward the action. And then, incredibly, he began to speak Hamlet's lines! The bum was Nichol Williamson!

There he stood, a few feet in front of me. I was electrified. This was far beyond acting. I knew that anything could happen as the play proceeded. And that this was the atmosphere that was needed if Hamlet was to kill somebody and the stage were to be littered with bodies by the end. Nichol Williamson could have murdered someone that afternoon. I was alert in my seat. My Bronx street vibes were shouting "Danger!"

He held this level throughout the play. There was no distance between him and Hamlet. You forgot this was an actor playing a role. By the end of the play, when Hamlet dies, I began to weep. It was like someone I knew had been killed. I couldn't stop crying. Completely spaced, I walked outside into the sunny late afternoon and found myself drifting north on Times Square. I didn't know or care where I was going. It was like a trip. The art had knocked the sense out of me. Left me exhilarated but without charts. Then, stopped at a corner, I saw a black face peering into mine as if she were looking into a well. I stepped back a notch and looked back at her. She was bemused and smiling. She looked kind but worried about me. Pretty, overly made-up, about six feet tall in her exaggerated white boots, her tiny red plastic micro-skirt, her halter top. A Times Square prostitute. She was looking into my eyes and she began to laugh. "Where you *been*, Daddy?" she said.

"I don't know," I replied honestly, still dazed.

She laughed like crazy, good-naturedly. As she began to walk away, she turned back and looked into my eyes again and said quietly, with feeling, "Take care of yourself, Daddy."

"I will," I said, grateful for the good advice.

When I returned home, I told Charlotte all about the afternoon and I raved, "I know the secret now of good acting. You have to own the strength to suppress your ego completely, to not let the audience know you are any different from the character you are playing. If you play a stupid violent man, you have to make the audience believe you actually are stupid and violent. They have to dislike you. You the actor. They have to believe you are revealing your real self. Nichol Williamson . . . it was like an acid trip. There was nothing there of his ego. I got a contact high. Anything was possible. I mean it. He held nothing back."

A couple weeks later, I read in the *Times* that Williamson had cracked during a performance in Boston. He had thrown some of the furniture around, wrecking the set and had to be restrained. They stopped the performance and put him in a mental hospital.

EARTH: LOVE IT OR LEAVE IT

For a month in the summers of 1969 and '70, we rented a tiny, one-room log cabin, set off by itself on a lake just north of Fitchburg, Massachusetts. A friend of ours from Charlotte's college days, Richard DeLisle, had purchased a house with forty acres of land at the end of a small road nearby. Behind the house, a lawn lined by birch trees sloped down to a brook. The perfect, peaceful, isolated spot to drop acid. Richard and his wife Margie didn't do psychedelics, but some days we house sat for them. Charlotte would wander around in her djellaba, tripping in the grass, playing her flute, looking like a pre-Raphaelite angel. Once, on acid, I turned toward a lovely little birch tree and I felt a strong, loving bond between us. I realized how much I liked trees. They were so harmless. So nurturing, with their shade and fruit. In a way, they seemed a higher life form than us. They had less desire. They were content to stand there for centuries with the soft wind floating their hair.

I approached the tree and for the first time, really, I saw that it was alive. Of course. Living undulations swelled through its limbs. It was actually an extension of the earth, like the antenna of an insect. When I moved over to touch it I could see its branches rippling, like thick, stationary snakes, the life force pulsing unmistakably down its branches. I took one of the vibrant branches in my hands and I rubbed it round, giving it a massage. I could feel the living ripples in my hands, traveling from the trunk outwards. I could feel how happy it was to be touched and massaged. I continued on the other branches I could reach, encircling each with my fingers and caressing it with my hand, back and forth, with and against the flow of its own energies that were moving like muscles.

I loved this little tree. We were connected on some other plane. Anytime I returned, high or not, I walked over to the tree and I spoke to it and massaged it.

We were surprised at the log cabin one morning by the appearance of Charlotte's former professor Louis Shepard along with another English professor we knew. They had come to offer me a job in English at Fitchburg State for the fall. Tenure track. Since I had a book coming out this meant tenure, security for life, medical and dental, nice retirement pension. Louis had it all planned. We could keep our rent-controlled apartment in the Village as a *pied-à-terre*. I was stunned. Very grateful that they thought highly enough of me to make this tempting offer. I wanted to teach at a university like Fitchburg. Practically free, lower class kids, undergraduate emphasis, no Ph.D. orals or dissertations. It was hard to pass up. I was not really an American. Americans had no fear of starvation. When they heard horses hooves they thought of a classy person out for a ride on the bridal path, not that the Cossacks were coming. But now I was a going to be a novelist. I had been playing it safe for my entire life. Even after I dropped out, I had completed graduate school and the Ph.D. so I would have something to fall back on. How could I go back to the academy when my life as an artist was just beginning? It was time to turn down security for life. That seemed to be part of the bargain in order to become an artist.

A week later, at the local diner in Ashburnham, Mass., near the log cabin, after Charlotte and I ordered breakfast, a tall, thin, hippie, maybe twenty years old, sat down next to me at the counter and just started talking. "If I ever get my hands on that Timothy Leary, I'll kill him," he said, but without a lot of emotion.

"Oh, yeah?" I said.

"Yeah. I dropped acid twelve times, man. Everything was cool. No problem. Then I take it the thirteenth time. Whoa." He was shaking his head in troubled disbelief. "I don't know man. I don't know what's real anymore."

"I don't either," I said, quietly.

"So what do you do?"

"I follow what the Zen Masters said. 'When you're hungry, eat. When you're tired, sleep.' I can't say that I have the answer. I mean about knowing what's real or not . . . . But I don't know, man. I'm finding it's not so essential right now."

The young guy was interested. I was taking him seriously. I wasn't judging him. He relaxed a little. I told him about my trips and my thoughts about them. That he was at the beginning of an ancient and honorable path if he chose to see it that way.

At one point he began complaining again and I couldn't resist one of my home-made jokes. He was railing about Art Linkletter, an unctuous, nationally famous, daytime TV host whom President Nixon had appointed a national drug advisor because he claimed (falsely) that his daughter, who had committed suicide, had jumped out of a window on LSD. "Didn't you hear?" I said. "They replaced Art Linkletter. He's not the drug advisor anymore."

"He's not?"

"No, they replaced him with a guy who claimed he had two daughters who took LSD and jumped out of windows."

He thanked me when we left. Said I had given him a lot to think about. It felt good to connect with a stranger and to feel that I was beginning to find a way to put my experiences to use. My friends tell me that I have a rare characteristic, that people come up to me in public places and tell me their life stories or ask me deep questions. I have no way of judging this, but my friends insist on it.

Whenever I would go to the museums on the Upper East Side of Manhattan, I would stop at the Horn and Hardart Automat for lunch. The Automat was pretty much the only place my family took me to eat out when I was young. Now, with all the wrenching changes in my life, I liked this tie to the past. I would even order exactly what I had eaten when I was a kid: Salisbury steak, baked macaroni, creamed spinach and beets in their special sauce. On one occasion a woman, about twenty years older than I, dressed in Bronx fashion, sat down at my table and began to weep.

"Are you OK?"

"My psychiatrist just kicked me out after five years. This is the third one." She began to bawl. "You're in pretty bad shape if even your psychiatrist won't even talk to you."

"You seem OK to me," I said.

She told me her life story. Actually, I found it interesting. It turned out that she lived in The Bronx with her mother, and she had been a big fan of Billie Holliday. She had even befriended Billie after a while. I couldn't see why a shrink wouldn't help her out. After an hour, I saw that she had stopped crying and was even showing signs of sparkling life.

"Well, I better go now," I said. "It's been good talking to you."

She looked a little disappointed and said tentatively. "Gee, I had a really good time talking to you. Do you think . . . I mean, now that I can't go to my shrink, maybe, we could meet here each week?"

For a second the craziest idea passed through my mind. Maybe I could come to the Automat every week and eat my favorite food and start a business–psychotherapy at the Automat. I'd probably be good at it and I could eat the fabulous baked beans, and the delicious pumpkin pie you took out of the vending outlets in the wall.

I was going to make a joke about it, some black humor, but I realized I would hurt her feelings. Her self-esteem depended on the fact that I had taken her seriously and listened to her. So I simply told her that I lived downtown and maybe we'd meet here sometime if the Gods willed it. She smiled as I left.

"Life imitates art."
Oscar Wilde

After seeing a show of cubist paintings in an early afternoon, I returned home and dropped acid by myself. I had always been working when I took the acid, trying to find a path, to hook into the holy dynamo. Now I would just have a good time by myself. After an hour I looked out my window and to my amazement, the buildings on my block were all cubist. I laughed like crazy. I laughed and laughed and I realized I was completely happy. For no reason. And that it wasn't so much the drug that was illegal, but I was illegal. I was the snake in the woodpile of our worldview, I was happy without having earned my joy by hard work and money. If they knew about me, the authorities would put me away for a long time. I began to shout, but just low enough so that the people outside couldn't hear me. "Call the police! Call the police! There's a man here who's happy for no reason."

I looked through the smog toward the Wall Street towers, inside them everyone running around like crazy, shouting about stocks and percents and all, the traffic outside on the Village streets spewing fumes down below, all the chaos of "reality," young people in costumes from other ages, drugged heads, crazy cabbies, the cubist apartment houses, the whole glorious mess of New York City in the late Sixties, and I became even happier. I had the radio on, and in the news break, Governor Rockefeller suddenly appeared, his voice recreated exactly by my talented speakers, and he was stating unequivocally, with great anger and determination, that everything was under control and he was in charge. "I'm the governor of this state!" he insisted. I laughed even harder as I thought of the mechanical governor of a car, keeping it under control, and it seemed hilarious to me that there was a man in Albany, my father's nemesis, Nelson Rockefeller, and somehow he thought he was the governor, and now he had appeared in my living room while I was on acid and he was reassuring me that he was in control of everything. All this made me even happier, sitting there at the top of my old building, by my window, with my pal Shep.

I listened to rock for a while, good old lovely bashing harmonic rock with its screaming and sadly singing guitars. I listened to Mountain, one of my favorite New York groups whom I caught at the Fillmore whenever I could, led by Felix Pappalardi, a tall Italian guy with a ramrod straight back and a big smile, who looked like an Italian organ grinder with his monkey, Leslie West, a 300 pound Jewish guy from Queens who had changed his name from Leslie Weinstein, and who waddled around the back of the stage like a drooling, preliterate animal in a buckskin vest with fringes, high on some kind of Western American kick, playing out his American dreams in songs of wagons leaving the city for the forest. Occasionally, he would look to Felix, and Felix would laugh and nod yes, and Leslie would take a solo, the guitar singing over Corkey Laing's organ chords, and Leslie played with such an innocent and beautiful lyricism, you knew only a Jewish guy from the New York boroughs could romanticize America that way and play love songs to it from his suffering Yiddish soul. I wondered if he knew that Nathanael West, one of my favorite novelists, had changed his name from Nathan Weinstein back in the Twenties, when he had left De Witt Clinton, my high school. I wondered whether Leslie

West had modeled himself after Nathanael West. I hoped so. I thought he and Mountain were among the underrated artists of that period.

Of course, all this was before the Seventies, when Felix Pappalardi drove his wife crazy by his philandering, until she shot and killed him.

Then I slowed the trip down and played Bach, the old master, to my mind the height of human achievement in the arts. But after a while I turned off the phonograph and I lost myself in the gorgeous, loving, marigold light.

THE DANGERS OF ROGER WILLIAMS

While we were at the log cabin in Massachusetts, we had turned our apartment over to Paul and Gloria, two hippies who lived in a studio in the basement of our building. For two months I hadn't even known there was an apartment down there until I wondered why this couple kept going down to the boiler room. They had little money, so we donated our airier, lighter apartment to them for a month each summer, although our place in July also resembled the Sahara.

Paul and Gloria were from Brooklyn. They had graduated from one of the city colleges and were spending a kind of extended honeymoon in the Village. They weren't committed to a new world, but wanted to enjoy the old one. Soon Gloria would become pregnant and they would move back to Brooklyn.

The second summer we did this, I had just bought a copy of Crosby, Stills, Nash and Young's record, *Déjà Vu*, one of my all-time favorites. I liked CS&N very much, but they added a little too much sugar for my Bronx tastes. With Neil Young's dark, brooding unpredictability and childlike passion, they were perfect, representing all sides of the Sixties' crystal. Like all records I cherished, I tried to take care of it. I saved it, the way I would save the cherry candy in the Chuckles' pack when I was a kid. I didn't want to be part of the disposable world. That was over.

Paul and Gloria came into the house, adored the record, laid it onto the phono, set the repeat function on, and played it for a month. When we came home it looked like the bottom of a frying pan.

I guess I couldn't hide the disappointment on my face. It wasn't the money. The record was worth nothing compared to the value of the apartment that we had loaned them for free. Paul picked up on this and invited us for dinner at The Ninth Circle, a restaurant down the street where he worked as a waiter.

He brought us a large steak dinner with all the works, and then when he handed us the bill he had only charged us for the dessert. I felt uneasy about this. This wasn't what we were supposed to be doing. Becoming more agile and crafty consumers. But there was no way to object without causing a possible scene that might cost him his job, so we took the present as offered.

I thought about this a lot. When he offered another free dinner, I turned him down. I wanted to live a life less tainted than the ones tendered by the blind and addicted culture, but there was a thin line between being pure and becoming a Puritan, a line I was wont to cross at times. I remembered the fate of Roger Williams. When the church in Boston decided to admit to membership young people who had not had the prescribed religious experience, doing this for practical reasons because the children of the visible saints were needed as members to keep the church going when the original sanctity of the immigrants faded, Williams had objected. This led to his traveling south with his wife and founding Providence, Rhode Island, where they could keep their church unsullied by backsliders. Yet even here people were not pure enough, so Roger Williams wound up taking communion only with his wife and I'm sure he watched her carefully as well.

With Charlotte and me spending so much time together, and me being so judgmental, I could see my imprint in this portrait. Thus, I had no choice but to accept when Paul appeared a few days later with a gift of several pounds of hamburger he had stolen from work. He said he couldn't eat it himself, because he and Gloria were vegetarians. What could I do? I didn't want to hurt his feelings. What the hell.

WAITING FOR KAREN

In my later years in New York the chronology becomes more fuzzy. I remember a weekend in Washington at my brother's. I spent Saturday running around the downtown area as part of some large demonstration. The protests were becoming more rowdy as we realized that we had no power to stop the war. I had watched Richard Nixon's first speech after his election. During the campaign he had asserted that he had a "secret plan" to end the war, which was bullshit of course, but I hoped that he was so cynical, he would simply blame the war on the Democrats and pull out. (One of my favorite protest signs read, "Pull out, LBJ, like your father should have.") Nixon's anti-communist credentials were impeccable. They later made it possible for him to approach an accord with China. He didn't have to fear, as did the Democrats, that he would be accused of being soft on communism, as the Democrats were blamed for "losing China" in 1949. Charlotte saw the look on my face as I turned off the TV that night in early 1969. She'd been reading.

"What'd he say?"

"The war's going to continue for at least four more years. Thousands will die."

She looked at me sadly. Turned back to her book.

On the weekend in Washington, somehow we wound up being chased by the police over to Pennsylvania Avenue. And there it was. The White House. All along the curb between us and the White House, they had lined up buses, dozens of them, parked touching each other, like some crazy modern example of a medieval wall around the castle. We had not given a thought to rushing the White House but I realized that we were making an impression. They had gone to all that expense and trouble to protect themselves against us. They were worried about us. We had more power than we thought.

I remember attending a party with Charlotte and my brother Mark and Lucy after an earlier protest in Washington. Our friend Richard DeLisle from Fitchburg, Mass, had met a terrific young woman, Margie, whom he would soon marry. Margie's family somehow owned a diamond mine in Pennsylvania but she was the most friendly, gentle, unassuming, unpretentious person you could meet. She had a fabulous new hot car that her family had given her, but I noticed that when the conversation turned to automobiles and someone asked her what she drove, she nonchalantly said, "A Chevy." She had an apartment in Georgetown.

Everything was quite civilized, we stood around sipping cocktails and wine, when suddenly a rich guy, Lance, perhaps twenty-one years old, drinking white wine heavily, sporting a crew cut and a white knitted tennis jersey, very varsity, suddenly, for some reason no one could discern, slapped Margie hard, right in the face, crack!, tearing off her earring, blood spilling from her ear. This was so inappropriate none of us could believe it for a couple seconds, but by the time Margie gave out a little scream and began to cry, my brother Mark had already tackled Lance, a full-bore, head-on tackle like Sam Hough the great Giants' linebacker. Lance went down, hard, my brother on top of him. I and others joined in, piling on Lance. You could hear Margie sobbing as she ran into her bedroom. But under the pile, as Lance struggled fruitlessly with us, we could also hear him. He was furious at us, trying to shout, but our pressure made it hard for him to breathe. He spat out his outrage as he twisted to free himself: "Get off me, you fuckers! You're on my tennis arm, you bastards! Goddamn it! You're on my fucking tennis arm!"

(Yes, Scott Fitzgerald was right. The rich are different from you and me.)

THE FACE OF GOD

As I waited for Karen, I continued to experiment with acid. Ken Kesey on the West Coast had compared acid to the new frontier. Wasn't that where writers were supposed to go? To the frontier of experience. And report back to the rest of the tribe. Didn't we need outside information at a time like this? A time of real cultural trouble. Stuck in a bad trip. Weren't writers descended from shamans?

I didn't think acid was "the answer." I didn't think anything was "the answer." The twentieth century was a reverberating testament of what was wrong with thinking in terms of an "answer." I kept insisting to myself that if the acid vision was "real," at least as real as any other vision was "real," then someday I should be able to see it without the acid. But I was learning so much from my trips. I saw myself as a human experiment. It was too early to stop. Way too early. The temple dancers of this ancient technology were just beginning to remove their veils for me.

Once, during a trip, I became possessed by a Thoreau-like desire to get to the bottom of things, for better or worse. I needed to see the face of God. God the Judge. I needed to find out who would judge me at the end. What was I up against at the termination?

I found myself in empty space. Without reference. I looked up and demanded to see the face of God. I trembled as I said this. I knew little of Judaism, but somehow I understood that this apple was really forbidden. Like looking into the sun. But I pushed ahead.

A kind of moon appeared, far away. There was a face in it. I felt a quick chill. It swooped down towards me, growing swiftly larger as in a cartoon. A ring of steel with thin rubber stretched across it like a round drum. The hemisphere was alive. A moving face pressed into the rubber, as if the source of the face were on the other side. As the moon approached and then halted, I could see the face quite clearly. It was my face! It looked back at me. Alive and peering straight at me from close by. My chest froze as if I were breathing crystals of ice. I stared in dumb, fearsome wonder. I saw immediately what this meant. I would be judged, in the end, by my own face. I looked at the face. It was so terribly weary. Cranky and tired and angry. I realized, terrified, that was an accurate picture of me. This was a face that was tired of life. Angry at the world. At everyone. A face that had been disappointed too many times. I realized with absolute certainty that I would not want to be judged by that face. I wouldn't have a chance.

At the same time, I recognized the answer. I would have to change the face. I would have to soften and learn compassion. I saw that this was what Jesus meant, when he said: "Judge not lest you be judged." Mine was not a face that you could allow into heaven. Somewhere in each of us there was a sense of simple right and wrong. We would judge ourselves. By the standards with which we had judged others in our lives. I would have to change. It would be a long process. But I would have to learn to forgive. To love my enemies. There was no choice. Even if it took lifetimes.

I began to weep at how tired and harsh I had become. The face lifted up and moved away slightly like the moon in a cartoon. Then, like a computer animation in 3D, it rotated slowly on its axis. I could see there was no head behind it. It was just a hollow hemisphere with a living face in the rubber on the one side. Now I could see the back of the face; it was all a show. When you got beyond God the judge, there was a space without judgment. A large bright space, with no forms, but not empty of light and of love. I saw that all the Gods were merely forms. They were higher than we were. They were between the light and us. They glowed with the light, and we could see the light coming through them. But behind them was the pure light that looked like a halo in the pictures of the Hindu Gods. This was what the Zen masters meant when they said, "If you meet a Buddha kill him." Keep moving forward, beyond all images, toward the formless light.

Somehow I understood that eternity was not a linear sum of a lot of years that went on forever. Eternity was beyond time. Eternity was no time. I began to weep with happiness. I could see that in the end, somehow, everything is OK. Forever.

But then I remembered my hard face. My ugly judgmental face. I would have to change that sour puss before I died. It wasn't going to be easy.

TERRY'S WORLD

Being mayor of a block wasn't easy. Terry had to spend a good amount of his time sitting at his tenement window just to the side of his stoop in order to keep track of the gossip, proselytize for Prez, and reassure the residents of the neighborhood that someone was in charge. Julie was often gone for rehearsals, so he did have a lot of free time. Julie was one of the principal performers in the theater associated with the Judson Baptist Church on Washington Square. Because she could sing as well as act, she performed in modernist, avant-garde plays the theater specialized in, like *Four Saints in Three Acts* by Gertrude Stein and Virgil Thompson. Then she won a featured role on Broadway in *Minnie's Boys*, a play about the Marx Brothers. Julie gave us comps for the show and afterwards took us backstage to meet Shelley Winters, the star.

My life was continuing in its Alice in Wonderland quality. Back in The Bronx, the only contact I had had with the theater was seeing my mother go to a Broadway musical once a year with her Mah-jongg group. Now here I was, backstage, making sophisticated conversation with Shelley Winters and trying to disguise the fact that I was a Mah-jongg baby from The Bronx. I liked Shelley Winters, by the way. There was something of the good sport about her, with a strong life-force and a sense of humor that was appealing. You felt she could take a joke.

Besides his stoop on the block, Terry inhabited an outside, somewhat magical world and during the years we lived on Grove Street, he introduced me to it. Once he asked if I would accompany him uptown. There was something he wanted to show me. We rode the IRT up to 107th Street and he led me to a large old, four-story, brownstone type building: the Nicholas Roerich Museum. I had never heard of Roerich, much less his museum. Apparently I wasn't alone in my ignorance, because when we entered the dark, old building, there were no other visitors. Two old-world style, elderly ladies appeared, perhaps in their eighties, in black dresses, the keepers of the museum and Roerich's flame. You could see how much they liked Terry. They greeted him effusively by name, and buzzed about him, asking how he was doing and so on, as they turned on the lights. They were delighted when he introduced me.

It turned out that I liked Roerich. He was one of those *fin-de-siècle* Tolstoyan Russian idealists who spoke in words that began with Capital letters: Education, The Spirit, World Peace, Youth, Art and so on. He had done set design for Diaghelev but he specialized in painting, generally in pastels. Of course, being a favorite of Terry's, he was not going to be on the map of art history, but rather followed an eccentric byway, painting mostly in tempera in a somewhat crude, but direct and soulful style. He had done his most important work in the Himalayas. Arrayed as a kind of mandarin Taoist teacher, he looked like the archetypal Eastern wise-man, and in a way he was, with his paintings of the heights of the Himalayas, the snow-capped peaks caught at sunset with pink and mauve and lilac tones. If you looked carefully, you might see a lone eremite, sitting outside his cave at a little fire, almost invisible amidst the vast and gorgeous surroundings. These were spiritual pictures, but also portraits of people who had left the social plane and were just barely still in the world.

Terry stood there smiling, watching my response. He was so vulnerable in his way, that I wouldn't have told him if I didn't like the paintings but fortunately, I did. He had given me something precious and he was delighted.

Terry took me on various of these expeditions. Once up to Times Square, where, in a large loft on one of the cross streets, he introduced me to the best saxophone repair man in New York. (And thus, by implication in the U.S.) The man gave Terry a big delighted bear hug. They each addressed each other as "Prez," as a sign of the utmost respect. Terry took me right behind the counter and showed me around. He was perfectly at home. You could tell he frequented the establishment because he knew some of the horns that were being rebuilt. ("This one belongs to Sonny Rollins," he said.) I knew how much Terry was honoring me with these visits. There was no one else he would trust with his valuables.

Once he led me down to a street just south of the Village Gate nightclub where the Village turned poor and immigrant filled. In the middle of a block with no other stores, there stood a little abandoned grocery with clouded-over windows. It looked deserted but on closer inspection, like a palimpsest, it revealed a dusty little Tibetan store. I was astonished. There were no Tibetan stores in the U.S. in the Sixties. Most of us had never even seen a Tibetan. It was like finding a yak in New York. Yet there in the dark, amidst Buddhas and Tibetan artifacts, sat a young man, perhaps early twenties, clearly a Tibetan, and when he saw Terry he burst out into a big smile and rose to greet him by name. He was so happy to see Terry, and the whole situation was so dreamlike, that I wouldn't have been surprised if they had begun to converse in Tibetan.

You never knew which oblique angle Terry would be coming from. Julie had a wide variety of friends in the world of culture and the theater and she often took Terry along to meet them. Julie had a wonderful disposition. Terry could be temperamental, but I can only remember her with a big smile on her face. Once they returned from having had lunch with Richard Howard, the fastidious, elegant poet and intellectual, the leading translator of French poetry and literature into English in America. Terry laughed. "Richard says to us, 'Where do you eat when you're in Paris?' and you should have seen his face when I told him, 'Oh, we buy baguettes and wine, Daddy, and we eat on the nearest curb.'" Terry began his Model- T laugh, "Har Har Har Har," and then his eyes brightened with tears as he giggled, unable to contain himself as he thought of Richard's horrified expression.

Once I met him coming up the block carrying an unfamiliar saxophone case. He was already laughing as he began to speak. "I was over at Marjorie's art gallery. Someone had left a saxophone there. When the guy never showed up to claim it, Marjorie gave it to me. I was bringing it home till I saw a little kid up at the corner." He nodded there with his head. "So I call the kid over and I give him a saxophone. He takes it and runs around the corner, but there was something funny about it, so I ran up to the corner myself and peeked around it and there he was, throwing the saxophone into the garbage!" Here he began to laugh again, "Har Har Har," like a young Gabby Hayes, at this kid throwing a valuable saxophone in the garbage.

Terry could be very sensitive about certain things, especially where saxophones were involved. He carried the insecure vulnerability of the autodidact. This led to a skirmish with Michael Kranish, a follower of one branch of the European left, I believe Trotsky. Michael didn't live on the block but hung out there with us on Terry's steps. He was a slight, somewhat frail young man, maybe twenty-five, with his feet not planted firmly on the ground. In fact, though learned and intelligent, he was scarcely on the Earth at all. Michael wore a wispy beard and unkempt hair and runny nose. He seemed to hardly pay attention to his clothes at all, as if his mother bought old fashioned secondhand clothes for him and dressed him in the morning while he contemplated philosophical issues on another plane. He was less an American than a New Yorker. In fact, although he was not religious, the place he really belonged was a Torah study group in Poland. He was completely unathletic, the kid who gets picked last in the schoolyard, gets stuck out in right field, and then hit on the head by a fly ball.

I liked Michael. He was smart and knew a lot and I liked his impracticality as well. He worked for his father; it was hard to see where else he might have labored or what his career might be. But he was honest and had a basically sweet nature; it never occurred to him to manipulate his self-image or to lie, and this ultimately got him into trouble with Terry.

Michael had a surprising stubborn side. Although the wind always was threatening to blow him down, nonetheless he went his own way. Like when he inherited a few thousand dollars and opened a book store in Brooklyn. He rented a storefront in the bottom half of a residential building on a block with no other stores, a half block from a neighborhood shopping street. Of course, this presented problems with visibility and foot traffic but Michael figured out a way to make the store look really nice so people would notice it: He had completely covered both the display windows on either side, and the window in the door with brown wooden shingles. When our gang from the block subwayed out there for his opening day party, we saw a small sign saying Bookstore over the door, but it looked like there had once been a store there and that now it had been shingled-over and reincorporated into the residential building.

Now not only was there no foot traffic, there was no way to know that there was a store there at all, even if someone did happen to walk past.

We all drank the punch and it was really good to see Michael's face glowing with happiness but the venture was doomed from the start. I bought a large expensive book just to help him out. It still stands on my bookshelf, thirty five years later, unread. This whole venture was a pity in motion, because Michael did have good taste in books, and I liked him a lot.

He was forced to close the store a couple months later. Perhaps this led to the contretemps with Terry. Soon everyone was talking about it.

The incident had begun with words over Prez. Terry had assumed that he and I were destined to keep Prez's reputation immaculate and his memory alive. I liked Prez, respected and even loved him, but actually Charlie Parker was my main man. Prez was really a man of the Thirties and Forties, the World War II generation of my parents and their friends that I was rebelling against. It took me many years to rise above my fears of being trapped in the coffin of my family. Terry sensed this but we never spoke of it. I simply supported him in his Prez discipleship, and I was grateful that he continued to give me rare Prez records and to educate me about Prez and those who followed in his gliding footfalls. I knew how sensitive he was about Lester and how easy it would be to hurt him. And I did have vast admiration for Prez, his playing and personality.

But one day, as Terry was sitting on the top of the steps, not at his window, presiding over us, a confab of about a dozen jazz musicians, hippy chicks, intellectuals (including Michael), Terry went on a bit too long about Lester and Michael snapped, in his innocent manner, "Prez, Prez, Prez, that's all you ever talk about, man. That's just your own ego trip, projected onto Prez. There's lots of great jazz musicians. This is just idolatry." Well, there was a certain amount of truth to this, but as in all religious quarrels, this was more about the canon and theology and heresy rather than a rational argument and it quickly escalated. Bill, a fine jazz musician, in his thirties, and more objective about the matter, later told me that his whole body stiffened, knowing Michael had gone too far. Terry moved toward Michael and began shouting about Prez, saying that Michael didn't know his ass from his elbow about jazz. Michael foolishly stood up to him, brandishing two thousand years of Talmudic logic and no common New York street sense, until Terry dramatically pronounced the

Ukase: "You're banished from the steps, man! You hear me? You can no longer sit here on the stoop with us. You've abused your privileges. You hear me, motherfucker?"

Michael was stunned. He began to laugh, aghast but trying to make light of this. As if it were some ridiculous joke, beneath them both. "You can't banish me from the stoop, man. This isn't your stoop. This is a public gathering place. Like a fucking inn or something, man. This isn't yours. You don't even own the building. Why don't you face it, man? You're just a crummy tenant in a crummy building."

Now, Terry rose to his full football player height. "You came onto my stoop, and you insulted my Prez, Daddy. You've gone way too far." They were both on the sidewalk now. Terry made a motion as if he was scattering chickens off the porch. "Beat it, jerkoff. And don't let me catch you here again."

But of course Michael turned toward him and began to dispute, as if Terry were a moron. "But, But, you can't banish a person from a *stoop*!" Then boom, Terry put both his hands on Michael's chest and gave him a rough shove backwards almost launching him into the air. I noticed that Terry had been careful, even in his fury, not to hurt Michael, but Michael was so light and awkward, he staggered backwards, twisting as he stumbled onto the concrete sidewalk. He lifted himself up, still angry, but careful now, incredulous that Terry hadn't understood this was a debate about legal and common law points and not a plebian fistfight to be decided by mere force. Michael backed off, saying, "You're crazy man. You're nuts." Then with disdain, "This isn't your stoop." But he kept backing off and then turned and walked away, as Terry stood there glaring at him, looking seven feet tall.

Later, when no one was around, and I spoke to Terry about this, gently indicating to him indirectly that he'd gone too far without actually saying so, knowing that he understood what I was saying. He looked a little forlorn but he refused to back down, "There's certain things you can't say, Daddy. You can't hurt my feelings like that. This is my stoop. Everyone knows that and everyone is welcome, but you can't assault me like that. I've got feelings too."

Every few weeks I brought this matter up lightly but Terry wouldn't yield. "Come on, Terry, of course it's your stoop. But with Kranish, you know, man, it isn't right, he cherished his time with all of us here." Terry would nod "no," stubborn as a boulder. "He doesn't even live on the block, Daddy. Let him go to his own block and make his own stoop."

"But Prez, it's *Michael*. You know how he is. He didn't mean anything." But Terry wouldn't yield. For months. And I knew how much Michael missed sitting with us on the stoop. He didn't have a surfeit of pals. One day I was walking down the street talking to Michael and we reached the stoop. Terry was inside at his window, so he couldn't swat Michael. I took a chance and stopped and continued to talk to Michael, but on the sidewalk in front of the stoop, not on the actual steps. I knew Terry would respect me and not interfere. And gradually he joined the conversation, while Michael, picking up on what I was doing, knew enough not to venture onto the actual steps. Slowly after that Michael rejoined our "café," but he never again said anything negative about Prez. Terry never really forgave him. When Terry threw a party for the block in the First Class Lounge of the Queen Elizabeth II when he and Julie were leaving New York, he didn't invite Michael.

I last saw Michael a couple years later when Charlotte and I invited him to visit us in our funky little house on a quiet dead-end road just outside the limits of the small northern California town of Sebastopol. On the night he arrived, we had a lively conversation about Fidel and Karl Marx and such. The next morning I was working on my writing, so Charlotte suggested Michael walk into town. "Just go out the door, turn right on the road, and walk about three-quarters of a mile, and you'll be at the center of the town." Michael drifted out of the house. Charlotte had a funny feeling about this; after a few minutes she walked up the street about a hundred feet where she saw Michael in our neighbor's driveway, facing away from her, staring at the closed garage doors.

Michael!" she laughed. "What are you doing in the driveway?"

He turned around, befuddled. "Oh, is that what this is, man?" He chuckled. "I thought it was too soon to be the town."

MAX

The roaches were all over our apartment. You would return at night and flip on the light and it was like a roller derby without a rink. Scurry Scurry Scurry, take the A train as Betty Roche might sing it. I didn't mind so much when they emerged one at a time. I had grown up with roaches in The Bronx. I just pretended it was always the same roach, my pet, Max. But now this was beyond even Bronx limits.

Charlotte couldn't bear for us to kill them. The horrible exterminator with his bombs! The pain! The violence! They were living creatures as well. She did find an organic spray that would flush them out. But what next? I had a plan. She sprayed. We kept the light off. Then we charged, flipped on the light, and I appeared with the vacuum cleaner and the hose attachment and swept them up, off the walls, the floors, running around swooping them up off the ceiling while Charlotte shouted, "Over there! Over there!" We did this several times. We sucked up about 800 cockroaches into the vacuum bag. It was winter. A cold wave. Below freezing. I tied up the bag and set it on the roof. They would freeze to death. About as painless a death as one could imagine for a roach, and no left over toxic fumes for us to breathe. We both prayed for them and wished them a better incarnation next time.

REINCARNATION

The idea of reincarnation is beyond the pale for most modern people, like some disease Shirley MacLaine picked up in the Andes. Yet Voltaire had it right, when he asked whether it is really more strange to be born twice than to be born once.

Humor can say so much that is true, since both humor and truth are based to a large extent on incongruity. I love the old joke that defines an atheist as one who doesn't believe in God and hates him. This joke points out the great verity that most people reject God on honorable moral grounds. The amount of evil and suffering in the world drives them away. But by rejecting God in this manner, they have already fallen into the power of the myths of the people they think they are opposing: That "God" is a man, a kind of old fashioned tribal leader, that God is the God of the Bible, and that He created us and sent us here against our will, that He has been responsible for the almost infinite instances of suffering and death, and that the only "reasonable" alternative to this position is the cold, random, Darwin, big bang world in which we find ourselves located. (Most atheists and agnostics who think they don't believe in anything believe quite strongly in the reality of the everyday world.)

When well-meaning people present their modernist view to me, I always answer, "God told us not to come here. He begged us not to come." [I speak of "God" in this way as a convenience rather than divagating into talk about "the living light" or such.] Granted this is only a "novel" I am presenting to unbelievers, but is it any less possible than either of the popular alternatives: fundamentalist religion or fundamentalist science? There are a million stories to explain being and suffering, but we have fallen into an impoverishment of the imagination. A patriotism toward tragedy, a compound fracture of mind, a self-destructive anger toward God that we can't let go of, all because we are married to the wrong stories.

Reincarnation is a "novel" that attempts to explain the ways of God to man, to account for evil and suffering in the world within a structure that is just and finally auspicious. We came here because we chose to come. Now we find ourselves here, like the man who goes into a Market Street double feature and then wonders why he is inside a smelly theater caught up in all these insipid little dramas, these adrenalin producing machines, when he could be outside on a beautiful afternoon. But we choose to stay. Most of us are choosing to be incarnated every minute of our lives. Somehow we feel there is a reason why we came here and there are things we still have to learn. And as long as we still have desires, we will choose to come back, again and again, until the last desire is burned out and we return to "Go," to the peace that passes understanding. Then, perhaps after eons, it all starts again.

[Once, I was asked by my class whether I cared about my reputation as a writer after I died, and I answered, "As much as I care about what people are thinking about me in my dream last night." This was somewhat hyperbolic, but not all that much.]

Is reincarnation "true"? How can one know? It's like the Zen master who was asked by the Emperor of China whether there was life after death and replied he didn't know. "But you're a Zen Master," said the Emperor. "Yes but not a dead one," responded the Zen Master. I do know that our inherited world view works to filter out hints of a universe of infinite possibility, a world of living unpredictability, unforeseen mercy, ever fresh mystery, and everlasting love.

SEX REARS

Walking home from the subway one afternoon, I saw Terry up ahead coming out of his building with his arm around Nicolette, a pretty, spicy, young hippie, maybe twenty years old. They kissed warmly at the foot of the stoop. Terry was barefoot, wearing only jeans and a T-shirt. Nicolette had the warm, blossomy smile of the recently fucked. They kissed again, both beaming. Nicolette drifted off toward Bedford Street.

When Terry saw me, he was laughing.

"What?" I said, smiling already as I knew he had a story.

"Nicolette!" he said, shaking his head, fondly. "She comes into my house, the door isn't locked, she knows Julie is gone for the weekend, I'm sitting on the floor playing this Wardell Gray LP. She walks up to me, pulls her dress over her head, and she's got nothing on underneath. *Gounish.* Nothing. I look at her amazed, Daddy. She still hasn't said a fucking word. She puts her hand into a kind of hitchhiking position with the thumb sticking out, she reaches down and puts her thumb into her snatch! She leaves it there for a second, then she pulls it out, holds it up in front of her face, licks it, turns to me, smiles, and says, 'It's ready.'"

I think it's fair to say the Sixties had never worked out a consistent attitude to sex, its pulls and its pushes, its silky allure and sweaty complications. Denis de Rougemont schematized this into a continuum between the antipodes of Don Juan, who desired to sleep with every woman, and Tristan, who stood for finding all women in one woman. I was more comfortable with the latter approach, although I had trouble with nagging horniness. Tristan was certainly the Romantic one. I found it easy to turn women into sex objects at a distance, but up close I couldn't help but see them as suffering subjects. (In the Buddhist sense, that we are all suffering here on earth.)

Actually, I didn't want to sleep with Nicolette, but I found it hard to admit this, even to myself; it seemed to detract from my masculinity in some Fifties' way. I wanted to love everyone, but I had a difficult time trusting them on an individual basis; I carried an old, Jewish, Bronx sense that people might turn unconscious and dangerous, and I was somewhat ashamed of the fact that I didn't like being sexually intimate and vulnerable with women until I got to know and trust them.

Yet, although I was less promiscuous than many, I loved being with my Sixties pals, the generosity, the warmth, the sense of being a persecuted minority together. We wanted to avoid the uptight, steel-glasses, hard-edged, squash playing, disciplined, repressed, do your duty way of life. (We saw it as leading one to project his dark energies onto others rather than attempting to integrate them into his overall personality). We felt that we had a moral duty to let out energy, to dance, to loosen up and shine, to have fun, fun, fun. And what times we had, even going way out there into acid space together, helpless together, risking not only our sanity and our lives, but our immortal souls. But I still did not fully believe in the liberating powers of sex. Capitalism would be able to ride that bucking bronco, taming it and integrating it with the other beasts in its corral. Sex would be co-opted into an instrument of TV ratings. Even though I couldn't see the full extent in which this would be realized—the Howard Stern vulgar use of women as sex objects, the transformation of taste by which a perpetually adolescent attitude toward sex became confused with adult tolerance and sophistication among would-be cosmopolitan urbanites

I struggled to stay faithful to Charlotte in spite of the '60s imperative to trash bourgeois morality. [Although it occurs to me that staying faithful and married for life is not exactly a bourgeois trait these days.] I was enamored of the idea of finding your true partner and abiding with her through eternity. (Isis and Osiris!) This romantic notion would fall when my resistance collapsed in California in the '70s, after my book came out and smart, funny women began to hit on me, something I could never have imagined before. When the light of the counterculture waned, all the old cockroaches crawled out of the walls—my unfulfilled teenage fantasies of dark sex-goddesses and blonde, California, surfer girls with a talent for writing poetry.

After a year of running wild, I would realize that I was being driven by cultural expectations more than hormones, and that sleeping around wasn't for me. Being monogamous had proven more difficult than I had anticipated, although I have to admit that I probably did better at it than most of the great historical figures, and authors, and gurus I looked up to.

A SIMPLE HORATIO ALGER STORY

In the fall of 1970, Karen invited me up to her office to review her suggestions for the book. I was a nervous jitter-head by then, having not seen her for months. What would Karen want? I had liked her when we'd met, but I didn't really know her. And what would happen to my soul when I gave up my point of opposition to this rabid society?

Karen had done me a favor during the summer. She'd recommended me to an Italian man from Venice who'd been a set designer for Fellini movies. He desired to direct a film on his own. She arranged a meeting between us at his apartment. He was very cordial and charming, but he merely had vague ideas on the order of an affair between a young American and an older Italian woman. There was really nothing substantial there for me, but I enjoyed talking with him. Made me feel like a real writer.

I remember he was playing a record softly in the background which I recognized as Vivaldi. "Oh, I love Vivaldi," I had said, to begin the conversation. "Yes," he smiled. "He's from my home town." This amazed me. I had thought of Vivaldi as a name outside of space-time, one of the immortals, like a statue in the NYU Hall of Fame colonnade in The Bronx. But now I realized Vivaldi was a guy, like me, with a hometown. I wondered how it would feel to imbibe high culture from your surroundings when you were young. To have Vivaldi's house down the street from where you lived.

Karen apologized for making me wait so long for the book. She offered to take me out for a proper author's lunch to celebrate. "Come on, I'll treat. It's on Dial. We'll go to a posh restaurant." I wasn't ready for a posh restaurant. I wanted to talk about the book. Not to be distracted by waiters or food. I would have really preferred a luau where everyone ate with their hands. I didn't want to join the decadent lunch crowd while my brother-in-law was locked up somewhere in a mud hut in Asia. I was too apprehensive about her response to the book to celebrate.

I showed up in my customary bum clothes, torn jeans, a work shirt. A nattily dressed man was seated with her, just rising to leave. I recognized him as John Simon the famous theater critic. Karen introduced us as he left. We shook hands. I remember his finely tailored gloves. I asked Karen if we could dine at some inexpensive restaurant where we'd be left alone. She smiled and took me to a place across the street that specialized in salads and hamburgers and was above concern about table cloths. I ordered the first carafe of red wine and a cheeseburger. We began to go through her markings in the text and to drink. Soon we were both drunk. I was relieved to see that Karen had meant what she had said. She had not changed the substance of the book. Merely pointed out excesses of poetic language, inconsistencies of character, and such. She was going to help me! Of course, we didn't get through much of the book, just a sampling, but I could see it was going to be OK. I objected in a couple places and she just said, "Think it over. You'll make the final decision. But I'd change it if I were you." Six months of worry and potential anger were dissolving with every minute. With every glass of wine. Karen was right. It was a time to celebrate. We drank another carafe of red wine. We were laughing as we staggered back to her office.

I see now that I was living out the real American success story. Poor guy from the nowhere Bronx becomes an American novelist. But in the crazy context of the Sixties, it was like a Horatio Alger story as played by Dennis Hopper. In Hollywood, if you talk about "selling out" they don't understand what you mean. It would be as if you were suddenly speaking Croatian. But at that time in the counterculture, selling out was as dangerous as LSD. Success in the straight world was a sign that you were endangering your soul. I thought about this all the time. Some nights I felt I should not publish at all. Suppose I succeeded and attained a real voice in the society. Leo Tolstoy had stood up to the Czar of Russia, telling young people not to respond to the draft and the Czar had hesitated to touch him. (In part because he was a nobleman and his aunt was a lady-in-waiting to the Czarina.) Of course I wasn't Tolstoy, and the times had changed, but the Sixties were an era when you could still believe that a writer could make a difference, could serve as a role model and change people's lives. How to behave? How to carry this responsibility toward one's audience and one's *soul*? (A term which might seem silly nowadays, but which would have made perfect sense to Turgenev, or Dostoevsky or Tolstoy, the giants at the head of the line of spiritual writers that I, a neophyte, aspired to.)

I read the *Bhagavad-Gita*, the ancient Hindu holy book and I took my answer from there. Do not do it for your petty, selfish ego. For the old dreams that incubated during those lonely nights walking the dangerous, concrete, gray-lonely streets in the Bronx; dramas of wealth and power and fame in a Technicolor world. Do it for Krishna. Do it for that unconditioned, pure, center of your deepest self. Do it unselfishly as part of a Karma Yoga, a yoga of service, what the Buddha called right work. That's why I had been so nervous about Karen's response, and why I had not changed the book for Bob Gottlieb. I had to keep this pure or I could not live with myself.

Being a writer in America was a difficult path at any time. I understood how many good, worthy, young people had taken up this task and failed, and how few had succeeded. How dangerous it was for you whether you made it or not. You wouldn't want to be in the business of selling life insurance policies to American writers. I can name thirty heroes and heroines right now, off the top of my mind, who died unnatural deaths by alcohol, drugs, shooting oneself, jumping off ships, or illness caused by negligence or poverty. Many had lost their way before they died. That was the greater danger. As Ken Kesey had said, once that big spotlight shines down on you, it's hard to step out of it.

The three contemporary writers who had most influenced me as a young man, Kerouac, Salinger, and Purdy, had all retreated and gone into hiding. I brooded over the sad news that in Kerouac's case it was too late. He died of drink in Florida. He had had his problems in life, but when you read what he wrote about the golden eternity, you knew he had gone there when he left St. Petersburg.

CUTTING

Tolstoy had said that rewriting is cutting, but I was reluctant to remove many of my "pearls" as I worked on the book with Karen. The rewriting went surprisingly fast. Karen hadn't asked for much, and most of what she asked for was reasonable, so I could easily go through a hundred pages of manuscript a week. Later I would be sorry that I hadn't taken more of Karen's advice. In retrospect, although some people see this as my best book [the *New York Times Book Review* ran a photo of me with my long hair in a red, white, and blue headband, and called it 'an honorable attempt at the great American novel'], I think it was an honorable attempt, but with emphasis on the *attempt*. I am painfully aware of the cuts I could have made to tighten the text and speed its movement and clarify passages that are more obscure than necessary. But Karen was a good sport about all this, always tactful in leaning on me.

A few times, we worked on the book at Miles Davis' house, a four-story, brownstone style pad on the upper West Side. Miles had the first two floors, Karen an apartment on the third floor, and Richard Pryor's wife lived on the fourth. I never met Miles during these sessions, but I picked up from Karen that he was having trouble with cocaine and that she had had to come to his aid on occasion. I was never clear about Karen's relationship with Miles, but it was obvious they were at least close friends, not merely landlord and tenant.

HIPPOS AND DIVAS

Late in 1970, Karen moved to a nice older apartment house in the same neighborhood as Miles. Karen had told me that Miles had become too difficult with his cocaine troubles, and such. We were working on the book at her new place one afternoon, shortly after she had settled in, when the phone rang. I heard Karen talking. "No Miles . . . I don't think so, Miles . . . We're editing a book here." I could see that she was trying to be reasonable but that she liked Miles and was giving ground and smiling as they spoke. She turned to me. "It's Miles. He wants to come over and watch us work." She shrugged and laughed as if dealing with a spoiled but beloved child. "What do you think? You think we could work with Miles here? He sounds pretty coked up."

Time stopped for a second. I had reached one of those turning points which had been entering my life of late. Miles Davis wanted to come over and watch me work.

He was high on coke. It was obvious we wouldn't really get much work done. We would do coke with Miles. Miles was being disruptive and irresponsible of late and losing it. Who knew where this might lead?

I was not a great fan of cocaine, but that wasn't the problem. I was simply stunned into stasis. Miles! Irwin Licker had been imitating him for years. We all had imitated him. He was the icon we prayed to in the late-Fifties. This was like receiving a phone call from Picasso or Matisse. How could he be coming over to watch me? The motorcycle was moving too fast. I was scared. I sputtered out to Karen, trying to be cool, "I don't know. From what you've been saying about him over the past couple months, I don't think we'll get much work done."

Karen immediately came back down to her rational self, no doubt remembering why she had moved out of Miles' house. "No, I don't think so right now, Miles," she said into the phone, gently. "We've really got to do this work."

They spoke for few moments more, quietly, then Karen hung up. "I'm glad you said that," she said. "Really. Miles has been impossible lately." We returned to editing the book.

For decades I cursed myself for that failure of nerve. How could I not have met and partied with Miles? I knew he would have liked me. I liked him and his music. I knew how to be liked by people when I wanted to be. How could I possibly have been so craven? So Bronx. This story became part of my legend. When a scholar wrote a book on batboys and Jerome Klinkowitz told him I had waved Willy Mays off a fly ball during batting practice when I had been batboy at the Polo Grounds, Jerry also related this Miles story to him, and the professor wrote that I was possibly the only person in the world ever to have waived off both Willy Mays and Miles Davis.

Now, in writing about this, I see something else that was at work. I did love Miles' music. The Gil Evans and "Milestones" and "Kind of Blue" classic Miles. Miles and Coltrane and Cannonball, and "Porgy and Bess" and "Sketches of Spain" and the great live "Miles at Carnegie Hall" with the Hank Mobley solo on "So What." But now Miles was no longer on the same wavelength. I couldn't have won him over so easily if I were honest. He was yielding to a kind of *Playboy* magazine materialism that I could no longer follow. The thousand dollar slim Italian suits, the boxing and Maseratis and treating chicks like shit. And I didn't really like Miles' music right then. The "Bitches Brew" era. I could respect that he was trying to move on from classic Fifties' jazz, but I found I wasn't listening to these new records despite my understanding of why he went there. I was no longer into worshiping divas, the great geniuses who disdained to look at their audiences, the great individualists who walked off the stage after their own solos. I was moving beyond the old inherited hierarchies, the bull hippo who had to be king of the beach.

I was moving towards a more democratic conception of art and the relation of the artist to his audience, to women, and democracy, and materialism. I was coming into a certain independent sense of who I, the son, was.

Miles was not a poor boy overcome by the presence of riches, and fame, and beautiful women, and the best aristocratic possessions. His father was a dentist. He went to Julliard. He was of a higher social class than I. Nonetheless, as I look back, I see his legacy as even greater than I had thought it would be. One of the greatest musical bequests that anyone has left us in the twentieth century. Miles suffered greatly and gave us so much, and I have regretted a thousand times not meeting him that day.

Hadn't I discovered that the most intense, fearsome, controversial artists were often lonely and quite nice when you approached them civilly with respect? Nina Simone was reputed to be angry and unapproachable, but when I, as a student, went up to her at the Village Gate and asked her some questions about her playing, she was as friendly to me as she could have been. And Coltrane, though playing himself to death with frightening fire, was always so polite and generous when I would address him at Pep's in Philly, between sets during the Saturday afternoon jam sessions. And back in the early Sixties, when I went to the ballet for the first time with my college pal Dan Heyman, we had a great time, but afterwards we decided to move to more familiar territory, heading away from geometry of bodies to the felt math of jazz down at the Five Spot on the Bowery where Ornette Coleman was playing with his Quartet with Don Cherry. Ornette was the most controversial figure in jazz at the time. The public didn't get what he was playing, his disharmonies and free rhythms. Even the jazz musicians were putting him down for coming too close to that thin Harlem River that separated improvisation from fraud. Ornette was as frightening a figure as I could have imagined. I saw him as terrifyingly abstract, stubborn enough to fight a two front war at once. Yet when he finished the set, and he was climbing down from the little bandstand behind the bar, I couldn't resist asking him about the new saxophone he was playing, the famous plastic one that he had brought back from England and thereby created a hurricane of vilification. Symphony Sid was detailing the controversy every night on his jazz show. Ornette turned to me and looked into my eyes, and suddenly I saw, with amazement, that he was an innocent, he was just playing his music and somehow couldn't really understand why everyone was so upset. He said to me in the sweetest voice, with a shy smile, "It's right over there." He indicated the bandstand. "Why don't you go and pick up it and see how it feels." He smiled at me again as he passed. I looked at the bandstand. There was no way I was going up there to touch the most famous saxophone in the world. But I learned a lesson about artists that night.

I was learning every day. The trick was to stretch my self-image gradually, so it wouldn't tear apart. If Miles had called again a month later, I would have said yes. But he never called again.

However, I did say yes at the jam sessions at Casey's Restaurant on Monday nights. Casey's sat just north of Sheridan Square. After the diners departed, a small jazz group would form around the beautiful, large, grand piano across the aisle from the bar: David Amram on French horn, Jeremy Steig on flute, the painter Larry Rivers on tenor, the novelist Frank Conroy on piano, with one of several excellent bass players. Sometimes Charlie Mingus would arrive and actually play a bit of bass. Here I saw his charm, without the public rage that he often carried. His sweet smile. Usually there would only be about eight or ten people left in the place. The meal was over, the businessmen and tourists gone. Perhaps Norman Mailer and his ex-wife Adele, the one he had stabbed when he had run for mayor and gone crazy. Sometimes Paul Desmond. A few other recognizable artists and musicians at the bar. Some random music lovers who had stumbled upon this treat.

David Amram was a musical genius. He collected instruments from around the world and played them all. He could knock out tunes on his head with his knuckles. He had been the first Composer in Residence under Leonard Bernstein at the New York Philharmonic. He had written the sad, haunting music I had loved for Archibald MacLeish's play, *Job*, when I had seen it on Broadway as a student.

Most of all, he was a rare person of generous high spirit. He wrote the music and was featured in the beat film that Jack Kerouac had written and narrated, *Pull My Daisy*, with Allen Ginsberg, Gregory Corso, and Larry Rivers. He was a living link to that beat world that I had idolized. Jeremy Steig was a well known jazz and rock flautist who recorded with his band, "Jeremy and the Satyrs." They were both fabulous musicians. And there they were, playing with Charlie Mingus, just for me, and Mailer and Adele, and Desmond, and a few other hip people after hours. They did this each Monday. I knew I would be returning every week. Wait till Charlotte heard what I had stumbled onto, just wandering around the neighborhood at night!

Frank Conroy was the hot writer in New York that year. I had liked his first and only book, *Stop Time*. Three years older than me, he wrote stories for the *New Yorker*. Conroy was handsome in a doomed, Scott Fitzgerald kind of way.

Karen told me that Bob Gottlieb had given him a huge advance on his next novel, the largest advance on an unwritten serious novel in history. He drank and raced around Manhattan in a sports car at night. There was something desperate about him. He liked money and rich women. For some reason Karen and he were having a feud. He had received famously splendid blurbs for his book from Mailer and Styron. Karen told me that beforehand "he followed them around so closely that everyone called him Mailer's wallet."

But after their set, he sat next to me at the bar and began to talk. I found him to be a wonderful guy. I loved his piano playing. Just the way I would want to play if I studied some piano. He was no Oscar Peterson. He didn't have the chops. He was a writer. But he had soul. He played beautiful chords, feeling his way deeply into the sounds. He played simple songs, like jazz versions of Beatle tunes, but he played them with feeling and beauty. We spoke about *Stop Time*. He told me the publishers had trouble deciding whether to present it as a novel or a memoir. (Karen later told me she thought this hurt the sales.) He said that everything in the book actually happened. I told him I was going to be a novelist as well. We talked about details of his book; he filled me in on some of the characters.

When he returned to the stand for the next set, a young guy at the bar struck up a conversation with me. He was a student of David Amram's at Rutgers. A nice guy who loved jazz. David Amram came up to us at the music's end. He invited the student to join him and the others for a little party at his apartment which was just a couple blocks away. Then, with his large spirit and intuitive understanding of a situation, Amram turned to me and smiled: "Why don't you come, too?"

David Amram's apartment was unpretentious and warm. We were all in a large living room scattered with musical instruments and objets d'art collected in his travels. I felt like we had been transported into *Pull My*

Daisy, which I had seen as a message from an alternative universe, an unthinkable place in which people who might understand me lived. Now I was an insider. Inside the movie. Making conversation about politics and art while watching myself with amazement.

[Jack Kerouac had died a year before. He was a fine artist, and a loveable person with a beautiful soul. I don't know if I could have become a novelist without his example. He understood Eastern religions, but also Christianity in its deepest, Dostoevskian sense as a religion of ultimate forgiveness and love. His vulnerability and success invited attacks from those who were more anchored in the world of manners and social reality, like John Updike, Herb Gold, and Truman Capote, attacks that surprised and burned him like dry ice. He really did know about the space of pure being within, but there was no getting around the fact that he had isolated himself and had drunk himself to death at age forty-seven, a slow, legal suicide. What had gone wrong?

The Buddhists speak of "attachment" as a negative term, a clinging to something or someone you feel you can't afford to let go of. A suffocating closeness that prevents you from seeing the object of your attachment clearly. (Later I would come to see that attachments stand between you and the light, even the last attachments, those to gurus and forms of God.) Kerouac's problems seemed to be related to his attachment to two objects: his mother, and an old dream of an America that no longer existed. Kerouac's America was a land of Mom and innocence, apple pie and ice cream. He couldn't adjust to a new America in which Dad had split, and Mom held two jobs, and corporations provided the apple pie and ice cream, along with a deadly cargo of preservatives, pesticides, cow-hormones, trans-fatty acids, and cholesterol.

He was furious when the protestors burned the American flag. The flag to him was still being raised by the heroes in Iwo Jima. He couldn't accept that the halls of Montezuma and the shores of Tripoli were the sites of oil deposits.]

Next Monday, Charlotte accompanied me to Casey's. She loved it there as I knew she would. Soon she was taking jazz flute lessons from Jeremy Steig.

The musicians from Casey's, with Charlie Mingus on bass for the evening, played a benefit at the Fillmore East on a weekday evening.

Here the other side of Mingus appeared, juvenile, angry, some part of him permanently stuck in a hurt space. He made faces and stupid gestures and blew up balloons and let the air out behind the other soloists, making weird, obscene noises as they played, particularly behind Jeremy who was the most difficult of the group to get along with. But back at Casey's things went on as usual. I was astonished later, when I heard that Frank Conroy had taken the job as Director of the Literature Program of The National Endowment for the Arts in Washington, D.C. Then he moved on to the most prestigious position in the Creative Writing field: Director of the influential Writers' Workshop at the University of Iowa. He never did write that novel for Gottlieb. I guess he felt he needed a stream of money. He had moved straight toward the centers of power and prestige. How would he survive dealing with college administrators and rich alumni? And teaching students who wrote in much more complex styles than his own?

Three decades later Charlotte, who was living in Cleveland, told me that he had finally written a second novel and she thought it was terrific. I had my doubts. Perhaps Charlotte was biased in her judgment, seeing the book through the rose-colored glasses she employed to look at the good old days of her life. When I read the book, *Body & Soul*, I was surprised to see that it was not like something out of the sophisticated and heady Writers' Workshop, but rather a book that could have been written a hundred years before, by Dreiser or Fitzgerald. Yet I dug his quiet, sincere, soulful immersion in his work, similar to the way he had played tunes like "Norwegian Wood" on the piano. The book moved me. Somehow he had resisted the influence of his own writers' workshop and had written a book that was simple and touching. No contemporary novelist can write about music like Frank Conroy.

[Years later, he turned up singing in the chorus and writing the notes for a CD by a young jazz singer I like, Karrin Allyson.]

His novel about music was not a great financial success. He died at the age of 69. Like F. Scott Fitzgerald, he was handsome, charming, and incredibly talented, and yet he seemed weak in the face of money and glamour and social prestige. He was the author of two novels. I wonder what he could have become if he had taken a different path in his life.

PLAYING IN CONCERT

When it was time for her debut, Charlotte invited me to the year-end concert of students at her music school. I had never been to the school, and she had never played in public. I looked forward to it. She was to play Bach. I had always loved Bach. Charlotte's playing his flute music every day had made him seem a member of our household. Charlotte and I also loved Mozart, and since we had never been to the Metropolitan Opera, we had gone up there to hear *The Magic Flute*. We liked the opera but not the surrounding social scene—people in expensive fashions standing at the bar, trying to appear classy. It reminded me of a *bar mitzvah*.

One evening, listening to Mozart on our phonograph late at night, I said to Charlotte, "I wonder what percentage of people are real geniuses? Do you think it stays the same at all times?"

"Yes," she said, with surprising assurance.

"And what percentage is that?" I said, teasing her.

"Ten percent."

"How'd you come up with that number?"

"God always takes his tithe," she said, quietly.

Another time, I said to her, "You remember in the Gospel of John, it starts, 'In the beginning was the Word'?"

She nodded. I continued, "Well actually what God said to John was, 'In the beginning was the *Void*.' The Light, the formless. But John thought that because God had a Jewish accent, when God said, *Void*, he was really trying to say, *Word*. So John mistranslated it to *Word*."

She looked at me for a second and then laughed in that way she did when I went really off the wall, a laugh that was 90% amused and 10 % psychiatric.

I was seated in the auditorium early at the local music school, watching as the rest of the audience arrived. Virtually all were couples in their thirties. I wondered about this, until the lights went down and the students marched out single file across the stage. They lined up and took a bow. Charlotte was the last one out. She was a foot taller than any of the other students who were mostly about eight years old. She had on a beautiful dress she had crocheted and wore a big smile across her face.

It was basically a children's concert. The audience was filled with parents. Somehow they all liked Charlotte. She was being a good sport about her odd position.

Each kid played. They were all counting the beats and missing notes but they were delightful and we all enjoyed hearing them. At the end, the teacher introduced Charlotte. She came onto the stage, seeming even taller than usual by comparison with the kids, looking so pretty with that big, self-effacing smile. She picked up her flute and began to play, and out came that big gorgeous sound and that blues timing and black sensibility that she had tuned into when still a young girl in Idaho, that gospel-music-derived approach she brought to everything she played, and suddenly the whole audience quieted and kind of gasped. She played so beautifully and simply that I kept wishing Bach was there too, because I knew he would really have liked the way Charlotte was recreating the gift he had given us. He would see that while she was smiling shyly, she was actually concentrating fiercely, and playing passionately for God. The audience applauded like crazy when she finished.

PREVIEW OF COMING ATTRACTIONS

As 1970 proceeded I felt that something was coming to a close. The Sixties in New York? My life in New York as well? The straight world was too sad to return to. I couldn't go back to my family. I stood out there like an opposable thumb. And it seemed the happier I became, the lonelier I became. I couldn't talk to my old Bronx or college friends about what really mattered. I feared they would apply the psychiatric model. It was the only model they had for what was happening to me. I was a nice guy, too sensitive for the world. I'd cracked.

But something more was ending. America? Nationalism? The world was too dangerous and small for the unlimited materialist aims that drove American capitalism and imperialism. Hannah Arendt had shown that if you were going to behave in the manner required to hold and maintain an empire, you needed racist assumptions that allowed you to dehumanize the people that you were robbing and killing. It was too late for this. The weapons were too powerful and becoming too widespread. An age of human history was dying. You could hear its screams and moans in the machinery all around us.

410

We were thinking more often of San Francisco. Charlotte and I had visited there briefly in the spring. Charlotte's boss gave her a week off so we could drive a station wagon across country to his son, visit for a couple days, and then fly back. We slept in the back of the wagon one night on a bluff on the side of the road in Wyoming in a lightning storm, looking down at the John Ford landscape from our makeshift bed, as we drank wine and the lightning shot down in streaks to the earth, no one in sight for miles.

We visited the Page Street menagerie in the Haight. Our dear friends. Rochelle now living with them. They all tried to convince us to move out there. It was not easy to find arguments against their wishes. We dropped in on Irwin Licker, on Lower Haight Street, in his own apartment which he shared with his trumpet. Still clutched to him like his idea of Miles. Irwin was always easier to deal with than his pal from The Bronx, Joel, at the lamp store in the Village, or his older brother. Marty was still in Canada. Irwin seemed content but quiet. Stoned and lonely.

I couldn't imagine this was the last time I'd see him. He would soon be dead. They said it was asthma.

We stayed with Jim and Paulette Saunt. They had moved to Lagunitas, a beautiful little town at the edge of civilization in western Marin. Practically next door to a glorious redwood forest which reached toward the wide Pacific Ocean. We had had the steel door installed in our apartment, so it was especially startling and funny to learn that their house no longer had a door. It had fallen off. They'd hung a quilt from the doorframe.

Jim was fun to talk to. He would converse on a large matrix of subjects: black music, jazz, blues, Nietzsche, Mahler, Otto Graham, Rodin, Eric Clapton, George Szell, Balzac, Kandinsky, Lou "The Toe" Groza, Brahms. Anything from Rimsky-Korsakoff's *Russian Easter* to The Cleveland Indians' Luke Easter. He was often quoting Yeats in those days. Art meant a lot to him. Passionate about all his enthusiasms and opinions, he hoped to be a sculptor someday. He was playing B.B. King records all the time and had bought tickets to take us to see B.B. in San Francisco. The entire visit built up to this climax. We all got drunk that afternoon, but especially Jim. The first act was a group we hadn't heard of. They weren't that good. The leader kept trying to compensate for this by moving up to the front of the stage and saying directly to the audience, "You *are* the beautiful people." Jim hated this. It was too forced, un-hip, and commercial, like a TV show. B.B. King has said that it was the response of the hippies in San Francisco that made him see that he could actually be appreciated by a white audience, which he had not believed possible before. But I guess this was one of his first shows on that path because, as great a seminal genius as he was, I'm afraid he played his standard straight white people's show for us. Jim and I saw this immediately. Jim began to drink more from the bottle of Jack Daniels he had snuck in. It was not only that the show was directed toward straight, white people, but that Jim had recommended it. Jim's taste and esteem were at stake. He kept drinking and hoping for a breakthrough but it never occurred.

Somehow we staggered back to Lagunitas, Jim angrily denouncing the concert and apologizing to us all the swerving way. Jim kept repeating with drunken disdain, "You *are* the beautiful people! You *are* the beautiful people!" He ran into the house, took his stack of B.B. King records, carried them out behind the house, set them on a wide tree stump, picked up a large ax, and chopped all the records to bits. Then he passed out.

When we left California, Charlotte and I both knew we would be coming back someday to stay.

MR. LICKER REGRETS

In September 1970, Marty Licker showed up in the Village, back from Montreal. A quick, raucous, banging exploded onto my steel door. Shep went crazy. I struggled to quiet him down. I was shocked to see Marty, gaunt and crazed, his eyes popping out as he ran past me into the apartment, puffing from the climb up five flights of stairs, expelling frantic words, way beyond sentences and pronouns: "Starving. Food. Need food." I rushed to the refrigerator and handed him a yogurt and a spoon. He pretty much scooped the whole cup down his gullet in one move, some of the white yogurt and fruit sliding down his lips onto his chin. "You want another one?" "Yeah, Yeah," he grunted like a beast. I quickly handed him a second cup. He swallowed this one in two or three scoops, still panting.

"When did you get back?"

He didn't answer but blasted past me, blurting out, "Soon. See you, soon. Gotta run," as he flew out, slamming the door.

He did show again about two weeks later, in a more stable state, but still off balance. He had stitches in the right side of his forehead. This time I sat him down and made us some tea. It turned out that he had been deported from Canada. "I like the Canadians, you know, but it's a little boring up there. It's like America without black people, man. But you know, I'm a fast runner, right, Jug? (He was the only one who still called me by my Bronx street nickname.) "I could take you any day, right? Don't deny it. Come on."

I didn't deny it. It was true. He hadn't been all that fast but he was faster than I was. "Come on, Jug, I'll race you right now, we'll see who's got bragging rights for Nelson Avenue." He was serious. He began to rise. I laughed. "Hey, you're right," I said.

"That's the story, morning glory," he said. "I ran circles around you."

"Only when I was twelve. When I was fat. But what happened to your head?"

"Oh, man, I was up in the old neighborhood, and over at Jerome Avenue I saw this young Puerto Rican guy with a young chic that was sooo beautiful. As they passed, I reached over and gave her a kiss and man, this guy, he goes crazy on me, shouting I'm a motherfucker and all that shit so I told him, look, man, 'a thing of beauty is a joy forever,' John Keats. . . ."

"So what'd he hit you with?"

"A fucken big Coke bottle. Bam! They took me over to Morrisainia. Can you believe it? Old Morrisainia hospital. It's still there. I told them I was OK, I'm a Marine, but you know the cops, always play by the book." Suddenly he brightened and began to laugh. "Remember that time I found a dead pigeon and reported it to the cops. I went over to the station. The 44th." He began to laugh louder. "Fuckin sergeant, he says, 'Forget about it,' but I stand up to him and I say, 'Forget about it? I found this dead pigeon in the street and I want to fill out the proper forms.' So he says, 'Look, just throw it down the sewer,' but I'm getting his goat now, I can see it, so I say, 'There must be forms for this.'"

"And that's when they threw you out into the street," I added and then we're both laughing. The old stories. The Bronx *Odyssey* and *Aeneid*.

"Hey, my man, the old Jug," he said, and I saw pride in his eyes at his sharp student. He always considered himself my teacher and he was in a way. The wounded doctor. But I could see that with time Marty's tea was turning bitter.

413

"What happened in Canada?"

"Well, you know, those Canadians, they're nice but a little slow on the foot paths too, man, so I found out if I could sit near the door in a restaurant, I scarf it down, and then, whoosh, I'm out the door like fuckin' Lou Brock, I'm gone, but in this one place I ran right into a cop coming the other way and he brought me down man, like Andy Robustelli, bam! I gotta hand it to him, I'm not the easiest guy in the world to bring down in the open field. Anyhow, they put me in the joint and one of the other prisoners man, a Canuck, he insults the old U.S. of A. so I let him have it, and then all the Canucks they pile on me and beat the shit outta me, and the next thing you know, I'm on a bus at the border at midnight and it's all bright as shit there with all the fuckin' lights at the American side, you know the crazy Americans, and this John Wayne schmuck he comes up to me with his uniform and all, the fuckin' sheriff, you know, Dodge City and all that shit, so I start shouting, 'I did it! I confess! I'm guilty!' and other cops come running over and they grab me and cuff me and they say, 'What'd you do?' and I say, 'I dunno, but with all the cops and the guns and the lights, I *feel* so fuckin' guilty I must've done *something*,' and then they whack me and all the *tsuris* starts up again, I mean why me, man, always me?"

I fed Marty and shared some tea. He was staying over on the rankest part of Avenue C with someone I didn't know. "Where's Marquel?" he asked. "And where's David and Valerie and the kids?"

"Marquel left town. I don't know. Maybe she's back in Idaho. And David and all, they're over on the lower East Side somewhere. I miss the kids. They were so cute, man. Real survivors."

"I'm going back to New Orleans. Maybe talk to Tennessee Williams. Can't take any more winter." He stood to go. Reached over and gave me a big hug. "Thanks Jug. You always were OK. You always took care of your old teacher." I had to laugh. We both knew he was only eleven months older than me.

"I remember that triple you hit at Babe Ruth Field," I said, as he walked out the door into the hallway. I knew that would make him feel good. That was one of his big successes in life and I knew he was proud of it. Babe Ruth Field was the Waldorf Astoria of sandlot stadiums in The Bronx, right across from Yankee Stadium. Paid attendants kept it perfectly groomed and only the best teams could get permits to play there. Our team, the Philtons, had played there once, and Marty had come through that day with a big hit, a ground ball down the first base line that he had somehow legged out for a triple. I could still see him chugging over to third base like he was running for his life with that crazy, tilted, rigid way he ran, his head leaning over to the right side, his eyes looking up toward the sky.

As he disappeared down the stairwell, Marty nodded happily and he gave me a warm smile.

I never saw him again. He died in New Orleans.

I HEART UNIVERSITIES

> *"I perceive now that the real attraction of the intellectual life . . . is its easiness. It's the substitution of simple intellectual schemata for the complexities of reality . . ."*
>
> Aldous Huxley

Whenever I went to Philly to see my friends, I stopped in to see Professor Murphey. I had madly mixed feelings about professors at the time. I was still furious at my teachers at Penn, but at the same time, now that I was no longer in their power, I couldn't resist a stubborn affection for them. Professor Murphey was adamant in pursuit of his ideals, but otherwise, he possessed a boyish charm, an easygoing sense of humor that was difficult to resist. He was so smart and learned that even if one disagreed with his totalizing project, one could learn so much from talking to him because he asked deep questions. And when he spoke, you could trust what he said, because he was very hard on himself. I remember once talking to him about non-Euclidean geometry. He had explained to us that geometry was deductive, it couldn't be falsified by comparison with the world. Instead, you would posit your axioms and rules and play out the consequent system that these brought forth. It was assumed that any other system than the Euclidean, which seemed to match our world, would falsify itself by producing internal contradictions.

No one spent much time examining this until the early eighteenth century when the Russian mathematician Nicholai Lobachevski actually tried positing that two parallel lines *would* eventually meet and worked out the implications. To his and everyone else's amazement, this did not lead to a contradiction, but simply an alternative system. Non-Euclidean geometry. There was no longer a single privileged and unique geometry, there were plural geometries. This seemed a theoretical curiosity, but not long afterwards, when Albert Einstein conceived of curved space in his relativity theories, he presented a situation in which parallel lines would eventually meet, and there was Lobachevski's geometry waiting to be applied to the "real" world.

I spoke to Professor Murphey about this one day, and told him there seemed to be an analogue to this in black humor, when it changes the conventional axioms we apply to life in our culture and logically works out the implications. For example, in *Catch 22*, Yossarian makes the assumption that his real enemy is the United States, that *they* are the primary danger to his life, that he is surrounded by people who are supposedly fighting for freedom but are unconscious, with no sense of the real situation or their actual motives. I also used Thelonius Monk as an example. On first hearing, his music might sound disorganized and random. On further listening you realized his playing stemmed from a system that was very logical and carefully worked out, but began with different axioms about what was beautiful and harmonic. It wasn't bad music. It merely presented us with a different universe of music, one with slightly "off" chords and a sad, almost defunct progression, playing "between" the keys in a way that was, from one angle, more appropriate to a dying civilization than the old, accepted modes.

Although I was determined not to open my heart to professors, or to lend authority to anything they said, I remember how happy it made me when Professor Murphey smiled. He saw what I was getting at, in my metaphorical manner, and I could see he was enjoying talking to me.

A SHADOW HISTORY OF THE WORLD

During the past few years I had been astonished to locate a compelling subterranean history of America, in which the U.S. talked about freedom and democracy, but was an expansionist imperialist power allied with dictators and vacuuming resources from poor peoples around the world. It was a history in which corporations talked about the benefits of the free market while limiting competition whenever it threatened to arise.

(Of course, on the other side, the Soviet Union talked about 'The People," but put them in gulags whenever they spoke out, until the whole country collapsed from lack of feedback.)

Shadows were appearing all around me in unexpected places. Some of them Jungian shadows, the unacknowledged parts of the personality which people separated themselves from and projected onto scapegoat figures. The hippies intentionally provoked this, in a way, becoming America's Jews, inviting the taunts of "dirty hippie" with our wild hair and torn or outdated clothing. We saw the main culture as murderous, ad-driven zombies, and we looked for ways to separate ourselves. We wanted to be able to tell our children we had had a "good war." To separate ourselves from the passive "good Germans." But what couldn't capitalism co-opt? It was becoming clear that stockbrokers could smoke pot. They could grow their hair slightly longer when it became hip and fashionable to do so. But they couldn't dress as failures or bums. That was going too far, even though the clothing industry could seize upon tie-dyed garments and jeans and make them expensive and fashionable for a season or two. Here lay one of the positive possibilities for LSD. Perhaps acid was something that the straight culture couldn't integrate into its materialistic worldview. That was our hope.

Now I chanced upon a shadow history of visionary drugs, a hidden story kept from us and even from the people who taught us. Mind-expanding drugs had been incredibly important throughout human history on the planet. But drugs were demonized and their place in the human story was rarely acknowledged, even by most of the liberal intellectuals and professors. The very term "drugs," rather than, say, "magic substances," or, "the flesh of the gods," was indicative of a political angle that had already prejudged the case.

Professor Murphey, to his credit, had once jokingly told us that Karl Marx had said that religion was the opiate of the masses, but that when Marx was writing, in the nineteenth century, it was actually opium that was the opiate of the masses. (In the form of laudanum, tincture of opium, the perfectly legal and popular "mother's little helper" at the time.) Yet the accessibility of cross-species plant information and mystical visions of the "other" were never incorporated into his own thinking at the time; Professor Murphey accepted the basic cultural assumptions about reality, although he wanted to circumvent received prejudices and cultural conditioning in order to arrive at an objective truth. I felt that we young people were contacting something that lay in the penumbra around science, some "other" or, why not say it, some God that didn't want to be measured, that refused to be tamed, that resisted being tagged and delineated and tweaked or tortured into offering responses that were repeatable as science demanded. There was something that was alive and larger than we were, more powerful and more merciful. Something that teased us with predictability but that ultimately would not submit. I didn't want it to submit. I didn't want to trade eternity for twenty extra years of old age, although science had its mercies and its saintly practitioners as well. Thinking about science, I remembered an old comic strip, *Mutt and Jeff*. Jeff is looking for a quarter at night, on his hands and knees in the gutter under a lamppost. Mutt says, "Where did you lose it?" Jeff points to the darkness up the street. "Then why are you looking over here?" Mutt says. Jeff answers, "Because it's lighter here."

Some of us had been taught that Coleridge wrote "Kubla Khan" after an opium vision, but not that human life, and especially artistic life, has been saturated with drugs, especially in the past two hundred years, and that drugs have influenced our heritage of great art, our classical music, our poetic imagery, our paintings and even our science (cf. Humphrey Davy, Michael Faraday, William James et al. getting stoned on nitrous oxide). Virtually all the noted poets of the Romantic period (except perhaps Wordsworth) experimented with drugs. Drugs were a way back to the intuitions that preceded the enlightenment and the industrial revolution. A way of contacting the primordial counterculture that the Christians had tried to exterminate by killing the "witches" who also used drugs. Hans Peter Duerr has shown in *Dreamtime* that the word "hag" for witch derives from *haguzza*, which goes back to "hedge," the barrier between the medieval town and the dark woods. The hag was the woman who lived on the fence between the two worlds, Civilization and Mystery. She was the descendant of the shaman, who kept alive the old medicines and visions and stories of the tribe.

Coleridge himself was a friend of the beautiful poet and actress of the previous generation, Mary "Perdita" Robinson, who wrote poetry about opium before he did. And this line stretched back before that to the Netherlands in the seventeenth century. Was it merely an accident that just at the moment that Dutch ships began coming back from the East Indies with tons of hemp, a new quality of light appeared in Dutch painting, a fascination with the beauty of the everyday? I'm not merely talking about the most famous, Vermeer with his golden light and his slow working habits, and Rembrandt and Franz Hals and Jan Steen, but literally scores of excellent painters (Gerard Terborch, Carel Fabritius, Emanuel de Witte, Jacob Van Ruysdael, Pieter De Hooch, Nicholas Maes, Pieter Saenredam, and Gabriel Metsu, to name just a few) surfaced all at once among this small population at the far corner of the world.

The nineteenth century French also experimented. The *Club Des Hachichin*s in Paris and their friends included Baudelaire, Flaubert, Theophile Gautier, Delacroix, Gerard de Nerval, while the next generation boasted Verlaine and Rimbaud with his talk of derangement of the senses. Were they any different from Jack London in California or Stephen Crane and his friends in New York at the turn of the century, hanging out in opium parlors? In the twentieth century, with the Surrealists and Walter Benjamin and such, it becomes unnecessary to list any further; in the second half of the century virtually every serious young aspiring writer would experiment with drugs. At mid-century, those like Henri Michaux and Aldous Huxley centered much of their thought on these issues but this information and the questions they raised never filtered into the serious academic thought of their time. Hermann Hesse experimented with hashish, and I remember when Dwight Macdonald said Hesse was silly, but to me this only made Dwight Macdonald seem silly. Suddenly he moved out of my Pantheon, from a freedom fighter to a nervous bookish guy who walked like a penguin.

All of these species of alternative visions had adherents who had persisted and, in ceremonies in the woods at night, or rituals in the mountains or jungles, or in documents hidden for millennia in caves like Nag Hammadi in Egypt, they had succeeded in passing down these precious outside viewpoints. Was this what Thomas Pynchon was alluding to in *The Crying of Lot 49* when he imagined a secret postal service kept alive through the ages?

> *"And so, in the fullness of time it has fallen on me, a retired banker, to be so greatly daring and to submit to the intellectual world a new theory of Soma's identity."*
> R. Gordon Wasson

In 1955, R. Gordon Wasson, former vice-president of J.P. Morgan, mycologist, (later a research fellow at Harvard and a trustee of Barnard College), and his Russian mycophile wife, Valentina, a pediatrician, went into the virtually unexplored tribal areas in the mountains of Mexico and found the legendary secret mushrooms at the heart of pre-Colombian religion that the Church had tried to stomp out. They were the first white people to be a part of these rites, secret for centuries. Wasson's article on this (which he later regretted) in his friend Henry Luce's *Life* magazine was influential in beginning the world-wide movement of psychedelic voyagers to Mexico.

Wasson's book, *Soma: Divine Mushroom of Immortality*, pointed out that the oldest holy books of India (and probably the world), the Vedas, were based on visions provided by a substance they called Soma, "the flesh of the gods," and Wasson provides convincing evidence that the Soma they speak of was a psychedelic. Soma (a term Huxley borrowed for his *Brave New World*) is portrayed in the Vedas as a means to seeing the gods and sometimes as God itself. There are debates now about whether Wasson identified the correct psychedelic; he thought it was a mushroom, amanita muscaria (fly-agaric) brought down from the North by the Aryans; many today have other suggestions such as the Persian haoma, a psychedelic whose visions informed the Avesta, the holy book of the Zoroastrian religion in what is now Iran, but in spite of these debates virtually everyone agrees that Soma was some form of psychedelic.

Today we see the ancient Greeks as the fathers of western civilization, reasoned argument, and democracy, but we are coming to realize they used psychedelics in a controlled ritual in the secret Eleusinian mysteries whose taboos have never been revealed. We know that the experience of the initiation took one into contact with death and the members came out of this experience with a different attitude toward life and death and their place in the universal schema. Whatever the substance was (probably an ergot of rye similar to the one that caused St. Vitas Dance and mass freak outs in the Middle Ages), we know it was portable, because the young Athenian general and general nuisance Alcibiades was censured with horror for using it at home in a party that mocked the ceremonies. Alfred North Whitehead said that all of Western philosophy is a series of footnotes to Plato, but we can now see that Plato and the other Greek fathers of our civilization had access to the psychedelic vision. Perhaps that's why their work is so much deeper than our own. To me, LSD stands for Little Slice of Death. I took LSD to practice dying. (Losing my ego.) The ancients had access to a world view that included experience in dying, the great sadness of experiencing the loss of an entire world dissolving in oceans of time, a view of the universe from the eternal outside, and the possibilities this offered for thinking, since death is the mother of meaning.

> *"We have drunk the Soma; we have become immortal; we have gone to the light; we have found the gods."*
>
> Rig Veda (c. 1000 B.C.)

SECRET SIGNALS

Grove Street was fairly deserted on a sunny afternoon. Terry and I were walking towards Sheridan Square. Suddenly Terry began making weird, stylized, ancient-Egyptian movements of his hands, almost as if a couple mosquitoes had gotten into his clothing. He continued to look straight ahead. I thought he was going crazy.

Then I noticed across the street, coming the other way toward us, a middle-aged, black man, nattily dressed in a dark suit and tie. He seemed oblivious of us, but when Terry stopped his movements, the man began to make similar movements, like a third base coach giving signs, using his arms as well as his hands while he continued to look straight ahead, as if oblivious of us. I was struck dumb momentarily. It was like two people were having a fit simultaneously on the same street.

When the man stopped signaling, I noticed Terry, still not acknowledging him, picked up his strange ballet of secret movements. I looked across the street when Terry left off and the black man started up his eccentric behavior again. Throughout this entire oblique and secret dance, they both continued to walk and to avoid looking directly at the other.

As the black man passed us, Terry shouted toward him out of the side of his mouth, "Charlierouse!" The man, continuing down the street, gave a quick little surreptitious smile toward us as he walked on.

I looked quizzically toward Terry as we proceeded on our way. "That was Charlie Rouse," he said.

Charlie Rouse was the great, world-famous saxophonist who had played with Monk for years.

"Charlie Rouse?"

Terry nodded happily. He offered no explanation. I guess none was needed. What could you say? I had somehow witnessed a ritualized sign language for those who could hear.

MOVING ON

Our little apartment was often filled to bursting with our pals, especially our friends from San Francisco. Rochelle Gatlin was there for weeks at a time, sometimes with her pal Ward Hoalton, other times by herself. Once, their roommate Bev showed up (without her wooden wheel chair) accompanied by a new boyfriend named Lou. Bev had named him "Lou-coo-ca-choo." Lou was a California mountain man. He reminded me of a slightly squat Terry, with his high-flying attitude, whiskers, long blondish hair and football player shoulders. Rochelle later told me she didn't like to hang around with him because his house was filled with guns, but I kind of liked him.

They had come across country in a camper with Lou's bulldog. There was something of the bulldog in Lou's aspect as well. They also brought across a jar of parsley soaked in PCP. PCP ("Peace") was supposed to be an elephant tranquilizer. Normally I'd be hesitant to try a drug that was reputed by the TV news to make people crazy and give them superhuman strength, but I could see that Bev and Lou were sane, although you could see that they were not really healthy. Like speed, the weeks on the drug were beginning to take their toll. Still, it was obvious that just trying it couldn't really hurt. Besides, it was fun to be bad. If the "good" people were crazy and destructive, it was almost a duty to have fun. It seemed so obvious that the government leaders with their uptight lives and rimless specs and the military officers who spent their evenings polishing their belt buckles were transforming all that repressed energy into aggression.

PCP was close to what we were looking for: a psychedelic type drug that you could take without going on a complete trip. The four of us sat around a candle on our dining room table smoking the parsley. Colors turned phosphorescent. The air was filled with love. I loved these people, driving around the country on PCP with their bulldog. I loved all four of us. We had just met Lou-coo-ca-choo, but I loved him already, and we hardly knew Bev, but she was Ward and Rochelle's roommate so she was family. It was so great to go outside on PCP and wind up at the Italian Street Fair down in Little Italy, with all the rides and colors and movement and food.

And it was fun the next night, on PCP at the top of the Empire State Building at dusk. Oh the soft blessed lights of the city. And when that group of Dutch tourists asked me to point out where Harlem was, how could I resist telling them how great the city was and giving them a kind of tour from the heights, along with a short history of my city? I was in heaven and amazingly they had a great time too. I could see it. They were laughing and kept trying to prolong my talk with more questions.

But after a couple days, Charlotte and I knew it was time to stop. This drug wasn't good for you. Over time it would thin you out and wear you down. Bev had lost too much weight. Though she seemed to be having a good time.

In the fall of 1970, Rochelle Gatlin and Ward Hoalton showed up from the Haight Ashbury. They stayed for a couple weeks. We loved living with them, like an idealized family. They kept imploring us to move to San Francisco. Rochelle had even taken out a subscription to the Sunday *San Francisco Chronicle* for us. Rochelle was struggling to remain inside the system, much as I had been torn apart when I had been finishing my dissertation. She was actually making a small living as an astrologer. Ivy League doctoral dissertations seemed like another century, another planet from the vantage of the Haight. The professors were like demented people from central casting who thought they had power. Rochelle had worked so hard to keep going and to finish. She had us all in the sway of James Agee. We were all reading Agee and learning about the figures in his life. Especially the book of his letters to his kind and generous mentor, Father James Flye, back in the Thirties. Father Flye seemed like the kind of older figure we all wanted to connect with in this time of generation gap.

Rochelle ventured to Philadelphia on the train to find out the fate of her dissertation. She had the same advisor I did. She returned home a couple days later and began to weep. She cried and cried. She couldn't stop. They had done the same number on her that they had done on me. Rewrite, reorganize, do this, do that, start again. Perhaps it was just normal behavior in normal times but these weren't normal times. Rochelle was spent. She had nothing left. In spite of the encouragement from her corner men, she couldn't come out for the last round. After all the years of being the most conscientious student, the long path from the working class of Torrance, California to the Ivy League was finished. She cried out her insides for days. Then she gathered herself together and moved towards her new life as an astrologer in San Francisco.

I was torn apart by Rochelle's struggle and grief. I knew how close I had come to suffering the same fate. Perhaps it was just some crazy final determination, some fear inherited from my father, that had enabled me to go one more round. I was infuriated by her fate and in a moment of passion I wrote to her:

> To Rochelle – In dealing with Dial, I've come to face, for the first time, the real depth of the indecency Penn laid on us. _Everyone_ there. They're actually _worse_ than the NY intellectuals. They're disgraceful. I will never forgive them for what they did to us.

Seeing Rochelle, who had looked so radiant and filled with hope in San Francisco, drawn down into the slough of grief and failure until she no longer could deal with what she saw as the East Coast systems and values, watching her give up her life dreams, turned Charlotte and me towards California even more strongly. I added in the letter to Rochelle:

> I think we've passed a critical point. We both want to move to California. There is no twentieth century. There is only the 19th and the 21st. . . . New York is the beautiful flame of the conflagration of the 19th century imagination. It is a tragic heroine in the moonlight. A scarlet neurosis.
> We want to sing in the sunshine.

That fall (1970) Jim Saunt came for an extended visit. Jim was our guide to the West. He was the leader of the wagon train. He had dropped out long ago. He was always trying to sell us on joining him and Paulette. Several people had already followed them out there from Cleveland. Jim was outside the career trip and normal mentality. Often he would call from California and just play a new record over the phone, Clapton or Hendrix.

Thus, I was astonished to discover, when we took him up to Massachusetts and we dropped acid at Dick and Margie's place, that in spite of the fact that he looked like a biker, and had been taking hard drugs at times for years (they had gotten him out of the draft), he had never tried acid. Could it be that on our own, while still negotiating with the system, in a certain way we had gone further out than he had? He went down to the brook by himself, and sat there for a hours just gazing into the rills of clear water.

Later, at sundown, he came back to the house and told one-liners, for hours, purposely bad one-liners, pretending that he thought they were funny, pretending to be a bad comedian, "The King Of the One-Liners," making an umpire's safe sign after each remark. I thought he was funny, though he did go on for a long time, but he scared Margie since he was big, a kind of biker, and she had never met him before, and he clearly wasn't behaving in a normal manner.

Jim kept insisting that we join them in California. We went to a couple plays in New York and he kept saying in regard to the spectators, "These people aren't your brothers." I knew what he meant. He was referring to the people who were trying to become hip by growing mutton chop mustaches and letting their hair and sideburns grow but who kept much of the old mentality. I thought this audience was bad for writers I respected like Kurt Vonnegut and Bruce Jay Friedman, because it tempted and almost forced them to include some "below the belt jokes" in their plays to keep the audience interested in the deeper aspects of the writing.

Jim did make a good impression on Terry because of Jim's authentic love for jazz and the way he kept quoting Yeats. After Jim left, Julie asked Terry whether he'd heard a certain record, and Terry replied, "That's like asking whether Jim Saunt knows Yeats."

"Who's Jim Saunt?" Julie said.

"Soon you'll be asking me, 'Who's Yeats?'" Terry said.

Jim and I talked for hours about my moving out west. Much of our conversations centered on the idea of family. We were both devastated by the realization that our families could no longer understand us. That they would sacrifice us if the government asked. We wanted to form some new kind of family. This is part of the reason why we on the left called each other "brother" and "sister." Jim was still close to his family in an unacknowledged way, especially his mother. I didn't recognize how close until we moved in with him and Paulette. His mother would send him money and would bail him out of any situation, figuratively and then later, literally. He had always had a two-sided life in Cleveland, and now, to a degree, it was continuing.

But I knew he was right when he said I needed to move on with my life. New York City was not the place to be if you wanted the space to create countercultural forms of life. New York was the place you went to if you wanted to get to the top of things, not if you wanted to get to the bottom of things.

BLACK POWER

Black people have usually been very nice to me and I have always listened when black people talk, because I know that in general black people have suffered more than I and that those that have not been driven crazy often have a kind of Dostoevskian wisdom that finally emerges from suffering. This is apparent in the presidential voting patterns, since, in my opinion, black people have been right more that any other group in America. You can't fool them with white tricks and the canned ravioli of political rhetoric. They had to understand white people better than the whites themselves, or they would have been Darwined-out before they reached the voting age.

Nonetheless, I was sorry when the blacks moved away from integration and the ideals of Martin Luther King Jr., and toward separation, although I could understand their reasons for doing so. I wasn't a Communist, but Angela Davis always made a lot of sense to me in her diagnosis of what was going down. The cops might crack our heads and gas us white kids, but they were *shooting* the black rebels.

After Dr. King was shot, and then later Fred Hampton and the others, the black people who had been trying for half a century to impress the whites with their ability to think and be civilized, suddenly looked at the situation—the whites now using poor colored people to murder other poor colored people on the far side of the world—and they said, collectively, "Civilized? Why I been wastin' my time tryin' to impress you, Fool?"

And they were right, I guess. We white folks *talked* rebellion, but they were in a more revolutionary situation. Still, in spite of the social services that the Black Panthers provided in Oakland, I was never comfortable with their mechanical military tactics and formations, though it did get the whites' attention and added to their fear that the country was getting out of control. This was positive in my mind, since I was convinced that the whites would not respond to anything except a perceived threat to their self-interest.

No longer did I head up to Harlem. I missed the great jazz records for sale, and the shows at the Apollo theater—Jackie Wilson before he was shot, singing "Lonely Teardrops" ("just say you will, say you-oo wi-hill"), Joe Tex diving off the stage into the orchestra, Screaming Jay Hawkins with his orange sneakers when such a thing was unheard of, Count Basie, Ella Fitzgerald, Oscar Peterson and the rest. And I missed that great feeling of being part of an interracial scene that was going to turn around this country and make it a beautiful place by integrating its institutions, and, as my fellow Clinton High graduate James Baldwin suggested, integrating the black side of each white person into a larger personal self. I miss Dr. King and his sweet philosophy, the real Christianity, though I did come to realize that I'm not a full pacifist. As my mother said, correctly, "You push Jerry, he moves back, you push him again, he moves back, you keep pushing, he'll keep moving back, but when he backs into a wall, he will fight."

I haven't been in a fight since the sixth grade, but I would have fought in World War II.

SYNCHRONICITIES

I loathed the Vietnam War but it was apparent to me that the war was merely a symptom of a deeper disease. I came to think that the heart of the problem lay in the collision of pre-atomic thinking with the atomic age. This had been bothering me in the Army and was still upsetting me. The entire world was going to have to change if the human race was to make it through the next centuries. And this transformation was going to be most difficult for those people and nations that had benefited most from the previous structures of authority, economics, and belief.

I thought that we needed a revolution in consciousness. We needed to fight this revolution nonviolently with our wits. We needed to dig out the roots of the old culture, its enslavement to the search for happiness outside of ourselves, its grasping for objects, its materialism and nationalism. We needed a renewed reverence for the universe, a respect for nature, a humility toward the Mystery in which we breathed every day, if we were to survive as a species. We needed to reconnect with the Love at the center of things, which we could hardly even imagine any longer after this horrendous century. But how could this change come about when even the brightest people couldn't see the roots of their own culture and core beliefs?

I knew the fundamentalist Christians believed that they had found something for themselves, a story, experience, or faith that they found satisfying, but they had clung to it, had became "attached" to it in the Buddhist negative sense of fearful clinging or hungry grasping. Instead of working with this larger vision against their egos, they had entangled their egos in it, decided it was the "Real," and the only "Real," and that they wouldn't be satisfied until everyone else affirmed their belief by accepting it as the only "Real." Their mistakes were easy to see, but it was more difficult to see that modern secular people had also invested their egos in a particular system of seeing and operating, and that they had received many benefits from this, and they had decided that this was the "Real."

(Yet there was a difference. While many students and book lovers had given up part of their youth, studying into the night, deferring gratification, reading book after book, trying to honestly understand the world around them, many of the born-agains had lazily spent their youth in self-indulgence and were now trying to make a virtue of having read only one book, insisting that it contained all the truth they needed to know. Many of them were now taking an unearned stance of moral superiority over those who had had the humility to study.)

How could we leap outside the culture and see it from the outside? It wouldn't require all of us. There were underground theories circulating which claimed that once a small critical mass of monkeys on an island learned something, Bam!, suddenly the whole tribe would change. It seemed to me that we needed a revolutionary vanguard among the young people who were still open to being transformed. And how were they to attain a viewpoint that superceded the old culture's conditioning? At that time there seemed to me to be only one possible answer while the daily killing continued: Acid. Desperate times required desperate measures. How else could we get outside and see that culture was hypnosis, all cultures?

I found myself thinking about what Carl Jung had called "synchronicities," meaningful coincidences, events tied together outside the normal realm of cause and effect. It did seem significant that right at this critical moment in history, a substance had turned up which appeared to de-culturate one for a day, to allow one to actually see the limits of science, and competition, and war, and to glimpse the benefits of tolerance, and cooperation, the ultimate brotherhood and sisterhood of humanity, the presence of some kind of living God or Goddess or Wholeness, and the possibility of making a world of meaning and love.

I came to think that acid and the atom bomb were connected in some non-ordinary way. Both acid and the H-bomb were too powerful for the planet. LSD was perhaps better left alone, like a genie in a bottle. Yet with the H-bomb out of the bottle, I thought that perhaps acid was the antidote to the bomb, sent here by the gods to provide the boost to consciousness and to our sense of human connectedness that we would need to survive on the earth in the atomic age. That was one reason I gave to myself for dropping acid repeatedly. It seemed my job as a writer. My unwanted fate.

Then I began to notice strange synchronicities: in all the millennia of human history, isn't it strange that acid and the bomb arrived within a year of each other? In 1938, Albert Hoffman, a Swiss chemist for Sandoz, isolated LSD-25 while doing other work, but discarded it as useless. He said that of all the many substances he had rejected, years later he was strangely drawn back to this particular compound, tested it again and wound up accidentally taking humanity's first acid trip in 1943, just when the work on the atomic bomb was being accelerated. I asked myself, isn't it strange that both LSD and the bomb are based on discoveries of German-Swiss scientists named Albert (Hoffman-Einstein)? Both devices dissolve what is solid and turn it into energy.

The bomb releases the energy bound in matter; acid releases the energy bound in ego, in personality structure. Matter is frozen energy. Acid as well as atomic fission or fusion turns matter into energy. Acid reveals that one's stable world is actually energy given form by the imagination, by one's will or thought, or more often by the categories of the culture. Both the bomb and acid work in the fundamental transmuting space between matter and energy.

And then I noticed that while acid is actually an artificial magic mushroom, the bomb is also signified by the mushroom.

My thinking about synchronicities between LSD and the atomic bomb was a pre-Enlightenment, pre-eighteenth century way of thinking, going back to the age of faith and religion. Though this mode of thinking could be suggestive and helpful at times, it was clear to me there could be no going backwards to the pre-scientific age of superstition and authority, the old "I'm right, you're wrong" style of thinking which is associated with so many organized religions. It was too late for that. We had to move forward to a more tolerant, post-scientific age. At least this was my "novel."

But I wasn't sure where science would fit into this schema. I found it hard to focus on what I loved about science: Albert Einstein and Neils Bohr, Charles Darwin, Ignatz Semmelweiss, Marie Curie, on the uses and mercies of science, all the kids who were walking around who would have been crippled by polio when I was young, antibiotics, magnificent telescopes and spaceships, all those scientists and engineers who worked anonymously for the betterment of mankind. I was angry. Angry at those people who had turned science into a new religion in which the beautiful scientific method had been hijacked to support a belief system in which "God is dead," propounded by a philosopher-prophet who soon went mad. I was angry at the men who used the ingenious electrical engineering marvel of television to lie to us every night. I found it hard to think straight about science. Every time I tried, my thoughts circled round to the war: The Boeing B52s, the Monsanto agent-orange, the Dow Chemical napalm, the thousand people who had been killed that day.

I was struggling to avoid letting my face be inhabited by the terrible God of judgment and wrath. The angry face in the "moon." My face. I had to remember the God of Love. Cold eye, warm heart. I had to stay conscious, remain awake, and remember the merciful living light that I had seen for myself. I had to remember that anger never worked for me, that I had to keep forgiving, myself as well as others, even amidst the daily maiming and killing.

"our own self was so pure and perfect that we required nothing else. We required nothing else to make us happy, for we are happiness itself."

Swami Prabhavananda

FILM

There is little doubt that Ingmar Bergman was one of the great filmmakers of all time. He took the Swedish film of his predecessors, Victor Sjöström and Mauritz Stiller, and he turned it into a classic international body of work. His films were usually dark and slow, but in *Shame* (1968) he went beneath tragedy to pure no-megawatt darkness. Not even enough opposition for melodrama. He went beyond classic Noh Drama to simple no drama. We all knew that his movies were affected by the months-long Swedish midnight, but early in his career, in his comedies, he had also remembered that the Swedish summers were all daylight. Now in *Shame* he had given in to depression and despair. I remember saying to people, "Why doesn't someone put him out of his misery? Turn him on! Take him out dancing!" But Bergman could never get any traction off the counterculture. He knew the old ship was sinking, but he was going to stay on board and record the social and personal devastation that ensued. The life boats were below, but he wouldn't jump off the fifty foot pole. He moved on to making movies in which women slashed their cunts with broken glass. This made perfect sense within the assumptions of the old culture. That was when I stopped attending his films.

I began to rate movies on whether they made you stronger or weaker. Did they make you more fearful of non-ordinary reality? Of ordinary reality? In the traditional secular, modern culture, life had no meaning or mooring. The great artist was the one who could face this. Anything positive was sentimental. The operating aesthetic was: the deeper you go, the darker it gets. Bergman was the champion here. He would fix his gaze on the black and stay there without consolation. That's why he was considered a wiser and more profound artist than the rest of us. But I was asking my friends whether it was true that the deeper you go, the darker it gets? I would say, "Yes, it does get darker for a while, but if you keep digging, don't you ultimately come out in India?"

Film. That was our alternative university. In the years in the Village when I had no real job and could walk easily to eight cinemas, how much of my day did it consume to run over and catch a film? I took a course in the early history of cinema from the underground filmmaker, Jonas Mekas. Somehow he obtained access to prints of movies like *Nosferatu*, and *The Last Laugh* with Emil Jannings, and *The Cabinet of Dr. Caligari*, and showed them to about eight of us in a loft in the area of small industry that was going to become Soho when the Village leaked south.

The new films were a university in themselves. The films from abroad. What a time it was for foreign film! Truffaut, Goddard, Resnais, Agnes Varda, Robert Bresson, Jaromil Jires, Claude Chabrol, Eric Rohmer, Marguerite Duras, Fellini, Antonioni, De Sica, Bertolucci, Pasolini, Bunuel, Lindsay Anderson, Milos Foreman, Jan Nemec, Ivan Passer, Evold Schorm, Jiri Menzel, Jan Kadar, Vera Chytilova, Miklos Jancso, Vatroslav Mimica, Akira Kurusawa, Satyajit Ray, great anti-colonial films from Africa like *Mandabi* (The Money Order) by Senegal's Ousmane Sembene, and Gilles Pontecorvo's still-great classic, *The Battle of Algiers*. (It was a couple years later that I would connect with Herzog and Fassbinder and my favorite, Yasujiro Ozu.)

Paradoxically, unlike fiction where I wanted to avoid at all costs a simple growing-up novel, in film I loved black and white, low-budget, heartfelt stories of adolescence and early maturity. Among my favorites in this regard were the early films of the Polish boxer/director Jerzy Skolimowski, or, to a lesser degree, the early films of Sweden's Bo Wilderberg, before he moved to gorgeous color (the anti-Bergman?). I loved foreign films. They sprouted in the neighborhood theaters like blessings. Once there was a double feature at the Fifth Avenue Cinema from Bulgaria. How can I explain how far away and shut off Bulgaria was then? It was more obscure than North Korea today. No one was allowed in or out. How could I not go? I discovered that there were still film buffs in that Stalinist fortress of Sophia, not merely agents with poisoned umbrella tips. And they had managed to see Truffaut and Goddard and to send out two gentle, lovely films. The world was coming together through these stories and images of light and sound. Our brothers and sisters in Eastern Europe were sending us hidden messages over this secret switchboard. Like when Dusan Makaveyev from Yugoslavia, in *The Love Affair*, had two young people making love in a small, spare room, and over the bed, in the corner, you can see out the window where all the older people, many in uniforms, are marching in the street to patriotic songs in some ridiculous, irrelevant parade.

The most influential of these filmmakers on my own work was Jean Luc Goddard. Goddard used a plethora of post-modern devices, interrupting the narrative with political signs, winking at the audience with sly references to film history, talking to the actors over the camera, asking them how their characters feel about what was happening to them, and the like. He brought a sense of fun and unpredictability to the screen that resembled jazz in its improvisations (although this had its risks, as in films like *2 or 3 Things I Know About Her*, in which the playfulness didn't work and became excruciatingly boring). What Goddard offered to me was a sense that my work of art belonged to me, and I was free to do what I wanted with it. If I wanted to violate the accepted forms, to address my mother in the middle of a book, to mix seriousness and farce, to mock the conventions of the novel in a novel, so much the better. And if someone resented this, tough! In one hilarious scene in Goddard's *Les Carabiniers*, the oafish peasant soldiers go to the movies for the first time, and one of them, Michelangelo, leaps up when a naked woman appears in a bathtub, runs onto the stage and attempts to get into the bath with her, pulling down the screen. This not only works on the level of anti-war farce, showing the soldiers as idiots, but on a more sophisticated level it comments on viewers' tendency to identify with the action on the screen rather than detaching themselves in a kind of Brechtian manner in order to understand that what we are seeing is not a picture of "reality," but images that are constructed and subject to manipulation. The scene mocks the disasters that ensue when one completely suspends his disbelief. Of course this is all done with a wink to Goddard's cineaste audience who, like him, are way too hip for this naïve approach to film, and it also references the old stories (true or not) about audiences at the birth of cinema running from approaching trains when they appeared in the first films by Lumiere. The best moments in Goddard's films are rebellious, playful, funny, literate, and most of all, free. Goddard gave us permission for our art to follow our pleasure rather than some notion of duty (i.e. traditional form.) (Duty smacked too much of patriotism.)

But what about America? Where were our films? There were a few independent American filmmakers who had broken through to a small degree: Shirley Clark, John Cassavetes. (*Shadows*! One of the greatest American films of all time.) Films like *Nothing But a Man*. Perhaps I liked the small European films because they were so un-Hollywood. But one of the strengths of Hollywood is that they will back anything that promises to make money. And somehow, *Easy Rider* snuck through. I went to see it immediately. On Times Square! It caught on like an arson fire. Of course. This was a real American film made by people from our counterculture. Peter Fonda, Dennis Hopper, Jack Nicholson. They had all done acid. This was not a European allegory, subtle and slant, it was a direct acid head-butt at America. Yet the film was American, even in its imperfections. And the music. It was *our* music! Up on the big screen. There had been a couple acid films before. Nicholas Roeg's terrific *Performance* with Mick Jagger, and even his *Walkabout* seemed acid-influenced, but *Easy Rider* was really American, far out, made by us. The wonderful era of the Seventies in Hollywood, with all the young directors taking chances, began at that moment. It gave us hope. We were initiating and expanding so many new ideas: Earth Day for ecology. Small cars. Small is beautiful. Alternative energy. Alternative medicine (promoted by former acid heads like Dr. Andrew Weil.) Body work. Eastern religions. Yoga. Organic and locally grown food. (Alice Waters). Dean Ornish diets for the heart. Spacey and radical comic books. The future practitioners and advocates in these and a dozen other fields were products of our beloved counterculture.

SO LONG, DON BYAS

In the summer of 1970, Charlotte and I walked over to the Village Vanguard to see Don Byas, one of the great tenor players of the 1930s and '40s. Don had played with the best and held his own, Bird, Prez, Hawkins, but in 1946 he moved to Europe and stayed there. In 1970 he had come back for a visit, now almost unknown in his own country.

Don was playing with Roland Kirk's group. I had seen Kirk play years ago when my old pal Tom Baruch from back at RPI had turned me on to him. Tom was working for Batelle Labs in Columbus, Ohio where Roland got his start. Roland was blind. He had a small entourage that led him around including a woman midget who held his hand.

There were aspects of a novelty act to his playing, since he often played three saxes at once. (He had re-discovered extinct sax-like instruments: the "manzello" and the "strich.") But you had to be careful not to be fooled. Roland Kirk was a powerful player and a real presence, as Don Byas found out that night.

Don Byas was dying. He was only about sixty, but he looked older, frail, thin, lost. On the stage with Kirk's group, he seemed disoriented. Roland Kirk played like a monster that night. No one could have kept up with him. Strong and fierce, he used his circular breathing to play without stopping for a breath, like a crazed bagpiper. He brought back memories of Coltrane in his abandon and ferocity. Poor Don Byas, who had blown away Prez and Bird at times, was blown away himself this time. He was TKO'd.

After a long set, Don wandered our way. He knew no one in the club. He made eye contact with Charlotte and myself. We asked to buy him a drink. He sat down with us, a really sweet guy; more like eighty than sixty, he looked unhealthy, lacking vitality, but there was something nice, modest and shy about him. He said that he was afraid of New York. He once had known people in Harlem and was protected, but they were all gone. After his twenty-five years in Europe, Harlem, where he was staying, seemed like a dangerous place to him. He said he had been forgotten in America. We told him we hadn't forgotten him. He kept talking in a haunted manner about being alone and unprotected. Charlotte and I succeeded in bringing his spirits up just a little through our attention and obvious affection, but he kept nodding his head sadly. In a way he reminded me a little of Charlotte's father, lean and un-citified. Then, just before the second set, he turned to me and he said, shyly, "I really have no friends in New York. Especially any women friends." Then he added painfully, nodding toward Charlotte, "Do you think I could borrow her to stay with me for a few days while I'm in town?"

"Borrow her?"

"Yeah, you know. I just can't bear being by myself up in Harlem." He hesitated a second, then he added, painfully, "I'll pay you money if you like."

He said this so sweetly and awkwardly, that Charlotte and I turned toward each other and we both burst out laughing. We were laughing like crazy. And then Don Byas also started laughing, even though the joke was on himself. We all were laughing, and I said, "Don, you can't buy a guy's wife like that. You've been gone too long."

"I know," he said, with a kind of sweet, dying innocence. "I'm sorry. I just got overcome by my loneliness."

We bought him another drink. We both looked fondly at him as he drank it.

He died two years later in Amsterdam.

> *"The real illusion is separateness."*
> Ramón Sender Barayón

BREAKTHROUGH

We all know that an object cannot be in two places at the same time, but what about a subject?

One Saturday afternoon, Charlotte and I decided to drop acid together. I don't recall the early part of the trip except that I was using "the sword of my intellect" to cut through any illusions that appeared. I wanted to go out there and find what was beyond the illusions. Then I found myself on a kind of cloud, floating in an isolated space outside of ordinary space and time. In fact there was no time. I had no idea how long I was there.

Norman Mailer in *The Deer Park* says that sex is time. This is correct so far as it goes, but in my experience it is a sub-category of the more general observation that desire is time. Time is a kind of anxiety we feel when we don't want to be where we are. Nietzsche said that all joy wants eternity. That is, if we are perfectly satisfied, we won't be imagining other situations we might rather be in. If you are in Hawaii, at a perfect sunset, why think about anywhere else in the world? You're already there. It's when we are dissatisfied that our imagination runs wild, driven by desire, and we find ourselves feeling the anxiety we call time.

On the acid trip, I suddenly found myself up on that beautiful white cloud in this pure, soft, white light. I felt better than I ever had before. I did not have a single trouble or care. In fact, I came to realize that I didn't have a body. In a sense I was the cloud and the light. My subjectivity was there, but not my limited self. I saw that when you really reach your goal, you aren't handed all the answers, but the questions disappear. I was simply and profoundly happy in a way I had never known before, and I had no desire to change, or to advance, or to go anywhere. I was beyond trouble, or loneliness, or separation, or pain. Just this cloud and this bright, benevolent, mystical light.

I can't say after a time, because I didn't feel any time, but eventually I began to realize I had to come back to the earth. I looked down from the ceiling position into the room, and I saw Charlotte and myself sitting next to each other like two kids on the floor, our backs leaning up against the wall. I looked down at us and to my amazement, still perfectly happy, I realized that I didn't know which one I was. I understood with a start that I could go down and enter either one of us and pick up my life where I had left off, taking on the body and memories of that person and thus, his or her identity as well. Identities were like movies that were placed in the projector over the same light. I was not Charlotte or Jerry, but here is the amazing part: I was still me. There was something completely familiar about who I was—the "person" looking. Then I got it—the Atman, the embodied form of Brahma or God. Now I knew the answer to all those people like Ayn Rand who asked: what was the point of losing your ego to get to realization? Who would be there to realize and enjoy it? The answer was you. You would be there. But a "you" that was larger than your particular ego, larger than your name, deeper and more familiar in a way. This was your original face, the one you had before you were born! The same "person" was looking out of every life and identity, was underneath each life's story and scars.

I zoomed slowly down toward the center of the two of us and then the consciousness branched off to the right and I entered the body of Jerry. I was Jerry this time. I had a body and an individual identity again. I was sitting of the floor next to Charlotte against the wall. I felt terrible.

My body was so weighty and stiff. A sack of blood and bones that I had been lugging around for thirty-three years. And the equally noxious weight of all my memories and desires and fuck-ups and disappointments. My history and my body and my ego. The dragging triplets.

I felt like crying, like a baby just born. Gravity was so heavy. I saw why the Buddha had said that life was suffering. Having a body was suffering. Any body. Having an ego was suffering.

But as I sat there, I came to understand what I had been given. What I had learned. I had contacted the ONE. And it was me. But not Jerry. And it was you. But not your name. And eternity was not a lot of years but no time. I thought of the Zen story about the man who stabs a fly on his abdomen with a dagger. You couldn't kill someone else. Ultimately the same "person" is looking out of each of us. Not-suffering was beyond loneliness if you followed the path all the way.

I looked at Charlotte sitting next to me. Had I been her at the beginning of this trip and now become Jerry? I felt a great love for her, *shlepping* around that bag of tissues and chemicals. Trying to remember who she really was.

I looked around our humble room which I also loved. So sad and beautiful, so brave in its particularity. I remembered from an earlier trip that the world is indeed just a dream, but now I realized: *What a dream!!!!*

My heart filled with love for all of humanity. I knew once again that somehow everything was OK, maybe not on earth, but somewhere higher. Everything and each one of us was OK forever. There was a part of us that had never been born on the earth, a part so deep that it had never been touched by any of the sadness, or pain, or confusion of life, but was still shining at our center in all its pristine and jewel-like clarity, and it would always be shining, a core of us that was more familiar than our name, and that glowed with a soft golden and silver light that was alive and could not be distinguished from love.

> *"The body of God is composed of the substance of light."*
> Pythagoras

THE TAX MAN

I thought deeply about this last trip before I went back to my daily life. Somehow I seemed to have backed into a Hindu creation myth in which the One says, "I," and this posits something that is "not-I" and thus begins the world of duality, subject and object, the world and the observer, all the parts in the drama played by the One.

At the same time, I did have a life to return to.

I often enjoyed hanging out at the store with Rigo and Guillermo. We had a continuing problem for a while with the state tax office. Not much money was involved but it had to be cleared up. Yet I found it impossible to connect with the woman agent who kept calling the store when I wasn't there and then not answering my calls.

Until I realized the solution: No one neglects calls from a doctor. And wasn't I a doctor? A doctor of philosophy, granted, but didn't people have problems with their philosophy? And wasn't I certified to help clear them up? The guys in the store were laughing when they overheard me call the tax woman and identify myself as "Doctor Rosen." But they were amazed when she picked up the phone. She proved to be a middle-aged woman who was exceedingly respectful, and when, to their amazement, we solved the problem in five minutes, I had the last laugh.

Until the next week, when they began chortling as I arrived.

"What?" I smiled uneasily. "What's going on?"

They both were giggling, as Rigo said, "Your girlfriend's been calling all week."

"Girlfriend?"

"Yeah. The one at the tax office. She's been calling every day and leaving messages for you. She wants you to help get her nephew into medical school."

MY MOTHER COUNTRY

BRRRNNNNGGGGG!

When I answered the phone and heard my mother speaking in a guilty, whiney voice, I knew I was in for trouble.

"Jerr, Charlie and I have been talking. We think Rigo is taking."

What?"

"He's taking."

"Why do you say that?"

"Of course he's taking. Anyone would. You're too naïve. You've always been too good for the world."

"So, suppose he's taking a bottle here and there? Or he doesn't ring one up after he sells it. So what?"

"*So what?*"

"Yeah. After Dad died, the store was closed. It was worthless. Now it's been giving us each a small steady income for almost four years. Rigo's responsible for that. If he leaves, the store has to shut down. So what if he takes a bottle or two?"

"What?!! Are you crazy? See, that's what Charlie and I were saying. You're too good for your own good. Don't you understand? It's *our* store. Rigo is *taking*!!!!"

"But we're all taking. I work one day a week and I take bottles and a small salary, too. Mark comes home from the Army and he takes a case of wine. You don't work at all and you get a small check each week from a store that you closed down as worthless. All because Rigo is willing to go there and stand up for us night after night and risk getting killed there. We owe him a lot."

"You see? That's crazy thinking."

"Look, Ma, Rigo isn't an idiot. He knows that he has a great position at the store. He works like crazy, but he makes twice as much as he would as a clerk in another store. He tells people he owns the place and it gives him status in the community. The point is Rigo knows that if the store doesn't make a decent return, you'll shut it down again. So he's very careful to keep it profitable and to make sure we're happy. We have an unwritten agreement. It's worked for four years and if we leave it alone it'll continue to work. Rigo and me, we understand each other. He's not a dope."

"But he's *taking*!!" Here her voice lost its singsong manner and the stiletto came out from its shield. "Jerry, we're putting in an inventory system."

"What?" I began to chuckle. "An inventory system? It'll never work. There are hundreds of different items. Rigo's already running the store pretty much on his own after Guillermo goes home each day. This'll double his work. The store is shaped like a square. All the bottles are on the walls, right behind all the customers. There's no way to stop them from taking a bottle here and there, and even with your whole complicated inventory system, if there's a couple bottles missing every week, there'll never be a way to tell if Rigo took them or the customers."

"We're putting it in."

"And all you'll do is make Rigo furious because of the extra work, but mostly because he'll be losing face. You're telling him, that after he's been risking his life for you and running the store successfully for four years, that you don't trust him."

"We're not saying we don't *trust* him."

"And then he'll get so mad, he *will* steal! Believe me. There are ways to beat the system and he'll find them. He's no dope."

"I didn't say he's a dope. And you, you're the smartest boy in the world, I always said that. But maybe it's time . . . time that we began to run the store. Charlie and me."

"What?!"

"It looks so old. It needs a new look. It needs to be classy. It needs some new energy. Some real business sense. Like we're thinking about getting open refrigerator cases to set in front of the walls and we'll put chilled French wine in them."

"What?" I was almost laughing but it wasn't really very funny at bottom. "Ma, you don't know anything about wine. You've never had a glass of wine in your life. We don't need that kind of thing. The store is in a slum. The only chilled wine we sell is pints of muscatel and Thunderbird to winos for fifty cents. We already have the old refrigerator Dad had. That's all we need."

"We're gonna change all that."

"Ma, face it. Now that price fixing is off, Macy's buys cases of scotch at a volume discount and sells a bottle for a penny profit to get people into the store. We can't compete with that. We're a mom and pop corner grocery store that sells to drunks and lazy people. The only way we can compete is to keep our expenses *down*."

"Well, we're going to be running it now. That's all I can say."

"So that's what you called to tell me? That you're taking the store, after I saved it and ran it and made a success of it when you gave up on it. And now you're taking it from me."

"Taking it? Who said anything about taking it from you?"

"Isn't that what you're saying? That you and Charlie will be running it, and I won't be involved or getting my little check from it."

"Well, that's what we'll be doing, but don't say we're taking it from you."

"But isn't that what you're doing?"

"Jerr . . ."

"Isn't it?"

"How could I be taking the store from you? I'm your mother. I love you. How could I take anything from you? Don't you realize that you're my whole life? That I only live for you. You're the only thing I care about in the whole world. My life centers around you. If anything happened to you, I would die, don't you realize that? I would give my life for you in a second. So how could I be taking something from you?"

"So you're not going to run it?"

"I told you, we're going to run it. And that's that. And you can move on. But don't say anything about my *taking* it from you. That's crazy talk." Now she was hurt and shouting. "How can you accuse me of something like that. I'm innocent! I don't have a selfish bone in my body. Don't you understand? I'm innocent! I'm completely innocent!"

I surrendered. I wished her well, and quietly put down the phone. Maybe it was time to move on in my life. Maybe it *was* time to move on geographically as well. Maybe she was right in a way.

THE DOCK OF THE PAY

So they fired me and began to run the store themselves. My mother was no longer a widow with a drowned liquor store in a slum, a store that I was keeping alive by administering CPR. Now she was the owner of a classy store once again, and she had a husband with a Cadillac who had demonstrated his love by purchasing a huge diamond ring for her and several new pink outfits. It was as if all the tragedies in her life had never occurred: the deaths, the failed investments, the whole concatenation of terrible occurrences that eventuated in the burning down of the Bronx. That was all behind her and forgotten. It was time for a new beginning.

My mother and Charlie installed an expensive inventory control system. Rigo was hurt and furious. They drove over there in the big Caddy that looked like a hearse with fins. The kids didn't like Charlie and scratched the fenders with iron nails.

They borrowed money to install wine coolers and stocked expensive European wines. In one year the store went bankrupt. Rigo and Guillermo and his brother Miguel lost their jobs. My father's liquor store, the one that had supported me throughout my ambiguous childhood, was closed down forever.

PEACE

In the future, about a decade after I left New York, I would receive a phone call from my mother in Florida. She spoke in a whiney voice. I knew that something was wrong.

"Jerr, I've got a problem."

"What's that, Ma?"

"It's Charlie. He comes home from work, and he plops down in his chair. He doesn't shop, he doesn't do the wash, he doesn't take out the garbage. No, he just plops down."

"But Ma, the man is dying. He has incurable cancer. The doctors have given up on him. Yet he keeps on working full time. And why? Because he still hasn't been able to pay the debts he took on to buy you the diamond ring and the red Caddy. He's working twelve hour shifts, three days a week, on his feet for that whole time at the convertible bed store. You're a dozen years younger. You're in perfect health. You have nothing to do all day, and he comes home after twelve hours on his feet, and collapses into his chair, and you want him to go shopping or to do the wash?"

There was a short silence. And then my mother said, quietly, still unconvinced, "I guess you get used to certain things."

My mother lived to be ninety-three, isolated and confused, not understanding why a person like herself, so filled with love for all people, received almost no phone calls or visitors. [Does this remind you of any particular nation-state?] Sometimes when disoriented and frightened she would lie down on her bed and cover herself with money.

How had this happened? I remember her in photos in her album. The bright little girl at PS 4 in the East Bronx. The one with the dark bangs, and the impish smile, and the radiant look that says: I know I'm only visiting this neighborhood. I know, already, I've got a higher destiny. A dazzling future.

And the photos of her in high school. With the girl's basketball team. In the album with her varsity letter. The prettiest girl. The athlete. The dancer. The American.

Again the distant look, the vistas of possibility. The photos of her from the *New York Post*, so pretty and shining, on the rail of a ship: "Showbiz Hopeful!" Her stories about how she had danced in theaters in Manhattan, and had gone to Boston to dance in a chorus line. She was so grateful when her father overruled her mother and decided to let her go. After all, he and my grandmother had sailed here as kids from Poland. At least she could speak English. She could read and write. She would make it back from Boston.

But she was a follower of her brother Mac. The handsome one, the American who was destined for Hollywood. Of course, her parents were sweet, going to that crazy little storefront orthodox synagogue rather than the new large brick conservative ones that were as large as churches and were springing up all over the neighborhood. She knew her father was respected by his tenants, and served on the synagogue board, and donated coal from his buildings to heat the little storefront in the winter. But that was part of the old world. America was a chance for something new and wonderful.

The photos of her marrying my father, with his gaunt, hungry look, uncomfortable in the hanging suit and tie, looking like the skinny Frank Sinatra. With all his hopes of going into the real estate business with her father.

The photos of her with me as a baby at the pool at Starlight Park in the East Bronx, the starlight of hope still sparkling in her eyes. How had all this happened, the Depression, the Nazis, World War II, the sudden death of her father, her mother's subsequent catatonia and death, her kid sister's disintegration and death at thirty-nine, her brother Mac's drinking and philandering, her brother-in-law Lenny's arrest and death in prison, the lost investments in South Bronx real estate, the liquor store crash, her husband's despair and death at fifty-six, her son Mark's great success as head of a 250 person Wall Street law firm and then his death at forty-eight, her other son Jerry's giving up a million-dollar career to marry a *shiksa* and become a hippy?

Her culture and society had not provided my mother with the resources she would need to handle all of these blows, and they defeated her. She

444

felt that her disappointments and pain gave her license to adopt a short-sighted, pleasure-principle calculus for the rest of her life. A corporate-encouraged narcissism that drove most of her relatives away.

But I know that there was a place inside my mother that was never tarnished by her life on the earth. A core that is still shining and will always be shining. She is a young soul. Unlike myself, she will accept many more lives here on the earth. And maybe in the next one the liquor store will thrive, and 400,000 people won't be burned out of their homes in the Bronx.

I know that someday, maybe in thousands of years, she will be seated peacefully near the warm, loving light of God. I know that my father and brother will be there, too. And you will be there as well, along with every victim of the vicious and criminal holocaust.

I understand that this is merely my "novel." But what is your "novel"? And who wrote it?

> *"What is the point of an art whose practice does not transform me?"*
>
> Paul Valery

[At times, on acid, I have performed an experiment by assuming, that like atheists and certain Buddhists, I don't believe in any "novel," that there is no overriding scheme in the universe, merely a parade of phenomena. Acid is a very good way to inhabit assumptions fully and to ride them quickly forward to see where they ultimately lead. Each time it has been clear to me that this assumption about there being no "novels" is also only a "novel." In fact, it seems to me that most atheists, who think they don't believe in anything, actually believe quite strongly in the reality of the everyday world (which they experience in the forms they have inherited from their culture). In my own experience, when you let go of all the forms and beliefs you bring to it, the world begins to move and come alive. This can be very frightening because you have relinquished control, but it is also liberating, since it is a good way to practice dying, and to see that ultimately, when you really do have to let go of your ego and all control, you will be all right, you will be supported, you won't fall out of Being.]

445

FROM MY LETTERS—NOVEMBER 1970

When people ask me why I am moving to northern California, I tell them that if you want to be a freak, you might as well join the circus.

As the time came to leave New York, I thought of how much I had changed over the past four years in Greenwich Village. In general I would say that now, as I write, I am less judgmental, more accepting than I was then, but my basic values were formed in that period, and I continue to hold many of them today. I paid a high price for this stubbornness. Once we moved into the post-Sixties era, the culture asked those who dropped out to pay a fee to re-enter. It was like the Fifties, when you had to renounce your leftist "misspent youth" in the Thirties. Except the Fifties were led by a real General, Eisenhower, while all the postmodern Eighties would be able to come up with was a guy who played a general in the movies. It was not that Reagan avoided danger by spending World War II in Los Angeles. He often put himself in life-threatening situations by driving on the Hollywood Freeway. Later, I was aghast when I heard that the Republicans wanted to put Ronnie's face on the money. But after a while I came to feel that maybe it was appropriate.

Reagan had been selling his genial smile, his corn-fed, Midwestern charm for his whole life. To Hollywood. To General Electric. To the Republican Party. So was it any surprise when we saw him in Germany, selling his surface appeal to the Germans, smiling his empty smile and laying a wreath at the Bitburg Cemetery where they had buried the Nazi storm troopers, the S.S.? You had to be glad he hadn't been a German in World War II.

Now, to get admitted back into the culture, all you had to do was "kick a hippie." You had to admit publicly you were wrong. The Sixties were wrong, the youth were the self-centered "me generation," and it was the Sixties, not the corporations and the media and advertising, that were the cause of virtually all that was wrong in American life. If you complied, you could be admitted back into the "real world," the economy based on greed and addiction: addiction to shopping, to oil, to prescription drugs. You could join a population of corporate-controlled addicts trying to export freedom to the rest of the world, especially to areas that sat on oil reserves. And the adults wonder why their kids are going to zombie movies.

You could see it all coming down the pike. The denial about Vietnam. Blaming the length of the war on the protestors for "encouraging North Vietnam." (Even Allen Ginsberg joined in here. Just as when the punks became popular, he claimed to have been the first punk.) Then the opinion makers claimed that we hadn't really lost, it was just that we were too good and we hadn't really tried. All this was preparing the nation for a next time. Oddly, the military did learn from Vietnam. They were embarrassed and faced the truth that in the future we should not get involved in a war unless our people were strongly behind it, we had clear and limited objectives, and a detailed exit strategy. When we invaded Iraq, it was Colin Powell, the old Vietnam general from the South Bronx, who tried to wise-up the hawkish ideologues running the government, the civilian draft dodgers who had avoided Vietnam. In a great irony of history, it now turned out that war was too important to be left to civilians.

I continued to protest in 1971. I was trying to save the soul of America, to be able to have the history books say that at least some young Americans fought back against the government war machine. I didn't realize that the victors really do write the history. Now the high schools teach that the Sixties were the worst decade in American history, when, for some unexplained reason, the kids turned selfish, took drugs, and ran around naked and sex crazed. Vietnam never happened.

The single best-selling serious novel by and about a member of the Sixties generation was *The World According to Garp* by John Irving. This narrative describes the life of a baby boomer, but somehow this book about a child of the Sixties era does not mention rock and roll, drugs, Vietnam, anti-war demonstrations, campus riots, the civil rights struggles, the black power movement, Eastern religions, Kent State, any of it. No wonder the American people loved it. Here we don't need a Stalin to force us to rewrite history. We do it willingly ourselves. And not merely for money.

Decades later Philip Roth played this card with his novel, *American Pastoral*. He portrayed the Sixties as a time of innocent, well-meaning, anti-war parents, *Saturday Evening Post* folks who only had their kids' best interests at heart, while the ungrateful kids, for no reason, had gone nuts, turned violent, and were bombing and killing people.

Of course, this projection, this weird mirror image of the world, was given the Pulitzer Prize. And the sad part of this is that I don't believe Roth created this warped picture of a decade to satisfy his audience, or to garner a large advance. I think he had actually come to believe it.

[I don't like to write about my fellow novelists, but I had to do it here to make a point about the Sixties. Like the Christians and the Moslems, I think we novelists often quarrel because we have so much in common.]

[Most of the novelists appreciated today, Roth, Joyce Carol Oates, Jonathan Franzen et al., are brilliant at depicting the grim prison of the culture, but they seem to have forgotten that the really great novelists like Tolstoy and Dostoevsky went beyond mapping the jail and offered plans for escape.]

FEAR OF DOMINOES

America was becoming a nation in which the political and the major corporate leaders who appeared on TV lied to the people all the time. A ruling class without shame. They would lie if you asked them about the weather. The majority of the people were becoming stupefied, their brains frazzled by the decades of TV ads that worked to confuse and infantilize them. They feared to comprehend the fact that everyone on TV was lying. Falling dominoes. They worried that their whole world would crash if they entered the post-modern age and accepted the fact that the world they were being presented with was a sham. The strange part of this was that even most of those who were lying, or reporting the lies without questioning them, couldn't face this either. They had gone unconscious long ago.

Professor Larzer Ziff wrote a book, *The American 1890s*, in which he claimed that the 1890s were the first decade of the twentieth century. This was the decade of major bloody strikes, riots, anarchist bombs, assassinations, outside (European) agitators, uppity women like Emma Goldman, crusading muckrakers, and the appearance of young writers like Stephen Crane, Frank Norris, Jack London, and Harold Frederick, writers who went "downtown," smoked opium at Chinese opium dens, married prostitutes, questioned the corporations, and dropped the pose of Victorian civility. This was followed by the quieter next decade, 1900-1910, when things calmed; Crane, Norris, and Frederick were dead, the Progressives and the government worked to mask their power and to temper the industrial conditions to a degree, while literature turned once again to books by the now more respectable older novelists, Henry James, Mark Twain, William Dean Howells.

This, it seems to me, is also a map of what happened in the Sixties. The Sixties were the first decade of the twenty-first century. Circumstances forced a generation to see that the old ways would no longer work in the world. That we were becoming a nation that someday was going to spend more on gas guzzler SUVs than on educating our kids and then believe we were involved in the Middle East because of our altruism.

The people with power wanted to stay in the Fifties. That was where their expertise lay. Many of the brain-damaged TV audience thought that the TV was telling the truth; some thought even the soap operas were real. (Ray Mungo's senile grandmother thought she was dating Liberace and would dress up each week for his program.) How could the public understand that we were headed for a day when 99 percent of the experts who told them about stocks on TV were wrong, a large percentage of them blatantly lying? That the stock market was a devious machine for taking money from widows in Idaho and alchemically transposing it into condos in Manhattan? Is it so strange that young people raised on thunderstorms of movie sex and violence, when given power over non-western people in a prison in Iraq would use them for homemade porn movies. Didn't everyone desire to be a film director? Hadn't they seen all this on the Howard Stern show?

We were determined to refuse to see that in a world saturated with weapons of mass destruction, we were going to have to learn to see what we had in common with other people and not treat other races as if they were savages or idiots, there to help us maintain our wasteful lifestyle. We were not ready to learn that the mentality that killed all twenty-five million buffalo for sport could no longer serve us. That there was nothing we could poison that wouldn't blow back onto ourselves. That the body was not merely a machine and the mind not merely a computer. That these were inadequate metaphors.

THE IDEAL CAPITALIST DRUG

You knew the Sixties were doomed when Max's Kansas City emerged as the fashionable new hip hot spot where the bohemians met the money. Located a little north of the Village on the way to the garment district and Madison Avenue, Max's was where the counterculture met the world of fashion and advertising, a kind of canteen for Andy Warhol's factory. Andy was a witty genius in his way, with a touch of Oscar Wilde, but whereas the Zen Masters had spoken of "cold eye, warm heart," Andy focused primarily on the former.

Max's was an oasis in time on the way from the Village to Studio 54, where pre-Raphaelite notions of beauty would yield to the manufacture of glamour. Where acid rock transmuted into glam rock. Once fashion and the fashionable entered the scene, the poor had to leave. No more the simple Kerouac ethos of the holiness of poverty and the American hobo. The word green had passed once again from a symbol for nature into the house of money and envy. You could only serve diamond-studded jeans and expensive work shirts in so many ways. Americans were heading out on the fashion trail that would lead from an imitation of Paris to Paris Hilton.

Max's was the graveyard of radical dreams. The red shift into impotence and self-indulgence. Where psychedelics yielded to cocaine. I avoided Max's like the plaque.

[Yes, *plaque*! It's a joke on the "beautiful people."]

Cocaine was the ultimate American capitalist drug: it was expensive, it didn't teach you anything, it was white. I tried cocaine a few times but it wasn't for me. In November 1968, Al Goldstein published *Screw*, a vulgar sex newspaper that modeled its form on the counterculture weeklies. *Screw*'s circulation quickly jumped to 150,000. Soon after this the *Rat* began its decline into factionalism. The women no longer wanted to work with the men. Much to the women's surprise, the men gave them the paper. This left most of the technical staff with no affiliation. Marvin, the business manager, a lively guy but never a purist, hired them and started up a rival sex newspaper that quickly became successful though not as popular as *Screw*.

Marvin was temporarily in the money and he could be generous with it. Often we all convened downstairs in our building at Bob Eisner's apartment to smoke a little dope or drink a couple beers while listening to rock records on a Friday afternoon. (Bob was now substitute-teaching students with learning disabilities in the New York public schools. I remember how happy he was when he brought his guitar to school and found that a somewhat autistic child was a kind of musical genius. With no lessons, and hardly able to speak, the child could repeat on the piano anything Bob played or sang.)

Now our little gatherings were enlivened at times by Marvin's sharing a little coke with everyone. I didn't like the way I behaved on coke. Out on the street afterwards I was more verbally aggressive than normally. If someone was rude to me, I would tell them off, much to my surprise. Coke seemed to me to be the right drug for Hollywood but not for the counterculture. As my friend, the rock musician Jerry Long would later tell me in California, "Coke is God's way of saying you have too much money." After a few trial runs, I stopped taking it. Most of the kids from the *Rat* weren't really into it. As I said, it could be fun but it didn't teach you anything.

[Once, in the Seventies, however, in San Francisco, I went by myself to a small club in North Beach to see the band of Buddy Miles, the rock drummer. I sat at the bar next to an African-American man, about my age, sharply dressed in suit and tie. He struck up a conversation with me. We talked about music and books and quickly hit it off. After a while, he said to me with a twinkle in his eyes, "Suppose, hypothetically, you met a guy at a bar, and you connected with each other, and were having a good time, and he offered you some really good coke. What would you say?"

I was surprised to hear myself quickly say, "I guess I would say, 'OK.'"

He smiled and stood up and signaled me to follow him. Downstairs we entered the men's room and stood inside one of the toilet stalls as he pulled out a vial of coke and a little spoon. It struck me at the time, as we took hits, how strange it was that I, now a professor, was hiding inside a toilet stall in North Beach doing coke with a stranger, hoping the cops didn't come in and take us to jail. But I trusted my instincts with this man and I was right. Here I saw the charm of coke, because the second set was fabulous, much better than the first; in fact the coke was so good it made me think that the band and everyone else in the club was also high on coke. Now, looking back to that era, I think that there was a good chance that everyone else in the club *was* high on coke. But I never did coke again.]

DANGEROUS ASSUMPTIONS

The following statement by Robert Brustein, who was the theater critic for the *New Republic* back in the day and one of the smartest and most learned of the reviewers (he had recently become Dean of the Yale Drama School), exhibits the unexamined assumptions of even the best of the respectable thinkers of the time. (He is defending civilization against what he sees as the formless, anarchic, anything goes, postmodern, Artaud and hippie-influenced theater of people like Richard Schechner, Julian Beck, and Tom O'Horgan.) "For all these developments are the by-products of a culture that has lost its confidence and its direction, a culture for whom the herd instinct has begun to manifest itself as a defense against loneliness and frustration. But there is another defense against these terrors, which we owe to the Greek way of thought. It is found in the capacity to live without salvation, to accept the hard consequences of being human, to develop a tragic sense of life. What great art shows us, and particularly the theatrical art of tragedy, is how to endure with courage and strength in the face of the emptiness of life."

Yet instead of the "emptiness of life" of Professor Brustein, Yale's expert on Greek drama, let's look at the words of Plato himself:

> *"having got rid of the foolishness of the body we shall be pure,*
> *and have converse with the pure, and know of ourselves, the*
> *clear light everywhere."*

Plato

There is no longer a felt need for the dean to justify terms like the "emptiness of life." It is merely assumed by him and virtually everyone who reads him. There is no need to question the murderous mess that the civilizations he is defending have gotten themselves into. There is no mention, or probably even any knowledge on the part of the Yale dean and defender of the Greeks, that the Greeks themselves used psychedelics in

452

the secret Eleusinian Mystery ceremonies, which they claimed gave them a meaning for their lives and a victory over death.

The Dean of the Yale Drama School was not going to put his eye to Galileo's telescope and see for himself whether Jupiter's moons really moved.

> *To Bruce and Riki Kuklick—"Luckily we missed the last smog emergency . . . the air problem seems to have touched something vital in people—everyone's talking about leaving the city."*

I HEART NEW YORK

In the spring of 1971 you knew the Sixties were fading fast in New York. It was not going to be a hippie heaven with cheap rents, and flowers in your hair, and fruit falling from the trees, and people sleeping in their cars during the winter because they were living a life of voluntary poverty. I would always love New York. In future years, when I came back to visit, as soon as I stepped on the street my accent came back and my attitude returned. New Yorkers were tough, though often friendly. They would not have an easy time learning to trust their "brothers," letting go of the tragic view, and greeting the world on the subways with smiles and optimism. I knew this because I was a New Yorker myself.

Boston had been founded by religious zealots, Philadelphia by Quakers, but New York had been founded by the Dutch; always multicultural, tolerant in its way, but a lively, energetic, business city at heart. The very geography of Manhattan had been leveled and carved up into square, numbered blocks for the convenience of realtors. Now, as the Seventies began, and the culture headed toward irony, glamour, wealth, individualism, *sauve qui peut*, the city returned to its time-honored ways and means.

New York was just too hard to live in, too cold in the winter, too damn big to harbor a culture of stoned idealists. There was a riot I recalled in which thousands of anti-Greek Albanians fought against thousands of anti-Albanian Greeks over at the U.N. near Forty-second Street. Albania at this time was an isolated, little Stalinist enclave. No one had gone there or come out for decades. Even the Russians couldn't go in. How could there be thousands of Albanians in New York, organized and hating the Greeks? The hippies and our peace and love were not going to take over this city. I had grown up in New York, and lived there for decades, and I had never met an Albanian. Yet there were probably as many Albanians in Gotham as there were dedicated hippies.

Already the Rockefellers and their pals were planning to destroy a venerable neighborhood of electronics shops to raise up twin monstrous skyscrapers down at the foot of Manhattan, buildings that would dwarf the rest of our beautiful skyline and make it appear to be *smaller*! If the Sixties were to be preserved, it would have to be on a kind of seed farm in Northern California. New York could absorb everything.

In a way, I wasn't sorry that pot was still illegal. If we were to have a counterculture, we would need an economy. Money from parents in Indiana was ultimately corrupting. Yet you couldn't run a modern economy on tie-dyed shirts and turquoise jewelry and macramé. At least illegal pot made it possible for something of an underground economy to exist in this one sphere. The culture had demonized "dope dealers," not differentiating between the small time pot sellers and idealist psychedelic distributors as opposed to the large international cocaine and heroine cartels. Instead of regulating and taxing pot, they turned it over to us. Billions of dollars.

In my own experience, the small time dope dealers were highly respected individuals in the counter community. They were taking great risks to provide us with consciousness-raising herbs and spores. In fact they weren't even really "dope dealers," but usually friends, generous with their wares and honorable in most areas of their lives. Unlike many of the straight, moral, upstanding citizens, few were interested in pursuing the killing in Vietnam. My own acid supplier was a nice young guy, Joe, who pretty much gave it away while driving a cab for a living. He was a sleepy, gentle soul from the Midwest who lived in the East Village with his old lady, Sharon, a pretty, soft-framed spiritual girl who lined their little apartment with quotes from Kurt Vonnegut on the wall and often came over to hang out with us. They charged a dollar for a hit of acid and sometimes donated a joint to smoke as well. The demon dope dealer was a kind of projection of the shadow of the capitalist hero.

After a fabulous free concert we attended with them in Tompkins Square, I wrote in my journal that New York was impossible, but when it worked it was magic. There was no greater feeling than seeing the poor residents of a ghetto smiling. New York outrage often carried a bit of humor. Like after the concert, I saw that someone had carefully painted a large, colorful sign on the side of a tenement: "FUCK YOU (From me to you)."

THE SOUND OF ONE CYMBAL

One doesn't have to invent symbols, the gods will bestow them. Bill Graham announced that he was closing the Fillmore East. This was like the falling of the Temple in Jerusalem. And then, even more to the point, about the same time, early in 1971, Terry and Julie's building was designated to be rebuilt and improved, but from their standpoint it might as well have been condemned, as they would have to move and the stoop would be destroyed. This was the end.

It was time for the oceanography of retrospection. What memories New York, my native city, had given me: The art shows, often so much more rich and wonderful than I had imagined beforehand: Matisse, Picasso, Milton Avery, Georgia O'Keefe, Claude Monet, Cezanne, Jean DuBuffet, Claus Oldenburg, Jackson Pollock, Willem DeKooning, George Segal, David Smith, Franz Kline, Robert Motherwell, Helen Frankenthaler, Jasper Johns, Roy Liechtenstein, Robert Rauschenberg and the rest; the trips to the museums to see old favorites like the Vermeers and the skies of John Constable at the Frick; the Met, the Guggenheim, the Whitney, the Brooklyn Museum, the MOMA with Charlotte for lunch in the sculpture garden. Memories of The Brooklyn Academy of Music; the old Madison Square Garden of my youth on Eighth Avenue and Fiftieth Street near Sam Goody's record store; the Alan Freed rhythm and blues shows at The Brooklyn Paramount and Loew's Paradise in The Bronx; The Apollo Theater in Harlem; the walks across the Brooklyn Bridge at twilight; late night meals with Charlotte and Bob and Gil Eisner in the basement at 17 Mott Street their favorite noodle joint; knishes at Yonah Shimmels bakery below the Village; the dinosaurs at the Museum of Natural History; The Hayden Planetarium; jaunts uptown to the Museum of the American Indian way up near where the Polo Grounds used to stand. Ten cent beers and twenty-five cent hamburgers at Grants on 42nd Street, a bar so wild and crazy they had their own police force—two uniformed guards and one was a lieutenant! (I found out later that Jack Kerouac also liked to drink there.)

I remembered the night Terry and I went up to the Garden to see Pistol Pete Maravich play. And the time I took Charlotte to the Golden Gloves. "I like the sub-novice," I told her, and in a short time she saw what I meant when one fighter went into the ring for his first fight but forgot to take his glasses off.

And the time I was sitting with Terry along with Paul and Gloria on my stoop, when an old man with a sprightly walk and a friendly demeanor approached wearing a clerical collar. Terry leaped up and said, "Jerry, I want to introduce you to Father Flye." The man opened into his big smile and shook my hand. Father Flye! James Agee's mentor in the Thirties! How could this be? Could he still be alive? But there he was, still in the flesh, as young in spirit as ever. And how did Terry know him? I loved the Village in so many ways, but one of the most appealing was the way it kept putting you in touch with a long tradition of dissent and artistic experiment in America.

> We talked of Agee. He loses time when Agee is concerned, moves back into memory-space. Flye is beautiful. A Zen-gentle saint with a stiff-stick broken back hunch-hobble walk and giggle. Wow! He's like a child. Very bright and he told us some of Agee's poems, just stood on the stoop and recited for Terry and me. Paul and Gloria didn't listen, got off on their own rap, while the ninety year old crook-back elf with a slightly southern tang to his speech beautifully recited three serious Agee poems—a child sleeping who will someday have to awake . . . . I was struck dumb by the innocence, the come-from-God Reality of it all. This hatless, beaming, red-faced, little Episcopal priest, reciting James Agee's poems on my stoop. And giggling as he told us a poem which ends something like, "So that's what it means to be an American veteran/ I'll never fight another war, unless they start a better one." Then giggling till tears came into his eyes. It was a beautiful moment and I was sorry that only Terry and I could

see it. Paul and Gloria were oblivious to it all. But then Gloria offered Flye an apricot, dried, and he took it and put it in his mouth and smiled at her and left. We each give what we can and take what we can swallow.

A couple days later I told Terry on the street that I was thinking about teaching next year but I was nervous about it because I had never taught before. He said, quickly, "What do you think you've been doing out here on the street every day, Daddy?"

I remembered the time shortly after another ineffective election day when I took some psilocybin, and I was amazed to notice that the handle on my toilet was the same shape as the handle on the voting machines.

I remembered the annual Avant-garde Arts Festivals, organized by Charlotte Moorman, the topless cellist, and Nam June Paik, the great TV artist whose statue of the Buddha watching himself being televised live on a TV set right in front of him was one of the great works of the century. One year they held the weekend festival on the Staten Island Ferry. We rode back and forth like in the poem by Edna St. Vincent Millay, mixing with the bemused commuters who couldn't figure out what was going on. I watched their faces as the twenty piece Sun Ra Orkestra blared out its dissonance right there on the ferry. One year they held the festival on the backs of flat bed trucks moving slowly along the roads winding through Central Park. I saw the looks of fear and horror on the faces of the well-dressed tourists, out for an evening of sophistication and class in New York, dining al fresco in the garden behind the beautifully lit Tavern on the Green, and here comes the Sun Ra Orkestra, on the back of a truck, Sun Ra at the electric keyboard in his metallic space suit making exaggerated gestures with his hands as he leads his orkestra of twenty black men screaming angrily through their horns, improvising furiously. You weren't sure they were all playing the same song but somehow it kept coming together.

All these vagrant memories touched me and left me saddened. I knew I would never be coming back to live in New York. How had I not seen that being reborn also involved a dying?

I remembered a day on which I couldn't work on my book. I was totally blocked, so I went out for a walk on a cold, wet afternoon, over to soggy, wind and rain-whipped Washington Square Park where, in a large window in the Loeb Student Center at NYU, I saw a vision, an angel. I moved toward her. I recognized Toshiko Akioshi, playing with her trio, in the warm and softly lit student lounge. I quietly entered, made my way to the front, sat at her feet and watched what a real artist looked like in the act of creation. I remained there, entranced, until the little concert was over, and then I thought, "I want to be like that." I walked home through the chilly drizzle and began to write again with renewed energy.

I remembered the times we picketed against the war at the foot of Manhattan down by Wall Street. Leafleting the Staten Island Ferry, or blocking the draft induction center at Whitehall Street. The day when we rioted at the draft center, and the police chased us, and we kept moving and blocking traffic as we made our way through the streets in the general direction of uptown. This went on for hours. The police were going crazy. Any time they thought they had us cornered, we would disperse, move into stores, pretend we were shopping, or head in another direction, across town.

Slowly we made our way north. They picked us off a few at a time, but we continued to tie up traffic and generate confusion, until we arrived all the way up at Madison and about Fifty-fifth Street after about five miles of running and walking, confrontations and escapes, perhaps twenty of us left. The Tactical Patrol Force, the biggest cops with the biggest clubs, surrounded us and made a vindictive charge. A church stood there, next to a huge hole in the ground for a new skyscraper. All the idealistic young people dashed into the church yelling, "Sanctuary! Sanctuary!" I dove under some construction machinery. The exhausted cops ran by me into the church and beat the shit out of the kids, while I walked quietly to the subway.

And I remembered some of the wonderful plays that I had seen at La Mama, and Café Cino, and the rest, especially in our neighborhood, the neighborhood that Jane Jacobs lived in and used as a model for a good urban environment in her classic *The Death and Life of American Cities*, a rare masterpiece of common sense. On Bleeker Street, I saw Jean Genet's *The Balcony*, in which a revolution kills off the chief justice, the bishop and the general, so they substitute three nobodies who had been dressing up and playing these figures in a whorehouse, and, to the astonishment of the three—a gas man, a CPA, and a milk man—the public accepts them and cheers them until they have to realize that even the originals they envied were basically whorehouse clients in costumes. And Eugene Ionesco's *Amedee or How to Get Rid of It*, also on Bleeker Street, great art incorporated into one's ordinary neighborhood life, produced and performed down the street by neighbors. Here an old couple sits in the living room with a mysterious corpse in the bedroom. They try to avoid it but it grows larger until giant legs with giant shoes break through the wall and slowly begin to fill up the space of the stage, like the mounting dead in a senseless war.

And I remembered the time at Karen Kennerly's office when she had been going on about how much she loved Eugene Delacroix and then had made me happy when she said, "I recently realized that your book is structured like Beethoven's *Hammerklavier Sonata*, the way it starts to stutter near the end." I bought the record on the way home, having never heard the piece before.

And I remembered the night I walked home along Christopher Street at two a.m. and saw a man in drag approaching, laughing and pushing a baby carriage. As he passed, I glanced into the baby carriage and there was another man in there, sucking on a bottle and also laughing like crazy.

I could tell these stories all day, for what is New York if not the world's greatest collection of anecdotes?

A NEW ETHOS

Jim Saunt had been talking about family and communal living in which we would subsist according to an ethic of unselfishness and togetherness, where all of his friends would inhabit separate houses in the country on the land we owned in common, and we would have a central building in which we could share the utilities, so I was startled to learn that he and Paulette were having deep trouble, that they were barely back together after splitting up for a while.

> *Dear Jim . . . Regards to Paulette. . . God I hope you two get it together. But if it's not in the cards, I hope you two get it together individually . . . .*

And later:

Dear J and P— . . . You Two Hold On! It'll be easier when we get there.

CHEMICAL LOGS

In the deep winter of 1970-71 we journeyed up to Fitchburg, Massachusetts, to take a farewell trip to the house of our pals, Richard and Margie DeLisle. They had married, lived in Georgetown for a while, then in Greenwich Village for six months before they bought the estate in Massachusetts. While in New York they had provided one of our most vivid memories of our years in the Village by taking us to a performance in the loft of Robert Wilson who was then directing his *Byrd Hoffman School of Byrds* on Spring Street in lower Manhattan. Robert Wilson would become world-famous for his operatic productions like *Einstein on the Beach* (with Philip Glass), but then he was just starting out, a young man from Texas with ambitions to integrate the arts and investigate space and time. The neighborhood around the loft was deserted on a Saturday night. Inside, about forty of us sat on folding chairs. Saw horses were set at the front of the loft, with a plank suspended between each pair. One by one, half a dozen people came out and climbed up onto the planks and just swayed there, slowly, up and down. One participant was a boy, another a very old lady. A person sitting near us whispered, "That's his grandmother. He flew her in from Ohio." This added another dimension to the spectacle, that he had put his past, his own relatives, up there, slowly moving up and down as in a surreal dream. As Dr. Johnson said about Milton's *Paradise Lost*, "None wished it longer," but there was something eerie and haunting and true about this, something unforgettable.

After the swaying stopped, we all proceeded downstairs where a flatbed trailer waited, covered with hay and pulled by a horse. We climbed onto the hay wagon and shared bottles of hooch. I had brought one and passed it to the people around me. Someone indicated the driver and said, "He's a farmer. They got him from New Jersey." We moved slowly around deserted lower Manhattan, drinking, on our late-night hay ride. You could only do something like this in Manhattan. That was the point. This was all so anti-Manhattan and yet also so only-in-New York.

We drove up the Bowery and then into a small, dark alleyway that ended in a kind of hidden square surrounded by tall empty warehouses. A rock band was set up in the corner, playing songs by Cream. We began to dance in the De Chirico space. Then, about seven stories above our heads, on top of the old, windowless buildings, we saw them—the Byrds. It was like a Batman movie in Gotham City. They had capes and hoods and were running around on the roofs, wings spread wide, soaring against the moonlit, silver-clouded sky. *The School of Byrds.* While the band played screaming Eric Clapton. I had to remember to breathe. This was the greatness of New York, though only about forty of us were there to see it.

Richard DeLisle was now teaching high school English. He and Margie were not real dopers, but because this was a special occasion, a farewell trip, Richard dropped acid with us and Margie smoked some strong pot which she was unaccustomed to. She was to be our guide but unfortunately the pot disabled her. We talked about various things as the acid came on, in particular about a chimney fire that had burned down a nearby house recently. I knew nothing about chimneys. Never had possessed a fireplace. I was an apartment kind of guy. When you were cold you banged on the riser steam pipes, and if you annoyed the super enough he might send up some heat.

The weather was frigid. A foot of snow slept on the ground. We remained in their lovely old house, sitting around the large fireplace, tripping on the flames dancing a gavotte upon the chemical logs.

There's no way of knowing how long we sat like that but suddenly POP-BANG the logs exploded. A large roaring fire leaped up into the chimney. "Chimney fire!" Richard shouted as he leaped up. We turned toward Margie for a reality check, the only one not on acid, but she was discombobulated, stoned and confused. Charlotte was in her own world somewhere else in the house. Richard and I ran into the kitchen, turned on the faucet, and began a series of frantic dashes with filled kettles from the sink to the fireplace in the living room. We would throw the water on the logs, they would hiss and sizzle and go out for a few seconds, and then flare up into flame once again. It was impossible to tell "objectively" how serious this was, but it seemed like there was a kind of demon in the fire. It was not going to go out until it had burned the house down.

Acid makes it possible to think in parallel (like Google search), to see many possibilities at the same time. While we were running back and forth like madmen with the water, I saw that from the acid point of view that this didn't matter that much. It seemed like a movie, one of the infinite holographs shown against the space of infinity that God displays, with central casting providing "cops," and "a President in Washington," and other distractions to pass the time. This was the acid vision, the archaic spiritual vision that we would need when we were dying, so we could remember that what was ending was a kind of "movie" and we were returning to our spiritual home.

At the same time, even on acid, while running with the kettles of water and shouting and participating in the crazy chaos, I could see this fire from the earth point of view. I could imagine vividly the beautiful old house burned down, and the four of us on acid in the bitter cold and snow outside the smoking ruin, trying to deal with the firemen and the terrible ramifications of this disaster if we didn't get the fire put out. I could imagine Margie's sadness. This was the dilemma of the acid vision in a nutshell. It did not help you function in the day-to-day exigencies of the world, but you needed it or something like it to resist the culture's tendency to turn death into the dark villain of a melodrama. I ran frantically with the pots of water. At that moment, I realized that I wanted nothing in the world more than to save Richard and Margie's house.

The earth was the world of the Two. It was difficult to remember the world of the One. (Let alone to communicate it to others!) That triumph over death, the feeling of safety and well-being outside of time, forever. Our culture had opted for life at any cost. We had separated life from death and repressed the knowledge of death from our consciousness, although it was there in our bones and tissues, causing who knows what illnesses within us and what bizarre outward behavior. Even the so-called Christians wanted to extend life for every last minute when the patient was in agony.

Finally we put the fire out. We sat there uneasily, surveying the doused logs for any further outbreak. They still seemed to be alive in some crazy way. I couldn't relax. I put on my coat and asked Richard to assist me. Using the tongs and shovel, we carried the logs, one by one, outside and set them down in a small pile in the snow. We returned to the warm house, but

I was still shaken and uneasy. I kept moving to the window and checking to see that the logs were truly extinguished.

After a while, I went outside, took each log in the pile away from the others and set it separately in the snow, so that if it did burst into flame again, it couldn't ignite the others and start a large blaze.

The fire had shaken us and colored the rest of our trip. Although nothing untoward occurred, we still were riding on frightening might-have-beens in our vivid imaginations and acid dreams. Richard kept asking me, "What does this mean, Jerry? What does it all mean?"

I shrugged my shoulders because sometimes Richard had been prone to do this with me, to give me the metaphysical authority to define the situation, when I wanted him to make up his own "novel." Richard and I were sitting opposite each other, still tripping to a degree, at the long wooden dining room table. Margie made a large punch bowl of red Jello and set it between us. Richard turned to me and said one more time, "What's it mean Jerry? Tell me." Quickly I picked up the large bowl of red Jello and I said, "OK, if you want me to be Jesus, I'll be Jesus," and I dumped the entire bowl of Jello over my head. Strangely, as the red Jello ran down through my long hair and in rivulets on my face, I felt like Jesus in a way, with the blood running down from a crown of thorns. At the same time I felt good.

Richard was startled for a second. Then he began to laugh like crazy. Everyone began to laugh like crazy. I tried to play the straight man, but I couldn't help but join them. We all were laughing and roaring as the gooey mass of Jello ran down my face and onto my clothes. Somehow I had managed to change the space of our trip. From that point on the trip was OK. I had committed a kind of Zen act that broke the chill that the doused fire had left behind. I had simply done it. I didn't know why. But somehow it was the perfect thing to have done. I guess that's what made it Zen. But at the time I was as startled as everyone else.

Thinking about all these acid questions over the years, I concluded that on acid or not, there was no substitute for compassion. The Bodhisattva is supposed to be the one who, although beyond desire himself, reincarnates in order to work to reduce suffering on the earth. There seemed to me to be no higher reason to be alive than to reduce suffering. But later I came to see that if compassion is to result in effective behavior, clear seeing is required, seeing of oneself as well as the world. Cold eye, warm heart.

A couple decades later, I called Richard and Margie from California. Their oldest son had been in critical condition for about a year from a mysterious illness that none of the best doctors in Boston could diagnose. Now, just as mysteriously, he was healed and back in the world again. Richard wasn't home. Margie was normally diffident, but this night she stayed on the phone for almost an hour. She spoke to me slowly about her family in a deep, heartfelt, almost unearthly voice that seemed to come from another, more true zone of human feeling than normal discourse. She quietly reviewed her life, talking about each of her four teenagers for about ten minutes apiece, telling me their attributes and moral qualities. Why she was proud of them, why she thought she had done a good job with them, and why she felt that each was ready to lead an independent, valuable life on earth. [This proved to be true.] She then spoke about Richard, how he was a respected chiropractor, beloved in their town of Leominster, Mass. He had taken up the path of Advaita Hinduism. When she said goodbye, she left me stunned. I felt like I had gotten a contact high from someone on a trip, someone egoless and without the necessary defenses to live on the earth. I was shaken and elevated, as I had been when I had seen Janis Joplin perform or Nichol Williamson as Hamlet. I was so high I couldn't sleep or come down.

When my wife Marijke came home from work at the mental hospital at one a.m., she looked at me and began laughing. "Are you on acid?" she said, knowing I hadn't done any psychedelics for years. I explained to her about the call. "That was the most moving telephone call of my life. There was something in Margie's tone. I can't explain it. It was like getting a phone call from someone in another dimension."

I stayed up pretty much the rest of the night. Too high to sleep. The next morning, out of a clear sky, Margie died of an asthma attack. She was 52.

WHERE THE BUFFALO ROAM

It was time to say goodbye to New York with love, to hitch up the wagons and move on, to the strains of Leslie West's anthem, "Theme for an Imaginary Western."

Terry and Julie held out longer than anyone else in their building.

The two of them seemed like characters in a Bernard Malamud novel, living alone in a large, decaying tenement. Like the older jazz musicians who had lost their fame and living wages to the younger, less skilled, rock musicians, Terry continued to resent rock and to fulminate grumpily against it from time to time. But one day when I met him coming down the street with his saxophone case, I could see he was in a good mood. "Where you been, Daddy?" I said. I liked to imitate his speech. I knew he liked it, too.

"Oh, I played over in [someone's] studio." And then, unable to hide his pride, he said, "I played with a group of guys. Johnny Winter was on lead." Johnny Winter, the great and famous Texas albino blues and rock guitar player. "Johnny Winter?" I said, ribbing him a bit. "Can he play?"

"Oh, he can play," Terry said, nodding begrudgingly.

But when I smiled, he added, laughing triumphantly as he left, "But he can't sing worth shit!"

Yet Terry and Julie couldn't hold out forever. Eventually they took a large settlement and decided that as long as they had to move, why not go to England and use it as a base to travel? So this was to be the end. The entire block seemed cast in gloom clouds and November shadows though it was actually the beginning of Spring, 1971.

The day before they were to leave, Terry came walking down the street from the direction of the subway with his horn. "Where you been, Daddy?" I asked.

It turned out he had been up all night, drinking. At four a.m. he had carried his horn and a camera onto the subway and had journeyed to Queens to try to find Prez's grave. The cemetery was closed; it was still dark when he arrived as he had planned. He climbed over the fence and set out among the thousands and thousands of graves looking for Prez. When the sun rose he still hadn't found him, nor when the cemetery opened for the day. Luckily, he encountered a gravedigger who knew where Prez was buried. Terry located the grave, placed his tenor saxophone on the dirt in front of the gravestone, and took a photo. Later he gave me a copy of the picture.

He was going to bed, but with a twinkle in his eyes he asked me in to look at something in his apartment. I followed him to his living room, now completely unfurnished. He pulled back the curtains covering a window that faced directly onto the flat, brick, solid wall of the next building, a newer structure that had been erected within about one foot of Terry's side window, completely closing it in. I couldn't understand what he was up to. With a big smile he asked me to wedge my head between the two buildings to look at something in the other wall. In the other wall? What was he talking about?

But he seemed serious. I pushed my head out of the blind window and wedged my head between the two walls, moving it slightly to the left until I saw it. There were several bricks missing in the newer wall. This formed an open space, a kind of cave in the wall. And there, in the cave, Terry had set up an entire small Tibetan village. You couldn't see it from his apartment. You had to wedge your head between the walls. I was amazed. He had little Tibetan houses, and a temple and little prayer flags. All in the semi-darkness, in the little invisible hole in the wall between the two buildings. I pulled my head out and looked at him with astonishment. He was completely happy, blissfully standing there glowing with pride. Then he began to laugh so hard he couldn't speak for awhile, but finally he managed to say, "Right now they're gonna renovate this old building, but someday, in maybe a century or two, they'll tear this place down, and can you imagine the look on the workman's face that finds this? A centuries' old, tiny Tibetan Village in a cave in the wall of a twentieth century building in New York." He began to cackle again, "Can you see his face when he shouts out to the other workers, 'What the fuck, man? What the fucken fuck?'"

QE II

Terry and Julie sailed for London on the Queen Elizabeth II. They threw a going away party for themselves in the First Class Lounge. Since they invited virtually the whole neighborhood, it was a party for all of us actually, a kind of farewell to the Sixties in Greenwich Village. I looked forward to seeing the huge ship. I had loved it in my youth when my father took me with him to the Lower East Side to buy cheap underwear. As we drove along the West Side Elevated Highway, I would marvel at the great liners, the Cunard Queens, The Ile de France, The Italian and Dutch liners, stacked up pier after pier, rising high out of the water, so close you could almost touch them. I had even seen the sunk Normandy lying on its side. But I had never been inside a liner.

I expected a kind of Titanic as I had seen it in the movies, with lots of carved wood and old world elegance, but this new ship was more like a Hilton Hotel. Life was filled with small disappointments like this. Like the Metropolitan Opera, everything that was supposed to be classy turned out to be a *bar mitzvah*.

But there was Julie, grinning, in a lovely cocktail dress, playing a society lady in a Marx Brother's movie, and there was Terry, sipping champagne, wearing his usual smoking jacket from the Salvation Army, and there were all the actresses from the off-Broadway theaters and the Alka Seltzer commercials, the avant-garde dancers, the jazz musicians, the poets and writers, the failures, the dreamers, the stalactites and stalagmites, the Trotskyites, the whole crazy crew.

We stayed as long as we could on the ship. We didn't want to let the Sixties go. Terry told me that the previous night he had called Kenneth Rexroth in San Francisco.

"You know Kenneth Rexroth?"

"Not, really, Daddy. But I told him I spoke to him once in a record store. I said to him that that time I hadn't read his books so I didn't know what to say to him, but now I had read his books and I did know what to say, and that I wanted to tell him I was leaving the country and moving to England."

"What'd he say?"

"He laughed. We had a nice talk."

Terry gave me a big drunken hug, kissing my cheek like my uncle Mac used to do as he whispered in my ear, "Check next to your bed when you get home, Daddy."

When I checked beside my bed, there was a saxophone case with an alto sax in it. A farewell present. I knew the alto was a good one. I knew Terry would have searched carefully for it and had it repaired up at the sax shop in Times Square. I knew I was part of his dream. That someday I would play like Bird, and he would play like Prez, and we would blow together.

The next morning, as I passed Terry's deserted building I looked over at his window where he used to sit beside the stoop, and there, against the inside of his closed window, he had pasted a best-selling, life-sized poster of the top half of Swami Satchidananda.

Years later I would study with Satchidananda who was a proponent of practicing hatha yoga not just for stretching and flexibility, but as a means of maintaining a healthy and pliable body which would not distract one from one's true work which was sitting in meditation and doing service to others. But at that time all I knew about Satchidananda was that he had been the Swami at Woodstock, blessing the Festival, and that his photo had appeared on this large, well-known poster that made him look like a child's vision of God. Now here he was, in Terry's "seat" in the window, right beside the stoop. And then, with astonishment, I realized that he looked like an older version of Terry. With his whiskers and shoulder length hair, and the twinkle in his eyes, damned if he didn't look just like Terry. The wise-guy, our Prez, had pulled another fast one, and left us all laughing every time we walked by his stoop.

THE PRODIGAL SON

About five years later Terry showed up at my door in San Francisco. He carried no bag, just a saxophone case. I was living with my second (and present) wife Marijke in a semi-basement flat in the Hispanic Mission District. Terry was accompanied by a big, rough-looking, unshaven guy with torn pants that showed his ass in the back. They were both reeling drunk. Terry kept referring to the guy as "This n_____," although the guy was white. He had driven Terry up from San Diego. He seemed a nice enough guy, a kind of follower of Terry. He had a drink with us and then continued on his way because Terry was being rude to him.

Terry stayed for a few days and we caught up with each other's lives. Terry and Julie were no longer together. When I asked him what had happened, he said he had these Buddhist offering bowls he had picked up in India and, "When I was out of town, she wouldn't even put water in my offering bowls, Daddy." I knew that just meant it was too painful to talk about. Terry said he had started a house-cleaning service in San Diego called "Wandering Brooms."

I said, "India?" He told me that he had read these books he loved about Buddhism and Hinduism by a German who had moved to India and become a monk, Lama Govinda. So he and Julie had visited India from England. He desired to tell Lama Govinda how much the Lama's books meant to him. They made it to the Himalayas and walked upwards until late one afternoon they actually made it to Lama Govinda's house. His wife (Mrs. Govinda?) answered the door. "Yes?" she said, puzzled to see these two westerners in this corner of the Himalayas.

"My name is Terry Kelsey from Greenwich Village."

"Yes?"

"Well I don't want to bother the Lama, but I just came here to India to tell him that I read his books and I really dig them."

There was a long silence. Then she said, again, gently, "And . . ."

"Well, like I said, I don't want to bother the Lama. I just wanted to thank him. What he wrote . . . it meant a lot to me."

Terry turned, joined Julie, and began to walk off down the hill.

"Well, just a minute," she called after him, smiling. "I can't just have you wandering around the Himalayas like this. At least you should have the opportunity to thank him in person. Why don't you come in for tea with us?"

So that was how Terry got to meet Lama Govinda.

Now he was drunk each day. By evening he was near unconsciousness. We took him to a party in the Castro. He was rude to people, staggering around and calling white people by the N word. When we took him home he fell down in our foyer, grabbing drunkenly for Marijke to regain his balance and accidentally striking her hard in the face.

The next day I was going to ask him if maybe he should move along for now, but I didn't need to. When he awoke, he poured a glass of Cutty and told me he'd have to be leaving. Then he told me a story about Ben Webster, one of the three great tenor men of his era along with Prez and Coleman Hawkins. He had seen Ben in Amsterdam just before Ben died. Ben and Terry had shared some drinks together during Terry's visit, and Terry stopped by Ben's hotel to say farewell on his way to the airport. "Ben was outside and he looked terrible. Worse than terrible, Daddy. Worse than dying. He said to me, 'Wanna come up to my room for a wink, T?' That's what he called a drink. A 'wink.' I told him, 'No thanks, Ben. I gotta catch my plane. I've already had a few winks today.' Of course Ben, he'd already had more than a few winks that morning. We said goodbye.

I knew it was for the last time. As he turned to shuffle off to his room, I began to cry and I said to him, 'I'll never forget you, Ben,' and he said to me, 'I'll never forget me either.'"

Terry had a little smile on his face as he said this. He was trying to keep from crying. He helped himself to a couple winks of Cutty and then stood up. "There's one thing I need to show you before I go, Daddy." He walked into the living room and indicated I should follow. Closing the door behind us, he took out his tenor saxophone. He turned his back to me, wouldn't look me in the eye, put the horn at a forty-five degree angle like Prez, and he began to play. *The Man I Love*. A soulful ballad by George and Ira Gershwin. Terry donated that raspy, breathy Prez sound that he had down perfectly. He played the whole song, slowly, beautifully and with deep feeling, while I stood there dumbfounded. Terry had done it. Terry was playing just like Prez! When he finished he turned toward me shyly, still not looking into my eyes, waiting for my response. "You got it," I said. "You really got it, Daddy. Now you could play with Bobby Timmons."

He opened into a sweet smile, his eyes all red from the drinking which had taken over his life, and he nodded yes. He knew he had it down. And now I had confirmed it. The President was still alive. He nodded again, put his horn in the case, turned to me, still smiling shyly, gave me a hug, and walked out of my life.

[In the Nineties, I heard that Terry, drinking and strung out on heroin, had toured Scandinavia playing with the great tenor saxophonist, Dexter Gordon.]

STREET KIDS

I was ready to leave but I knew I would always be a New Yorker in the way that my wife Marijke will always be Dutch. One last instance of this occurred when Karen Kennerly invited Charlotte and me to a dinner with her and her current partner, the novelist Jerome Charyn.

Jerry Charyn was from The Bronx, Claremont Parkway, near my old neighborhood. He was a couple years older than I, but much older in terms of savvy and experience. He had gone straight into literature after college, teaching and writing. He seemed to be at home in that world, wanted to innovate within it. I liked him. I'm sure he opposed the war, but he had a more moderate, mature approach to things than I did. Jerry's brother was a cop and he seemed proud of this. He was very serious about his work. I wasn't surprised to learn years later that he was teaching at Princeton along with Joyce Carol Oates.

When we arrived at Karen's apartment, she showed us a manuscript for Jerry's newly finished novel, lying by itself in an empty dresser drawer. I reached down to look at the first page but Karen screamed, "No, No, don't touch it!" I pulled my hand away as if it had been booby-trapped. Karen closed the drawer, saying, "He can't stand it if anyone touches his manuscript." She laughed embarrassedly. "He'll know," she added, fondly. "I don't know how, but he'll know." I later heard that Karen was seeing Donald Barthleme, but you could see at that time how much she cared for Jerry Charyn. While we waited for Jerry to arrive, she told us proudly, again laughing, that when he sold work to Hollywood he made a stipulation in his contract that under no circumstances would he ever have to actually come to the West Coast and set foot in Los Angeles.

The four of us strolled up Broadway for about a mile to a small Chinese restaurant. On the way home I saw just how much of a New Yorker Jerry was. And myself as well.

The evening was warm. We had lingered at dinner. We enjoyed walking leisurely down dark and deserted Broadway in the 70s and 60s, prolonging our farewell, since this would be the last time we met, as Charlotte and I were leaving in a couple days. Karen was absorbed in conversation with Charlotte, Jerry and I were reminiscing about The Bronx. When we reached Karen's apartment building and said our farewells, Karen commented, "Wasn't that a lovely walk after dinner on this fine spring night," and Jerry said, "Yeah, except for that little stick of dynamite up in the Seventies."

"What?" Karen and Charlotte both said together.

"Over on the left," I said. "Down the block towards Amsterdam Avenue."

"Ready to explode," Jerry said.

"I'm glad we got out of there when we did," I said. "That was really going to be violent.

"All those teenagers there on that dark street. They were mad as hell at each other," Jerry said.

The women looked at us puzzled. Were we making this up to tease them? Then they realized we were stone serious. Karen from out on Long Island and Charlotte from Idaho had been walking along in glamorous Manhattan, discussing something animatedly, and hadn't seen a thing, But the two novelists, still Bronx street kids in their souls, while continuing our conversation, had, without saying a word about it, been keeping track of everything that was going on in the dark streets for blocks in every direction. Both of us had seen the volatile situation, read it quickly, and made the same decision, walking a little faster, ushering the women to safety along with ourselves, efficiently getting us all out of there without attracting attention before the gun shots started, all the while continuing to talk to each other about post-modern literature.

SCIENCE TO SILENCE

Was I also leaving science behind? Science had been my first love and you never lose that feeling, even though we had broken up when I had caught her selling herself for big money to soldiers at the military base. I was at war with science, but only a part of me. There was also a side of me that still respected science. I wouldn't admit this to myself, but it would come out whenever I encountered bad science or factitious social science. Yet I still felt that science was part of this hubris in which we were drowning, especially those attempts to control the world through technology and social science methods. I understood the value of statistics in understanding our world and its history, and the usefulness of social science methods in putting together a story of our past when they were applied to the vast mountains of data compiled by the government and others, but I felt we needed to be humble in the face of reality. God entered us through our wounds. The light came in through the cracks in the structures we had built, both inside and outside ourselves. We needed to be able to leave the civilized precincts of the ego to wander in the dark woods and bring back boons to our people. We needed mystery larger than our linear functionalist conceptions in order to breathe. To avoid asthma of the imagination, we needed to see the spaciousness of the universe which meant looking outside at night. Down here on the abused Earth, much of the light that we required was only visible in the dark.

[Over the years, I began to soften my opposition to science and to those who practiced it. I still believe that the purely objective point of view deserved to be attacked from all sides as it was in the Sixties. That it is to a large degree a claiming of authority for a system and point of view that benefits white, male, western, middle-class people. That, for example, there is no way to say which substance is a "drug" outside of a cultural context. Peyote is a drug for us, a sacrament for the Huichols. Of course our point of view gives us power in the present world, but that does not mean it is true, or ultimately satisfying.

As I grew older, I came to recognize that my old Bronx friends who had become hard working physicians, not thinking about themselves as holy, just diligently carrying around their pagers, teaching young doctors at Stanford Medical school, or going in to Morrisainia Hospital in the South Bronx every day to help the poor, were also following a path that the Buddha would have called "right livelihood." When medicine saved my life many years later, I was grateful to my oncologist, a brilliant young woman who had studied hard, come here from India, and was attempting so earnestly to help me.

But I never went back to the modern worldview which saw life as an accident surrounded by nothingness, and mind as merely an epiphenomenon of the brain. To paraphrase Richard Grossinger, if natural laws produced all this, cockroaches and Albert Einstein, and *schnorrers*, then natural laws were something far more interesting and mysterious than we normally assumed.

Just as I think I'm not a Jew until I meet a Nazi, I think I'm not a scientist until I meet someone who doesn't think straight and violates the rules of evidence. Now I view the world of science as a kind of precious operating room that has been improved by each generation and passed down to us. It is our job to keep it uncontaminated. We need such a space. It can save lives and reduce pain. It needs to be sterile and intensely lighted so it can serve its function. But you wouldn't want to live in such a room. To spend your life there and limit your horizons to its boundaries. That would be like living in a world of perpetual daylight in which you couldn't see the stars, and name them, and connect them into images and stories.]

[Over the years, I also came to recognize how difficult it is to be a good parent and spouse today. I admire those who succeeded at it. I had a lot to learn in these areas. (Although I was probably as good at it as most of the great authors, thinkers, and social activists whom I admire.) And what strength and stamina it takes just to earn a living and support a family in this age, which I see as the start of the slope of America's long relative decline in the world.]

Ernst Becker wrote a good book, *The Denial of Death*, in which he says that all of our activities, all we've invented and all we've built, our whole civilization is part of a denial of death. I think he's right, but I don't limit myself to his solution, which is the best our culture has to offer: to accept the inevitable end and tough it out. If you read Philip Roth's book about the death of his father, this is basically where he has arrived: Grin and bear it. In fact, this is where the world of modern intellectuals in general sits.

Ken Kesey said that the aim was to learn how to function on LSD. I don't think so any more. I think the aim is to function with the acid vision in mind while not on LSD. And if one doesn't want to go near the acid vision, I would say the aim is to at least examine the assumptions of our culture and to admit when one is hypnotized by them.

That is one of my goals in writing this book. To point out the ways in which we are all hypnotized, by unexamined scientistic assumptions as well as by other cultural beliefs and values.

Do we harbor a need to inhabit a world larger than the one offered by our secular culture? Can we move forward to a post-modern world that is different from the intellectualized, denatured, post-modernism that the academics have captured and exhibited in their Ph.D. dissertations? Can we remember that Michel Foucault, one of the fathers of post-modern thought, and to some, the greatest philosopher of the second half of the twentieth century, came to San Francisco in his last years and took acid for the first time, after he had written most of his powerful books. He was incredibly surprised and moved; he realized this changed everything. He had to stop writing for two years to try to come to terms with what he had seen.

I have learned from my own experience that there is a viewpoint from which you can see that nothing can ultimately harm you, or anyone else, and that even if the whole universe blows up, everything will finally be all right. In fact, the universe already has blown up. And yet here we are.

LAST DANCE

On the Sunday afternoon before we left, my brother Mark and Lucy, always generous, threw a farewell party for us. Mark, now out of the Army, was working for his father-in-law, a successful lawyer, in Manhattan. Their main client was the Newhouse newspaper chain. Lucy taught gifted children. She had been a gifted child herself, going through her senior year in high school (as did Mark) at the age of fifteen. Mark and Lucy lived with little Lauren in a nice, unpretentious house north of the City in Westchester County. Everyone was at the party. Friends, family, neighbors from The Bronx.

A sweet sadness lay over the backyard like humidity. I knew I would never see many of these people again. Already we were losing touch with those on the rim of the family. The great uncles and third cousins from Poland. My mother's relatives, "The Brooklyn Bergers," a tribe of rowdy moving men who showed up drunk at weddings. And my great aunts from The Bronx, Yettie and Bertie, along with my mother's sharp dressing cousin with the trimmed mustache, "Snappy" Sylphin, and his shy daughter, Mona.

I was sad. A little grumpy and paranoid. Besides Mark and Lucy, virtually everyone there was indifferent to the war. Some supported it. I kept thinking of my brother-in-law Rod, dead or in a prison hellhole. Why didn't anyone care about him? It was clearly time for Charlotte and me to leave for someplace far away. Innocent statements and gestures irritated me. I was on media overload. Civilization overload. The war seemed like it would last forever, circling around us like the planet Mars, easy to ignore if you chose to. It was futile to talk about it with the old Bronx crowd. Why couldn't they see that however it turned out, America would never be the same? A great dream was dying. And not just a national dream. A world dream. That was the way I saw it back then.

Little unconscious remarks irked me. One man admonished me sharply for saying the word "bitch." He nodded toward his three year old daughter, absorbed in playing with a toy on the other side of the room, paying no attention to our low key conversation. A cousin said that she was going to buy a training bra for her thin, nine year old daughter, playing innocently in the back yard. Everybody was rubbing me the wrong way like a hard rubber eraser. People I had known for my whole life, and whom I felt much love for, now seemed to believe they were speaking sincerely, but when they opened their mouths TV commercials came out.

I told my mother the good news I had heard from Karen Kennerly. She had hired Paul Bacon, one of the two most noted book jacket designers (along with Milton Avery) to do the cover of my book. Unlike many of the book jacket designers, Bacon was not only really good, but he was known to actually read each book he worked on. Karen had given him the manuscript. He called and told her he thought it was a terrific book. In fact, he liked the book so much, he told Karen he was going to design the back of the jacket as well, for no charge. Karen was delighted. This was quite a rare compliment. And he was the first person outside of those at Dial who had actually read the book.

I thought my mother would be happy to hear this sign of success, but she looked worried. "Are they going to have your picture on the back of the book?"

"I guess so."

Now she looked upset. She just stared at me.

"Ma . . . ?"

She smoothed my hair to the side with her hand. "You have such beautiful hair. Why do you ruin it?" She paused, then added, "Why don't you let me get you a tube of Alberto's VO5?"

The perfect symbolic moment arrived just before we left. I was talking to Duane, the son-in-law of Charlie Rosenberg, my mother's second husband. I had known Duane and his family back in The Bronx. Everyone here was connected through networks of relations and marriages. There were no degrees of separation. Duane's brother Sammy had married Ethel, the daughter of Mrs. Scharf, a stuttering, very kind, European immigrant who had baby-sat for me and thought I was a genius. When I was a kid and she would see me on the street, she would run up to me and begin kissing me on the top of my head and saying, "Oy, is d-d-dat a J-J-Jerry! Is d-d-dat a J-J-Jerry!"

Duane was a tough street guy from the East Bronx. He aspired to the lower middle class. He had let his sideburns grow in the new fashion but he was old fashioned in every other way. I respected his work ethic. He was up in the dark every night to make it to his job at the Bronx Terminal Market where the fruit and vegetables and meat came in each morning on the trucks. Then sometimes in the evening he would work at the trotters at Yonkers Raceway, selling pari-mutuel tickets from a booth.

I stood alone in the living room with Duane. He said, smiling, "So, Jerry, ya gonna California." I nodded yes. I could see he thought I was nuts. He pulled a monster stogie out of the vest pocket of his yellow sport jacket and moved to light it. Lucy, happening by, ran up to him. She smiled. She knew Duane and she knew there was going to be trouble. He wasn't going to take any guff from a woman, especially any "new age" guff. "Duane," she said, self-consciously, gently, "would you mind very much taking your cigar onto the deck? We don't smoke inside the house."

Duane was dumbfounded. He smiled. A crazy smile. He had no idea how to respond to this. Was she kidding? He turned to me, trying to read my reaction to see if this was a joke. Lucy almost had to laugh. She read the entire situation perfectly. Duane was trying to figure out how a man acted in this situation. They both kept smiling. Lucy said, very gently, trying to keep from laughing, "I mean it Duane. Really. Could you please just smoke it outside?" She indicated the people on the deck behind the French doors. Duane was still holding an unstruck match in his hand, smiling now like De Niro in a Mafia movie, when you're not sure whether he's going to shake his head and back off, or he's going to break out into a wild laugh and shove his wine glass into your face.

Duane nodded a couple times, as if to say, "So that's the way it is with you," and then he slowly lit the cigar right in front of Lucy, looking her straight in the eye. He took a long, long drag, held it in, enjoying it, and then, still smiling, he blew the whole lung full of bad cigar smoke right into Lucy's face.

Lucy was frustrated, but she had to laugh. Like World War I, one small incident threatened to explode into full-blown warfare, but she saw the humor in the situation. Since Duane was her guest, she turned and continued her walk to the deck. A look of satisfaction permeated Duane's face. He held the cigar up in the air, admiring it as if it were a rare Cuban. He turned to me, and with a slight smile of victory still on his face, he said, "So, Jerry, ya gonna California . . ."

[My brother-in-law Rod Mayer was never heard from again. After the war his co-pilot, Dave Wheat, was repatriated, but forty years later Rod is still one of the MIAs. An old Vietnamese nurse who lived in the area where

Rod was shot down was recently questioned by a Vietnamese-American
search team. She said she had attempted to save the life of an American
pilot who had parachuted into a nearby field at about that time, but he was
too badly injured, and after a few days he died. All she remembered was
that he was very tall. Rod was six feet four.]

[In high school shop class in Lewiston, Idaho, Rod had once constructed
a solid, heavy wooden record cabinet which still sits in my living room.
Like everything Rod did, it was built to last.]

> *"That's the way I makes my songs.
> I makes it by what happened to me."*
>
> Lightning Hopkins

ANOTHER RUSSIAN NOVELIST

I envy authors like Tolstoy and Dostoevsky who still had a living
spiritual tradition in which to plant themselves when encountering the
modern secular world. I set off on a search for certainty through science
and wound up immersed in a world of mysteries within mysteries, but a
world that is not meaningless. I began in The Bronx, but I entered realms
that are beyond the reach of language, places that are so beautiful and filled
with kindness that when you get there, you forgive God for everything
you have been through in the ghastly twentieth century–the crimes, the
wars, the Holocaust, all of it. At that moment, the thousand hurts and
humiliations that have been inflicted upon you every day, and those that
you have inflicted on others, simply drop away like a heavy old robe
you've brought to the beach, and you move forward toward the gorgeous
and infinitely merciful light. You just do it. There isn't any question about
it.

And you realize that, in some deep part of yourself, you always knew
this was how it was going to end.

MAKE THE SUNSET LAST

Charlotte and I took a station wagon from a place on Times Square where
U-Drive someone else's car across country. Although the proof editing of

my novel was not completed, we decided to move west in early April 1971. Karen said that we could finish up the work by mail and phone.

Shep was a good sport about the drive across country, lying in the back of the wagon with the cartons of records that were too delicate to ship. Our friend Betsey Dingman (of the Dingman sisters of Troy), now married to my RPI pal Tex Eidinoff, had a dream of Charlotte and me crossing the country in a covered wagon. I was caught up in the fantasy, calling the car a "covered station wagon" and shouting "get the wagons in a circle" whenever we pulled into a diner to eat.

I would miss my friends, my old RPI buddies and their wives who had continued to come down to the Village to visit us throughout our four years there, although they didn't sleep on our floor like my pals from San Francisco and Penn. This voyage west was a mythic turning point in our lives. I knew I would never be coming back to live in New York. I desired to become a new person. I made Quixotic resolutions, like the goal to always give more than I took from each person I met or taught. I wanted to clean my karma and thus prepare for when I died. I didn't want to come back to Earth again.

We drove leisurely across. The U.S. was not a grid of superhighways yet. You glided right through the center of the little towns for thousands of miles, often on two-lane roads. The town centers were alive, giving you a chance to interact with the different subcultures and people. They had an Edward Hopper kind of dark, fragile beauty.

I used the time to think about how far I had come in my life, since I had been fulfilling a Horatio Alger dream of wealth and upward mobility. In many ways I knew less now than when I started. Questions filled my mind and heart. How did you learn to see the acid visions, the holiness and magic, the timeless love and infinite beauty of the universe, without the acid? Would meditation ultimately be able to replace the drugs? What did you do about medical care, when you'd come to distrust the medical-industrial complex, the hospital bureaucracies and mega drug corporations? And what about your food, when you'd seen through giant agribusiness with its pesticides and hormones and the corporations that boiled and canned and processed and preserved your food?

I had discovered another parallel secret history: The influence that Eastern philosophy had on Western thinking in the Romantic age.

Nineteenth century German idealistic philosophy is suffused with Eastern wisdom as is the thought of Emerson, Thoreau, and Walt Whitman, and those they influenced. All were educated by books which derived ultimately from the psychedelic vision. Yet how often was this acknowledged?

Mircea Eliade, the world expert on shamanism and famous professor of religious history, opined that the use of visionary plants and such represented a decadent period in the history of a particular sect or religion. But for most people who were actually trodding this arcane path, Eliade's conclusion was completely opposite to what our senses were telling us. Could a great expert like Eliade be completely wrong? On the war in Vietnam the experts had been wrong again and again. In Eliade's case, I came to learn that he had definitely been wrong at least once before: when he supported the Nazis. It was obvious that religion was based on the visions of seers. We could tell that the visions we were exposed to were in the same realms that gave birth to the venerable holy books. God was still speaking to those who had the courage to listen. It was when the sacred was institutionalized and mediated by an organized priesthood that the visions were lost and religion degenerated.

Perhaps at this level there are only "novels," but often even our best teachers didn't realize that alternative "novels" had been censored, lost, or forgotten. Yet it is dangerous to swim in these waters. To the degree that life is seen as a dream or a hallucination (maya), an ill-informed person might take this as a license to kill. Of course this is a complete misunderstanding of these visions, since their message is that you would be only killing yourself, and that the visions present a basis for a higher morality of cooperation and mutual understanding, of treating the other as if he were yourself. This was the basis of my hope that these visions might be useful in the atomic age when no other path seemed possible in the long run. But people are all too prone to misunderstand (c.f. Alcibiades again).

And on the individual level, too early and uninformed contact with these visions can drive men mad. It is important to remember that the Greek mysteries were secret in their substance, a secret unrevealed over millennia. The Jewish Kabala mysteries were for centuries only taught to family men over forty under the assumption they would be the educated and experienced and responsible elite capable of handling the powers offered.

480

And in the world of international relations, how could an enlightened people survive in a world of greedy, amoral nation-states? Aldous Huxley took up this question in his novel, *Island*, a book which fails as a novel, its characters are stick figures being used by the author as mouthpieces, and thus they can never achieve independent vibrant life on their own terms, but the novel does succeed in presenting a portrait of a well-thought-out utopian society and the perils it would be subject to.

In *Island*, Huxley shows us an edenic island in the Pacific where society is run intelligently with the aim of supporting people on their way to enlightenment and awareness. Children are taught a world view that works against the ego that separates each of us from the others, and from the All. Mynah birds in the trees are taught to continually say "Awake," and schools offer initiation into psychedelic states so students at the proper level of development can actually *see* the reality of what they are being taught. Unfortunately, as Huxley was too honest to hide, the world of modernity and modernization can't let this happen. Oil is discovered on the island, the unhappy people on their sister island which has already been developed, join with international forces and with greedy people on the edenic island who have been infected by modern goals and they bring the paradise to an end.

Yet what other goal makes sense in an age of weapons of mass destruction, other than to leave the age of nationalism, and yes, even the American dream and visions of America as the country of God, and move toward a multi-cultural future? And what argument can question consumerism and empire, if it is not based on some alternative to a materialistic philosophy?

I was delving into deep water here. Water over my head. When I became fearful or felt a tendency to panic, it was comforting to look out toward the horizon and see my friends who were farther out than I was. My old Bronx pal, Marty Licker, my new friend from Grove Street, Terry Kelsey, and my fraternity brother, Jim Saunt and his wife Paulette out in California, my pal from Grad School Rochelle Gatlin in the Haight, all swimming along, somewhat awkwardly but still afloat.

"From every sentence, deep original and sublime thoughts arise, and the whole is pervaded by a high and holy and

*earnest spirit. In the whole world . . . there is no study . . .
so beneficial and so elevating as the Upanishads. They are
destined sooner or later to become the faith of the people. "*
Arthur Schopenhauer

The trip across the country was uneventful except in New Mexico
where the State Police kept stopping us and searching the car for drugs.
They wanted to let us know hippies were not welcome in their state and
they succeeded admirably.

*April 1971: To the Kuklicks—UNLEASH CHIANG KAI
SHEK! We have moved in with Jim and Paulette Saunt. We
live in the hills outside of Fairfax [in Marin County] in a
valley actually between the hills with a garden in our backyard
over a creek. At the end of our [little] road (1/2 mile away)
civilization stops. There's a 30 foot waterfall and deer etc.
Bela Bartok chased one in there last week. (He's Jim's huge
German Shepherd.) We have a large bedroom with white
roses hanging outside our window . . . . Charlotte is fine,
doing part-time office work and selling cherries with a group
of hippies from trucks alongside the road . . . . Everything is
new and functioning. You go to the bank and they give you
a ball point pen and a cup of coffee. And no waiting lines .
. . . Last Sunday we saw a performance of "Playboy of the
Western World, " on top of Mt. Tamalpais, above our town.
We had to drive through the clouds to get there and were
in the sun above the clouds watching the play. The Pacific
Ocean is just over the mountain. Miles of deserted beaches.
Perhaps the most striking thing here is how friendly everyone
is and how content and peacefully happy the people seem.*

[If I wanted to tell you in one sentence, now, what I like about living in
Northern California, I would say: Our plumber also does psychotherapy.]
We all lived in a rented, old, wooden, ranch-style house, set in a
surrounding garden off a virtually deserted road. Little Claudio, three, had
the third bedroom. Paulette's brother Rocco, nineteen, lived up the street in

a garage with his girlfriend, Thais, a pretty young woman with long silky platinum hair who had come out with him from Chicago. Their landlord lived in the main house while his teenage daughter lived in the backyard in a geodesic dome in a tree. Rocco and Thais had no money. They sold cherries from Oregon along with Charlotte and others. Rocco practiced his guitar, sometimes played in his little rock band for a few bucks, and followed Jim like a loyal dog.

Paulette's youngest brother, Perry, sixteen, showed up in June. Like Rocco a few years before, he had left school in Chicago and simply took off for the Coast and the shelter provided by their sister. Paulette was famous for her good heart. She took care on any waif who came along, and continued to do so throughout her life, step-daughters, unwanted nieces, they all showed up when they needed shelter and succor. Perry moved into a tent in the back yard.

Jim's sister Honey was teaching at the tough, Latino, Mission High School in San Francisco, which was a long stretch for a Jewish girl from Shaker Heights. But the students loved her. The guys had formed a revolutionary group of Brown Berets and she was a kind of unofficial "faculty advisor." She went up into the hills for days on maneuvers with them, and then they would all show up and stay in our backyard. I didn't know what they did in the hills and I was afraid to ask.

Steve and Karen Whitelaw, two wealthy friends, had followed Jim out from Cleveland. With their two young children they lived down the road in a large barn-like house in which they threw great parties. Steve Whitelaw was very smart and hyper-energetic. He had gone to Cornell and then to grad school at MIT, studied science and history of science and was a varsity swimmer. Then he had returned to Shaker Heights and worked for Karen's father in his beauty parlors. Steve advertised on TV and expanded the business into a chain of beauty parlors worth millions, then sold his share and followed Jim out to California looking for adventure. Karen was a bright, nurturing person who also had lots of energy. She was small and filled with good will. We called her "Mighty Mouse."

Steve was more of a wild man than a business man. He had a tenuous relationship to the counterculture. Perhaps his connection was based more on anger at America than on any belief in an idealistic future. On his capitalist side, he immediately began to buy houses, fix them up, and sell them or rent them. After a while he had about 160 rental units in the area. He employed Rocco and Perry to do odd jobs for him. He opened a stand at the Marin Flea market where he had Rocco selling illegal eight-track tapes along with large stolen cans of eel meat. I based the character of Wheeler in my *Carmen Miranda Memorial Flagpole* on Steve who would go along with anything that promised to be interesting or funny. He was funding a booth for the State Fair that the gang was making when we arrived. It was mostly Paulette who was doing the work. Paulette had degrees in painting and art history back in Ohio. She would do acid and paint these beautiful water colors of flowers and plants. She could do anything of an artistic nature. When Jim needed new clothes for his court case, she took some material and quickly sewed him a beautiful suit.

Now she was sewing a large tent. Everyone was pitching in. Using music and slides and colored lights they were going to take the audience in the tent on "A Trip." Somehow they got all this together. It wasn't a very good simulation, but it did cohere sufficiently so that they didn't lose too much money and none of the customers shot them, which wasn't bad for a group of stoned amateurs.

Quinn Wilson and Linda had been living in our room before we arrived but they had broken up and moved out. Quinn was a tall thin, bearded man with long hair, about my age. A student of history in the graduate school at Berkeley, he taught at the local J.C. He was a good historian. I liked to talk with him. He knew a lot and saw through things. But he was fed up with the culture and he dropped out to become a carpenter. Linda was a pretty woman with dark hair, in her twenties, with a shining smile. I heard that the man she was now seeing was a local, small-time dope dealer. They were always around the house along with Quinn's sister Sally and her husband Roger, a physicist, tall and lanky and bearded just like Quinn. [Sally would live her life as an elementary school teacher, Roger as a physics professor at San Francisco State University who donated some of his spare time to do the books for free for a beloved local bookstore.]

Honey Saunt was hanging around often, in fact she hooked up with a nice, quiet, bearded local man, Corkey, a handyman. Ultimately they occupied the tent in the backyard, while Paulette's younger brother Perry moved in with little Claudio. The Whitelaw's kids were often there as well as Lucy, their babysitter, a swimming champion who had dropped out and joined the tribe. Honey's closest pal, Sara Cousins, the daughter of Norman Cousins, editor of the *Saturday Review,* was also at the house a lot, along with an architect who wore women's makeup and his wife, and other drop-outs and fellow travelers like Marilyn Marioni, the wife of Tom Marioni the conceptual artist, and their little son Miles. In fact, like the chemical logs that wouldn't be extinguished at Richard and Margie's house in Massachusetts, there was a continuing party at the house that would simmer and seem to die from time to time, but would always ignite again come the weekend. Neighbors, friends, relatives, kids, dogs, brown berets, total strangers, everyone was welcome to join in. (One morning we woke up and found a Hispanic man sleeping in the bathtub. No one knew him so we just let him sleep and he disappeared after a few hours.)

What we hadn't counted on was that our friends in San Francisco, Rochelle, Ward, Ken, Beverly with her wheelchair and the rest, didn't fit in with Jim's scene. They preferred that we visit them. This was supposed to be one big family, at least in my imagination, but in my desire for harmony I hadn't noticed that the gang on Page Street lived a minimal lifestyle while Jim lived a maximal lifestyle. On Page Street the house was practically unfurnished. The large kitchen and living room were almost bare. Bev didn't even have a chair since she wheeled around the house in her wheelchair. Everyone was stoned all the time but the rooms were spotless. Even magazines and books were kept in the neat individual rooms. There were no dogs or kids or rugs or chaos. Just quiet stoned conversation around a pot of tea.

Jim and Paulette's house was hardly minimal. Everything Jim did was larger than life, his dog, his stereo, the old piano, the rugs, the drums and tambourines and rattles that lay scattered all over the living room amidst the children's toys, dog toys, books on the floor, pots of flowers, bottles of wine, brandy, malt liquor, joints, and so on. The house teemed with chaos and life. People were often making music. Rocco would play lead guitar, Charlotte flute, Perry was musically gifted and he would chord on the piano, I would play rhythm on blues harp if I could find the right key, and the rest of the tribe and neighborhood and local musicians would pitch in on various percussion instruments or strings or horns if they could.

Paulette would honk along on my alto sax. If art was a way of making chaos out of order, this was art. Anyhow, it always felt good and we had a great time.

The Page Street gang in the Haight kept their distance. Jim took up too much space for their tastes. And they sensed, rightly, that he was beginning to unravel. I was starting to see that it wasn't so easy to create a family or a communal living arrangement. This was clearly not our house. Jim and Paulette were renting from the landlord and, as friendly as they were to us, we were renting from them and it was still their house. Charlotte was upset that no one had taken her around and pointed out what was hers, like making some space for her things in the bathroom. Little things bothered her, like when Jim and Paulette were having their weekly brunch with eggs Benedict and they asked her to run to town to get them some more cheap champagne. And I was upset because Bela Bartok wouldn't let Shep out of the bedroom. We had to keep the dogs apart in the house. It was Bela's territory and he would charge Shep if given the chance. Poor Shep was unhappy and confined to our bedroom much of the time.

Jim was beginning to run into trouble over his work life. He wanted to take up the line his family had been in, but on a smaller scale. Welding gates, banisters, spiral staircases. Rocco would be his assistant. He had searched for an appropriate, cheap, nearby, fire-proof place for months and finally found one owned by an older local lady. But at the last minute, she backed down and gave it to a friend. Jim was crushed. He wanted to move beyond air-guitar and begin his business. He even had a name for it: The Better Smith, which was a translation of T.S. Eliot's dedication of *The Waste Land* to Ezra Pound. Now all those months of looking had led to a dead end.

Jim was accustomed to charming his mother and having her back him up in all situations. He had transferred his filial feelings and expectations to this woman who had rejected him. This drove him crazy. He could not imagine she could turn him down. He sued. This lead to a series of court appearances that pushed him toward despair. Especially when he realized that the woman was a friend of the judge who called her by her first name, while Jim was the outsider from back East, the hippie trouble maker. He didn't have a chance, yet he invested more time and hope into the case. He began to go nuts.

He drank all day and played his stereo full blast. Jimi Hendrix, Johnny Winter, really loud blasting music with a heavy beat. One night an angry man showed up at our door. He was screaming that he lived on the other side of the creek in the valley behind our house and he couldn't stand it anymore. The stereo had been going full blast for thirty hours. We turned it down. Jim began to search again for a rental but he was still sulking. Twice he welded on our deck, set the bushes on fire, and almost burned the house down. We were all relieved when he found a place in San Anselmo and moved his equipment over there.

Actually, I had been having an idyllic time of it. During the mornings I studied grammar. I had cut elementary school when they taught us the fundamentals, and I wrote mostly by ear, but this wouldn't be good enough for a college composition teacher. Every day the weather was perfect, maybe eighty degrees, low humidity, a breeze off the ocean and through the redwoods, not a cloud in the smog-less, pure blue sky. In the afternoons I would drive over to the state park and join the young people at a sheltered waterfall for nude swimming. Everyone was so cool about this. It was delightful to get to know your neighbors without clothes. We all shared joints and cold beers. My own little Eden. This ain't The Bronx, Jerr.

We were cool about many things in those days. We were like a threatened minority, an endangered species. We had to care for each other. Charlotte and I would venture into the city each week to see our friends. One evening they took us to a large old hall for some kind of reception party. They were invited by a friend of theirs, a Filipino painter named Leo Vallador. Friends of friends were welcome in those days. As we entered the high-ceilinged hall, we encountered two silver trays, one with glasses of champagne, the other with perfectly rolled, large, bomber joints. In the kitchen area at the rear of the room stood a line of older Filipino women turning out delicious Filipino food all night, noodles and satay and such. With a hip band at the front, and stoned guests from different nationalities and races dancing as a group, it was like magic had come down to earth.

In June I received a phone call from Karen Kennerly. *Partisan Review* had bought a section of my novel. An electric thrill ripped through my body. Now my novel couldn't just disappear. It would have to be reviewed. It was becoming real. In my mind, since the Thirties, *Partisan Review* had been the leading journal of leftist intellectual thought in the world. It was true that I had lost some of the rosy picture I'd once had of New York intellectuals. For example, Dwight Macdonald, one of my earlier heroes, had said that Hermann Hesse was "silly." This made me furious. Hesse was too schematic and allegorical in his earlier novels, but *Steppenwolf*, *Siddhartha*, and *Magister Ludi* were not "silly." I remember thinking that Dwight Macdonald was silly in his trying to preserve his turf, to attack the world he couldn't grasp or venture into. Just like John Updike and Herb Gold and Truman Capote had attacked Jack Kerouac.

But *Partisan Review*! Now I knew why I was so moved by the image of the bum who had wandered into a Broadway theater and had found himself on stage speaking Hamlet's lines. It was a metaphor for my life.

Jim and Rocco settled into Jim's garage-like shop. They were able to charm Marin housewives into hiring them. They had low prices, they were drunk and disheveled, dressed in torn and burned clothes like bums and Jim would quote Yeats. They were irresistible.

The summer was heavenly. Often my friends from both the Haight and Fairfax would get together in San Francisco for a march or demonstration. On serious issues like the war we were all united and willing to take risks together. Once a week our household would drive into Sausalito to attend a classic French movie at a school. Sometimes in the late afternoon we would drive over Mount Tamalpais to the coast. Route One ran near the town of Bolinas, but every time the State put up a sign at the turnoff, the residents would tear it down. They didn't want tourists to know the town existed behind a hill. Bolinas was a bit too far for most commuters, requiring a run up the side of Mount Tam on switchbacks. It was more suited to rich artists and people on welfare. Robert Creeley lived there, along with Richard Brautigan who later shot himself there. [Brautigan's daughter Ianthe wrote a good book about him when she was my student.] Grace Slick lived there, but the house of hers that burned down was back over the hill in Mill Valley.

Bolinas was two blocks long. The residents had put old couches in the road on the main street as if it were a café. There were a couple bars, a bookstore, a library, a café, what more could you want? Jim and Paulette and Charlotte and I and Claudio would buy steamed clams and ale and take them onto the deserted beach at sunset. I was learning how to slow down. I yearned to be an easy-going guy who enjoyed hanging out but that would not be easy. The dropouts, failures, disability guys, and real dopers were much better at it than I could ever be.

The house next door to us belonged to a nice woman in her forties who made a little money as a masseuse. She had a large swimming pool in her backyard right below our deck, with a little separate sauna house across the pool from her home. After a sauna, her clients would often lie around the pool without clothes. In the fall, a young man showed up, Chris, long blond Jesus hair, spacey blue eyes, a sweet, far-away smile. He came over and introduced himself. It turned out he was her son. He had been living in the desert on fruits and nuts. Now his mother was going away for a few weeks and he was going to house sit. He invited us to use the pool anytime we wanted. "The pool belongs to the people," he declared.

He declared this to many people. In town and country, over hill and dale. He declared this to the multitudes in the town park, to the people living there in tents, and to those living in buses besides the park. We took him up on this and joined the nude bathers. Quickly the number of bathers began to multiply. Chris then said he was going to throw an unending party for the whole town. "The house belongs to the people." Everyone came. The party went on for days, in the house and out, in the pool and sauna, people sleeping wherever they could find space on the floor or the grass. Some people were clothed, some were nude. That was one of the nice things about California. No one cared what you did. There were no fixed rules. I, as always, represented moderation and the golden mean: sometimes I wore clothes, sometimes I didn't.

Everything was cool. But after about five days strangers began to show up. Then a woman's purse was stolen. The vibes changed. But the festivities continued. Until the eighth day of the party, when the sauna burned down.

Even Chris had to admit the party needed to come to an end. When Chris's mother returned she was admirably forgiving of him. That's the way the people of Marin were back then. Loose and tolerant. Non-judgmental. They were mostly affluent homeowners or broke hippies; neither had to worry much about money. It was a pleasure to be around them. Chris had meant well. His mother respected idealists.

THE SHACK

In October, after I had begun teaching part-time at Sonoma State University, about forty miles to the north, Charlotte and Shep and I jammed much of our stuff into my old clunker, Rusty, the decrepit VW bug we had purchased from a hippie. We would come back for the rest. It was like driving in a metaphor. We still believed we were going to change the world. We had to. I knew that even northern California had a kind of winter, and that before long the rainy season would begin. Somewhere up ahead we might break down or get bogged in the mud and then the serious rotting and the rusting would begin. But there didn't seem to be any alternative.

Somehow we had located a community of African-American farmers that had moved to the land outside of Santa Rosa after the Civil War. The shack we rented from one of their families was spare, the size of a garage, four tiny rooms in a bare field of five acres of tall sun-browned grass. (It hadn't rained in months.) Our landlords kept up the farming tradition by planting a beautiful vegetable garden. When we went to pay the rent, they often gave us a large bag of carrots or Swiss chard.

We were set just south of Santa Rosa and Sebastopol on a flat plain that reminded me of Kansas except that you could see Sonoma Mountain in the distance. We were a long way from Greenwich Village. Our bathtub emptied though a rubber hose that ambled down through a hole in the floor into the backyard where it sat in an evergreen patch of grass. Once a frog crawled up the hose and we found it in the tub in the morning.

Over the hills to the west lay the Pacific Ocean, endlessly rocking. If I had gone any farther away from my family, I would have been in the sea.

As soon as Charlotte and I got settled, we took some psilocybin (the active ingredient in psychedelic mushrooms) to consecrate our new home. The sky was lovely with low floating clouds, various shades of gray and silver, furry and lazy like sheep in wolves' clothing over the flat plain. We dragged our mattress (no one used beds in those days, just a mattress on the floor) and set it down in the field of tall grass beside our house. We pulled our comforter over us and lay there still, looking up at the heavenly sky. Shep came over and lay down beside us on the grass. We didn't give a thought to what the folks in cars might think as they drove by on the county road. (Actually named Stony Point Road.)

We connected shortly with two hippie couples who rented down the road. One pair, Abner and Emily, were long-haired, young, country people who had become a-political hippies. One night they were coming home on the freeway with Abner driving on LSD and Emily asleep when a cop pulled them over. Abner hadn't realized he was going five miles per hour. He exited the car and stood there on the edge of the highway. The cop came over and asked him why he was leaning on a tilt. "Because of the hill," Abner said. "But there is no hill here," the cop said, puzzled. Somehow Emily got them out of it and drove Abner home. They were nice folks. I was sorry when their trailer burned down.

The other couple had a pet lamb in their large kitchen. I had never seen a whole lamb up close before, just lamb chops. I liked its large hoofs. But I knew little about animals and was not comfortable when a group of big steers wandered up to our cabin. I had seen steers stampede in Western movies in the Ogden Theater when I was a kid, and I didn't feel secure in the tiny house when they were around. After we moved out, someone built a large house beside it, and turned our shack into a garage.

Sonoma State was located just outside the town of Cotati which sat at the conjunction of three old Indian roads. Cotati didn't have a town square but a large town circle. Nothing square could exist in Cotati. The town was a center of the late Sixties back-to-nature movement, stuffed with dropouts from Berkeley, artists, writers, hippies, back-to-the-landers, freaks, environmental activists, political radicals, dopers, welfare cheats, geniuses, students, communards, the whole tribe. Cotati would have been the spiritual home of everyone in "The Great Lebowski." When my student and pal and soon to be famous writer Kate Braverman, the Queen of Metaphor, showed up running from some beef with the law, she named Cotati "The Land of a Thousand Comebacks." Cotati made the national news in 1971 when the hippies took over the town, electing the daughter of the local grocery store owner as mayor and dropouts as a majority of the city council. Their reign was cut short however, when the mayor and half the new city council were arrested one night trying to break into the police station to steal the bags of pot the police had seized in raids.

At my job interview for the English Department at Sonoma State, the hiring committee had begun by asking me what would be my first act if I was given a composition class, and I responded, "I would enter the room and set a dictionary on fire." They laughed. I couldn't believe it. I was going over. This had to be the place for me. Then I heard rock music from outside. It turned out this was Peace Day. Sonoma State was a kind of country annex of Berkeley. A new state college, expanding rapidly, friendly to the countercultural students. In fact many of the students were Berkeley dropouts going country. And many of the profs were Berkeley and Stanford Ph.D.s. Only a handful of buildings had been erected. No dorms. Some of the students, residing in old trucks and buses, had formed a stoned encampment in a corner of one of the large, half-empty parking lots. The college went along with it. Then the students asked for showers and bathrooms. Again the college was going to comply, but when the students insisted on co-ed bathrooms the school had to desist because it was known Governor Reagan hated the place and this might give him ammunition to shut it down. Nonetheless, the school and the students negotiated a deal with a farmer across the street who let the little village move into "Sonoma Grove," a tuft of trees that remained an improvised hippie-student sanctuary for years. You could get stoned just by driving past with your windows open.

After about a half hour of my job interview, the sounds of the Peace Day festivities drifted into the room. One of the committee, Professor J.J. Wilson, said, smiling, "Maybe we should adjourn. I'm sure you'd rather be out at the party." She'd read my mind. [J.J. Wilson was a Virginia Woolf scholar, one of the founding mothers of feminism in California. She became a friend, as did Karen Petersen who, together with J.J., was writing the classic text, *Woman Artists*.]

Four bands were appearing that day in a field behind the music building. Sonoma State was known for outdoor concerts. The weather was generally good and one of my attractions to the school had been programs on New York's PBS-TV of free concerts of the Grateful Dead and The Jefferson Airplane there in the grass. Sonoma State was one of the few American universities in which the students never rioted in the Sixties. Never. They knew the administration was on their side and they appreciated it.

At the festival, several hundred people listened to the music and danced in the field while they passed around gallons of red wine and bomber joints. Some of the students were dressed in costumes from other eras, many were hardly dressed at all. I was handed a joint by a beautiful young woman wearing only a volley ball net. I wondered whether, in my new status as potential professor, I should smoke the joints with them. The Country Joe Band with Barry Melton began to play. There wasn't a cloud in the sky. Everyone was smiling and sharing. How could I say no?

I shared a joint with a student who told me laughingly that the local paper was feuding with the school because an art professor had brought finger paints into class and asked for volunteers to pull down their pants and paint with their asses. Of course everyone volunteered. He also informed me that the student government had gone to the reservation of a local Indian tribe and surrendered. When the older Indians came forth and asked what they meant, the Student President said, "Look, it's your land. The white people stole it. We want to give it back. You can have the university as a start." The Indians were gracious and amused but they politely declined. Then the student government dissolved itself saying they had no real power anyway. [For years the school had no student government, no athletics, no fees. No one seemed to mind.]

Sonoma State was the school for me. The student newspaper was called "The Stony Point Gazette." The Chairman of the English Department took me under his wing. He told me to he wanted to hire me. Sam Bullen was a Stanford Ph.D. specializing in Charles Dickens. Later he told me there was something in my writing that reminded him of Dickens. He had been born a Mormon and had asked them to excommunicate him. They said, "Just don't show up anymore." He said, "No, I want to be excommunicated."

Sam's wife had converted to Judaism. One day when I was typing in the kitchen, Charlotte rushed in with a strange, anxious look on her face. "It's the Department Chair's wife. She's at the door. She's selling soap powder." Charlotte shrugged her shoulders, her face set somewhere between a laugh and a person watching a car crash. The antics of the straight people always scared Charlotte. She could never get in tune with their customs and rituals.

"*What*?"

"She just showed up here. She has these big boxes of laundry soap powder. They're expensive. What should I do?"

"Buy them," I said. "Buy anything she has. If she's selling tropical fish food, buy it."

Now Charlotte relaxed and began to laugh. "But we don't have any fish."

"Just buy whatever she has and then when she leaves throw it away."

Now we were both laughing. We would have no shortage of laundry soap for a long time.

Sam was a great guy. A rare generous soul who mentored me for several years. I still miss his kindness. I never realized how much he meant to me and to the department until the department fell apart and disintegrated into petty bickering after he died, when he poured lighter fluid on himself and set himself on fire at a barbecue.

After my Sonoma State interview, I delayed talking to any other universities. Soon I was hired for part-time teaching which was what I wanted. When I had taught a semester, they asked if I would be interested in full-time teaching but I declined. It would be a terrific position, in the wine and hippie country just north of San Francisco, but I wanted to try to support myself as a writer. My book hadn't come out yet. In any case, I would want to pay for myself. As a matter of principle I didn't want to take welfare or be supported by my wife.

I wanted to live in a shack with no luxuries. I didn't want to be a member of the First World. Didn't want to carry the weight of that guilt. I only desired what everyone else in the world could have without oppressing others or despoiling the environment. I wanted to leave the earth pretty much as I had found it. [I kept this up for twenty years, living in a semi-basement flat in San Francisco's Mission District for sixteen years with my second and present wife, Marijke, who was from Rotterdam, bombed out and burned to the ground like much of The Bronx. Come to think of it, San Francisco was also burned down in the earthquake of 1906. Perhaps that's what life on earth was: rebuilding things after they've burned down.]

[Marijke is a psychiatric nurse, the perfect occupation for a writer's wife. We finally bought a little house in a working class, Hispanic neighborhood in San Francisco. I figured what the heck, there's enough wealth in the world for me to have a small house. A decade later, during the dotcom boom, the neighborhood became somewhat fashionable among the hip young people and the house quadrupled in value. Oh well . . .]

I loved going in to teach every day. You never knew what was going to happen. I particularly loved my encounters with original students, students who lived in chicken coops and communes and alternative realities. One of my favorite students wrote off-the-wall stories that I knew were autobiographical. One day she approached me at the start of a class and said, softly, "Can I please leave a little early today?"

"What's up?"

"I brought my boyfriend along today, but he's real shy and he ran away. Now he's over near the Student Union hiding in a bush."

One of our students, Sara Howard, a woman in her twenties who still wore the name of the leading African-American university her family had founded after the Civil War, worked at the county mental hospital. (Her brother had had a bout with a mental hospital after he called the police from California and "confessed" to shooting President Kennedy back in 1963, but that's another story.) Sara arranged for the university to act as a kind of half-way house to mental patients before they were released. As the motto of the time was "Why Not?" it seemed like a good idea. I took two of the young men into my writing classes. It worked out OK in a way. One said his name was John Hawkes. He claimed to be the son of Norman Mailer. I liked him. At least he had read a lot of novels and he regaled the class with anecdotes about his "father." The other was quiet and never volunteered to read his stories to the class. One day we all asked him to read. He complied with a story about a young man who winds up being kidnapped to San Francisco's Chinatown. The story moved along satisfactorily up to this point, but after he was handed over to the locals, the rest of the dialogue was in Chinese. Or should I say "Chinese." He was Caucasian, and had never given any signs of ability with languages. His language sounded Chinese in a way, but in a way it didn't. None of us wanted to ask him about it, since he was quite shy and he seemed to be taking a chance in reading to us.

It was difficult to grade stories such as this. I was glad we had a new grading system that permitted grades of pass/fail or incomplete. I liked the option to award an incomplete grade. I thought it was evidence of the influence of India on our culture. In India there was no hell, no grade of F at the end of your life. You either passed and moved along, or you got an "Inc" and had to take your life again.

Once I assigned Tom Wolfe's *The Electric Kool Aid Acid Test* to a literature class. I thought I would be cooler than the class but I was wrong. In those days we held some classes at students' houses. A young, bright, beautiful student I liked named Jo suggested we hold the class at her house. Jo was nineteen and fun, self-confident and smart, but sometimes she could be a wise-guy. The class held fifteen people: ten young hip students, and five very nice, fortyish, straight women from Santa Rosa. One of my favorites among them was a flautist whom the other women called "Tweety." Jo always referred to them as "the little old ladies from Santa Rosa," although they weren't little or old.

Jo welcomed us with glasses of Kool Aid. We all smiled. As we sat around Jo's living room, discussing the book about Ken Kesey's journey with the merry pranksters around the United States in a psychedelic painted bus while on acid, driven by Neil Cassidy himself, I began to notice something strange. Jo and her friends. What was it? Then, with a start, I realized what was happening. The class was on acid!

Jo had spiked the Kool Aid! I myself wasn't tripping. But I knew the kids were. I panicked. Immediately called for a break. Signaled Jo to follow me quickly into the kitchen. "Are you nuts!" I barked in her face.

"Jerr," Jo said, completely unflustered beneath her sly smile. "It's cool. Don't worry."

"Don't worry? You can't dose those nice ladies. Are you nuts?"

Jo laughed. "Jerr . . . What do think I am? Didn't you notice? There are two pitchers. One that's electric for the electric people and one that's straight for the little old ladies from Santa Rosa. Don't worry so much. I've got everything under control."

"Yeah, but you're on acid," I said, almost having to laugh myself at the craziness of it, now that I realized the older women were safe.

Jo just smiled and went back to the class.

Sure enough there were two pitchers. So I resumed the three-hour class as the younger students began to get off. Yet strangely enough it worked out. Probably because of the magic of the time. The older women had a great time, perhaps just imagining the younger kids had had a few drinks before coming to the class. They had no idea most of the class was hallucinating, although I could see it quite clearly, even though I was preoccupied in praying fervently for the class to end as soon as possible.

Finally the class did actually end. I left the house in a better mood once I realized I wasn't going to be fired or jailed. The young kids remained behind. Later Jo told me they all took off their clothes and squeezed into the bathtub at about the time the sun came up.

FINALS

The chilling rains came in December. I decided to hold my final class in a bar. I wasn't too sure about this, but the class suggested it and even the women from Santa Rosa went along. Things were different then. There was a smoking room in a local high school where the kids could get stoned under supervision. But we faculty still received memos from our boss, the big chief in Sacramento, Ronald Reagan. It was hard to know where to draw the line.

I wanted to be the opposite of a state bureaucrat in my teaching, to work with each student individually, to create a new, more generous and further out personality for myself, to work against my ego. At the same time I wanted to keep my job, and thus I had to act straighter than I really was, although I doubt that I was really fooling anyone. Yet I was also supposed to be a wild and crazy novelist. How could I refuse to have the final class in the new women's bar that had opened up in Cotati, a block from the central part of town, behind a funky corrugated building that held about three or four stores that no one patronized?

The students were getting drunk together. Everyone was telling me it had been a great class and most were arranging to take further classes with me. What was there to worry about? How could I not get drunk with them? After all, most of them were over the legal drinking age. They could handle themselves. I needed some red wine to burn off the chill. Besides, I wasn't their parent. When the class ended, my *in loco parentis* responsibilities ended as well. Didn't they?

According to this logic, when the class actually did end, and the students gave me a round of applause, wasn't I supposed to become a novelist again? We all continued to drink together, into the shadows of the rainy evening.

Then one student, Darryl, a sweet thin guy, long dirty-blond hair, maybe three or four years younger than I, asked me to come out to his car to try this fabulous Thai stick he had run into. I was new to this novelist trade, my book wasn't out yet, but what would Jack Kerouac or Ken Kesey do? Somewhat reluctantly, but in part because I was concerned about keeping up my image as a far-out guy, I joined him in his car which sat in the unpaved, wet, rutted area that lay between the building and the road and served as a parking lot. There was little light, just a sodium lamp down in the town proper.

It was interesting to me and a little scary, getting wrecked out of my mind with one of my students in an old car. Darryl wasn't lying about the weed. He looked at me proudly as I spaced out into a kind of acid venue, the result of all those years of trying to go into orbit on just pot. I always thought of the Buddha saying, "Let go, what are you holding onto? Your ego? The town? The universe? Get lost."

We were both lost when I heard a knocking and saw a face that seemed very far away at the window. It was another student. "Come quick," he was saying on Mars. There's a real problem. There's been a crash. Tweety . . . "

A crash? What crash? Suddenly I realized what was happening My parents had been right. I was fucked. I had been given responsibility by the society and I had failed to assume it. All those years of study would be thrown away. I had to function but I couldn't. I could never function on dope. The cops would soon be here. I was too fucked up to make believe that I was a professor. I tried to wait, hoping the excited student would go away to some other planet, but Darryl, my partner in crime in the car, jumped out and said, "Come on, let's go."

They both looked at me. I figured I'd better go with them. The rain had thinned into drizzle, but the night was dark and it was hard to make out what was happening on the other side of the lot. The whole class was standing there in a semi-circle, looking at an old American car that Tweety had backed into. Her own vehicle was barely dented, but she had crushed in the door of the other car.

There was nowhere for me to hide. I kept saying a mantra to myself, "Maintain." And then the class, as one, turned toward me. Apparently I was the still the parent. Jo said, "We asked at the bar, but no one knows who owns the car. What should we do?"

They waited for an answer. I was trying to remember what town and state I was in. The people and surroundings looked familiar, and I knew

I was their teacher somehow, but was this Fitchburg or California? I was filled with terror. I had to do something before the police arrived and found out that the class was drunk and I was in Massachusetts.

Then I had an inspiration. It came in the form of a tenth-of-a-second flashback to an image of my brother Mark and my father getting out of my father's '47 Buick in The Bronx. I was twelve, my brother eight, my father was furious and my brother abashed, looking down at the ground, holding a baseball in his glove. They had just come back from Brooklyn where my father was visiting his brother Abie. My father was yelling, "I told this kid a thousand times, don't play catch with a hardball in the street. You'll break a windshield. But no. I'm in the house with Abie, so he's a goddamn wise guy. Bang. There goes a goddamn windshield." I looked at my brother, his eyes not meeting mine. "But here's the worst part," my father said. "You wanna hear the worst part? He doesn't even run. No one knows him, but he just stands there." He looked toward my brother. "He stands there and waits for the goddamn cops!! Didn't I tell him a thousand times, 'If the cops are coming, run!' but no, he just stands there and he waits for the goddamn cops!" My father had seemed to be pleading his case up to the Gods.

I looked toward the class and before I knew it, I heard my self saying to Tweety, who was in her forties with large eye-glasses and short hair, one of the nicest people you could imagine, "Look, we're never gonna find this guy. We can't wait here all night. Just take off." When this got no immediate agreement from the class, I added, "It's only a scratch."

Here I saw the difference between me and the Americans, straight or stoned. They were all looking at me in shocked disbelief. They hadn't been chased out of Europe by the Cossacks. They hadn't grown up with some maniac trying to wipe their people off the face of the earth. They hadn't been tortured in Bronx lots because some idiots thought you had "killed their savior," whatever that meant. They hadn't had their home city burned to the ground for reasons no one could understand. They believed in fair play. They were aghast. I was fucked.

One student, Phil, stepped forward. "A scratch!!! She smashed in his whole door. She's got to leave a note."

Somehow here, at that moment, stoned as I was, my muse (perhaps my father in heaven?) stepped in and spoke though my mouth, improvising quickly with great certainty, "Well *of course* she's got to leave a note! That goes without saying! That's what I meant." And I bent forward as if I was looking at the door more closely from another angle. "Let's see if anyone has a plastic bag in his car. Then we can write her name and address and all on a piece of paper, and put it in the bag under the windshield wiper, and when the other guy comes back tomorrow, it'll all be cool. The insurance'll take care of it. That's what we pay them for, right?"

I looked up. The whole class relaxed as if they all were saying, "Whew!" at once. They were smiling again. One guy said, "We thought you were just telling her to split and get out of here." "Hit and run" a young woman added. "Hey!" I said in the Bronx manner, which could mean anything. I put my hands out, palms to heaven, which was an Italian gesture that meant, "What am I, a fucken idiot?"

When everyone had left, I stood in the lot with Daryl. We both relaxed and smiled. I felt another wave of phenomenology come over me. Where we were was real, but where were we? "That was far out weed," I said. He laughed proudly as if I had praised a story he had written.

"You all right?" he said. "You think you can find your way home?"

"Yeah," I said. "I'm cool. But just answer me one thing."

"What's that?"

"Are we in California?"

He laughed like crazy. He thought I was joking.

ACADEMIC POLITICS

Teaching certain subjects was difficult for me because I had not been an official English Major. At times I found myself teaching courses I hadn't taken. I also needed time and energy to work on my own writing since, having grown up in The Bronx, "proper" English was in some respects a second language to me. I could never use words like "wry" or "rueful" without feeling somewhat like a showoff or social climber.

I was lucky in my students who generally rated my classes amongst their favorites. When I took the job, I decided that I was going to attempt to give them the same class they would have received at Penn or Princeton. This was not really possible because of my heavy teaching schedule—eventually 200 writing students a year. (I told the students that the reason that Ivy-League schools were so expensive was because the semesters there were shorter.) But I think I was able to give many students the unforgettable experience of being in contact with their creative potential in a free and supportive atmosphere in which many of them produced work that was interesting and worthwhile. I always kept in mind that writing was part of life, and thus the class had to be about the world outside of literature as well. One can teach content as well as technique. A writing class is a wonderful opportunity to challenge the basic assumptions of the culture that the students drag into class. One's aims in literature can be related to one's aims in life.

AMERICA THE BEAUTIFUL: FROM GOTTLIEB TO SHINING GOTTLIEB

Robert Gottlieb was on the East Coast, continuing with a brilliant career that would lead to his running the *New Yorker* and later editing Bill Clinton's autobiography. Meanwhile, on the West Coast, another Gottlieb, Lou, had taken a different path. Lou Gottlieb had been raised in LA where he studied atonal music and composition with Arnold Schoenberg. Then he formed the Limeliters, a highly successful folk group in the Fifties, but he found that he was always sick and traditional medicine couldn't help him. When he started taking LSD the illness went away, so he used the money from the Limeliters to buy some land in Sonoma County, which he opened to the people and deeded to God. There were two major American communes near my shack: Wheeler Ranch and Lou's Morningstar Ranch. I was surprised by the kind of people I met from these communes. Ramón Sender Barayón became one of my closest friends. He later married the teacher and social reformer Judy Levy who worked for peace between the Jews and Palestinians. Fluent in Spanish, she was a beloved teacher in San Francisco's Mission District. Ramón was the son of the great Spanish novelist, Ramón Sender, who was nominated for the Nobel Prize. When Ramón Sr. was chased out of Spain during the Civil War, his wife tried to join him, along with Ramón, who was two, but the Fascists caught her and shot her. No wonder Ramón became a peacenik and communard and made his living as "Zero the Clown." Ramón wrote an excellent book about his mother, *A Death in Zamora*, and composed electronic music. Another musician on the commune who was also a student of mine, Vivian Gotters, performed Bach on the harpsichord and wrote about Bach for me in her writing classes.

There was more to communal life than stoned classical musicians strolling nude on the countryside. You could see that the easy years were over and the Sixties, even here, were in decline. As the Haight sunk into heavy drugs and despair, refugees from the carnage showed up at the communes. The county authorities were not happy with the communards flowering in their quiet rural area and busted them by declaring that their teepees were in violation of the building codes. Lou Gottlieb also ran into trouble because he had deeded the land to God. When a woman was hit by lightning in Arizona, legally an "act of God," she sued him to seize the land from God as damages. This further added to the legal troubles which would eventually bring the commune down.

The communes were an experiment in egalitarian living. All the former participants that I know continue to look back on them with affection and pride. Many consider those years the best of their lives. When they get together, it is immediately apparent that the deep bonds between them have endured. As Ramón Sender says in a Zen-like aphorism, "It's very easy to keep a dirt floor clean."

I liked many of the communards very much, and I loved my counterculture students, but there were also some stoned hippies in Cotati who evoked more ambivalent feelings in me, though they did some wonderful things. For example, led by an older drop-out from LA named Vito, along with his old lady, Suzie Cream-cheese, the hippies built (with questionable legality) a neat redwood bandstand in the center of town, a beautiful work that has provided a venue for decades of music and recreation for the entire area.

Yet the LA dropouts raised my hackles at times. They hung around the university and they seemed to have, as my friend the poet David Bromige called it, "a stonier-than-thou attitude." They wandered around the campus like a colorful gypsy tribe with their naked kids trailing behind them, shitting on the grass. Charlotte hooked up with them. I thought they were a bad influence on her. They existed on a spectrum that joined hippie with LA hipster.

The counterculture wasn't perfect, but I would never be a straight person again. The dilemma I would struggle with for the rest of my life was not yet completely clear to me: I loved my old friends, and I always would love them, but I couldn't live in the "normal," mainstream culture. And I didn't want to. It was toxic to me. The materialism was too dense. I couldn't see the Light. It was not my aim to fly around the world to fabulous hotels for extravagant meals while hungry people lay outside on the sidewalk. Wherever I slept at night, I could hear the Earth crying.

Yet I was beginning to see that I wasn't a complete stoner like Charlotte, smoking weed from morning to night, 24/7, wake and bake. I liked to get high, but I also liked to be straight when I worked. When I didn't work, I missed the weekends. I hated to admit this, even to myself. I preferred being straight most of the time and then getting stoned or sometimes dropping acid for spiritual explorations. I was becoming a writer, but I felt I lacked the courage to be a Jack Kerouac who was one of my idols. Later I found out that even Jack Kerouac wasn't "Jack Kerouac." That we had confused him with Neil Cassidy. [When I suggested this to Carolyn Cassidy, she agreed. Kerouac was very brave and he traveled far, but he did spend most of his time at home, in Queens, in his bedroom at the house of his conservative, Catholic mother.]

When Charlotte and I got settled, we put in for adoption of a baby. With our long hair and old clothes and our domicile that was basically a garage, we feared the initial interview, but when the social worker showed up with long blond hair down past his shoulders, a colorful shirt, and a large Mickey Mouse watch, I knew we were home free. A year later we were given a six week old boy. I named him Jesse. I wanted him to have an unpretentious American name, a western name with a hint of the outlaw about it. Today Jesse is a welder in Ohio with a good sense of humor. [Oddly enough, it was through Jesse that I finally ended my own Vietnam War by making peace with my former mother-in-law, Bessie Mayer of Lewiston, Idaho. Bessie lost her son Rod in Vietnam and had become a fervent supporter of the hideous war that tore our family apart, but years later when her husband Joe passed away, Bessie "adopted" little Jesse who was being raised in far from ideal circumstances by Charlotte and Jim Saunt in Ohio. Seeing that we had similar aims, we began to cooperate in helping out Jesse when we could. It was here that I saw my ex-mother-in-law's true generosity and sense of caring for others. Somehow, years after my divorce from Charlotte, Bessie and I became friends and we were able to put the war behind us.]

Sometimes in northern California the sun shines all day in a perfect blue sky that clouds don't know about and the fog has forgotten. I was inside our shack, grading some student papers, Shep was outside, a few feet from the front step, sleeping in the brown grass. Then a nice neighborhood woman, in her forties, driving on our almost deserted street, lost control of her car and drove off the road, panicked, sped sixty feet across the level flat land in front of our house, ran over Shep and killed him. The woman wasn't drunk or on drugs, it was just one of those things, a mystery. She took a step out of her car and folded over, collapsing in the grass near Shep who was dying. I found myself trying to take care of her as well as Shep. She felt so bad, she was sobbing away there in the grass. I felt sorrier for her than I did for myself, after all, she was the one who had done it. But after I got her together and forgave her and sent her on her way, I felt a devastating wallop of hollow sadness inside myself. How could this have happened? Shep had been through it all, the Village, the Sixties, the trek across the prairies to California to start a new life. He was part of the plan. I wanted Shep to be there when things began to brighten and change.

I took Shep to the vet and left him there. Then came the hard part. I went home and sat there for hours thinking about how I was going to tell Charlotte when she returned from work. I planted myself on our stupid old St. Vincent de Paul couch, thinking about how devastated Charlotte was going to be when she walked in the door smiling and I had to tell her. I thought about all the wisdom I had accumulated about death and all, and it helped a great deal, but it still hurt so bad while it was happening. I knew Shep would be OK somewhere. I took out a Beach Boys record and played "Good Vibrations" a couple times, but it wasn't the same, listening to it without Shep.

Charlotte came home after midnight. I told her quickly. Looking at my face, she had no doubt I was telling her the truth. She sat on the couch and wept. She just wept and wept, her head hanging limply on her shoulders. She wept all night.

Charlotte had a close relationship with animals, having grown up on a farm in Idaho. Shep and I, though, we were city people. New Yorkers. We felt safer in urban areas. We always knew that in a place like New York there were so many people that if someone was going to shoot someone, or run someone over while he was sleeping, it would usually happen to someone else.

Charlotte worked two nights a week typesetting the *Pacific Sun*, a liberal weekly newspaper. She was a swift typist and being a former English teacher she could proof-read a bit along the way. Sometimes she didn't come home until two a.m. Often I was in the little shack by myself. The fog would come in from the Pacific which rolled just behind the low hills to the west. The soft fog would sheath our valley from light and sound, enclosing us in a down comforter. No cars would appear on the road. There were no houses especially close to our tiny home on the big blanketed plain.

I was often lonely on the empty California land. But some evenings, as I sat there, I would stop grading papers and I would feel a kind of pure happiness. Sometimes, on acid, I would feel that I was at the center of the wheel, that the great wheel of the universe was turning around me. That I had no desire. That I was already at the sweet, peaceful center of everything, the place of no needs, neither inside nor outside of myself. But it's funny, whenever I tried to put that feeling into words, or even thought about it in words, I found that I was no longer there at the center.

It was as if language begins to break down as one leaves the earth. Like the Great Wall of China, language was from the world of the Two. But acid could take you into the world of the One.

When the Zen masters admonished us not to mistake the pointing finger for the moon (enlightenment), could it have been language they were indicating? At a certain point simple sentences begin to shred. Sentences like "It's all a dream," are not enough. If it was only a dream, why was murder obviously wrong? As you traveled into space, you came to a zone where only myths and questions remained. And Zen koans, with their many-sided, crystalline responses. And then you reached a place where language itself dropped away.

I drove down to visit my friends in Marin just before the landlord sold Jim and Paulette's house and they had to leave. Rocco was sitting alone in the darkening living room, picking out some chords on his guitar. A cigarette with a long ash dangled from his lips. His eyes were totally stoned, a pint can of malt liquor beside him on the floor. His clothes had holes in them from the welding. His hair was long and unkempt, covered on top by a bandana folded into a triangle like a house painter. If you didn't know Rocco, you might think he was a tough guy. He would have been played by Jean Paul Belmondo in a French movie. He looked like a bum, or a hood, but he was amazingly innocent, buoyed by dreams of being a rock musician and filled with ready gratitude to anyone who treated him right. Actually, from the back, he was easy to mistake for his sister Paulette who was also short and had similar dirty blond hair.

Rocco's face lit up when I walked in. He stopped picking the guitar and said, "Ay! Wait'll you hear what the fuck happened, man." He dragged on his cigarette and took a long swig of malt liquor.

I sat down beside him and he continued, speaking out the side of his mouth, slurring his words. "I'm with Jim driving along Sir Frances Drake in the van, man, and there's this American guy standing beside the road hitching a ride, but listen to this, man, he's got this huge turban on his head. I mean huge, man, white, all wrapped around and everything, man. I thought to myself, whew, this guy's really out there, man. Then we're driving along and I thought, man, I know that guy. Who is it? Then I realized man, holy shit! It's my fucken brother Perry! Can you believe it, man? My fucken brother Perry is out there in these fucken robes and a fucken *turban*, man! I mean Jesus Christ, man, suppose one of my friends saw him!" He shook his head with a kind of slow woe. He smiled a bit but he wasn't really kidding.

Some time later, Quinn, the historian/carpenter, invited us all to his house warming. He'd built a beautiful A-frame house out in Lagunitas near where the redwoods began. Mostly one large room with a loft for sleeping. Quinn was living with a young woman named Lotus who was a dancer. She wasn't a great conversationalist, but as long as the rock music was blasting on the stereo, and everyone was getting wrecked on wine and dope and dancing wildly in the large central room, Lotus was in her element, happily one of the centers of attention. It was when the music changed to quiet jazz, and Quinn brought out the trays of food and the white wine, and we all chatted about art and politics, that Lotus found herself out of the water so to speak. I could see she was unhappy. She was about nineteen and had little to say. Then suddenly she had an inspiration. She began to do cartwheels around the room, somehow managing to avoid crashing into the guests at what had become a cocktail party. Everyone simply continued to talk and nibble at the food, trying to accommodate her, as Lotus happily cartwheeled around the room, again and again, for what seemed like an hour, whirling between us like a planet gone mad around a collapsed sun.

As the Sixties wound down and people tried to try to pick up their lives, things began to change for our friends. Lotus and Quinn split up. I heard a rumor that she went to Brazil and was kidnapped by pirates on the Amazon.

Paulette's youngest brother Perry moved to San Francisco where he became a disciple of Sri Chinmoy. He lived in an ashram in the city, and he cooked at Carlos Santana's vegetarian restaurant. After a couple years he took off his turban, left the religious life, and returned to school. He studied economics at Berkeley and Harvard, achieving a Ph.D. Today he is running a large African country for the IMF.

Rocco and Jim drank more and experimented with heroin. Jim ran off with Lily, a single mother and heroin user, and Rocco lived with them. Rocco told me Jim was never a "real junky," but when Jim almost OD'd in the men's room at Macy's in San Rafael, and he was arrested, and was put into a drug rehab facility, Rocco returned to Chicago where he lived with his mother and took a job as a "parkee." Not long afterwards, he drank himself to death. Before he left California, he had called me and asked to borrow some money. I agreed to give it to him but I couldn't bear to look at him, he was so sad. My friend, the beautiful, witty poet Karen Elizabeth Gordon and I bumped into him one night and she said his face looked like "raw hamburger." (This was before Karen became famous for writing funny, erotic grammar books for the *New York Times'* publishing company.) I told Rocco I would leave the money in my mailbox. The next day he had taken the money and I never saw him again. I remember how happy he was the time his band got a good gig playing at a festival in a park. Whenever he would talk about that day, he glowed with rare joy. It was so great to see Rocco shining. And I recall how we used to drive around Marin, and he would toke at his joint, and sip on his malt liquor, and then he would lean back in his seat and look up at towering Mount Tamalpais and nod his head with satisfaction, and say, "The Big Chief. The Big Chief is still up there, man."

People think the Sixties ruined a lot of lives, but actually while it lasted the counterculture floated a lot of special people who couldn't get a toe hold on life in the mainstream society. My pal Rocco was one of them.

Rochelle Gatlin continued to delay her dissertation while she drew astrology charts and taught part-time at San Francisco State. Then she fell in love with a visiting Englishman who invited her to emigrate and join him in Plymouth. She gave up her job, her cheap room in the flat in the Haight, sold her furniture, and took off in the lane of love. When she arrived in England, things didn't work out. The guy hadn't been straight with her. She returned to San Francisco and took a tiny apartment on a poor street in the Mission, living in poverty for years, surviving on jobs here and there, a class of teaching, an editing job. With the encouragement of Bruce Kuklick, now an important professor at Penn, she finished her Ph.D. Then she wrote an excellent book on the history of women in America since 1945, emphasizing the liberating effect the Sixties had had on many women. Eventually she was given a full-time position with long teaching hours at the local, excellent junior college. Now she teaches hundreds of poor students a year. I sat in on her class. She's a fabulous teacher. She still lives in the same little flat in the Mission. Somehow Rochelle backed into a life of honorable poverty and Buddhist meditation and teaching the poor.

Her ex-husband Ken Gatlin moved back to Northern California, to the town of Eureka, where he and Ward Hoalton had originally come from, up near the Oregon border. Ken remarried and became a strict Christian.

Ward moved to a room in a house just outside of Oakland, where he continued his Spartan lifestyle, cleaning houses for a meager living.

Jim's sister Honey and Corkey emigrated to Israel. Corkey converted to Judaism at Honey's request. In thirty years there they raised three children. Then they ran into financial problems and they moved to Cleveland. Corkey, with his usual generosity, taught my son Jesse many of his valuable skills in construction and carpentry. Corkey got a job as a "Super" in an apartment house that came with a free apartment. Then he had a heart attack. Honey and Corkey split up. He returned to northern California. She took a job teaching poor kids in a mixed-race neighborhood as she had done in San Francisco's Mission District. Back to a life of public service and right livelihood.

Karen and Steve Whitelaw divorced after a few years. Each married quickly and amazingly each new spouse died shortly thereafter at an early age. Steve married again, a second French woman. He moved to the South of France and became an expert scuba diver. Later he bought each of his two kids a million dollar house in San Francisco. Karen Whitelaw moved to Mill Valley, married again, and became the Director of the large San Francisco Jewish Community Center.

Jim and Paulette's son Claudio played trumpet in the San Francisco all-city high school jazz band. He took a degree in history at Columbia, Phi Beta Kappa. He did graduate work at Oxford, and took a Ph.D. at Duke. Now he is a professor and award-winning author, an excellent historian with books out from Oxford and Cambridge University Presses on Native American history and border history at the intersection of cultures. Border history! Sounds like the story of our lives.

Paulette kicked Jim out, moved to San Francisco with Claudio, and married Jerry Long, a sweet guy, shaved head rock musician, former motorcycle racer from Missouri. She managed his band for a while, then took a job as receptionist for two aged women pediatricians. I gave her my alto sax. They allowed her to play it at her desk when there were no patients in the office. Somehow she managed to put Claudio through all those universities on her own, without Jim's help. Jerry Long formed a duo with a nice guy named Vice-Grip who worked in a hardware store, wore a vice-grip as a tie, and was said to sleep in a coffin. Vice became locally famous later on when he donned a tuxedo and fronted a big band in the retro-swing craze.

After about ten years, Paulette and Jerry split up. Jerry married a nice woman, Phobi, a manicurist who some people said was a Borden's heiress. Jerry taught her to play bass and added her to his new band. I saw Claudio, on vacation from university teaching, playing trumpet with them one New Year's Eve at a wild club on Haight Street.

Paulette next married Shep Pollack, the former president of Philip Morris. She became a patron of the arts. Shep became Chairman of the Board of ACT, San Francisco's leading repertory company. There is a plaque to their generosity in the basement of the ACT theater, given after they donated an elevator in the wake of the deadly earthquake of 1989. Paulette has returned to her original field, painting. She is now a fine abstract painter who recently had an impressive show at the San Francisco Italo-Americano Museo.

Who could have imagined that Charlotte would wind up in Cleveland with Jim Saunt? Jim and Charlotte and I all had trouble handling my success. Once it became clear that the counterculture was dying and that my fifteen minutes of fame was only going to last for five or six minutes, I ran wild for six months. I behaved stupidly, trying to make up for my lonely, haunted high school years by sleeping around with the "California Girls" I had heard about on Beach Boy records. Once I found out that some of these "girls" were funny and smart and that, unbelievably, now that I had somehow become "a novelist," they wanted to sleep with me, I couldn't resist. I lost it and behaved badly.

When we were teenagers, I had a cousin Arnold in Brooklyn who was arrested for following women home from foreign movie theaters. Arnold had been beaten as a boy by his parents. He was gaunt and shy, bent over like a question mark. The police saw that he was harmless and ultimately let him go, but that trope, the wounded, lonely boy, the ultimate outsider staring at another world he would never enter, a world symbolized by sophisticated gentile women of a higher class, lived inside of me even into my early thirties. In California I was given the opportunity to realize my teenage dreams. But I quickly realized that these dreams were not mine. I was no longer a teenager. It was difficult to admit that this path wasn't for me, it seemed square to think that way, but I couldn't shake the sense of guilt, the notion that I was selling out Charlotte, committing adultery, that it would lead to a false marriage based on lies.

I had hurt Charlotte and acted like a fool for six months. Then I stopped. But she needed to express her equality so she ran around for six months. We tried an open marriage but that was hopeless. I suggested that we return to monogamy and I completely stopped outside liaisons. But even after we gave up sleeping around, it was difficult to stitch our marriage back together. Life was different now in the Seventies. I felt that the price of admission to Charlotte's world was failure. In the Sixties, failure had served as a red badge of courage. Now with the culture returning to the Fifties' values, failure seemed more like a wound. Charlotte had been at home in a world of failure and no ambition. She'd been a kind of star. Now anyone who achieved anything, my new friends—poets, novelists, artists, professors, psychologists, historians—were all "too bourgeois." When they came to the house, she would go into the bedroom and not come out. One of the prices of writing books was the risk of success. She kept saying she would never change. She would never leave the summer of love. She said she didn't need me. She would marry Mr. Welfare. I told her that I hoped he gave her as much money for dope as I did.

After we moved to a railroad flat in the Mission District of San Francisco, she left her job at the newspaper, worked part-time at Jesse's child care center, and began to hang out with Jim Saunt. He was out of rehab but still shooting heroin, writing bad checks to his friends, and stealing from them. Once he broke into Steve Whitelaw's house and made off with Steve's clothes. I knew Charlotte and Jim were close when I came home from work one day and found that she and Jim had cut their arms and mixed their blood. Charlotte said that now they were "blood brothers."

It was hard to know how to respond. Our world was collapsing. The American people were beginning their long denial about Vietnam. Hope was dying. It was hard not to forgive your friends. I knew I needed some forgiveness myself. We were all in trouble. Charlotte was getting more stoned, out of control. Anytime I said to Charlotte that I thought we would have to change to fit the changed circumstances, she said that meant I didn't love her. But when I said we should split up, she wouldn't accept that either.

Finally I got her an apartment. I moved Jesse and her down the block. All of us were astonished when she hooked up with Jim. I never imagined they would move to Cleveland, that Jim would stop using heroin, and they would join a conservative synagogue. That they would take their children to temple every weekend. That Charlotte, who had started out to be a nun and then had transformed into an acid queen, would convert to Judaism. That she would keep kosher. Nothing un-kosher could enter her house except her pet pig that followed her wherever she went. (At the same time that she was playing Mozart and Bach in the Shaker Heights Symphony, she had a goat living on the roof.) They inherited money when Jim's parents died. They bought a nice older house and acres of land in the countryside outside of Cleveland. They moored a cabin cruiser on Lake Erie for family weekends, and they kept horses. Jim put on over a hundred pounds and stopped rooting for the Cleveland Indians because, as he put it, "Who can root for a bunch of spics?" They voted for Ronald Reagan, opposed welfare, supported Israel and hated Arabs.

Yet at the same time their whole family was also living a shadow, biker-style, grunge life, soaked in weed and booze, hot merchandise, motorcycles, Chicago blues, and trouble with the law. They had inherited Jim's family's structural steel business. They peopled their operation mostly with part-timers—dopers, ex-cons, thieves, guys fleeing warrants, crack heads from the inner city, and their own children. Each of their three children spent time in jail. Charlotte was surprised.

They ran the steel business for about twenty years before it went bankrupt. Then they opened a smaller steel shop, Rosie's (named after Rosie the Riveter), that lasted about five years. They let go of the horses and the boat.

Charlotte took custody of her two African-American grandchildren and raised them while her daughter was in prison. She and Jim took them to synagogue. Charlotte made sure they had Hebrew lessons so they could say the four questions for Jim at Passover. Charlotte became a vegetarian, thin as a reed. Jim endured a long series of illnesses and died at sixty-five.

I like to think of Charlotte, still wearing second-hand clothes, probably stoned, playing her beautiful Haynes flute for a couple years in the Shaker Heights Symphony (the flute she had bought in Greenwich Village just before we left New York), glowing with pride at her valedictorian teenage daughter playing violin beside her in the string section, in the time before the period of arrests and addictions and rehabs and jails began.

Jim Saunt was a charismatic, intelligent, irresponsible, and very spoiled man. One person will remember him giving us energy, art, laughter and soulful music, while another person will remember him behaving treacherously and inflicting wounds that have still not healed. In some cases these will be the same person. When I say he left a very mixed legacy, I will probably disappoint both those who have fond memories of him and those who are still furious with him. I hope he gets another incarnation in which his many good qualities win out.

Charlotte remains in Cleveland with her children and grandchildren. Like many young Americans of their generation, Charlotte's kids endured a confused and dangerous adolescence that lasted into their twenties.

They're good kids at heart, I've always liked them, and it gives me great joy to see them growing up and beginning to take strong steps toward a more stable and fruitful life. I know they're going to make it. Our son Jesse is working full time as a skilled craft welder. Charlotte and Jim's daughter Jamie went back to college, graduated with A grades, and is studying to become a social worker while working at Cleveland's House of Blues. Their son Zolie is a musician-songwriter who has just sold his first songs to a singer, a former Playmate of the Month, and he will play on her CD.

Charlotte lives simply, striving for a spiritual life in a material world. She is still a vegetarian and an active member of her synagogue. She prays for peace and does many good deeds for the people around her. Her favorite Hindu God is Ganesh, the elephant who helps to move immovable objects. She has added blues harp and Indian flute to her repertoire of instruments. She is currently setting Hebrew prayers to ancient Hindu melodies that she sings to her African-American grandchildren at bedtime.

God's blessings on Charlotte and her family. The German-Catholic, Idaho farm girl who aspired to be a nun has traveled a long way from her birthplace on the Snake River.

"Living's much more difficult than Sanskrit or chemistry or economics."

Aldous Huxley

A NEW WORLD

I was often lonely out on the California plain, especially as the dream of the commune in the country with all my friends began to fade. I didn't know that I was entering a different world, and I was on the verge of making many colorful and charming friends. The publication of my first book in 1972 shook everything up. Jim Saunt was very disturbed by the fact that suddenly I was speaking about the Sixties on TV in Boston and at Yale University. He felt my book had gotten it all wrong, that the book shouldn't be taught, and he made a secret list of everything that he thought was off the mark about it.

I didn't find out about this until much later, but I was making new friends like Andrei Codrescu who showed up in the area after Israel ransomed him when the Ceausescus wanted to throw him out of Romania. Andrei is now famous for his years of radio commentaries on "All Things Considered," and his movie, *Road Scholar*, in which he was filmed driving a Cadillac across country and having adventures, but I hope his fans remember that he is a poet first, a worthy member in the line of Romanian surrealists. Andrei used to say things like, "I feel like a Swiss cheese in a hailstorm of knives."

Andrei moved to Sonoma County, the Russian River, where he became the leader of a ragtag bunch of funny and talented young poets. Pat Nolan had come from Montreal and married the poet and bus driver, Gail King. Now he sat beside the river each day, elevated his spirits and wrote little Chinese poems in the manner of Li Po. Keith Abbott was another of the gang. He was a big, gentle, lumberjack kind of guy from the Northwest who followed his fellow Tacoma native son Richard Brautigan in his playful writing style, and at times, even worked for Richard, trimming trees on Brautigan's Montana ranch. Keith is now teaching at the Buddhist inspired Naropa University in Colorado. Jeffrey Miller from Detroit was another of Andrei's followers, but Jeffrey's life was tragically cut short in his early twenties in an auto accident up along the Russian River. Andrei took a long time to get over this. He believed in Jeffrey's talent and I knew why when I recalled a line Jeffrey had written in my class when Patty Hearst was in all the papers with her machine gun: "Patty Hearst, her inky-black newspaper eyes."

I liked hanging with Andrei. Our backgrounds were similar in a way. When younger he had studied math in Moscow. After he was deported, he lived for a while in Italy. Andrei was always grateful that the Italians had taken him in. He loved the Sixties and he had an immigrant's love for America, but sometimes its behavior would disturb him. He would attack Communism directly, telling me it was much worse than I imagined. After a time I came to see that he was right. With America he would usually limit himself to a wry remark in his Transylvanian accent, like, "Tell me Jerry, don't you think Italian men dress much better than Americans?"

Andrei ultimately wound up in New Orleans, justly famous, but I remember one afternoon before he left when Charlotte and I were living in a dark railroad flat in San Francisco's Mission District. Andrei and I were chatting quietly over a can of beer in our tiny living room which Charlotte had completely covered, walls and ceiling, with bed sheets she had tie-died in psychedelic fashion. A soft breeze came up and the whole room began to breathe around us like a lung. Suddenly Andrei leaped up and screamed out, "I can't stand it anymore, it's too crazy." He ran out the door and disappeared down the street. This amazed me. Andrei was one of the wildest guys I knew. I guess that living in a lung was weirder than I thought. The next morning I found an unopened bottle of ale on my window sill. I knew Andrei had gotten drunk, felt guilty, and had come back in the middle of the night. Seeing we were asleep, he had set it there for me.

The Sixties had faded in northern California, but the era hadn't really died until the fall of 1980 when Reagan was elected and some idiot shot John Lennon. Perhaps one could say that the Sixties were a flowing out to the rest of America of the values of the San Francisco Bay Area. A wisp of the Sixties survived in places like Sonoma State. I was fortunate in having an office mate Helen Dunn, who was simpatico with my temperament, a funny, generous, Irish lass who told me that an Irishman had invented the lawn chair: Paddy O'Furniture. Thus she didn't mind when a former student of mine, Brant Secunda, showed up with a Huichol shaman. Brant had left school to hike into the mountains of Mexico where he apprenticed himself to Don José, an aged peyote wizard who taught Brant the ancient rites and ceremonies. One day Brant showed up with Don José, who was 102 years old, about three and half feet tall with a withered arm and the sweetest smile I had ever seen. Brant said, "You are my two teachers. I wanted you to meet." It turned out that Brant and Don José were traveling around California together, sleeping on people's floors. It occurred to me that Don José had been using peyote for eighty-five years. And here he was, not speaking a word of English, hitchhiking around America with a young guy with little money at the age of 102. Whew! You never knew where you would wind up when you went to work at Sonoma State in those days.

Karen Elizabeth Gordon was a grad student. She was always funny and smart and would say little poems like (approximately): "During the day he worked at an auto body shop/then at night he would bang out my dents." She knew I would get the teeth reference in "dents." I knew Karen would get her own poetry published, but I didn't imagine she would be discovered by Times Books and turn this into a career with her erotic and funny grammar books.

Sherril Jaffe was one of our part-timers' gang for a while. This was just about the time she wrote her first book, *Scars Make Your Body More Interesting*. Sherril was married to my partner in the writing program, the poet David Bromige. One night at their house I was sitting across the kitchen table from Sherril and Karen. We were all stoned and they were right under a hanging lamp that shone off their hair and made them look like angels. I took a kind of mental photo of the moment, because Karen and Sherril began to shoot one-liners back and forth at each other on such a high level of wit and learning it was astonishing to watch it, like viewing a badminton match in fast motion. I recognized that at that moment I was with two of the wittiest women in the world, and they were inspiring each other to incredible heights I might never hear again.

When David Bromige returned from his night class, he convinced Sherril to bob her head in her famous imitation of a boiling egg. My familiar loneliness was not present at that moment.

[Sherril has written eight books. Karen moved to Paris and wrote about a dozen books including *The Transitive Vampire: A Handbook of Grammar for the Innocent, the Eager and the Doomed*. Andrei has written numerous books: poetry, novels, essays, autobiography, collections from his magazine, *Exquisite Corpse*, among others. David Bromige has written thirty-three books.]

After Sherril and David divorced, she married Alan Lew, a poet, graduate of Penn and Iowa Writers' Workshop, who ran the Berkeley Zen Center. Alan went on to become a rabbi, the head of the largest conservative synagogue in San Francisco. He would write books on Judaism and Zen and would establish the only meditation center attached to a synagogue in the world. David Bromige would marry a former Sonoma State student, Cecelia Belle, who introduced the late night movies on TV. Cecelia would go on to establish, direct, and find annual funding for a valuable psychological counseling center for high school students in Sonoma County. She now employs twenty people

David would later win the Western States Book Award for a lifetime of poetry. I was lucky to have him as a partner. David credited me with saving his life one time. He had gone catatonic. Sherril came to fetch me in a panic. He was completely under the quilt and no one could get him out. I cleared the room, sat on the foot of his bed, and quietly began to tell him the funny stories that he, a Londoner, loved about my childhood in The Bronx. I saw the covers beginning to stir. David was laughing. He couldn't help himself. After a while he sheepishly came out. Ever since he has credited me with saving him. I helped him again during the period when he thought he was being followed by disciples of the guru George Gurdjieff for some reason, although he had never had any contact with them. I told him that it wasn't true. "Guys like you and me, we're not important enough to be followed." It seemed to help him a bit.

[Once my pal Barry Gifford (*Wild At Heart*) told me he was being stalked by a woman fan. "Really?" I said. "Jerr, everyone gets stalked from time to time," he answered nonchalantly.]

David Bromige introduced me to the world of language poetry. I was not a poet. I never felt that my final aim was the language, but something beyond the language. Once David asked me why I didn't write more poetry and I cracked him up by saying, "I respect poetry too much to write it." Sometimes funny things would just pop out of my mouth before I had a chance to think about it. When I did a reading with Robert Hass (this was before he became Poet Laureate of the U.S.), he read some translations he had done from *The Inferno* about Dante and Virgil. By chance I followed by reading a piece that included a friend of mine named Virgil, back when I was twenty-two and worked for Boeing in Seattle. I told of how Virgil was a young man, an obliquely wise African-American bass player from Seattle who was sleeping on my couch. Virgil played terrific jazz "bass" by humming and strumming his nose. I described how once, when we were drunk at a club in Vancouver, Virgil sat in on a real bass, but he kept playing the same note over and over until he broke the string, and then he lost his shoes. Somehow I turned to Robert and heard myself saying, "When a guy named Virgil shows up in a work of art, you know you've got to listen to him," and I watched incredulously as Hass laughed so hard he almost fell out of his chair.

Although David Bromige was raised in England, he came to us via Canada. He prided himself on being nobody's fool. He had been suspicious of people since his childhood during the bombing of London. "The Germans tried to kill me when I was a boy," he once said to me. But he was a romantic about poets and poetry and language. He did readings from his work around the world, but I think he was especially touched when Sonoma County named him as Poet Laureate.

He won many awards in both the U.S. and Canada. Once he was given an award at a dinner in LA hosted by Xerox. When I asked him how the dinner went, he said, "Fine. But everyone from Xerox ordered the exact same menu." David was the best book reader I ever met. He could read quickly with great retention, seeing everything from twenty angles. He could really concentrate. Maybe because he literally thought words were more real than life. He could take a book from your bookshelf and read the whole thing in a couple hours. Of course, he might not return the book, but that's another story.

Early on, Ntozake Shange showed up and joined us part-timers at Sonoma State for a couple years. Ntozake was a bright, stylish, hip, former Barnard girl who was commuting up from San Francisco where she was just beginning to perform at bars, working out the rudiments of her *for colored girls who have considered suicide when the rainbow is enuf*, the play in which she would star and take to Broadway where it made her famous. Zake was a lot of fun. She had a vivid imagination, which did not help with her driving. For one thing, she had worked out a roundabout way of driving up to SSU that added about twenty miles to the trip each way, because she said the Golden Gate Bridge was too narrow for cars to drive on. Once she got a flat tire while speeding along the freeway. When she heard the FLAP FLAP FLAP and felt the car pulling toward the side of the road, she panicked because she thought that a helicopter had landed on the roof. Zake was an original. She was talented, versatile, steeped in American culture and especially jazz and black culture. I was happy when her gifts were recognized in New York.

I always tried to reach out to my students. Many repeated my classes again and again. One young writer, Jerome Reiter from Kansas City, was with us for so long that he called himself "the only student with tenure." A student from Eritrea was very shy in a lit class I taught until I told her to talk about *Hedda Gabler* for the class in Eritrean. She laughed but she began to speak in Eritrean. The class loved it. Shortly afterwards, when she began to speak in English, I had her give the class a short history lecture to explain why the Eritrean language was sprinkled with Italian words.

David Bromige and I were a good team. We swung with whatever came through the door and we had many colorful students. I loved most of my students. I was more honest with them, in front of a class and personally, than I was with many of my colleagues in the English Department.

I could tell endless anecdotes of my students who so often gave us stories that came straight from the heart, funny and sad stories that might never be published in this wicked Babylon, but stories that came alive while they read them, and no doubt live in people's minds today. I'll just mention two more: Natasha Littletree, who died recently, was crippled with one of those nerve diseases where you can't move and can hardly speak. She guided her wheelchair with her finger, weighed hardly anything, and sometimes had to be carried to class. But she came every week. She was always prepared, did twice the work of anyone else, tried to speak to give feedback on other stories. After a while, she had taken so many of my classes that I could act as translator for her to the class. She also organized the Native American students on campus and became advisor to the university president on matters of race, as well as winning several elected offices. Once, she asked me to certify to Social Security that she deserved continued funding for her tuition because she was heading towards a successful career that would pay her well as a published novelist. Of course no one could say this honestly. But I said it. I thought that if America, the richest nation in the history of the world, wouldn't pay a few bucks for this valiant woman's attempt to get an education, then it was so much the worse for America.

Vicki Contreras had the same disease. Vicki came to us from Mexico, was about twenty, small and very beautiful with long black hair and huge, soulful, sparkling, black eyes. Like Natasha Littletree, she was similarly paralyzed. Yet she wheeled around campus in her wheelchair directed by her finger, and she always showed up and added so much light to our class with her beautiful and holy stories. But I worried about her, completely vulnerable as she returned to the dorms in the twilight on the near-deserted campus after class. When I asked her if she was safe, she said, "Dy-ess. I yam safe." She looked up at me, smiled helplessly, and added, "I play to the Virgen Mary to plotect me."

I still worried about her, but it turned out she was right. No one ever harmed her. In fact, my friends Jan and Gerry Haslam (he wrote about his people, the Oakies, and struggled to put the Great Central Valley of

California on the literary map) took her into their big family for a while and looked after her.

I see writers as people who felt rejected as children and then became writers so that they would continue to be rejected and thus would always feel comfortable and in familiar circumstances. I had my share of rejections, but with heroes like Natasha and Vicki around, I was never able to feel sorry for myself for very long.

> *"Even as the heart is mourning its loss,*
> *The soul is rejoicing at its find."*
>
> Sufi saying

MOVING ON

In the traditional *bildungsroman,* the young hero leaves the provinces (the outer boroughs) and heads for the capital (Manhattan) where he achieves great success, triumphing over the elite of the culture on their own terms and ending up in a penthouse, the "princess" (a beautiful actress?) on his arm, looking over the city he has taken as it sits below them, shining in the night. This isn't my story. (Actually it's Woody Allen's.) I could no longer play this role, although I didn't see this clearly at the time. I couldn't live in the old stories. They made me sick. They all seemed to be noir tales. Nightmares of speeding toward a dead end in a '49 Ford with a needy, demented guy at the wheel.

I had a lot to learn. And perhaps more to unlearn. Yet I knew I had found my path. I knew there was a place beyond suffering, and it had to do with softening the ego, letting go of desire, a process of subtracting more than one of adding, but I also knew it was going to be difficult to communicate this to other people. This knowledge was not going to be welcomed by people attached to the old culture or to their egos, especially their religious egos which are the most difficult to lose. And most likely my path was somewhat unique, not suited to most. A kind of shamanic path that even in the old tribes was only followed by a few. But surely, there were others around me who were secretly traveling on parallel paths.

And throughout this process, I was glad that my Fifties friends stuck with me. They didn't mind that I had wild hair hanging down to the small of my back, or that Charlotte had taken to wearing a kind of toga that she had constructed out of an old bedspread she had found twisted into a tree beside the road. Budding millionaires, future captains of industry, we always stayed in touch. Friends like Ed Segal, the CEO of Metron Technologies on the NASDAQ, and Serge Abend, the chief patent attorney at Xerox Parc, would show up at my various basements and shacks, not willing to let me go. I was very lucky in my old pals. They are still like my family to me. We may agree to disagree, but over the years I think we've all learned the great lesson that friendship goes deeper than ideology.

It took me many years and much pain before I realized something that they helped teach me: There are millions of methods to work against the ego, millions of paths toward the goal of this work. Yoga means union. It aims to unify one's smaller self with the Self that is beyond the limits of ego, the Self that is larger than the universe. Or universes. What prevents this unity is the hard shell of ego, our own little Defense Department. We fear that if we lose our little ego, we will go mad or die. I found through my own experience that this is not the case. It is terrifying to endure this experiment, this flirtation with death and madness. Not many will follow. Yet the knowledge that someone else did it might not be unwelcome for those on a similar path.

I never took on a guru, but I might have been less lonely if I had realized earlier the benefits of associating with a *sangha* where you could spend time with others who had somewhat the same world view. I did learn from many teachers, among them Swami Satchidananda, who eventually came to look like Toltsoy in Tolstoy's shamanic phase, when he dressed like a peasant and was taught by a peasant cobbler how to make shoes; I learned as well from the Swami's woman disciple, my good friend Swami Vimalananda, Director of the Integral Yoga Institute in San Francisco. Swami Vimalananda passed on Satchidananda's teachings about other yogas, ways of working against the domination of ego: Hatha Yoga (stretching), Japa Yoga (repeating a mantra), Bhakti Yoga (devotion), Jnana Yoga (thinking), and especially Karma Yoga, (service, doing good, living within the model of cooperation and treating others as if they were yourself.)

In fact, perhaps there are as many yogas as there are people, yogas of a thousand different modes of meditation, prayer to a thousand gods and goddesses, standing on a pillar in the desert, eating and drinking and smoking concoctions of visionary plants and fungi, numberless combinations and permutations of yogas. I am certain that there are people all around us unconsciously moving slowly along their own paths, doing the yogas of sitting still quietly and not harming anyone, yogas of staying awake all night to help a sick child, of sacrificing to educate that child, yogas of giving to charity, yogas of helping the lame, the weak, and the blind, yogas of starting businesses that provide employment for people, yogas of worrying that you might have to lay someone off, yogas of smiling at customers in your job as cashier, yogas of discovering medicines that will reduce suffering, of inventing devices which will entertain and make life easier for people, yogas of providing the money and means for those who can make these discoveries, yogas of baseball players practicing bunting, yogas of people sitting alone at night hoping their friends won't find out that they are secretly praying for the world; so many secret yogis and yoginis, each working in his or her own way against the selfishness we are all born with, heading toward a better reincarnation, perhaps in an easier dream. I remembered a war protestor who told me that his father said to him, "Vietnam doesn't matter. Why don't you wake up? The only thing that matters in the world is money." The poor young guy was astonished into silence. But I knew that with my dark sense of humor, I would have answered, "Then why don't I kill you and take your money?" Of course he didn't kill his father. They both knew that money wasn't the highest value. Yet I also knew that we were approaching a time when we had to change or die.

I knew there was a part of us that had never been born into this dream and was always, even right now, at peace. And I knew it was necessary to stay grounded in this peace inside ourselves if we were to live in peace in the world. I knew that part of my task was to stay in touch with this knowledge and to attempt to bring it into the world.

We lived each day in the world of the Two. (The "ten thousand things" the Hindus and Buddhists called it, which was just another term for "multiplicity.") This world might eventually turn out to be just a dream that we wake up from, but it was a long and often painful dream. I thought that when students reach this position—when they say that the world is maya, an illusion—that's when the Zen master hits them with a stick. That is to say, this may be a dream, but it can really hurt. In the world of the Two, we had to work on our insides but also on what was outside. This would be good for our spiritual practice as well as beneficial to the emerging new reality. It was easy to be a Zen Master on the mountain.

After one particularly peaceful night, I awoke the next day to learn that the U.S., led by Kissinger and Nixon, had invaded Cambodia, a small impoverished Buddhist nation completely on the other side of the world. (This was shortly before Henry Kissinger won the Nobel Peace Prize.) I knew there would be a protest in Berkeley, at the former People's Park, an empty lot owned by the university near campus that protestors had seized and turned into a homemade park for the kids of Berkeley, built by joint (yes, joint) community labor, everyone contributing his talents and sweat, a beautiful idea that had come to fruition until the university joined with Governor Reagan to take it back, destroyed the park and paved it over, turning it into what we called "People's Parking Lot." Reagan had already sent helicopters over the campus and gassed the students. The authorities, Reagan and the university administration, wouldn't give in easily. They had shot and killed one young man, James Rector, a bystander on a roof on Telegraph Avenue, when they had taken back the park by force in the first battle.

It was time to come down from the mountain. I mounted my trusty steed, Rusty, the VW Bug, the rusting wreck of a wonder-car, and headed south. It was time to face the guns again and take a risk for our communal future.

At the freeway entrance I saw a pretty girl, maybe eighteen, hitchhiking, wearing a T-shirt and little chopped off jeans. Although I was up near Santa Rosa, fifty miles away, on a highway that didn't go to Berkeley, somehow I sensed she was headed there. I pulled over. "People's park?" she said. I nodded. She opened the door, then ran off to the bushes behind her. Returned carrying a six-foot long battle ax.

"Whoa!" I said. We both laughed. "Hey, I'm not driving through the national guard troops with a battle ax," I said, still laughing.

We both recognized that reason was on my side. Yet emotion was on her side. So we made a rational decision: I would drop her and the ax off a couple blocks before we encountered the troops.

At People's Park, sure enough many of the students had axes and were chopping up the asphalt. I joined a line of hippies and students who were passing out pieces of the parking lot, Chinese style, in a human chain, and piling them up in the street. After a short while I saw the girl hitchhiker. She gave me a big smile. She was chopping up part of the parking lot with her ax. After perhaps a couple hours the entire surface of the parking lot was lying in the street. Grass and dirt appeared from under the pavement. The park was a park once more.

Then the troops arrived, in formation, advancing slowly against us, coming north on Telegraph Avenue. Right near where they had shot James Rector. We taunted them. Young people threw objects at them. They pointed their rifles and began to fire at us. We retreated. I picked up a rubber bullet. We slowly moved back. There was a lot of cursing but the battle was never fully joined. We had already won the day.

And there was a meeting of the Berkeley City Council that night that we were all going to attend. They were voting on a resolution for the City of Berkeley to make a separate peace with the National Liberation Front of Vietnam. Everyone in the movement across the country was aware of this vote. It would be a great symbolic triumph and a terrific way to embarrass the government. To meet with the NLF in Paris or somewhere and sign a treaty on international TV. To show the world that not all Americans had gone crazy.

The auditorium was large, with the City Council behind a table on the stage. Nine people. The spectator's seats were full and the aisles jammed. People were out in the lobby trying to wedge themselves in. Everyone was in a festive mood. The adrenalin from tearing up the parking lot and being shot at by the troops was still flowing in our arteries. A contingent of witches sat together in the back, faces painted white, emitting special weird chants. Everyone was ready to go. Our triumphant day was going to continue. This might be the start of something.

The meeting somehow proceeded in the midst of earnest interruptions from members of the audience, strange witch mantras, wild shouts, laughter and jeers, the usual tribal sounds of the Berkeley holy menagerie. My spirits were up. The Council looked frightened. Then they took the vote. One by one with cheering and booing the Council members let their position be known. The vote was a tie. Four to four. There was one voter left. He took the microphone and explained in a reasonable tone that he had spoken to the City Attorney and was informed that the vote was illegal.

Berkeley couldn't make its own foreign policy. It was subject to the laws of the United States. So he was forced to vote no.

A shocked silence ensued. No one had expected this. Then one tall thin young man, wearing a dress and earrings and high heels, leaped up onto the stage and snatched the microphone roughly away from the councilman. The young man turned to the audience and screamed into the mike, "I hereby accuse the Berkeley City Council of inciting a riot!" He turned towards the fearful Council behind their table, looked over his shoulder at the audience like a lieutenant leading his troops into battle, and shouted, "Come on gang, let's riot!" As he waved them forward, he moved toward the table, turning it over right onto the City Council members. As one, the Council members grabbed their briefcases and ran out the back door as the audience flooded over the rim of the stage and began to wreck everything they could get their hands on.

I loved this. This was the most exciting moment in the Berkeley City Council since that night on TV that Jim Saunt had told me about when the mayor had dragged a large garbage bag onto the stage and announced proudly that this was just some of the marijuana the Berkeley police had seized from people they had recently arrested, and a young man had leaped onto the stage, grabbed the mayor, turned to the TV cameras, and shouted, "I hereby make a citizen's arrest of this man for possession of marijuana!" He attempted to pull the mayor off the stage. A wrestling match ensued over the garbage bag of pot until the young man, still shouting, was carried away by the police. It was the funniest moment on TV until the time when a reporter during a demonstration in San Francisco asked a young black man what he thought. The young man turned towards the camera and said, "Wait a minute! This is TV? Live TV? I can speak on live TV right now and everyone can see me?" When the reporter said, "Yes," the young black man approached the camera, put his face right into it, and shouted, angrily, "Nixon, I know where you live. I'll get you Nixon. I know where you live."

After the wrecking of the auditorium stage, the audience proceeded toward downtown Berkeley to wreck some more. It was only windows. Unlike the legal violence of the government, nothing permanent would be damaged or maimed. But I'd had enough excitement for the day. I had a fifty mile drive back to my shack among the steers and sheep, but this time without the charming girl with the large battle ax.

I didn't realize it, but I was moving into a different strata of society. An unstable world of brilliant and crazy writers in which a person would be a drunk one day and a millionaire the next, or a millionaire one day and a drunk the next. In which two of my women pals would be nominated for the Pulitzer Prize, and when their books didn't sell that well suddenly they were gone, to Buffalo and Arkansas. In which two women friends from India would suddenly be famous and formerly famous writers would shoot themselves. I would publish seven books that were the subjects of four European university dissertations, I would speak about my work at leading universities around the world, but one incident I recall was perhaps the most emblematic of the writer's life: I sat on a panel, "Handling Fame and Fortune as a Novelist," with two of my novelist friends, Sara Vogan and Floyd Salas. We had each written about four novels and had each won some plaudits and prizes. As we spoke to a large, attentive audience, it came to me that all three of us were broke. Sara had lost her publisher and was drinking heavily. Floyd told me that the Navy was following him and had poisoned his dog. Floyd was small but he was a fighter. He said, "Writing is fighting." He had made it out of the Oakland hood and he was somehow able to barely keep things together by teaching a class in writing at San Quentin and coaching the Cal-Berkeley boxing team. Sara had ushered for a rock concert the night before. She wouldn't take my suggestion to go to AA. "Too religious," she said. "Then teach!" I said. She had been offered the co-chair of the writing program at the University of Oregon in the hip town of Eugene. "I'll die before I'll teach." She stubbornly insisted on being a pure writer. She drank herself to death a couple years later at the age of forty-two.

There were multitudes of writers in the Bay Area. I met most of them and befriended many. If you were going to believe in something, you could do worse than devoting your life to art. Yet I had still been in touch with that loneliness at my center, even in the art world, even with many friends in each of the social worlds I inhabited. It took me many years before I could acknowledge that the emptiness that I often felt at my core was actually an openness, an opening to the Light that has never been touched by the pain of the world, the living, merciful Light that is beyond any possible loneliness.

But I didn't know any of this yet. Back in 1971, Dial Press kept postponing my publication date. They were aware the Sixties were waning. As the draft faded, the summer soldiers and sunshine patriots were coming back into the society with its mainstream Fifties' values. There would be little market for a book like mine. Dial allocated no money for publicity. Finally they agreed to publish the book on the last day of the fall list, February 29, 1972. I looked at my calendar to be sure there *was* a February 29th that year. The book didn't sell that well, but it received some wonderful reviews. The *New York Times Book Review* gave it an almost full-page favorable notice (rare for a first novel), the *Milwaukee Journal* called it "the best book of its kind in several years." A syndicated article that appeared in six newspapers chose it as one of the ten best books of the year. But after a while it faded away.

The Eastern religions tell us that although we can't control everything that happens to us, we do have some control over our response. One fall day in 1972, right after Nixon had creamed McGovern in the election, a few months after my book was published, I decided to drive "Rusty" down to San Francisco to see my friends. I put on my psychedelic, tie-dyed, T-shirt, set my red, white and blue headband on the crown of my head, and shook out my long hair down below my shoulders. I could see now that my book's life was coming to an end. Karen Kennerly had left Dial Press for a career as Executive Director of the American branch of PEN, the worldwide writers' organization. There was no one at Dial to look after the book but it wouldn't have mattered. America was climbing back into the cocoon of denial. A novel can't get any traction without publicity and the lack of a budget was impossible to overcome. I had become a novelist as a way out of the world of buying and selling. I hadn't realized that a writer had to sell his book himself. Now I understood how Arthur Miller could have written such an astute play about a salesman. A writer was a kind of salesman, one of the last true entrepreneurs. Like Willy Loman, you might meet the mayor of Providence, but if the public stopped smiling, you were on your own.

But I didn't mind. I marveled at how I could be living in such a lovely place with a job I liked. I felt a great peace descending upon me. I knew the sound of one hand clapping but I didn't realize that I knew it.

"I myself have traversed it [the realm of the Tao] this way and that; yet still know only where it begins. I have roamed at will through its stupendous spaces. I know how to get to them, but I do not know where they end."

Chuang Tzu

I knew now that I wasn't a true stoner, wasn't straight, and strangely enough wasn't moderate. I wasn't sure where I fit in. I would never be a Biblical creationist, but I also would never be pure atheistic Darwinist even though it was obvious that species changed and living things evolved. Everywhere I looked around me I saw signs of design and intelligence, if only in the laws that Darwin was the first to notice.

I drove south under a gummy sky, a thousand shades of gray looking like they had been badly erased. Winter was coming. You could smell the coming months of chilly rain in the air. But for most of the year there were these beautiful birds and trees and flowers. I didn't know their names because we didn't have things like that in The Bronx. I had always feared that if I didn't make it out of The Bronx, I might land as a checker at the A&P. Now I had found a path in life, a way with hope and beauty. I didn't know that I had decades of hard work ahead of me, extracting the barbs my culture had placed in me, working against my desires and lifelong habits, suffering numerous regressions and making mistake after mistake, but even if I had known this it wouldn't have made any difference. I wasn't afraid of work, as long as I had a direction and a purpose. Now I had found a shining goal. And I didn't have to believe in it. I had seen it.

And how lucky I felt to have been part of one of the few movements in world history in which people banded together and worked nonviolently for a dangerous moral and spiritual cause that would stand the test of time. Young and somewhat spoiled and humanly flawed as we were, we had attempted to put aside careers and to work against our egos because the hungry greed and corruption and waste and mindlessness and lies around us made us sick. We had attempted to rise above outdated nationalism, manufactured patriotism, and shallow materialism, to work against racism, and sexism, and homophobia, and most of all to stop a murderous and immoral war that was making us ashamed to be Americans. Following teachers like Gandhi and Dr. King and Cesar Chavez we had stood up against the guns and bayonets in the name of a principle, that love was more powerful than greed and fear. They cracked our skulls. They shot us (they broke in and assassinated Fred Hampton in his bed at night), they gassed us and jailed us, young women and men, but we kept coming back, 99 percent of us nonviolent. We succeeded in bringing down a president and finally, after a decade, by sheer guts and wit and persistence, we forced the greatest military machine in the history of the world to yield.

We had also stood up to the powerful forces of consumerism and materialism, we made the connections between the economy and addiction, we stopped going to beauty parlors, we recognized the link between big cars and foreign intervention, we moved beyond discarding last year's fashions and the habits of buying things in hopes of moving up in social class. We saw how our consumption habits were raping the earth and fouling the air and despoiling the seas for our children, how we were arming dictators and training their armies so they could keep their people down in order to provide us with cheap imports of goods we didn't need.

We had given the world millions of idealistic young people, most of them women, who had decided to live simply and to become teachers and nurses and librarians and social workers as a way of devoting their lives to the service of humanity, the path of karma yoga. We had brought different ways of thought, Buddhism and Hinduism and Taoism, shamanism and magic to the mainstream Western discourse. We had understood that people in power made the laws in their interest, and we honored people who broke those laws in the name of a higher principle, priests like the Berrigans who had gone to jail for destroying draft board records, government employees like Dan Ellsberg who risked years of jail to release classified information that undercut the rationale for the war, and CIA agents like Philip Agee who revealed that they were teaching the agents of our dictators how to torture people. We saw through the fog of lies of the politicians of both parties and the bullshit of the media. We made the connection between Yale and Harvard and Wharton and the slick advertising that was designed to enslave our children. For a brief time we saw through it all.

Unlike the somber, methodical Communists we had learned that it was OK for a protest to be festive, that we could avoid becoming a mirror image of those we were opposing by staying light and flexible, by including music and dance and comedy and having fun, by admitting that we didn't have scientific laws to justify ourselves and by flirting with Mystery.

I was so proud to have been part of this movement. I had not one single regret that I had given up a lucrative career and joined it. It taught me so much and nourished my soul, offering me the finest times of my life and thrusting me into one of the greatest episodes in history. Somehow an entire generation had awakened for a while. And I was there. I would always be proud of this. I was a part of it with my brothers and sisters.

"Work out your own salvation with diligence."
The Buddha's Last Words

I drove easily, sat back, relaxed, with Santana's "Samba Pa Ti" on the tape deck. I thought to myself if only Shep had been there with me, riding shotgun by my side. I turned onto the north-south freeway and bit into a golden Sebastopol apple, a famous Gravenstein. For several months a year you could pick them up when they fell off the trees. With my fragile job and no money, it was comforting in the Russian-Jewish neighborhood of my soul to know that if you kept your wits about you, it would be difficult to starve in California.

As I drove along, I thought of possible futures for the world. I knew history was depressing and often didn't seem to have a meaning, but I believed that you had to keep trying to change things. And that you might be more effective in changing history if you remembered that the real meaning you were looking for lay outside of history. At least that was the way I saw it. Of course I was aware that the counterculture appeared to be dying, but I believed it would come back to life. It had to. There was no other way forward that I could envision.

I could no longer go back to my old ways of seeing and thinking. I couldn't believe there was no North Dakota. I had been to North Dakota.

Two centuries ago Shelley had said that poets were the legislators of mankind. Now advertising copywriters, martini drunk and tormented, were the legislators of mankind. And they were paid by the same hungry and confused souls who paid the official legislators in Washington, also drunk and confused. Reality was so much larger and more vital and magical than our conceptions. We had measured it to death, an inch at a time. The world had once been enchanted. It sang with meanings. The music was still in the air if you listened. And the gods could also speak to us by silence. You could hear it at times when you really quieted down.

It was clear to me by now that we might not succeed in changing the world for quite a while. But as I drove leisurely down the western edge of the great continent in the direction of the lovely city of San Francisco, watching the rain beginning to fall on the little windshield of my rusty bug, listening to Santana on my eight-track tape, I was glad about what I had done, and I was sure that my life was going to be a beautiful trip while it lasted.

> *Everyone has a shadow*
> *Except the Sun.*
> *She simply shines.*
> *She doesn't need a reason.*
>
> Gerald Rosen

THE END

Printed in the United States
145407LV00008B/55/P

9 781882 260188